DESTINY
BETRAYED

DESTINY
BETRAYED
Second Edition

JFK, CUBA, AND THE GARRISON CASE

James DiEugenio

With a preface by Lisa Pease and
a foreword by William Davy

Skyhorse Publishing

Skyhorse Publishing books may be purchased in bulk at special discounts for sales
promotion, corporate gifts, fund-raising, or educational purposes. Special editions can
also be created to specifications. For details, contact the Special Sales Department,
Skyhorse Publishing, 307 West 36th Street, 11th Floor, New York, NY 10018 or
info@skyhorsepublishing.com.

Skyhorse® and Skyhorse Publishing® are registered trademarks of Skyhorse Publishing,
Inc.®, a Delaware corporation.

Visit our website at www.skyhorsepublishing.com.

10 9 8 7 6 5 4 3 2

Library of Congress Cataloging-in-Publication Data is available on file.
ISBN: 978-1-62087-056-3

Printed in the United States of America

To my mother, Flo (1924–1991)
With sorrow and regret that you weren't
here to see this book published.
Rest in peace, forever.

Contents

Preface   ix

Foreword   xi

Acknowledgments   xv

1. The Legacy   1

2. The Education of John F. Kennedy   17

3. Bay of Pigs: Kennedy vs. Dulles   34

4. Kennedy De-escalates in Cuba   57

5. New Orleans   77

6. Witches' Brew   101

7. On Instructions from His Government   117

8. Oswald Returns: Strange Bedfellows   151

9. Jim Garrison in 1966   167

10. Garrison Reopens the Kennedy Case   175

11. Inferno   220

12. "Shaw Will Never Be Punished"   260

13. Anticlimax: The Shaw Trial   286

14. Garrison Must Be Destroyed   312

15. Blakey Buries the Case   325

16. Mexico City and Langley   346

17. Washington and Saigon   365

18. Denouement   382

Notes   398

Bibliography   453

Index   459

Preface

Not all conspiracies are theories. As grown-ups, we need to learn to decouple those terms, which have been irresponsibly glued together since 1963.

I grew up with conspiracies. I watched Congress investigate Watergate and Iran Contra. I saw high-level government officials repeatedly tell us Iraq had "weapons of mass destruction," only to learn that that information was false. I was a juror on a conspiracy trial. Conspiracies happen.

So why do some conspiracies get investigated while others get covered up? This volume will help you answer that question.

I first encountered *Destiny Betrayed: JFK, Cuba and the Garrison Case* in an independent bookstore, on a shelf labeled simply—and appropriately—"Intelligence." Within the first few pages, I knew I had discovered something special. I had read a handful of books on the assassination of President Kennedy by that point, but this was the first book I read that put the events squarely in their historical context. I experienced a "light bulb" moment, seeing the convergence of factors that led to Kennedy's death.

The book also explained why the erudite Jim Garrison I met in Garrison's own wonderful book, *On the Trail of the Assassins*, did not match the image of him that the press was presenting. The picture of a crazed district attorney hell-bent on prosecuting an innocent man never rang true to me. Here was a district attorney who, in my opinion, had done the right and honorable thing, something that had not been done to that point: treated the assassination like the prosecutable crime it was. He called in witnesses. He arrested Clay Shaw, a prominent citizen, on charges of conspiracy to kill the President because of strong evidence. He took his case to trial. And yet, Shaw was found not guilty. What happened?

In this volume, James DiEugenio connects the dots to explain why Garrison's case fell apart, who undermined it, and how those players connect to the circle of people who had been manipulating Oswald long before the Kennedy assassination took place.

If you want to understand how a lie can be perpetrated for almost fifty years, read this book. DiEugenio deconstructs, through declassified government records, personal interviews, and careful analysis, how high-ranking members of the CIA—through their allies on the Warren Commission and the House Select Committee on Assassinations, with the help of FBI Director J. Edgar Hoover, and the FBI's and CIA's assets in the mainstream media—derailed not just Garrison's investigation but *every serious attempt* to investigate John F. Kennedy's assassination.

Greatly expanded and rewritten from the original edition, this book shows us how our past has been deliberately rewritten to hide the important truth of who killed President Kennedy and why.

This is not "conspiracy theory." This is the factual history of how the investigations into the assassination of President Kennedy were deliberately and provably subverted. DiEugenio exposes the mechanisms that enabled the conspiracy and cover-up to take place.

But this book is not just about our past. If we don't learn not only what happened, but how the cover-up was effected, then not only did they get away with it, but the same operational template can be run again.

If you never punish a criminal, will the criminal voluntarily stop committing future crimes? Of course not. The same is true when the criminal is a government official. It's long past time we started demanding that people be held accountable for high-level crimes and cover-ups. Accountability matters.

And why are we, the people, so gullible? It has often been said that people *prefer* to believe a conspiracy killed Kennedy because such a consequential act demands a consequential reason. But consider the reverse. Why would anyone in their right mind *prefer* to believe that members of their own government had Kennedy killed and then covered it up? Who would *choose* to believe that? Isn't that why the lies persist? We *want* to believe our government would never do such a thing, even when the facts scream otherwise.

But the truth doesn't have to be scary. A cover-up is like a magic trick. Once you understand how it was accomplished, you can never be fooled by it again. That's why this book is so important. It dissects the magic trick. You may feel you're losing your innocence, but you'll only be losing your naïveté.

Jim Garrison stepped up, did the right thing, and was pilloried for it. It will take many more people with the courage to do what Garrison did, to risk ridicule and defamation, in order to rescue our future. But with each new recruit, the truth becomes more obvious and less of a struggle to defend. That's where you come in.

It is too late to hold some of these people accountable in their lifetimes. But it's not too late to hold them accountable in the eyes of history. "Who controls the past controls the future," wrote George Orwell in his prescient book *1984*. By restoring to us the *real* history of these events, this book offers us the power to choose a different future. Let's accept the gift and do something useful with it.

—**Lisa Pease, coeditor of *The Assassination*s**

Foreword

Like millions of others in 1992, I too was caught up in the buzz created by Oliver Stone's 1991 film, *JFK*. Primarily based on New Orleans District Attorney Jim Garrison's 1988 book about his investigation into the assassination of President Kennedy, *On The Trail of the Assassins*, Stone's film generated controversy, legislation and a lot of ink.

Unlike a lot of the movie going public though, I had already studied the JFK assassination and the Garrison case for more than ten years and so had a little easier time separating the wheat from the chaff—and there was a lot to digest. In the wake of the film, a spate of books, magazines, newspaper columns, and TV specials flooded the market.

One day at the newsstand, I picked up a copy of *Cineaste* magazine that was devoted to the topic of *JFK*, the film (Vol. XIX No.1, 1992). That issue featured many interesting articles by the likes of Christopher Sharrett, George Michael Evica, and—Garrison's editor and Stone's—cowriter, Zachary Sklar. But what caught my eye was an ad on page 22 announcing the release of a new book on the Garrison investigation called, *Destiny Betrayed: JFK, Cuba, and the Garrison Case*. I have to admit, I greeted it with skepticism. Other than Paris Flammonde's book, *The Kennedy Conspiracy*, and Garrison's own volumes, little of note had been written about Garrison, and one had to be wary of the mountain of disinformation and shabby scholarship surrounding the case. I was somewhat relieved to find out that the book was being brought out by Garrison's publisher, Sheridan Square Press, and had been endorsed by both Stone and Sklar. Yet I still had a nagging feeling as I had never heard of the author—James DiEugenio. Somewhat reluctantly I mailed my check off.

I needn't have worried. I remember that the book arrived as I was house sitting for my parents and had plenty of reading time on my hands. I devoured the book from cover to cover and then read it again. I was impressed by the way the author deftly placed the assassination and the subsequent investigation into their appropriate historical context—something sorely lacking in the field to this day. The writing flowed logically and the depth of the information in the endnotes section alone could have been another book in itself. The bibliography is still a valuable resource to this day. But the meat of the book is what ultimately matters and there DiEugenio didn't disappoint. Jim took the Garrison case to new heights with diligent interviewing, new areas of research and plain old-fashioned shoe leather—having driven his battered Toyota from coast to coast.

At the 1993 Midwest Symposium in Chicago, I got to listen to Jim speak and meet him—albeit briefly. Two important events occurred in the immediate aftermath of that conference. Jim and some of his West Coast colleagues went on to form Citizens for the Truth about the Kennedy Assassinations (CTKA) and its in-house magazine *Probe*. The second event was that I got to meet Peter Vea. Peter was a volunteer worker at the Assassination Archives and Research Center (AARC) in Washington, D.C., who specialized in the Garrison probe. The AARC was started by attorney Bud Fensterwald who had been close to Garrison in his lifetime and was now being run by preeminent FOIA attorney, James Lesar. The AARC was a huge repository of the former New Orleans DA's files as well as Paris Flammonde's working papers, numerous unpublished manuscripts, and more. As a D.C. suburb resident, I was a regular "customer" of theirs and was down there every Saturday and a lot of weeknights as well. Peter took note of my interest in all things Garrison, and we became fast friends and colleagues.

Around this time as a result of hearings in the House and the Senate, legislation was passed to induce government agencies to release all Kennedy assassination-related documents—a classification left purposefully vague to compel agencies to release anything close to a Kennedy-era document. (To say compliance has fallen short of expectations would be an understatement as agencies are still withholding millions of pages of material.) A declassification review board was established (ARRB) to oversee the process. But before the members could be approved by Congress, many agencies did a massive data dump, and the National Archives was now home to millions of pages of material that had been held on to for decades by the CIA, FBI, DOD, the House Select Committee on Assassinations, the Church Committee, et al.

Researchers now had an avalanche of materials to pore through, and Peter and I took on that task, with our primary focus being New Orleans. During subsequent conversations with Peter, I found out that he had gotten to know Jim DiEugenio at the Chicago conference and had maintained contact with him since. In fact, he was going to join Jim on the southern leg of Jim's latest coast-to-coast summer research odyssey. When Jim and Peter returned to the Washington area, they rang me up and we met at an Italian restaurant in Chantilly, Virginia. After lunch, we convened at my house where I shared my now burgeoning file collection with Jim. As Jim and I got to know each other better, we found we had other areas of mutual interest as well (cinema for example). We too became fast friends and stayed in contact.

In the spring of 1994, Jim and a CTKA colleague, Dennis Effle, returned to Washington for a series of CTKA related meetings, and I put them up at my house. During that time, we started laying the groundwork for a two-week research blitz tour planned for that summer in New Orleans. That trip yielded numerous interviews with many key witnesses and cemented a relationship with Jim Garrison's sons that allowed us unprecedented access to boxes of the late DA's public and private papers. A follow-up trip in 1995 by Peter and me augmented an already colossal archive. By that time I had started writing for Jim's publication, *Probe*, and had amassed so much new material that I wrote a monograph titled *Through the Looking Glass*. It was published in a comb-bound edition and was printed and distributed exclusively by Jim and CTKA. I later expanded that work into book length and published it as *Let Justice Be Done* in 1999. As *Destiny Betrayed* had been my inspiration, I had only one person in mind to write my foreword and Jim graciously wrote that wonderful opening essay.

While the years saw the cessation of the print edition of *Probe*, CTKA's online site picked up the slack, far surpassing any comparable web sites put out by the so-called "new media." Jim's (and others') contributions to the site are always insightful, informative and entertaining, whether it is keeping the public abreast of new work in the research community or reviewing a worthy new book in the field. At the same time, CTKA pulls no punches in taking the piss out of authors of shabbily written and lazily thought out volumes (e.g., those by Waldron, North, et al., but it is Jim's ten-part demolition of Bugliosi's bloated, pompous *Reclaiming History* that is the site's magnum opus). Not to be overlooked, *Probe*'s earlier articles proved to be so popular that an anthology, edited by Jim and Lisa Pease, titled *The Assassinations* was released by Feral House in 2003.

So, we now come full circle to the rerelease of *Destiny Betrayed*. Rest assured this is not some crass attempt to cash in by reprinting old material and just slapping on a new preface. This is a reboot—a total rewrite from start to finish. Because of the timing, Jim did not have the benefit of having all of the new file releases at his disposal when the first edition was published—Jim more than makes up for it here. His chapters on the Bay of Pigs and Vietnam alone produce more insight and correct more historical wrongs than whole volumes on the subjects. At the same time he pumps new life into the chapters on Garrison and New Orleans. The chapter dealing with the National Security State's interference with Clay Shaw's perjury trial is as compelling as it is frightening. The writing is masterful throughout, the pacing is brisk and the information invaluable—just what you would expect from an author at the top of his game (but sadly what you too often *don't* get).

Destiny Betrayed belongs in that pantheon of books that have changed history and will stand the test of time. I'm just thankful to Jim that I was along for the ride.

—**William Davy**

Acknowledgments

For the rewritten and expanded version of this book, I should thank Len Osanic who got me in touch with Tony Lyons and Skyhorse Publishing. They made the decision that the book was worth republishing, and they let me almost completely rewrite it to reflect the current state of research in the field.

The new information this book contains is largely reliant on the work of the Assassination Records Review Board (ARRB). That body operated from 1994–98. That agency created a unique declassification process that reversed the prior Freedom of Information Act law. Now the restricting body, whether it be the CIA or FBI, had to show why the document *should not* be released. Therefore, much new information, about two million pages worth, concerning the murder of President Kennedy has now been declassified. Once that process began, two friends of mine, Peter Vea and William Davy, began searching through these documents at the National Archives. They forwarded much of the most interesting material to me. We then organized two trips to New Orleans in 1993 and 1994. There, we did many interviews, established contact with several helpful people, and searched more archival repositories.

From 1993–2000, I was part of a journal called *Probe Magazine*. This periodical covered the major assassinations of the sixties and the new developments in those cases. Illustrious researcher Lisa Pease and I edited this journal from 1995 onward. We published many articles based on these documents. And it is from those writings that much of this new material, especially on the Garrison case, originates. We had many, many authors—too many to list here—contribute distinguished articles to that journal. This book could not exist in the form it does without that major and enduring contribution to the literature in the field.

CHAPTER ONE

The Legacy

"The Soviet Union was playing one of the greatest gambles in history . . . We and we alone were in a position to break up the plan."

—*Dean Acheson*

The events that exploded in Dallas on November 22, 1963, had their genesis in Washington on a February day in 1947. In a distant but very real sense, it was John Kennedy's resistance to the policy begun on that day that killed him.[1]

On February 17, 1947, H.M. Sichell, assistant to Lord Inverchapel, the British ambassador to Washington, sent a message to Dean Acheson.[2] The ambassador wanted to talk to Secretary of State George Marshall, but, since Marshall was out of town, the diplomats spoke instead to Acting Secretary of State Acheson. They told him the British were experiencing difficulty "administering" Turkey and Greece. For one thing, Britain was unable to quell Greek leftwing partisans in their civil war against rightwing monarchists. Indeed, the formidable strength of domestic leftists and economic havoc in both countries put the British in an unprecedented position. Still reeling from the economic effects of the war and already in need of a large loan from the United States, Britain was in no position to maintain its military involvement or extend aid to either country. The two diplomats impressed on Acheson their fears that a communist, neutralist, or even nationalist victory in the area would change the power structure in the Middle

East, India, North Africa, and Italy. Their implication was obvious. England was stepping down as a "superpower," and America must fill the vacuum.

From this watershed meeting, three epochal events ensued: the United States assumed leadership of the West; any hope of avoiding the Cold War was lost; and the initial steamrolling impact of the domino theory—the view that if one nation falls to communism, all those nearby will follow suit—commenced.[3]

A month later, on March 7, President Harry Truman stood before Congress to request 400 million dollars in aid for Greece and Turkey. The request was overwhelmingly approved, for Truman couched it not in humanitarian terms, but in the terms he had received it: without it, the free world would end. With this, the Truman Doctrine was born and the Cold War became irreversible.

On June 5, after Truman's request was expedited, Secretary Marshall made a complementary speech at Harvard outlining the administration's intent to extend massive economic aid to the rest of Europe.[4] The expressed reason was to rebuild the shattered continent, to ensure its survival against a Moscow-led communist victory. The real reason was to reconstruct Europe's ability to buy American exports, so as to avoid either a depression or socialist advances.[5] The overall request was for 17 billion dollars. A special session of Congress was called, and funding for the Marshall Plan was approved, despite considerable opposition.[6]

If the resulting economic isolation did not cause Josef Stalin and the USSR sufficient worry, the forthcoming Brussels Pact, signed by England, France, Belgium, the Netherlands, and Luxembourg, certainly did. It was a military pact formed in the name of thwarting communist aggression. It led to the formation of NATO, which added other nations, particularly the United States.

But the crucial year for us is 1947. In the context of the onrushing Cold War, one telling piece of legislation completed the construction of a national security state: the aptly named National Security Act. Signed on July 26, 1947, this law established the National Security Council to oversee all U.S. intelligence operations, created the Central Intelligence Agency, and gave the Director of Central Intelligence (DCI) the leadership of that agency.[7]

The odd thing was that the least discussed part of the act was potentially the most important: the intelligence functions of the CIA. It was not until the end of the congressional debate that they were even addressed. Congress had been preoccupied with the question of the jurisdiction of the CIA, specifically that it have no domestic purview. The head of the FBI, J. Edgar Hoover, emphatically concurred.[8]

Once these matters were decided and CIA responsibilities were ostensibly restricted to a foreign domain,[9] the Agency was delegated five functions: to correlate, evaluate, and distribute intelligence; to advise the President's National

Security Council on national security matters; to recommend ways to coordinate various intelligence departments; to perform "additional services of common concern" for the government-wide intelligence community; and to perform *"such other functions* and duties related to intelligence affecting the national security as the National Security Council may from time to time direct"[10] (emphasis added).

The last clause was the key to Pandora's Box. Indeed, "other functions" became the linchpin for future covert and paramilitary operations, although the legislative history of the law shows that the phrase was not intended to justify those types of acts. It was meant to cover unforeseen circumstances. Congress never considered secret warfare or international coercion.[11]

As with every other aspect of the anticommunist national security state, this bill passed with alacrity. And six weeks after Truman signed it, the CIA was founded. The first DCI was Navy Rear Admiral Roscoe Hillenkoeter.

At first, the Agency had neither the skill nor the experience to extend its reach to overseas coercion.[12] But it learned quickly from its British cousins, first the SOE and then the SIS.[13] After setting up Radio Free Europe in 1950 and Radio Liberty in 1951, it went into partnership with the SIS in the Baltic republics of Lithuania and Estonia, but, due to Soviet counterintelligence and Agency incompetence, these first forays into covert operations failed. But two things happened that expanded the range and success of the fledgling agency: First, there was the Mao Zedong's (Tse-tung's) communist victory in China in 1949.[14] Second, there was the outbreak of the Korean War in 1950. With these two events, the Cold War went to another level, and the power, range, and skill of the CIA were greatly expanded. Bases were opened everywhere, especially in the Far East. Old intelligence officers from World War II were re-recruited. Expenditures were multiplied. Dummy fronts to conceal CIA operations were opened. Resupply operations were enhanced. By 1953 the Agency had over 10,000 employees.[15]

Dulles, McCloy, and Reinhard Gehlen

But there is more to the story of the birth of the CIA. Out of the ashes of World War II emerges an episode so dark in tone, so epic in scope, so powerful in its connotations that it was a state secret not exposed to any significant extent until the 1970s. And it sheds much light on the genesis and excesses of the Cold War and the national security state.

As World War II drew to a close, many high-ranking Nazis, recognizing that defeat was coming, began to plan their own escapes. One was Reinhard Gehlen. He did not cut an imposing figure when he turned himself in to the victorious U.S. troops in May of 1945; and, over his protestations, he was immediately shunted off to a prison camp.[16]

Gehlen had been a commander in Hitler's Foreign Armies East, responsible for German military intelligence throughout Eastern Europe and the Soviet Union. In addition to intelligence work, he had created a network of fascist paramilitary groups to fight the vaunted communist threat in Eastern Europe. And by 1945 he was a potentially major player in any anti-Soviet agenda.

Gehlen had surrendered, calculating that the best way to save himself was to offer his formidable intelligence organization to U.S. intelligence as a bargaining chip. He was sure that when the right people realized who he was, the fear in the Allied camp of the communist threat would induce the Office of Strategic Services (OSS), America's wartime precursor of the CIA, to consider his offer seriously.

Allen Dulles did not disappoint Reinhard Gehlen. Dulles was chief of the Berlin OSS office, under General William Donovan. He had been dreaming of incorporating Gehlen's operation since 1944.[17] Plans for a post-war, allied, anticommunist intelligence organization had been in the works since then. Donovan and Dulles had been against the official policy of prosecuting all Nazi war criminals and had said so to Roosevelt.[18] Indeed, Dulles kept the details of his plans secret from Roosevelt and then Truman. Both Donovan and Dulles, it seemed, saw Gehlen's organization as a prime asset in their scenario for a postwar CIA.

By late summer of 1945, Dulles had finished his negotiations with Gehlen. In September of 1945, Gehlen and six of his aides were flown to Washington by Eisenhower's chief of staff, General Walter Bedell Smith (another future DCI), for high-level meetings. The Gehlen Organization was transferred, and on Gehlen's terms.[19] It remained intact and under his control, "justified" under the rubric of mutual defense against the communist menace.

The United States agreed to finance and support the new network until such time as a new German state would take it over. In 1949, Gehlen signed a contract worth five million dollars a year to work for the CIA.[20] And in 1950, High Commissioner of Germany, John McCloy, appointed Gehlen as adviser to the German chancellor on intelligence.[21] Ultimately Gehlen would become the chief of intelligence of the Federal Republic of Germany. It was an incredible deal. Gehlen got everything he could have asked for. (In addition, this extraordinary agreement was what allowed men like Klaus Barbie and Josef Mengele, to escape to South America.[22]) From the ruins of defeat, the virtual head of Hitler's intelligence became the chief of one of the largest intelligence agencies in the postwar era. A man who should have been imprisoned and prosecuted for war crimes[23] became a wealthy and respected official of the new Germany.

By consummating the Gehlen deal, Allen Dulles accomplished two things. First, he signaled that the hallmark of the coming national security state would be anticommunism. Morality, honesty, common sense, these would all be sacrificed at the altar of this new god. Second, he guaranteed that the future successor to the OSS, the Central Intelligence Agency, would be compromised in a strange way: it would be viewing the new red threat not through American, but through German—indeed Nazi—eyes, an incredible distortion, since in essence Gehlen was selling Hitler's view of the Soviet Union and communism. Not coincidentally, this was a view that dovetailed with Dulles's. Morality fell by the wayside; in Dulles's words about Gehlen, "He's on our side and that's all that matters."[24] Finally, we see that Dulles had no compunctions about overriding orders from above when he felt that *his* vision of national security was at stake.

This was the line that Dulles sold Truman at the birth of the Agency, the same line Dulles implemented as Eisenhower's Director of Central Intelligence. It is one of the more glaring ironies in recent history that future CIA Director Allen Dulles was appointed to the panel that investigated the circumstances of President Kennedy's murder. If there were a plot that involved and exposed any part of the national security apparatus, Dulles would doubtless hide the trail in order to cover up a crime of this superstructure, which he himself had helped construct. This is an important part of our story since, as we shall see, Dulles was the single most active member of the Warren Commission.

The Dulles Brothers and the Cold War

In 1953 General Dwight D. Eisenhower took over the White House. Although his public image was that of an avuncular, charming old man—a university president and citizen-soldier—he was in reality a hard-nosed Cold Warrior, adept on the international stage of power plays and intimidation. Eisenhower had developed a healthy respect for espionage and secret operations through his experience in World War II with the SIS, the French Resistance, and the OSS. He firmly advocated and implemented the full use of this type of agency in a wide variety of roles. In 1952, the Democratic Party's response to the communist threat, commonly named "containment," was inadequate, according to the Republican Party. In the presidential campaign, the GOP ridiculed the idea of keeping the Soviet empire confined, of merely parrying future expansion and waiting for the communist world to collapse. Its spokesmen advocated something more radical and dangerous. Sometimes it was termed "liberation." Sometimes it was called "rollback." Either way, it meant that the U.S. should go beyond resisting future Soviet advances. It should actively begin to free those people it considered already enslaved by communist doctrine and power.

While Eisenhower never clearly embraced this policy, he came close.[25] He had no problem with its endorsement by Secretary of State John Foster Dulles or Vice President Richard M. Nixon. But secretly, Eisenhower agreed with containment. After all, he had been in conference with Truman and Marshall right at its creation in 1947 during the Greek-Turkish crisis. And during the Hungarian crisis of 1956, when Ike was urged by advisers like Nixon and Dulles to intervene directly against Soviet tanks and liberate Hungary, he chose not to.

Although he stopped short of rolling back the communists, Eisenhower was a dedicated practitioner of an active containment policy, at any price, in any place, or at the slightest provocation. His tool was the CIA. And the frequency and the alacrity of its use was greatly aided by the fact that his Secretary of State's brother, Allen Dulles, became CIA Director in 1953. Although Eisenhower came to his Cold War stewardship through mostly ideological eyes, with the Dulles brothers, the Cold War was more complex, sophisticated, and monetary. Prior to becoming part of the American foreign policy establishment, both brothers had worked at the giant New York corporate law firm Sullivan and Cromwell. John rose to managing partner and Allen became a senior partner. Here they served huge overseas clients like United Fruit and DuPont. In 1932, Allen saved a rich oil and mineral field for the wealthy Mellon family of Pittsburgh when he rigged the Colombian presidential elections by bribing one of the candidates.[26] With his prior experience in the State Department, where he had worked before going to Sullivan and Cromwell, Allen became quite proficient at the art of secret operations. When he became part of the OSS in World War II, he honed these skills even further. With these years of experience, when he became CIA Director, he was ready and willing to make huge changes in the philosophy and actions of the Agency. As some have written, it would not be improper to state that Allen Dulles revolutionized the CIA. The two previous Directors, Roscoe Hillenkoeter and Walter Bedell Smith, were military men. They generally believed that intelligence should be used to supplement military action. But Dulles's broad background in the State Department, the OSS, and at Sullivan and Cromwell gave him a much wider and more daring vision of what the CIA could be and do.

But we should add one other ingredient to what Dulles brought to his vision of the Agency. In his service to the upper classes at Sullivan and Cromwell, Dulles and his brother both worshipped at the altar of ruthless corporate Realpolitik. In other words, for these two men, the Cold War was more than about just ideology and the domino theory. It was about American versus Russian dominance in the resource rich Third World. With Allen Dulles, the acronym CIA came to stand for Corporate Interests of America. No method was discarded in his pursuit of their ends. Indeed, during his administration, the CIA perfected the art of the covert, paramilitary operation. As one study stated, "Probably at no time since World War II has violence—especially on a militarized level—in the execution of covert American foreign policy been so widespread as during the Eisenhower administration. Especially was this so with respect to U.S. relations with Third World countries."[27] In 1953, at the service of British and American petroleum interests, Eisenhower authorized Operation AJAX to undermine the nationalist government of Prime Minister Mohammad Mossadegh in Iran. The Dulles brothers cooperated on a plan for his removal with the British. The Shah, previously a constitutional monarch, fled the country at the time. With Mossadegh's overthrow, he now returned as a brutal dictator, and decades of Arab resentment in the Middle East ensued. In 1954, at the request of United Fruit Company, Allen Dulles's Operation SUCCESS caused the overthrow of the progressive Jacobo Arbenz government in Guatemala; again, decades of brutal, military-backed governments followed. It was during this Central American intervention that Allen Dulles gave an opportunity to men like Howard Hunt and David Phillips to cut their teeth in the art of government overthrows. In 1957, an attempt to overthrow Sukarno in Indonesia nearly destroyed his neutralist state and pushed him into forming an alliance for nonaligned countries—that is, those nations who wished not to be tied to either the Russians or the United States in terms of the Cold War. In Vietnam, the Dulles brothers helped construct and maintain the government of Ngo Dinh Diem in the south. They backed Diem's refusal in 1955 to agree to elections mandated by the Geneva Accords, the pact that ended the first Indochina War in 1954.[28] In 1960, Allen Dulles warned against an imminent communist takeover of the Congo and authorized a 100,000 dollars fund to replace the country's first prime minister, Patrice Lumumba, with a "pro-Western" group. This triggered a chain of events ending in Lumumba's assassination.[29]

All of these actions were aimed at controlling these Third World governments so that they would not be able to exercise their own free will in using their own resources for their own public good. This made it easier for American businesses to profit from exploiting friendlier leaders, some of them brutal dictators but backed by the USA nevertheless.

American Imperialism in Cuba 1925–1957

Finally, there was Cuba. Ever since the controversial, and increasingly despotic, rule of President Gerardo Machado in the twenties and thirties, there had been two poles of political power on the island. The first was decidedly leftist, as far left as communism. And this movement appeared to have certain ties to the Soviet Union. The second pole of power was a common one in Latin America after the Spanish were defeated and departed the continent: the upper classes, who allied themselves with the military. Going back as far as Machado's regime of 1925–33, a major figure in that alliance was then Sergeant Fulgencio Batista. And it is important to note here that as early as 1925, "officers from virtually every branch of the Cuban armed forces . . . had attended various military academies in the United States."[30] The combination of worker unrest, with withdrawal of American support, led to a military coup that ousted Machado; a coup in which Batista was an important figure. The problem was that the State Department did not really like Machado's successor, Ramon Grau San Martin.[31] Grau tried to enact certain programs benefiting the working class, like an eight-hour day and a minimum daily wage for sugar cane cutters. But, understanding what had happened to Machado, he also tried to maintain ties to the military. This turned out to be a difficult balancing act. Grau was overthrown in a military coup in 1934. This coup featured the newly self-promoted Colonel Batista.[32]

The second military coup in two years shifted the political spectrum in Cuba decidedly to the right. This movement was accented by the "massacres that accompanied the repression of political strikes involving thousands of workers" in 1934 and 1935, and helped wreck "the organs of mass democratic control, devastated workers' movement, and consolidated military rule in Cuba."[33] For the next twenty-five years, Batista took a powerful role in the Cuban state. He himself served two terms as president: from 1940 to '44 and from 1952 to '59. His two terms bookended a second term for Ramon Grau San Martin and a four-year term for Carlos Prio Socarras. But even though those two men were more moderate than Batista, they could only maneuver within the boundaries that Batista himself had already set with the remaining remnants of the left.[34]

Batista was so friendly with American interests that he lived in the USA when his first term expired. He shuffled back and forth between a hotel room at the Waldorf-Astoria in New York and his home in Daytona Beach, Florida. He returned to Cuba to run for his second term. But when it appeared he would be defeated, he staged another military coup to place himself in power again. The United States welcomed this power grab and recognized his government.[35] In his second term, Batista was much less accommodating to the progressives on the island. Therefore, between 1954 and 1956, new foreign investment in Cuba quadrupled.[36] One of the highest growth industries was the American dominated tourist resort business. Large tax breaks and other subsidies resulted in the construction of 28 new hotels and motels. Some projects, like the Havana Hilton and Havana Riviera hotels, had direct state financial assistance during construction.[37] Batista was so accommodating to American businesses that in 1958 he declared Cuba a tax-free haven. In other words, if an American company wanted to place its headquarters in Cuba, it would not be subject to state taxes.[38] By the end of 1958, the total book value of American enterprises in Cuba was the highest of any state in South America, save the then Standard Oil dominated nation of Venezuela.[39]

What made it all worse for nationalists in Cuba was the fact that, from 1952 through 1958, Cuba imported anywhere from 60 to 65 percent of its total needs from American sources. This caused the state to run large negative trade balances, which, in turn, Cuba had to finance through short-term borrowings via Wall Street and the International Monetary Fund.[40] But the familiar result was that the debt was not eliminated—it was just turned over. But the loans kept coming since Batista himself was so friendly and accommodating to American businesses. Because of this favoritism, enterprises like Moa Bay Mining Company cultivated ties with high-level Batista officials.[41] As one CIA operative stated, if you had a business problem, all you needed to do was get a call into Batista and he would fix it for you.[42] And this aid and cooperation extended over to the American Embassy, which did all it could to furnish help in obtaining both the contacts with Batista and a favorable business outcome. Both American ambassadors to Havana in this time period—Arthur Gardner and Earl T. Smith—were told to get along with the dictator: "We were not to do anything to overthrow Batista, but to support Batista as the Government of Cuba that we recognize."[43] And since Smith himself was very close to these business interests, he cast a blind eye to the mushrooming labor unrest, unemployment, and poor living conditions of the working class. This dissatisfaction was magnified by the growing corruption and bribery in government, not just from American capitalists, but also from the American mob—led by Meyer Lansky and Santo Trafficante—which had strong interests in the Havana resort hotels, and also the gaming industry and prostitution, which operated through them.

One company that Smith was close to deserves special interest here since it touches on various tangents to be discussed later. Smith, who had no previous diplomatic experience, owed his appointment largely to New York multi-millionaire John Hay Whitney. A year before his appointment, Smith had made large contributions to a Republican finance committee that Whitney had chaired. Whitney, in addition to owning the *New York Herald Tribune*, was chairman of a company called Freeport Sulphur. Freeport had various operations inside of Cuba. These dated as far back as 1932.[44] Two of these that are relevant to this narrative are Nicaro Nickel Company and the aforementioned Moa Bay Mining Company. Moa Bay would develop a nickel processing facility in New Orleans. In 1960 former Ambassador Smith was accused in the American press of negotiating a large tax reduction for Moa Bay with Batista at the behest of Whitney.[45] Although this dubious dealing was denied by Smith, it had been previously discussed in the Cuban press in early January of 1959. Smith resigned his post shortly after his work for Moa Bay and Whitney was exposed. CIA officer David Phillips's later protege Antonio Veciana—the man who said he saw Phillips with Lee Harvey Oswald three months before the assassination—received his intelligence training in Cuba in a building that housed both a Berlitz School and a mining company. And it is here, at this time, that Phillips appears to have met and recruited him.[46] Further, while in pre-revolutionary Cuba, Phillips knew Julio Lobo, a Cuban banker who contributed money to the setting up of the Cuban exile group in the USA called the *Directorio Revolucionario Estudiantil* or DRE. Fellow CIA colleague Howard Hunt later told the House Select Committee on Assassinations that Phillips ran the DRE for the Agency. The DRE is a group that Oswald would later have a strange encounter with in New Orleans in the summer of 1963.[47]

The Fall of Batista

Because of his mission statement—to get along with Batista in the name of American enterprise—Smith slighted the growing uprising on the eastern part of the island. In fact, some diplomatic cables from Santiago warning of this growing rebellion were actually doctored at the American embassy in Havana in order to discount this growing threat.[48] In fact, even in 1957, when 31 American Marines were kidnapped by the insurgents, the State Department favored negotiation rather than armed intervention.

It was not the Dulles brothers, or Eisenhower, or Vice-President Richard Nixon who first began to focus on the growing weakness and corruption of the Batista regime. It was the press and Congress. In the summer of 1957, the *New York Times* did a series of extensive interviews with mid-level trade union officials in three major cities in Cuba. The report discovered that the majority were politically anti-Batista. And on the eastern part of the island, in Santiago, the working class was characterized as being in "open revolt" against the government.[49]

But further, as Batista grew more and more unpopular and had to resort to more suppression and torture tactics by his paramilitary secret police, there began to be a debate in Congress as to whether or not to keep on extending military aid. This began in early 1958, and the focus on human rights and the brutality of what one senator called a "fascist dictatorship," forced many congressmen to, for the first time, reconsider Eisenhower's unqualified support for Batista. Some went as far as to call for an immediate halt to American military assistance to Cuba, plus a withdrawal of all military missions there. By the middle of 1958, even the State Department began to see that there was a serious problem in Cuba. For at this time, Batista sustained a serious defeat in his attempt to suppress the rebellion led by Fidel Castro and Che Guevara.[50] Some at State recommended that Batista resign, and a broad based transitional government be appointed. But Batista would not cooperate. Instead he staged phony national elections, which isolated him even further from the populace.[51] In the face of this obstinacy, the CIA began to devise desperate tactics to stave off a Castro victory. One alternative was to arrange a meeting between wealthy U.S. industrialist William Pawley and Batista. The goal, with Howard Hunt as the mediator, was to release from jail a former Batista opponent, General Ramon Barquin, in hopes that he could displace Batista and provide a viable popular alternative to Castro. Neither of these tactics came off as planned.[52] After Ambassador Smith informed him that the U.S. could no longer support his government, Batista decided to leave the country on New Year's Eve, 1958. No one knows how much money Batista embezzled and took with him. But estimates range well into the nine figures. On January 8, 1959, Castro and Che Guevara rolled their army into a jubilant Havana.

As we have seen, Eisenhower and the State Department were slow in recognizing just how bad the Batista regime really was and how potent the rebellion against it was. Eisenhower was also a bit slow in realizing who Castro—and the even more radical Che Guevara—really were, and what they represented. On January 15, 1959, the American Embassy in Havana wired its first dispatch to Washington describing the new government. It characterized it "as basically friendly toward the United States and oriented against communism."[53] This view should have been undermined by what Che Guevara had told the CIA about a former Batista agent now under his control. Jose Castano Quevedo had been second in command of BRAC, which stood for Buro para Repression de la Activivdades Communistas. This was Batista's own Gestapo service. Suggested to him by the Dulles brothers, BRAC was meant to hunt down and then torture, maim, and frequently kill suspected communists.[54] BRAC headquarters was immediately seized by the rebels as a symbol of everything evil about the former regime. Quevedo was now imprisoned and was about to be summarily executed. What made him even more despicable to Che Guevara was that he had been one of the many Batista officers trained in the USA. When the Agency asked him not to place Quevedo before the firing squad, the revolutionary replied that if he did not kill Quevedo for being a former Batista lackey, he would do so because he was an American agent.[55] Although the State Department seemed to be wrong about the sentiments of the new regime, the CIA was certainly getting a different take on the antipathy held by Che Guevara toward Batista's former northern ally.

But if the United States had any hope of having friendly relations with Fidel Castro, those hopes were soon quashed by American policies quickly instituted against him. Because Batista's programs had left the government shackled by debt, and because he had also looted the treasury, Castro and Che Guevara needed the extension of credit in order to make their new programs work. But since most of these new policies were aimed at providing relief for the poor and working class and, on the other hand, cancelling the American owned Cuban Telephone Company's 1957 rate increase, these extensions were not immediately provided.[56] In fact, private banks were calling for a quarantine of credit toward Castro until the USA learned all the facts about the new government. And these private banks advised international agencies, like the Export-Import Bank, to do the same. This initial reluctance to extend a hand included a freeze out by the White House. When Castro visited New York in April of 1959 to address the American Society of Newspaper Editors, Eisenhower seriously contemplated not granting him a visa. He eventually backed off that stance but proudly wrote that, "I nevertheless refused to see him."[57]

On this trip, Castro and his entourage did meet with some lower-level Treasury and State Department employees, and discussions about loans and credit did take place. But Castro had given his aides prior instructions to not formally request any funding on this visit. He wanted the exchange to be a process by which he could gauge the kind of aid that America was willing to grant his new government. The general idea put forth by the American side was that assistance was contingent on Havana's ability to negotiate an IMF stabilization loan.[58] Castro understood what this meant. And he knew that to agree to this would amount to a betrayal of his revolution. For as John Perkins has described in his book *Confessions of an Economic Hit Man*, these types of loans almost always mean that the general populace will experience lower wages, price increases, and social welfare budget cuts, and further, that the client state will stay in debt and that the American dominated International Monetary Fund would have a growing influence on the client's domestic policy agenda.

The American Empire in Cuba Falls

When Castro returned to Cuba, he then proposed his first major piece of reform legislation. This was the agrarian reform law, which was announced in May and passed on June 3. With this law, Castro was now indelibly marked as both a communist and an enemy of the United States.[59] The goal of the law was to redistribute land in order to provide for more efficient agricultural production. The maximum land allotment in area was capped at 995 acres. Any property over this size was expropriated by the state, and the owner was compensated for it. The problem was that the compensation price was set by previous tax records. Since most owners had deliberately discounted the worth of their property to lower tax payments, they could not now challenge the records without exposing earlier tax evasions. Most of these expropriations did not touch American interests. But Washington perceived this move as a precursor of what was to come. And when Cuba asked for advice on the program, the American embassy deliberately kept its proper distance.[60]

But this law was not just a watershed event in regard to Cuban-American diplomatic relations. It also created the first serious tensions on the island between Castro and Che Guevara, on one side, and the more conservative members of the Cabinet, plus the upper and professional classes, on the other. Philip Bonsal, the new American ambassador, took notice of this split and immediately cabled Washington about it: "Opposition to the government among middle and upper classes is mounting as a result of the agrarian reform law, and the Embassy has heard numerous reports that counterrevolutionary plots are germinating."[61]

This antagonism accelerated in June and July of 1959 when the Cuban government seized 400 of the largest American- and Cuban-owned cattle ranches, amounting to about 2.3 million acres. Several months later, Castro seized a Moa Bay Mining plant that processed nickel ore. In reply, the American Congress allowed various denunciations of the new Cuban regime by former Air Force Chief Pedro Diaz Lanz.[62] The United States now began to make threatening noises about its largest bargaining chip with Castro: it would lower its purchases of sugar unless sound and sure compensation was meted out. In the face of this, Castro and Che Guevara did not flinch. In early November, American agricultural and mining properties in Oriente and Camaguey provinces were seized. This included properties owned by large businesses like Bethlehem Steel, International Harvester, and King Ranch.[63] With this, the so-called "fact gathering" phase with the new regime was over. The businesses that had been at risk were now petitioning the State Department for action to salvage their investments. How angry were these businessmen who were now losing tens of millions of dollars? As Jim Garrison later discovered, Charles Wight of Freeport Sulphur appears to have instigated an assassination attempt against Castro.[64]

Therefore, in the fall of 1959, there began to be discussions about what the American response to these confiscatory actions would be. As a result, representatives from the CIA and State Department came up with a plan which was approved by President Eisenhower in March of 1960. It should be noted here: the approval of the plan came one month after Castro signed an economic agreement with the Soviet Union, thus ending the American monopoly of the island's trade.

The War Against Castro

The March 1960 plan amounted to a secret war against Castro.[65] The U.S. would first isolate Cuba diplomatically and economically by breaking off relations, embargoing the island, and urging other countries to do the same. It would also launch a propaganda drive against Castro, culminating in the clandestine recruitment of Cuban exiles. These policies were to be kept secret because they would offend Latin-American sensitivities by the raw display of American might. But the new Secretary of State Christian Herter (John Foster Dulles had died in May of 1959) recommended that the new leftist regime in Cuba be eliminated by the end of 1960.[66] In other words, for Herter, Eisenhower, and Allen Dulles, there would be no living with Castro and Che Guevara. In the span of one year—like Mossadegh and Arbenz before him—Castro was now marked for an Allen Dulles manufactured CIA coup. Especially now that Castro and Che Guevara had both expressed interest in spreading the revolution into other areas of Latin America. Also, by the end of 1959, many of the more "responsible" members of Castro's Cabinet had been replaced by leftist ideologues. For instance, Felipe Pazos was no longer head of the Cuban National Bank. The Argentine guerrilla, Che Guevara, now helmed it.

As these former civil servants were retired, they and former members of Batista's military were recruited by the CIA. One such officer who did so was David Phillips, who had been stationed on the island before the revolution. He wrote that, "In meetings with Cuban officials, I found some disillusioned with the drift toward communism and recruited them as intelligence sources for the CIA."[67] The Agency was now in the process of creating a "third force" consisting of the Cuban refugees and exiles who had fled the revolution. In the face of Castro's confiscation of property, thousands of middle- and upper-class Cubans had left with whatever wealth they could smuggle out. Most settled in the American Southeast: Florida, Georgia, Louisiana. Many had only one goal in mind after their resettlement: working for the immediate overthrow of Castro's communist government. With this new covert plan approved by Eisenhower, they and the White House shared a mutuality of interest.

One example of a former Batista civil servant who was recruited by the Agency was Sergio Arcacha Smith. Arcacha had served as a Cuban Consul in various outposts in South America, Europe, and the Far East under Batista. He then went into private business in Venezuela managing the Lago Hotel in Caracas. He then worked public relations for American businesses in Latin America, for which he earned excellent fees. He even paid a visit to the Rockefeller founded International House, a body meant to encourage international trade and globalization.[68] In 1959, Arcacha decided to leave Cuba.

He landed at the Alvin Callender Naval Air Base in Belle Chasse, Louisiana. Two Navy jets ferried the former diplomat, his family, and furnishings into the USA.[69] An Office of Naval Intelligence reserve officer—and friend of Guy Banister and Clay Shaw—Guy Johnson, arranged the drop off. Arcacha then became part of a CIA-backed Cuban exile group along with his friends Jose Miro Cardona and Tony Varona. Both Miro and Varona had served as Prime Minister of Cuba. All three men would become involved with the Eisenhower originated Bay of Pigs invasion.

As it turned out, the murder of Fidel Castro was also on the anti-Cuba agenda. At least for the CIA. The actual assassination attempts were made public by the Church Committee investigation of the CIA in 1975. Senator Frank Church and his staff had access to the Inspector General report on this subject prepared at the request of President Johnson in 1967. Some of the methods proposed were of the Keystone Kops variety. They included attempts to use poison cigars and ice cream sodas, chemicals to make Castro's beard fall out, and even the use of a poisoned seashell at his favorite skin diving beach. But there is little doubt that the CIA wanted someone to get close to Castro and assassinate him. In attempting this, they reached out to the Mafia. As mentioned earlier, the mob had been earning large profits in the hotel and resort business in Cuba. But months after gaining power, Castro decided to shut these down also. But in 1959, Castro actually imprisoned Santo Trafficante at the Tresconia detention camp on the outskirts of Havana. This was an easygoing prison, which allowed visitors. One of these visitors to Trafficante was reported to be Jack Ruby.[70] Which makes perfect sense since one of Ruby's close friends, Lewis McWillie, had reportedly worked for Trafficante in one of his Havana casinos.

Realizing that the mob was probably interested in getting their lucrative hotel/casino business back, the CIA made contact with private investigator Robert Maheu.[71] In the fall of 1960, Maheu got in contact with mobster John Roselli. Roselli then arranged a meeting for Maheu with Chicago don Sam Giancana and Florida godfather Trafficante. The letter said he had a contact on the island who could probably get the job done.[72] But the contact got cold feet about feeding poison pills to Castro. Trafficante then suggested Tony Varona who still had contacts in Cuba. This scheme entailed a man who worked in a favorite restaurant of Castro feeding him poison pills. But Castro stopped going to this particular establishment.[73] This failure ended the first phase of these assassination attempts—all of them prior to the Bay of Pigs invasion— thus leaving Castro in place to lead the opposition to that perfect failure.

As 1959 bled over into 1960, the USA and its allies tried to organize a banking boycott of Cuba. The State Department actively tried to block loans from Europe to Cuba. And they explicitly stopped in place a large Dutch,

French, and West German loan transaction to Castro. Therefore, with nowhere else to turn, in the first half of 1960, Cuba now signed trade and credit agreements with communist countries like China, Poland, and East Germany.[74] By backing Castro into the communist orbit, the planned isolation of Cuba was now becoming a self-fulfilling prophecy. Predictably, Eisenhower now said that Castro was beginning to look like a madman, and something had to be done about him. He even mused about blockading the island.[75]

In March of 1960 there was another important meeting at the White House about Castro. Dulles and his special assistant on Cuba, Richard Bissell, met with the president to discuss a Guatemala-type incursion against Cuba.[76] There were four main parts to the plan: creating a credible government-in-exile; launching a full propaganda offensive aimed at both Cubans in exile and those on the island; creating an on-island guerrilla unit sympathetic to the government-in-exile; and creating a paramilitary force outside Cuba to precipitate action.

Eisenhower approved the plan but insisted that all four parts be in place, especially the first, before he would initiate hostilities. Dulles thought this would take about six to eight months. Eisenhower wished to get rid of Castro before he left office. But if he did not, he felt that Richard Nixon, who both enthusiastically supported the plan and, as White House Cuba Project action officer, knew its details, would succeed him as President and carry it out well.[77]

Unfortunately for Eisenhower, Nixon, and Dulles, Jack Kennedy's election in 1960 was a big surprise.

CHAPTER TWO

The Education of John F. Kennedy

*"In the matter of the Batista regime, I am in agreement with
the Cuban revolutionaries. That is perfectly clear."*

—*President Kennedy to Fidel Castro, November of 1963*

It is difficult to imagine two major politicians as seemingly different as Dwight David Eisenhower and John Fitzgerald Kennedy. Their superficial differences are easy to list. Eisenhower was a traditionally conservative Republican. Kennedy was a liberal Democrat. At the time, Eisenhower was the oldest President to hold office, while Kennedy was the youngest ever elected. That age difference was visually dramatic: the former general was partly bald, white-haired, wrinkled, and stooped; Kennedy was youthful, with a full head of wavy, brown hair; he was effervescent, vibrant, with fashion-model good looks.

In the 1960 election, the Kennedy brain trust was well aware of these differences and worked assiduously to take advantage of them. Indeed, the idea of the "New Frontier" theme was created at the nominating convention in Los Angeles, when, with more than 50,000 in attendance, then Senator Kennedy accepted the nomination with these words: "We stand today on the edge of a New Frontier—the frontier of the '60s—a frontier of unknown opportunities and perils—a frontier of unfilled hopes and threats."[1]

Kennedy was challenging an image of eight Republican years of apparent security and quietude or, as one commentator has termed it, "years of excitement cushioned in complacency."[2] For Kennedy seemed like a new kind of liberal—well-informed, dynamic, moderate, fiscally prudent, yet one who could reach across lines of class and politics to create a consensus. Unlike Adlai Stevenson or Hubert Humphrey, Kennedy could not easily be pigeonholed by the Republicans.

But if there was one area where Kennedy and Eisenhower seemed to intersect, it was in their response to the communist threat. For all his freshness and energy, Kennedy was a prudent politician. He knew that to be branded soft on communism would be to invite political oblivion. Throughout his career, he had carefully cultivated anticommunist credentials, even on domestic issues. For instance, when he first began investigating labor issues in the House of Representatives, he targeted communist membership in American unions.[3] During the Senate voting to censure McCarthy for witch-hunting against the army, young Kennedy carefully dodged the roll call, failing to phone in his vote from his hospital bed. It was Kennedy's fence-sitting on the McCarthy issue that cost him the support of the liberal paragon, Eleanor Roosevelt, in his drive for the vice-presidential nomination in 1956.[4]

In the 1960 campaign, Kennedy was strong on national defense, claiming a huge missile gap existed between the U.S. and USSR. (In fact, the "gap" was decidedly in our favor; the U.S. had a ten-to-one advantage in missiles, and the Soviet Union had cut its military budget by one-half between 1955 and 1960.[5]) He was strong on defending the tiny islands of Quemoy and Matsu off the coast of China against the Chinese Communists—a crisis that had been all but extinguished by that time.[6] Most of all, he was tough on Cuba. In the famous election debate against Nixon, Kennedy used the Cuban issue like a billy club. When Nixon attacked the Democrats for "losing China," Kennedy shot back that Nixon was in no position to accuse anyone of not standing up to the communists, since his administration had allowed a communist takeover ninety miles off the Florida coast.[7]

Kennedy was even more specific in his prescriptions for dealing with Castro: "We must attempt to strengthen the non-Batista democratic anti-Castro forces. . . . Thus far these freedom fighters have had virtually no support from our government."[8] This was not accurate. As we have seen, Eisenhower had sanctioned formal backing of the recruitment and formation of anti-Castro forces and the attempted creation of a government in exile. During the winter of 1959–60 there were actually paramilitary operations of Agency-supervised bombing and incendiary air raids piloted by Cuban exiles.[9] It is hotly debated just how much Kennedy knew about the Bay of Pigs preparations during the campaign. Allen Dulles briefed JFK on the operation twice, once in July and again in September. Dulles has stated that at the first meeting only generalities were discussed and the only clandestine operations he revealed were radio broadcasts. Dulles did not reveal the substance of the second meeting, but after it, Kennedy went on record in two speeches in support of the freedom-fighting forces in exile.

Then, on November 18, president-elect Kennedy received a fuller briefing from Dulles on the proposed invasion. Again, it seems that specific details were not discussed. But Kennedy appears to have developed other channels both inside and outside the government to gather information on the planned operation.[10] In any event, Kennedy then showed some affinity with Nixon and Eisenhower about the need for alternatives to Castro. In 1960, whether because of or in spite of these similarities to the Nixon-Eisenhower positions, JFK won the closest election victory in American history. Out of nearly 70 million votes cast, Kennedy won by a bit over 100,000. The electoral vote was a more solid 303–219.

But below the level of campaign rhetoric, John Kennedy was not simply a more youthful version of Eisenhower. This was especially marked in his attitude toward the communist threat in respect to what was becoming known as the "third world," those developing former European colonies just achieving their independence.

In the 1950s, there was massive conformity in American politics about counteracting alleged communist infiltration or expansion into so-called free or neutral areas: it must be prevented, no matter what the price or circumstances. Since 1946, this attitude was increasingly vehement, explaining in large part the intensity of reaction to Castro's leftward turn in Cuba. Despite its internal differences, the communist world was portrayed as a hulking monolith, poised to enslave a precarious free world. Soviet actions right after World War II, the Alger Hiss case, the Rosenbergs' alleged theft of atom bomb secrets, the activities of the House Committee on Un-American Activities—of which Nixon was a member—the wild accusations of Senator Joe McCarthy, all these and more seemed to paralyze rational analysis and, ironically, give the lie to the self-proclaimed serenity of the golf-playing Eisenhower and the era taking his name. But what ensured a rigid, overwrought, knee-jerk reaction was the juggernaut of the domino theory.[11]

Like most political boilerplate, the theory had some relation to fact. After World War II, every Eastern European government had gone communist. All but Yugoslavia were closely allied with Stalin. Extrapolating from this, jingoists postulated that this chain reaction would be repeated if another country in any other area were to fall to communism. The peculiar relationship of the Soviet

Union to Eastern Europe, Stalin's legitimate fear of Germany,[12] the fact that China went communist under totally different circumstances and by itself in 1949,[13] the indigenous nature of most Third World liberation struggles—all this was ignored or distorted in this oversimplified, self-serving theory. Once the dominoes started falling, there was no telling where they would stop: the Philippines, Australia, Hawaii, maybe even San Diego.

Eisenhower was an avid believer in the domino theory. During his administration, one domino after another seemed to be constantly falling. After the French defeat at Dien Bien Phu in Vietnam, a treaty organization had to be formed or "the whole anti-Communistic defense of that area [would] crumble and disappear."[14] The democratically elected Arbenz government of Guatemala had to be subverted, or it would endanger Central America all the way up to the Rio Grande: "My God," Ike told his Cabinet, "just imagine what it would mean to us if Mexico went communist!"[15] The U.S. could not even "lose" tiny islands like Quemoy and Matsu "unless all of us are to get completely out of that corner of the globe."[16] He even postulated that the threat must be met in Vietnam or the dominoes would fall across the Pacific to Australia.[17]

This was a frightening scenario for politicians to ponder. Who would want to be responsible for the loss of whole areas of the globe?[18] And who better to broadcast the alarm than the aged eagle who had saved us from the barbarous Nazis?

As we have seen in the intervening years, the Communist Bloc was not a monolith, nor did the domino theory describe the real world; although the fear of it and of "losing Vietnam" led Lyndon Johnson into both national and personal tragedy in Southeast Asia. At the time there were some scholars and politicians (and many ordinary people) who were bold and imaginative enough to think of the world as more than just bipolar, free versus enslaved, and who wished to penetrate the surface of this new constellation of ideas and how they worked—especially in the third world.[19] One such person was John Kennedy.

Kennedy had always held a strong interest in and curiosity about foreign affairs. His first published book, *Why England Slept*, was an analysis of the reasons for that country's reluctance to face up to Nazi aggression prior to 1939. In 1951, Congressman Kennedy toured the Far East. According to his biographer, Herbert Parmet, it changed him a great deal: "He returned highly critical of . . . British and French colonialism . . . It enabled him to understand the potency of nationalism as a force more significant than communism and as something utilized by them to gain their own ends."[20]

But Parmet actually underplays the impact that this tour had on Congressman Kennedy. He also fails to detail what Kennedy actually did, where he visited, and who he met on this trip. In the author's view, this is a key part of the story, because it explains why Kennedy did what he did in his first year in office. Its an element that is too often ignored or slighted, both in books about John F. Kennedy—for example Chris Matthews's recent biography, *Jack Kennedy: Elusive Hero*—and, even worse, in volumes dealing with his assassination. This part of his biography helps delineate what made Kennedy's foreign policy unique in comparison to what came before (the Dulles brothers) and what followed afterwards (LBJ). It should be dealt with in some detail.

1951: Kennedy, Colonialism, and The Cold War

By early 1951 Kennedy had decided that he would not remain in the House of Representatives for another term. He had set his sights on the Senate seat held by Massachusetts incumbent Henry Cabot Lodge. But in order not to be characterized as a local or provincial politician, he knew he had to broaden his scope of interests. This meant that he had to set a higher profile in international affairs. So Kennedy's camp decided he should take two well-publicized foreign excursions. The first was, quite naturally, to Europe. The second one was a bit unusual in that his itinerary consisted of places like the Middle East, India, and French Indochina, including Vietnam. While in Saigon, he ditched his French escorts and decided to seek out the best and most honest reporters and diplomats. He wanted to find out for himself just what the violent conflict between the French colonizers and the Vietnamese was really all about. And further, if the colonized populace had any chance of winning the struggle.[21]

While in Saigon, Kennedy met an American diplomat named Edmund Gullion. Gullion advised Kennedy that France's Indochina war to hang onto Vietnam was not really about democracy versus communism. For the Vietnamese it was really about a choice between colonialism and independence. He impressed upon Kennedy that the Viet Minh rebellion in the south, supervised by northern nationalist leader Ho Chi Minh, could not be extinguished by France since too many Vietnamese were willing to die rather than stay a colony of the Europeans. France could not win such a long and brutal war of attrition.[22]

There is no doubt that his talks with Gullion and others had a strong impact on Kennedy's thinking about both the Cold War and the Third World struggle for independence. Robert Kennedy, who accompanied his brother on this journey, later said that the seven weeks they spent in the Far East had a major effect on Kennedy's foreign policy views.[23] And, in fact, its effect was shown in speeches Kennedy made upon his return to America. Speaking of French Indochina, he said, "This is an area of human conflict between civilizations striving to be born and those desperately trying to retain what they have held for so long." He later added that, "the fires of nationalism so long dormant have been kindled and are now ablaze. . . . Here colonialism is not a topic for tea-talk discussion; it is the daily fare of millions of men."[24]

It is worth noting here that Kennedy also took time to criticize his own State Department for what he thought was its lackadaisical approach to the true issues in the area. He pointed out that too many of our diplomats spent too much time socializing with and then serving the short-term goals of our European allies instead of "trying to understand the real hopes and desires of the people to which they are accredited."[25] What makes this last remark unusual is that young Kennedy was criticizing both a Secretary of State and a sitting president from *his own party*—Dean Acheson and Harry Truman. He then went even further and questioned the wisdom of the USA in allying itself with "the desperate effort of a French regime to hang on to the remnants of empire."[26] And, in fact, this was true. As historians of the Vietnam conflict know, the American commitment to that war began in 1950. This is when Truman and Acheson chose to recognize the newly propped up French proxy government in Vietnam led by their stand-in Bao Dai. In other words, Kennedy was not playing political favorites. Since Gullion, at the time Kennedy met him, was working for Acheson, Kennedy understood that the views of both parties about the Cold War in the colonial world suffered from a lame orthodoxy. Kennedy was so impressed by Gullion that he brought him into his administration when he was elected president.[27]

The first Indochina War, between France and Vietnam, lasted from 1946 to 1954. Already depleted by the impact of being overrun and then occupied by the Nazis, France could not economically sustain this long and difficult colonial war. In fact, it became so unpopular that native born French soldiers were not even asked to serve there. Other parts of the declining French Foreign Legion, from as far away as Madagascar and Tunisia, were made to supply troops. And by 1952, the USA was footing the bill for a large part of the war effort. So much of it in fact, that America reserved veto power over whether the French could enter into peace negotiations with Ho Chi Minh. And, in 1952, America exercised that option. Dean Acheson exerted pressure upon France not to attend a scheduled meeting with Viet Minh negotiators in Burma.[28]

On July 1, 1953—a year before the fall of the French empire in Vietnam—Kennedy spoke on the floor of the senate about why France would not win the war: "the war can never be won unless the people are won from sullen neutrality and open hostility to support it. And they never can be, unless they are assured beyond a doubt that compete independence will be theirs . . . at the war's end."[29] The following year, Kennedy tried to explain that Ho Chi Minh and the Viet Minh were popular because they were seen as conducting an epic battle against French colonialism. Whether they were communists or not was not the point. For, in Vietnam, they were first seen as liberators.[30]

Needless to say, Kennedy's advice was not heeded. He understood this. So in May of 1953 he wrote a letter to then Secretary of State Dulles. He asked him forty-seven specific questions about what the aim of American involvement in Vietnam was.[31] The following year, he got his answer—in rather dramatic fashion.

In March of 1954 Commander Christian de Castries's French garrison at Dien Bien Phu was being surrounded and trapped by the brilliant Vietnamese General Vo Nguyen Giap. The French asked the United States for help. Days of consultation ensued. John Foster Dulles argued to extend aid. Vice-President Nixon was also predisposed to send help. In fact, Nixon began a lobbying campaign to convert the press and congress to a hard line on the issue. The idea was to prevent the French surrender. At any cost.[32] The contemplated solution was to send in over 150 air sorties, code named Operation Vulture, to relieve the French garrison. The operation was to be topped off by the use of three tactical atomic weapons. When Senator Kennedy got wind of this, he again took to the floor of the senate and had what was perhaps his first defining national moment. He wanted to know how "the new Dulles policy and its dependence upon the threat of atomic retaliation will fare in these areas of guerrilla warfare." Then, during the actual siege, he again took the floor and said, "To pour money, material, and men into the jungles of Indochina without at least a remote prospect of victory would be dangerously futile. . . . No amount of American military assistance in Indochina can conquer an enemy which is everywhere and at the same time nowhere, 'an enemy of the people' which has the sympathy and covert support of the people."[33]

Eisenhower decided not to commit to Operation Vulture. But the day after Kennedy's speech, he announced that America would not retreat from its commitments in Indochina. He added that to do so would lead to a domino effect in Southeast Asia. Therefore, in September of 1954, John Foster Dulles organized the Southeast Asia Treaty Organization (SEATO), to protect that area of the world against further communist encroachment. But further, in the summer of that year, Dulles commandeered the American presence at the Geneva Accords. This served as a settlement conference for the first Indochina War. The conference agreed to a temporary partition of Vietnam between north and south in preparation for national elections in 1956. This would lead to unification under one leader. But the unification never came off. Although the USA orally supported the treaty, it did not actually sign the agreement.[34] Eisenhower and Secretary of State Dulles then used this as a pretext to actually subvert the accords. It was a two-pronged strategy. First, as the Eisenhower administration would do with Cuba, the U.S. "began an economic boycott against the North Vietnamese and threatened to blacklist French firms which were doing business with them."[35]

Then, in an act that would have epic American repercussions for two decades, Director Allen Dulles sanctioned a huge CIA operation to find an alternative leader for the South and to prop him up with American support. The man Dulles placed in charge of this Agency effort was veteran black operator Edward Lansdale. Lansdale engineered a huge psychological covert operation to bolster the American discovered leader of South Vietnam, Ngo Dinh Diem. Eisenhower and the Dulles brothers realized that Ho Chi Minh would overwhelmingly win any national election.[36] So now, with the CIA's help, Diem seized complete power in the South. He then announced that there would be no unification elections in 1956. Yet Diem proved so unpopular with the peasants in the countryside that, as early as May of 1956, Eisenhower had to send 350 troops as military advisors to protect him. John Foster Dulles actually crowed about this. In what is today a startling statement, he said, "We have a clean base there now, without a taint of colonialism. Dien Bien Phu was a blessing in disguise."[37] As Senator Kennedy feared, Secretary of State Dulles had been secretly planning for the United States to assume the French role in Vietnam. This therefore became President Kennedy's problem in 1961.

In 1956, Senator Kennedy attempted to make some speeches for the campaign of Democratic presidential candidate Adlai Stevenson. By this time he had seen that both parties were missing the point about independence for the Third World. Kennedy was now even more convinced that the nationalistic yearning for independence was not to be so quickly linked to the "international Communist conspiracy."[38] When Kennedy made some speeches for Stevenson he used the opportunity to attack the Manichean world view of the Eisenhower-Dulles administration. But he also alluded to the fact that the Democrats were not that much better on the issue:

> The Afro-Asian revolution of nationalism, the revolt against colonialism, the determination of people to control their national destinies . . . in my opinion the tragic failure of both Republican and Democratic administrations since World War II to comprehend the nature of this revolution, and its potentialities for good and evil, has reaped a bitter harvest today—and it is by rights and by necessity a major foreign policy campaign issue that has nothing to do with anti-communism.[39]

Again, Kennedy was not playing political favorites. But the content of the message was too much for even that liberal paragon Stevenson. His office now requested that Senator Kennedy make no further foreign policy comments associated with the candidate's campaign.[40] But Kennedy did not let up on John Foster Dulles, or Richard Nixon. He strongly objected to the "us or them" attitude that would not let a Third World nation be neutral or nonaligned. And then be allowed to choose a middle ground in the Cold War. And he also objected to the self-righteousness with which people like Dulles expressed this stark choice. John Foster Dulles's string of bromides on the subject, such as, "godless communism," and the "Soviet master plan," were met with this response from Senator Kennedy: "Public thinking is still being bullied by slogans which are either false in context or irrelevant to the new phase of competitive coexistence in which we live."[41]

1957: Kennedy Attacks Eisenhower on Algeria

In 1957, Kennedy again attacked the presiding foreign policy establishment of Eisenhower, the Dulles brothers, and Richard Nixon. And again, the issue was over French colonialism and American willingness to support it. Instead of Vietnam, the location this time was the colony of Algeria on the north coast of Africa. France invaded the territory in 1830 and, after a brutal imperial war, Algeria became a colony in 1834. But in 1954 a rebellion broke out. Having just lost in Vietnam, French Premier Pierre Mendes was not going to now give up Algeria, which was much closer to the homeland and was actually considered part of France. By 1957 France had 500,000 troops in the country to suppress this ferocious rebellion. Because the Algerian rebels fought guerrilla style and out of neighborhood cells, the war degenerated at times into torture, atrocities, and barbarism. When these were exposed, it split the French nation in two and eventually caused the fall of the Fourth Republic and the rise to power of Charles de Gaulle.

On July 2, 1957, Senator Kennedy rose to speak in the Senate chamber and delivered what the *New York Times* was to call the next day, "the most comprehensive and outspoken arraignment of Western policy toward Algeria yet presented by an American in public office."[42] As historian Allan Nevins later wrote, "No speech on foreign affairs by Mr. Kennedy attracted more attention at home and abroad."[43] It was the mature fruition of all the ideas that Kennedy had been collecting and refining since his 1951 trip into the nooks and corners of Saigon. It was passionate yet sophisticated, hard-hitting but controlled, idealistic yet, in a fresh and unique way, also pragmatic. Kennedy assailed the administration, especially John Foster Dulles and Nixon, for not urging France into negotiations, and therefore not being its true friend. He began the speech by saying that the most powerful force in international affairs at the time was not the H-bomb, but the desire for independence from imperialism. He then said it was a test of American foreign policy to meet the challenge of imperialism. If not, America would lose the trust of millions in Asia and

Africa. He then pointed out specific instances where the USA had aided the French effort there both militarily (through the use of weapons sales) and diplomatically (by voting to table the issue at the United Nations). He attacked both the administration and France for not seeing in Algeria a reprise of the 1954 Indochina crisis:

> Yet, did we not learn in Indochina . . . that we might have served both the French and our own causes infinitely better had we taken a more firm stand much earlier than we did? Did that tragic episode not teach us that whether France likes it or not, admits it or not, or has our support or not, their overseas territories are sooner or later, one by one, inevitably going to break free and look with suspicion on the Western nations who impeded their steps to independence.[44]

He later added that, "The time has come for the United States to face the harsh realities of the situation and to fulfill its responsibilities as leader of the free world . . . in shaping a course toward political independence for Algeria."[45] He concluded by stating that America could not win in the Third World by simply doling out foreign aid dollars, or selling free enterprise, or describing the evils of communism, or limiting its approach to military pacts. (This last was a direct knock at John Foster Dulles, who specialized in setting up these kinds of regional alliances against the Soviet Union.) He then said the true appeal of America to these emerging nations "lies in our traditional and deeply felt philosophy of freedom and independence for all peoples everywhere."[46] This speech ignited howls of protest, especially from its targets—Eisenhower, John Foster Dulles, Acheson, and Nixon. The latter called it "a brashly political" move to embarrass the administration. He further added that "Ike and his staff held a full-fledged policy meeting to pool their thinking on the whys underlying Kennedy's damaging fishing in troubled waters."[47] Eisenhower complained about "young men getting up and shouting about things."[48] John Foster Dulles commented that if the senator wanted to tilt against colonialism, perhaps he might concentrate on the communist variety.[49] Jackie Kennedy was so angry with Acheson's disparaging remarks about the speech that she berated him in public while they were waiting for a train at New York's Penn Central.[50] Kennedy's staff clipped newspaper and magazine responses to the speech. Of 138 editorials, 90 were negative. Again, Stevenson was one of Kennedy's critics.

But abroad the reaction was different. Reporters from both England, like Alistair Cooke, and France, like Henry Pierre, comprehended that to consider the speech a political blast was to ignore its content and its intent, because Kennedy knew what he was talking about. Even the popular French magazine, *Le Monde*, wrote on July 10 that, "The most striking point of the speech of Mr. Kennedy is the important documentation it revealed and his thorough knowledge of the French milieu." Kennedy now became the man to see for visiting African diplomats, especially those from nations breaking free from the bonds of European colonialism. And as things proceeded, and the war dragged further on, and the French government fell, more and more commentators came to see that Senator Kennedy was quite wise in his observations. Eric Sevareid noted on CBS radio, "When Senator Kennedy a year ago advocated outright independence for Algeria, he was heavily criticized; were he making the same speech today, the response would pretty surely be different in considerable degree."[51]

But the speech had even more impact than that. As Alistair Cooke noted, the way the speech was perceived by the White House, and the derogatory comments made by its occupants, had now vaulted Kennedy's profile into high relief in Europe. He was the man pointing out their dogged and doomed attempts to hang on to fading empires. In America he had made himself the Democrat that Eisenhower had to "do something about." He was now the one Democratic hopeful that the Republicans were uniting to scorn. Cooke incisively concluded, "It is a form of running martyrdom that Senators Humphrey and Johnson may come to envy."[52] Cooke was correct. For five months after making the watershed Algeria speech, on December 12, 1957, *Time* published its first cover story on Kennedy. It was titled, "Man Out Front."

Every book about Kennedy's assassination ignores virtually all of the above. In my view, one cannot. For example, as author Henry Hurt has documented, while the Warren Commission was in session, in April of 1964, the French government requested information from the FBI on the whereabouts of one Jean Souetre. Souetre had been associated with the numerous attempts to murder Premier Charles de Gaulle. In fact, a whole paramilitary network had sprung up over de Gaulle's attempt to settle the Algerian war at the bargaining table. They killed thousands of French and Moslem Algerians, and attempted to kill de Gaulle dozens of times. This group was called the OAS, or Secret Armed Organization. It turned out that not only had Souetre been in the United States, he had been in *Fort Worth* on the morning of November 22, 1963—the exact place where President Kennedy was that morning. When Kennedy went to Dallas and was assassinated that afternoon, Souetre was there also.[53] As just pointed out, it was Kennedy's powerful Algeria speech that helped collapse the Fourth Republic and brought de Gaulle to power. As Hurt writes, it does not appear that the Warren Commission was ever cognizant of the French request for information on Souetre. In fact, the CIA documents that reveal that request, and the fact that Souetre was picked up within forty-eight hours of the assassination, were not declassified until

1976. When they were, further research revealed that Souetre had developed contacts with radical rightwing elements in Dallas and New Orleans, and also with anti-Castro Cubans.[54]

But beyond giving a motive to certain possible suspects, one cannot understand Kennedy's policies when he took office in 1961 without understanding this important background information. For once in office, Kennedy did break out of the Eisenhower classic Cold Warrior pattern, especially in regards to the Third World.

1961: Kennedy Breaks with the Cold War Consensus

Congo is the second largest country in Africa, and one of the largest in the world. It was first colonized by Leopold II of Belgium in the 1870s and formally annexed in 1885. Leopold's regime was one of the most barbarous in colonial history. The great export at the time was rubber, and if the natives did not meet quota they were maimed by having a limb amputated. Adam Hochschild, in his book *King Leopold's Ghost,* estimates that perhaps as much as half the population of the country was decimated during Leopold's reign, which lasted until 1908. Leopold's colonization was so brutal that it became infamous. The British exposed it in a report, and Joseph Conrad wrote a classic novel, *Heart of Darkness,* about it. International opinion was so outraged that the Belgian parliament decided to take over administration of the state from the king.

By 1960, a native revolutionary leader named Patrice Lumumba had galvanized the nationalist feeling of the country. Belgium decided to pull out. But they did so rapidly, knowing that tumult would ensue and they could return to colonize the country again.[55] After Lumumba was appointed prime minister, tumult did ensue. The Belgians and the British backed a rival who had Lumumba dismissed. They then urged the breaking away of the Katanga province because of its enormous mineral wealth. Lumumba looked to the United Nations for help, and also the USA. The former did decide to help. The United States did not. In fact, when Lumumba visited Washington in July of 1960, Eisenhower deliberately fled to Rhode Island.[56] Rebuffed by Eisenhower, Lumumba now turned to the Russians for help in expelling the Belgians from Katanga. This sealed his fate in the eyes of Eisenhower and Allen Dulles. The president now authorized a series of assassination plots by the CIA to kill Lumumba.[57] These plots finally succeeded on January 17, 1961, three days before Kennedy was inaugurated.

His first week in office, Kennedy requested a full review of the Eisenhower/Dulles policy in Congo. The American ambassador to that important

African nation heard of this review and phoned Allen Dulles to alert him that President Kennedy was about to overturn previous policy there.[58] Kennedy did overturn this policy on February 2, 1961. Unlike Eisenhower and Allen Dulles, Kennedy announced he would begin full cooperation with Secretary General Dag Hammarskjold at the United Nations on this thorny issue in order to bring all the armies in that war-torn nation under control. He would also attempt to neutralize the country so there would be no East/West Cold War competition. Third, all political prisoners being held should be freed. Not knowing he was dead, this part was aimed at former prime minister Lumumba, who had been captured by his enemies. (There is evidence that, knowing Kennedy would favor Lumumba, Dulles had him killed before JFK was inaugurated.[59]) Finally, Kennedy opposed the secession of the mineral-rich Katanga province. The secession of Katanga was a move very much favored by the former colonizers, Belgium, and their British allies. Thus began Kennedy's nearly three year long struggle to see Congo not fall back under the claw of European imperialism. This story is well captured by Richard Mahoney in his milestone book *JFK: Ordeal in Africa*. As we shall see, whatever Kennedy achieved there, and it was estimable, was lost when Lyndon Johnson became president.

In Laos, on the last day of 1960, Eisenhower had commented to the Chairman of the Joint Chiefs of Staff, "we cannot afford to stand by and allow Laos to fall to the Communists. The time may soon come when we should employ the Seventh Fleet, with its force of Marines."[60] To which General Lemnitzer replied that the proper units had already been alerted. The communists in this case were the Pathet Lao, who were allied with the forces of Ho Chi Minh. They were attacking the Royal Lao Government and its army, which was allied with provincial Hmong guerrillas. These latter groups were all supplied with money, weapons, supplies, and trainers by the CIA and the Pentagon. As this December 31, 1960 meeting ended, Eisenhower reiterated that Laos could not fall, "even if it involves war in which the U.S. acts with allies or unilaterally."[61] Further, if there were a coalition government, the Pathet Lao were not to be included. In a meeting with president-elect Kennedy on January 19, 1961, Eisenhower stressed how important Laos was in the overarching duel with the Soviets. If no political settlement was possible, the outgoing president advised JFK that the USA must intervene. Laos was the key to Southeast Asia, and if we did not act, it would endanger Thailand, Cambodia, and South Vietnam. He said it would be fatal to allow the communists as any part of a new government; and if we had to act unilaterally, then we should do so.[62]

When Kennedy entered office, he quickly let it be known he was very interested in a political solution in Laos.[63] At his first press conference, Kennedy said that he hoped to establish Laos as a "peaceful country—an independent country not dominated by either side."[64] He appointed a task force to study the problem, was in regular communication with it and the Laotian ambassador, and decided by February that Laos must have a coalition government, the likes of which Eisenhower had rejected out of hand. Kennedy also had little interest in a military solution. He could not understand sending American troops to fight for a country whose people did not care to fight for themselves.[65] He later told Richard Nixon, "I just don't think we ought to get involved in Laos, particularly where we might find ourselves fighting millions of Chinese troops in the jungles. In any event, I don't see how we can make any move in Laos, which is 5,000 miles away, if we don't make a move in Cuba which is only 90 miles away."[66]

He therefore worked to get the Russians to push the Pathet Lao into a cease-fire agreement. This included a maneuver on Kennedy's part to indicate military pressure if the Russians did not intervene strongly enough with the Pathet Lao. The maneuver worked, and in May of 1961, a truce was called. A few days later, a conference convened in Geneva to hammer out conditions for a neutral Laos. By July of 1962, a new government, which included the Pathet Lao, had been hammered out.[67]

In Vietnam, within two weeks of his inauguration, Kennedy encountered a proposal left by the outgoing administration for a stronger commitment to South Vietnam. This was presented to him by two men. One would end up being the resident hawk in the Kennedy White House, Walt Rostow. The other was the man who the Dulles brothers had originally sent to Vietnam to prop up Ngo Dinh Diem, General Edward Lansdale. Lansdale presented to the president a grim report he had prepared for the Eisenhower administration. It painted a dire picture of continuous communist encroachment into South Vietnam.[68] This marked the beginning of an unrelenting campaign by several Kennedy advisers to get the new president to commit American combat troops to Saigon. The attempt occurred no less than nine times in 1961. Each attempt was parried by Kennedy.[69] It all culminated in a week-long debate in the White House in November, 1961. Kennedy's response to the fact that all his advisers wanted him to send in combat troops is memorialized in a memorandum made by Vice-President Johnson's military attaché, Howard Burris. The Burris memo deserves to be paraphrased at length.

After Secretary of State Dean Rusk requested full support for an American commitment to South Vietnam, Kennedy vigorously argued against committing combat troops. Kennedy stated that, unlike with Korea, the origins of the this conflict were unclear. Kennedy said Korea was a case of pure aggression from the north. The conflict in Vietnam was not so clear cut. Therefore, even leading Democrats would have a hard time defending such a position in public. The USA would also need its allies since such a program would undoubtedly lead to much controversy. He then added that much manpower and material had been spent there already and yet there was little to show for it. And, before that, the French had spent even more with very little success. Kennedy explained that this was because guerrilla warfare in the jungle was very difficult to fight, especially with an enemy who was nowhere and everywhere at the same time. When others tried to divert his thought process, Kennedy returned the discussion to what would be done next in Vietnam, not whether or not the U.S. would become involved.[70] Kennedy's ultimate decision was to send in 15,000 American advisers to help South Vietnam fight the war.

Kennedy's arguments for direct nonintervention clearly hark back to his 1951 conversations with Gullion in Saigon. Interestingly, as Gordon Goldstein points out in his book *Lessons in Disaster*, when Lyndon Johnson began his policy of escalation in 1965–66—that is, the direct insertion of tens of thousands of American combat troops—he drew succor knowing that former president Dwight Eisenhower would back him in that policy. In fact, Eisenhower wanted LBJ to request that his entire Cabinet resign as soon as he took office.[71] Eisenhower then unhesitatingly backed Vietnam commander William Westmoreland's recurrent calls for more ground troops. Eisenhower even went as far as saying ". . . he would use any weapons required, adding that if we were to use tactical nuclear weapons, such use would not in itself add to the chance of escalation."[72] This rather shocking contemplation of the use of tactical atomic weapons shows that Operation Vulture was only shelved because Vietnam was a foreign war at the time.

But as several authors have shown, Kennedy was insistent that he was *not going* to insert American combat troops to fight the Vietnam War. And with Goldstein's book about National Security Adviser McGeorge Bundy, we now have on record that all three of Kennedy's chief military advisers—Bundy, Secretary of Defense Robert McNamara, and General Maxwell Taylor—concurring that this was not going to happen with Kennedy under any foreseeable circumstances. And, in fact, it did not. At the time of Kennedy's death, there was not one more American combat troop in Vietnam than when he was inaugurated. As we shall see, this changed with remarkable speed once Johnson assumed office.

The giant island archipelago of Indonesia had been colonized by the Netherlands in the late 1500s, and then dominated by the private Dutch East Indies Company for the next 200 years. In 1798, authority over Indonesia was switched back to the Netherlands, which retained control until the Japanese invaded the huge mineral rich country in 1942. When Japan was defeated, nationalist leader Achmed Sukarno declared Indonesia an independent country. But British army units soon began landing in Indonesia. They wanted to help the Dutch restore their colonial empire there. Sukarno and his Moslem Vice-President Moham-med Hatta tried for a diplomatic solution. This proved unpopular and a guer-rilla war followed. International pressure finally made the Dutch cede control over to Sukarno in December of 1949. But the Dutch decided to keep hold of the eastern island of West Irian.

Sukarno and Hatta tried to keep Indonesia a neutral in the Cold War. This way, the nation would be free to follow its own interests in its foreign policy. There were two prominent American-based oil companies at work in Indonesia at this time. They were both part of the Rockefeller owned Standard Oil empire: Stanvac and Caltex. Internally, these holdings were balanced by a large communist party called the PKI, which usually was loyal to Sukarno. In 1957 there was an assassination attempt on Sukarno. He blamed this on the Netherlands and used it to take control of the last Dutch business holdings in Indonesia. The CIA, which was already funneling money to the opposition, blamed the murder attempt on the PKI.[73]

The large influence of the PKI, Sukarno's seizure of the Dutch interests, and his desire to "go it alone" in his foreign policy now made him a target for another overthrow attempt by the Dulles brothers. As one CIA officer later wrote, the first step was to manufacture intelligence reports about Sukarno in order to generate alarm in Washington.[74] When the American ambassador to Indonesia then wrote that he disagreed with these CIA assessments about Sukarno, John Foster Dulles had him removed and replaced with someone more amenable with his brother's intentions.[75] In late 1957, Allen Dulles secretly visited Indonesia to organize support for the upcoming coup attempt. This would use army officers, plus civilians who were bought off by the Agency, in order to arrange attacks on various islands. But the overarching goal was to make it appear as a local uprising. Not one in any way sponsored by the United States.

This cover story was demolished on May 18, 1958. During a bombing run that was part of the phony uprising, CIA pilot Allen Pope was shot down. He had enough American ID on him to prove that he was in the employ of the American government.[76] Since Pope's bombing run had killed many civilians, Sukarno was able to use it as evidence that it was the USA that was killing innocent Indonesians. This helped turn the tide with both the Indonesian populace and the army. Spurred on by this propaganda victory, Sukarnos's loyal forces now stopped the CIA-led rebellion. Prior to the Bay of Pigs, this was the Agency's single largest failed operation.

Three months after his inauguration, President Kennedy decided to invite Sukarno to the United States. Sukarno was at first reluctant to come, but he later relented. Since Kennedy wished to discuss the issue of Pope's imprisonment, he asked Dulles for the report on how Pope became a prisoner of Sukarno. Dulles gave him a redacted copy of the internal CIA report.[77] But even in this form, Kennedy understood what had occurred. After reading it, he exclaimed to an adviser, "No wonder Sukarno doesn't like us very much. He has to sit down with people who tried to overthrow his government."[78] Well prepared, and sympathetic to Sukarno's dilemma in relation to the USA, Kennedy managed to pull off a mutually beneficial meeting. He broached the idea of Sukarno freeing Pope, and he also arranged for a team of economists from Tufts University to come up with a plan on how economic aid could best be extended to Indonesia in nonmilitary ways.[79] When, in 1962, at the direct request of Robert Kennedy, Sukarno agreed to release Pope, President Kennedy now took the lead in helping Sukarno talk the Netherlands into returning West Irian to Indonesia. This was an issue that Eisenhower and John Foster Dulles, in deference to the Netherlands, had kept bottled up at the United Nations.[80] President Kennedy now made this transfer to Sukarno a priority. He sent his brother and veteran ambassador Ellsworth Bunker to personally visit both Sukarno in Indonesia and the Dutch at The Hague to hammer out an arrangement. In 1962, this agreement was approved at the United Nations and signed into law.[81]

As the reader can see, in all four cases—Congo, Laos, Vietnam, Indonesia—not only did Kennedy break with previous policy, but he actually went beyond that. In the cases of Congo and Indonesia, he endangered relations with European allies in order to favor emerging nationalist movements led by local leaders. Movements and leaders who had been perceived by Eisenhower and the Dulles brothers as to be either communist or communist leaning. In the cases of Laos and Vietnam, unlike Eisenhower, he simply did not believe either place was crucial to the national security of the United States. And therefore, neither was worth sending American troops into action. And because of his understanding of the forces of nationalism in emerging colonial nations, Kennedy was not enthralled by the dangerously flawed domino theory. Which, it should be noted, was not actually originated by John Foster Dulles, but by the Democrat Dean Acheson.

CHAPTER THREE

Bay of Pigs: Kennedy vs. Dulles

"That little Kennedy, he thought he was a god."

—Allen Dulles

The Bay of Pigs invasion of Cuba was first designed during the last year of the Eisenhower administration. It was meant to be the culminating action of the battle plans that originated in the White House in March of 1960. It was originally drafted by the CIA's guerrilla warfare expert Jake Esterline as a small-scale infiltration plan.[1] The idea was to unite with a larger group of dissidents on the island. It was thought this could be done since there was a group of anti-Castro rebels in the Escambray Mountains that this landing force could locate and unite with.[2]

This design was called the Trinidad Plan and had been approved by Eisenhower on March 17, 1960. It consisted of a group of 500 trainees and 37 radio operators. The CIA-trained Cuban exiles could be used as an invasion force, or as infiltration teams. But Esterline noted that any successful paramilitary operation would be "dependent upon widespread guerrilla resistance throughout the area."[3] In other words there had to be a significant number of resistance forces already on the island to recruit from. For even if all five-hundred men went in, this would not be nearly enough to combat Castro's standing army, plus his reserve forces.

Somewhere around the time of Kennedy's election, this concept was changed. A cable from Washington directed a reduction in the guerrilla teams to only 60 men. The rest of the exiles began to be formed into an amphibious and airborne assault strike force.[4] This may have been caused by Castro's aggressive internal war to eliminate any opposition forces to him inside of Cuba. By the end of 1960, all dissenting newspapers had been closed, and radio and television stations were under strict state control. Neighborhood spy teams had been set up to turn in counter revolutionary suspects. And thousands of them had been jailed.[5] The main organized counter revolutionary group on the island, UNIDAD, advised the CIA it was not yet ready to support any large military actions. Another factor impacting this decision was the difficulty the CIA had in supplying dissidents on the island by aerial drops. Only four of the thirty drops were successful.[6]

Therefore, in late 1960, CIA Director of Plans Richard Bissell altered the concept. It went from a slow, clandestine build-up of guerrilla forces to an overt assault which consisted of an amphibious landing of a strike force accompanied by aerial bombing. The idea now was to *trigger* an uprising, instead of preparing for one in advance.[7] The budget of the operation now tripled.[8] As Inspector General Lyman Kirkpatrick noted in his highly critical report: as the operation expanded, it reached a point where it simply was not plausibly deniable.[9] But yet, even with this, the departing Eisenhower still recommended the project to president elect Kennedy. He said all was going well with the plan, and he urged Kennedy to continue with it.[10] In fact, Eisenhower had broken off relations with Cuba on January 3.

Once this switch in concepts occurred, the preparations now became large scale. Kirkpatrick's report is highly circumspect of the preparations for the personnel. He criticized the training the Cuban exiles received in advance of the assault. For instance, the supervisor in Guatemala, which was one of the main training bases, never got written instructions from CIA HQ as to what type of training he was supposed to carry out. Kirkpatrick noted that the training in New Orleans was also confused, and the supplies never arrived as planned.[11] As we will see, CIA Officer David Phillips was likely involved in the training in New Orleans, as was David Ferrie.[12] There was also a diversionary element to the plan. This aspect was also trained in New Orleans.[13] Yet, in a mystery that has never been fully explained, this diversionary landing never came off.[14]

In the face of all these logistical and tactical problems, the CIA was still telling President Kennedy on March 1, 1961 that, "The Cuban paramilitary force if effectively used has a good chance of overthrowing Castro." And, in fact, one of the techniques used to prod a reluctant Kennedy into going along with the plan was to say that if the USA waited any longer, the Cuban military would be greatly strengthened and much harder to dislodge.[15] Another technique the Agency used was to tell Kennedy there would be a "disposal problem" with the Cubans. That is, what would America do with thousands of Cuban exiles who had been primed and ready to invade their homeland and take it from this Communist usurper?[16] When a skeptical Kennedy would ask Dulles and Bissell probing questions about tactics, Dulles would ultimately reply that he felt more confident about this operation than he did the operation against Guatemala in 1954.[17] (As we will see, there is strong evidence that, not only was Dulles prevaricating here, but he knew he was doing so at the time.) But no matter how hard the Agency tried, Kennedy was never enthusiastic about the plan. When Arthur Schlesinger asked him what he thought about the invasion, Kennedy replied that he thought about it as little as possible.[18] And Dulles understood Kennedy's distance. He later referred to the CIA invasion plan as "a sort of orphan child JFK had adopted—he had no real love and affection for it."[19] Therefore, he and Bissell knew they had to boost his enthusiasm for it, by any means necessary. In the middle of March, about one month before the invasion, the CIA gave Kennedy one of its most boldly tendentious reports of all. It said that Castro's popularity was diminishing and that only 20 percent of the public supported him. It further said that many Cubans thought Castro would fall soon. Worst of all, it predicted that if a real fight against Castro were to begin, 75–80 percent of the militia units would defect.[20] The true facts indicated the opposite: Castro had just rounded up the last of the active resistance groups hidden in the Escambray Mountains.[21] Therefore, when the invasion occurred, not one resistance fighter from the island ever got to the beach. In other words, there was no real, organized dissident force for the invasion to unite with at all.

Kennedy also asked: What would the force do if it got pinned down on the beach? Dulles and Bissell replied that they would then "go guerrilla." But yet, the guerrilla-style training had never really been part of the training camp curriculum. And the new location for the invasion was separated from the mountains by eighty miles of swamp. How could any surviving force trek that far if they were under fire?[22] Yet according to Arthur Schlesinger, who was in the White House at the time, it was the contingency of "going guerrilla" that ultimately convinced Kennedy to go along with the plan.[23]

In the middle of March, Kennedy asked that the original plan, with a landing at Trinidad, be changed. He thought that it too much resembled "a small-scale World War II type of amphibious assault."[24] He requested an "unspectacular landing" with minimal, if any, air support. The idea was to land small groups, or cadres, which were thoroughly prepared for guerrilla operations. In fact, at one meeting in February, Kennedy asked, "Could not such a force be landed gradually and quietly and make its first major military efforts from the mountains—then taking shape as a Cuban force within Cuba, not as an invasion force sent by the Yankees?[25] So clearly, Kennedy did not like the CIA's frontal assault plan. Further, and this was to be a point of heated controversy after the operation failed, Kennedy's revision envisioned air operations only *after* the landing force had secured a beachhead.[26] In light of this, the CIA therefore switched the landing site from Trinidad, in the center of Cuba on the south coast, to Playa Giron, which was slightly west. One of the specific reasons this site was chosen was because, "The beachhead area contains one and possibly two airstrips adequate to handle B-26's."[27] But it became obvious that the CIA needed some air cover to land their strike force version of the plan, and they insisted on this. Yet even under those circumstances Kennedy still resisted. He asked Bissell, "Do you really have to have these air strikes?" To which Bissell replied that they would work to have minimum noise from the air and that Cubans on the island would join in an uprising quickly[28] Another reason that the Playa Giron site was chosen was because there were no known "enemy forces (even police) in the area, and it is anticipated that the landing can be carried out with few if any casualties and with no serious combat."[29]

If there were to be "few casualties" and "no serious combat" then Dulles and Bissell must have been anticipating the element of surprise. Two things tended to mitigate this idea of "surprise." First, numerous stories on the guerrillas's training in Guatemala began to appear in the American press: *The Nation* ran an editorial in its November 19, 1960, issue; pictures appeared in the *Miami Herald* the same month; in January 1961, a detailed account finally made the front page of the *New York Times*.[30] Then, on March 17, one month before the invasion, that paper actually predicted an invasion of Cuba.[31] Any Castro spy or sympathizer—of which there were many in the U.S.—could have sent him any of these articles. Beyond that, Castro was getting intelligence reports about riots taking place in Guatemala over the training of the Cuban brigade there.[32] Secondly, in direct contradiction of the above, *there was* a police force at Playa Giron the night of the invasion.[33] That force relayed a message to Castro. And Castro—who had placed his army on high alert in early April and placed his troops near probable landing sites—quickly deduced that this was the awaited invasion and not a diversion. Within ten hours he had his regular troops at the beach. In fact, Castro had been informed as to when the last landing ship had left Guatemala.[34]

We should note here that there was a political element to the plan. The CIA project officer, Tracy Barnes, had appointed E. Howard Hunt to piece together a group of leaders who, if the invasion succeeded, would then constitute a new government in Cuba.[35] Hunt, now reunited with his Guatemala coup colleague David Phillips—who was director of propaganda on the project—was happy to be working again with his old chums like Phillips and Barnes. As he himself noted, it was "a cadre of officers I had worked with against Arbenz."[36] In fact, Hunt was informed that Phillips—who had been stationed in Havana for three years prior to the revolution—had already been at work on organizing Cuban students, women, and professional groups against Castro.

As anyone who has studied him knows, Hunt was quite conservative in his politics. A former cohort said that, "Howard was a regular rightwing nut" and a big backer of McCarthy in the fifties.[37] Therefore, like certain business organizations we have mentioned, he proposed killing Castro in 1960 as a part of the operation.[38] This murder reflex came from two things. First, his vehement Cold War attitude, which is exemplified by the following: "There can be no peace and security in the Western Hemisphere until communism is eradicated from Cuba. This can only be done with force of arms—and time is running out."[39] It also stemmed from his experience from the overthrow of Jacobo Arbenz a decade earlier. As Larry Hancock has amply demonstrated, assassination was clearly a part of that operation, which Barnes, Allen Dulles's Golden Boy, also was project officer on.[40] After analyzing the evidence in newly declassified documents of the successful coup, Hancock writes: "Clearly . . . CIA field staff were very much involved with the subject of assassination and actively involved in preparing surrogate personnel to carry out political eliminations."[41] Further, the Agency had prepared an assassination manual in advance as part of the project. The manual had an organization chart showing how elimination teams would work during the coup. At a meeting of the coordinating team in March of 1954, three months before the coup, there was a discussion of the killing of fifteen to twenty top Guatemalan leaders using trained assassins from the neighboring Dominican Republic.[42] Therefore, from this previous experience, Hunt understood that assassination was something not just to be tolerated, but planned upon.

Because of this outlook, as the CIA evolved its political front (originally called the Frente Revolucionario Democratico, or FRD) for the operation, two things became prevalent. First, these men were to be mostly figureheads. As both Arthur Schlesinger and Lyman Kirkpatrick have pointed out, the Agency looked upon these men with condescension. Kirkpatrick concludes in his internal Agency review that the political leaders visited the brigade recruits only one time, in March.[43] Kirkpatrick then goes on to comment that this was an example of the Agency's "high-handed attitude toward Cubans that became more and more evident as the project progressed."[44] He then says that this attitude contributed to the state of mind of the exiles that this was really an American project, not a Cuban one. And since this was the case, the Agency pitched many of their written FRD propaganda manifestos at investors and bankers. Therefore, Kennedy adviser Schlesinger asked: How could they be expected to win the hearts and minds of the working class? Especially since Castro had been trying to help those men and women for the two years he had been in power.[45] Further, at least one of the leaders, Jose Miro Cardona, asked Schlesinger on April 12 why he, a Cuban exile leader, did not know any specifics about the plan.[46] This was just five days before the launch of the invasion.

When Hunt was added to the political arm of the operation, the name of the Cuban political group evolved into the CRC, or Cuban Revolutionary Council. Its main members were Miro, Tony Varona, and Manuel Artime (the last was extremely close to Hunt). And a second point now becomes more obvious. As Kirkpatrick writes, this was essentially a centrist spectrum, which eventually tilted right when Ricardo Rafel Sardinia was added in August of 1960.[47] This was by design. One internal CIA report stated that the Agency had "plenty of flexibility to choose the Cuban group we would eventually sanction as a provisional government."[48] In January of 1961, with Hunt now firmly in control of this aspect, another report stated that it was the Agency rather than the Cubans who were making all plans and decisions: "We have charted five different lists of proposed assignments for any future provisional government of Cuba and are compiling biographic data on those Cubans who might be utilized by us in forming a future Cuban government."[49] This last statement seems even stranger upon reflection. Because it seems to say that it will be the United States that charts out both policy and the people leading it if the invasion succeeded. In other words, it faintly sounds like a return to the days of Batista. And, although Kirkpatrick does not cite the author of the memo, the language and attitude seem reminiscent of Howard Hunt, who, with the exception of Artime, thought little of the leaders. And, in fact, Hunt himself writes in his book on the subject, *Give Us this Day,* that he was in charge of escorting the CRC exile leaders into a liberated Havana and staying on as an adviser after the first post-Castro elections.[50] Further, according to Hunt, until Kennedy was inaugurated, Richard Nixon was the action officer in charge of the Bay of Pigs at the White House. Any bottlenecks would be cleared by his representative General Robert Cushman, and Hunt could call Cushman anytime. Nixon, and his friend, the wealthy industrialist William Pawley, clearly favored more conservative recruits for the operation. And this is how Hunt was gladly proceeding. Until Kennedy was inaugurated.

At that point, Schlesinger, with Kennedy advisers Richard Goodwin and Chester Bowles, now recommended that the CRC become more liberal. The man they wanted for that liberal position was Manolo Ray. Ray was a civil engineer in Cuba who turned against Batista in 1957. He formed a highly effective underground movement against him, and when Castro took charge, he appointed Ray Minister of Public Works. Ray resigned when Castro began to nationalize industries and expropriate land. He now formed a resistance movement against Castro. In November of 1960, Ray left Cuba and entered the USA. Because he was considered to the left of the other CRC leaders, Artime and Hunt strongly resisted him. In fact, in the coming years, there would be a rivalry between Artime and Ray. Hunt despised Ray so much that when one of the directors of the CRC supported his joining the group, Hunt essentially expelled him.[51] But Kennedy insisted on including Ray in the CRC. He even had Bissell call Hunt to make sure it happened. This was something Hunt could not tolerate. Therefore, near the eve of the invasion, Hunt resigned his post rather than work with Ray. He moved over to the propaganda arm and worked with his friend Phillips.[52] But interestingly, Hunt writes in his book that this was just for him to get away from Ray. If the invasion had succeeded, he was still to fly with the CRC into Havana.[53]

The number of CIA employees and Cuban refugees involved in the April 17 invasion exceeded 3,000. As stated above, Dulles and Bissell assured Kennedy of its success. But from the beginning, the assault devolved into a debacle.

The fact that the planes used in the preliminary bombing expeditions on April 15 were owned by the United States was exposed. And since Castro understood an attack was coming, he had dispersed his Air Force over several sites so that no one sortie could eliminate them all.[54] Therefore, that mission failed to eliminate the T-33 jet fighters, which were active with machine guns two days later when the actual invasion began. Allegedly due to heavy waves, the diversionary landing near Guantanamo Bay could not take place. The main invasion force at the Bay of Pigs landed successfully, but two ships were sunk, with ammunition, communications gear, and aviation fuel, crippling radio contact among the exiles.[55]

But the two biggest mistakes were in the Agency's predictions of Cuban responses. Dulles and Bissell had told Kennedy it would take days for Castro to get troops, artillery, and tanks to the front. They also had stated that large numbers of Cubans would join the brigade once it landed. Both assertions were wrong. The Cuban people rallied to the island's defense, and, as stated above, large forces were deployed against the invaders within ten hours. In fact, by that time, the invasion force was already outnumbered. And Castro already had tanks and mortars at the front.[56] Conversely, and in a complete reversal of what the CIA told Kennedy, not one sympathizer reached the shore to aid the exile army. In fact, Castro later crowed how the relatively small amount of people in that area completely backed him.[57]

Just how bad was the planning for the operation? If anything, the coruscating Kirkpatrick report may understate it. Former Castro Air Force Chief Pedro Diaz Lanz had been a favorite of both Hunt and Phillips. But they could not find a position for him in the invasion in 1960. Out of the blue, he was recalled by the CIA in March of 1961. He was told to create a small landing force of about 160 men. When the CIA told them to leave for Cuba to land at Oriente province, some of them did not even have one week's training. Worse, they were not told of their landing site until they were at sea.[58] Worse still, no one was awaiting them upon their arrival. When Diaz Lanz sent a reconnaissance patrol ashore, they found that instead, there was a large Cuban force lurking there. They retreated. Diaz then radioed back to the CIA and asked for an alternative landing site. There was none for them. Diaz actually called this utter incompetence "complete treason."[59]

After twenty-four hours, Castro had enough infantry and armor at the front to prepare to polish off the brigade.[60] By April 19, forty-eight hours after the initial landing, the invasion force was completely frozen, unable to advance at all. With no beachhead secured, and in fact with Cuban tanks shelling the beach, the rest of the supply boats now retreated well over fifty miles offshore.[61] By the end of the second day, two of the three landing zones had been taken by Castro's forces.[62] Deputy Director Charles Cabell went to analyst Victor Marchetti and told him there were Soviet MIGs strafing the landing force. He tried to get Marchetti to relay that message to the White House. Cabell hoped to use this piece of false information to get Kennedy to send in Admiral Arleigh Burke's naval task force, which was about ninety miles off the coast of Cuba at the time. Marchetti refused since he knew by previous information collection that there were no MIGs in Cuba at that time.[63] Even with that fact in mind, there were still appeals to Kennedy to send in air power. He decided against direct U.S. intervention. But then, the CIA overruled Kennedy. They gave orders to fly missions to bomb Castro's airfields. But according to Kirkpatrick and Peter Kornbluh, fog prevented the pilots from locating the targets.[64]

In the midst of this disaster, the CRC was sending out messages—many of them penned by Hunt and Phillips—saying that Castro's regime was about to fall.[65] In reality, on April 19, less than seventy-two hours after the initial landing, the last part of the brigade in the last landing zone surrendered. Since the supply ships were stationed well over fifty miles offshore, the resupply effort was considered futile. This final force, with ammunition running out due to both the sunken and distant ships, was confronted with thousands of regular Cuban troops and several tanks.[66] When the invasion was defeated, U.S. ships ferried some survivors back to Florida. Castro captured more than 1,200 soldiers. Over a hundred members of the brigade were killed. On April 21, Kennedy stated in public that he took full responsibility for the failure. But in private, the very next day, he commissioned a White House inquiry led by General Maxwell Taylor into what had actually happened.[67] Taylor's report was filed in June. Kirkpatrick's report was filed in October. In November, Kennedy fired Dulles, Cabell, and Bissell.[68] What were the grounds?

One of the most interesting aspects of the Taylor Commission report is the testimony of Allen Dulles. Dulles understood that his job and career were on the line. Therefore his answers to difficult questions were evasive. When Admiral Arleigh Burke asked him if the responsibility for the conduct of the operation was not all at CIA, the following dialogue appeared:

> Dulles: But that was done by military personnel.
> Burke: But not under our command structure.[69]

General Lyman Lemnitzer, chair of the Joint Chiefs at the time, also scored Dulles on this point. When asked if he "or the Joint Chiefs were the defenders of the military aspects of the operation, or was it the CIA?" Lemnitzer replied that "The defenders of the military parts of the plan were the people who produced it and that was the CIA. We were providing assistance and assuring the feasibility of the plan."[70]

Dulles also tried to take back his and the CIA's earlier promises about the key component of internal uprisings that would aid the strike force. He said that in the revised plan, this was not so crucial. Robert Kennedy pounced on this denial:

> Kennedy: Then what was the objective of the operation?
> Dulles: Get a beachhead, hold it, and then build it up.[71]

Kennedy was flabbergasted at this reply: "How could you possibly do that—take 1000 or 1,400 men in there and hold the beachhead against these thousands of militia?" Later on, Dulles was further exposed on this point. For both Secretary of Defense Robert McNamara and Secretary of State Dean Rusk said the operation was reliant on the contingent uprisings. In fact, Rusk said that "the uprising was utterly essential to success in terms of ousting Castro."[72] When General Shoup, the Marine Commandant, was asked the same question, he said dependence on the uprisings was absolute; the operation's ultimate success relied on them. When Shoup and Lemnitzer were asked for the source of the intelligence on the uprisings—for which the ships were loaded with 30,000 extra rifles—both said the intelligence came from CIA.[73] So clearly, Dulles was prevaricating on this point.

The Taylor Commission then caught Dulles in another lie. Both Dulles and Bissell had told the White House that if the landing failed, the option was to "go guerrilla." The Taylor proceedings spent much time adducing this point. Dean Rusk said that if there were not an uprising, he had been told the landing force would head for the hills. He was then asked, "Was the point made that this area had not been used for guerrilla operations in this century?" Rusk replied that he did not recall that point being made.[74]

Lemnitzer said that he had been informed by the CIA that this was the contingency option also. In fact, he actually said, "Every bit of information that we were able to gather from the CIA was that the guerrilla aspects were always considered as a main element of the plan." He was then told that President Kennedy had that same impression, but the commission had discovered that this possibility never existed. Lemnitzer replied, "Then we were badly misinformed."[75]

In a rather surprising development, it turned out that not even the troops were informed that they were to go to the hills and fight guerrilla style if the landing failed. Two Cuban exiles testified that there was no plan to retreat to the mountains and fight like guerrillas. In fact, such an option was never even mentioned to them.[76] When Dulles was confronted by this above testimony, he was then asked: How could the troops have gone guerrilla without training or instruction? His reply was startling: "I wouldn't wholly buy that. These people had a cadre of leaders—20 percent to 30 percent would be the leaders. They knew about guerrilla warfare. The guerrillas in World War II never had any training until they got into a guerrilla operation."[77]

In other words, the brigade members were supposed to invent techniques as they went along. These are the gyrations of a man frantically treading water to (unsuccessfully) avoid going under. And for good reason. One of the most significant witnesses undermining Dulles's oversight of the plan was Hunt's nemesis Manolo Ray. As author Michael Morrisey points out in his analysis of Maxwell Taylor's report, it seems that the CIA never really wanted what Kennedy actually envisioned, a true guerrilla-style counterrevolutionary force in the Escambray Mountains of central Cuba. For instance, Ray wanted the CIA to aid in his plan to take the Isle of Pines, a large island off the southwest corner of Cuba, thereby freeing political prisoners located there and maintaining a good geographic launching pad for raids on Havana and also to unite with rebels in the Escambrays. Ray testified that the Agency never supported, or seriously entertained, these guerrilla tactics.[78] As previously stated, much of this is probably due to Hunt's sneering and imperious attitude toward Ray. Ray went on to tell the commission that he—and others—were never for the strike-force plan. Ray wanted to use his contacts on the island, especially in the labor movement, to cause genuine uprisings that would unite with tactically trained guerrillas. Then came a colloquy that harks back to the CIA's control of the political arm and Howard Hunt's political philosophy. Ray stated that: "Another thing that was wrong with the plan was the fact that many of the elements of the invasion force represented the old [Batista] army. We felt that it was wrong to give the impression that the old army was coming back, and we protested."

In fact, in Ray's eyes, even the leader of the brigade was a Batista man:

> Q: Did you approve of Pepe San Roman as the commander?
> Ray: No. Everyone knew that he liked Batista. His brother had also fought against Castro in the Sierra Maestra.[79]

One of the points that Morrisey brings up about the failure of the invasion and the inability of the CIA to coordinate things properly with the White House is this: Where was Allen Dulles while the disaster was happening? After all, he was the Director of the Agency at the time. This was really his baby, since he was one of the first to declare Castro an enemy of the USA. Dulles chose to be in Puerto Rico on the day of the landing. But further, in the two major reports about this operation, there is no record of him phoning in from there to contribute instructions or relieve bottlenecks and confusion. For all intents and purposes, while his operation was collapsing everywhere, it was his deputy, General Charles Cabell and Director of Plans Bissell who were running the operation. As we have seen, Cabell tried to get Victor Marchetti to fabricate a story about Russian MIGs in Cuba. But further, as Morrisey notes, these two men made two serious errors in judgment. When Dean Rusk gave them the opportunity to phone President Kennedy about air strikes from Nicaragua the morning of the invasion, they declined. Then, on the third day, when the brigade was running out of ammunition, Cabell had the opportunity to request naval assistance in escorting supply boats to the front. The CIA refused to make any request. And this marked the end of the invasion.[80]

Yet, on April 19, when the invasion was now defeated, when the operation he had been preparing for over a year was now in tatters, Dulles appears to have met with, not President Kennedy, but Richard Nixon.[81]

As Morrisey asks in his essay, could such a string of errors and incompetence, such confusion, such rudderless leadership, could this all be just happenstance? Or was there something else at work underneath it all? As both Larry Hancock and David Talbot have noted, there was important information that was kept from the White House about the operation. In 2005, a primary source CIA history on the invasion was finally released to the public. In it was a November 1960 CIA memo prepared for Bissell that said that "our concept . . . to secure a beach with airstrip is now seen to be unachievable, except as joint Agency/DOD/CIA/Pentagon action." Peter Kornbluh states that this memo demonstrates, five months in advance, that the Agency knew it could not achieve a beachhead without direct Pentagon intervention. But they went ahead with the project anyway. But more to our point, there is no evidence that Bissell ever forwarded this to President Kennedy.[82] Colonel Jack Hawkins, the Marine amphibious expert detailed to the project by General David Shoup, wrote a similar memo. This one centered on the number and type of planes to be used, and the number or air sorties to be flown. Again, there is no evidence that this memo ever got to Kennedy's desk. It stopped with Bissell.[83]

But Hawkins and Esterline go even further in this vein. Esterline states that he was never present at any high level White House discussion of the project. As he should have been. He and Hawkins later concluded that this was most likely deliberate. And in their absence, Bissell had given unfounded assurances to Kennedy about two key elements of the plan. First, that in its revised form it would still be plausibly deniable. Second, that it would need minimal air support. Hancock states that Bissell had many opportunities to misinform Kennedy. As the discussions about the project were heating up, he had thirteen "off the record" meetings with the president from January to March of 1961.[84]

In the wake of this strategic and tactical incompetence, this arrogance and superiority toward Cubans risking their lives, this maneuvering to keep crucial information from President Kennedy, the CIA hatched a cover story. It was essentially this: the operation failed not because of them, but because of Kennedy. How was it the president's fault? The Agency and its media assets now created the myth of the "cancelled D-Day air strikes." And since both Lyman Kirkpatrick's CIA Inspector General Report and the White House's Taylor Report were both classified for three decades, that myth began to gain ground. Before dealing directly with that controversial issue, let us address the point that Kirkpatrick makes early in his review. For the sake of argument, let us assume the CIA launched the D-Day air strikes and they managed to knock out all the jet fighters on the ground. What situation would that have left for the exile army? As Kirkpatrick notes, the 1,500 man army would no doubt have eventually "been crushed by Castro's combined military resources strengthened by Soviet Bloc-supplied military materiel." Later on, Kirkpatrick enumerates the size of this combined force at 32,000 regular army troops supplemented by a 200,000 man reserve militia.[85] In other words, the exiles were potentially outnumbered by a ratio of well over 100 to 1.

But yet, it seems clear in both reports, and from other sources, that these D-Day air strikes were to be launched *only from a strip secured within the beachhead*. Which meant that the invasion force had to capture and maintain a protected beach zone large enough to contain an air strip. In fact, the CIA agreed to this. In their revised version of the plan, delivered on March 15, they mention it at least three times.[86] For instance, this March 15 memo reads that air operations over Cuba would be "conducted from an air base within territory held by opposition forces." Later, in describing the sequence of the actual military landing, the memo reads, "The second phase, preferably commencing at dawn following the landing, will involve the movement into the beachhead of tactical aircraft and their prompt commitment for strikes against the Castro Air Force." Then, a couple of sentences later, it reads, "the whole tactical air operation will be based in the beachhead . . ." Therefore, it is clear that the CIA understood this fact a month before the invasion began.

In furtherance of this declassified information, Kirkpatrick's report contains an interview with Hawkins. He states that once the Trinidad Plan was revised, Bissell told him that the State Department and Kennedy had imposed new restrictions, one of them being they had to capture an airfield from the first day for air operations.[87] Therefore, from this testimony, we know Bissell understood this requirement. In the Taylor Report, it clearly states that McGeorge Bundy, Kennedy's National Security Adviser, told Cabell the night before the brigade landed that there would be no D-Day air strikes unless they were launched from a strip within the beachhead.[88] Importantly, it was *at this point* that Bissell and Cabell now went to Dean Rusk to argue this point. This sequence also jibes with what Robert McNamara told Noel Twyman for his book *Bloody Treason*—that is, the CIA *came back* to the White House and asked for this D-Day air raid from outside Cuba. It was not in the revised plan. Finally, on April 16, when the idea of a D-Day air strike from Nicaragua came up with UN representative Adlai Stevenson and Dean Rusk, Kennedy specifically said he was not signed onto that decision. It was his understanding that any further air strikes would come from inside the beachhead.[89] So, with these declassified reports, the evidence on this issue is compelling.

In light of this information, there is an interesting letter contained in the newly recovered files of the Garrison investigation. In it, *Fortune* reporter Charles Murphy is writing to veteran black operator Edward Lansdale. They are corresponding over an article Murphy had penned entitled "Cuba: The Record Set Straight." Murphy writes that after this article appeared—in which he blamed Kennedy for the failure at the Bay of Pigs—JFK stripped him of his Air Force reserve status. Murphy added that this really did not mean that much to him. For his true loyalty was not to President Kennedy, but to Allen Dulles.[90] As we will see, it was through compromised reporters like Murphy that Dulles got his cover story out. We will later see that— among other things—Dulles switched the blame for the failure from himself to JFK. Since the Kirkpatrick and Taylor reports were classified, the cover story took hold. Until now.

From the evidence adduced above, one could make a strong case that Kennedy was being misled by both Dulles and Bissell about the chances of success for the operation—that he was being given all the wildly optimistic reports, but he was being deprived of crucial information about the liabilities of the operation. Was this done in a deliberate attempt to mislead him into committing to the project? If so, was it because Dulles and Bissell knew it could not succeed unless it had direct American military forces involved? Today, we can firmly say that this was the case. Unfortunately, the public had to wait over two decades to read the evidence.

In 1965, Dulles was preparing a magazine memoir about the Bay of Pigs. He got so far as writing some notes about it. He then decided against it. But many years later, his coffee-stained notes were discovered in his papers at Princeton. In them, Dulles finally admitted that he had a secret agenda for leaving Kennedy misinformed. He wrote that he never raised any objections when Kennedy insisted that there be no American troop commitment to the operation, or that the invasion be deniable, or quiet, or it should rely on internal uprisings. He then explained why:

> We did not want to raise these issues . . . which might only harden the decision against the type of action we required. We felt that when the chips were down—when the crisis arose in reality—any action required for success would be authorized rather than permit the enterprise to fail. . . . We believed that in a time of crisis we would gain what we might have lost if we provoked an argument in advance.[91]

In other words, by misleading Kennedy into committing to a project he really did not want to commit to, Dulles would place him in a position where he would either have to swallow a humiliating defeat or reverse his public pledge of April 12: "There will not be, under any conditions, an intervention in Cuba by the United States armed forces."[92] In Dulles's eyes, all the deceptions about "going guerrilla," about the D-Day air strikes, about the Cuban masses rallying to the exile beachhead, these were all justified in his Machiavellian world view. He then tried to rationalize his justification:

> I have seen a good many operations which started out like this B of P, insistence of complete secrecy—non-involvement of the U.S.—initial reluctance to authorize supporting actions. This limitation tends to disappear as the needs of the operation become clarified.[93]

This essay, by Lucien S. Vandenbroucke, was not published until 1984. At the time, the publication, *Diplomatic History*, gave Bissell an opportunity to reply. Bissell admitted that he and Dulles "had allowed Kennedy to persist in misunderstandings about the nature of the Cuban operation."[94]

But it's actually even worse than that. Because back in 1964, four of the exiles involved in the activity told reporter Haynes Johnson that the CIA had anticipated that Kennedy might pull back from the operation at the last minute. If that contingency arose, their handler told them to put on an act as if they had imprisoned the officers involved. They should place an armed guard at each CIA officer's door, cut off all communications, then go the landing site and proceed anyway.[95] This is how intent Dulles and Bissell were in putting Kennedy's back against the wall.

There is little doubt that, by the time both inquiries were completed, Kennedy had understood he had been duped. In fact, he said as much to his friend Paul Fay. He stated that when he first came into office, he was appalled by the lack of judgment some of the military had shown. Being a former Navy man, he had looked up to these officers who placed the many ribbons and medals they won on their uniforms; he assumed they had higher qualifications than the rest of us. He now thought he was wrong in that perception. He would not instinctively follow their advice in the future. He then alluded to the Bay of Pigs: "They wanted a fight and probably calculated that if we committed ourselves part way and started to lose, I would give the OK to pour in whatever was needed."[96]

As we have seen from Dulles's notes, Kennedy was correct. But Dulles did not like his darker and duplicitous side being exposed. In addition to putting out a cover story through Murphy, he seemed to have some personal animosity toward Kennedy. When he was doing the preliminary work on his magazine essay on the Bay of Pigs, *Harper's* sent over a young writer named Willie Morris. In the midst of one discussion they had about Kennedy, Dulles surprised Morris by blurting out the following comment, "That little Kennedy, he thought he was a god." Morris wrote many years after, "Even now those words leap out at me, the only strident ones I would hear from my unlikely collaborator."[97]

With what was in the two reports, Kennedy felt he had no choice except to take drastic action. Action, which as we will see, Eisenhower very likely would not have taken. But before doing so, he consulted extensively with a scion of the Eastern Establishment, Robert Lovett. Lovett had been a friend of his father, Joseph Kennedy. Under Eisenhower, the elder Kennedy had worked with Lovett and David Bruce on a forerunner of the Foreign Intelligence Advisory Board. This was a civilian panel meant to monitor the activities of the CIA. Both men were stunned at what Dulles had done to the Agency. They felt it was a perversion of what Truman had meant it to be: an intelligence and analysis center. When Robert Kennedy served on the Taylor committee, he called Lovett as a witness. After RFK died, biographer Arthur Schlesinger found Kennedy's notes and a remnant of a report Bruce and Lovett had written among his papers.[98]

Lovett told the Cuban board of inquiry that "Bruce was very much disturbed" by the CIA's actions. "He approached it from the standpoint of 'what right have we to go barging into other countries, buying newspapers and handing money to opposition parties, or supporting a candidate for this, that, or the other office.' He felt this was an outrageous interference with friendly countries." The report therefore captures Dulles's cavalier, unfeeling attitude— probably garnered form his days at Sullivan and Cromwell—about sending young men of privilege abroad to engage in adventures with a blank check in hand. Bruce went as far as to deride Dulles's actions as irresponsible "King Making," all the while ignoring what the CIA was really supposed to do: col- lect, collate, and evaluate the best intelligence possible. They further scored the system Dulles installed, which rewarded success and ignored failure, with no system of justification or control. As long as a covert action was deemed as frustrating the Russians or keeping a country pro-Western, it was given the go- ahead. Approval was almost always a "pro-forma" matter, done over lunch by a small inner group. The result was that, "no one, other than those in the CIA immediately concerned with their day to day operation, has any detailed know- ledge of what is going on." This meant that the CIA's covert action arm exerted unilateral influences on American foreign policy. And at times, not even the U.S. ambassador in country knew about it beforehand. The writers believed that what had happened "could not possibly have [been] foreseen" in the legis- lation of 1947 and 1948. And they blamed lack of oversight as being "responsible in a great measure for stirring up the turmoil and raising the doubts about us that exist in many countries of the world today."

The report also pointed out that the way Dulles organized the CIA allo- wed covert action programs to consume 80 percent of the budget. Further, the National Security Council (NSC), exercised little or no control over covert action. The CIA's Directorate of Plans "is operating for the most part on an autonomous and free-wheeling basis in highly critical areas." At times this was truly lamentable since "the operations being carried out by the Deputy Direc- tor of Plans are sometimes in direct conflict with the normal operations being carried out by the Department of State." A perfect example of this was the CIA coup attempt against Sukarno in Indonesia. John Allison, the ambassador, opposed the coup attempt. So Allen had his brother at State remove Allison. The new ambassador was kept largely in the dark about the CIA plans. The coup failed, greatly alienating Sukarno from the USA. Lovett and Bruce— and Joseph Kennedy who was also on the advisory board—continued to press their case against Dulles until they left. In their last report they wrote that "the CIA's concentration on political, psychological, and related covert action activities have tended to detract substantially from the execution of [a] primary intelligence-gathering mission. We suggest, accordingly, that there should be a total reassessment of our covert action policies."

Lovett told the Cuban board that, "I have never felt that the Congress of the United States ever intended to give the United States Intelligence Agency authority to conduct operations all over the earth." Lovett's report and testimony held great sway with the Kennedys. In fact, Joseph Kennedy was so impressed by working with Lovett that he urged JFK to offer him a top job in his Cabinet. Kennedy did, but Lovett declined. After his Bay of Pigs testimony, President Kennedy called Lovett in for a private meeting. He told the president that the CIA was "badly organized, dangerously amateurish, and excessively costly." It had to be re-organized, which wasn't possible with Eisenhower as president and Dulles as Director.

There can be little doubt that Lovett's testimony and his relationship with Kennedy's father helped convince JFK to fire Dulles, along with Cabell and Bissell.

But was there something even more nefarious buried deep inside the Bay of Pigs? Something that Dulles could never, ever admit to? There were hints of it in Kirkpatrick's report and in Arthur Schlesinger's book *A Thousand Days*. In Kirkpatrick's report he writes that the CRC (the ultimate council Hunt had formed—and then temporarily left) was held up during the invasion at an airfield in Miami, Florida. The author says they were held under "strong persuasion" while the CIA wrote the bulletins sent out under their name.[99] In his book, Schlesinger is more straightforward since, on Kennedy's orders, he actually visited them there when the operation appeared to be failing. They were held inside a safe house while, "Young American GIs, their revolvers conspicuous in holsters, were patrolling their grounds."[100] But further, as Manolo Ray told Schelsinger, they were being held incommunicado with the outside world. No information was coming into them, and they were not allowed to talk to anyone outside. When Kennedy learned of this house arrest, he was shocked. Like many other things, neither Dulles nor Bissell had told him about it.[101] It was only when Schlesinger told Kennedy about their detention that they were released under his orders.

It turns out Schlesinger was not revealing all he knew about the Cuban detention in his book. On June 9, 1961, a little less than two months after the disaster, Schlesinger wrote a memo to Richard Goodwin, another liberal White House aide whom Hunt detested. Schlesinger had been talking to Sam Halper, a *New York Times* journalist who specialized in Latin America at the time and had excellent contacts with the Cuban exiles. Halper told Schlesinger that the CIA had set up something called Operation 40 to run parallel with the Bay of Pigs. It was to be helmed by one Luis Sanjenis. It was named after the 40 original operatives assigned to it. But it later expanded to 70 persons. The ostensible purpose of it was to administer liberated territories inside Cuba after the invasion succeeded. But Halper had learned something different about it. The man in charge, a CIA officer named Felix, had trained the operatives in methods of third degree interrogation, torture and general terrorism. The Operation 40 group consisted of the most conservative members of the exile community. The liberal exiles came to believe that "the real purpose of Operation 40 was to 'kill Communists,' and"—reminiscient of the death lists in Guatemala in 1954—"after eliminating the hard-core Fidelistas [on the island], to go on to eliminate first the followers of Ray, then the followers of Varona and finally to set up a right-wing dictatorship, presumably under [Manuel] Artime," who, as we have seen, was the one exile leader closest to Hunt both personally and politically. These suspicions were so well founded that Tony Varona later fired Sanjenis. But Sanjenis then set up his own office with CIA support.

Picking up on Operation 40, Larry Hancock writes that Sanjenis was closely associated with David Morales and the counterintelligence group he had set up against Cuba. Morales, as we shall see, was a veteran black operator who worked with both Theodore (Ted) Shackley at the Miami CIA station and David Phillips. Morales's job was also to create an intelligence force for the new government of Cuba. Sanjenis had been trained under Morales and his so-called AMOT group. This group had prepared files on all the CRC leaders and all the brigade members. But further, they had also gone into Cuba to do surveillance work on the leaders of Castro's government.[102] If Hunt was to supervise the construction of a post-Castro government the CIA was to set up in Cuba, then there can be little doubt that he knew about Operation 40. As mentioned above, we have seen that in the 1954 CIA coup in Guatemala, which Hunt and Phillips participated in, lists of those to be killed afterwards had also been assembled. The two, who were now much higher in the command chain, were repeating a pattern. In fact, in a memo written by CIA Officer J. C. King on May 19, 1961, Ray told King that he was afraid if the invasion was successful, his followers would also be killed in the mopping up operation code named Operation 40. It may be that this deep and hidden agenda is what made Hunt discount all of Ray's appeals to use his underground forces in the invasion. In fact, Hunt actually belittled that underground by saying it did not exist. And he also admitted in his book that he was writing the communiqués for the sequestered CRC, and further, the house arrest was aimed at Ray.[103]

If this information is accurate, and among others, Trumbull Higgins, Warren Hinckle and William Turner stand by it, then Kennedy was not just being lied to about the actual operation and its chances for success.[104] He was also being betrayed about who would be running Cuba if the invasion succeeded. Under Hunt and the CIA, it was not going to be his favorite, Manolo Ray. It was to be Hunt's favorite, the much more conservative Manuel Artime.

There is no doubting the personal impact of the failed operation on Kennedy. He incriminated himself afterwards: "How could I have been so stupid as to let them proceed?" He also called it, "the worst experience of my life."[105] According to James Blight in the film, *Virtual JFK,* Kennedy afterwards went through a period of mild depression. In a surprisingly candid series about the CIA, Tom Wicker of the *New York Times* quoted Kennedy thusly: "President Kennedy, as the enormity of the Bay of Pigs disaster came home to him, said to one of the highest officals of his administration that "he wanted to splinter the CIA in a thousand pieces and scatter it to the winds."[106] He did not go that far of course. But he did take steps to try and bring the CIA under control. First, after firing Dulles, he pointedly brought in someone from outside the Agency to take his job. He appointed John McCone as CIA Director. McCone had been a businessman who made a fortune in the steel industry and in ship building. He then worked as chairman of the Atomic Energy Commission, which is where President Kennedy got to know him. In other words, he had no ties to the so-called Old Boys network which had helped form the Agency in the forties. Second, Kennedy also sent out diplomatic orders that the highest ranking official in any foreign country was to be the ambassador, and policy was to be run through him and not the CIA. Kennedy felt that he would now control things abroad through the State Department, bypassing the CIA, which he did not trust, since as Lovett had told him, the Agency would not clear its clandestine operations either with State or the ambassador in the field.[107]

Third, as John Newman notes, National Security Action Memoranda (NSAM's) 55, 56, and 57 were the direct result of the Taylor Report. Kennedy approved of their drafting on June 28, and they were worked on by Taylor himself.[108] NSAM 55 was directly delivered to Chairman of the Joint Chiefs Lyman Lemnitzer. JFK was angry that the Pentagon had not delivered a trenchant critique of the Dulles-Bissell invasion plan. So from here on in he wanted their advice "to come to me direct and unfiltered." He also added that he wanted their input into military and paramilitary operations of the Cold War.[109] As both John Newman and Fletcher Prouty have noted, this was a real cannon shot across the bow of the CIA. Allen Dulles had instituted these types of paramilitary operations previously, and the CIA had run them almost exclusively. As Newman describes it, NSAM 55 was "the opening shot in Kennedy's campaign to curtail the CIA's control over covert paramilitary operations."[110] The other two national security memoranda flowed from the first one. NSAM 56 was an order to make an inventory of paramilitary assets and equipment the Pentagon had on hand and then to measure that against the projected requirements across the world and make up any deficit. NSAM 57 stated that all paramilitary operations were to be presented to the Strategic Resources Group. That group would then assign a person and department to run it. The CIA was only to be involved in paramilitary operations "wholly covert or disavowable," and then only if they were within the Agency's "normal capabilities."[111] Clearly, Kennedy never wanted the CIA to touch a project the size and scope of the Bay of Pigs again. As Newman then sums up, "The consequence of these presidential directives was the first significant chink in the CIA's covert armor since its creation."[112]

Fourth, Kennedy decided to move his brother in as a kind of ombudsman over certain CIA operations dealing with Cuba. Any offical CIA action against Cuba had to be ultimately approved by a Special Group on which Robert Kennedy served. As we will see, certain CIA officers did not appreciate this at all.

David Phillips described his reaction to the Bay of Pigs in his 1977 book called *The Night Watch*. He said he came home from headquarters, and his wife tried to feed him, but he couldn't eat. He then fell asleep. He woke up but still could not eat. He went outside with a portable radio and listened to reports about the invasion disaster. He then began drinking. With nothing in his stomach, he began to vomit. He then began weeping. His wife called him inside, but he would not go. She brought a blanket out for him, and he wrapped himself in it. Phillips said he cried for two hours before vomiting again.[113]

Phillips went further about what he really thought in his discussions of the matter with his Cuban recruit Antonio Veciana. Veciana described Phillips— who he knew as Maurice Bishop—as extremely frustrated. He stated that the disaster at the Bay of Pigs was caused by President Kennedy because he had withheld air support for the invasion force.[114]

Hunt was less melancholy and more condemnatory. He began *Give Us This Day* with this blast, "No event since the communization of China in 1949 has had such a profound effect on the United States . . . as the defeat of the U.S.-trained Cuban invasion brigade at the Bay of Pigs in April 1961."[115] He then went on to say, "Still, and let this not be forgotten, Lee Harvey Oswald was a partisan of Fidel Castro and an admitted Marxist who made desperate efforts to join the Red Revolution in Havana." Hunt then says if Castro had been toppled, there would have probably been "no assassin named Lee Harvey Oswald."[116]

Hunt had nothing but scorn for the Maxwell Taylor investigation. He said its aim was "to whitewash the New Frontier by heaping guilt on the CIA."[117] At this point in his career, Hunt was now detailed to Dulles's personal staff. His job was to help answer queries from Taylor's committee. In describing the firings of Dulles and Bissell, Hunt said they were made "scapegoats to expiate administration guilt." And after watching Dulles go through this investigation, Hunt described Dulles's fate at the hands of Kennedy's investigation as that of a "remarkable man whose long career of government service had been destroyed unjustly by men who were laboring unceasingly to preserve their own public images."[118] Hunt went so far as to admit that he and Dulles reviewed the proofs of the above mentioned *Fortune* article by Charles Murphy on the Bay of Pigs before it was published. And further, that Hunt actually worked on the article for two days and furnished Murphy with classified background information for the piece.[119] And what an article it was.

The Murphy-Dulles-Hunt piece begins by stating that Kennedy had been an ineffective president so far. The reason being because, unlike Eisenhower, he did not know how to manipulate the levers of power.[120] Although the article is supposed to be about Cuba and the Bay of Pigs, Murphy and his (secret) co-authors spend the first few pages discussing Laos. They clearly believe that Kennedy erred in seeking a diplomatic solution there. They call the fact that he did not take a military stand there, a "reversal." To top it off, they then say that Laos is now "finished"—when in fact the Pathet Lao did not take power there until fourteen years later. They then imply that because of the Laos diplomacy, Ngo Dinh Diem of South Vietnam, a stout friend of the USA, is now under siege by "murderous communists." In pure Eisenhower-Dulles Domino Theory hyperbolic style, the article then states that because of this "loss of face," from the Philipines to Pakistan, the world is now under challenge. In one of the most jarring statements in this startling article, the authors then write that because Kennedy took the diplomatic route in Laos, he then *had to take* the military alternative in Cuba. As we have seen, this is specious. For, from the beginning, Kennedy was not going to commit American forces into Laos. And the Bay of Pigs operation is something that he had to be deceived into going along with. But there is one more statement in the beginning which should be noted. The authors write that it was really Prime Minister Harold Macmillan, while on vacation in Key West, who convinced Kennedy not to commit to Laos.[121] This is a key point of the essay. The idea is to paint Kennedy as a man who can be easily influenced by advisers who really are not up to fighting the Cold War against the communists. In other words, Kennedy is really a man who had no backbone on this issue since he had no vision of the actual conflict. The author has been at pains in the preceding pages to show this is wrong. He did have a vision, except it was not Allen Dulles's vision.

The article now goes on to strike at two targets. First, quite naturally, it states that Kennedy reneged on the D-Day air strikes.[122] As we have seen, in light of the declassified record, this is simply not supportable today. But what is interesting is that in his later book, *Give Us this Day*, Hunt writes something different. There he says that Deputy Director Charles Cabell actually stopped the D-Day strike from proceeding.[123] In fact, he writes that Cabell stopped that sortie because the operation was only granted one air strike! The discrepancy between his two versions labels Hunt's work with Murphy as "black propaganda"—that is, a deliberate deception—which is what he and Phillips specialized in. And this stroke appears to have been directed by Dulles since, on his own, Hunt wrote something different, and more true to the facts.

The second target of the piece is the liberal coterie around Kennedy—Richard Goodwin, William Fulbright, Adlai Stevenson, and Arthur Schlesinger. In other words, the bunch that made Hunt swallow Manolo Ray. In fact, what the trio does here is insinuate that the original Dulles-Bissell plan was tactically sound and approved by the Pentagon.[124] When, as we have seen, Bissell deliberately kept the White House in the dark about a memo saying that the military chiefs believe the plan would not succeed without direct American intervention. Then the essay states that this original plan was "dismembered" by Kennedy's liberal advisers.[125] (They actually include Dean Rusk in this group.) They then say it was Rusk who caused the original plan to be moved from Trinidad to Playa Giron. They also say that Kennedy had actually approved limited direct American air power from a carrier task force to be used.[126] Towards the end, the piece actually tries to say that it was Adlai Stevenson who caused the D-Day strike to be called off. At the very end, when they quote Kennedy saying that there were sobering lessons to be learned from the episode, they clearly insinuate that the president should not have let his "political advisers" influence operational decisions. Since Dulles later confessed that he never thought the operation could succeed on its own, but he thought Kennedy would save it when he saw it failing, this appears to be nothing but pure deception on his part, delivered through his instruments Hunt and Murphy.

This was clearly the beginning of the CIA's counterattack—led by the man who would now be fired for his prime role in that deception—against Kennedy for finding out the truth about the operation. Kennedy now ended Dulles's intelligence career, which extended back to World War I. The article is crucial in two ways. First, from where it was published. Henry Luce's Wall Street–aimed magazine had clear influence on the Power Elite, the wealthy classes who had so much influence over politics and communications. Second, extending downward, people like Hunt and Phillips would now use this disinformation scenario to influence the Cubans against Kennedy by depicting him as an amateur who let himself be buffeted about by some unrealistic dreamers who had no idea of the stakes involved in the Cold War against communism. As we shall see, in that regard, the essay turned out to be all too effective.

The reader will note that the author has spent some time and length in reviewing the Bay of Pigs debacle. This has largely been done in light of the declassified information now available. In addition to showing how the CIA manipulated Kennedy, how the inquiry afterward resulted in the ending of three intelligence careers, how Kennedy then tried to take control of the CIA, and how certain Agency officers were emotionally impacted by the aftermath, there is one more reason this author devoted this much length in chronicling the episode. That is because many of the characters we will soon encounter were either directly or indirectly involved in that operation. In addition to Dulles, Hunt, and Phillips, there are David Morales, David Ferrie, Clay Shaw, Bernardo DeTorres, Sergio Arcacha Smith, and Guy Banister. And as we shall see, in the famous Sylvia Odio incident—which the Warren Commission unsuccessfully tried to deny—the Cubans attempting to frame Lee Harvey Oswald told Sylvia that Oswald thought that the exiles should have killed Kennedy after the Bay of Pigs. The person they were telling this to, Odio, was a follower of Manolo Ray. In telling the true story of Kennedy's murder in light of the declassified record, it is hard to overestimate the importance of the failed invasion at Playa Giron. Because of the cover story that Dulles and Hunt circulated, many of the operatives involved never forgave Kennedy. And as we shall see, there is evidence that some of them were in Dallas that day, perhaps in Dealey Plaza.

CHAPTER FOUR

Kennedy De-escalates in Cuba

"This blockade and political action, I see leading into war.
I don't see any other solution. It will lead right into war.
This is almost as bad as appeasement at Munich."

—*General Curtis LeMay*

After the Bay of Pigs debacle, there was a flurry of memoranda concerning what to do about the "Cuban problem." The military disaster, and its attendant huge international embarrassment, now created something that likely would not have existed if the invasion had not occurred. The blizzard of memoranda began on April 20, the day after the defeat. McGeorge Bundy's assistant Walt Rostow wrote to Kennedy and Secretary of Defense McNamara and stated the problems the USA now faced on the island. Two days later, on April 24, Rostow again sent a memo to McNamara pressing him on solutions to the "Cuba problem." He listed all the perceived dangers, but now he appended possible solutions to these problems. His solutions included a blockade of the island and "an invasion of one sort or another" as a way to unseat the regime. He also asked that contingency plans be written up for an American invasion. Two days after this, McNamara received a memo from the Joint Chiefs of Staff about various military options against Cuba, including a blockade and an invasion. This memo contained a rough outline for a plan to invade Cuba. Similar memos followed from the CIA and presidential assistant Richard Goodwin. The two Rostow memos set the tone for the ratcheting up of armed resistance to the "Castro Problem." On May 2, 1961, Tracy Barnes sent a memo to Dulles in which he outlined a possible program of "infiltration and exfiltration of individuals" into Cuba and "sabotage of shipping and small raider operations." This last was the option the administration eventually settled upon: the beginnings of the "secret war" against Cuba, which would eventually be called by its code name, Operation Mongoose.

The progress toward Mongoose was accelerated at a meeting of the National Security Council on the fifth of May. There it was decided that the CRC would be continued, that the aim of American foreign policy should be to oust Castro, and that Cuban nationals should be encouraged to enlist in the U. S. armed forces.[1] That same day McNamara wrote a memo suggesting special forces training for these Cuban volunteers. On May 9, Barnes, Bissell, and J. C. King met to discuss where this training would take place and what the plans for sabotage and raiding would be. Incredibly, even though Manolo Ray had the best underground movement in Cuba, it was agreed that the CIA would have no dealings with Ray unless the CRC membership approved. On May 19, members of the CRC met at the State Department where they were advised that they would continue to be supported in their various endeavors. But further, that a program for exile paramilitary trainging was being worked out. On that same day, the CIA submitted a paper entitled "Program for Covert Action aimed at weakening the Castro Regime." In essence, this five-part paper was to become the operational outline for Mongoose. By June 22, Dean Rusk was in receipt of a memo which outlined the recruitment and training of the exiles to be used in Mongoose. Yet in this memo, it appears that Ray had decided to leave the CRC. As the memo describes it, the withdrawal of Ray "deprived it of its most liberal . . . element and has shifted its center of political gravity appreciably to the right." In July a report was delivered stating that Castro had received much military supply from Russia. Therefore, this had contributed to a "major buildup of ground and air forces there."

By November, after seven months of a memo frenzy over the "Cuban problem," Kennedy seems to have decided on a middle ground between those who wanted a full-scale invasion and those, like Chester Bowles, who wished to do little or nothing. It is around November 3 that the project got its code name Mongoose. In his notes entered for November 7, Robert Kennedy described the planned action as "espionage, sabotage, general disorder run and operated by Cubans themselves. . . . Do not know if we will be successful in overthrowing Castro but we have nothing to lose in my estimate." The man who Maxwell Taylor and Robert Kennedy chose to run Mongoose was the legendary Edward Lansdale, the Air Force Brigadier General who had made a huge name for himself in Asia and the Pacific as a covert operator of boldness and imagination.

The operation was to be supervised by a committee called the 5412 Special Group helmed by Maxwell Taylor and RFK. It was a multi-department operation between State, Defense, and the CIA. The main CIA representative on the Special Group was William Harvey. The Cubans were to be stationed on the campus of University of Miami, the station itself was code named JM-WAVE. Day to day operations there were to be run by station chief Theodore Shackley and his Chief of Staff, David Morales. Lansdale's intent was to build a resistance movement in Cuba, step by step, and by different means: propaganda, infiltration, exfiltration, surveillance, spies, raiding attacks, etc. Lansdale felt that within a year he could pinnacle the operation into a general uprising. Kennedy authorized the plan on November 30.[2] In February of 1962, Ted Shackley arrived in Miami to begin the program.[3]

By all accounts, Lansdale's campaign—in which he had tens of millions of dollars, and hundreds of Cubans to call upon—was not successful. As Clark Clifford once noted, "We sent teams at one time or another into Cuba to try to get information. They were all rolled up. . . . and we never heard from them again."[4] The effort was further hindered not just by Castro's internal security forces, but by the fact that there was no American embassy on the island. In Agency vernacular, Cuba was therefore a "denied area," with no diplomatic base. As one commentator noted, "The people inside the country were not in a position to really change the course of the Cuban Revolution. Without an embassy, without being able to talk to people outside" their usefulness was limited.[5] Another problem Lansdale could not surmount was that Castro had delivered on many of his promises. Therefore the masses of the public were not dissatisfied with him. Or as one CIA report stated, "the Castro regime has sufficient popular support and repressive capabilities to cope with any internal threat likely to develop within the foreseeable future."[6] Further, some of the operations were bungled. A raiding party to destroy a bridge was met by Castro forces. An attempt to blow up a copper mine was deterred by a leaky ship.[7] Some of Lansdale's more ambitious schemes were to poison the turkey population and incapacitate sugar harvest workers via chemical warfare.[8] Another was to fire star shells into the night sky from a submarine as part of a plan to stage a Second Coming of Christ. This was to inspire the Catholics to overthrow the communist, possibly atheistic, Castro. But none of it seemed effective.[9]

When Lansdale specifically mentioned the October 1962 target date for an uprising, an officer working under Richard Helms—who had replaced Bissell as Director of Plans—wrote on the timeline, "With what? We haven't got any assets. We don't even know what's going on in Cuba."[10] In this way, many CIA officers now began to resent Lansdale. They thought of the former advertising man as something of a "con man" and a mystic. As Cuban scholar Morris Morley states, through 1962, Mongoose "performed largely as an intelligence collection body by infiltrating teams into Cuba."[11] After another thwarted operation in late August, Lansdale presented a plan to the Special Group to target strategic production in mineral areas like copper, nickel, and petroleum. His memo also suggested, "encouraging destruction of crops by fire, chemicals, and weeds, hampering of harvest by work slowdown, destruction of bags, cartons, and shipping containers."[12]

By this time, the Special Group had become skeptical about Lansdale's grandiose designs and his ability to fulfill them. Therefore the committee had now become apprehensive about sabotage proposals. But the CIA representative on the Special Group, William Harvey, now grew angry with the Kennedys. Harvey began to see that Mongoose was not going to be successful. (As David Talbot writes in his book *Brothers,* this may have been the Kennedys' concept from the start.) In fact, Harvey thought the brothers were "fags." And after serving on the Special Group, he grew resentful about RFK and called him the "little fucker."[13] Eventually the conflict grew to "the point where Harvey considered RFK's 'amateur' actions were endangering operations and lives." Harvey came to despise Bobby Kennedy, because he began to feel that some of his acts were actually not just counterproductive, but those of a traitor. He concluded that the Kennedys should not be running Operation Mongoose.[14]

It was probably these feelings toward RFK and Lansdale that caused the CIA to reactivate the plots to kill Castro. According to the CIA's Inspector General Report, this happened in April of 1962. The report states that Harvey got in contact with two CIA officers associated with the first phase of the plots and asked to be introduced to Johnny Roselli.[15] Harvey seems to have been prompted for this by Deputy Director of Plans Richard Helms in early fall of 1961. Harvey was to formalize a plan to deniably assassinate foreign leaders. One of the first things Harvey did was to arrange two meetings with British Counter Intelligence Officer Peter Wright. Harvey was joined at these meetings with a man we have yet to encounter, but who will strongly figure in our narrative: CIA Chief of Counter Intelligence James Angleton. Both men began to quiz Wright about "delivery mechanisms" for assassinations. Wright recalled that Harvey asked him what he personally thought of Castro, while Angleton took copious notes.[16] In fact, the reason Angleton was there is contained in Harvey's notes of his meeting with Helms, where Helms originally tasked him with the function. After noting that the planning should include angles for blaming the Russians or Czechs, and how a phony CIA 201 personality file had to be set up, forged, and backdated, Harvey concluded the review of his conference with Helms with the note to talk to "Jim A" about the matter.[17]

Harvey then arranged to have poison pills to be picked up by him at CIA HQ. His accomplice, Roselli, then had them delivered to Tony Varona, who allegedly had contacts in Cuba. Varona also asked for arms and equipment needed for support of his end of the operation. Harvey passed this request to Ted Shackley, Chief of JM-WAVE. Shackley procured the equipment. This included explosives, detonators, 30 rifles, 25 handguns, 2 radios, and 1 boat radar set.[18] For several months, from May of 1962 to February of 1963, Roselli and Harvey waited for any positive word of success from Varona. But none ever came. Harvey than asked Helms if he could have one last meeting with Roselli to close out the arrangement. In June of 1963, Roselli visited Harvey in Washington, stayed as a guest in his domicile, and went out with Harvey and his wife for dinner.[19] As the reader can see, even though the operation did not succeed, the two became friends. This has led some people to believe that this relationship was maintained through the fall and winter of that year. And may have been of use in the murder of President Kennedy.

Before leaving the subject of Mongoose, mention should be given to another operation that—as with the Castro assassination plots—the Kennedys did not sanction. This was Operation Northwoods. It was proposed by the Joint Chiefs of Staff in March of 1962. It was to be planned and implemented as part of Mongoose. It was to be carried out by the Pentagon. The Northwoods proposal was finally declassified in November of 1997 by the Assassination Records Review Board (ARRB). This was the body set up by the executive branch and congress to declassify all records related to President Kennedy's murder. Northwoods is what is known in spy jargon as a "false flag" operation. That is, provocations would be performed by disguised American agents, and the resultant violent actions would then be blamed on your targeted enemy, in this case Cuba. The purpose being to cause enough popular support for an armed intervention to depose Castro.[20] The ideas offered up to do so were to stage a phony attack on the U.S. military base at Guantanamo on the west end of Cuba; blowing up an American ship in Cuban waters; sinking a boatload of Cuban refugees off the south coast of Florida; and having a jet disguised as Cuban shoot down an American jet liner.[21] The list went on for pages. As the reader can see, some of these seemed to entail the killing of innocent civilians. Kennedy rejected it out of hand. But it is important to remember the "false flag" concept: using American agents disguised as Cubans in a violent act to provoke a retaliation against Castro. As the reader will eventually see, that is what seems to have happened in the Kennedy case.

As noted, the Special Group was growing disenchanted with Lansdale's grandiose schemes, which did not come close to achieving the objective of unseating Castro. But Mongoose was actually terminated by something unforeseen when the project originated: the attempt by the Russians to insert nuclear weapons into Cuba.

1962: Kennedy Avoids Armageddon

In July of 1962, the Defense Minister of Cuba, Raul Castro, had visited Moscow for two weeks. Afterward, the CIA received reports of Soviet freighters arriving in Cuba with military cargo on board. They then got reports of "military equipment arriving at Cuban ports and moving to interior areas under Soviet guard."[22] In August, there were reports of a military parade in which Castro had displayed Soviet built MIG fighter aircraft.

In September, there were more reports of Soviets moving around equipment. CIA Director John McCone thought these may have been defensive Surface to Air Missiles (SAMs). But he cautioned President Kennedy that it was hard to distinguish SAMs from medium-range ballistic missiles (MRBMs), which were offensive. When asked about this issue, the Russian ambassador Anatoly Dobrynin told Robert Kennedy that the Soviets had no intention of placing offensive missiles in Cuba.[23] But then, Republicans in the Senate began to state on the floor that the administration was looking the other way as the Soviets made a forward rocket base out of Cuba. Kennedy was forced on the defensive by these charges to explain what he would do if this was the case. On September 13, he said that if Cuba "should ever . . . become an offensive military base of significant capacity for the Soviet Union, then this country will do whatever must be done to protect its own security and that of its allies."[24] And, in fact, contingency plans were then drawn up by the Defense Department for an invasion of the island.

On October 14, at the request of John McCone, a U-2 reconnaissance aircraft flew high over Cuba snapping photographs of the terrain below. McCone wanted more data to determine if the Soviet materials were for defensive or offensive missiles. On October 15, the analysts at the CIA's photographic analysis center examined the photos and began to discern missiles that looked more like MRBMs than SAMs. By late that afternoon, the determination was made that they were MRBMs. This information was then passed on to the top level of the CIA, and McGeorge Bundy was alerted to the discovery. The deliberations concerning what to do about the missiles began on October 16 at 11:45 A.M.

It should be noted here that Kennedy had a taping system installed at the White House in the summer of 1962. The reason being that he did not like the fact that, in the wake of the Bay of Pigs disaster, many people involved had leaked information that was not consistent with what had actually been said and done.[25] It took a very long time, but these tapes were eventually transcribed. And today, there are two books based on these transcriptions.[26] Consequently, we can base a review of this momentous event on what was actually discussed rather than on the more usual historical standard, personal memoirs. From the beginning, when Kennedy asks Dean Rusk to speak, the options presented to him are military in nature. Rusk states the options are either a quick air strike or a slow build up of troops in Florida.[27] Maxwell Taylor, now Chair of the Joint Chiefs, also opted for the surprise air strike. He was then backed by both Secretary of the Treasury, Douglas Dillon, and Bundy. Deputy Secretary of Defense, Roswell Gilpatric, then went even further: "I suggest, Mr. President, that if you're involved in several hundred strikes, and against airfields, this is what you would do: pre-invade."[28] In other words, in addition to bombing the missile sites, an occupying force would be sent in. The first mention of a blockade was made by Kennedy in relation to stopping further missiles from coming in and therefore limiting the amount of air strikes necessary.[29] Robert Kennedy then brought in the issue of how much collateral damage would be done, that is, how many lives would be lost in air strikes. This is a point that JFK returned to in later meetings by asking probing questions about how accurate the bomb runs would be and how many civilians could be killed. Therefore, within two days, a consensus led by McNamara, Rusk, and RFK began to move away from air strikes and invasion to a blockade, which would then leave the next step up to Soviet Premier Nikita Khrushchev.

On October 19, Kennedy had a meeting with the Joint Chiefs of Staff. Kennedy got into a back and forth with the hawkish Air Force General Curtis LeMay. LeMay was infamous for his firebombing strategies of Japanese cities, which left tens, perhaps hundreds of thousands of civilians dead. LeMay frowned upon the blockade option. He also looked askance on Kennedy's worry that if he invaded Cuba, Khrushchev would take over West Berlin. LeMay predicted the opposite effect: "If we don't do anything in Cuba, then they're going to push on Berlin and push real hard because they've got us on the run."[30] LeMay, who was never one to mince words, then went even further. To show his utter disdain for the blockade concept, the World War II veteran actually brought up something rather bizarre. He said, "The blockade and political action, I see leading into war. . . . This is almost as bad as the appeasement at Munich."[31] LeMay was now comparing Kennedy's preference for the blockade with Neville Chamberlain's giving away the Sudetenland to the Nazis, which encouraged Hitler to invade Poland. Although not expressing themselves in such extreme figures of speech, the rest of the chiefs of staff agreed with LeMay. LeMay then brought up Kennedy's September 13 comment about how seriously he would take the Russians making an offensive base out of Cuba, "I think that a blockade, and political talk, would be considered by a lot of our friends and neutrals as being a pretty weak response to this. And I'm sure a lot of our own citizens would feel that way too. You're in a pretty bad fix, Mr. President."[32] To which Kennedy replied that unless he had not noticed, LeMay was in there with him. Before Kennedy left he closed with, "I appreciate your views. These are unsatisfactory alternatives."[33]

As startling as this dialogue was, what followed after Kennedy left the room equaled it. Marine Commandant David Shoup told LeMay, "You pulled the rug right out from under him. Goddamn." LeMay laughed and said, "Jesus Christ. What the hell do you mean?" Shoup replied with, "He finally got around to the word 'escalation.' That's the only goddamn thing that is the whole trick. Go in and get out and get every goddamn one." To which LeMay replied, "That's right."[34]

Many writers have used the LeMay-Kennedy dialogue to show just what a divide there was between the military leadership and Kennedy about Cuba. But what fewer commentators have noted is the meeting between President Kennedy and selected congressional leaders three days later. Kennedy summoned 20 of them to the White House right before he was to go on television and broadcast his implementation of a blockade to the public. Included were Senators William Fulbright and Richard Russell and Representatives Carl Vinson and Charles Halleck. After Kennedy previewed his speech, Russell disagreed with the decision. He said the time had come to "assemble as speedily as possible an adequate force and clean out the situation. . . . A war, our destiny will hinge on it. But it's coming someday, Mr. President. Will it ever be under more auspicious circumstances?" Fulbright was also for a full invasion, "an all-out one, and as quickly as possible." Vinson said that the USA should go in with as much force as possible and get it over with quickly. Only Halleck offerd to support whatever decision was made.[35] A day after meeting the congressional leaders, Kennedy and his brother met privately. They were clearly shaken by the saber rattling of the Chiefs and the representatives. They agreed that the blockade was the least they could have done. If not, Kennedy would have been impeached on some trumped up charges. JFK also revealed his distaste for the air strikes as needlessly ratcheting up the tensions.[36]

Contrary to popular belief, the crisis did not halt once the blockade was created and the Navy started stopping ships. For the Russians continued constructing the missiles already on the island and, in conjunction, camouflaging the sites. So although the appearance was that the crisis was solved, in reality it was not. And by this time, about ten days into the episode, the tide was turning towards the Joint Chiefs. Even former soft liners like McNamara were talking about dislodging Castro and installing a new government.[37] It is important to note here that at around this time, both Khrushchev and Kennedy decided to go around their advisers. (The specially assembled group for Kennedy was called the ExComm.) On October 26, the Russians had a KGB agent under journalistic cover meet with ABC News correspondent John Scali. The message Scali carried was that the Russians were amenable to a diplomatic solution. The core of the deal was that the Soviets would remove the missiles if Kennedy pledged not to invade Cuba.[38] About five hours later, a long, emotional telegram was received at State from Khrushchev that generally aligned with what Scali had relayed.[39] While this was occurring, Robert Kennedy was meeting privately with another Soviet intelligence agent Georgi Bolshakov, and also Soviet Ambassador Anatoly Dobrynin.[40] Between the assurances given in this back channel and Kennedy's reply to the Khrushchev cable, a deal was announced. Kennedy would pledge not to invade Cuba, and the Russians would remove the missiles. Kennedy gave assurances through the back channel that he would later remove Jupiter missiles from Turkey and Italy that were aimed at Russia. It is important here to discern a future pattern. For Kennedy also went around his militant advisers when he was formulating his policy to withdraw from Vietnam, and also to create a back channel to Castro in 1963 for reasons of a rapprochement.

Kennedy's performance—which seems masterful today—was too cautious and diplomatic not just for LeMay, but for William Harvey. As we have seen above, Harvey was in contact with Johnny Roselli through the latter half of 1962—that is, at the time of the Missile Crisis. Although Harvey was not in on the ExComm deliberations, as supervisor of Task Force W, he largely ran the CIA's part of Mongoose. Therefore he was privy to intelligence surveillance out of JM-WAVE during the Missile Crisis. Roselli left the west coast and was either in Washington or Miami for the week of October 19–26.[41] He very likely was meeting with Harvey. These days overlap with the Missile Crisis of October 15–28. And it was during the latter part of the Missile Crisis that Harvey did something baffling. He dispatched three unidentified boat missions into Cuba, to be supplemented by the parachute dropping of 50 Cuban exiles.[42] What their purpose was has never been explained. But because of Harvey's probable meeting with Roselli at the time, one of the boats may have included an assassination team.[43] When Bobby Kennedy learned about this, he was enraged. He ordered the boats called back. He was told this was not possible, which reveals that they were probably on some kind of segregated radio frequency. If so, Harvey deliberately arranged this. Robert Kennedy demanded that Harvey be terminated. Harvey angrily retorted that if JFK had not lost his nerve at the Bay of Pigs, the Missile Crisis would not have happened.[44] McCone understood that, with that comment, Harvey's career had just imploded. But Richard Helms decided to soften the blow. He only removed him from Task Force W and then transferred him to Rome. Before departing he had his last dinner with Roselli in Washington. But also, his CIA colleagues had a going away bash for him. One of the party activities was a spoof of Shakespeare's *Julius Caesar* with Harvey in the lead. When the act concluded, someone asked: Who played Brutus? Harvey replied that it was Bobby Kennedy.[45]

Before leaving the Missile Crisis we should make two more observations. First, President Kennedy had learned his lesson well from the Bay of Pigs. This time he included persons whom he had the utmost trust in during the deliberations: his longtime assistant Ted Sorenson and his brother, Attorney General Robert Kennedy. When he felt stifled by extreme hawks, he used his brother to create a back channel to the other side. Finally, Kennedy never felt that the reason Khrushchev installed the missiles was to protect Cuba. He always believed that they were a chess piece from which the Soviet premier could demand a deal over West Berlin, which was located inside of the Russian satellite of East Germany. And he voiced this concern several times throughout the deliberations. Further, the sheer size and power of the deployment is out of all order to neutralize either Mongoose or an invasion. The deployment included 40 land based ballistic launchers, including 60 missiles in five missile regiments. The medium range missiles had a range of 1,200 miles, the long-range ones, 2,400 miles. In addition, there were to be 140 air-defense missile launchers to protect the sites. Accompanying them would be a Russian army of 45,000 men with four motorized rifle regiments and over 250 units of armor. There would also be a wing of MIG-21 fighters, with 40 nuclear armed IL-28 bombers. Finally, there was to be a submarine missile base with an initial deployment of eleven submarines, seven of them capable of launching one megaton nuclear warheads. In addition there were low-yield tactical nuclear weapons for coastal defense in case of an invasion. In other words, the Soviets could now hit approximately one hundred American cities with all three legs of the nuclear triad: rockets, bombers, submarines. This, in essence, was a first strike capability. It dwarfed the 15 outmoded Jupiter missiles in Turkey.[46] But it would have proved a great bargaining chip to get the U.S. out of West Berlin.

But the point is that in this instance—as with the Bay of Pigs—when most everyone urged him to bomb and invade the island, Kennedy did not. This probably harks back to his days in Saigon with Edmund Gullion. Kennedy resisted using direct American intervention in what he considered a country coming out of generations of foreign imperialism. As we have seen, in this instance, much of the imperialism was American in nature. Kennedy was painfully aware of this fact. He brought it up with Fidel Castro the following year in their negotiations over renewed diplomatic relations. But the point should be made: the hawks in this administration—Harvey, LeMay, Dulles—had now seen Kennedy bypass two perfect opportunities to rid America of the "Cuba problem." By the end of the Missile Crisis, they must have felt that if Kennedy had not acted by then—with Cuba nearly a nuclear base aimed at America—that he was not going to act ever. (As we will see, they were correct.) The Cuban exiles felt the same way. Kennedy's no-invasion pledge was shattering to them. As one investigator discovered, whenever there were gatherings of exiles in safe houses or at training camps, the word "traitor" was now used in relation to JFK.[47] Therefore, if the Castro regime was to be dislodged, they themselves would have to provoke that action.

1963: Kennedy's Rapprochement with Castro

At the time, and with most historians, the Missile Crisis rated as the high point in Kennedy's exercise of public foreign policy. He and Khrushchev had used direct and back channel communications to thwart nuclear extermination. And Kennedy now began to build on that development. Notwithstanding the media's Cold War triumphalism, JFK began to move toward a lowering of the nuclear threat and Cold War tensions with the Soviets. This included establishment of a direct Kremlin/White House hotline and negotiations toward a nuclear test ban treaty. Kennedy had navigated very difficult terrain in reaching an accommodation that managed to remove the missiles and bombers from Cuba. Yet, because there was a rift between Castro and Khrushchev—the Russians barely consulted Castro over the resolution—Castro did not allow on-site inspection of the removal.[48] Inspection was to be done by overflight photography. This allowed a loophole for Kennedy's enemies to launch a provocative and secret operation into Cuba. And finally, within weeks after the resolution of the crisis, Kennedy decided to pull the plug on Operation Mongoose and began moving toward a possible accommodation with Castro.[49]

As Peter Kornbluh pointed out in late 1999, the origins of the back channel between Kennedy and Castro began with the rift between Cuba and the Soviets after the Missile Crisis. New York lawyer James Donovan had been Robert Kennedy's chief emissary in negotiating the release of prisoners taken by Castro at the Bay of Pigs. In January of 1963, he alerted American intelligence officials that he had heard through Castro's personal doctor, Rene Vallejo, that Castro had broached the topic of establishing diplomatic relations with the USA.[50] To show how interested Fidel was in this, Vallejo even invited Donovan back to Cuba for a private visit for extended discussions with Castro himself.[51] The State Department told Donovan to tell Castro that if he wanted to proceed with discussions, he needed to break relations with the Soviets first. When Kennedy learned of this request, he overruled it. McGeorge Bundy wrote in a memo, "The President does not agree that we should make the breaking of Sino/Soviet ties a non-negotiable point. He doesn't want to present Castro with a condition the he obviously cannot fulfill."[52] Bundy added that Kennedy felt we needed to be flexible in our approach to this topic. The memo also stated that Kennedy was really interested in this, and it should be held close to the vest.

Donovan did return to Cuba. When he arrived back in America in April, he was debriefed by the CIA. John McCone then wrote Kennedy that "Castro knew that relations with the United States were necessary and that Castro wanted relations developed."[53] Kennedy was so fascinated by this that he met with McCone privately. The CIA director stated that he would be sending Donovan back to Cuba at the end of April. Following Donovan's return from this second meeting with Castro, McCone "characterized Castro's tone as mild, frank, and conciliatory." He also noted that Castro understood that a viable Cuba, an economically strong Cuba, required conciliation with the United States. This is what he wished, but it was hard to attain. And he could not get any real answers about it from Donovan.[54] Castro was obviously hinting that he felt the exploratory stage had ended. He wished to proceed to the second step with someone who actually represented the administration's wishes on how to get there.

At this stage, the reader should note a potential problem, which more than one commentator has previously pointed out. When Kennedy vetoed the State Department on having preconditions accompany the back channel talks, he requested that these discussions be held close to the vest. But yet, the CIA seems to have been aware of Donovan's actions from the beginning. And, in fact, had debriefed him on his second return from Cuba. So clearly, the upper echelon of the Agency was aware of the genesis of this potentially epic breakthrough in American/Cuban relations. For what Kennedy was now doing was not just ruling against invading the island, not just dismantling Operation Mongoose. He was now doing something that had been unthinkable a few months earlier. He was exploring ways to reestablish relations with Cuba after four years of nothing but hostilities with the revolutionary government of that communist island. And the CIA, which had sponsored the Bay of Pigs invasion, had a large hand in Mongoose, and, in league with the Mafia, had tried to murder Castro, was now aware of it. They would not take this lying down.

In mid-March of 1963, the militant Cuban exile group Alpha 66 called a press conference in Washington. They announced an attack on a Russian freighter in a Cuban harbor and a resultant firefight that ensued. Years later, the exile group's leader Antonio Veciana told House Select Committee on Assassinations (HSCA) investigator Gaeton Fonzi why this had occurred at this time. He told Fonzi that the attack and the press conference had been deliberately planned by his handler, Maurice Bishop. Veciana told Fonzi that "The purpose was to publicly embarrass Kennedy and force him to move

against Castro."⁵⁵ During and after his tour with the HSCA, Fonzi convincingly demonstrated that Bishop was David Phillips. Phillips had arranged for
two government officials to appear with Veciana to give his press conference
an air of legitimacy. Phillips arranged for this raid to happen at an opportune
time for himself. Kennedy was away from Washington in Costa Rica trying to
build support for his new Cuba policy. Therefore, because of the press conference, the *New York Times* noted that the White House "was embarrassed by
the incident." It further noted that Kennedy's party in Costa Rica telephoned
several times for reports on the situation.⁵⁶

A few days later, the *New York Times* reported another attack on a Russian
ship near Cuba. The Russians now made a formal protest to Washington and
ambassador Anatoly Dobrynin met with Attorney General Robert Kennedy.
As a result, it was decided that the Justice Department would aid in an effort
to push these kinds of exile raids off the mainland.⁵⁷ This was also done in
furtherance of Kennedy's pledge taken at the end of the Missile Crisis not
to invade Cuba. Therefore, the Justice Department, FBI, Coast Guard, and
Immigration and Naturalization Service (INS) were employed by the Kennedys to make arrests and seize contraband involved in these raids. Two
cities in which these raids were prominently enacted were Miami and New
Orleans. These were two cities also heavily involved with both the Bay of
Pigs and Operation Mongoose. The Kennedys then beefed up this task force
and the *Times* reported that "The action followed the Government's announcement last weekend that it intended to 'take every step necessary' to halt
commando raids from United States territory against Cuba and Soviet ships
bound for Cuba."⁵⁸

In reaction to these seizures and arrests, in mid-April, Jose Miro
Cardona now resigned from the CRC. According to sources around him,
the FBI concluded that Miro was disgusted with Kennedy's new policies
toward Cuba. After returning from a high-level meeting in Washington,
Miro concluded that "the United States policy is now one of peaceful co-
existence with Communist Cuba."⁵⁹ Summarizing the CRC's feelings toward
this new turn in policy, Miro said for the record, "To hell with it." Miro continued that the reaction against the new policy among the exiles "was very
bad against the United States" and the exiles now feel that "the U.S. is now
committed to a policy of peaceful co-existence with Communist Cuba and
have been abandoned in their fight."⁶⁰ Miro's resignation was accompanied
by a symbolic gesture reported by the Associated Press on April 18 from
Miami: "The dispute between Cuban exile leaders and the Kennedy administration was symbolized here today by black crepe hung from the doors of
exiles' homes."⁶¹

In fact, while Miro was voicing his extreme displeasure with the administration's turn, JFK was reassuring the Russians he would keep his pledge. In an April 11, 1963 letter from Kennedy to Khrushchev, the president wrote, "I have neither the intention nor the desire to invade Cuba; I consider that it is for the Cuban people themselves to decide their destiny. I am determined to continue policies which will contribute to peace in the Caribbean."[62]

In fact, as declassified documents now show, the clandestine effort against Cuba in 1963 was minimal. When William Harvey was sent packing after the Missile Crisis, Desmond Fitzgerald took over the Cuba desk at CIA. In a review of covert operations against Cuba made for the Johnson administration, Fitzgerald stated that there were only five raids authorized against Cuba in the second half of 1963, less than one per month. By the end of 1963 there were only three groups of commandos left, amounting to about 50 men. Fitzgerald admitted that with this size force, any covert operation to impact any real change in the Cuban government was simply unrealistic.[63] Fitzgerald later wrote a similar letter to Bundy in which he thoroughly discounted Manuel Artime's Central American operation against Cuba. Fitzgerald said, if he were lucky, Artime got off one raid every three months.[64] It seems that at the very least, if Kennedy was running a two track "carrot and stick" operation against Castro in 1963, there were very few sticks being meted out.

In late spring of 1963, Castro now continued the back channel through a different source, ABC news reporter Lisa Howard. In a very long interview with her, Castro was clear about his desire for some kind of melting of tensions with America. He also approved of Kennedy's cracking down on the exiles' raids into Cuba. When asked how any kind of relaxation of tensions could occur, Castro replied that steps in that regard were already being taken. Howard wrote about this interview in an academic journal. In this article she was even more specific about what Castro had said. She wrote that he was willing to discuss the following: Soviet personnel and military hardware on Cuban soil, compensation for nationalized land and investments, and the question of Cuba as a launch pad for communist subversion in the Americas.[65] Howard urged the White House to send a quiet emissary to hear Castro out on even more specifics. Although Kennedy was attuned to doing so, the CIA was not. CIA Director McCone opposed Howard's approach to Cuba and wrote "that no active steps be taken on the rapprochement matter at this time."[66] McCone may have been influenced in this by Director of Plans, Richard Helms. On May 1, 1963 Helms produced a memo to McCone in which he recorded every step made by Castro to make a détente between the two former belligerents a reality. From McCone's negative reaction we can see how Helms must have felt about this back channel.

But Kennedy disagreed. In 1975, during the Church Committee hearings into crimes of the intelligence community, William Attwood, an aide to the United Nations delegation, testified that he was chosen as an emissary for the White House in the Kennedy/Castro back channel operation. Attwood knew both men. He had written a two-part article on Castro for *Look* magazine in 1959. He had been a speechwriter for Kennedy and also his ambassador to the West African country of Guinea. As he stated in a September 1963 memo to Kennedy and his boss at the UN, Adlai Stevenson, he had enough rank to make Castro think the talks would be serious, but he was not well known enough to be easily noticed in his comings and goings. The negotiations were about to enter into high gear. By this time, Kennedy tried to freeze out the CIA and conduct his own diplomacy through private channels: Howard, Attwood, Cuban ambassador to the UN Carlos Lechuga, and as we will see later, French journalist Jean Daniel. But, Helms already knew the previous steps. And the National Security Agency was intercepting hundreds of calls per month from the USA to Cuba. Further, as Arthur Schlesinger notes, the CIA had wiretapped the Cuban counsel's phone at the UN. And in October of 1963, Vallejo—the man who started it all—now became a subject of interest to the Mexico City CIA station. Further, there is information that one of these CIA messages about Vallejo refers to a point of contact between him and an asset of David Morales' AMOT counter intelligence group out of JM-WAVE.[67] In other words, Morales' counterintelligence group may have had a basis for knowing about the back channel.

William Attwood later addressed the issue of what the CIA and Cuban exiles would do if they learned about the back channel. He said that if the CIA had found out about the back channel, it would have trickled down to the exiles and their gung-ho type handlers "who had been involved in the Bay of Pigs. . . . I can understand why they would have reacted violently. . . . This was the end of their dreams of returning to Cuba and they might have been impelled to take violent action. Such as assassinating the President."[68]

Attwood would have been apprehensive, maybe fearful, if he knew that *there were* Cuban exiles who appeared to know about the negotiations. While with the HSCA, Gaeton Fonzi interviewed many anti-Castro Cubans. One of them was Rolando Otero. Otero told the HSCA that the word being passed around Miami was that "Kennedy was a communist. He's against us, he's messing up the whole cause."[69] Otero went on to say that something big was being planned for the late summer or fall of 1963. Fonzi did all he could to find out Otero's source for this information. It turned out to be one Bernardo DeTorres.[70] DeTorres was a member of the Bay of Pigs invasion brigade. He was wounded and then captured. He was released from prison in December of 1962. Upon his return to Miami, he quickly rose up the ranks of the exile leaders to become a CIA favorite. Another exile with more specific information about why "something big" was being planned was Felipe Vidal Santiago. In a raid into Cuba in 1964, Vidal was apprehended by the Cuban internal security forces. He was tortured and then executed. While being interrogated, Vidal revealed a rather interesting piece of information. He began talking about what he had been doing in the fall of 1963. According to Fabian Escalante, a high officer at that time in Castro's G-2 forces, Vidal talked about his intense effort to communicate a key message to the other exiles at that time. That key message was that Kennedy had opened up negotiations with Castro and further, that President Kennedy was going to get the Soviets out of Cuba and try to establish normal relations with the revolutionary government. When that happened, the exile cause would be doomed.[71]

Operation TILT exemplified the desperation felt by the Cuban exiles and their allies in the summer of 1963. This was a renegade project. The Special Group inside the White House, headed by RFK, did not authorize it.[72] This was a June 1963 infiltration operation that was meant to bring back two Russian officers from Cuba. Once returned, they would testify how all the nuclear missiles on the island were not yet gone. In advance of the project, individuals like the wealthy industrialist William Pawley and John Martino—a close ally of the exile community who had served time in Castro's jails—and exile groups like Alpha 66 shopped the story in advance. In fact, a reporter from *Life* magazine was a part of the boat mission to Cuba. And even though the Special Group did not authorize the project, Theodore Shackley of JM-WAVE provided logistical support for it. The mission was a complete failure. In fact, the Cubans who went ashore never returned. And it is doubtful that the two Russian officers ever existed. But it shows just how badly Kennedy's opponents wished to upset his evolving Cuba policy.

But it may have been worse than that. In a visit to Washington in April of 1963, CRC leader Miro had asked Kennedy for 50 million dollars and permission to launch a new invasion of Cuba. At a press conference on April 17, Miro said that this request was turned down. TILT may have been part of a larger operation to instigate an invasion. For in the *Miami Herald* of June 20, 1963 a story led with the statement that 500 Cuban commandos had landed in Cuba and that this was the beginning of a campaign to liberate the island and that this information was generated by Tony Varona of the CRC, the new leader of that group after Miro had resigned after his meeting with the Kennedys. But two days later, that same newspaper carried an article bannered with "U.S. Skepticism on Cuban Commando Raid Grows." This article said that if there was any landing, it could not have been anywhere near that large. One day later, *The Miami News* carried an article saying that the "invasion" was a hoax. Later FBI reports confirmed this was a hoax done with the tacit approval of other CRC members.[73] And, in fact, even after it was exposed as that, certain members of the CRC still tried to sustain the fraud. After the FBI transmitted this information, the CIA came to agree the invasion was a hoax and concluded it was appended to TILT. Further that there were no Soviet contacts on the island.[74] After this dangerous attempt at provocation, the CRC lost its 80,000 dollars per month U.S. subsidy.

There was another way of provoking action of course. That was to reactivate the Castro assassination plots. In March of 1961, a CIA officer in Mexico City met with a dissatisfied member of Castro's government named Rolando Cubela.[75] Allegedly, Cubela had been overheard talking about eliminating Castro. In August of 1962, he was given some training by the CIA but refused to be polygraphed. This put his mission on hold.[76] It was taken off of hold in the early fall of 1963. Meetings took place in Paris with Cubela. Cubela insisted on meeting with a senior U.S. official in order to make sure that what was being attempted had the sanction of the American government at the highest levels. Cubela, whose code name was AM/LASH, suggested a meeting with Robert Kennedy.[77] This was not possible since the CIA was hiding these plots from the Kennedys. So on October 29 Desmond Fitzgerald went instead. Meeting Cubela in Paris, he said he was a friend of RFK. Fitzgerald's decision on impersonation and deception was discussed with Richard Helms. The Inspector General Report specifically states it was not cleared with the Kennedys.[78] Once given assurances, Cubela requested high powered rifles to kill Castro. Although there is some evidence that this was considered, the Inspector General Report states that he was actually given a poison pen device. The actual poison being Black Leaf 40. The delivery was reportedly made in Paris on November 22, 1963.[79]

As Arthur Schlesinger stated, the whole episode with Cubela raised serious questions. The resumption of the plots took place when, at the very least, Helms knew about the back channel and the change in policy. Schlesinger concluded that "it was a studied attempt to subvert national policy."[80] He then went further and agreed with Attwood, "Undoubtedly if word leaked of President Kennedy's efforts [in the back channel], that might have been exactly the kind of thing to trigger some explosion of fanatical violence. It seems to me as a possibility not to be excluded."[81]

This last comment seems an appropriate note on which to conclude our summary of what actually did happen with the back channel. Through Howard's communications with Castro, Attwood got a message that Castro wished to talk to Kennedy's emissary directly. He would send a plane to

Mexico to pick up the official and fly him to a private airport near Vera-
dero, where Castro would talk to him alone. The plane would then fly him
back.[82] Howard added that Castro wished to talk directly with Kennedy's
representative, but would not rule out sending an emissary if necessary. In
September, Kennedy then had Howard arrange a meeting between Attwood
and Lechuga under the cover of having a party at her house. Attwood told
Lechuga that Stevenson had authorized him to talk to the ambassador and
he would be flying to Washington in a few hours to inform Kennedy of the
feasibility of a rapprochement between the two countries.[83] Attwood continued that Kennedy felt that a change had to be made in the relations between
the two nations. It would not happen overnight, but a start had to be made.
Lechuga replied that Castro had wanted to make a new start with Kennedy,
but the Bay of Pigs had rendered that futile. But he had liked Kennedy's American University speech of that summer urging peaceful co-existence. Both
men pledged to keep in touch about developments since both leaders now
knew the other was interested in an official visitation. The next day, Attwood
reported on this to Robert Kennedy. RFK felt Attwood going to Cuba was
too risky. The negotiations would surely leak out then. He wanted to know
if Castro would be willing to meet elsewhere, perhaps at the UN. He told
Attwood to pursue the matter with Lechuga.[84]

Kennedy and Attwood then took a dramatic next step. Attwood now
arranged a new channel. Knowing that his friend, French journalist Jean
Daniel, was going to interview Kennedy and then proceed onto Cuba to talk
to Castro, he alerted Kennedy to Daniel's itinerary. Thus, a historic conversation took place on October 28 between Kennedy and Daniel. Kennedy wanted
Daniel to tell Castro that he understood the horrible exploitation, colonization,
and humiliation the history of Cuba represented and that the people of Cuba
had endured. He even painfully understood that the USA had been part of this
during the Batista regime. Startlingly, he said he approved of Castro's declarations made in the Sierra Maestra Mountains. He added, "In the matter of the
Batista regime, I am in agreement with the first Cuban revolutionaries. That is
perfectly clear." Daniel was somewhat taken aback by these sentiments. But,
Kennedy continued, the dilemma now was that Cuba—because of its Soviet
ties—had become part of the Cold War. And this had led to the Missile Crisis.
Kennedy felt that Khrushchev understood all these ramifications now, after that
terrible thirteen days.

The president concluded with this, "but so far as Fidel Castro is concerned,
I must say I don't know whether he realizes this, or even if he cares about it."
Kennedy smiled and then ended Daniel's instructions with this: "You can tell
me whether he does when you come back."[85]

Daniel then went to Havana. On November 19 Castro walked into his hotel. Fidel was fully aware of the Attwood/Lechuga meetings. He was also aware of Kennedy's briefing of Daniel. He had found out about this through Howard. In fact, he had told her he did not think it would be a good idea for him to meet Attwood in New York. He suggested that the meeting could be arranged by picking up Attwood in Mexico and flying him to Cuba. Castro also agreed that Che Guevara should be left out of the talks since he opposed their ultimate aim. Attwood said that Lechuga and he should meet to discuss a full agenda for a later meeting between himself and Castro. This was done per Kennedy's instructions, and JFK wanted to brief Attwood beforehand on what the agenda should be. The endgame was now in sight.

Daniel was unaware of the above when Castro walked into his room for a six-hour talk about Kennedy.[86] After Daniel relayed Kennedy's message, Castro spoke thusly, "Suddenly a president arrives on the scene who tries to support the interest of another class." Clearly elated by Daniel's message, Castro and the journalist spent a large part of the next three days together. Castro even stated that JFK could now become the greatest president since Lincoln.

On the third day, Daniel was having lunch with Fidel when the phone rang. The news about Kennedy being shot in Dallas had arrived. Stunned, Castro hung up the phone, sat down, and then repeated over and over, "This is bad news . . . This is bad news . . . This is bad news." A few moments later, when the radio broadcasted a report stating that Kennedy was now dead, Castro stood up and said, "Everything is changed. Everything is going to change."[87]

Castro was correct. Attwood would later write that what it took eleven months to build was gone in about three weeks. By December 17 it was clear that President Johnson was brushing it all aside. Retroactively, Attwood came to conclude that it had all really ended in Dealey Plaza. He finalized his thoughts about the progress made up to that point with this sentence, which is quite appropriate to this discussion: "There is no doubt in my mind: If there had been no assassination, we probably would have moved into negotiations leading toward normalization of relations with Cuba."[88]

The author has tried to show here how Kennedy's foreign policy concepts differed from Eisenhower and the Dulles brothers and how those ideas were resisted. We should add one more important piece of information before leaving that topic for now. As noted above, Howard Hunt greatly admired Allen Dulles. And, in fact, he was detailed to him after the Bay of Pigs debacle. Together, they tried to shift the blame for the Bay of Pigs disaster to Kennedy. But there is another man who was even higher up in the CIA who admired Dulles perhaps even more than Hunt. In fact, he revered him. In his holographic will he called Dulles "The patriot."[89] Counterintelligence Chief James Angleton was appointed to his position by Dulles. His sponsorship of Angleton "was the key factor in the untrammeled growth of Angleton's internal authority."[90] In life, jealous colleagues named him "No-Knock" Angleton, since, unannounced, he could walk into Dulles's office almost anytime he wished. In death, Angleton exhibited his devotion by actually carrying his mentor's ashes at Dulles's funeral.[91] Angleton could not have been very glad to see his friend, colleague, and benefactor from OSS days forced to leave the office he had nearly unlimited access to.

After the Bay of Pigs, Angleton was tasked with conducting a review of Cuban intelligence and also helping to create and train a more competent intelligence corps to serve the CRC.[92] This would have brought him into contact with both Morales and his AMOT service, and David Phillips who—as we will see—was moved to Mexico City and tasked with conducting anti-Cuba operations from there.

As we have seen, the more militant wing of the Cuban exile community actually thought Kennedy was a communist for winding down the secret war against Castro and considering a diplomatic approach to Cuba. There was no more reactionary an anti-Communist than James Angleton. Angleton thought that the Soviets had actually installed about 30 communist sympathizers as either heads of state, in high-level political positions, as foreign intelligence officers, or even CIA officers. This included Lester Pearson of Canada, Olof Palme of Sweden, Willy Brandt of West Germany, Harold Wilson of England, and Averill Harriman of the United States.[93] As we have seen above, both Harvey and Angleton were tasked by Richard Helms with exploring techniques of assassinating foreign heads of state.

Allen Dulles left office in late November of 1961. Five months later, Lee Oswald and his Soviet wife notified the American Embassy in Moscow that they planned on leaving Russia to return to the USA. The reader should take passing notice of this fact. Because as we will see, in the declassified files of the ARRB, there exists much evidence to show that, at the very least, James Angleton had a strong interest in Lee Harvey Oswald. At the most, Angelton was his control officer. In light of that, in the summer of 1963, Oswald, in a move that has never been fully explained, relocated from Dallas to New Orleans. We shall now begin to move our focus there in order to elucidate some of the fascinating evidence the Warren Commission would ignore about what Oswald did while in the Crescent City. Jim Garrison would later be convinced by this evidence that Oswald was being manipulated in advance of the assassination. As we will see, for this discovery, he would be targeted by James Angleton.

CHAPTER FIVE

New Orleans

*"Oswald is a patsy. They set him up. The bastards have done
something outrageous. . . . They've killed the president."*

—Gary Underhill, November 23, 1963

In retrospect, both the giveaway and the key was always New Orleans. It seems strange that no one picked up a pattern at the time. But as we shall see, the official investigatory agencies weren't really looking for anything suspicious.

The Woman Who Foresaw the Assassination

Very late on November 19, 1963, at a bar on U.S. Highway 190 near Eunice, Louisiana, a woman got into an argument with two men she had driven up to the saloon with. The seedy bar was called the Silver Slipper Lounge, and the bartender was named Mac Manual. Eunice is due west of Baton Rouge, northwest of New Orleans.[1] Rose Cheramie was a woman with quite a shady past, one which dealt with drugs and prostitution. On this night, she was involved in a heroin deal with the two Cubans who were with her. Their journey had begun in Florida and was scheduled to end in Dallas. But at the Silver Slipper, she got into an argument with the two men who were scheduled to meet a third party at the saloon. The argument got heated, and Manual and the two escorts threw her out. She then started hitchhiking on 190. She was hit by a car driven by one Frank Odom.

Odom then delivered her to Moosa Memorial Hospital in Eunice.[2] On November 20, Lieutenant Francis Fruge of the Louisiana State Police received a phone call from Mrs. Louise Guillory, the hospital administrator. She knew Fruge worked the narcotics detail, and she felt that Cheramie, who was addicted to heroin, was going through withdrawals.[3] Fruge drove to the hospital. When he got there, he encountered a middle-aged white female sitting down in the waiting room outside emergency. She was only partly coherent. The reason Guillory had called was because Moosa was a private hospital, and Cheramie seemed bereft of funds. Fruge took Cheramie to the Eunice City Jail and then attended the Eunice Police Department's Annual Ball. About an hour later, a police officer came to the function and told Fruge that Cheramie was undergoing severe withdrawal symptoms.[4] Fruge then called a local doctor who suggested a sedative. Dr. Derouin then suggested she be taken to the state facility at Jackson. Fruge now called for an ambulance from Charity Hospital in Lafayette, and he accompanied her to Jackson.

According to Fruge's deposition for the House Select Committee on Assassinations, it was in the ambulance that Rose began to relate her fascinating and astonishing tale. Calmed by the sedative and, according to Fruge, quite lucid in demeanor, she began to respond to some routine questions with some unusual answers. She told Fruge about the trip from Florida to Dallas to deliver the package of heroin. But she also said something almost omniscient: That the two Cubans had talked about killing Kennedy in Dallas.[5] Fruge did not take this very seriously. He considered it to be, at least partly, the ravings of a junkie. Once delivered to Jackson, Fruge left. He then told a cohort on the force, Don White, about what Rose had told him.[6] Fruge may not have taken her seriously at the time, but according to a doctor interviewed by the House Select Committee, Rose predicted the assassination before it occurred on November 22.[7] A nurse by the name of Charlie Wilbans also talked to Cheramie.[8] A couple of days later, the same doctor to whom she told her miraculous prognostication talked to her again. She told him a remarkable detail: she had worked for Jack Ruby. The fact that she predicted the assassination in advance spread through the hospital. Dr. Wayne Owen, who had been interning from LSU at the time, later told the *Madison Capital Times* that he and other interns were told of the plot in advance of the assassination.[9] Owen told the same newspaper that Cheramie had also revealed the name of one Jack Rubinstein in advance. Owen did not understand the significance of this until he learned that Rubinstein was Jack Ruby's real name. When Owen learned that Ruby was Rubinstein, he grew quite concerned: "We were all assured that something would be done about it by the FBI or someone. Yet we never heard anything."

Once Kennedy was killed in Dallas, Fruge reversed himself on Cheramie. He called the hospital in Jackson "and told them by no way in the world to turn her loose until I could get my hands on her."[10] So, on November 25, Fruge interviewed Cheramie again. He found out her Florida journey with the two men had originated in Miami. Also, that the men seemed to be a part of the conspiracy rather than just cognizant of it. Cheramie's child was being held as ransom so that she would play her part in the drug deal. After the heroin transaction, she was to proceed to the Rice Hotel in Houston under an assumed name. Houston is in close proximity to Galveston, the town from which the drugs were coming in. From there, they were to escape to Mexico. Fruge had the heroin aspect of Cheramie's story investigated. Every part of it checked out from the correct ship name coming into Galveston to the reservations under a false name at the Rice Hotel.[11]

On November 26, Fruge flew Cheramie from Louisiana to Houston. In the back seat of the small Sesna 180, a newspaper was lying between them. One of the headlines read that the investigators had found no connections between Ruby and Oswald. When Cheramie read this, she started to giggle. She said that Ruby and Oswald did know each other. She understood this from working for Ruby.[12] Fruge then had his superior call Will Fritz of the Dallas Police to relay what an important witness Cheramie could be in the Kennedy case. Fruge then told the HSCA what happened next: "Colonel Morgan called Captain Fritz up from Dallas and told him what we had, the information that we had. . . . And there was a little conversation. . . . He turned around and told us they don't want her. They're not interested."[13] Fruge then asked Cheramie if she wished to tell her tale to the FBI. She declined. She did not wish to involve herself further. With this, the Cheramie investigation was now halted. Rose was released, and Fruge went back to Louisiana. Her potentially explosive story was now put out to pasture.

The story could possibly have been even more explosive than Fruge thought. For on November 28, 1963, a Margaret Kay Kauffmann of Martinsburg, Pennsylvania, told the FBI that her mother had recovered a piece of paper in the leaves beneath her porch. It was a trailer advertisement. In handwriting scrawled across the top left was the name of a club called the Silver Slipper or Silver Bell. In the top middle of the page was the name Lee Oswald. On the top right was the name Rubinstein. In the middle was the name Jack Ruby and at the bottom was the name Dallas, Texas. A Cuban doctor named Julio Fernandez often burned trash in their backyard, under her balcony. The paper with the names on it was found about 20 feet from his last burn. Fernandez's brother had been the captain of police under Fulgencio Batista.[14]

Martin Pushes Banister over the Edge

Guy Banister told Guy Johnson about a week before the assassination, "If I'm dead in a week, no matter what the circumstances look like, it won't be from natural causes."[15] As we have seen, Johnson was the reserve Office of Naval Intelligence officer who had aided the arrival of Sergio Arcacha Smith from Cuba into New Orleans. On November 22, in the company of Joe New-brough, Banister had stopped at a print shop where he learned about the assassination of President Kennedy in Dallas. He said, "Now all we have to do is kill Earl Warren and the country will clear up."[16] Once cozily ensconced and drinking at the Katzenjammer Bar, he then said, "I wonder why Bobby wasn't included."[17]

Banister was joined at the Katzenjammer by his associate Jack Martin. Martin was one of the so-called investigators who did detective work for Banister's office whenever an assignment would come in. Later on, back at the office, a quarrel developed between the two men. According to Banister's secretary Delphine Roberts, Martin was standing in the office in proximity to where the files were kept. Banister then accused Martin of absconding with several files and hiding them in his coat. Martin said something he should not have: "What are you going to do, kill me like you all did Kennedy?" Banister then started to pistol whip Martin's face with a .357 Magnum revolver. Martin felt that Banister would have killed him if not for the intervention of Roberts, who pleaded with him not to shoot him.[18] Banister relented. He shoved some money in Martin's pocket and told him to go to a doctor or hospital. As Martin walked out, he stopped back at the bar he and Banister had been drinking at. He remarked to the bartender, "The dirty Nazi bastards did it to him in Texas and to me here!"[19] Martin was treated for his injuries at Charity Hospital.[20] Martin also called the police about the assault. But in addition, he called Presley Trosclair Jr., a police intelligence officer, to report the incident. According to Bob Buras, a former New Orleans police officer and HSCA investigator, no ordinary person could get through to Trosclair about such an incident. The report was written by Francis Martello, another interesting fact. For, as we will see, it was Martello who interviewed Oswald after he was arrested in a curious street disturbance in August of that year.[21]

Local FBI agent Regis Kennedy, along with his partner on the Cuban exile beat Warren DeBrueys, knew much about New Orleans, Guy Banister, and Lee Oswald. Garrison investigator Andrew Sciambra learned that Kennedy thought Banister was the key to everything that happened in New Orleans and further, that he was in on everything from the beginning to the very end. Kennedy also believed that Martin *did* actually steal some of Banister's CIA files and that is what caused the assault.²² Confirming part of this was Mary Brengel, a part-time secretary in Banister's office. She said that when the news came on the radio that Kennedy had been shot, Delphine Roberts was elated. For the HSCA, Brengel said that she came to believe that both Banister and Roberts had some prior knowledge of the assassination.²³

But, interestingly enough, Martin now began to talk to and send letters out to law enforcement officials about David Ferrie, not Banister. (This is probably because he feared being assaulted again.) On the twenty-third, he told the New Orleans police that Ferrie owned a rifle similar to the one used in the assassination; that Ferrie and Oswald were in the same Civil Air Patrol unit; at the time of the assassination, Ferrie was headed for Texas; and that Ferrie had Oswald's library card on him the day Kennedy was killed.²⁴ In a November 25 letter to the FBI, Martin said much of the same about Ferrie, except that he added a couple of interesting points. First, Ferrie was getting mail from Cuban people Oswald was connected with, and second, Ferrie was dumped by Cubans because of his pro-Castro activity.²⁵ Since there is no record of Ferrie doing anything pro-Castro, could Martin have been talking about Ferrie's knowledge of and/or participation in Oswald's pro-Castro activities that summer? On the twenty-fourth, Martin got in contact with Herman Kohlman of the DA's office in New Orleans.

Although the New Orleans police did not think there was anything interesting about Ferrie, they were almost certainly either wrong or being deliberately blind. For in the wake of the assassination, Ferrie was doing something that was more than faintly suspicious. In fact it could be noted that, as prosecutors like Vincent Bugliosi like to say, Ferrie was showing "consciousness of guilt." For it appears he was trying to confiscate evidence that he was ever associated with Oswald. Within the space of five days, he did this at least three times. Oswald's former landlady in New Orleans told several sources, including the HSCA, that Ferrie was at her door in search of his library card. He thought he may have loaned it to Oswald and wanted to retrieve it from his room. Even though Oswald had left New Orleans two months previous, Ferrie was looking for it now. But, as William Davy has noted, what is so startling about this testimony is that Ferrie was at her door on the day of the assassination, *before* he left for Texas.²⁶ After Ferrie returned from that state, he was at it again. He went to see a neighbor of Oswald, a couple named Eames. Ferrie had heard that her husband saw Oswald at the library. He wanted to know if Mr. Eames ascertained whose card Oswald used there.²⁷ Then again, on November 27, Ferrie was on the phone calling the home of a past member of his Civil Air Patrol unit. Roy McCoy was not there at the time, so his wife answered the phone. She said Ferrie asked about any pictures McCoy had at his house that depicted his past membership in Ferrie's CAP unit. Ferrie said the meetings he helmed were held at the New Orleans Airport. Ferrie also asked her if the name "Oswald" was familiar to her. McCoy called the FBI about this incident. He told them that he thought that "Ferrie was seeking information about Oswald and photographs of Oswald to show that he was not acquainted with Oswald,"[28] which is an appropriate description of what Ferrie was up to in the days after the assassination. The obvious question that no one ever got to ask David Ferrie about this was: Why?

Ferrie's Old Friend Lee Oswald

David William Ferrie was born in Cleveland, Ohio, in 1918. He was educated in Catholic schools like St. Patrick's Elementary and St. Ignatius High School, from which he graduated in 1935.[29] His father, James H. Ferrie, was a captain in the Cleveland Police Department and later became a lawyer. After graduating, Ferrie then went to John Carroll University, another Catholic institution. Ferrie got good grades there, but he decided to leave after his junior year to become a priest. Therefore in 1938 he entered St. Mary's Seminary in Cleveland. He studied there for three years. But the year before he was to graduate, he had a nervous breakdown. After he recovered, he tried to return, but St. Mary's did not want him back. He reportedly had, a problem with authority.

Ferrie now shifted his goal to becoming a teacher. He enrolled at Baldwin-Wallace College in nearby Berea, Ohio. In 1940–41 he did his student teaching at Rocky River High School located in a suburb of Cleveland. A department chair, interviewed years later about Ferrie, said he was a poor teacher. She also criticized his character as being "tricky, a bluffer, shrewd, and probably a liar." She also added that he seemed to have "a particular interest in the younger students, more than a teacher should have."

At the conclusion of his student teaching, Ferrie seemed to understand it was not for him. So he tried again to become a priest. In August of 1941, he enrolled at St. Charles Seminary in Carthagena, Ohio. While there, his father bought him a plane, and David learned to fly. But in 1944, on the eve of his graduation, the seminary refused to allow him to continue his studies. After spending six years trying to become a priest, Ferrie had now failed not once, but twice. This was obviously a terrible blow to him.

There was an unsigned memo at St. Charles which explained why this had occurred. The anonymous author noted that although David had started out there well, he later began to have social problems. After gaining a position of leadership, he began to exhibit an instability of character. This manifested itself in growing conflict and jealousy, back-stabbing, self-pity, exaggeration, manipulation, threats, and contempt of authority. There was no one grand event, but rather an accumulation of infractions that led the elders at the seminar to believe Ferrie would not fit in as a leader of a religious community. The final and most debilitating point against him was this: "When corrected, his attitude seemed to be that the rule should be changed rather than he should be forced to observe it." So on November 27, 1944, he was dismissed.

David now began to see a psychiatrist. And it resulted in a period of relative stability for him. He resided at home while teaching English and aeronautics at Benedictine High School, a Catholic boy's school in Cleveland. It was here that Ferrie also began his long relationship with the Civil Air Patrol. And around this time, Ferrie began to be seriously interested in the Cold War and fighting communists. He tried to secure an Air Force commission by writing President Truman's Secretary of Defense Louis A. Johnson. In the letter, Ferrie accented both his flying and instructional skills with young pilots: "and by God, they will get into action and kill those Russians—they should have been wiped out years ago. When am I going to get the commission, when the Russians are bombing Cleveland?"[30] When the commission was not forthcoming, Ferrie tried writing the Air Force directly, in similar terms, "There is nothing I would enjoy better than blowing the hell out of every damn Russian Communist, Red, or what have you. . . . I want to train killers, however bad that sounds. It is what we need."[31] In 1948, a string of serious misconduct episodes in the CAP culminated in him leaving Ohio. In one instance, Ferrie flew a grounded plane after dark and with no lights from Columbus to Cleveland. Upon his landing, he said he was an officer in the Air Force. This almost got him dismissed from the CAP. In 1950 two CAP cadets reported that Ferrie, as their instructor, had them visit a bordello in a nearby town. Facing dismissal, Ferrie negotiated a transfer to Louisiana. When the Louisiana branch asked for his Ohio file, the Cleveland office found it missing, but could not prove it had been stolen.

So in 1951, David Ferrie arrived in his new home of New Orleans. He moved into the storied French Quarter and was soon living on Bourbon Street. Ferrie had some productive years there in the fifties. He landed a good job with Eastern Air lines, learned to fly large passenger jets, and was eventually promoted to the rank of captain. With much downtime, Ferrie began to study things of interest to him like biochemistry, psychology, and hypnotism. He continued his involvement with the CAP and rose to the rank of captain. It was here that Ferrie met the young Lee Oswald.

In 1955, a classmate of both Oswald and his friend Ed Voebel interested the two adolescents into joining the local CAP.[32] Oswald was fifteen at the time; Ferrie was more than twice his age. There were two troops in New Orleans: One was at Lakefront Airport (Lakefront Squadron), and one was at Moisant

Airport (Eagle Squadron). Oswald began attending meetings at the former location. But later in the summer, he shifted to Eagle Squadron. Eagle appears to have been a renegade CAP unit created by Ferrie after he got in trouble again with the authorities over his dubious activities.[33] He encouraged them to drink, took them on unauthorized flights in his Stinson Voyager plane, and taught them "mouth-to-mouth resuscitation."[34] He gave his cadets the impression he was studying medicine at Tulane University, which he was not. He also led overnight encampments at Keesler Air Force Base in nearby Biloxi, Mississippi.

But Ferrie also told his cadets that he was going to control their outside activities and their future destinies. Two former cadets said that Ferrie convinced four of them to join the Marines.[35] Robert Boylston told the HSCA that Ferrie gave him over a thousand dollars to attend Loyola University in New Orleans and never once asked for it back. Boylston recalled that Ferrie was always talking about secret orders of a military or intelligence nature. In 1958, Ferrie said he had secret knowledge of the Lebanon Crisis, where Eisenhower sent troops to secure the Beirut International Airport when Lebanon was being threatened by Syria and Egypt. In 1960 he said he knew about secret orders about Cuba. When he was wounded in 1960 or '61, Ferrie said it was on a flight over Cuba. In 1961—after the Bay of Pigs—Ferrie talked a great deal about a "group" who knew what was going on in America and was going to take care of it. Boylston said that when Ferrie's drill team went to Dallas for a competition, Ferrie gave them a name to call. They did, and the man set up reservations for them at a motel. Ferrie flew back on an Air Force C-47. Ferrie told Boylston that he was never to talk about their training at the lake, even if "it" didn't go. Boylston did not know what "it" was. And he did not want to know. But he felt that "some of the people around Ferrie, and Ferrie, were not playing when they talked about "taking care of something."[36]

In 1993 proven plagiarist Gerald Posner wrote in his discredited book *Case Closed* that there was no credible evidence that Oswald knew David Ferrie. This is and was ludicrous. It turns out that Ferrie was correct in his fear that there was a photo of himself with Oswald from the CAP. The photo surfaced in 1993 and was shown on the PBS *Frontline* special about Oswald. Former Moisant CAP member John B. Ciravalo Jr. discovered it.[37] But beyond that, there were several witnesses who put the two men together in New Orleans. Posner deliberately avoided mentioning this evidence, because it was easy to find. It was also easy to discover that, in addition to absconding with evidence that demonstrated the relationship, Ferrie was lying about not knowing Oswald. In his FBI interview of November 25, Ferrie named Jerry Paradis as an instructor in the CAP in 1954–55. Ferrie told the Bureau that Paradis could tell them that Oswald and Ferrie were never in the same unit together. Yet when Mike Ewing of the HSCA interviewed Paradis, he told him that he was surprised that the FBI never interviewed him about the matter since, "I sure could have told them when Oswald and Ferrie were in the CAP." He stated that "I specifically remember Oswald. I can remember him clearly, and Ferrie was heading the unit then. I'm not saying that they may have been there together, I'm saying it is a certainty." Paradis, who was then a corporate lawyer, said Oswald first attended meetings at Lakefront, but when Ferrie left Lakefront to start up a troop at Moisant, Oswald followed him there.[38] This was echoed by CAP member Anthony Atzenhoffer, who was a platoon sergeant and frequently called the roll at meetings. He told Ewing that he was sure Ferrie and Oswald were at Moisant together at the same time. He also recalled Voebel being there with Oswald.[39] (To further show the kinds of connections Ferrie had at the time, Atzenhoffer added that Ferrie tried to recruit CAP students for "experiments" at Tulane Medical School.)

George Boesch was another cadet who recalled Oswald as one of the twelve to fifteen students who attended meetings at Moisant Airport when Ferrie was the instructor.[40] Colin Hamer, now with the New Orleans Public library, also attended meetings at Moisant Airport, which were run by Ferrie. He recalled Oswald attended these meetings helmed by Ferrie that summer of 1955.[41] Ferrie himself later admitted to teaching Oswald in the CAP. In June of 1964, Thomas Lewis Clark worked for Ferrie at his filling station on Veteran's Highway. After Ferrie sold that station, Clark continued to work with him at Saturn Aviation. On one occasion, Ferrie and Clark discussed Lee Oswald. According to Clark, Ferrie said that he had been Oswald's instructor in the CAP.[42] So it was only natural for Oswald to look up some of his former CAP friends when he returned to New Orleans in the spring of 1963. As we shall see, this is what happened.

But the David Ferrie that Oswald met up with again was not the same man from 1955. Towards the end of the fifties, Ferrie caught a disease called *alopecia totalis*. This caused his hair to fall out in clumps. Before long, all the hair on his body, including his eyebrows and eyelashes was gone. He hand fashioned a crude wig for his head and used grease pencils to draw in ersatz eyebrows. As the fifties ended, Ferrie began to further grow his violent political temperament. He finally fulfilled this by becoming a contract agent for the CIA, flying missions over Cuba.[43] Ferrie developed an obsession for the regime of Fidel Castro. This led him to become more intertwined with the Agency and its underground Cuban exile community in New Orleans. He bombed targets inside of Cuba at the request of former Cuban Congressman Eladio del Valle. Del Valle was linked to the CIA, Santo Trafficante, and Senator George Smathers.[44]

But in the early sixties, two things happened to Ferrie that managed to turn his life in New Orleans upside down. First, along with Sergio Arcacha Smith, Ferrie was part of the CIA training and preparations for the Bay of Pigs. When that operation fizzled, Ferrie was devastated. Secondly, he got into trouble with his CAP duties that ended up costing him his pilot job at Eastern Air Lines. One night, Ferrie got intoxicated and, trying to impress a young man, he borrowed a plane and went for a joy ride. He flew very low to the ground, at treetop level. FAA officials were awaiting him at the airport when he touched down. They set in motion an effort to pull his pilot's license.[45] Ferrie also was expelled from the CAP. He insisted on sleeping in the cabin with the teenage cadets, and threw a beer party on the beach for the troop. Both were violations of CAP rules. Once he left the CAP, Ferrie started his own flying club for teenage boys, holding meetings at his home. Ferrie eventually was dismissed from Eastern Air Lines. As Jerry Paradis told the HSCA, he knew Ferrie was quite bitter about losing his job, which was well paying and allowed him to live a comfortable life. For instance, in 1961, Ferrie was living in a three-level house near New Orleans International Airport, where he worked. Ferrie lived with his mother on the main floor. This is where he held air patrol meetings. The top floor was David's domain. It contained a medical library, a psychiatric couch, and medical equipment like microscopes. In the basement were the sawed-off remains of a World War II fighter plane, which Ferrie used as a teaching tool to simulate flying for his students. When Oswald recontacted his old friend in 1963, Ferrie apparently could not afford the house anymore. He was living in a second level apartment on Louisiana Avenue Parkway in uptown New Orleans. As we shall see, in this time period, Ferrie grew more and more obsessed with Cuba and fighting communists.

Clay Bertrand Hires a Lawyer for Oswald

Dean Andrews was a short, roly-poly New Orleans attorney who walked with a jaunt and spoke in an offbeat manner, using words like "Daddy-o" and "cool cat" and "my man."[46] It was hard to see exactly what he looked like because he wore a set of oversized sunglasses through which he could see the world but no one could see him. He wore them constantly, indoors and out, no matter what the weather.

Andrews was not an upper-echelon, corporate lawyer. He had a small office in an older office building and was not above letting clients and friends buy him lunch. Heavyset, he suffered from a heart condition, which he did little to counter. Much of his practice dealt with morals charges like pro-

stitution—including homosexual prostitution—and he also did immigration
work. He did not deal with deep-south high society, which might help explain
his demeanor. It certainly explains his clientele, which included many Hispa-
nics and poor whites. In the summer and fall of 1963, both groups called on
him for services that would lead him into unwanted prominence, and later
into perjury.

Sometime in late May, a group of young Hispanic youths, or as Andrews
called them, "gay Mexicanos," were brought into his office. They were with
a slender white man of medium height.[47] Andrews knew the man who had
sent the "gay Mexicanos," a Clay Bertrand. He agreed to represent the
youngsters on charges of lewd behavior. During his testimony, Warren Commission counsel Wesley Liebeler asked if by "gay" he meant they were homosexual. Andrews replied they were. After the youths left, the other man—Lee
Oswald—stuck around and chatted with the attorney about some of his own
legal problems: his military discharge (which had been lowered to undesirable
because of his defection), his own citizenship, and the citizenship of his Russian wife. Andrews told him that they were not serious problems. They would
be easy to solve. Some Oswald could handle himself. He advised him where to
get the proper forms and how much it would cost. Andrews said that Oswald
visited his office three to five times that summer. Once was with one of the gay
boys who accompanied him the first time. He said he also saw him leafleting
downtown on Canal Street. Interestingly, Oswald told Andrews he was being
paid to do a job.[48] Andrews did not see Oswald again after that time.

Liebeler noted that Andrews was appearing under a subpoena that compelled him to bring any documents relating to his work with Oswald. Andrews
replied he had none since his office had been rifled right after the assassination.[49]

A few months after meeting Oswald, Andrews was in the hospital. He
received a call from an acquaintance named Clay Bertrand.[50] Bertrand called
him occasionally to defend his friends who, like the young Latins, got involved
in minor scrapes or morals charges. Andrews told Liebeler that he assumed
that Bertrand was the man who sent him the young boys and Oswald. Unlike
most of his other clients, Bertrand was not lower class, poor, or indigent. He
was well off, educated, respected. He occupied a different social stratum, so
much so that Andrews rarely saw him, "he is mostly a voice on the phone."[51] He
was calling Andrews now because he knew someone in Dallas who needed his
services. It was the man with the previous citizenship problem. His name was
Lee Oswald, and he was accused of murdering John F. Kennedy.

In an interesting yet little noted part of this interview, Liebeler—who had
reviewed all the FBI documents on Andrews—asked the witness if he recalled

telling an FBI agent if Bertand had come into his office with Oswald.[52] Andrews did not actually deny it. He said that he did not remember it. Which is interesting because, right after this, Andrews said that he had seen Bertrand about six weeks before, and he had run away from him. Liebeler then asked if Bertrand was simply a figment of his imagination. To which Andrews replied that this is what the FBI wanted him to say. And he had been badgered by them so much that he told them to "Write what you want, that I am nuts. I don't care."[53] And it is clear that, as we will see, Andrews was being worn down. As Liebeler later noted, in his December, 1963 FBI report he described Bertrand as being six foot, two inches. Yet on the day of his testimony, July 21, 1964, he said he was five foot, eight inches. Clearly, Andrews was trying to discount his ability to ID the man. But there is little doubt that Bertrand did call him to defend Oswald. For Andrews then called a lawyer friend of his named Monk Zelden to go to Dallas for him instead. Zelden let him know he would not be going because Oswald had been killed.[54]

The Clinton-Jackson Incident

Banister pistol whipping Martin on the day of the assassination after Martin cast aspersions over his role in the JFK murder; David Ferrie searching frantically to see if Oswald had his library card or if there was a picture depicting him with the accused assassin; Clay Bertrand calling Dean Andrews to defend a previous client he likely had forwarded him and who was now accused of killing President Kennedy. All of these incriminating events took place in New Orleans within a few short days after Kennedy was killed in Dallas. Perhaps no one noticed a pattern in these seemingly unconnected events because the individuals involved seemed themselves so unconnected. But if the authorities had dug a bit deeper and traced their travel and their associations in the New Orleans area that summer, they would have found such a connection: a time and a place that linked three of the main characters and (more than) several credible witnesses who could have testified to their association.

Edwin Lee McGehee was a town barber in Jackson, Louisiana. It was late summer and as the afternoon rolled on and the temperature decreased, he decided to turn off the air conditioning.[55] He then walked over and opened the door to his shop. He was alone so as he returned inside, he plumped down in his barber chair. As he did, he heard—but did not see—a car pull up and then a door slam. A young man who McGehee had never seen before now walked inside. Upon entering, the visitor said "A barbershop is a good place for a haircut and some information." As McGehee got out of the chair, the young man slid into it. Edwin began to clip his hair, and the customer now asked if there were any jobs available in Jackson. The barber replied that there were few opportunities. Oswald suggested the local hospital. The formal title of which was the East Louisiana State Hospital. Informally it was called "East." (This is the same mental hospital Rose Cheramie was taken to.) The barber said, "Do you know that is a mental hospital?" Oswald acted surprised, "Oh?" Recovering, the young man now queried the barber, "Do they have all kinds of jobs over there? Such as an electrician job?" Edwin said they likely did. But he then added that if he wanted to secure employment, he would probably have to get a reference from a local political representative. In that regard, Edwin recommended he see his friend Reeves Morgan who was a state legislator from the area. Oswald got up and complemented him on the haircut. McGehee then gave him directions to Reeves Morgan's home. Edwin also told him that it probably would help if he was a registered voter in the parish. If he did that, he would have to go to the voter registrar's office in nearby Clinton. After the young man left, McGehee went to the sink to wash his hands. Looking through the window, he could see that the car that pulled up was now gone. For New Orleans DA Jim Garrison, Edwin identified his customer that day as Lee Harvey Oswald.

It was now evening and the air was thinning out. There was no trash service at his rural Jackson home, so Reeves Morgan decided to burn some trash in his fireplace. His son Van was playing outside in the front yard. His daughter Mary was in the house.[56] From his front window, Reeves saw the headlights of a car pull up the driveway of his home. A knock came to his front door, and the young man was let in. As the visitor stepped inside and began speaking, Mary walked by him to the freezer on the front porch.[57] He introduced himself as Lee Oswald. He asked Reeves if he could assist him in obtaining a position as an electrician at the hospital. The local representative replied that he could not place him ahead of his Clinton and Jackson constituents. Morgan then advised him that he would probably have to take a civil-service test, and if he were a registered voter in the parish, that would give him some extra points on it. Oswald then left and Morgan heard the car drive away. Young Van, who had been playing outside, recalled being impressed by the length and look of the car, which he recalled as a black Cadillac. He thought they must be important people. He also noted that the driver of the car, who stayed inside it, had a shock of white hair.[58] Reeves Morgan later identified this visitor to Jim Garrison as Lee Harvey Oswald.

Clinton and Jackson are neighboring small agricultural villages about 90 minutes northwest of New Orleans in Feliciana Parish. That summer of 1963, the civil rights movement was picking up steam everywhere in the South, and in Clinton a major drive to register voters, sponsored by the Congress of Racial

Equality (CORE), was taking place. The tension between the Afro-American CORE workers and the local whites had been demonstrated in a series of articles in the *Baton Rouge States Times* in mid-August.[59] Most of the town's adult population was out on that September day. They congregated around the registrar's office. Blacks wanted to prevent any intimidation by whites to stop African-American registration; whites were checking on any possible outsiders rolling into town to organize and encourage the drive.

They were concerned, therefore, when—following Reeves Morgan's advice—the large black Cadillac drove into Clinton in the midst of the CORE registration drive. One of the first to notice the car that morning was the local CORE leader, a man named Corrie Collins.[60] The conspicuous car parked across from the registrar's office on Helena Street. Collins watched as a young white male emerged from the back of the car and entered the registration line. Oswald was notable not just because of the car he arrived in, but because, aside from Estes Morgan, he was the only white man to try and register that day.[61] In tongue-in-cheek acknowledgement of their singularity, while waiting in line, Morgan told Oswald that they would probably not get to register that day since they were white. Oswald replied that he was probably correct.[62] Henry Brown, another witness to the incident, said that the wait got so long that Estes Morgan actually sat in the car at one point.[63]

The local registrar was a man named Henry Earl Palmer. He was open only two and a half days per week, on Thursday, Friday, and Saturday morning. Palmer opened at 8:30. On this day, at about 10:30, he decided to go downstairs to buy a cup of coffee.[64] As he did, Palmer could not help but notice Oswald in line. And he also noted Collins watching the black Cadillac. Town residents like Andrew Dunn, James Bell, Charlotte Greenup, Verla Bell, and William Dunn all noted the car. Greenup later said that the car stayed there for hours.[65] CORE worker James Bell was asked why he so vividly recalled the car. He said that, "When you're working for CORE, you begin to try to read people and automobiles as fast as you can."[66] Robert Thomas noticed the car with "white men in it." Eddie Lee Spears recalled the black car in Clinton with three white men sitting inside.[67]

Henry Burnell Clark was a twenty-nine-year-old grocery clerk who had just stepped out in front of the Stewart and Carroll store a little before the noon hour. He saw "coming from the direction of the bank, east of the store, and walking in a westerly direction toward me, a tall man in a dark business suit. . . . He approached facing me, to a distance of about ten or twelve feet from me, and stepped off into the street." Clark then said that he entered the black car parked at the curb. Clark had a solid memory of this man since, "He reminded me of a movie actor I remembered seeing on the screen, and because he was unusually tall, standing well over six feet."[68] In fact, when Jim Garrison read Clark's description, he wrote the name of actor Jeff Chandler on the back of it. But further, Clark also recalled a strange looking individual using the pay phone that day. He remembered him because of his "unusual hair" which, "stood up in all directions on his head."[69] When shown photos of Clay Shaw and David Ferrie, Henry Burnell Clark positively identified them as the respective men that he clearly remembered.

Palmer and Elizabeth Graham later noted that they thought Oswald talked to two females. One was Gladys Palmer and the other was Gloria Wilson.[70] Palmer now walked over to local sheriff John Manchester. He told Manchester that he should get an ID on the driver and a license check on the car. As a result, Manchester walked over to the black Cadillac, around it, and asked the driver to show him some identification. The driver took out his driver's license. As Manchester handled it, he asked him what his business was in the area. The driver then told him that he was a representative of the International Trade Mart in New Orleans. Manchester did not know what this was. So he then asked him if he had anything to do with the voter registration drive. The driver said that he did not. Manchester decided he was not there as an outside influence. Looking over the license, the sheriff asked him what his name was. The driver said it was Clay Shaw. This corresponded to the driver's license. Manchester was satisfied and walked away.[71] Manchester would later also identify the passenger as David Ferrie. He then walked over to Palmer and told him what he had found out from the brief interview. Palmer, like Manchester, was puzzled by what a man who worked for the International Trade Mart would be doing there.[72]

As Verla Bell noted, the black auto stayed around for hours. In mid-afternoon, Palmer set about on another shift of processing applicants. When he finally got to Oswald, Palmer asked for identification papers. Oswald produced what Palmer later called "separation papers" from the Marines. These had a local address in New Orleans on them. This, of course, made it hard to believe that Oswald would drive over a hundred miles just to register to vote in a parish he did not inhabit. Consequently, Palmer now asked Oswald where he lived. He said he lived at the hospital. Palmer now asked him who he was living with there. There is confusion as to how Oswald replied. Palmer said, "He told me— I'm not positive about this name—but I think he said, Doctor Person."[73] In the journal that *Life* reporter Richard Billings kept on the Garrison investigation, he wrote that Garrison had determined that Oswald said he was living with a Cuban doctor named Frank Silva.[74] What is astonishing about these replies— whichever is correct—is this: Both men *did work* at East at that time. For when the HSCA subpoenaed a list of doctors employed from that hospital in 1963, both a Malcolm Pierson and Frank Silva were on it.[75]

The obvious question then becomes: How did Oswald know the names of these men? Or if he did not, how did Shaw or Ferrie know them? One possibility is this: According to Cuban intelligence, Silva was active in the anti-Castro cause in the New Orleans area. Silva was Cuban-born and from an upper-class family. He was actually associated with Tulane Medical Center at the time.[76] Tulane was located in New Orleans. Dr. Alton Ochsner, who was on the board of, and Chief of Surgery at, Tulane Medical School, was a friend of both Shaw and Banister.[77] In fact, at the New Orleans Public Library, there is a photo of Shaw sitting at a small table with Ochsner.

Another way that Oswald could have known these names was through a mutual acquaintance of Shaw and Ferrie, Sergio Arcacha Smith. Both Cuban intelligence and Garrison's investigators discovered that there was a connection between the two Cuban refugees. Dr. Robert Heath, Chairman of Tulane University Medical School's Department of Neurology and Psychiatry, became infamous for using LSD and electrode implantation in his research. Many of the people he worked on came from East Louisiana State Hospital, where an entire ward was dedicated to his work.[78] East doctor Alfred Butterworth (whom this author interviewed shortly before his death) told the author that he had seen both Ochsner and Silva while he was there. Butterworth also revealed that Tulane University had a special psychiatric unit at the hospital, where they secretly administered LSD.[79] This is important background to the following information. During his inquiry, Jim Garrison came across a witness who had attended a gathering at Dr. Heath's home. There the following event occurred: Dr. Silva introduced the man to the former local representative of Howard Hunt's CRC, Sergio Arcacha Smith.[80] Pierson was a former narcotics offender who, according to HSCA subpoenaed records, listed Silva as a reference in his job application.[81] It is hard to believe that, left to his own devices, Oswald would have known that either of these men worked at the hospital. If either of these more logical options is accurate, it gives the incident even more scope and depth.

But here lies an ironic miscalculation on the threesome's part. For Palmer then asked Oswald his purpose in registering. Oswald replied that he wanted to get a job at the hospital. He had been told previously that he had a better chance to get such a position if he was registered. Palmer said this was not the case: "I know people out of Mississippi that are working at Jackson." At which Oswald turned, walked out the office door, and returned to his car. After he closed up that day, Palmer went to buy something at the local drugstore. There he met with Gloria Wilson, who he thought had talked to Oswald earlier. She alerted him to the fact that Oswald had left in the black Cadillac with the two cohorts inside.[82]

For Jim Garrison, and the HSCA, Palmer would identify Shaw and Ferrie as the occupants of the car, and Oswald as the man he talked to about registering. Further, at the Clay Shaw trial, Palmer personally demolished the disinformation story constructed by Shaw's defenders that it was Guy Banister, not Clay Shaw, who was the driver of the black Cadillac. To assistant DA Andrew Sciambra, Palmer stated he knew Banister from before 1963. When asked if Banister was in the car that day, he replied that he was sure he was not.[83]

Oswald and Shaw were also reportedly seen by two people at the Clinton Courthouse. And from there, these two witnesses said the duo went on to the East Louisiana State Hospital.[84]

This is undoubtedly what happened. Bobby Dedon, a receptionist at the hospital, directed a man she would later identify as Oswald to the personnel office.[85] Maxine Kemp recalled the Oswald application form since she actually saw it.[86] She also knew of another employee there, Dale Booty, who had seen the file.[87] And Aline Woodside said the same thing.[88]

How to explain this strange, almost dreamlike trip? What was Oswald doing looking for a job in Clinton, away from New Orleans, when he did not drive? Why was Shaw there? What was the well-dressed, dignified, upstanding representative of upper-crust New Orleans doing in this sleepy hamlet with these two characters from the opposite end of the social spectrum?

Now that we know a bit more about Ferrie and Oswald, perhaps the Clinton trip of that motley trio is a bit more clear. It helps explain Oswald's surprise on learning that the hospital was a mental institution. The trip was not his idea. He had not checked it out. He was likely given the names of Silva (or Pierson) through his two cohorts. Who, at least, had lived in New Orleans for years. Who would have thought that one day soon, one of the trio would be asking Dean Andrews to represent another of the threesome in the murder of President Kennedy. For, as we will see, Dean Andrews knew that Clay Bertrand was only an alias. The caller's real name was Clay Shaw.

Nagell Tries to Stop the Assassination

In the summer of 1963 there was someone trying to connect all these signs *before* the assassination took place. Incredibly, working essentially by himself, Richard Case Nagell came very close to finding out what would happen. But according to his biographer, in the end, he couldn't convince Oswald of what was happening to him. And then when he failed at that, he couldn't bring himself to kill the man he now regarded as a friend.

Jim Garrison referred to Nagell in these terms: "Richard Case Nagell is the most important witness there is."[89] No serious and objective writer in the field can disagree with that to any great extent. If Nagell was not the most important of the cooperating witnesses, he was certainly in the top five. In 1981, the late Bud Fensterwald of the Assassination Archives and Research Center wrote that "Nagell is probably the only vital individual who knew the details of the assassination and is still alive."[90] Even though the Warren Commission had an FBI report on Nagell that said he had met Oswald only socially in Texas and Mexico City, there is no record of anyone on the Commission ever interviewing him. (As we will see, their meeting was anything but social.)[91] Nagell did try. He wrote two letters to the Commission saying he had knowledge of both Oswald and the conspiracy—in advance of the assassination.[92] Either someone intercepted the letters or the Commission was not interested. Since, as we shall see, Nagell was in prison at the time he wrote the letters, the former is a distinct possibility. As we will later see, the first law enforcement officer interested in what Nagell had to say was Jim Garrison. Almost four years after Nagell discovered what was going to happen to President Kennedy. This is shocking because, as Nagell's biographer notes, at the time he was arrested in El Paso in September of 1963, Richard Case Nagell had in his personal effects a near duplicate of Oswald's Uniformed Services Identification and Priveileges Card. To be clear, he himself had a card like that, but he also had a card with Oswald's photo inset on it.[93] It is understandable that this may have not set off any alarms two months before Kennedy was killed. But one would have thought that someone in the judicial system would have recalled this the day Kennedy was shot and realized its potentially immense significance. For one difference between the Oswald card Nagell maintained and the one Oswald had was that the photo was different. The photo from Oswald's card appears borrowed from another card. And on the other card, Oswald's alias of Alex J. Hidell is used. At the very least, this would indicate that Nagell had to have been quite close to Oswald prior to the time of his arrest. Nagell even had other things showing a mutual interest with Oswald: the same names in each man's notebooks, Cuba-related leaflets (from the same pro-Cuba group Oswald commandeered), two tourist cards for Mexican entry (one in the name of Aleksei Hidel), and miniature spy cameras.[94] One would have thought that, on the day of the assassination, the legal authorities would have wondered how Nagell came into their possession. Especially when, upon being apprehended, Nagell said, "I would rather be arrested than commit murder and treason."[95] Recall, this is two months before President Kennedy is murdered. How did Nagell know such a thing was going to happen? And how did Nagell know so much about Oswald? And, as we shall see, David Ferrie?

In 1953, at the tail end of the Korean War, Nagell attended the Monterey School of Languages, a Defense Department institution for the accelerated acquisition of foreign languages. (As we shall see, Lee Harvey Oswald very likely attended there also.) After this, Nagell worked for Army Intelligence, doing surveillance on suspected domestic communists.[96] In the winter of 1955–56, Nagell was first recruited by the CIA. In late 1956, Nagell was transferred to a secret intelligence group called Field Operations Intelligence (FOI). This group was involved in what intelligence operators call "black ops": assassinations, kidnappings, blackmail, etc.[97] FOI operated in the Far East, so Nagell worked in Japan. It was there, in 1957–58, that Nagell first encountered Lee Harvey Oswald. Nagell wondered why Oswald was seen outside the Soviet Embassy in Tokyo. So he arranged to be introduced to him under an assumed name. Nagell and Oswald had girlfriends at the Queen Bee, a famous nightclub in Tokyo.

In late 1959, after leaving FOI and the Far East, Nagell returned stateside to a civilian job. But he still freelanced for the CIA. Specifically, Nagell worked for the Domestic Intelligence unit.[98] This is significant because, as we shall see, this unit would later be formalized under Tracy Barnes as the Domestic Operations Division, with Howard Hunt allegedly a major player.[99] After a shooting incident on his job, Nagell left and secured a Mexican tourist card in Los Angeles. He visited a friend of his at the Hotel Luma in Mexico City. In 1966, in a letter to his sister, Nagell hinted at how important this visit was to him: "If it does eventually become mandatory for me to touch upon the events leading to my sojourn in Mexico in 1962 . . . (where and when it began), I shall do so, but only subsequent to being granted immunity from prosecution."[100]

Nagell later told his friend Art Greenstein that in 1962 he was now under control of the CIA. His mission was to serve as a double agent for the Agency in an operation against the Soviet Embassy in Mexico City. The timing of this mission was near the outset of the Missile Crisis. And since these types of operations were the domain of David Phillips—who manned the Cuban desk in Mexico City—Nagell hinted to Greenstein that Phillips had been an accomplice on this project.[101] This becomes interesting in regards to what happens next. For it was after the completion of this project, when the Missile Crisis was over, that Nagell learned about a plot to kill President Kennedy. And he learned of it in his double agent status through the KGB.[102]

In October of 1962, a Soviet contact of his told him that he had heard that a Cuban exile group named Alpha 66 had been talking about a plot to kill JFK, because the group had gotten wind of Kennedy's pledge about not invading Cuba which resolved the crisis. As Gaeton Fonzi later revealed, the leader of Alpha 66 was Antonio Veciana. Veciana named his CIA handler as

Maurice Bishop, who Fonzi demonstrated was Phillips. Nagell had just begun his preliminary inquiries when, in an unprecedented move, he was called to the Soviet Embassy. He was now told that the JFK plot was not just a rumor. And the Soviets were worried that part of the plot's design would be to blame them for the murder.[103] He was further briefed on the matter and given a sheath of pictures. One of the photos was of Oswald. The Russians were suspicious of him because of his defection to Moscow, though, at this time, not in relation to the plot to kill Kennedy. Nagell left Mexico on October 21, 1962. His friend Greenstein asked Nagell if he would be hearing from him in the future or reading about him in the papers. Nagell replied that he would. Greenstein followed up with, "Something big?" Nagell responded more prophetically than he could have possibly known with, "Yes . . . something big."[104]

Nagell first went to Dallas to check up on the status of Oswald. He found the supposed communist in the midst of the counterrevolutionary White Russian community. From here, Nagell went to his first point of interest: a Cuban exile group that planned on blowing up the Orange Bowl where Kennedy was to speak to the prisoners released from Cuba in the Bay of Pigs exchange.[105] In fact, the Miami Police Department had a report that said a local Cuban was overheard saying on the night JFK spoke that "Something is going to happen in the Orange Bowl."

Nagell then did some important follow up work in Miami. He was checking on an alleged relationship between former Cuban congressman Eladio Del Valle and former Cuban diplomat, and present New Orleans Cuban Revolutionary Council representative, Sergio Arcacha Smith.[106] He was also checking on an associate of Arcacha's friend David Ferrie. This shows what a remarkable investigator Nagell was, as Oswald had not even moved back to New Orleans yet.

In April of 1963, Nagell moved to Los Angeles, since Alpha 66 had opened up a new chapter there. Here he picked up the scent of another attempt on Kennedy's life, scheduled for June. The focus of the plot was a man named Vaughn Marlowe, who was an executive officer with the Los Angeles branch of the Fair Play for Cuba Committee.[107] This was the same organization that Oswald was now leafleting for on the streets of New Orleans. Marlowe wrote Jim Garrison in 1967 telling him that Nagell had been following him at that time for reasons foreign to him.[108] Nagell later revealed why he had been tailing Marlowe, and again it proves his acumen as a detective. Marlowe was being considered as a fall guy by a member of Alpha 66. This Cuban would later visit Sylvia Odio in September of 1963.[109] Nagell discovered that the scene of the crime was to be the Beverly Hilton hotel where Kennedy was to stay for the LA premiere of the film *PT 109*.

Two important things now happened to Nagell. He now learned that somehow the Cubans he was monitoring knew about both Kennedy's attempt at rapprochement with Castro and his attempt at warmer relations with the Soviets. Nagell did some digging into this and found out how the back channels talks were escalating from the summer to the fall. And he thoroughly understood how his targets would feel about this, especially in light of what they considered Kennedy's failure at the Bay of Pigs. He also knew that these now desperate men would feel they had no choice but to alter this new Kennedy/Castro agenda.[110] With this new information, Nagell began to exclusively monitor the plot that would take Kennedy's life. At this time, Nagell told a friend of his, John Margain, that Oswald was being set up by the CIA and the Cuban exiles.[111] As Nagell told Greenstein, one of the personages integral to this setting up of Oswald was David Ferrie.[112] Two others were the two men who were to visit Sylvia Odio. Two others were Arcacha and, in all likelihood, Carlos Quiroga. Quiroga was suspected by Garrison of supplying Oswald with pro-Cuba literature, and then lying about it by saying he was really infiltrating Oswald's alleged group. When Garrison had him polygraphed, Quiroga was asked this direct question. When he replied he was trying to infiltrate Oswald's group, the machine indicated deception. He also was being deceptive when he said that he only talked to Oswald once, and that Oswald did not know Sergio Arcacha Smith or Guy Banister.[113]

This information dovetails perfectly with a piece of evidence that Nagell had stored away in a secure place with a friend. This was a tape recording of four men, speaking primarily in Spanish, but some of the time in English. This discussion concerned a plot to assassinate Kennedy. Two of the men were Arcacha and a man who Nagell would only identify as "Q," almost certainly Quiroga.[114] Nagell was now told to concentrate on this New Orleans Cuban exile cabal.[115] He would find out that Ferrie knew both the Cubans who showed up at Odio's apartment door in Dallas.[116] He also discovered that on the fringe of the plot was an Oswald double who went by the name of "Leon." Leon Oswald worked only with the anti-Castro Cubans and, unlike Lee, made no attempt to appear pro-Castro.[117]

By late August and early September, Nagell understood he was in the midst of "something big." Except he did not know where the actual denouement would take place. He went to Mexico to try and contact his CIA handler. He failed. But his KGB liaison told him to try and separate Oswald from the conspirators by telling him he was being duped. If this was not effective, and the plot seemed heading forward, he should terminate Oswald.[118] As Nagell later said, if anyone wanted to stop the assassination, it was the KGB. But Nagell could not convince Oswald he was being victimized, and he could not bring himself to kill him. He therefore expected to be eliminated himself. He even began to suspect he was used by the CIA to confuse the KGB about the end-game of the plot.[119]

Nagell wrote a letter to the FBI warning them of the plot. He then thought of leaving for Europe. Instead he drove to El Paso. He was suppo-sed to meet a contact with someone across the border in Juarez. He did not. Instead he went into a bank in El Paso ostensibly to purchase some American Express checks, since he was being paid through them by the CIA.[120] There, he decided to fire shots in the bank that deliberately did not hit anyone. Thin-king he would only be tried on a misdemeanor, he thought he would be able to produce evidence in court showing the machinations of the plot. But he was not allowed to mention American Express in court; he was charged with a felony, and some of the evidence he had in his car disappeared. Therefore, the plot proceeded.

Did Gary Underhill Know Who Killed JFK?

The remarkable thing about the above events is that they all happened either in advance of the assassination—Rose Cheramie, Clinton-Jackson, Nagell; the day of the assassination—Banister beating Martin; or within just a day or two after the assassination—Bertrand's call to Andrews, Ferrie searching for his library card. They all appeared to originate in and around New Orleans. But there was another episode that occurred in the northeast, which supp-lied a connection with these local events to Washington. Like the above, this remarkable incident was also suppressed.

On the evening of November 22, 1963, Gary Underhill was a deeply troubled man. What he had learned, and the fact that *they knew* he had learned it, were too much for him. He had to escape. Once he was out of Washington, he could regain his equilibrium. Then he would decide what to do. He had friends in New York he could talk to without fear of the word getting back to Washington.

He arrived on Long Island the next morning.[121] His friend Robert Fitzsim-mons was asleep. He and his wife, Charlene—Bob called her Charlie—were about to leave on a long trip to Spain that day. When Underhill learned of the trip, he said, "You're going to Spain? That's the best thing to do. I've got to get out of the country, too. This country is too dangerous for me now." He paused and added, "I've got to get on a boat, too. I'm really afraid for my life."[122]

Charlene Fitzsimmons realized something was wrong with the usually rational and objective Underhill. But Underhill insisted he had not been drin-king. It was the Kennedy assassination, he explained. It was not what it seemed to be. "Oswald is a patsy. They set him up. It's too much. The bastards have done something outrageous. They've killed the President! I've been listening and hearing things. I couldn't believe they'd get away with it, but they did!"

Charlie did not know what he was talking about. Who were "they"?

"We, I mean the United States. We just don't do that sort of thing! They've gone mad! They're a bunch of drug runners and gun runners—a real violence group. God, the CIA is under enough pressure already without that bunch in Southeast Asia. Kennedy gave them some time after the Bay of Pigs. He said he'd give them a chance to save face."

He could tell Charlie did not believe him. "They're so stupid," he continued. "They can't even get the right man. They tried it in Cuba, and they couldn't get away with it. Right after the Bay of Pigs. But Kennedy wouldn't let them do it. And now he'd gotten wind of this, and he was really going to blow the whistle on them. And they killed him!"

"But I know who they are. That's the problem. They know I know. That's why I'm here. I can't stay in New York. Can you put me up?"

Charlie reminded him they were leaving for Europe in a few hours and would be gone for months.

"Well, maybe I can go with you."

Charlie was frightened now. Recovering, she said he could stay there for a few hours. When Bob came down, he might let him have the key to the place for a few days.

Underhill mulled it over for a few seconds. "No, that's all right. Maybe I shouldn't leave the country." He turned toward the door. "I'll come back in a couple of hours. Bob will be up by then." He walked out without saying where he was going. It was the last time the Fitzsimmonses would see their troubled friend.

John Garrett Underhill knew whereof he spoke. He had attended Harvard and then served in military intelligence during World War II.[123] His family had been active in military-political affairs for a long time. Underhill himself was an expert on limited warfare and small arms. After the war he had shuttled back and forth between special assignments for the CIA and consulting for Henry Luce at *Life* and *Fortune.* He had had a strong influence on Luce's views of both World War II and Korea.[124]

Underhill was close to top military brass and higher-ups in the CIA,[125] and had voiced his fears about these people to another friend, Asher Brynes,[126] a writer for *The New Republic* who also knew Underhill's estranged wife, Patricia.[127] Underhill did not leave the country after his visit to the Fitzsimmonses. He returned to Washington and began quietly to investigate the assassination. He spoke about it to Brynes.

On May 8, 1964, Brynes visited Underhill's apartment. When no one answered, he walked in, to discover Underhill in bed sleeping. As he approached his friend, he noticed that his face seemed discolored. It had a yellow-green hue.[128] Brynes drew closer and saw a bullet hole in his friend's head. Underhill was dead and had been for days. Yet no one in the apartment house had heard a gun go off. Odder still, Underhill had been shot behind the left ear and the gun was under his left side, yet Underhill was right-handed.[129] Despite these strange circumstances, the coroner ruled the death a suicide. Brynes was disgusted with the conclusion, but did not pursue the matter. Patricia Underhill would not talk to anyone about her husband's death and refused to turn over any papers he may have written concerning the assassination.[130]

Each one of these events was concealed, discounted, or tampered with by the authorities. And the Warren Commission did nothing with them. Therefore, they laid dormant for four years.

CHAPTER SIX

Witches' Brew

"Obviously something was going on . . . they were trying to put a cover on it. The idea behind it was cover, cover, cover . . ."

—Gordon Novel describing Banister's preparations
for the Bay of Pigs

In the immediate aftermath of the assassination, Oswald seemed less a person than a projection of our own personal demons and our disdain for the image of Dallas: nouveau riche, coarse, rightwing, and redneck—the only big city that pelted and spat upon then U.N. Ambassador Adlai Stevenson. And so with Oswald.

Due to the shock of the assassination and the biased and shallow reporting, the picture we received of him, the one the general public retains, is foreshortened, superficial, and, in light of the current record, distorted. Unfortunately, Oswald had no opportunity to correct it. The Dallas police made no stenographic record or audio recordings of his twelve hours of questioning.[1] He requested legal counsel, but ended up with none. Then his life was snuffed out while he was literally in the arms of the police. Oswald never admitted shooting anyone, which would seem odd in the wake of a politically motivated crime. What most people remember is the image that was heard and seen and read over those two days of incarceration and accusation: a poor, white non-conformist who was a warehouse worker at the book depository in front of which the Presidential motorcade passed. Whatever was known about his past, beyond the commonly reported events of his time in the Soviet Union and his military service, seemed reduced to a single photo-image: film clips of him in dark clothes passing out "Hands Off Cuba" flyers in downtown New Orleans. That picture seemed to sum up the case: a lonely figure in dark clothes, passing out communist literature as people walk by. Oswald's sponsoring organization was the Fair Play for Cuba Committee. The Committee did exist, based in New York City, but oddly, Oswald was the only member of the New Orleans chapter. The address stamped on the literature was 544 Camp Street.

In its multitude of glaring omissions, the Warren Report never got to the bottom of the intriguing mystery of 544 Camp Street. If Oswald was the only member of the organization, why did he use that address, the Newman Building? It was not his home address. If he was making about a hundred dollars a month and spending about sixty on rent, how could he afford an office?[2] For that is what the Camp Street address was, an office building. If he did not rent space there—as the owner of the building, Samuel Newman, said—did someone rent a room for him or lend him an office to use?[3]

This mystery could have been solved by looking through one of the FBI reports submitted to the Warren Commission. The report is a nine-line summary of an interview with former FBI agent Guy Banister, the detective who beat up his assistant, Jack Martin, on the day of the assassination. The address given in the report for Banister's office is 531 Lafayette Street.[4] Newman's office building was located at the corner of Lafayette and Camp. If one entered on the Lafayette side, the address was 531; if one entered on the Camp side, it was 544. In J. Edgar Hoover's (deliberately) evasive inquiry into the assassination, he tried to cover up this point from both the Warren Commission and the public. Not long after the assassination, New Orleans special agent Harry Maynor drafted a message that was changed before it arrived at FBI HQ. This message was directed to Director Hoover. Scratched out, but still visible, are the words, "Several Fair Play for Cuba pamphlets contained address 544 Camp Street."[5] Also, when the FBI forwarded its very few and skimpy reports on Banister to the Warren Commission—in which they did not question him about Oswald—they failed to use the 544 Camp Street address. They used the alternative address of 531 Lafayette.[6] This may have some significance. For the Commission did print one flyer Oswald had been distributing that summer that included the Camp Street address. It was the famous pamphlet written by wealthy New York activist Corliss Lamont entitled "The Crime Against Cuba."[7] So even if the Commission had tried to connect the two addresses, they would have a hard time doing so.

Why did FBI Director Hoover attempt to conceal any relationship between Guy Banister and Oswald? Because, as with David Ferrie, it is difficult to reconcile the politics and activism of Banister with the image of Oswald as presented in the Warren Commission. In fact, some would say it is not possible to do so. Banister, who died of a heart attack in 1964, was a compelling character. He spent a large part of his life in law enforcement. Born in Monroe, Louisiana, in 1901, he attended LSU and Soule College in New Orleans. He began his career as an investigator for the Monroe Police Department and then received an appointment as a patrol officer in 1929.[8] He quickly became assistant to the Chief of Police and, a year later, he became Chief of Detectives. In 1934, Banister was sworn in as a special agent of the Bureau of Investigation, the forerunner to the FBI. At that time, this agency was run by Hoover. He was first stationed in Indianapolis. In 1935 he relocated to New York City. It was here that Banister developed his interest in surveilling and rooting out communists. This was through his colleague George Starr. Starr spoke fluent Russian, as his father had trained race horses for the Czar. For years, Starr was Hoover's designated leader in conducting investigations of communist subversion. In fact, he taught these techniques to fellow agents. One was Banister. As Banister rose in the Bureau, he began to supervise other agents doing this kind of inquiry. And what is important here, he also developed informers within leftist ranks. As he referred to them, "they were counterspies sent in to report on the activities of the Party members."[9] Banister was to specialize in this activity for Hoover for seventeen years.

From New York he transferred to Newark. He then became Special Agent in Charge (SAC), that is running the office, in Butte, Montana. During the war, he juggled between Oklahoma City, Minneapolis, and Butte. In January of 1954, he became SAC of the Chicago office. In a move that has never been fully explained, he retired from the FBI at the end of 1954. He moved back to New Orleans and was hired by Mayor DeLesseps Morrison to run Internal Affairs and clean up a corrupt police department. He was then promoted to Deputy Superintendent of Police. In 1956 Morrison appointed him to a much more natural position. He was to prepare a study on the influence of communist subversion in New Orleans. This was to be done in conjunction with rightwing Senator James Eastland's Senate Internal Security Sub-Committee. It was at this time that many of Banister's worst traits began to surface. He was an extreme racial bigot, and his politics were near neo-Nazi. For instance, he was closely tied to the state Sovereignty Committee, a very conservative group that was anti-integration and McCarthyite in its anti-Communism. In March of 1957, at the Old Absinthe House in the French Quarter, Banister's violent nature ended his career on the police force. Apparently, at least a bit drunk,

Banister drew his gun on a bartender and said, "I have already killed two men and another wouldn't make any difference."[10] About a year later, he set up Guy Banister Associates, his own private investigation firm.

His business was first located in a small office on Robert E. Lee Boulevard. But Banister then moved to the Balter Building. As William Davy notes in *Let Justice Be Done*, that building was named after its owner, Colonel Buford Balter, who was another extreme right winger.[11] In fact, according to a 1962 FBI report made by Banister employee Dan Campbell, Balter partly financed a trip by American Nazi leader George Lincoln Rockwell to New Orleans. One of the purposes of the meeting was to discuss a merger between the Rockwell group and the Klan.[12] It would seem that one reason Banister's office was housed there was, since his political philosophy was in tune with Buford Balter's, he probably could get a good deal on a lease.

For the evidence indicates that Banister did little, if any, detective work himself. This became clear at an early date. Joe Oster was a friend of Banister's from the local police force. Banister hired him as investigator and treasurer. Oster quit when he found himself doing most of the work and Banister not taking advantage of potentially lucrative investigations.[13] Garrison investigator George Eckert found another source that said Banister's friends never bought the idea that he had separated himself from the government. He accepted fees for investigatory services that were well under the going rate. He then maintained "connections with sources, which provided him technical assistance."[14] In that regard, Oster recalled that Banister could actually pick up the phone and talk to J. Edgar Hoover.[15] This is an important point in regards to the FBI cover up about Oswald's flyers mentioned above. Oster recalled that Banister also got less and less choosy about who he hired. At first he stuck with FBI veterans like himself. But he later got less discerning, since he spent most of his time building his file system of perceived Communist sympathizers in the area. For instance, Banister published something called *Louisiana Intelligence Digest*. This publication stated that the civil rights movement was a communist front and ridiculed President Kennedy for being soft on communism since he supported the movement.[16] Banister testified before a Special Committee of the Arkansas State Legislature, where he claimed that Communists were behind the riots that followed the integration of the Little Rock, Arkansas, public school system.[17] Some of Banister's later behavior can be attributed to his firing from the police force by Morrison. His sister-in-law later said that Banister's termination "had a great emotional effect on Guy. . . . He started drinking pretty heavy at that time . . . and he started having family problems. He left his wife Mary Wortham, and moved out." His former wife had him placed in a hospital for observation, where it was revealed he had a series of small strokes.[18]

When Oster left, he was replaced by Vernon Gerdes. Gerdes also said he saw the American Nazi Rockwell with Banister.[19] As noted by more than one author, Sergio Arcacha Smith's office for the CRC was located in the Balter Building when Banister was there.[20] Since Arcacha Smith's group was part of the Cuban exile political front set up by the CIA for the Bay of Pigs invasion, Howard Hunt was also seen at the Balter Building. In fact, Joe Oster later said that when he was there with Banister at the Balter Building, there were phone calls coming in from the CIA, and he heard the name Hunt mentioned.[21] Banister employee Joe Newborough also stated that Banister was a conduit of funds for the CIA.[22]

In 1961, preparations for the Bay of Pigs were ongoing. As we have observed, Phillips and Hunt were major parts of that preparation. We have noted evidence for Hunt's presence in New Orleans with Sergio Arcacha Smith, and probably with contacts to Banister. What about Phillips? Is there any evidence of his contacts in New Orleans at this time? In 1969, Gordon Novel—a man we will revisit later—sued *Playboy* magazine over comments Jim Garrison had made about him in his interview in the issue of October 1967. In a deposition Novel gave for that lawsuit, he mentioned a meeting he had with Arcacha Smith in 1961. Novel met Arcacha in a New Orleans hotel on the recommendation of Ed Butler, the director of the Information Council of the Americas, a rightwing, CIA-associated propaganda outfit. Arcacha Smith wanted Novel, an electronics wizard, to help him put on a New Orleans based telethon exposing alleged atrocities by Castro in Cuba. Novel seemed agreeable, so Arcacha invited him to a second meeting on the subject. This was at Banister's office in the Balter Building. This time the two were joined by Banister and a Mr. Phillips from Washington.[23] Novel had never seen Phillips before. But he was impressed by the ease with which Phillips commandeered the meeting. Phillips went through a written agenda from a typewritten sheet. The subject was to raise funds, but more importantly, to get the city of New Orleans behind the Cuban cause. Phillips said he was with Double-Check Corporation. This was later exposed as a CIA front to hire American pilots who flew at the Bay of Pigs. From his background as a CIA propaganda specialist, and the description Novel gave of him, authors Lisa Pease and William Davy have concluded that this was David Phillips.[24]

In this deposition, Novel also described the efforts by Banister, Arcacha Smith, and David Ferrie to prepare for the Bay of Pigs assault. One of the things Ferrie did was to train Cubans at both Abita Springs, north of Lake Ponchatrain, and the Belle Chasse Naval station, south of New Orleans. Ferrie told a CAP colleague of his that the equipment for the training there was coming in from both the State Department and the CIA through Sergio Arcacha Smith.[25]

In 1967, the CIA tried to make sure the training at the site would remain secret to Jim Garrison. Therefore, there was an inventory and history done on the training grounds. The CIA memorandum says the site was opened on February 12, 1961, with the first Cubans arriving about a week later. About 300 Cubans were trained there over a six-week time period. They were tutored in demolition, communications, and UDT (underwater demolition). And in fact, part of the Bay of Pigs invasion included underwater demolition teams landing on the first morning, each led by an American contract employee.[26] Another group of Cubans Ferrie trained as a strike force was sent to Guatemala on March 22, 1961 to join the landing Brigade. The memo closes with this: "...the training camp was entirely Agency controlled and the training was conducted by Agency personnel." The author, who seems to have quite a close understanding of what went on there, was David Phillips. The memorandum appears to be written for James Angleton.[27]

Arcacha Smith wrote a letter to Ferrie's superiors at Eastern Air Lines asking for paid leave for Ferrie so he could devote more time to the CRC.[28] This was denied. But Ferrie's vacation coincided with the Bay of Pigs invasion. And when it occurred, Ferrie was at Arcacha Smith's home.[29] Where they were likely getting reports about the progress of the landing. In fact, Arcacha Smith was so plugged into the CIA and the Bay of Pigs operation that he actually had films of the failed operation that he and Ferrie would watch at Arcacha's home.[30]

But there is even more proof that Banister, Arcacha Smith, and Ferrie were involved in the Bay of Pigs invasion. In his deposition, Novel states that when he was in Banister's office there was always ordnance of some type there, and he specifically named "Daisy Cutters," fuses for aerial bombs.[31] Also, Arcacha Smith sent him, in a clandestine manner, looking for ingredients to conduct chemical warfare. Further, Novel said that Arcacha Smith was always in contact with Miami. And he was always talking about the "new government" that would be constructed in Cuba after Castro was ousted. In fact, the famous Houma raid—the trip to obtain heavy explosives from a bunker on the giant French Schlumberger Company lot in Houma, Louisiana—was for the Bay of Pigs invasion. Banister arranged for a key to the bunker to be mailed to Novel. Later, Novel met with Arcacha Smith and Ferrie at a hotel. Arcacha Smith told Novel to go to Ferrie's in a couple of days. When Novel arrived at Ferrie's, he saw a huge map of Cuba on the wall, more incendiary fuses, and white mice. Novel showed Ferrie the key, and Ferrie said to return in a couple of nights dressed in black. The night Novel returned, about eight of them, including friends of Ferrie's like Layton Martens, and drove a laundry truck due east to Houma. They were outfitted with state-of-the-art walkie-talkies, which Novel said were so powerful they had to be of government issue.[32] When they got to the bunker, it was full of explosives like grenades, mortar shells, bazooka shells, and .30 caliber machine gun shells. The container crates were marked "Interarmco," an arms company with proven ties to the CIA. The Agency had lent these explosive devices to Schlumberger since that company had backed the OAS rebels versus Charles de Gaulle during the Algerian struggle, which was now coming to a close.[33] Jim Garrison discovered these arms were transferred to both Ferrie's apartment and Banister's office for later use in the Bay of Pigs invasion. And there was testimony that Banister's office contained dozens of crates of grenades, land mines, and "unique little missiles" in April of 1961.[34] Some of the ordnance might have been also stored in rented warehouses. For Banister also asked Novel to find him large empty buildings. Retroactively, Novel became sure about their involvement in the Bay of Pigs. Because the day after the invasion failed, Arcacha Smith called on him to perform another mission: he asked him to find some blood.[35]

Banister was also associated with another outlet to the OAS rebel group, local attorney Maurice Gatlin. Gatlin was an attorney who, from the 1940s, was an obsessive anti-Communist. In fact, he appeared to know about the overthrow of Arbenz in Guatemala a year before it happened. He even offered to brief Assistant Secretary of State John M. Cabot about it.[36] Gatlin had helped organize a group of communist "pushback" organizations throughout the world. The one in New Orleans was called the Anti-Communist League of the Caribbean. Banister was a member of the group. And after Arbenz was overthrown, Banister employee Allen Campbell told the author that both Ferrie and Banister were instrumental in training the new regime's army and security forces.[37] In fact, Banister had sent Campbell to Guatemala under the cover of conducting an air show to check on their proficiency. And like Banister—with Allen and his brother Dan Campbell—Gatlin was active in recruiting young men to become informants on the left. One of Gatlin's recruits was Tulane student William Martin, a man who Banister also knew, and who will figure in our story later.[38] Gatlin also likely knew Howard Hunt since he attended an anti-Communist conference in Guatemala in 1958 arranged by him.[39] On October 5, 1960, Gatlin wrote a letter to the *New Orleans Times Picayune* in which he praised Banister for the seizure of a supply of Jeeps being sent into Cuba. Gatlin liked to boast about his undercover work for the CIA. He once stated to a friend that he was going to Paris to give a large amount of money to the OAS to finance an assassination attempt against de Gaulle.[40]

Banister's intelligence work for Sergio Arcacha Smith and the CRC also included the tracking of Castro loyalists in the New Orleans area. Somehow Arcacha had gotten hold of what he called a "code book" from the local Cuban consulate before the USA had broken relations with Castro. He gave it to

Banister in hopes that one of his intelligence agency contacts could decipher it.[41] He had also prepared a list of Cuban students that he thought were loyal to Castro who attended colleges in the New Orleans area. The list went to Banister and Gatlin to track in case they were counterintelligence agents for the revolutionary regime.[42] Arcacha understood how important Banister was in this regard, since Banister was involved in both the exfiltration and infiltration of anti-Castro Cubans into and out of the island.[43] This was done because, outside of Miami, New Orleans had the highest number of Cuban refugees in the USA.

This leads us to Banister's legendary filing system, which he boasted about as being the best and most extensive in the state. One of the things that helped Jim Garrison find out what Banister was really doing in New Orleans in the late fifties and early sixties, and how Oswald was actually associated with him, was the DA's discovery of an index to this system. The topics were things like Ammunition and Arms, Anti-Soviet Underground, Civil Rights Program of JFK, and Dismantling of Ballistic Missile System.[44] But the location of at least some of the actual files would also have revealed that Banister was part of a local intelligence network. For in the eighties, New Orleans advertising representative Ed Haslam was asked to do some work for a new radio program that seemed to be sprouting up in support of the Reagan administration's war against the Contras in Nicaragua. One of the leaders of this group, which was being supported by the local rightwing financial oligarchy, off-handedly showed him boxes of files that he said had belonged to Banister.[45] In the nineties, Haslam ventured down to New Orleans again on a research trip with a correspondent for PBS, which was doing a special about Oswald. Haslam and the correspondent walked into an office for a taped interview about Oswald and his fateful summer of 1963 with Ed Butler, a man who participated in a debate with Oswald that summer. Haslam now recognized Butler as the man who—a decade previous—was starting up the new radio channel and had shown him Banister's files.[46] As we have seen, Butler had worked for the local anti-communist propaganda shop INCA in the sixties. He was also the man who originally referred Novel to Sergio Arcacha Smith.[47] From this piece of evidence, plus all we have previously outlined, it is clear that Banister was really not interested in doing private-eye work in New Orleans. He hired men like Oster, and later people like David Lewis and Jack Martin, to perform the occasional gumshoe work which came into the office. And this provided the cover apparatus for him to do the things he was actually interested in at that time, which were an extension of his previous communist surveillance work he had done in New York with his mentor, George Starr. Except that, as we have seen, Banister was now not hampered by being a domestic FBI agent. He was now free to perform actual offensive operations outside the boundaries of the law, knowing that he would be protected since his former colleagues at the FBI were told not to interfere with CIA operations against Cuba.[48]

But there would likely not be much to worry about from local FBI agents Warren DeBrueys and Regis Kennedy. Since they both spoke fluent Spanish, these two men were Hoover's trusted agents on the anti-Castro, Cuban scene in New Orleans. Garrison had learned from an informant that DeBrueys was so involved with Banister, Ferrie, and men like Sergio Arcacha Smith, that he operated out of a special office at the Customs House near Canal Street.[49] Regis Kennedy was the FBI representative to the Friends of Democratic Cuba, a peculiar organization we will discuss soon, which appears created by Banister and Sergio Arcacha Smith.[50] Orestes Pena told the House Select Committee on Assassinations that he saw Oswald with both DeBrueys and Customs agents leave the restaurant he worked at and go to the Customs House.[51] The Bureau felt this information concerning DeBrueys and Oswald was so sensitive that, on the eve of the HSCA being formed, they had Pena's files destroyed.[52] For, as we shall see, there is evidence that Oswald was an informant for the FBI, and his handler was DeBrueys.

Obviously, Banister was well known to just about every aspect of the intelligence community in New Orleans. In fact, there is evidence that Banister had heard of Oswald before he even arrived in New Orleans in the summer of 1963. This is the famous Bolton Ford incident, which occurred on January 20, 1961, the day President Kennedy took the oath of office. Two men, one a powerfully built Latino, the other a thin Caucasian man, encountered employees Oscar Deslatte and Fred Sewall at the Bolton Ford lot in New Orleans. They wanted to buy ten Ford pickup trucks for an organization called Friends of Democratic Cuba. (The reader should note, this is about three months before the Bay of Pigs invasion.) The Latin man called himself Joseph Moore, but he said the bid had to be in the name of "Oswald." The Caucasian man said that Oswald was his name and he was the one with the cash. They both told Deslatte that there should be little profit made on the transaction since it was for a patriotic cause.[53] Deslatte then printed the name "Oswald" and Friends of Democratic Cuba on the bid form.[54] When Kennedy was assassinated, Deslatte called the FBI, and they came by and picked up the form. This piece of information was included in the FBI documents handed to the Warren Commission. But it was not fully declassfied until many years later as part of a much longer FBI report by DeBrueys. And when it was declassified, the actual order form with Oswald's name and Friends of Democratic Cuba was not included in the report.[55] DeBrueys, who wrote a long summary report on Oswald in which this episode was included, had to have known the significance of the Banister/Oswald connection far in advance of the assassination.

Obviously, this could not have been the real Oswald since he was in Russia at the time. When Garrison found out about who was involved with Friends of Democratic Cuba, a clue began to emerge about how his name was involved from such a distance. It turns out that the FDC was an organization largely created by Ferrie's friends and colleagues Sergio Arcacha Smith and Banister. Its ostensible purpose was to raise funds for the anti-Castro cause. But no significant funds were ever raised. Therefore the organization appeared to be some kind of dummy front. Martin McAuliffe was a member. He owned a publicity agency that did work for the CRC. Bill Dalzell, who was a CIA contact and knew Clay Shaw, was also part of it. And as we mentioned, Regis Kennedy was also an FBI representative for the group.[56] Garrison had information that the FDC was really an undercover operation done in conjunction with the CIA and FBI to ship equipment and persons in and out of Cuba.[57] Considering the incident was three months before the Bay of Pigs, that makes sense. To this day, no one knows for sure why Oswald's name was used, or how it was obtained. But a distinct possibility is that it likely came from Ferrie. For in 1961, in his letter to Eastern Air Lines requesting paid leave for Ferrie, Arcacha Smith had nothing but effusive praise for the intricate work Ferrie had done with his group of Cuban exiles.[58]

After Banister and Arcacha left the Balter Building, they went to 544 Camp Street, sometimes called the Newman Building after its owner Sam Newman. By the time that Banister moved there, his secretary was a woman named Delphine Roberts. Roberts was of a piece with Banister when it came to rightwing politics. On April 16, 1962, the *New Orleans Times Picayune* carried a story describing a Catholic Church being picketed by three women. One of them was Roberts. The picketing was over the desegregation of Catholic schools. She had met Banister in 1962 when she was protesting from a booth on Canal Street that the American flag was not getting enough respect.[59] Off of this meeting, Banister hired her as his secretary. In her interviews with Jim Garrison, the diminutive Roberts was very tight lipped about her experience with Banister. For Banister had sworn her to secrecy in the wake of the Kennedy assassination. And he kept her out of the office until it blew over.[60]

Years later, with Banister dead, and with no threat of criminal prosecution, she started to reveal what really went on that summer at 544 Camp Street. She began this process with the HSCA, which suppressed most of her information. But field investigator Bob Buras did two interviews with Roberts in the late summer of 1978. In the first one, Roberts stated that Banister was very angry when he heard that Oswald was arrested with the 544 Camp Street address on his pro-Castro material. And he complained about this to both Sam Newman and building custodian James Arthus. She quoted Banister as saying, "How is it going to look for him to have the same address as me?"[61] She also said that Banister definitely had a file on Oswald. (In fact, one police officer who saw a remnant of Banister's files said they contained basic information on Oswald's activities in New Orleans.[62]) But in this first Buras interview she did not admit to seeing Oswald in person at the office.

The next month, Buras tried again, hoping he could get more information from her. This time, Roberts admitted to Oswald coming into Banister's office. She also thought she saw Marina there with him once. She told Buras that Oswald had a few private meetings with Banister where she could not hear what was being said. In this interview, she said that Arthus and Newman had let Oswald use a second floor room as his own office. Left unsupervised, this is probably how Oswald carelessly placed the 544 Camp street address on his Corliss Lamont authored pamphlets. And this is why Banister was angry with those two men. Later, investigator Scott Malone found a corroborating witness for Roberts. The aforementioned Mary Brengel told Malone that about two weeks after the assassination, Roberts told her that Oswald had been in Banister's office.[63]

Later on, Roberts reluctantly poured out even more of her story to author Anthony Summers. Summers also interviewed Roberts' daughter. The daughter said that she used a room at 544 Camp Street for photographic work. She said that she and a friend also saw Oswald at the address: "I knew he had his pamphlets and books and everything in a room along from where we were. . . . I never saw him talking with Guy Banister, but I know he worked in his office. . . . I got the impression Oswald was doing something to make people believe he was something he wasn't. I am sure Guy Banister knew what Oswald was doing."[64]

Like Mary Brengel, Consuela Martin did part-time work for Banister at Camp Street. She was fluent in both Spanish and English, therefore Banister used her as a translator of documents and pamphlets from English to Spanish and vice versa. Martin noted the large amount of Cuban exiles in the building, and also coming in and out of Banister's office. Martin had a separate office, and she said Oswald came to see her more than once to drop off things to be translated. Since his documents were pro-Castro and Banister hated Fidel, she thought Oswald was trying to locate pro-Castro sympathizers for Banister. This probably relates to the list of students Arcacha Smith had given to Banister. In addition, since her room was right next to Banister's office, she saw Oswald inside Banister's more than once.[65]

Dan Campbell was one of the young men who Banister used to infiltrate leftist student groups. Dan received 50 dollars per week for his services.

Campbell told the author that "Banister was a bagman for the CIA and was running guns to Alpha 66 in Miami."[66] Since Campbell was an expert marksman, one of his other duties for Banister was to assist Cubans in small arms training. He described Banister as a "frighteningly violent person" and the group of men at his office as "the worst kind of fanatics."[67] He recalled one day when he was at Banister's, a young man came in to use the phone: "I knew he was a Marine from his bearing and speech pattern the minute he walked into 544 Camp Street." The next time he saw this young man was when his image was on TV and he was accused of being the killer of President Kennedy. Campbell immediately knew something weird was afloat: For how could a working acquaintance of Banister's be a communist?

Allen Campbell, like his brother, also worked for Banister. On one of the days Oswald was distributing his literature nearby, Allen recalled Delphine Roberts returning to the office and complaining to Banister about Oswald distributing pro-Castro leaflets on the street. Campbell remembered Banister trying to reassure Roberts by telling her not to worry because, "He's with us, he's associated with this office."[68]

Former Banister investigator Vernon Gerdes later worked for attorney Stephen Plotkin. He told Plotkin that he had seen Oswald and Ferrie together with Banister. Plotkin later told one of Clay Shaw's lawyers he considered Gerdes a reliable witness.[69] Another former Banister gumshoe, Jack Martin, said he was introduced to Oswald by Ferrie in Banister's office. With Ferrie at the time was Sergio Arcacha Smith. Echoing Delphine Roberts and her daughter, Martin said that Oswald had his own room to work out of at 544 Camp Street. Further echoing Roberts, he said that Arthus knew about Oswald and absconded with his paraphernalia after the assassination.[70] Tommy Baumler was another former student who worked for Banister. He joined left wing college groups and reported back to the former G-man. Baumler was another Banister employee who was very reluctant about talking to Jim Garrison. But many years later, after being established as a New Orleans lawyer, he spoke to researcher Bud Fensterwald and told him that there was no doubt that Oswald had worked for Banister. Baumler also revealed how professional Banister's operation was in regard to this kind of double agent operation. For Baumler added that Banister was able to give out letters of marque—that is, a license to clear one with law enforcement officers—so that "if you are caught as a communist, the letter will clear you of communist leanings."[71]

William Gaudet did work for the CIA for a number of years. He had a virtually rent-free office in Clay Shaw's International Trade Mart where he published *Latin American Report*. He told the HSCA that "on one occasion he observed Oswald speaking to Guy Banister on a street corner."[72] Gaudet told

Anthony Summers that he also saw Oswald with Ferrie. And that another important person was Sergio Arcacha Smith: "I know he knew Oswald and knows more about the Kennedy affair than he ever admitted."[73] David Lewis, a former investigator for Banister, stated that he once met Oswald in the summer of 1963 in a restaurant housed at the Camp Street building. With Oswald was Arcacha Smith.[74] George Higgenbotham was still another of Banister's young men who infiltrated student organizations as a double agent. When the young infiltrator kidded Banister about sharing an office with people papering the streets with leftist leaflets, Banister snapped, "Cool it, one of them is mine."[75]

How widespread was this knowledge about the association of Oswald, Banister, and Ferrie in the summer of 1963? The Church Committee did a limited investigation of the performance of the intelligence community for the Warren Commission. One of the agencies they consulted with was the Immigration and Naturalization Service in New Orleans. In 1975, the committee conducted interviews with two INS agents, Wendell Roache and Ron Smith. They discovered that one of the functions the INS performed was to track Cuban refugees to see if they were in the USA legally. One of the people they ended up keeping files on in foreign nationals tracking was David Ferrie, since he was with the Cubans so often. They ended up discovering Ferrie working out of Guy Banister's office at 544 Camp Street. But they also discovered Oswald was there that summer too. Further—and corroborating Roberts, her daughter, and Jack Martin—they learned that Oswald had his own room at the building. These INS reports were quite extensive. The INS had dossiers on Ferrie's problems with his former employer Eastern Air Lines and also his proclivity for young boys. Both Roache and Smith concluded that, from what they could see, Jim Garrison had good intelligence sources and very good eyes and ears in the French Quarter.[76] After the assassination, Smith was transferred to Uruguay and Roache to Puerto Rico. When Roache finally testified before the Church Committee he said, "I've been waiting 12 years to talk to someone about this."[77]

Sam Newman, the owner of the building, was rather inconsistent in his stories to the FBI and the New Orleans Police. In a report of November 25, he told the Bureau that he rented space to the CRC in approximately March of 1963. He had seen these Cubans around Guy Banister's office previously. He thought one was Sergio Arcacha Smith. The CRC was there for only three to four months. Yet, two days later, to the New Orleans Police, he said that he rented space to these Cubans around fifteen months previous. They were there for only four to five months. They fell behind in their rent so he evicted them. From other evidence, it appears that the CRC was not located at 544 Camp while Oswald was working under Banister. But Arcacha Smith was in close contact with his old friends that summer.

In his testimony before Gary Cornwell, Deputy Director of the HSCA, Newman was a bit more candid, but still dissembled. When Cornwell asked him about Oswald being in his building, Newman acted like this was the first time he ever heard of it, which could not be true since he was interviewed by Jim Garrison about that subject.[78] When Cornwell told him that several people saw Oswald there, Newman now said that, if so, he had never rented any space to him. He then said he had a lot of people in and out, and he was not around there very much. In other words, since he was not there a lot, he could have missed him in the rush. Cornwell then asked Newman if he was aware of Oswald being arrested that summer while he was passing out pro-Castro literature. Newman replied in an interesting way. He said he knew that the address 544 Camp Street was on at least one piece of literature Oswald had upon his arrest. He said that this showed Oswald had to have been associated with the Cubans. When Cornwell delved into this further, Newman admitted that Banister had asked him to rent space to the anti-Castro Cubans. Cornwell then asked why would Newman assume that Oswald, who was pro-Castro, be associated with the anti-Castro Cubans in his building? Newman now said that Oswald could also have been in league with Banister—because Banister was such an odd bird, you never knew what he was up to. When Cornwell asked Newman how Banister reacted to Oswald placing the address on his literature, Newman said he was not aware of his reaction. He then said something contradictory: "Jack Martin can tell you about that. He was in Banister's office 90 percent of the time; every day almost."[79] Question: How could Newman know that Martin was there almost every day if, as he said previously, he was not there that much? The indications are that Newman knew more than he was admitting. And unlike Roberts, he never told the whole truthful story. We know this through the interview Roberts did with the HSCA. As we saw, she said that when Banister learned Oswald had used the Camp Street address on his literature, he got extremely upset—in the presence of custodian James Arthus and Newman.[80]

When the CIA—through Dulles and Hunt—blamed Kennedy for the Bay of Pigs failure, those involved in the operation had nothing but resentment for the man they were told had blown it all. Ferrie had piloted many missions to Cuba prior to the Bay of Pigs. Sometimes they were bombing missions; sometimes they were extractions of anti-Castro Cubans. Many of them were done on orders of Eladio Del Valle, a former Cuban congressman who was in league with the CIA and Senator George Smathers of Florida to dislodge Castro.[81] Now convinced that Kennedy had sold out his dream of walking into a liberated Cuba as a hero, Ferrie began to lash out at the president. In a speech before the Military Order of World Wars, he ranted on so disjointedly about how Kennedy had double-crossed the Cuban brigade that people walked out and he had to be escorted off the podium. He also sketched on a blackboard the mistakes that had led to the defeat of the invasion.[82] To others, Ferrie "became obsessed with the idea of Kennedy and what he was doing with Cuba."[83]

This antipathy toward Kennedy was something that Eastern Air Lines used in Ferrie's dismissal proceedings. Guy Banister, his loyal friend, showed up to testify on Ferrie's behalf. Banister knew about this problem Ferrie had about berating Kennedy in public. Therefore, he tried to dissemble and say that the target of Ferrie's tirades was President Eisenhower. But when he was alerted to the date of the Military Order of World Wars meeting, he admitted it was July of 1961. The following colloquy then ensued:

> Q: The Commander in Chief on that date was whom?
> A: It was President Kennedy wasn't it?[84]

Needless to say, Banister's efforts were not successful. Ferrie was terminated. He then went to work for Banister and moonlighted as an investigator for Carlos Marcello's local attorney G. Wray Gill. He also worked for the CIA as part of Mongoose.

When Operation Mongoose began, Ferrie let it slip that he was a part of "Operation Mosquito." Clearly a miscommunication, Ferrie meant Mongoose.[85] And there is no doubt that he was a part of this effort. The supposedly secret training camps for the operation included sites in Louisiana. One was at Lacombe, across from Lake Pontchartrain, directly northwest of New Orleans. Banister visited this camp. And he helped finance it.[86] It was on land owned by Bill McLaney, an old business friend of Jack Ruby's. Ferrie had been an instructor at the camp. His interests and talents fit right in there.[87] According to Anthony Summers, some claim that Ferrie brought Oswald to this camp. On July 31, 1963, the FBI raided a cottage near the Lake Pontchartrain site. There they confiscated a broad array of munitions: dynamite, bomb casings, fuses, and fuel explosives. McLaney, the camp's owner, planned to bomb oil refineries in Cuba. The FBI had been tipped off to this violation of the Neutrality Act and proceeded on the President's orders. They also captured some key players in the movement but, oddly, released them without filing charges.[88] As we saw previously, this was part of Kennedy's program of curtailing any renegade attacks against Cuba from American soil. As some authors have noted, as the White House severely cut back on these camps and attacks after the Missile Crisis, the Cubans and people like Ferrie began to accept funds from the radical right and the Mafia. This particular camp also supplied trainees for Manuel Artime's CIA-backed operation in Guatemala. There is evidence that one of the financial backers of the Lacombe site was Texas multi-millionaire H. L. Hunt, and the go-between may have been David Phillips.[89] The fact that these men were not charged encouraged them to repeat the action later. According to historian Michael Kurtz, there was a sighting of Ferrie, the Cubans, and Oswald at another camp in early September of 1963. They were dressed in military fatigues and carrying automatic rifles. They were conducting what looked like a military maneuver. This episode took place in a swampy area of Bedico Creek. Which, in 1963, was an undeveloped area with an inland body of water in Tangipahoa Parish, about fifty miles north of New Orleans.[90]

These are not the only references to Oswald being with David Ferrie at a post–Bay of Pigs Cuban training site. Delphine Roberts has said that Ferrie took Oswald on at least one visit to an anti-Castro training camp outside of New Orleans.[91] And, in fact, INS agent Wendell Roache stated that Ferrie took films of one of these exile training camps.[92] This may be a film that House Select Committee Deputy Counsel Robert Tanenbaum saw and talked about in an interview for *Probe Magazine*.[93] Tanenbaum stated that, "To the best of my recollection, we found that movie somewhere in the Georgetown Library archives." Tanenbaum, an experienced prosecutor, brought in witnesses to identify people he thought were Phillips, Oswald, and Banister.[94] This was confirmed upon multiple witness viewings. Or as he told the author, "Oh, yeah. Absolutely. They're all in the film." Since Phillips and Oswald were there, this is very likely the Lacombe camp.

As Mongoose began to dwindle down, Ferrie, and others, now grew even more resentful of Kennedy. For the first time, Ferrie mentioned to a young protégé a design to do away with JFK. But he never included himself in the plans. He talked about it in the second or third person.[95] Sometimes he went further and said that Kennedy "ought to be shot."[96] This was also echoed by Guy Banister who had been a CIA conduit of funds for the training camps.[97] In 1963, Banister bitterly commented to a colleague that "someone should do away with Kennedy."[98] Banister's fascist ideology was conducive to such things. He once pulled out his handgun and shouted, "There comes a time when the world's problems can be better solved with the bullet than the ballot."[99]

Considering the above, it is not at all surprising that in the newly discovered records of the House Select Committee on Assassinations, there are memoranda saying that custodian James Arthus suggested to Guy Banister that they send a dead pigeon to the White House.[100]

CHAPTER SEVEN

On Instructions from His Government

"Any attempt to explain what happened in Dallas must explain Lee Harvey Oswald. . . . He is not, to put it in simple words, an easy man to explain."

—*Robert Blakey,* Frontline, *1993*

If Oswald was being manipulated by Banister, Ferrie, and Shaw, then was he a true Marxist? Or, to look at it the other way, if Oswald were a true believer in the communist cause, why would he be associating with rightwing extremists?

Of course, it would not be necessary for Oswald to be a right winger in order to be useful to these men. In fact, who would expect them to be associated with a crazed Marxist? But at this point in his life—the summer of 1963—was Oswald a true Marxist and did his psychology fit into the profile of an assassin?

Of course, since he was killed by Jack Ruby in the basement of the Dallas Police Department, Oswald never had the opportunity to argue his case in court. The media and the Warren Report then seized on some of the facts of his life and some statements to prove the case against him. These included conversations with friends in the service, his alleged defection to Russia, his mailings for communist literature, his aforementioned distribution of pro-Cuba flyers, and the ensuing radio debate in New Orleans in which he defended Marxism. But does this collection of exhibits add up to a convincing indictment? Does it encompass all pertinent details and exclude other alternatives? For as we will see, the Warren Commission never mentioned any of Oswald's activities in New Orleans, which we have discussed in the previous two chapters. In the 888 page report, you will not see any mention of Guy Banister, Clay Shaw, David Ferrie, Oscar Deslatte, the Friends of Democratic Cuba, the Clinton-Jackson incident, or anything about the entire Bolton Ford episode. You will see a mention of 544 Camp Street, but this is only to say that the address appeared on a flyer Oswald was passing out when he was arrested. And this mention appears to have been done only to brand Oswald a liar. For the report then immediately says, "investigation has indicated that neither the Fair Play for Cuba Committee nor Lee Harvey Oswald ever maintained an office at that address."[1] This spurious statement is then repeated in Chapter 7, on page 408. The Warren Report deals with Oswald in New Orleans in three places: Chapter 6 (3 pages), Chapter 7 (6 pages), and in its Appendix 13 (5 pages).

It is interesting to look at how the Commission managed to keep Oswald out of 544 Camp Street. When one looks at the references for this statement, the reader will see a Secret Service report, an FBI report, and a local police report. The closest thing to actual pertinent evidence is an interview with Sam Newman. Who, as we have seen, never was really candid with anyone, and gave inconsistent stories. In other words, there was no real and rigorous attempt by the Commission to interview anyone who was at the location in the summer of 1963 on this key point. And, in fact, to support its negative argument, the Commission never asks the obvious question: If Oswald was never at 544 Camp Street, then why did he rubber stamp the address on this pamphlet in his possession entitled "The Crime Against Cuba"? For the address was stamped on the inside back cover. As noted above, unlike the Warren Commission, both Jim Garrison and the HSCA uncovered evidence that did place Oswald at 544 Camp Street.

To see just how valid the Warren Commission's inquiry was, let us consider some of the statements included in its negative argument. In one supporting document, Cuban exile Frank Bartes tells the FBI that Oswald was unknown to him.[2] This is bad even for the Commission. For as John Newman notes, Frank Bartes appeared *in court* with Oswald on August 12, 1963. This was at a hearing which resulted because of Oswald's fracas with Carlos Bringuier over leaflets he was passing out on Canal Street.[3] Bartes said he was in court in support of Bringuier. After Oswald pleaded guilty, the press started to ask him questions. Bartes got angry with the media and Oswald because the Cubans were not allowed to present their views. Bartes then warned an FBI agent that

Oswald was a dangerous man. Bartes was not just an FBI informant, but he went on to work for the CIA.[4] Any serious inquiry would have shown that Bartes was lying to the FBI about not knowing Oswald. Yet both the Bureau and the Commission accepted his lie.

In another dubious statement, the report states that, "The FBI has advised the Commission that its information on undercover Cuban activities in the New Orleans area reveals no knowledge of Oswald before the assassination."[5] Again, this is not supported by the facts we have just seen. Several Cubans knew about Oswald in New Orleans that summer. In another supporting document quoted by the Commission—an FBI interview with Sam Newman—he states that it was Jack Martin who brought him Sergio Arcacha Smith as a renter.[6] Yet, as we have just seen, Sam Newman told Gary Cornwell of the HSCA that it was Banister who brought him Arcacha. Another source that the Commission used to keep Oswald out of 544 Camp Street was a Secret Service report with James Arthus. As we have seen, this is the man who kidded Banister about Oswald being in the same building with him.[7] In a transparent attempt to keep Oswald out of 544 Camp Street when the Cubans were there, a footnote says that although the CRC was located at Camp Street, it moved out in early 1962, before Oswald's return from Russia.[8] As we have seen, Sam Newman did not tell the FBI or the police the CRC moved out that early. This particular falsehood appears to be simply manufactured.

This kind of performance shows one of the main weaknesses of the Commission: their reliance on the FBI as an investigating arm. But it also shows a related failing: The Commission's inability to then follow through and conduct a real investigation of its own. But the point is, almost the entire Warren Report biography of Oswald is constructed like this. That is, it is entirely superficial. It accepts certain events in passing, which any normal investigation would stop and ask questions about. It then avoids certain circumstances and relationships—like Clinton-Jackson, 544 Camp Street, the association with Ferrie—which will seriously dislodge the simple story that the Commission and the FBI wants so badly to maintain. But as we shall see, Oswald's life, which ended at age twenty-four, is anything but simple. In fact, one can argue that he was one of the most complex twenty-four-year-olds to enter the annals of history. With the releases of the Assassination Records Review Board, we can now begin to tell the story the Warren Commission could not.

A Fatherless Child

He was born in New Orleans in 1939 to one Marguerite Claverie. He had two brothers. One of them, John Pic, was from his mother's previous marriage to

Edward Pic in 1929. This marriage only lasted two years; but the divorce took almost a year and half to complete.[9] Afterwards, Marguerite Claverie began seeing an insurance collector named Robert Lee Oswald. Three weeks after her divorce from Pic was finalized in 1933, they were married at a church in New Orleans. A year later, Robert Oswald Jr. was born.[10]

For the next few years, the Oswalds lived in different residences in New Orleans. But then, in August of 1939, Robert Oswald Sr. died of a heart attack.[11] Two months later, in October of 1939, the fatherless Lee Harvey Oswald was born. Marguerite got a five-thousand dollar death benefit. But she was now responsible for three children, with no husband and without a steady income. Finding it difficult to support the three boys, she occasionally placed them in nearby orphanages, or left Lee with his aunt, Lillian Murret.[12] While working at a hosiery shop in the summer of 1943, Marguerite met Edwin Ekdahl. Edwin was an electrical engineer originally from Boston. Recovering from a heart condition, Marguerite took care of him, and they decided to marry. Edwin expected a change in his job location, so Marguerite moved to Dallas with her sons. After some hesitation, she married Ekdahl in May of 1945.[13]

In October of 1945, the couple moved to Benbrook, a suburb of Fort Worth. Something of note happened here, which the Warren Report does not mention. On Oswald's enrollment card at Benbrook Common School are listed two addresses: the Worth Hotel and 7408 Ewing. The family lived at neither. They were living in a rented home on Granbury Road. The family may have briefly lived at that Fort Worth hotel in the months preceding. But there was no reason for the Ewing address, because Marguerite would not live at 7408 Ewing for two more years. And Oswald's only attendance at Benbrook was 1945–46.[14] It is hard to believe that the Commission did not notice this odd discrepancy because they actually cite the records of that school in the report.[15] And two pages later, they mention Ewing Street as a 1948 address.

Marguerite suspected her new husband, correctly, of infidelity. They also began to argue about finances. They separated in 1946, reunited in 1947, and divorced in June of 1948.[16] After this divorce, Marguerite reverted back to her former name of Marguerite C. Oswald.

In October of 1948, John Pic wanted to join the Marine Corps Reserve. Yet he was only sixteen years old. Marguerite signed a false affidavit stating that John was seventeen years old and was born on January 17, 1931. (He was actually born in 1932.) John entered the reserve on October 24. He then quit high school and began working at a department store. It was at this time that Marguerite purchased the home in Fort Worth on Ewing Street.[17] By 1949, all three boys now attended Fort Worth public schools, since John had decided to go back and achieve his high school diploma. John was in high school, Robert was in junior high school, and Lee attended Ridglea West Elementary School. Marquerite held a series of jobs, usually having to do with retail sales.

New York City

In January of 1950 John Pic turned eighteen. He graduated from Paschal High School and decided to join the Coast Guard.[18] He was first stationed in New Jersey and would not return to Texas for nine months. In August of 1951, he married Margaret Fuhrman in New York City. He was soon assigned to port security at Ellis Island. He therefore moved to an apartment on East Ninety-Second Street in New York City. In July of 1952, without graduating high school, Robert Oswald joined the Marines. He soon left for San Diego.[19] This left twelve-year-old Lee at home with his mother in the house on Ewing. Lee graduated from Ridglea Elementary and now should have attended the brand new William Monnig Junior High in the fall of 1952. But instead, Marguerite now sold the house on Ewing and drove to New York City with Lee. Her reason for this was that she did not think Lee should be left alone while she worked.[20]

The visit began well enough. But when Marguerite disclosed that she thought Lee and herself should live with the Pics, relations soured. For Pic's wife did not take a liking to Marguerite.[21] Lee and his mother then moved to an apartment in the Bronx. (Which is where Jacobi Medical Center is located, a point that will be explained shortly.) Marguerite now again began taking jobs in retail sales stores like Lerner's Shops. And she and her son occasionally saw the Pics. Lee now began having truancy problems in the New York public schools. Other pupils teased him because of his "Western" clothes and Texas accent.[22] Lee complained to Marguerite that he wanted to go back to Texas.[23] Because of this problem, the Oswalds were to appear in Domestic Relations Court in March of 1953. Lee did not accompany his mother, and therefore a warrant was issued for him. He was eventually apprehended at the Bronx Zoo, where he called the attendance officer a "damned Yankee."[24]

On April 16, 1953, Lee and his mother appeared in court. Lee was judged a chronic truant. Therefore the judge remanded him to Youth House in Manhattan for observation for a period of three weeks.[25] He was interviewed by social workers and psychologists who delivered various opinions about him. (One of these observers, Dr. Renatus Hartogs, actually revised his opinion of Oswald after the assassination for his book *The Two Assassins*.) The recommendation from Youth House was that young Oswald be placed on probation, and that his mother be required to seek help from a family consulting agency.[26] From most indications, after this, Oswald's behavior in school generally improved and the truancy problem was alleviated to the point that Marguerite did not feel any more court appearances were necessary. But one more appearance did ensue in November. And the probation officer suggested using the Big Brother organization to provide a mentor for Oswald.[27] Marguerite called both the probation officer and the Big Brother group before deciding to return to New Orleans in January. She clearly did not want to return to court and risk having Lee remanded, which would have altered her plans to leave the city.

We should note some anomalies in the New York school records that the Warren Commission did not note. The most curious being that it appears that "the original sets of New York school, court, and psychiatric records disappeared while in FBI custody."[28] Only copies are available today. Yet, when Anne Buttimer of the ARRB surveyed the documentary record on this issue, she wrote that the Warren Commission was supposed to have the originals of these records.[29] Yet, it appears that what the Commission worked with was not original material. And further, the FBI did not do a complete job in their field investigation. Only one teacher of Oswald was interviewed and no schoolmates were.[30] Another oddity is that in the extant New York records, nothing appears to have been transferred from Forth Worth: no grade cards, no enrollment forms, and no transcripts.[31] Further, the records of his actual school attendance differ as to the number of days Oswald actually missed. In one set of records produced by the Commission, the truancy problem is quite serious. Yet in the New York School records, it does not seem very bad at all. In the former, he missed seventy-five more days of school in a ten-month period than in the latter.[32] Finally, when John Malone of the FBI wrote a report based upon the original records, he said that when Oswald left Youth House in May of 1953, he entered ninth grade at P. S. 44. Yet, the previous September, Oswald entered the seventh grade. How could he have been skipped through a grade if he was a chronic truant?[33]

Before leaving the subject of Oswald and his mother in New York, two other points of information should be noted—points which either the FBI or the Commission itself knew about. About a week after Kennedy's assassination, the FBI office in New York received a phone call from a Mrs. Jack Tippit. Mrs. Tippit had just received a call from a strange woman with a foreign accent. This woman wanted to know if Mrs. Tippit was related through marriage to the slain police officer in Dallas who Lee Harvey Oswald allegedly had shot. She replied that yes, they were distantly related. The woman with the accent now warned Mrs. Tippit not to go to the press with the information she was now about to disclose. She implied she was calling from a public phone so the call could not be traced. She also said she could reveal her name since she feared for her life if it ever got out. She said that she personally knew Oswald's father and uncle. They had come to New York from Hungary. They were communists. They had lived at Seventy-Seventh Street and Second Avenue in a section of

New York called Yorkville. They had been unemployed while she knew them. The communist party in America had supported them because they worked on communist activities. The unidentified woman gave Mrs. Tippit two names. When she did, her demeanor now became agitated and her speech more disjointed. One was Emile Kardos. She then mentioned the word "brother-in-law," a phrase which she repeated. The other name was "Weinstock."[34] Louis Weinstock, also from Hungary, was the head of the Communist Party in New York City in the early 1950s. Weinstock was also General Manager of *The Worker*, located in New York. It was a publication Oswald subscribed to and wrote to in 1962. There is no evidence the author could find revealing that the FBI tried to find Emile Kardos or investigated if any Oswalds ever lived in Yorkville.

The second point of information is perhaps even more interesting. And the Warren Commission clearly knew about it. To any student of the Oswald family, it becomes apparent that, at this time in her life, Marguerite was not at all financially well off. She was barely surviving on about 45 dollars per week as she went from job to job in retail sales work. Yet, while in New York, she hired a housekeeper to clean her one bedroom apartment. Her name was Louise Robertson. And she cleaned her apartment two to three times per week. Louise worked for Marguerite for about six weeks. During which time Marguerite told the cleaning woman that the reason she had brought Lee to New York was to undergo mental tests at Jacobi Hospital.[35] (Which, as noted earlier, is in the Bronx where Marguerite moved to after leaving John Pic's place.) When chief consul J. Lee Rankin of the Warren Commission asked Marguerite about this particular point—Jacobi Hospital—she replied in the negative and escaped into a defense of "normal" characterizations of Oswald as a boy who had puppies and a bicycle. She clearly was avoiding the broader context of the question. For mental tests did not have to deal necessarily with abnormal psychology. This utterly fascinating point was never brought up again.

Return to New Orleans

Following the Warren Commission biography of Oswald, the reader will now notice something rather odd. The author (attorney Wesley Liebeler) has just spent about four pages on Oswald in New York. He will now spend a bit more than half of that on Oswald's return to New Orleans even though Oswald stayed there for about the same length of time before joining the Marines. This seems odd because some very important things happened in this time period, which the Commission clearly discounts.

In January of 1954, upon her return to New Orleans, Marguerite Oswald first lived with her sister Lillian Murret on French Street in the Lakeview area.

The Commission then says that Marguerite's friend Myrtle Evans rented them an apartment at 1454 Saint Mary's Place. Oswald now attended Beauregard Junior High in New Orleans. He graduated in June of 1955 before attending Warren Easton High School that fall. He then dropped out, worked in New Orleans for the next eight months, and then moved to Fort Worth in early 1956.

But Robert Oswald said, on numerous occasions, that Lee attended Stripling Junior High in Fort Worth. He said this before the Warren Commission in 1964, in 1959 after Oswald's defection to Russia, and in 1962, upon his return.[36] Yet, according to the Commission, this did not occur. In fact, it could not have occurred since Oswald graduated from junior high school in New Orleans. This may be why the Commission deals with Oswald's intermediate schooling in New Orleans in just one paragraph.[37]

Yet, in 1993, Principal Ricardo Galindo backed up Robert Oswald. He stated that it was common knowledge that Oswald had attended Stripling.[38] In fact, a teacher, three students, and an assistant principal all recalled Oswald being there.[39] And here begins one of the strangest discoveries in the recent scholarship on the phenomenon of Lee Harvey Oswald.

In 1994 John Armstrong got in contact with Stripling assistant principal Frank Kudlaty. He asked him if Galindo was correct: Did Oswald attend Stripling Junior High School? Kudlaty replied without hesitation that he had. Armstrong then asked how he was so sure. Kudlaty's response was, "Because I gave his Stripling records to the FBI."[40] Kudlaty went on to say that on the Saturday morning after Kennedy's murder, he was contacted by his superior, Weldon Lucas, the school principal. Since he lived close to the school, he was to meet two FBI agents there. Kudlaty was there before the FBI was. He went and retrieved Oswald's file, which he briefly looked at. He noted that there were no trailing records—that is, records from his previous school, or a notice that Stripling had transferred records to his next school. He placed the file back into the folder. Once the agents got there, they asked for it. Kudlaty turned it over. They then left. Kudlaty locked up the school and went home.

Kudlaty's credentials are beyond reproach. After leaving Stripling, he became Superintendent of Schools in Waco, Texas. He stayed there until his retirement in 1987. When the State Department selected a group of school administrators to advise the Chinese government on education, he was one of those chosen to attend. He traveled to China in 1979.

One of the most disturbing aspects of Kudlaty's testimony is that the FBI *had to have known* Oswald attended Stripling ten years previous. Or else how could they have called Weldon Lucas the morning after the assassination? Yet, this information is not in the Warren Commission. Neither are the names of Frank Kudlaty or Wendell Lucas. And, as with the original school records from

New York, it appears the FBI misappropriated the file Kudalaty gave them. For it is nowhere to be found today.

The Warren Commission chose to believe Marguerite Oswald when she said her son began to read communist literature in 1954.[41] This was strongly disputed by Oswald's best friend at that time, Edward Voebel. He said that "I believe that's a lot of baloney . . . I am sure he had no interest in those things at that time."[42] Later he was asked specifically about Oswald studying communism at age fourteen, "Did you see any evidence of that when you were going around and associating with Lee Oswald?" Voebel replied firmly, "No, none whatever."

In 1955, an event would occur that would change Oswald's life. He would join the Civil Air Patrol and meet David Ferrie. This is how the Warren Report deals with that crucial topic: "He was briefly a member of the Civil Air Patrol."[43] And that is that. Even though in Volume VIII of the Commission volumes, two witnesses tentatively recalled Oswald being in the CAP with Ferrie as the commander.[44] We have already dealt with this key topic at length in Chapter 5. But we should note another aspect of it here. As we have seen with Ed Voebel, his friend did not recall Oswald reading any communist literature or expressing Marxist sympathies in 1954. This important observation is backed up by Robert Oswald: "If Lee was deeply interested in Marxism in the summer of 1955, he said nothing about it to me. During my brief visit with him in New Orleans, I never saw any books on the subject in the apartment. . . . Never, in my presence, did he read anything that I recognized as Communist literature."[45] Therefore the evidence indicates that the dabbling in Marxist literature likely began with Oswald meeting Ferrie.

Oswald dropped out of Warren Easton High School on October 7.[46] He brought a forged note to school saying his family was moving to San Diego. He then tried to join the Marines by claiming he was seventeen. (He had just turned sixteen on October 18.) There is a very interesting incident that occurred previously, in the summer of 1955, that foreshadows Oswald's eagerness to join the Marines. Marguerite recalled being visited by a man in uniform who she presumed to be a Marine Corps recruiter. This man encouraged her to let her son quit school and enter the Corps. As this was illegal at that time—Lee was fifteen—this man could not have been a legitimate Marine Corps officer. As more than one commentator has pointed out, this may have been Ferrie masquerading as a recruiting officer.[47] We have seen how Ferrie was active in recruiting young men into the service, and also how he had a domineering role in their lives. This incident likely influenced his mother to later make out a false affidavit about Lee's age to join the Marines. The subterfuge failed.[48] By badly underplaying Oswald's service in the CAP, and not even mentioning Ferrie, the Commission leaves out a key piece of the puzzle as to why Oswald was so eager to join the Marines illegally, as to have someone visit his house in order to do so.

The Warren Report then tells us that Oswald went to work as a messenger at Gerard Tujague's shipping company. Again, by never mentioning the Friends of Democratic Cuba, or the Bolton Ford incident, the report leaves out another key piece of key information. For Gerard Tujague was the vice-president of the Friends of Democratic Cuba.[49] In other words, the name "Oswald" could have been gathered through him. According to his mother, Oswald now began studying the Marine Corps Manual and waiting to turn age seventeen to join the Marines.

In July of 1956, Marguerite moved back to Fort Worth. She rented an apartment at 4936 Collinswood. Oswald now enrolled at Arlington Heights High School on September 6. He dropped out after only a few weeks.[50] This was in preparation for his joining the Marines the next month. Two other things happened around this time that should be noted. Although Oswald had been studying the Marine Corps Manual month after month, he tried to sell classmate Richard Garrett on communist philosophy, for which Garrett reported him to the principal.[51] The second interesting point is that on October 3, Oswald wrote a letter to the Socialist Party of America. He said he was very interested in their youth league and would like information on a branch in his region so he could join. He then closed with: "I am a Marxist, and have been studying socialist principles for well over fifteen months. I am very interested in your Y. P. S. L." (This last refers to the youth league groups.) The Warren Report makes almost nothing of these two incidents, or their timing. Yet, any honest investigator would have certainly arched his or her eyebrows reading about them. For in just a bit more than two weeks from the date of this letter to the Socialist Party, Oswald would be interviewed, fingerprinted, and measured for his later enlistment in the Marines.[52] It is astonishing that the Warren Report never mentions this jarring juxtaposition. Oswald was writing letters to the Socialist Party, and trying to sell his classmates on communism at the same time he was joining the branch of the service that was trained to fight and kill communists. Was Oswald a split personality? If so, the report does not say that. The inability to explain this dichotomy, or to even honestly acknowledge it, is one of the largest lacunae in the Warren Report.

Oswaldskovich in the Marines

Oswald was in the Marine Corps from October of 1956 until September of 1959. He served in three main geographical locations: the southeast United States, California, and the Far East. He served in boot camp in San Diego. In early 1957 he went to Camp Pendleton for infantry training (ITR). In March he went to the Naval Air Station in Jacksonville, Florida, for Aviation Fundamental School. This was the beginning of his training to be a radar operator. He took classes in basic radar theory, map reading, and air traffic control assignments.[53] This training continued at Keesler Air Force base in Biloxi, Mississippi. Keesler is home to the Air Education and Training Command and specializes in training students in such areas as radio communications and avionics as well as related electronics areas. Oswald was granted a security clearance to deal with confidential material at this time.[54] This is odd considering his relatively recent letter to the Socialist Party. But in light of the fact that Ferrie used to take his CAP students on bivouac maneuvers at Keesler—which he had to have clearance for—perhaps it is not so odd. In late June of 1957, after graduating seventh in a class of thirty, Oswald was given a certificate as Aviation Electronics Operator.[55]

In July he was sent to the Marines Corps Air Station at El Toro, California. That August he was sent to Yokosuka, Japan. It is necessary here to point out how the Warren Report deals with this next crucial step in Oswald's life. It reports that Oswald would now be "based at Atsugi, about 20 miles west of Tokyo. Oswald was a radar operator in MACS-1. . . . Its function was to direct aircraft to their targets by radar, communicating with the pilots by radio."[56] Somehow, the Commission cannot bring itself to state two important pieces of information about Oswald's new assignment. First, Atsugi was known not just as the home of the First Marine Air Wing, but as home of the "Joint Technical Advisory Group," jargon for its being the main operational base in the Far East for the Central Intelligence Agency. It evolved into that in the early 1950s, for operations into China and Korea.[57] The Agency's influence there expanded in the mid-fifties when the high altitude reconnaissance plane, the U-2, which had just become operational, flew out of Atsugi. The CIA had developed the plane through Lockheed Aircraft. There were three units in operation at this time, two flew out of the Middle East, and one out of Atsugi.

In the index of the Warren Report you will not find a reference to the U-2, or to Francis Gary Powers. Powers was the pilot of the U-2 that was reportedly shot down over Russia in May of 1960, while radar operator Oswald was there. It was this downing that fouled relations in advance between Eisenhower and Khrushchev for their summit meeting in mid-May. This was meant to be a momentous four-power summit between England, France, Russia, and the United States. Held in Paris and hosted by Premier Charles de Gaulle, Khrushchev disrupted it on May 16 by meeting separately with Harold Macmillan of England and de Gaulle before announcing a set of demands for Eisenhower to meet about the U-2 incident.[58] Eisenhower did not meet them, since they included punishment for those involved with the flight. Therefore, Khrushchev left the meeting and withdrew his invitation to Eisenhower to visit the Soviet Union after the summit. This is a meeting that Eisenhower had planned for many months in advance. In fact he and Khrushchev had met in the summer of 1959 and got along so well that they planned on negotiating things like a test ban treaty and the status of Berlin at the Paris summit.[59] It was supposed to be the capstone to Eisenhower's eight years in office.[60] He had meant it to mark a thaw in East-West relations, an opening which his successor could then develop further. It is an established fact that Dulles and Bissell had found ways to authorize flights by working around Eisenhower's instructions.[61] There has been a debate ever since over whether or not this particular flight was authorized by Eisenhower. Afterwards, he cancelled all U-2 flights.[62] Some have even speculated that it is this episode—the shootdown and its scuttling of the summit—that caused Eisenhower's famous warning about the military-industrial complex in his January 1961 Farewell Address. A speech that, in one draft, lamented his inability to achieve world peace.[63]

As John Newman notes, and the Warren Report conceals, one of Oswald's duties while in Japan was to actually guard the U-2 while in hangar. Oswald also used state-of-the-art radar equipment to track the plane.[64] Other members of Oswald's unit, MACS-1, recalled that they were stationed right next to the air strip where the U-2 would land. And they had special radar height finding technology, which could track the plane up to over 80,000 feet.[65] Now, the U-2 program was classified as Top Secret. Yet, as previously noted, the Warren Report states that the highest security clearance Oswald was ever granted was Confidential, two classes below that. As Newman notes, this does not seem credible in light of the new document declassification by the ARRB. In fact, some of Oswald's service pals have hinted that he did have a special security clearance.[66] For Oswald appears to have been part of Detachment C, a special technical unit that seems to have been part of the U-2 program. Further, he knew something that virtually no one else did: the U-2 was flying not just over Russia, but over China.[67] And this unit followed the U-2 as it went around the south Pacific to various trouble spots, like Taiwan and Indonesia. This is an important topic that we shall further discuss when Oswald defects to Russia.

Also, a strange but notable coincidence occurred that may be just ships passing in the night. Oswald arrived in the Tokyo area, just a few months after it appears Howard Hunt had left the area. Further, Hunt left Japan to at least partly work on the U-2 flights in Europe.[68]

As mentioned in Chapter 5, another notable point about Oswald in Japan is his meeting with Richard Case Nagell. Oswald had been seen outside the Tokyo Soviet Embassy by the National Police. He was walking outside the gate but then turned and went inside. Nagell knew it was Oswald since a friend of his on the force showed him the young man's picture.[69] Nagell then arranged to meet Oswald under an assumed name. He found out that Oswald's ostensible purpose at the embassy was to have some coins identified. But Nagell also found out that Oswald had also met with Colonel Nikolai Eroshkin. Eroshkin was under embassy cover but was actually a GRU agent. In America this would make him a military intelligence agent. Nagell states that the Soviets suspected Oswald of being some kind of surveillance agent almost immediately. What makes this even more interesting is that the CIA was involved in an attempt to get Eroshkin to defect to the American side.[70]

Another point that should be made about Oswald's stay in the Marines was his training in the infantry for marksmanship. Oswald was tested twice, once in December of 1956 and once in May of 1959. To put it mildly, he did not do very well either time. There are three classifications in the Marines. From highest to lowest, they are expert, sharpshooter, and marksman. On his first test in 1956, Oswald scored 212, which was two points above the minimum to qualify as a sharpshooter. In other words, he was in the lower ranges of the middle slot. In 1959, Oswald scored 191, which was 1 point over the minimum ranking for marksman. In other words, he almost completely slipped off the bottom of the scale.[71] The Commission realized it had a problem here and so they called in Marine Corps Major Eugene D. Anderson to try and explain why Oswald did so poorly in 1959. Anderson said that, "It might well have been a bad day for firing the rifle—windy, rainy, dark." Mark Lane looked up the true weather conditions that day. Like most days in Southern California, it was sunny and bright with no rain. The temperature ranged from 72–79 degrees.[72]

What makes this even worse is the observation by some of his colleagues in the service as to Oswald's general aptitude with a rifle. Henry Hurt interviewed dozens of Oswald's Marine Corps acquaintances. They all agreed that Oswald could not shoot. For instance, Sherman Cooley said, "I saw that man shoot. There's no way he could have ever learned to shoot well enough to do what they accused him of doing in Dallas." James Person, who later became a bank president, recalled the lack of physical coordination that contributed to Oswald being a poor shot on the rifle range.[73] In fact, Hurt did enough investigating on this point to learn that Oswald was actually called a "shitbird." That is someone who repeatedly failed his test and had to do it over and over. In fact, Hurt interviewed some Marines who said Oswald never did pass the test. But he was given a final qualifying mark so that he and the unit could continue with basic training.[74]

There is no way around describing what the Warren Report does with the above information. To show how candid and painstaking they were in their pursuit of the facts, as a way to disguise Oswald's poor performance before leaving the service, they actually repeated Anderson's fib about the bad weather on Oswald's scoring round in 1959.[75] They then quote two military men as saying that Oswald was an above average shot for a Marine, and an excellent shot compared to a civilian.[76] As Hurt demonstrated, Oswald was somewhat of a joke in this regard to his fellow Marines. Like many statements in the report it was made not because of the evidence, but in spite of it.

On October 27, when Oswald opened his locker, a derringer dropped out, discharged, and the bullet hit him in the left elbow. He was taken to a nearby hospital for two weeks and then, in April of 1958, he was court martialed for having an unregistered weapon.[77] He was sentenced to twenty days in the brig, fined 50 dollars and was reduced in rank. He was given a suspended sentence on the twenty days confinement, which was to be remitted in six months. In June of that year, Oswald was again court martialed for getting in a verbal altercation with an officer and pouring a drink on him.[78] He was again sentenced to the brig and fined. But because of the repeat offense, this time he had to serve his former suspended sentence.

In December, Oswald was transferred stateside to Marine Air Control Squadron No. 9 back in Santa Ana, California. There, headed by Lieutenant John E. Donovan, he was part of a ten-man crew engaged in aircraft surveillance.[79] And for the first time, the report now states that Oswald may have had a clearance higher than confidential. Which is surprising. Because the report is now about to describe something quite unusual. That is a marine whose "thoughts were occupied increasingly with Russia and the Russian way of life."[80] Yet, as Philip Melanson noted, his access now did not appear to become restricted. Even as he did things like study the Russian language and read Russian books for hours at a time. He also subscribed to the famous Russian newspaper *Pravda*. He even played Russian records so loudly that they could be heard throughout his barracks.[81] Oswald openly discussed Soviet politics and talked in Russian to his fellow Marines. His friends now began to kid him by calling him "Oswaldskovich." He kidded back by calling them "comrade." He now began to call Soviet communism "the best system in the world."[82]

This was in 1958—ten years after the fall of China to communism, five years after the close of the Korean War, and just four years after the McCarthy witch hunts. The Rosenbergs had been executed in 1953. Yet, there was no action taken against Oswald for any of this. Mail-room workers dutifully reported his leftwing mail. Nothing was done. Then in February of 1959, he did something that caused Jim Garrison to drop his pipe when he read about it in the Warren Commission volumes: Oswald took a mastery test in Russian.[83] As the DA described it, he had been on active or reserve duty for over two decades.

Neither he, nor anyone he knew, had ever taken a test in Russian. Further, as Garrison then commented, why would a radar operator need to educate himself in the Russian language? The Warren Report tries to minimize the impact of this startling examination by saying that he did not do very well on the test. But Oswald kept up his studies and improved drastically. One of Oswald's colleagues arranged a meeting for him with his aunt, Rosaleen Quinn, who was also studying Russian. Except she had been tutored in the language for over a year in preparation for a State Department exam. Quinn was quite impressed that Oswald now spoke Russian at least as well as she did.[84] Oswald tried to explain his marked improvement by saying he listened to Radio Moscow. Any language expert will tell you that one does not learn a language as difficult as Russian by listening to distant voices speak the language rapidly. One has to work at it slowly, piece by piece, so that one understands words and phrases enough to build context for both comprehension and spoken mastery. In other words, like Quinn, one must construct a controlled environment, perhaps with a tutor. Or perhaps in a classroom.

The latter appears to be what Oswald did. The report does not tell us this, but the Commission knew about it. In 1974, researcher Harold Weisberg finally received the transcript of the January 27, 1964 Warren Commission executive session meeting. Most of this session was spent discussing the issue of whether or not Oswald was a secret agent, since reports had already been circulating in the press about this possibility. During the meeting, Chief Counsel J. Lee Rankin mentioned that the Commission was trying "to find out what he [Oswald] studied at the Monterey School of the Army in the way of languages."[85] As Rankin phrased it, there is no question in his mind that Oswald was there. (And so was Richard Case Nagell.[86]) This may explain how Oswald improved his proficiency in a matter of months. Further, when the author interviewed Dan Campbell in New Orleans, he told me that he was part of a marksmanship team that would tour military facilities giving instructions and exhibitions. He gave one once at the same California base Oswald was at. He recalled it because the host officer had him sleep in Oswald's bunk since, as he told Dan, Oswald was hardly there at the time.[87]

It was in this time period, 1959, that another introduction is made to Oswald. He met another Marine recruit named Kerry Thornley. Although Thornley lived on another part of the base, and he only knew Oswald for a period of about two to three months, Thornley would became an important witness for the Warren Commission.[88] Whereas other soldiers acknowledged that Oswald was studying the Russian language, was interested is Russian culture, and was cognizant of the Russian governmental system, it is hard to find anyone who actually said Oswald was a communist. For instance, Jim Botelho was friends with Oswald and even took him home to meet his parents once. Botelho once told Mark Lane that he was quite conservative at that time: "Oswald was not a Communist or a Marxist. If he was I would have taken violent action against him and so would many of the Marines in the unit."[89] Marine David Bucknell told Lane that during 1959 Oswald and others, including himself, made a visit to the Criminal Investigation Division (CID) at El Toro. There they were pitched on becoming part of an intelligence operation against communists. Oswald made a few more such visits. He told Bucknell that the civilian recruiter those later times was his same intelligence contact at Atsugi. He then told Bucknell that after he was discharged, he would go to Russia as part of an American intelligence mission, and would return to America as a hero in 1961. Botelho later revealed his reaction to Oswald's journey to Russia. He said it was the talk of the base by all of Oswald's pals. Botelho said that none of the radio codes at the base were altered, even though Oswald knew all of them. Since Botelho knew Oswald was actually anti-Soviet, he suspected there would be no real investigation at the base. Two civilians later arrived. They asked a few questions, took no written statements, and did not tape record any interviews. Botelho concluded it was a CYA investigation: one done so the Marines could say there was an inquiry. When this occurred, Botelho said, "I knew then what I know now: Oswald was on an assignment in Russia for American intelligence."[90] If this suspicion was as widespread among Oswald's cohorts as Botelho implies, it may be why most of their statements collected in the Warren Commission are rather brief. In fact, many of them are perhaps a half page long. Most of them were not even heard by the Commission.

But of the ones who were heard, Kerry Thornley probably testified the longest. And he was the one who portrayed Oswald as an ideological Marxist. Consider this as possible motivation for the assassination: "This gets back to emotional instability and why did it occur. I do believe, to begin with, Oswald, how long ago he had acquired the idea . . . it was almost a certainty that the world would end up under a totalitarian government." And later, "I think he accepted Orwell's premise in this that there was no fighting it. That sooner or later you were going to have to love Big Brother . . . this was the central thing that disturbed him . . . he wanted to be on the winning side for one thing, and therefore, the great interest in communism."[91] And then, as the Commission does, Thornley says that although he was convinced Oswald was a Marxist, he could never have predicted his defection.[92] Thornley was also used as an amateur psychologist to portray Oswald as being a bit eccentric. For instance, he described Oswald as walking around with the bill of his cap down so he would not have to look at anything around him: "This is just an attempt . . . on his part, to blot out the military so he wouldn't have to look at it: he wouldn't have to think about it. In fact he made a comment to that effect at one time

. . . he didn't like what he had to look at."[93] Thornley's testimony, more than any other Marine cohort, set the profile for the Commission's portrayal of Oswald as a Marxist misfit and helped provide them with a reason for Oswald to murder President Kennedy. We will return to Thornley in our discussion of Jim Garrison's inquiry.

Let us close out our discussion of Oswald's military service with two fascinating and revealing episodes, which need to be examined in light of the declassification process. They are Oswald's application for entry into Albert Schweitzer College in Switzerland and his hardship discharge.

In mid-March of 1959, Oswald somehow picked up an application to attend Albert Schweitzer College (ASC). He applied for the spring term of 1960. As some commentators have noted, Schweitzer was a college in name only, since it offered no degrees.[94] It began as a lecture series by one Hans Casparis. Casparis then expanded the offerings with help from various individuals from the USA and also the Unitarian Church, which also played a part in its administration. In 1953, because of this financial outreach, Casparis purchased the former Hotel Krone in Churwalden, a five story, thirty-room building and announced the opening of the "college."[95] The location of ASC was odd. It was high in the Swiss Alps, fifteen miles from the industrial town of Chur. There was only one main road winding through the town and into the Alps. The school accommodated only thirty students, yet Schweitzer listed sixty-eight individuals as representatives and references of the college.[96] There was no bus or railway service to the village and no library, hospital, fire department, or police station. The college officially opened to students in the fall of 1955. Yet in the entering class of thirty, none were from Switzerland. This may have been deliberate, in order not to have to register or be accredited with the Swiss government. As we shall see the college was virtually unknown to Swiss authorities. In fact, when the FBI tried to find the place, it transferred the request to agents in Paris. Even they had never heard of it, so they contacted the Swiss police. It took the Swiss police two months to find Albert Schweitzer. If the idea was to keep a low profile, it was achieved.[97]

Since there were so few students attending, the school had to get by on donations from benefactors. The American Committee of Friends of Albert Schweitzer College was incorporated in New York but had its offices in Boston. The head of the American Admissions Committee was Unitarian Church Minister Dr. Robert Schact of Providence. It was Schact who cleared Oswald's application and sent it to Switzerland for final disposition.[98] When Marguerite Oswald wrote her son a series of letters in Russia in late 1959, she enclosed money orders. She got no reply except a returned letter. She was worried he might be lost. She alerted the FBI to the fact that she had gotten a letter from Casparis saying that Lee was expected there in April of 1960. He had been accepted and his application fee had been deposited. She was visited by FBI agent John Fain in April of 1960. Marguerite told Fain about the returned letters and how Lee was apparently lost in Russia. Now, J. Edgar Hoover began to search for Casparis and his college. This search occasioned the famous June 3, 1960, memo by Hoover saying that there is a possibility that an imposter is using Oswald's birth certificate. It turned out that Oswald never went to Schweitzer. But the question that remains, which the Commission never answered is: How did Oswald ever hear of this obscure institution halfway around the world while he was in Santa Ana? Because, as has been shown, the college did not advertise in the Christian Register from 1948–59.[99] Was it brought to Oswald's attention by Kerry Thornley? Thornley testified that he had been going to the First Unitarian Church in Los Angeles around the time he met Oswald.[100] Author George Michael Evica also explored the career of Hans Casparis, who wrote that he had graduated from three universities and lectured at the University of Zurich. When Evica contacted that university, they said he had never lectured there. He also had no reported degrees from any of the colleges he said he graduated from.[101]

Then there is Percival Brundage. Brundage was one of the three incorporators of Friends of ASC, whose purpose was to receive and administer money and properties for the benefit of the institution. As Evica notes, Brundage was a major Unitarian Church Officer from 1942–54. This was during the time period—during World War II and at the beginning of the Cold War—when the Unitarians were cooperating with first the OSS, and then the CIA. In fact, this association became so prevalent that by 1960 all Quaker/Unitarian welfare agencies were placed under suspicion by the KGB.[102] But further, in 1960, Brundage was also a signatory for the purchase of the Southern Air Transport airline by the CIA. In fact, he became one of the major stockholders of the company.[103] As many people know, this was an infamous CIA proprietary company that did major supply missions for the Agency in Southeast Asia and the Caribbean. Brundage was a director of the Friends of Albert Schweitzer College from 1953–58. The FBI visited the mysterious school in 1960 and 1963. The latter visit was part of the Warren Commission investigation of Oswald. Coincidentally—or not—Albert Schweitzer closed down in 1964, shortly after Kennedy's murder.[104]

Because Oswald never had the opportunity to stand trial, how he knew about and why he applied for this almost undetectable institution is one of the many mysteries of his short life. But it would appear to indicate that he knew months in advance that, after his Marine service was over, he would be emigrating to Europe. We will now examine how Oswald actually did leave the

Marines, for this aspect is almost as clouded in mystery as his application to an obscure "college" in Churwalden.

Oswald's military assignment was scheduled to end on December 7, 1959.[105] (It had been lengthened because of his confinement.) Yet, on August 17, he submitted a request for an early discharge due to medical problems his mother was having. With less than four months remaining on his obligation, and realizing there would be some kind of inquiry at both ends of the request, one would think there must have been quite an emergency at home. In another conspicuous failure, the Warren Report spends four sentences on this issue.[106] It merited much more attention.

One reason for a hardship or dependency discharge is so the enlisted man can be home to care for the ailing dependent. Once Oswald was discharged he spent all of *three days* in Fort Worth with his mother.[107] What makes this "dependency" discharge even more odd is this: Seven days before he was actually released, he applied for a passport. Obviously, no passport was needed to go to Texas. He stated on his application he may be traveling to Europe, among other places, including Finland. (This last, as we shall see, was significant.) On his application he mentioned his intent to attend ASC. His passport was issued six days later, the day before he left for Texas.[108] It would seem then that Oswald's actual agenda was not to care for his mother, but to hightail it for Europe using his application to Albert Schweitzer as a pretext. Once in Europe he would then leapfrog to Finland for easier access to his real destination, which was Russia. (For this is what actually happened.) When he did arrive in Fort Worth, he gave his mother a hundred dollars—which he could have mailed her—and then left for New Orleans, where he said he was going to get into the import-export business.[109]

Oswald began maneuvering for this early discharge on July 6th. That day he visited the Red Cross HQ at the Marines Corp Air Station in El Toro.[110] He told them that his mother had suffered an injury at Cox's Department Store in Fort Worth and had filed suit against the store. Yet his mother had worked at King Candy Company in the Fair Ridglea Department Store and her civil action was against them. But the suit was not filed until August 11, over a month after Oswald spoke of it. He requested a "Q" allotment be sent to her from his check, that is, a certain portion of his funds be dispersed to her. He then asked for supporting paperwork to begin his dependency discharge. The Red Cross in El Toro then got in contact with the Red Cross in Fort Worth. The Red Cross there got in contact with Marguerite. They learned that she claimed to have been hurt by a candy jar falling on her nose on December 5, 1958 while working the King Candy booth at Fair Ridglea Department Store.[111] Dr. Milton Goldberg examined her and said there was a laceration, but his X-rays revealed no fractures. But Marguerite kept on returning to him and complaining of ailments. Goldberg did more X-rays but could find no fractures anyplace. He concluded she had suffered no partial or permanent disability.[112] When the company filed its first notice of the injury, they said she would be out of work for one week. As we have seen, even though this injury occurred in early December of 1958, Oswald did not file for a "Q" allotment for seven months. Further, there is no evidence that Marguerite ever got any help with her injury from her son Robert who lived right there in Fort Worth.

On the day of the assassination, Dr. Goldberg phoned the local FBI office in Fort Worth. He told them about his treatment of Marguerite. He explained how he could not go along with her alleged injury for compensation purposes. He suggested two other doctors for her to see if she wished to pursue it. But he also added an interesting detail. He said he recalled that during the time he treated her, she said that her son wanted to defect to Russia.[113] Her first visit to him for a lacerated nose was on January 9, 1959. This was a full nine months before Oswald was formally discharged. It is six months before he reported to the Red Cross to begin his dependency discharge.

Marguerite went on to see five doctors total. Finally, her insurance company decided to cut off payments to her. This is when she decided to file a lawsuit against King Candy. She told the Red Cross on July 9 that this is why her son needed the hardship discharge, and this is why she needed the paperwork to follow through on it. The paperwork was completed, and Oswald filed his petition on August 17. On August 27, just ten days later, the board approved the petition. On August 31, it was directed that Oswald be released from active duty.[114] The House Select Committee on Assassinations did something the Warren Commission did not do. It interviewed the senior member of the board that reviewed Oswald's discharge. Colonel B. J. Kozak told them that, compared to the pro forma procedure the board gave Oswald, it normally took three to six months for a hardship application to be approved.[115] In fact, this was common knowledge among Oswald's Marine buddies. In his testimony before the Commission, Nelson Delgado stated that he knew Oswald was requesting a hardship discharge, but "it usually took so long a time to get a hardship discharge."[116] For some reason, it did not take long at all in Oswald's case: just two weeks.

Virtually everything about this discharge suggests it was a pretext to get Oswald out of the service early and on his way to Russia. Since, according to Rosaleen Quinn, he now spoke Russian well, there was no need for him to do any more military service, since he was not an infantry man, but an intelligence asset. The cover-up the Commission performed on this aspect of Oswald's life is typical of the quality of their work in exploring who Oswald was.

Oswald, Russia, and the CIA

Oswald departed Fort Worth by bus seventy-two hours after he got there. There is no record of him offering any kind of medical care for his mother. In fact, for part of his seventy-two-hour stay he visited with his brother Robert and his family.[117] (Predictably, the Warren Report does nothing to underline this seeming paradox.) Oswald then left Texas to go to New Orleans. He arrived on September 17 and went to the International Trade Mart. There he went to Lewis Hopkins of Travel Consultants. Hopkins also handled travel arrangements for Clay Shaw who managed the Trade Mart.[118] Curiously, Oswald stated on his passenger questionnaire that he was in the import-export business, which he was not, but Shaw was.[119] Oswald stayed at the Liberty Hotel, and he booked passage with Hopkins on a freighter called the Marion Lykes for 220.75 dollars. He wrote a letter to his mother in which he said that his values were different than his family's and, "Just remember this is what I must do. I did not tell you about my plans because you could hardly be expected to understand."[120]

Nelson Delgado told the Commission he could not quite comprehend how Oswald could afford to travel across Europe: "I couldn't understand where he got the money to go. . . . The way it costs now, it costs at least 800 dollars to 1,000 dollars to travel across Europe, plus the red tape you have to go through."[121] The late Philip Melanson expressed similar doubts. The author of *Spy Saga* noted that before his departure, Oswald's bank account showed a balance of 203 dollars, which is about what the ticket for his ship journey cost. It is possible that he stowed away over a thousand dollars. Or perhaps he borrowed the money from someone. But there is no evidence of that.[122]

His ship made two stops in France before departing for England. He landed at Southampton on October 9. He told officials that he planned on staying in country for a week before departing for college in Switzerland.[123] The report says that Oswald arrived in Southampton on October 9 and left for Helsinki, Finland—a country on his passport application—the same day. Yet Oswald's departure from England is stamped on his passport for October 10.[124] He arrived in Helsinki late on the night of the tenth. He then did something that the report just glides over: He checked into the Hotel Torni for a bit more than a day, and then the Klaus Kurki Hotel for over four days. Yet here, the official story arrives at another quandary. We have mentioned the problems that the financing of this long voyage presents for someone of the status of Oswald. Complicating this is the fact that servicemen in Japan at that time were paid in scrip redeemable at American bases.[125] Yet, when Oswald arrived in Helsinki, he stayed at a five star hotel. The Torni is the same hotel that housed U.S. President Herbert Hoover, President Mannerheim of Finland, Soviet Premier Aleksei Kosygin, the great Finnish composer Jean Sibelius, and Finnish aristocrats like Prince Bertil and Count Folke Bernadotte.[126] Upon its opening in 1931, it was billed as Finland's first skyscraper hotel. Its top floor holds art exhibitions monthly, and the hotel has an observation platform, which is the highest vantage point in Helsinki. It was also constructed with marble staircases and stained glass windows. Upon its opening, it was the leading hotel in the city, and it published its own newspaper.

During World War II, the Torni became an espionage headquarters for both the British and Soviets. In fact, the entire hotel was occupied by the Soviets from 1944 until 1947. Outside the edifice there is a plaque which states that "The Control Commission of the Allied Powers resided in this hotel during 1944–1947."[127] Clearly, no one from the Warren Commission visited this place. Retired British police detective Ian Griggs did. When the author met Griggs in Dallas in 2010, he told me that the Torni was roughly the Finnish equivalent of the famous Savoy Hotel in London. On his own, it makes absolutely no sense for Oswald to have stayed there. On his budget, Oswald should have been staying, at the most, at a Holiday Inn Express–type motel. Either someone told him about this, or he checked his wallet, did some figuring, and understood he was not even in Moscow yet. So on his second day he checked into the Klaus Kurki, where he stayed for four days. But according to Griggs, this second hotel is another high-class operation. It is located on Bulevardi, one of the best streets in town and is described as a "boulevard hotel." The two buildings are about 300 yards from each other. According to Griggs, the Torni is perhaps the number one luxury hotel in Helsinki; the Klaus Kurki is probably number two. If the Commission had described these two hotels in any detail, or furnished photos, any objective reader would have to ask: What was a guy with 203 dollars in his account doing at a hotel where, if he was in town, Nelson Rockefeller would stay at?

That question brings us to Oswald's purpose for naming Finland on his passport application. He was there to attain a visa to Russia. The Soviet Embassy in Helsinki had direct ties to Intourist, which was the Russian state-owned travel bureau. Therefore, they could arrange for a visa in five to seven days, which is usually how long it took for Intourist to arrange for suitable lodgings. On page 690 of the Warren Report, it states that Oswald "probably applied" for the visa on October 12 and received it on October 14. But according to his actual visa application, he applied for it on October 13, which means he got the visa not in forty-eight hours, which is what the Commission leads us to think, but in a startling twenty-four hours.[128] The Commission was troubled by the alacrity with which Oswald was processed. They asked the CIA to investigate. The Agency said that Mr. Golub, the employee who handled visas there, could issue a transit visa—one good for twenty-four hours—in a few minutes. But for a longer stay it would take about a week.[129] This really did not explain how Golub got Oswald his visa that fast since Oswald's initial visa was for a week. What the CIA did not tell the Commission is that the Russian embassy in Helsinki may be the only one in Europe where the officer was allowed to issue a visa in a matter of hours. A State Department dispatch of October 9, 1959 revealed that the American Embassy in Helsinki had direct ties to Golub. And they sent persons to him who needed a visa in a hurry. Golub then would call them back to alert them the mission had been accomplished.[130] None of this is in the Warren Report, where Golub's name is not even mentioned. Perhaps because it would indicate that someone was informing Oswald on how to proceed in advance. Further, Oswald was still indulging in his spendthrift ways. For Oswald purchased ten "tourist vouchers" at a price of thirty dollars apiece.[131] Oswald then left Helsinki by train on October 15 and crossed into the USSR at Vainikkala. The Russian speaking Marine, Oswaldskovich, was now where he wanted to be.

At this point it is necessary to do something that the Warren Report does not do: Place Oswald's supposed defection in a historical perspective. Prior to 1958, American defectors to Russia had been a quite rare phenomenon. But yet, in 1959, there had already been two defectors to the USSR, Robert Webster and Nicholas Petrulli. In 1958, there had been four.[132] By the end of 1960, the number had ballooned into the high teens.[133] Several of them had a change of heart and returned to America. Many of them followed the same route of entry into Russia as Oswald had done.[134] And, like Oswald, several of them were from the military.[135] To make things more intriguing, Webster had worked for Rand Corporation, which had close ties with the CIA. Rand was one of the first companies to sell technical products inside of Russia. And it was at such a trade fair that Webster defected. Both Henry Rand, who founded the company, and executive George Bookbinder worked for the OSS, the precursor to the CIA. Their Washington representative Christopher Bird was a known CIA agent.[136] And although Oswald was not supposed to have known about Webster, as he was arranging to leave Russia in 1961, he asked U.S. embassy officals about the fate of a young man named Webster who came to Russia at about the time he did.[137]

None of this important history is in the Warren Report. In fact, the names of Webster and Petrulli are not in the index. Which is surprising in light of the following fact: Webster met the nineteen-year-old Marina Prusakova in Moscow in 1959, before she met her future husband, Lee Oswald. And Webster spoke to her *in English*—a language Marina was not supposed to have learned yet. But which she spoke, albeit with a heavy accent.[138] Further, after the assassination, the address of Webster's Leningrad apartment was found in Marina's address book.[139] For, like Oswald being sent to Minsk, Webster was sent out of Moscow to Leningrad, from where he applied for an exit visa. It would seem more than happenstance for a nineteen-year-old girl—whose uncle worked for the Soviet version of the FBI—to meet two out of the three American defectors in all of Russia in a matter of months, especially when they were among the first defectors to Russia in many years. Further, Webster eventually took a common-law wife in Russia who was suspected of being a KGB agent. Webster informed authorities of his intention to defect two weeks before Oswald did the same. Webster left Russia a fortnight before Oswald left. Marina once told an acquaintance that her husband had defected to the USSR after working at a trade exhibition in Moscow. Marina had temporarily confused Oswald with Webster, for this is how Webster had defected.[140] All this says much about the probability of an American defector program in place, and Russian knowledge of it.

When Oswald got into the Moscow train station, he was met by his Intourist guide Rimma Shirakova. She took him to the Hotel Berlin and gave him a tour of Moscow. Oswald made it a point to tell Rimma he was in possession of classified information about U.S. airplanes.[141] He also said he wanted to apply for Soviet citizenship. She forwarded his request and told him he must write a letter to the Supreme Soviet,[142] which Oswald did on October 16.[143] On October 21, Rimma relayed the news that Oswald's request for citizenship had been turned down; therefore, he could be deported since his six-day visa would expire in a matter of hours. In his so-called Historic Diary, Oswald writes about an apparent suicide attempt and Rimma discovering him at 8:00 P.M. that night. This is all strange because Oswald was in the hospital at four that afternoon.[144] This discrepancy—and others—have led many people to think that the Historic Diary is not really historic, or a diary. The doctor who examined Oswald at Botkinskaya Hospital called the attempt a "show suicide," one made over his attempt at citizenship.[145] The actual cut was about two inches in length and shallow.[146] No major blood vessels had been severed so there was no massive loss of blood. In fact, no blood transfusion was necessary.[147] In fact he had cut his wrist with Rimma waiting for him in the hotel lobby. So he probably suspected that she would come up and discover him.

After this, Oswald was placed in the psychiatric ward of the hospital. During this seven-day stay in the hospital, Soviet intelligence authorities were in all likelihood reading reports from the hospital and from Intourist, debating about his fate, and deciding whether or not he was a genuine defector. This decision would come under the purview of the Second Chief Directorate of the KGB.[148] When he was released, Oswald was moved to the Hotel Metropole. He then decided to make a bold move. He would go to the American Embassy in Moscow to renounce his citizenship.

Richard Snyder was a former CIA employee who likely worked under diplomatic cover at the U.S. Embassy in Moscow.[149] He had long been on friendly terms with the Agency. For instance, in the mid-fifties while studying Russian at Harvard, he was used as a spotter for the CIA to recruit students into REDSKIN, a project designed to interview Russian speaking students and sign them up as legal travelers into the Soviet Union. Snyder was then working under Nelson Brickham in the Agency's Soviet Russia Division.[150] This background helps explain what Snyder did shortly before Oswald's arrival. Three days before Oswald showed up to renounce his citizenship, Snyder wrote a letter to a fellow State Department employee on his experience with American "defectors." Quotes are placed around that word because Snyder did so in this letter. And he was referring to the Webster case. He also writes about Webster violating Section 349 of the naturalization code, and this is how he lost his citizenship. Snyder writes that it is how thoroughly the renouncement of American citizenship is documented that is the key to losing one's citizenship. Therefore, quoting Talleyrand, he exercises some practical foresight is these cases. When Oswald met with Snyder (and officer John McVickar), as if he had read Snyder's letter, he handed him his renouncement note based on Section 349.[151] During this interview, Oswald made statements threatening to turn over radar secrets and information he had learned as a radar operator to the Soviets. He then added that he might know something of special interest,[152] which may have referred to the U-2. This was probably done because he suspected the embassy was wired by the KGB, which it was.[153] This disclosure would then give him a bargaining chip to stay in Russia. There is no other reason for him to say such a thing directly to American diplomatic officers. For he could have been detained and then charged for intending to give away military secrets. Or as Oswald's Russian friend Ernst Titovets has written, considering the intensity and pitch of the Cold War, something worse could have happened.

Neither Oswald's verbal or written request were sufficient enough to renounce his American citizenship. To do that, one had to file a "Certificate of Loss of Nationality" according to the Expatriation Act of 1907. This document would then be forwarded to the State Department for final dispostion. Although Oswald asked for these papers, remembering his letter of seventy-two hours previous about "defectors," Snyder did not give them to him. Snyder told Oswald to think it over and return in a couple of days. Because of Snyder's maneuvering, Oswald never signed the papers.[154] So he never officially renounced citizenship.

But, perhaps the most important and revealing thing about this Saturday morning visit is not what transpired in Moscow, but what happened as a result of it in Washington. Quite naturally, once the newspaper reports came into the U.S. about Oswald's defection, the FBI opened its file on November 2 for security purposes.[155] There were three other points where the information on Oswald came into Washington: the State Department, Office of Naval Intelligence, and the Navy office at the Pentagon. The first—since it came from Snyder—and last carried information about Oswald's threat to give up radar secrets. On November 3, the FBI found out about this threat also. Therefore, the Bureau now issued a FLASH warning on Oswald. That is, the FBI should stay on the lookout for Oswald's reentry into the United States under a false name.[156] All of this seems quite routine and normal. What is not routine or normal is what happened when the Navy memo got to the CIA.

On all the other pieces of information we have mentioned, the documents contain names and dates that make them easy to track. Not so at CIA. When the Navy memo got to the Agency, it went into a kind of limbo. After it finally surfaced, it went to James Angleton's CI/SIG unit—on December 6. Angleton was chief of counterintelligence. SIG was a kind of safeguard unit that protected the CIA from penetration agents. It was closely linked to the Office of Security in that regard. The question is: Where was it for the previous thirty-one days? Both this Navy document and Snyder's State Department cable went into a kind of "black hole" somewhere. In fact, the very first file on Oswald was in the Office of Security. Which is odd because the Oswald file should have gone to the Soviet Russia Division. It appears the black hole kept the documents from getting there when they should have.[157]

Further, there is no evidence that the CIA did a security investigation about the dangers imposed by Oswald's threat to give up radar secrets and something of "special interest." What makes this odd is that, as mentioned previously, Oswald even knew the U-2 was flying over China. The combination of this information from Moscow, plus the fact Oswald was in Detachment C, these should have triggered a damage assessment investigation in 1959. And the reconnaissance program should have then been adjusted accordingly. But there is no trace of such a contemporaneous investigation in the newly declassified CIA files.[158] What makes this hard to swallow is the fact that after Oswald defected, in May of 1960, the Gary Powers U-2 flight went down over Russia. Powers thought that "Oswald's work with the new MPS 16 height-finding radar looms large" in that event.[159] What is also surprising is that the Warren Commission never investigated this important subject. In fact, they avoided it. Because when called to testify, Oswald's Marine colleagues were not questioned about the U-2. John Donovan, who knew Oswald in the Philippines and discussed the U-2 with him there, and was later his commander at El Toro, was ready to talk about the matter at length. But the Commission was not. In fact, Donovan was briefed in advance not to fall off topic. Donovan was actually stunned by the Commission's avoidance of the subject. He asked his briefers afterwards, "Don't you want to know anything about the U-2?" The reply was essentially, no they did not. Donovan asked a friend of his who had testified, "Did they ask you about the U-2?" The response was, no they did not. Which is remarkable considering that former CIA Director Allen Dulles was a very active member of the Commission, and the U-2 had originated on his watch. Donovan was not questioned by the CIA about the U-2 until December of 1963. But this was probably a counterintelligence strategy, to see whom he had talked to and what he had revealed. That is probable because, after Powers was shot down, the CIA closed its U-2 operations at Atsugi. Yet, Powers did not fly out of Atsugi. The only link between Powers and Atsugi was Oswald.[160]

And this is not the end of the negative template at CIA about Oswald and his defection. Perhaps the most remarkable thing about Oswald's CIA files is this: His 201 file was not opened until *over a year* after his talk with Snyder and McVickar. That is on December 8, 1960. This gap seriously puzzled the HSCA. Their investigator Dan Hardway called Angleton's employee Ann Egerter about the matter. She did not want to talk about it.[161] According to the CIA, a 201 file is one of the most common files the Agency has. It is an information file on any person of interest to the Agency. This could be of operational interest, prospective operational interest, or of counterintelligence reporting.[162] By these criteria, Oswald most certainly had to be a person of interest. At the very least, after his meeting with Snyder and McVickar. So the HSCA, with the CIA's help, tried to neuter the issue by studying other defector cases. But this comparison is faulty since people like Webster and Petrulli did not imply a threat to surrender secrets about the U-2. In fact, when Egerter finally did open the 201 file, Oswald's defection was noted, but his knowledge of the U-2 was not. The delay in opening the 201 file was so unusual that the HSCA asked retired CIA Director Richard Helms about it. His reply was, "I am amazed. Are you sure there wasn't? . . . I can't explain that." When the HSCA asked where the Oswald documents were *prior* to the opening of the 201 file, the CIA replied they were never classified higher than Confidential and therefore were no longer in existence. This turned out to be a deception. Because many were classified as Secret, and author John Newman found most of them, since they were not destroyed. Further, the ones classified as Confidential were still around when the ARRB declassified them in the nineties.[163]

But the oddities about the CIA and Oswald are not yet ended. Although no 201 file was opened until December of 1960, Oswald was placed on the

Watch List in November of 1959.[164] This list was part of the CIA's illegal HT/LINGUAL mail intercept program, and only about 300 people were on it. It was supervised by Angleton.[165] This was at a time when Oswald's file was in limbo. It was not possible to find a paper trail on him until the next month. How could Oswald be, simultaneously, so inconsequential as not to have a 201 file, yet so important as to be on the exclusive Watch List? It is so odd as to be unexplainable. Unless the lack of a 201 file was deliberate. Because, clearly, someone in CIA knew who Oswald was and felt he was important enough to have his mail intercepted. When this writer asked author and former intelligence analyst John Newman how one could explain this in light of the fact that Oswald's first file was opened at CI/SIG, he replied that one possibility was Oswald was being run as an of-the-books agent by James Angleton.[166] In light of all the declassified information we have learned of in this section, this author knows of no better way to explain this dichotomy. Through these new discoveries, it would appear that either when Oswald was at Atsugi, or perhaps, as related by David Bucknell, during his interview with CID, he was recruited by the CIA. And since Angleton's principal (but not only) domain was counter-intelligence versus Russia, Oswald's Russian language training, his questionable hardship discharge, his Albert Schweitzer ruse, and his choice of Helsinki as an entry point, all appear planned for his Agency mission as part of the mushrooming false defector program to Moscow. This was a program that Snyder seemed all too familiar with—so much so that he made it easy for Oswald to regain his American citizenship.

Minsk and the KGB

In early January of 1960, Oswald was called to the passport office and given a Residence document, which was not the same as a grant of citizenship. He was given 5000 rubles and told he was going to Minsk.[167] Escorted by two new Intourist guides, he arrived there on January 7. And by January 13, he was at work there in a radio factory. His fellow workers could not translate his first name so they called him Alik.[168] (This is the first name Oswald would later use as an alias.) Further, he was granted a rent free apartment by the Mayor of Minsk, and given a rather generous salary of 700 rubles per month. This was supplemented with a Red Cross stipend of the same amount. In March, he was moved to a 60 ruble per month apartment overlooking a river which he called "a Russian Dream."[169]

Oswald had given interviews to American newspaper reporters Aline Mosby and Priscilla Johnson in which he clearly played up his attitude as a disillusioned expatriate. Consider some examples: "One way or another I'd lose in the United

States. In my own mind, even if I'd be exploiting other workers. That's why I chose Marxist ideology."[170] And also this: "I could not live under a capitalist system. . . . I will live now under a system where no individual capitalist will be able to exploit the workers. The forces of communism are growing. I believe capitalism will disappear as feudalism disappeared."[171] And this: "I started to study Marxist economic theories. I could see the impoverishment of the workers before my own eyes in my own mother, and I could see the capitalists."[172] Besides these B movie banalities, he also said he became interested in communism at age fifteen when, "an old lady handed me a pamphlet about saving the Rosenbergs."[173] The KGB likely had Oswald's room at the Metropole Hotel wired, since it was outfitted with an infra-red camera.[174] Once they heard this last, they must have arched their eyebrows in wonder. Oswald has to be talking here about his stay in the liberal New York City. But in 1954, when he turned fifteen, he was in New Orleans. And why would anyone be distributing literature on saving the Rosenbergs at that time? They had been executed in June of the previous year. Naturally, it appears that the KGB had reservations about Oswald as a genuine defector. They therefore shipped him out of Moscow to Minsk, about 450 miles southeast. Once he arrived there, he was a guest of the state so that he could be observed by them.[175] In fact, when the Minsk KGB chief received the Oswald file from Moscow, the first suspicion given as to his threat potential was that his former service in the Marines was alarming. For the KGB saw the U.S. military as a recruiting ground for intelligence agents. As hinted at above, they also thought his grasp of Marxist-Leninist theory was poor. They also felt that he spoke much better Russian than he let on.[176] Which as we saw with Rosaleen Quinn, he did. It appears he feigned not speaking fluent Russian so as not to reveal that he had been trained in the language for a mission. Also, if those around him did not know he was fluent in the language, they would not suspect he was surveilling them.[177]

The KGB chief picked a case officer to handle the Oswald case. The case officer then chose a network of informants with whom to surround Oswald. One of them was Pavel Golovachev, a co-worker at the Minsk radio plant who Oswald helped with his English. Pavel met with the KGB three or four times and they gave him assignments to do saying, "Try this out on him and see what he says."[178] This was supplemented by photographic and electronic surveillance.[179] Oswald realized that the KGB was suspicious. In fact, one day he and his friend Ernst Titovets started looking for electronic listening devices in his apartment.[180] He also realized that from Minsk, little of value could be adduced by him. But he did what he could with what he had. Since there was some radar instrumentation going on at the plant, he appears to have absconded with a radar detection device.[181] He wrote a very detailed summary of the radio factory, which former CIA agent Bill Boxley called "a beautiful example of an intelligence agent's casing report on the electronics factory in Minsk."[182] And in fact, according to former CIA employee Donald Deneselya, when Oswald was debriefed on his return to America, he gave a vivid description of this place, since the Agency was interested in maintaining files on all things technical and scientific in Russia.[183] (Of course the official CIA line is that Oswald was not debriefed.)

By 1961, Oswald began to exhibit the same disillusion with Russia as he had with America.[184] He complained about the similarity of the food at different cafes, and that it reminded him of the stuff he ate in the Marines. He also said that he was becoming increasingly conscious of just what sort of society he lived in. He talked about the constant state of fear the Soviets lived in and how this inhibited a girl he knew, Ella German, from loving him.[185] In one year, Oswald had reversed himself about becoming a Russian citizen. When called before the passport office in January of 1961, he was asked if he still wished to become a Soviet citizen. Surprisingly, he replied no he did not. But he wanted his residence permit extended for one year.[186] The next month, Snyder got a letter from Oswald asking for the return of his passport and saying he wished to return home to the USA. He reminded Snyder that he was still an American citizen, therefore he expected him to do all he could to help him get back home.

There was one major event left for Oswald in Russia. That was his meeting and whirlwind romance with Robert Webster's Leningrad-Moscow acquaintance, the rather mysterious Marina Prusakova. FBI agent James Hosty found out some interesting facts about Prusakova. Marina was born out of wedlock. She then acquired a stepfather who treated her harshly and favored his own children. She went to pharmacy school at age thirteen. Her mother died two years later, and life with her stepfather now became oppressive. She was kicked out of the pharmacy school, but they accepted her back, and she acquired her diploma at about age eighteen. In August of 1959 her stepfather forced her to leave their home in Leningrad. So she went to Minsk to live with her uncle Ilya. Ilya was a high ranking member of the Communist party and a Colonel in the MVD. This was an internal secret police roughly the equivalent of the FBI, and it worked closely with the KGB. In fact, both intelligence agencies were directed by the same people. Ilya's apartment was in a complex set aside for ranking members of the KGB and MVD. It was located across the street from the Surorov Military Academy. One of the building's tenants was the chief of the Belorussian Communist party. Marina became a pharmacist at a Minsk hospital. She also joined the Komsomol, or Communist Youth Party.[187]

In addition to this background, there is one other detail about Marina that should be noted. It is not in the Warren Report, since it was deliberately excised. After the assassination, James H. Martin became Marina's business manager. She told him about her life and activities in Leningrad prior to going to Minsk. She said she had known, and had access to, some of the important officials in Russia, and she also could frequent many government facilities. She said that she had once entertained the Ambassador of Afghanistan in his hotel room in Leningrad.[188] Martin later told the HSCA that when he related this story about Marina and the Afghan ambassador to the Commission, at that point, the interview was stopped and those comments were stricken from the record.[189] So in addition to not revealing anything about Marina and Webster, the Commission kept us in the dark about other possible interesting activities of Marina prior to her meeting Oswald.

Lee and Marina met at a trade union dance in mid-March of 1961.[190] She thought he spoke Russian with an accent, perhaps from the Baltic area. They arranged to meet again and they did, about a week later. This time he walked her home from the dance. Oswald then called to say he was in the hospital. He was having his adenoids removed. Marina visited him often there and, just like that, they decided to marry. And the MVD colonel, Ilya, agreed to it.[191] Although the Warren Report places this on April 20, the intent to marry notice was filed on April 10,[192] which makes the affair even more rushed. Within seven days of this notice, Marina was given permission to marry Oswald. This is a very fast time to grant permission to marry a defector. But the marriage took place, after a required waiting period, on April 30.

Some friends of Oswald's in Russia, the Ziger sisters—daughters of a foreman at the radio factory—had heard about Marina's curious past in Leningrad.[193] Whatever the reason, in a matter of weeks, Marina was allowed to marry a defector. And then she was allowed to leave Russia with him. George Bouhe was a member of the White Russian community in Dallas that befriended Oswald on his return to America. In an off-the-record conversation with the Warren Commission, he said that, after the assassination, he came to think of Marina as like a great actress; or perhaps he was fooled and she was a superagent of some sort. For he, and others, were "amazed at the ease with which Marina left the USSR, which we, who know the setup on the other side, is almost incredible. American, British, and other diplomats married Russian girls and it took them years to get their wives out." Bouhe then said that he asked the couple how they did it. The reply was, "Well, we just went to the right office and they said: 'All right, take it away.'"[194] In light of what Bouhe had just said, this is not credible. It would appear that something was being hidden. And some members of the Warren Commissison understood that.

Contrary to popular belief, not all the members of the Warren Commission were actively participating in a cover up. The unfortunate thing is that those who weren't were not in control of the Commission. Representative Hale Boggs,

Senator John S. Cooper and, most of all, Senator Richard Russell, had real doubts both about what they were doing, and what their conclusions should be. They also had doubts about the Commission's star witness, Marina Oswald. Therefore, on September 6, 1964 Russell led a small expedition to the hanger of a Naval Air Station in Dallas. Only three Commissioners were there. Let us call it the Southern Wing. Russell presided, with Boggs and Cooper in attendance. Chief Consul J. Lee Rankin was there with two interpreters. Notable by their absence were the three Commissioners who were, by far, the most active members of the Commission. Let us call them the Troika: Allen Dulles, John McCloy, and Representative Gerald Ford. These three clearly promoted Marina as the Commission's number one witness.

From the beginning of his examination of Marina, Russell makes two things clear. First, he has thoroughly digested the past record of her interrogations. This includes her relationship with Ruth Paine, who he once called Marina's alter ego and "one of the most charitable people we have."[195] Secondly, he has real doubts about her testimony. Especially concerning her husband, and about Oswald's real reason for going to Russia. He asked if Lee had told Marina that Russia was such a communist paradise, and that is why he was there, then why did he never attain Russian citizenship?[196] Some of Marina's answers not only make little sense, they are at odds with the record. She actually says that Oswald was unhappy with this living quarters and his wages.[197] This is absurd since as far as wages and living quarters went, this is as good as it got for Oswald once he left the service. Russell also probed for any connections between Marina and the KGB or the Soviet military. It turns out George Bouhe was correct. The CIA had written a memo in March 1964 that stated, "In practice, permission for a Soviet wife to accompany her foreign national husband is rarely given. In almost every case available for our review, the foreign national was obliged to depart the USSR alone and either return to escort his wife out or arrange for her exit while he was still abroad. In some cases, the wife was never granted permission to leave." Following this proven record, Russell asked Marina who she saw in the military to get her exit visa out of Russia. He then asked her: Did she know any other Russian citizen who left Russia with a foreign national?[198] Russell is skeptical about why she was allowed to leave Russia at the height of the Cold War. In fact, this line of questioning got Marina so defensive that she actually volunteered that she was never given any assignment by the Soviets or the Americans! Even though she was never asked that specific question.[199] In trying to discern a motive, Boggs asked her questions about how Oswald felt about Kennedy. He was so persistent in this line that he got her to admit she was thoroughly rehearsed on this point in her previous Commission appearance.[200] The questions also focused on Marina's facility with the English language. Russell seemed to doubt her need for an interpreter.[201] This last was a key point. The evidence is that Marina attended a vocational school until June of 1959. There is no indication she attended any English classes.[202] Yet, when she met Webster, Webster says she spoke to him in English. If this is so, the obvious question would have been: How did she acquire the language? And then: Why did she acquire it? For she was trained to be a pharmacist.[203] And this is what she says she worked at. But it turns out Russell was correct. For Robert Oswald later revealed to FBI agent Bardwell Odum that Marina did speak and understand English. And she also wrote the language.[204] That Russell could not fully demonstrate this is not his fault. His attempt here at a real cross-examination is the closest anyone came at the time to suggesting that Marina was a KGB agent who was planted on another agent, namely Oswald.[205] And this interview gives us a taste of what the Commission could have been if it was a real inquiry.

Going Home

In July of 1961, Lee Oswald went to Moscow to talk to Snyder about leaving Russia. He was trying to make sure that he would not be prosecuted once he got to America. He said he had "learned a hard lesson the hard way."[206] Because—as Snyder had planned—Oswald had not become a Russian citizen, or formally renounced his American citizenship, the embassy returned his passport to him stamped only for the USA. The next day, Marina accompanied Oswald and was interviewed by McVickar. This was to initiate her admittance to America as an immigrant.[207] They returned to Minsk to begin work with local authorities to leave the country. Because there were many others leaving the country, the couple was told it would take awhile to process their applications. In late December, Marina was called to the Passport Office and told the couple would be granted exit visas. From the time Oswald visited Snyder in July, to the time they got word they would be leaving, the process took less than six months. As George Bouhe said, in comparative terms, this was quite unusual.

The Oswalds had a child in February named June Lee. Although they had planned on leaving in March, they now postponed the voyage to take care of the infant.[208] Oswald also was applying for a loan through the State Department for the return trip. In May, Oswald quit his job and went to Moscow to sign the final papers. On June 1, Oswald signed a promissory note for a 435.71 dollar loan from the State Department. They then boarded a train for Holland and crossed out of Russia on June 2.[209] It should be noted here that Oswald's passport was stamped "Netherlands" on June 3, and Marina recalled having spent some time in Amsterdam, even though they departed from Rotterdam.[210] (Some commentators believe Oswald may have been debriefed in Amsterdam by the CIA.) On June 6, they boarded their ship the Maasdam and on the journey over, Oswald began to write a memoir about his time in

Russia. Their ship landed in Hoboken, New Jersey on June 13. They were met by one Spas T. Raikin of the Traveler's Aid Society. He had been contacted by the State Department to aid the Oswalds when they arrived.[211] Raikin was also a former secretary of the American Friends of Bolshevik Nations, an anti-communist lobby with extensive ties to the CIA and other intelligence agencies.[212] Raikin helped them apply for a federal loan, and took them to a hotel in Times Square. Robert Oswald wired Lee money for airline tickets. On June 14, Robert picked up the Oswalds at Love Field in Dallas.

The CIA has always denied Oswald was debriefed on his return from Russia—something that even Dan Rather finds hard to swallow. Their reply on this is that since he was a former Marine, it was the Navy's assignment. But Oswald had been separated from the Marines for two and a half years at the time of his return. His discharge had been lowered to undesirable status. He was, and would remain, a civilian. It was the CIA that carried on intelligence and espionage wars with the KGB at the time. And there is evidence today that Oswald was debriefed by the CIA. In 1978, Donald Deneselya—a man we have met before—was interviewed by the HSCA. He recalled receiving a debriefing report from the New York City field office about a Marine defector in 1962 who had just returned from Russia. The man who wrote the report was Andy Anderson. The Agency, as mentioned above, was quite interested in the radio factory the defector had worked in while in Russia. Deneselya reported to Robert Crowley, a close friend of James Angleton. Crowley had handled the Webster case. Deneselya talked to both Richard Schweiker of the Church Committee and the HSCA. Deneselya saw the report since his job was monitoring technical and industrial progress in the USSR and filing reports with the CIA's Industrial Registry branch.[213] Deneselya was interviewed for the 1993 PBS Frontline episode on Oswald. But his voice was drowned out by Richard Helms who insisted that the CIA had not debriefed Oswald. What the show's producers did not reveal is what happened when the cameras were turned off. John Newman was on the set that day. After Helms had delivered his speech about no CIA debriefing of Oswald, Newman asked him, "Mr. Director, what would be so bad about the CIA debriefing Oswald? Is that not your job? Doesn't it therefore look bad when you say you did not?" Helms thought it over a bit. He then told the cameraman to start rolling again. This time he would say that the Agency did debrief Oswald.[214] Unfortunately, PBS did not take him up on the offer.

PBS also did not reveal the text of a CIA memo that Newman discovered. At the end of a memo reviewing Oswald's probable return, the chief of the Soviet Russia division wrote, "It was partly out of curiosity to learn if Oswald's wife would actually accompany him to our country, partly out of interest in Oswald's own experiences in the USSR, that we showed operational intelligence interest in the Harvey [Oswald] Story."[215]

CHAPTER EIGHT

Oswald Returns: Strange Bedfellows

"The CIA claims not to have been concerned with Oswald prior to the assassination. But one thing is certain: Despite these pious protestations, the CIA was very much aware of Oswald's activities well before the President's murder."

—*Jim Garrison*, Playboy, *October 1967*

Upon his return to Texas, Oswald looked up Peter Gregory, a petroleum engineer in Fort Worth. Gregory, who was born in Siberia, also taught Russian at the public library. Oswald got in touch with him since he sought help in getting his memoir about Russia published. According to Gregory, the reason Oswald contacted him was he wanted help in securing employment as a Russian translator or interpreter.[1] On June 26, Oswald was interviewed by the FBI in Fort Worth. The interviewing agent was John Fain, who had tried to help Marguerite locate Oswald when she could not find him in Russia. Oswald was not cooperative or forthcoming. And unlike with the CIA, there was no discussion of the radio factory he worked at in Minsk.[2] Quite naturally, the discussion centered on who his contacts were in Russia, any information exchanged with the Soviets, and any attempt by him to become a Soviet citizen. Oswald rightly said he had not become a Soviet citizen, but he also said he never offered the Russians any information—which, as we have seen, according to Richard Snyder, was not accurate.

Peter Gregory had Marina give his son Paul Russian lessons twice a week.[3] In late August, Peter invited the Oswalds to his house for dinner and introduced them to George Bouhe. Bouhe was a leading light of the Dallas White Russian community. And here begins another oddity about Oswald that the Warren Report does not formally acknowledge. But Jim Garrison did. To the point that he ironically titled a chapter in his bestselling book, "The Social Triumphs of Lee Oswald." That irony is the comingling of this ostensibly communist couple with the conservative White Russian community in conservative Dallas. Let us look at one excuse given for this: Why would Gregory need to pay Marina to teach her son Russian, if in fact, he himself taught Russian? Through Bouhe, the Oswalds were introduced to Anna Meller, who was born in Russia; to Declan Ford, a consulting geologist and his wife Katherine; to Elena Hall who was also of Russian parentage; and to Max Clark and his wife Katya. Max was a retired Air Force Colonel and former security officer for General Dynamics. His wife was born Princess Sherbatov, a member of the Russian royal family.[4] The Clarks were once dinner guests at the Oswalds, with Marina cooking. It is hard to believe that no one at the Commission, in all the months they studied Oswald, ever raised an eyebrow to this jarring juxtapositon of warring ideologies that somehow was cozily conversing over dinner right in front of their rather incurious eyes. In fact, almost subconsciously, the authors of the report seem to realize that something is wrong here. For they begin to make excuses for why all these rightwing, traditional Russians would socialize with these leftist, revolutionary Russians. The report says Oswald became "increasingly unpopular" with this group. Why? Because of his self-centeredness and his treatment of Marina. Some even thought he was mentally disturbed. But they stuck it out because they felt sorry for Marina and her child.[5] The report then gets even more curious.

George DeMohrenschildt was also born in Russia of an upper class family. His father, a "marshal of nobility" served as both the czar's governor of Minsk, and director of the Nobel oil interests there before the revolutions of 1917. Hence George was sometimes called the Baron. He came to America in 1938 and spent the summer in Long Island, where he met the mother of Jackie Kennedy. He also was an oil geologist and member of the Dallas Petroleum Club. DeMohrenschildt was acquainted with George H. W. Bush. His acquaintance with Bush was through a man named Eddie Hooker, who the Baron had partnered with in an oil investment firm. Hooker was Bush's former roommate at Phillips Academy in Andover, Massachusetts.[6] DeMohrenschildt was a regular CIA contact from at least 1957. This was when he was interviewed by Dallas CIA station chief J. Walton Moore about a journey to Yugoslavia that he had just returned from. Moore tried to cover up his long and diversified relationship with DeMohrenschildt by writing a memo saying he only met with the Baron twice, once in 1958 and once in 1961.[7] But the HSCA found out then Moore had periodic contacts with George and saw him several times in 1958 and 1959.[8] The two actually socialized together. It was through Moore and Max Clark that DeMohrenschildt decided to befriend Oswald. For, as George told the Commission, he suspected that Clark was somehow connected with the FBI in his security work. And Bouhe confirmed this to him.[9]

Just before he passed away, DeMohrenschildt went further. He told author Edward Epstein that he had met Moore over lunch in late 1961. Moore had told him about an ex-Marine who worked at an electronics factory in Minsk. He would soon return to the USA and the CIA had an interest in him. In the summer of 1962, George said that an associate of Moore's provided him with Oswald's address in Fort Worth, suggesting he should meet him. DeMohren-schildt called Moore and asked that in exchange for his utility with Oswald, the State Department should assist him with an oil exploration deal in Haiti. Which later on, he received. Moore then encouraged him to go ahead and meet up with Oswald.[10] Which George then did. And although DeMohrenschildt denied this was a quid pro quo arrangement, that is what it appears to be. For as DeMohrenschildt said, "I would never have contacted Oswald in a million years if Moore had not sanctioned it."[11]

The Baron encouraged Oswald to continue writing his memoir about Minsk. And in the fall of 1962, he urged the communist defector to move to Dallas. So that he would be in closer proximity to the White Russian commu-nity. Oswald then quit his job at a welding factory to facilitate the move. Accor-ding to George's family, it was he who helped secure Oswald's next job at the graphic arts house in Dallas called Jaggars-Chiles-Stovall.[12] DeMohrenschildt told Moore that a typed draft of Oswald's memoir was now at his home. Not long after, there was a break-in at the Baron's apartment.[13]

Oswald's position at the graphics art company is another of the myriad examples of the Warren Commission camouflaging the almost mad paradox of Oswald's life. Consider his relationship with co-worker Dennis Ofstein. While there, Oswald developed a friendship with Ofstein, who knew a bit of Russian. Oswald showed Ofstein photos of military headquarters he had taken while in the Soviet Union. Oswald commented on them, making detailed remarks about ammunition, orders given the guards, and the deployment of armor, infantry, and aircraft in divisions. Even more revealing are the following notations in Oswald's address book alongside the address and phone number of JCS: "TYPOGRAPHY" and "micro dot." As Philip Melanson has noted, typography was a sophisticated technique of photographic reduction used by JCS in its advertising work. A micro dot is a method employed in espionage to reduce large amounts of printed information photographically down to the size of a period. The dot is then passed on in the text of a letter or document. This last process was unknown to the employees at JCS. It was explained to Ofstein by Oswald as "the way spies sometimes sent messages and pictures and so on, was to take a micro dot photograph of it and place it under a stamp or send it." Ofstein actually testified about this exchange to the Commission.[14] He came to believe that Oswald was with the U.S. government when he was in the Soviet Union. He deduced this because of Oswald's keen eye for detail in pointing out things in his photographs and also because of the above noted knowledge of comparative styles of military disbursements. He also told Ofstein that he never observed a vapor trail in Minsk, demonstrating the lack of jet aircraft there. But he did know that the Russians kept tanks north of the city. Ofstein deduced that Oswald's knowledge of Soviet military logistics was not confined to Minsk but extended to Moscow also.[15] Ofstein's fascinating testimony is not mentioned in the Warren Report.

But that it not the worst about Oswald at Jaggars-Chiles-Stovall. This company handled contracts for the U.S. Army Map Service.[16] And as author Henry Hurt later discovered, part of the work there appeared to be related to the U-2 flights over Cuba. In fact, Oswald's first day at work was four days before President Kennedy saw the first U-2 photos of missile silos on the island. According to Oswald's co-workers, some of them were working at setting type for Cuban place names on maps.[17] To point out the absurdity of this scenario is both simple, and by now, needless. Especially considering Oswald's background with the U-2, particularly the Powers shootdown. But by avoiding all this, the Warren Report does not have to explain it away. For another thing Oswald did there was to send examples of his photographic work to the American Communist Party newspaper in an attempt to secure work from them.[18] It is very hard to believe that the FBI, which had all of these groups infiltrated, did not know about this exchange of letters at the time they were sent. But perhaps no action was taken because, around this time—October of 1962—an inexplicable occurrence took place: The FBI closed its file on Oswald.[19] This is at the time the former communist defector was working at a Pentagon map-making company that appears to have been doing overflight maps of the U-2 over Cuba during the Missile Crisis. John Newman speculates that this may have been done because this was when DeMohrenschildt's relationship with Oswald was heating up. What makes this interesting is that the file will not be re-opened until March of 1963. The ostensible reason given for this by FBI agent James Hosty was that Oswald had just opened a subscription to a communist newspaper. Yet, when the Dallas FBI had previously learned of another similar subscription, it had closed the Oswald file. Newman notes that the reopening of the Oswald file coincides with George DeMohrenschildt leaving the Oswald circle for, first Washington, and then Haiti. This coincides with the report by Teofil Meller, husband of Anna. He told the Dallas Police after the assassination that he had "checked with the FBI and they told him Oswald was all right."[20]

In March of 1963, right before Oswald left Dallas for New Orleans, DeMohrenschildt eventually did get his oil consulting contract with the Haitian government, worth about 300,000 dollars.[21] The next month, he left the city, never to see Oswald again. In May, he met with CIA and Army intelligence officers to further his Haitian endeavor.[22] The Commission never really expressed any real reservations about DeMohrenschildt, or his association with Oswald. Jim Garrison did. He came to the conclusion Oswald was probably being "babysat" by DeMohrenschildt. That is, Oswald was being protected and kept in place while a mission was being prepared for him. But Garrison felt that this was done by George without any knowledge of what the end game was.[23]

In light of what was to happen to Oswald, one of the most important things that DeMohrenschildt did occurred right before he left Texas. Commission lawyer Wesley Liebeler discovered it when he asked Ruth Paine if Marina Oswald had ever mentioned DeMohrenschildt to her. Ruth answered with: "Well, that's how I met her."[24] That is, he introduced Lee and Marina to Ruth and Michael Paine. As one reads the interactions of this White Russian community with the Oswalds, it is fairly clear that they are trying to separate Lee from Marina. And, in fact, they actually did do that, temporarily.[25] But as we shall see later, Ruth Paine actually accomplished this for a longer interval and at a much more crucial time. Once Ruth was introduced to Marina, within two weeks she got in contact with her via a note. Then a week later she visited her in person. About a week after that, Ruth invited the Oswalds to her home for dinner.[26] Even though she and her husband were separated, Michael Paine was also on hand for this event. In fact, it was Michael who actually picked up the Oswalds at their home that night. And then something really strange happened. Ruth had known Marina for less than a month. They had seen each other three times. Yet, on April 7, "Ruth wrote a note to Marina (which she claims she never sent) inviting Marina to come live with her."[27] This is surprising not just because of the speed with which it was done, but also because the Paines were Quakers. But here Ruth is essentially trying to split off a wife, who she barely knew, from her husband. Two weeks after that, there was a picnic with the Oswalds. And near the end of April, Marina is staying with Ruth, while

Lee is in New Orleans in search of a job and a place to live. After Lee did find an apartment, Ruth drove Marina to New Orleans. She then returned home to Irving, and started a written correspondence with Marina which lasted all summer.

In light of the above, there can be little doubt that, almost from the beginning, Ruth was intent upon separating the Oswalds. In the summer correspondence, Ruth said that Marina mentioned she may have to go back to Russia. When Ruth heard this, she now, for the second time, invited Marina to move in with her.[28] But in July, Marina replied that her relations with Lee had improved and she would not be going back to Russia. That August, Ruth was traveling by car around the country visiting friends and relatives. She got a letter from Marina saying that Lee was now unemployed. Ruth then decided to stop off in New Orleans to visit the Oswalds on her way back home. She stayed with the couple for three days. It was decided that Marina would return home with Ruth so she could deliver her second child at Parkland Hospital. But yet, this was not altogether impromptu. It seemed planned in advance. Because "according to FBI interviews of Ruth's friends and family, Ruth had told everyone she was going to pick up a Russian woman in New Orleans and bring her home to live with her in Irving."[29] Ruth now achieved what she seemed intent on doing from the start. The Oswalds were finally separated, and they would stay that way until Lee's murder at the hands of Jack Ruby. What the purpose of this separation was, and why Ruth was so single-minded about it, these have never been explained. But by September 27, Marina was living with Ruth while Oswald was allegedly in Mexico. And, Quaker-like, Michael was committed to giving Marina financial support in order to stay there. When Oswald finally returned to Dallas, he got his new job at the Texas School Book Depository, an act in large part facilitated by Ruth Paine. The fact that the couple was separated, but Ruth had packed her station wagon with their things in New Orleans, meant that many of Oswald's belongings were now in her garage. Therefore, they were under her control at the time Oswald was apprehended. And Ruth and Michael Paine now became the source for much of the dubious evidence used to build a case against Oswald. At the same time that their true backgrounds and characters were being hidden by the Warren Commission. The reader will comprehend why their background was deliberately covered up by the Commission in Chapter 10.

Last Months

In late April of 1963, the Oswalds decided to move to New Orleans. Oswald said it was Marina's idea. The Commission said that the real reason was that

Marina wished to get him out of town because he took a shot at General Edwin Walker.[30] Yet Oswald was never even questioned about this shooting incident, let alone made a suspect in the case. It was only after Oswald was dead that the FBI said he had taken a shot at Walker.

When he arrived by bus in New Orleans, Oswald stayed with his Aunt Lillian Murret while looking for a job. He secured a position with William B. Reily Co. on May 10. This was a large coffee company which grinded, canned, bagged, and sold coffee. There are two interesting details the Warren Report leaves out about this company. First, it was located just two blocks from Guy Banister's office.[31] Second, as Jim Garrison notes in his book, only a stranger to the city would not be aware of Reily's support for anti-communist causes like Arcacha Smith's Crusade to Free Cuba and Ed Butler's right-wing, CIA related propaganda shop, INCA.[32] The Information Council of the Americas chief sponsor was another New Orleans rightwing patrician, Dr. Alton Ochsner. Through the author's field investigation in New Orleans, there is no doubt Banister knew Ochsner, and so did Clay Shaw. In fact, there is a photo in the New Orleans Public Library of Shaw with Ochsner.[33] Ochsner had a CIA clearance which appears to have originated in 1955.[34] The point being that if Banister wanted to salt Oswald away nearby in order to provide him a temporary cover, he could have easily done so by making perhaps one or two phone calls. What makes this even more probable is a conversation the author had with William B. Reily III in 1994. When contacting the Reily Coffee Company at that time, to inquire about any records left over about Oswald, the author talked to Reily. When asked about Oswald, he said, "What year was that assassination?"

But also consider this: There were a number of Reily's employeess who left after Oswald's departure for a peculiar destination. Oswald's superiors, Alfred Claude and Emmett Barbee, both left in July to work for NASA in eastern New Orleans. Two of Oswald's co-workers, John Branyon and Dante Marachini, were also later hired by NASA. Oswald himself told Alba he expected to be picked up by NASA.[35] Garrison suspected that they were moved out so as not to talk about Oswald's offbeat work habits. If this is so then it would suggest that, like Ochsner, Reily's company had intelligence connections. This was certified by a declassified document confirming that the company was of interest to CIA dating back from 1949. Further, it appears to have been assigned a contact number.[36]

After Oswald secured an apartment on Magazine Street, Ruth Paine drove Marina to New Orleans. Ruth stayed for three days, returning to Irving on May 14. In mid-July, Oswald was terminated from Reily for spending too much time at Adrian Alba's Crescent City Garage reading gun magazines.[37] On one occasion, Alba claimed to have seen an FBI agent handing a white envelope to Oswald while he was standing in front of Reily's.[38] As we have seen, Orestes Pena, proprietor of the Habana Bar, has testified to seeing Oswald there speaking to FBI agent Warren DeBrueys. As we shall see later, there is even more evidence Oswald was a likely FBI informant.

When Oswald moved to New Orleans, the FBI claims to have lost track of him until late June.[39] This is not credible. For Oswald was now writing the Fair Play for Cuba Committee—using his real name—an organization that was being infiltrated and surveilled by American intelligence agents. But in the initial stages of his local New Orleans program, Oswald used the alias Alek Hidell on his post office box and certain pieces of literature. FBI agent James Hosty wrote a May 28 report to his superior Gordon Shanklin saying that he learned Oswald had left Dallas in mid-May. He said that he then inquired at the post office and learned that Oswald had left no forwarding address. This is false, and Hosty likely knew is was so. Oswald *had* sent in such a card from New Orleans. That card is stamped May 14 per its arrival.[40] How could Hosty not have known this? His initial discovery of Oswald's absence was on May 15. Further, the FBI or the Warren Commission altered and switched Oswald's flyers in the Commission exhibits to eliminate knowledge that the FBI had to have known where Oswald was living in New Orleans before they said they did.[41] John Newman constructed a chart which graphs seven different instances in which—during this so-called "blind period"—the FBI should have known, not only where Oswald was, but about his dealings with the FPCC.[42]

A possible reason for this after the fact obtuseness is that Oswald was, in all likelihood, acting as part of the CIA's anti-FPCC program. Warren DeBrueys told the author that whenever the FBI was cognizant of such an Agency program, they were told to steer clear of it.[43] The fact that such a program was being run is one of the most important discoveries of the ARRB. Since it now helps to place Oswald's activities in their larger and more proper context. But perhaps even more compelling is who was running this program: David Phillips and James McCord.[44] That this key piece of information was kept classified for decades is one of the true abuses of the classification process, which relies so much on the excuse of "national security."

For this belated discovery also helps explain why the CIA ordered 45 copies of the first printing of Corliss Lamont's pamphlet "The Crime Against Cuba" in June of 1961. This is the year their counter intelligence program against the FPCC began.[45] This first edition sold out fast. In 1963, when Oswald was handing out the pamphlet, it was at least in its fifth printing. Yet Oswald was handing out the *first edition* in 1963. He could not have ordered it himself since he was in Russia at that time.[46] It is very possible that either Banister requested these from CIA, or someone like Phillips gave them to either Oswald or Banister as a part of the program he was running with McCord. But it should be noted that another reason the FBI was cognizant of this Phillips/McCord project is they were running their own discreditation operations against the FPCC. These were supervised by Cartha DeLoach.[47]

Hosty said that the FBI did not discover Oswald's address in New Orleans until the end of June. And this was not confirmed until August 5. By odd coincidence, that is the same day that Oswald now began to appear in public as an agent of the FPCC. Prior to this, he had been corresponding with the New York City FPCC office, opening a post office box, securing applications, printing up his own literature at Banister's, picking up special flyers at Jones Printing Company, dropping off flyers at places like the Tulane campus to root out leftist sympathizers, etc. The one exception to this was a very low profile picketing incident on June 16. But August 5 is when he began his public exhibition of street theater. Or as Newman writes, "the FBI's alleged blind period covers—to the day—the precise period of Oswald's undercover activity in New Orleans." On August 5, Oswald had visited Carlos Bringuier's clothing store. He offered to do something he had experience in: to train members of his Cuban exile group, the Cuban Student Directorate, or DRE. In other words he appeared as if he was anti-Castro. On August 9, Bringuier and two cohorts angrily confronted Oswald while he was acting pro-Castro. This is when he was passing out his Fair Play for Cuba literature on Canal Street. This created a minor fracas. And arrests were made for disturbing the peace. The arresting officer, Lieutenant Frances Martello described it as saying that Oswald "seemed to have set them up, so to speak, to create an incident, but when the incident occurred he seemed absolutely peaceful and gentle."[48] The idea that this incident was "set up" is fortified by the fact that Oswald described the incident to the national office of the FPCC on August 4, five days before it happened. In this letter he described being attacked by Cuban exiles in the street and then being approached by the police. He then added, "The incident robbed me of what support I had, leaving me alone."[49] Further evidence it was stage managed is that when he was booked, Oswald turned over the out of print Corliss Lamont pamphlet from 1961.[50] In other words, the evidence more than suggests that Oswald was acting out a scene he had written five days in advance, with props furnished to him by either Banister or Phillips.

After Oswald was arrested, something else not noted by the Commission happened. And although Martello told a different story about it to the Warren Commission, to researcher Larry Howard he said that Oswald handed a piece of note paper over to him. On one side were the Moscow numbers of the press agencies UPI and AP. Oswald pointed to a number on the other side and said,

"Just call the FBI." He added that he wanted to be interviewed by DeBrueys.[51] When the call came into the FBI office, DeBrueys was not there. So James Quigley decided to go to the jail and interview Oswald. Before he did, he had a young employee check the file indices on Oswald. William Walter did find an informant file on Oswald with DeBrueys' name on it. Walter later said that there was also a locked security file on Oswald with DeBrueys's name on that also.[52] This is further evidence that Oswald was known to the FBI during Hosty's blackout period. In fact, Oswald's landlady in New Orleans said that FBI agent Milton Kaack talked to her about Oswald three weeks after he arrived in New Orleans. When Anthony Summers called Kaack about this, the FBI agent cried, "No, no. I'm not talking. You won't get anything out of me."[53] And finally, after being transferred to Kansas City after the assassination, Hosty later told Church Committee witness Carver Gayton that Oswald indeed was an informant.[54]

And, in fact, if Oswald was actually a communist, why would he have his jailer call the FBI after his arrest? This is not something a genuine communist does. It is something that either an informant or infiltrator does. And this type of weird behavior typifies what Oswald did with the FPCC in New Orleans. Many decades ago, researcher Ray Marcus was a member of the communist party. In a 1998 interview, he told the author that they never did the things Oswald did in New Orleans. When they leafleted, it was always at night, leaving the papers in the doorway or the foyer of homes or apartments. This way the reader would not be seen looking at the literature. He could do it privately without any peer pressure being applied. This insight would apply even more strongly to a southern city like New Orleans. In fact, during the FBI investigation of the Kennedy murder, they learned of a source representing John Stanford, a secretary for the Texas Communist Party, who had told Senator Ralph Yarborough that he had solid information that Oswald was really a CIA agent.[55] In other words, not only did Oswald associate with right wingers and CIA types like Ferrie, Banister, and Clay Shaw; not only is it impossible to find any communists or communist cells Oswald associated with or frequented; but the communists around him thought he was an intelligence operative.

When Quigley finally wrote up his encounter with Oswald, he tried to say that he knew nothing about him before he talked to him. But yet, Quigley had looked over Oswald's Navy file in 1961.[56] This jailhouse interview lasted a long time. Estimates range from 90 minutes to three hours. Quigley produced a five page report. But, in keeping with FBI standard practice, the notes were destroyed.[57] There would seem to be at least some information that was left out. During the interview process, Oswald turned over some of his literature, and also an FPCC card which was signed by A. J. Hidell.[58] This last is significant since the Warren Commission tells us that Oswald mail ordered the rifle that he shot Kennedy with under this name. For now, the reader should note that Oswald allegedly ordered the rifle a few months prior to turning over this membership card. Yet, according to the Commission, knowing that the FBI now had this card, he would use this same rifle in the assassination.

The reader would think that this incident could not get any odder. Or suspicious. But it does. There was a court hearing on August 12. Bringuier showed up with someone who was not involved in the episode, one Frank Bartes. Even though it was Oswald who was the accosted party, he pleaded guilty and agreed to pay a nominal fine. Even though it was Bringuier who did the accosting, he pleaded innocent and the charges against him were dropped. This sounds as if it was arranged in advance. As we have seen, Bartes was associated with the FBI, and later the CIA. He told the press who had gathered that Oswald was a dangerous man. One month later, when the FBI interviewed him, he said the name Oswald was unknown to him.[59]

The next day, Oswald was in the office of the *New Orleans States-Item* trying to convince city editor David Chandler to give more coverage to the FPCC. Three days after this he reportedly called a New York City radio show asking to be a guest.[60] Then, on August 16, he was on the streets again. The unemployed Oswald first went to the unemployment office and hired a couple of young men on the promise he would give them two dollars for fifteen to twenty minutes of work passing out leaflets in front of the International Trade Mart. Why just for fiftenn to twenty minutes? Because very soon after, Jesse Core, Clay Shaw's right-hand man, phoned WDSU-TV about the "event." And they showed up. (It should be noted here, Shaw was friendly with the owners of this station, Edith and Edgar Stern.) George Higginbotham, who worked for Banister, saw the incident and walked over to Banister's office to tell him about it. Banister calmly replied, "Cool it. One of them is mine."[61] Although at his trial, Shaw denied he saw Oswald outside leafleting that day, there is a photo of him walking into the building and he is looking at Oswald and Oswald is looking at him.[62] What makes this even more interesting is that Core was at the previous Canal Street incident also. He picked up a Corliss Lamont pamphlet from Oswald and recognized the Camp Street address on the inside of the back cover. On August 19, from the Trade Mart, he mailed the pamphlet with a message to the FBI office in New Orleans. The handwritten message said, "Note inside back cover."[63] In other words, Shaw and Core were likely aware of the faux pas by Oswald. Was Oswald made aware of this also? Perhaps. Because a few days later, he was seen inside the Trade Mart.[64]

Before leaving these two leafleting incidents, it is worth making one more observation about them. In between the two filmed episodes, Carlos Quiroga—a mutual colleague of both Sergio Arcacha Smith and Bringuier—was sent by the latter to infiltrate Oswald's FPCC organization. Bringuier said that Quiroga brought with him a couple of sheets Oswald had dropped on Canal Street. But this story is suspicious on two grounds. First, both Bringuier and Quiroga told the Commission it took place after the Trade Mart incident, and second that Quiroga was just returning a few flyers that Oswald had dropped. But these are undermined by a neutral witness, Mrs. Jesse Garner, Oswald's landlady. She told the Commission that Quiroga was not there to deliver a few flyers. He had a stack of literature about five to six inches high. Second it was not after the Trade Mart episode. It was just after the Canal Street arrest.[65] If this information is accurate, then it appears that far from infiltrating Oswald's nonexistent FPCC—of which he was the only member—they were actually supplying him with the literature for the next leafleting event. What makes this even more likely is the polygraph exam given to Quiroga by Jim Garrison. Quiroga was asked about this specific point: "You have said you tried to infiltrate Oswald's "organization." Isn't it a fact that you knew his Fair Play for Cuba activities were merely a cover?" Quiroga replied in the negative. That response indicated he was lying. So did his negative response to the following question: "Is it not a fact that at that time Oswald was in reality a part of an anti-Castro operation?"[66]

After the Trade Mart incident, Oswald walked over to WDSU and was interviewed briefly by WDSU television and radio. Bringuier then called Bill Stuckey, a reporter who had a weekly radio program at WDSU. This interview was excerpted on his show "Latin Listening Post" on August 17.[67] Stuckey then arranged for a debate on August 21, between Oswald and Bringuier on a longer format show called "Conversation Carte Blanche." Prior to the broadcast, the FBI contacted Stuckey and read him large parts of Oswald's file, including about his defection. The last participant in the debate, Ed Butler of INCA was tipped off about the defection from his contacts on the House Un-American Activities Committee.[68] (Butler, as we have seen, would be the eventual custodian of Banister's files, and he was the man who put Gordon Novel in contact with Sergio Arcacha Smith and David Phillips about a New Orleans telethon.) When confronted with the damaging information about his defection—in other words that Oswald was not a neutral party, but a closet communist himself—Oswald did his best to parry it. He said that the Russian experience gave him the background to say that the FPCC was not communist controlled. Stuckey and Butler later returned to this aspect and kept Oswald on the defensive about his defection. Stuckey felt that the debate finished the FPCC in New Orleans because it had been linked to a man who had lived in Russia for three years and was a self-admitted Marxist.[69]

But Oswald slipped up during the debate, and someone on the Warren Commission noticed it. About two thirds of the way through the audio portion,

Stuckey asked Oswald how he supported himself in Russia. After saying he worked while he was there, Oswald says that he was "under the protection of the American government . . ." He then caught himself and said he was *not* under their protection. But in the transcript as produced in the Commission volumes, Oswald does not need to correct himself since someone altered his initial statement to say that he was *not* under the protection of the American government.[70]

This was the last public event Oswald did associated with the FPCC. These episodes are important to the case because of the extraordinary media coverage they captured. It was these films and tapes that were then played on television to incriminate Oswald as a communist in the public eye after the assassination.

In August, Ruth Paine wrote Marina again. She was hard at work trying to find a hospital for Marina to deliver her pregnancy. She was also arranging to see Marina after visiting her family in Philadelphia.[71] In September, Ruth did stop at the Oswalds. On September 23, after packing up their things, she drove Marina to Irving, arriving on the 24. On that same day, the Warren Report tells us that Oswald left for Mexico.[72]

Oswald returned to Dallas from Mexico on October 3. About ten days later, he took a boarding room in Oak Cliff. Marina was living at the Paines and gave birth to their second child on October 20. Lee would visit the Paine home to see his wife and children on weekends. The Warren Report states that Ruth Paine heard through a friend that there was a job opening at the Texas School Book Depository.[73] Ruth called supervisor Roy Truly at the Depository to arrange a meeting for Oswald. She then told Oswald about this arrangement that day, October 14. Lee interviewed on the 15th, and started work on the 16th. The Report tells us that the Oswalds were elated with his new job. What the Report does not say is that an offer for a better paying job came in before Oswald started work at the Depository.

When Oswald returned from Mexico he visited the Texas Employment Commission.[74] In reply to that visit, Robert Adams phoned the Paine residence on October 15 with a better job offer for Oswald than the one he took. Adams said he spoke with someone there about a permanent position as a cargo handler at Trans Texas Airport, a job that paid about 100 dollars more per month than the Depository. Adams said that he was told Oswald was not at home. He left a message that Oswald should call him about the job.[75] Adams called again the next morning. This time he was told that Oswald had taken a different job. Adams therefore crossed him off his list.

When Ruth Paine was asked about this phone call from Adams, she first said she did not recall it, but she eventually did. Yet she said she heard of it through Lee Oswald. Oswald informed her that he had high hopes for it but it had "fallen through."[76] This does not coincide with what Adams stated. He tried to notify Oswald twice, since the job was still available. The job offer from Adams paid about 30 percent more than what Oswald earned at the Depository. Therefore if Oswald had known about it, why would he not have taken it? Especially since Marina testified that Lee was not satisfied with the Depository job. He was searching through the newspapers for something better.[77] Needless to say, if whoever had talked to Adams had told Oswald about the offer, he very likely would not have been on the motorcade route a month later.

In November of 1963, two events occurred before Oswald died that confirm his status as an intelligence agent and his journey to Russia as part of a false defector program. Otto Otepka is a man whose name does not appear in the index to the Warren Report. Which is another of its grievous shortcomings. In light of what we are about to learn, Otepka should have had his own chapter. Otepka worked in the State Department as a security analyst in the Intelligence and Research Bureau.[78] In late 1960 he sent a memo to Dick Bissell at CIA for information on a number of American defectors to the Soviet Union. Bissell turned this request over to James Angleton's Counter Intelligence staff, but not to the Soviet Russia Division, which had jurisdiction over defectors. Further, as John Newman notes, many of Oswald's documents from this period bear the label CI/OPS which means Counter Intelligence Operations. This would suggest that Angleton had an interest in the defector program.[79] The eighth name on Otepka's list was that of Lee Harvey Oswald. Although Hugh Cummings actually sent the memo, Otepka originated the request. He sent it because neither the CIA nor military intelligence would inform him which defectors were genuine and which were double agents. When the CIA assigned the job to a researcher, they told her to work on some of the names, but not on others. One of the "others" was Oswald. When the CIA sent back its reply in late November, Oswald's name was marked SECRET.[80] It is very interesting that it is after this request from State that Oswald is finally given a 201 file. Thirteen months after his defection. One has to wonder: if Otepka had never made this request, would CI/SIG ever have opened a 201 file on Oswald? Or would his papers have remained in their private domain?

This request marked another milestone at the other end. Otepka, who had been an award winning employee, now saw his career slide downhill. And then both his career and his life become a Kafkaesque nightmare. He was first taken off of sensitive cases. Stories began to appear in the press that his job could be eliminated. He was asked to take another position in State but he declined.[81] He was then called before a Senate Committee to explain his methods for issuing security clearances. This happened four times in less than three years. He still would not resign or suspend his defector investigation. Spies, phone taps, and listening devices were then planted in his office.[82] His office started to be searched after hours and his trash was scoured for any of his notes. Even his house was being surveilled. Otepka could not understand what was happening to him. He could only conclude that the sensitive study of American defectors hidden in his safe was behind it all. That safe was later drilled into after he was thrown out of his original office and reassigned. Whoever drilled it then used a tiny mirror to determine the combination. The safecracker then removed its contents.[83] On November 5, 1963 Otepka was formally removed from his job at State. Later on, author Jim Hougan asked him if he had been able to figure out if Oswald was a real or false defector. Otepka replied, "We had not made up our minds when my safe was drilled and we were thrown out of the office." Just two and a half weeks after his forcible departure from State, Oswald, the man he had studied for months on end, was accused of killing President Kennedy. In nearly nine hundred pages of text, the Commission could not find room to tell this important and riveting story. A story that directly impacts on who Oswald really was.

The call Oswald made the night before he died probably demonstrates why Otepka had to be stopped. On Saturday night, November 23, Oswald tried to make a call to North Carolina. Two phone operators manned the Dallas jail switchboard. Whenever Oswald attempted to make a call, the operators were tipped off in advance. Then two plainclothesmen came into the switchboard office. In an adjacent room, the two men would monitor the call.[84] When Oswald came on the line, he gave one of the operators a number to dial. The operator wrote it down and passed it on. After it was passed onto the two men, the operator then told Oswald the number was unresponsive, even though there was no real attempt to dial out. The operator then hung up on Oswald and threw the number into the trash. Curious, the other operator later picked up the note paper out of the trash.[85] It contained the numbers of two men, both named John Hurt. When the HSCA investigated the affair they found out that Oswald was trying to call a man named John Hurt who lived in Raleigh.[86] John Hurt turned out to be a former military counterintelligence officer. When researcher Grover Proctor called him, he denied calling the jail or knowing who Oswald was prior to the assassination.

But here's the problem. Chief Counsel of the HSCA Robert Blakey later confirmed that the call was outgoing.[87] So Hurt's reply to Proctor was a cleverly worded non-denial: it was Oswald trying to call Hurt. Blakey added to the gravitas of the matter by saying, "It was an outgoing call, and therefore I consider it very troublesome material. The direction in which it went is deeply disturbing." But why would Oswald call Raleigh, North Carolina? Perhaps because the Office of Naval Intelligence (ONI) operated a base nearby at the coastal town of Nag's Head. Since Oswald received his language training in the

Marines, he would have been under ONI's authority at the time he defected. And according to former CIA officer Victor Marchetti, the Nag's Head base operated a training program for false defectors to be sent to the Soviet Union: "It was for young men who were made to appear disenchanted, poor, American youths who had become turned off and wanted to see what communism was all about."[88] The intent was to have the false defector be recruited by the KGB. Then you would have a double agent in place for whom to funnel disinformation through and receive information from. One could easily conclude that, in Oswald's time of crisis, he was trying to contact his handlers through a former, distant cut-out. He was the spy caught out in the cold: What did they want him to do? One could also conclude, as Marchetti does, that it was this attempted call that guaranteed his execution.

In the period of 1961–63, as we have seen, Howard Hunt was first working with Allen Dulles. He helped Dulles answer queries from the Taylor Commission about the Bay of Pigs. He then helped Dulles and Charles Murphy write their attack article shifting the blame for the Bay of Pigs from the Agency to President Kennedy. After this, Hunt did extensive work on the former Director's 1963 book called *The Craft of Intelligence*.[89]

But after this, Hunt appears to have been working for Tracy Barnes. Author William Davy went to see former CIA officer Victor Marchetti about a declassified document showing that Clay Shaw had a covert security clearance. He showed it to him and Marchetti commented with the information that it appeared that Shaw was actually working in some kind of domestic clandestine service.[90] This was called the Domestic Operations Division and it was being run by Barnes. As Marchetti said, Hunt was likely there also and they were getting into some very bizarre things, In reading his reply, its clear that Marchetti did not want to be specific about what Barnes and Hunt were doing.

CHAPTER NINE

Jim Garrison in 1966

*"I was perfectly aware that I might have signed my political
death warrant the moment I launched this case."*

—*Jim Garrison,* Playboy, *October 1967*

One of the many criticisms brought against Jim Garrison when his inquiry into President Kennedy's death was made public was this: He was doing it to advance his political career.[1] In fact, one newspaper even wrote that Garrison hoped to become Vice-President because of the fame to be garnered from his inquiry.[2] This is one of the worst things one can say about a District Attorney. Since it implies that he is willing to indict and prosecute someone only to advance his political ambition. This was only the beginning of a two year war of character assassination that would turn Garrison into a caricature and Clay Shaw into a martyr. As we will later see, in reality, it was this campaign of calumny that was politically motivated. And it was performed by some journalists of rather questionable ethics. The truth is actually the opposite. In pursuing his Kennedy investigation, Garrison threw away a political career of great promise. And along with it, the two offices he most aspired to: District Attorney and the U.S. Senate. This part of the story was not told to the public. We should relate it here.

Garrison's family hailed from Iowa. His father had an alcohol problem, which resulted in a criminal record. Therefore Jane, Garrison's mother, divorced him when young Garrison was barely six years old.[3] After this divorce, Garrison never saw his father again. Not knowing he was dead, Garrison did try and find him many years later. He broke down when he saw the authorities had written on a legal document that the man had "no family."[4]

Jane moved the family to New Orleans. There, Garrison graduated from high school in 1939. As a senior, he joined the National Guard. He then entered Tulane. But anticipating World War II, he dropped out after his freshman year to join the service. Garrison flew low altitude planes called "grasshoppers." These were meant to spot artillery targets. They were very dangerous to fly and had high fatality rates. Toward the end of the war, Garrison was in on one of the first details to liberate the German concentration camp at Dachau.[5] On his return from the service in 1946, he legally changed his name from Earling Carothers Garrison to Jim Garrison. He then entered Tulane Law School. And here he began to show symptoms of his military service. For he would suffer from dysentery and serious back problems for the rest of his life.[6]

By 1950, Garrison had earned both a law degree and a Master's of Civil Laws.[7] It is interesting to note what happened next. Garrison was fortunate enough to join a large law partnership called Deutsch, Kerrigan, and Stiles. He didn't like it. He quit and joined the FBI. (This motif, passing up a lucrative desk job for public service, will be repeated later.) When the Korean War broke out, Garrison reenlisted in the service. But he had recurrent nightmares about his previous grasshopper flights. On his first day at Fort Sill, he reported to sick call. From there he was dismissed within two weeks due to battle fatigue.[8]

Once dismissed, he returned to New Orleans and met up with his old law partner Eberhard Deutsch. Deutsch introduced him to Mayor DeLesseps "Chep" Morrison. Morrison was so taken by the young man that he appointed him to the Public Safety Commission that governed over Traffic Court.[9] Garrison's political career began with this appointment. He turned out to be an excellent and bold administrator who revolutionized that position. Garrison took the law seriously and fined those who did not show up in court. He also got legislation passed that gave him the power to suspend the licenses of those who habitually failed to appear. Consequently, in just a year, he nearly doubled the amount of revenue from traffic fines. In a preview of his future run-in with judges, he criticized those he felt were too lenient on failures to show in court. His administration was so successful that a new and separate traffic court, with it own judge, opened up.[10] Morrison offered his young protégé that judgeship. Garrison turned it down. He said he would rather be appointed an assistant to the District Attorney. Morrison complied and Garrison confided to a friend at the time that his ambition was to be DA of New Orleans one day.[11]

He served as an assistant DA from 1955 to early in 1958. And here we address an important point that was, as in Orwell, rewritten after Garrison's Kennedy inquiry went public. Many compromised journalists, plus Shaw's lawyers, felt it was necessary to portray Garrison as an irresponsible and reckless DA. Therefore, to aid this agreed upon objective, they stated that Garrison did not actually try any cases as an assistant. Even though Garrison alluded to his experience doing just that in his book, some people still uphold this myth.[12] In fact, in an interview in New Orleans in 1994, Irvin Dymond suggested that to this author. When asked if he ever faced Garrison in court, Dymond replied, "I don't think he ever tried a case." The implication being that his superiors did not trust Garrison to handle a trial. This is nonsense. Garrison handled a wide variety of cases: burglary, lottery operations, prostitution, homicide, and fraud.[13] This is unusual since, in most large cities, the DA's staff specializes in certain fields. Obviously Garrison was trusted enough to handle a wide array of cases. In fact, he was so trusted that by early 1958 he was made executive assistant. Then he did something that some people would call quixotic, but would foreshadow his behavior in the JFK case. When his friend in the office, Malcolm O'Hara, ran for election and won in 1958, there were charges of voter fraud. As executive assistant to incumbent Leon Hubert, Garrison supervised the investigation of the charges for the grand jury. He promised he would leave "no stone unturned."[14] He kept his promise. Which is a bit surprising. Because it cost him the first assistant job, which O'Hara had promised him if he won. His inquiry caused the election to be overturned and Richard Dowling was declared the winner.

Garrison now went into private practice and ran for a judgeship. He lost. He then secured a position in the City Attorney's office. From here, he had a good window on Dowling's practices. He did not like what he saw. Dowling sold off cases. In fact, David Ferrie bought one for 500 dollars.[15] Garrison decided to run for the office. In a televised debate in January of 1962, he did well enough to win the endorsement of the *New Orleans Times Picayune*. Garrison ran close to Dowling in the primary and this forced a runoff election in March of 1962, which Garrison won. He was helped by published letters showing that Dowling had been accepting contributions from strip club owners as part of a shakedown racket, one in which the police were also involved.[16]

Garrison delivered on his promise of reform. He allowed no police beatings of African-Americans. Refusing to enter into an alliance with the Catholic Church, he prosecuted priests for soliciting sex and for child abuse. (This is in opposition to what his successor Harry Connick did in the infamous Dino Cinel case.[17]) He vigorously pursued illegal lottery operations. He broke the gender barrier by bringing the first woman into the office, Louise Korns. He even went after his predecessor for selling off cases.[18]

Perhaps due to the timely exposure of Dowling and his ties to the strip club racket, Garrison quickly moved to perform a crackdown on the Bourbon Street "B" girl drinking business. In brief, this was a swindle in which a tourist was suckered into buying an expensive bottle of liquor. It was profitable since the split was 2/3 for the house and 1/3 for the "B" girl. When drinking by the glass, the girl's drinks were always diluted. In fact, when the mark was drunk enough, the girl's drink was replaced with water. The *Washington Post* described what happened next: "During the party, champagne at 30 dollars a bottle gets you all kinds of promises, and sometimes, a little more than promises."[19] Toward the end of the night, the waiter would start to shortchange the drunken guest after each champagne bottle. Inevitably, the mark would be led out in the wee hours of the morning, just about penniless. The house would then call for a cab.[20]

As evidenced by the Dowling contributions, the practice was usually condoned by previous DA's. And the police were also bought off, or sometimes they took a piece of the action. There had been prior attempts at breaking up this racket, but they were half-hearted ones that did not get far. And, in May of 1962, when Garrison began his version, many people doubted its staying power. One commentator said, "In this town a reformer is just an outsider who wants to get in on the inside. So he hoots and hollers and wins office. And gets gentled down."[21] But Garrison, the experienced administrator, had planned his crackdown in advance, both thoughtfully and effectively. First, since he did not trust the police, he hired many of his own investigators. The DA was going to use teams of undercover agents to sit down in these bars. They would be well dressed and well groomed, suggesting high rollers. They would make a record of their dealings, and then a day or so later, the DA would arrest all those involved. This method was terrifically effective. For example, in one night of these undercover operations, Garrison arrested 33 people.[22] Often, the DA would use civil court since he could get stiffer penalties enacted. It went on for months, stretching out over a year. At its peak, the DA shut down nine clubs in two days. Seven clubs were closed permanently.[23]

Over this extraordinary crackdown, unprecedented in the Crescent City, Garrison now got into a dispute with the local judges who had to sign off on expenditures for the ongoing campaign. The actual money came from a fines and forfeiture fund the DA kept. Garrison would have to make requests for the judges to sign off on a reimbursement or an expenditure. The dispute was multifaceted. One issue was whether or not the police or the DA should be operating this big of a vice investigation. Garrison felt that he had to since the police were too sullied to do something of this magnitude. Also, Garrison sometimes went from judge to judge to get a request approved. There was also the matter of the haphazard records submitted by Garrison's staff.[24] The dispute escalated when the judges called a temporary halt to the process. Garrison took out a personal loan to keep the crackdown going. The judges then threatened not to reimburse him. Further, they dismissed a case against three Bourbon Street clubs.[25]

The DA now began to engage in a war of rhetoric with the judges. This included two statements which were provocative in their overtones. The first was this: "The judges made it eloquently clear where their sympathies lie in regard to aggressive vice investigations by refusing to authorize use of the DA's funds." The second was: "This raises interesting questions about racketeer influences on our eight vacation-minded judges."[26]

The references to "vacation-minded judges" referred to the two and a half months off the judges had in the summer due to a Louisiana statute which pre-dated air conditioning. Although the air conditioning had been installed in the 50s, the judges still took the long vacation.[27] The insinuation about racketeer influences had some underpinning. Two of Garrison's assistants had drinks with one of the judges, Judge Haggerty, who would preside over the Shaw trial. Haggerty introduced them to Francis Giordano. Giordano was a Carlos Marcello associate. He complained to them that when Dowling took away their illegal gaming machines, he returned them. Garrison did not. "How come," Giordano asked?[28]

In the first week of November, 1962 the judges requested an ethics investi-gation of Garrison's office. Garrison then requested an independent probe of the judges' "real motives for blocking and ending our investigation of B-drinking and other vice in New Orleans."[29] It appears that this last remark—which clearly echoed his previous one about racketeer influences—provoked the defamation lawsuit to be filed on November 8. The judges also now demanded that each further request out of the fines and fees fund be signed off on by the majority of the judges. In advance. When the case went to trial, Garrison's lawyer asked for a jury to hear it. This was refused. When that happened the DA felt it was a hopeless cause. The judge's decision was handed down on February 6, 1963, with the DA on the losing end. He also lost the state Supreme Court appeal in June of 1963. In April of 1964, the case went to the U.S. Supreme Court. The month previous, the court had decided the *New York Times v. Sullivan* case in favor of free speech. This aided Garrison. The court sided with the DA, a decision Garrison always cherished.

After this decision, Garrison pushed the police to aid his campaign. His office and the police joined to raid two clubs operated by Carlos Marcello and his brother. The one Garrison raided was actually across the county line in Jefferson Parish.[30] He did this to goad the Jefferson County DA into doing something. Garrison then attacked the state Attorney General for being lax on the county.

Because of his campaign against Bourbon Street, and his controversial legal dispute with the local judges, Garrison had now raised his profile in the city, the state, and even garnered some national exposure. He was now about to use that capital to show that he was one of the most powerful politicians in Louisiana. He had already helped two judges get elected in New Orleans: Frank Shea and Rudolph Becker.[31] In 1964, he decided to show he had statewide influence. He backed John McKeithen, a dark horse, for governor. Of the nine candidates running for office that year, McKeithen was considered in the bottom half of the field. Garrison vigorously backed him, to the point of taking out a full page ad in the *New Orleans Times-Picayune*. Surprisingly, McKeithen won. Garrison now had an ally in the statehouse. If Garrison wanted to be Lieutenant Governor or Attorney General, the office was his. He never asked. According to a 1995 interview the author did with assistant Bill Alford, Garrison actually turned down the Lieutenant Governor offer when it came. At the time, he was too busy investigating the Kennedy case. The actual circumstances were this: Alford walked into Garrison's office. The DA was on one phone, with the receiver from another phone in the trash can. Alford could hear someone's voice speaking out of the trash. He asked Garrison who it was. He replied, "Its that damn McKeithen. He wants me to run for Lieutenant Governor with him. I can't get involved with that penny ante political crap while I'm investigating the Kennedy case!" Undoubtedly, if he had said yes to McKeithen, Garrison would have been Lieutenant Governor since McKeithen was so popular he ran unopposed in the general election. From there, Garrison could have easily been governor, and then realized his dream of being a senator. This incident should finally end the fabrication that Garrison was using the JFK case to further his career. Since that case actually ended a most promising political career.

Garrison's association with McKeithen also puts to death another baseless charge tossed around about him. Namely that he was somehow in bed with the Mafia. As we have seen above, Garrison went out of his way to raid a Marcello establishment in Jefferson County. In his raids on the Bourbon Street rackets, he shuttered bars that were either owned by Marcello or his associates.[32] But the grateful McKeithen offered Garrison something that further undermines this whole Mafia influence angle. Namely, he offered Garrison a free ticket to riches and retirement. He first offered him a state bank charter. Garrison turned it down. The governor then awarded it to another of his bigger backers. Who turned around and sold it for 750,000 dollars. The equivalent of 2–3 million today.[33] The governor then offered the DA a plum position as legal representative of a Savings and Loan. A desk job that would have made him a lot of money. He turned that down also. McKeithen then offered him state business as part of a large law firm that would later make him managing partner when he retired. Garrison turned that down also. Garrison really liked being DA.

When Garrison had backed McKeithen, his political power stemmed not just from the Bourbon Street battle. He had actually made his office into a much improved organization. As he once said about the legal battles with the judges, "All I want to do is run my own office. If I can't run it my way, I don't want it."[34] As we have seen, Garrison was a gifted administrator, so he ran his office quite well compared to Dowling. By 1964, each assistant was now made a full-time position, there was no moonlighting in private practice. Courts were now open every Friday. There was stricter foreclosure on bail bonds. These reforms, and others, produced results. In Dowling's final year in office, he had tried seventy cases and lost forty-two. In approximately eighteen months, Garrison had tried 101 cases and won eighty-six.[35] In 1965, the performance was even better. His office prosecuted twenty-two jury trials that year without an acquittal. Interestingly, both the *New Orleans Times Picayune* and Aaron Kohn of the Metropolitan Crime Commission backed his performance with accolades.[36] With his reformed office working at high efficiency, Garrison now went after the state legal establishment for the selling of paroles. He was so forceful on this issue that 13 lawyers resigned the Criminal Courts bar association upon hearing Garrison's evidence.[37] When the police attempted to prosecute a bookstore owner for selling James Baldwin's *Another Country*, the DA interceded with a powerful denunciation of censorship and managed to win the owner's release. This brought him the ill will of the White Citizen's Council. They accused him of being soft on "Negroes" and pornography.[38] Garrison also went after the state legislature for bribery. In 1964, Garrison won re-election and he revealed at this time that he wished someday to become a senator.[39]

It is important to add one other point about Garrison before his Kennedy inquiry was made public. The above would seem to make him out to be a law and order liberal. But that would actually be a mischaracterization. Garrison was surely a reformer but he was really a moderate. For instance he was anti-ACLU. He once said about that group that it had "drifted so far to the left that it is now almost out of sight."[40] He also favored the Cold War. In a speech he said that the United States had to act against Communist aggression in places like Korea and Vietnam.[41]

From the above, before his Kennedy inquiry of 1966, we can say that Garrison was a real reformer who was not at all afraid of taking on the local and state Establishment. We can also say he was pretty much incorruptible.

As a former resident of the area once said, "Jim Garrison? That guy cannot be bought for any price."[42] Money did not mean a lot to him. His job meant a lot to him. Third, he was a talented administrator who understood how to run a bureaucracy and instill pride in his office. This meant not just buying better equipment and tools, but making the surroundings more attractive. For Garrison spent much money on redecorating the DA's office. He also did not make political appointments to his staff. He recruited the top graduating law students from the local universities like Tulane and Loyola.[43] And there is little or no doubt from any quarter, Garrison could have gone about as high as he wanted to go in state politics. That is, until he decided to open his full court inquiry into the Kennedy assassination.

Not that he was not warned about this in advance. Pershing Gervais was a raffish scoundrel. Yet a man Garrison, who had poor judgment about people, employed and trusted for years. The realist Gervais tried to play Claude Rains to Garrison's Jimmy Stewart. He told the DA this one was not worth it. That he was signing onto a suicide mission in which he would be telling the world the American government was lying. Gervais said he was not one to enlist for what he called "kamikaze flights" since he had acquired "this habit of breathing."[44] Even though Gervais was correct, Garrison was not listening. As he told both Alford, and also Dutch television during his investigation, nothing else mattered to him.

It is important to draw this accurate picture in advance. If only to contrast it with the lurid portrait that the mainstream press would later draw of the DA. And also to show how certain entities and persons who previously backed the DA would later turn on him with a vengeance. And, in fact, they would now portray the man they had previously praised as a fine DA as a deluded, power mad megalomaniac; a Captain Ahab who would destroy an innocent man—Clay Shaw—to either find his Holy Grail and/or advance his political ambitions.

No commentator—except Gervais—pointed out what was really about to happen: Garrison was about to wreck his political image and reputation. In the process, he would lose the two jobs he always wanted: the District Attorney's office and the Senate.

CHAPTER TEN

Garrison Reopens the Kennedy Case

"The only way you can believe the Warren Report is not to have read it."

—Jim Garrison, Playboy, *October 1967*

Jim Garrison, the District Attorney of Orleans Parish, Louisiana, had actually begun investigating the assassination on November 25, 1963, four days before the Warren Commission had been announced. Even then, he was closer to the truth than the Commission. Unfortunately, Garrison did not pursue the matter as he could have.

Shortly after the ex-FBI man and private detective, Guy Banister, had pistol-whipped his employee Jack Martin into a hospital bed, one of Garrison's Assistant DAs came to him with some provocative information. Martin's tongue had been loosened by Banister's beating, and he had told a mutual acquaintance about a strange ice-skating and goose-hunting trip on the day of the assassination by David Ferrie. Ferrie had left New Orleans on the afternoon of the assassination with two young friends named Melvin Coffey and Alvin Beauboeuf. Driving 400 miles all night through a torrential rainstorm he first went to Houston. Ferrie gave more than one story as to why he did this. First, it was to relax.[1] The next was that it was to go goose hunting. Except downtown Houston is not a good place to hunt geese, which is maybe why Ferrie did not take any guns.[2] The trio arrived at the Alamotel early on November 23. The trio then said they went figure skating at Winterland Skating Rink. Yet Chuck Rolland, the proprietor of Winterland, said Ferrie spent two hours waiting near a pay phone. When it rang, he answered. After he hung up, he left with this two companions.[3] The trio then went on to Galveston where they arrived at around 9:00 P.M. at the Driftwood Motel. (A little noted problem is that the check in/check out times on the motel records conflict. That is, they appear to be staying at both places at the same time.[4]) Hurt and resentful, Martin cast the weekend excursion in a particularly dark light. Something about Ferrie being a "getaway pilot" in an elaborate assassination plot.[5]

Ferrie Lies to the FBI

Garrison had a slight acquaintance with all three characters named. He had known Banister when Banister was a policeman, and they had traded stories about their previous work in the FBI. Through Banister, he knew Martin. He had met Ferrie only once. After his election as District Attorney, the odd-visaged pilot had congratulated him on the street. At this point, Garrison was harboring no suspicions about any of these men. His next encounter with Ferrie, however, would change that attitude quickly.

On the weight of Martin's accusations and a previous police complaint record, Garrison sent assistants from his office to Ferrie's apartment. When they arrived, they found two young boys inside, waiting for Ferrie. They said he had left for a trip to Texas on the 22 and had not yet returned.[6] This was also Garrison's first knowledge of Ferrie's odd living conditions. The apartment had a collection of mice for Ferrie's cancer research, a batch of Army rifles and other military equipment, and a wall map of Cuba.

When Ferrie returned from Texas, Garrison brought him in for questioning. Ferrie's answers were a mixture of truth, lies, and subterfuge. He admitted going to Houston on the 22nd. He denied ever knowing or meeting Oswald. When Garrison pressed him on his reasons for driving to Texas through a fierce rainstorm, he gave the ice skating-goose hunting story described earlier (he once changed this to an interest in building a rink himself).[7] To Garrison, this was like driving 400 miles for a hamburger. The DA was also suspicious of Ferrie's nervous and evasive demeanor. On November 25, he decided to arrest Ferrie and turn him over to the FBI for questioning. The FBI disposed of him quickly when they determined his plane could not fly that weekend. Evidently they were not concerned that Ferrie would not need his plane in Houston and had already arranged for another plane to be waiting there.[8] Garrison automatically accepted the decision of the FBI, his former employer.

This was a mistake, because Ferrie lied through a large portion of his FBI interview[9] For instance, he said he never owned a telescopic rifle, or even used one, and further he would not know *how* to use one. This from a man who, as we have seen, worked as a CIA trainer for both Mongoose and the Bay of Pigs. Ferrie further said that he did not know Oswald and that Oswald was not a member of the CAP squadron in New Orleans. What is odd about this is that Ferrie named to the Bureau Jerry Paradis as drill instructor for the CAP. If the FBI had talked to Paradis they would have learned that Ferrie was lying. For, as we have seen, Paradis vividly recalled Oswald and Ferrie in the CAP. And if they had pursued this further, they FBI likely would have found the photo that Ferrie was worried about. The one depicting Oswald with Ferrie at a cookout in the CAP. Further, in that interview, Ferrie discusses both Jack Martin and Guy Banister. He says that Martin had charged calls to Banister's office. The agents failed to ask how Ferrie could know that unless he knew Banister and had been in his office. From there, the agents could have then discovered that Oswald had the address of Banister's office on his FPCC pamphlet that summer. Ferrie also said that he knew Sergio Arcacha Smith and his anti-Castro group from their stay in th̶ ̶B̶̲̅e̶r Building. But he never knew the group or Arcacha Smith from ̶ ̶ ̶ ̶̲̅et. And that he had no association with any anti Castro group from a man who admitted he was part of Mongoose.

shows us that the FBI was not interested in finding out who s and who actually killed President Kennedy, it is their failure nterview. For under Title 18, U.S. Code, Section 1001, it is a n FBI agent. If J. Edgar Hoover had really been interested in Ferrie would have been indicted for both lying to an agent ̶ ̶ruction of justice. He was not. Because Hoover was not interested.

Garrison Slowly Gets Back In

Most chronologies of the Garrison investigation say that the DA lost interest in the Kennedy case until, on an airplane trip on November 13, 1966 with Senator Russell Long, the conversation turned to the Kennedy assassination. There, Long made some comments that set off Garrison's curiosity about the case. And, in fact, even Garrison has essentially stated that this is what brought him back into the Kennedy case. Today, there is some contravening evidence that indicates that although this is true as a generality, it does not cover every instance in between. For having surveyed what was left of Garrison's files, the author noted four to five memoranda that fell in the time frame of 1965–66. When the author called Garrison's former Chief Investigator Lou Ivon, he said that there had been intermittent instances when Garrison would get interested in a certain aspect of the Kennedy case prior to the Long in-flight conversation.[10] As Garrison's first assistant John Volz related to Joan Mellen, this began with Garrison picking up a copy of the March 1965 issue of *Esquire* which featured a review of the Warren Report by illustrious critic Dwight MacDonald.[11] Comparatively speaking, MacDonald's critique was a mild one. But it did appear in a high profile national magazine.

Therefore, it seems Garrison never really lost interest in the case after he mistakenly turned Ferrie over to the FBI. He nurtured it along intermittently through 1965 and most of 1966. The plane conversation with Long was the capper which sent him into full investigative mode. He now began reading every book and article he could find on the assassination: Vincent Salandria, Harold Weisberg, Mark Lane, Edward Epstein, et al. He then ordered the Warren Report and its 26 volumes of testimony and exhibits. That was the clincher. Garrison's reaction was disbelief, or as he termed it, "the end of innocence":[12]

> It is impossible for anyone possessed of reasonable objectivity and a fair degree of intelligence to read those twenty-six volumes and not reach the conclusion that the Warren Commission was wrong in every one of its major conclusions concerning the assassination.

The DA decided to reopen his investigation. Oswald had been in New Orleans for over five months before going on to Dallas less than two months before the assassination. Garrison's initial assumptions about the assassination, about the probity of the Warren Report, the FBI inquiry, about his own brief investigation, all these were now in freefall. Garrison was now about to make a series of discoveries which would undermine the viability of the Warren Report. For as we have seen, there was a multitude of evidence indicating conspiracy in New Orleans. It was time to uncover the mystery of 544 Camp Street.

The Warren Commission had spent very little time on the New Orleans portion of Oswald's life. Commission lawyer Wesley Liebeler had interviewed some witnesses in Louisiana, and Ferrie's name had come up, but it had been disposed of quickly. (As mentioned previously, the testimony appears in Volume VIII with interviews of Edward Voebel and Frederick O'Sullivan, who testified they tentatively recognized both Oswald and Ferrie as CAP members.) Liebeler had also interviewed local New Orleans lawyer Dean Andrews, whose testimony, as we have seen, was quite interesting. But whatever the reason, the Report discounted his testimony. This seems unwarranted, if predictable, because Andrew's original story was buttressed by the testimony of three people: his assistant, Preston Davis; Eva Springer, his secretary to whom he told the story; and his colleague, Monk Zelden, whom he called and asked to help him in the case.[13]

But besides these and a few other bits and pieces, the only lead the Warren Commission left to Oswald's trail in New Orleans was an interview with Sam Newman. Newman was the owner of the building at 544 Camp Street, the address stamped on Oswald's pro-Castro pamphlets. The FBI dropped its investigation of this address when Mr. Newman said he rented no office there to the Fair Play for Cuba Committee and did not recognize Oswald's photo.[14] As we have seen in Chapter 6, Newman was not entirely forthright in any of his interviews. So this was another indication of lack of rigor by the FBI.

This was where the Commission ended its inquiry into Oswald's stay in New Orleans. It is where Garrison began.

544 Camp Street and the FPCC Agent Provocateur

Because the Oswald pamphlet with the address 544 Camp street is in the Commission volumes, Garrison decided to go down and inspect the building. Garrison realized that its other address was 531 Lafayette and recalled that Guy Banister's office had been there. This, of course, led Garrison to solving the Camp Street mystery and to establishing Oswald's association with Ferrie and Banister. Unfortunately—and this is what makes Garrison's failure to follow up his 1963 inquiry so crushing—Banister and his associate Hugh Ward had both died in 1964. Nevertheless, Garrison managed to get the title cards to Banister's files and uncovered his façade as a private detective. One of the files was entitled "Shaw," but its papers had disappeared within days after Banister's death.[15]

In reading the Commission volumes, Garrison became convinced that Oswald had been receiving intelligence training in the Marines. And that his learning of Russian was preparation for being part of a false defector program. Now he began to understand that after he was brought back to America, his next assignment was to act as Banister's agent provocateur in New Orleans against the pro-Castro FPCC. What Garrison could not know at that time— unless he knew what happened to Otto Otekpka—is that the false defector program was likely being run by James Angleton. And what he could not have known under any circumstances is that both the CIA and FBI were running counter intelligence programs against the FPCC and that David Phillips and Jim McCord were supervising that particular Agency effort.[16]

To certify Oswald as an agent provocateur for Banister, Garrison went back to his 1963 lead about David Ferrie, namely Jack Martin, who had worked for Banister. Martin had originally called Herm Kohlman, an assistant DA. Garrison now had Kohlman get in touch with Martin. Martin had contacted not just Garrison but the FBI back in 1963. He told the Bureau that Ferrie had known Oswald in the CAP, for he had seen a photo of the two together, and Ferrie may have hypnotized Oswald into shooting Kennedy.[17] So now, three years later, Garrison sat across a table in his office from Martin. After describing the November 22, 1963, physical assault on him by Banister, Martin now told Garrison about all the Cubans in Banister's office, along with David Ferrie, who he said practically lived there and how Banister didn't really do any detective work. If anything came in, he did it. Martin added, as several people knew, that Oswald was also there. Sometimes he would be meeting with Banister, and at times he would be talking to Ferrie.[18] But this is as far as Martin would go at this early stage. It was through his assistant Frank Klein that Garrison discovered that Banister's office was serving as a clearinghouse for anti-Castro Cubans involved in Mongoose. Klein discovered newspaper stories about the FBI crackdown ordered by Kennedy against anti-Castro training camps in 1963. Particularly the raid on the McLaney cottage, near Lacombe as outlined in Chapter 6.[19] When Garrison called Martin back in to show him that he now understood what the Banister office was about, Martin added a personage: Ferrie had introduced him to Oswald in Banister's office. With Ferrie at the time was Sergio Arcacha Smith, the local Cuban leader of Howard Hunt's group, the CRC. Further, agreeing with Delphine Roberts, Martin said that Oswald had an office in the building. And that James Arthus, the custodian the Commission had partly relied on to keep Oswald out of 544 Camp Street, had taken Oswald's paraphernalia after the assassination.[20]

The FBI and Shaw/Bertrand

Another important early witness for Garrison was Dean Andrews. The gravity of the plot was made clear to Garrison in his meeting with his old law school chum. Garrison was intensely curious about who Clay Bertrand really was. From 1963, when Andrews had first told the FBI of his phone call from Bertrand to defend Oswald, the lawyer had been backpedaling from his original story. Andrews almost begged not to be interviewed anymore. Andrews implied that he backpedaled because the FBI wanted him to change his story. He even denied knowing what Bertrand looked like, though he had seen him twice.[21] To Garrison, this meant that Andrews's original corroborated testimony was true. But due to his reception by the Commission, he had decided to tap dance away from it. For although Andrews's testimony lasts for 14 pages in the volumes, the actual Warren Report deals with him in one paragraph.[22] And in that one paragraph the name of Clay Bertrand is not mentioned; in fact, it is not in the entire Warren Report. And clearly, whoever wrote this part of the report was out to discredit Andrews. The anonymous author says that the witness was 1.) unable to locate records of Oswald's visits, 2.) investigation could not locate the man who called Andrews to go to Dallas to defend Oswald, and 3.) Andrews was under heavy sedation at the time of the call.

Again, this shows just how thoroughly preoccupied the Commission was in scapegoating Oswald. For Andrews had told Commission attorney Wesley Liebeler that his office was rifled shortly after he was released from the hospital and interviewed by the FBI after the assassination.[23] As per Andrews being under sedation at the time of the call, this is false. The FBI discovered that Andrews did receive sedation on that day, November 23. But it was at 8:00 P.M. in the evening. The call from Bertrand came in four hours earlier.[24] As per the FBI investigation not being able to locate Bertrand, as we shall see, that is because the Bureau never really wanted to.

Garrison invited Andrews to lunch early in 1967 and asked him Clay Bertrand's true identity.[25] When Andrews would not respond truthfully—he insisted he did not know what the mysterious Bertrand looked like—the conversation turned dramatic. Garrison grabbed Andrews's arm and warned him that he would take him before the grand jury and, if he dodged the question on the stand, he would go to jail for perjury. Andrews's response was equally intense. He told the DA that if he revealed the identity of Clay Bertrand, "It's goodbye Dean Andrews . . . I mean like a bullet in my head." Although Andrews was clearly upset, Garrison was adamant. He would still call him to testify. Andrews expressed this same fear for his life to Mark Lane, before Garrison interviewed him, and to Anthony Summers after Garrison interviewed him.[26]

The Search for Rose

In the early part of 1967, Garrison got his lead on the Rose Cheramie affair. A man named A. H. Magruder had spent the Christmas holidays of 1963–64 on a hunting trip with Dr. Victor J. Weiss. At that time Weiss was the Clinical Director of East Louisiana State Hospital in Jackson, Louisiana. The two were sitting at Magruder's home near St. Francisville when Weiss started to talk about Cheramie and her connection to the Kennedy case. Weiss told Magruder that he had treated Rose when she came to Jackson. She had told him she worked as a dope runner for Jack Ruby. She also said she had worked in a Ruby nightclub. She had been making a dope run for Ruby from Florida to Dallas. She did not want to do it but she had a young child who was being held. She told Weiss about being abandoned by her male cohorts, which is how she ended up at Jackson. She told the doctor that the president and other Texas officials were going to be killed on Kennedy's upcoming visit to Dallas. Weiss told Magruder that, like Fruge, he did not pay very much attention to these meanderings by the patient. But after Kennedy was killed, he went back to her. She now said, after Ruby had shot Oswald, that Oswald knew Ruby since she had seen them together at Ruby's club.[27]

Once Garrison got this explosive lead, he tracked it down. He discovered who Fruge was, and had him transferred from the State Police to his staff. The first thing he wanted Fruge to do was to find Cheramie. Fruge went to Jackson, found some records, and located her sister in Houston. The sister told her she was now dead. She had been killed in 1965 while on a small highway between Tyler and Dayward, Texas.[28] Garrison wanted to exhume the body but the local authorities would not let him. Garrison now instructed Fruge to find the saloon that Rose had stopped at before she was abandoned. This place was called the Silver Slipper and the bar manager was a man named Mac Manual. After visiting with him once, Fruge came back with some photos that Garrison had given him. Manuel identified the two men with Rose as Sergio Arcacha Smith and Emilio Santana.[29] In other words, the Cheramie lead went back to denizens related to 544 Camp Street. According to an interview the author did with Lou Ivon, in 1967, Santana disappeared into the Miami Cuban underworld.[30] Arcacha Smith reportedly moved out of New Orleans to Texas in late 1962. First he went to Houston and then to Dallas. But he visited New Orleans often to stay in touch with his former friends. Garrison tried to question Arcacha Smith in Dallas. He sent Jim Alcock and William Gurvich to do the questioning. But, as we will see, the Cuban exile leader said he would only talk to them if Dallas policemen were present. Garrison rejected that condition.[31] Arcacha Smith's lawyer said he might agree to be questioned as long as he did not have to go to New Orleans. On April 1, Garrison telegraphed an arrest warrant to Dallas for Arcacha Smith's role in the Schlumberger bunker raid in Houma. He was arrested and then released on a 1,500 dollar bond. Garrison then sent extradition papers to Texas, which Governor John Connally refused to sign. Because Connally did not sign them within 90 days, Arcacha Smith was released from the bond. Thus, one of the most suspicious characters in the entire case was allowed to escape serious questioning. And, as we shall momentarily see, the dark clouds around Arcacha Smith extend even further and deeper.

Nagell, Shaw, and William Martin

After Richard Case Nagell had been apprehended in the El Paso bank, he was legally railroaded. He was convicted for armed robbery even though there was no intent to rob anything. (He was sentenced to ten years, but he eventually ended up having that lowered to three years.) Even though he had a mimeographed newsletter from the FPCC, a Minox miniature spy camera, and a tourist card for entry into Mexico in the name of Aleksei Hidell. Even though on the way to the El Paso Federal Building he said to the FBI, "I would rather be arrested than commit murder and treason."[32] Further, at a preliminary hearing for Nagell, the defendant related to his arresting officer, a man named Jim Bundren, that he wanted to be caught. Bundren replied that he knew Nagell was not out to rob any bank. Nagell then said, "Well, I'm glad you caught me. I really don't want to be in Dallas." To which Bundren replied, "What do you mean by that?" Nagell answered with, "You'll see soon enough."[33] Bundren later concluded that the FBI understood a lot more about Nagell before his trial than they let onto.

Nagell tried to warn authorities about the assassination even while he was in prison. He wrote a letter to the Secret Service via the prison authorities warning them about an upcoming assassination attempt. The date of this letter was November 21, 1963.[34] Nagell, then wrote letters to J. Lee Rankin in 1964, and later Sen. Richard Russell in 1967. He told the senator he was surveilling Oswald in 1962 and 1963. And that Oswald had no significant connection with the FPCC. When the news of Garrison's probe broke in February of 1967, Nagell got in contact with his office from his Springfield prison. Garrison arranged to have one of the many volunteers that had flocked to his office interview Nagell. This was a lawyer named William Martin. This turned out to be one of the many errors Garrison made. For it later turned out that Martin was suspected of being one of the several CIA plants in Garrison's office. And his practice was located at Shaw's International Trade Mart.[35] Neither Nagell nor Garrison had suspicions about the man at the time of Martin's first interview with Nagell. Even though, as we have seen in Chapter 6, this is the same Martin that Maurice Gatlin had turned over to Guy Banister to spy on the left while a student at Tulane. Martin eventually became Chief Investigator for the Banister/Gatlin organization, the Anti-Communist Committee of the Americas.[36] The reason his office was at the ITM is because after he left Banister's organization he went to work for Shaw as the Director of International Relations and world trade at International House, the Rockefeller founded, sister organization to ITM.[37] It is at this point that Martin now began to be formally associated with the Agency.

Unaware of any of this at first, Nagell was quite open with Martin when he got to Springfield, Missouri to interview him. Nagell garnered from Martin that Garrison's working background concept was that the assassination had much to do with Kennedy's evolving policy toward Cuba, the failure of the Bay of Pigs, and how both of these had inflamed the Cuban exile community against him. Nagell replied, "That is absolutely right, as a general picture, but of course there are some fine points here and there that you have not covered."[38] Nagell went on to say that he would now tender evidence to Garrison that would all but certify his inquest. He told Martin that he had been able to infiltrate the assassination plot. To the point that he could "make a tape recording of four voices in conversation concerning the plot which ended in the assassination of President Kennedy." Nagell said that the tape was primarily in Spanish, although at times certain voices lapsed into English. When Martin asked who the participants were, Nagell replied that one of them was "Arcacha," and another Nagell would only identify as "Q."[39] Aracha has to be Arcacha Smith, and "Q" is very likely Carlos Quiroga. Quiroga, as we have seen, was not just associated with Arcacha, but also with Carlos Bringuier. But according to Sam Newman, Quiroga was actually Arcacha Smith's right hand man.[40] As we have seen in Chapter 8, Quiroga was likely supplying Oswald with literature for his FPCC leafleting display in front of Shaw's Trade Mart. And he also probably lied about this before the Warren Commission and also to Garrison's investigators. On Garrison's polygraph test, Quiroga also indicated deceptive reactions when asked two further questions. The first was, "According to your own knowledge did Sergio Arcacha know Lee Oswald?" The second was, "Prior to the assassination of the President, did you ever see any of the guns which were used in the assassination?"[41] These last two questions of course directly relate to what Nagell is speaking about, namely the setting up of Oswald in an assassination plot by CIA related Cubans. As per the tape, although there is some dispute about this, it appears that it was stolen in a burglary of Nagell's possessions, probably in 1964. What makes this unusual is that during the heist, it was the *only* object that the burglar stole.[42] Due to the handling of certain other documents between the two, and their future filing, by July of 1967, Nagell became quite estranged from Martin, and terminated any further discussions with him. And a few days after this, Martin then moved his office out of Shaw's Trade Mart and returned to "my private practice."[43]

As noted, Arcacha Smith left New Orleans sometime in late 1962. But, as Quiroga and others have indicated, he stayed in close contact with his former New Orleans colleagues after the move. As we have seen so far, Arcacha Smith directly relates to Howard Hunt and David Phillips through the CIA's attempt to launch an extension of the CRC in New Orleans. He was involved in preparations for the Bay of Pigs, to the point that he actually had films of the operation. He then relates to both Ferrie and Banister through his activities at 544 Camp Street. He relates to Clay Shaw since Shaw donated funds to the CRC and, during the Garrison investigation, Shaw made many direct calls to Arcacha Smith's lawyer.[44] We have now outlined evidence that directly connects Aracha Smith in a plot, involving other Cubans, to murder Kennedy and to set up Oswald as a patsy. As we will see later, there is still more evidence of Arcacha Smith's involvement.

Dischler, Fruge, and Lloyd Cobb

It is not certain how Garrison came in contact with the Clinton-Jackson incident. But it may be through the work of two law enforcement officers who were on leave to him. They were the previously mentioned Francis Fruge and an undercover agent named Anne Dischler. Garrison had them investigating multiple alleged appearances of Oswald in the Lafayette area.[45] And it was through that investigation that the two came in contact with John Rarick and Ned Touchstone. Rarick was a judge in the Feliciana parishes. Touchstone was a rightwing publisher. In 1964 barber Edwin McGehee told Rarick about the Oswald visit. Rarick then told Touchstone. An article appeared in Touchstone's *Councilor,* and through that exposure word filtered back to Fred Dent of the State Sovereignty Commission. Dent told Fruge and Dischler, who may have already seen the article.[46] Garrison now told Fruge and Dischler to transfer their effort from Lafayette to Feliciana. They did so with exceptional results. All the material discussed in Chapter 5, and more, was now at Garrison's disposal. But two key exceptions should be noted.

When Fruge and Dischler first visited with Henry Palmer in May of 1967, Dischler brought her tape recorder, but not her notebook. Palmer, who was the registrar at that time, pulled out a book, opened it and said, "Look, this is where Oswald registered."[47] According to Dischler, although Oswald's name had been written over, you could still see the capital "O," the space where "Lee H" had been signed, and the shadow of his name. When Fruge asked why Oswald's name had been written over, Palmer ignored the question. Later on, Fruge asked to come back the next day, for he wanted to copy the book. At this point, Palmer may have hinted as to why Oswald's name was written over. He told the pair that, at first, he and Sheriff John Manchester decided not to say anything about Oswald being up there. When Fruge and Dischler showed up the next day, the registration book with the remnant of Oswald's name in it was gone. Palmer expressed surprise but offered no explanation. Dischler never forgot that reversal.[48]

Second, someone took a picture of the black Cadillac as it was parked and its passengers were waiting for Oswald to register to vote. According to Dischler, it looked to her as if Shaw was in the driver's seat of the car.[49] Dischler had it in her possession and used it to help certain witnesses like Corrie Collins identify the suspects. But the picture was from a bad angle and the resolution was not good. Therefore, when Garrison tried to blow it up, it lost still more resolution. Therefore it was not submitted at Shaw's trial.[50]

One of the most fascinating things that Garrison discovered about this endlessly interesting episode is that three witnesses there remembered seeing Lawrence Howard in the town area. Howard was a physically imposing Latin who was vigorously involved in anti-Castro activities, including the training of paramilitary forces, at the time of Kennedy's death. This fact was widely known in the intelligence community. So widely that the FBI tried to (falsely) say that Howard was one of three men who appeared at the door of another exile activist, Sylvia Odio, in late September of 1963. Edwin McGehee said that he cut Howard's hair once. During their conversation, Howard said he worked at Marydale Farms.[51] Reeves Morgan said he saw Howard walking the streets of Jackson.[52] Both men identified Howard from a folio of suspect photographs shown to them by the HSCA. Further, Henry Earl Palmer also identified Howard as someone associated with Marydale Farms.[53] Howard himself admitted he was in Louisiana on the day Kennedy was killed.[54] Marydale Farms was owned by Lloyd Cobb, the president of the International Trade Mart; in actuality, he was Shaw's superior. Located just outside of Jackson, it was a sprawling 12,000 acre parcel that produced dairy goods. Cobb himself was a rightwing figure who had a CIA clearance to serve on a "cleared attorney's panel."[55] His brother, Alvin, was a close friend of Guy Banister. All this is made even more fascinating by information that Garrison did not know. When this author and William Davy traveled to Jackson in 1994, Reeves Morgan told us something that he said he had never told anyone else. He said that on the day of Kennedy's assassination, he noticed the caretakers at Marydale rounding up all the cattle there as if they were closing the enterprise down. When he asked them what they were doing, he was warned to forget everything he had seen at the farm if he wanted to maintain his health. When Morgan said this to us, it truly did sound as if he was letting go of an old and bottled up fear.[56] It would appear that Cobb's huge farmland was being used to produce more than just milk.

Garrison's investigation of the Clinton-Jackson incident went on for over five months. He came to conclude that the aim of the exercise was to get Oswald's name into the files at the hospital. Then have a contact at the hospital—maybe Silva through say Sergio Arcacha Smith—switch and modify Oswald's folder from the employment to the patient files. This would then certify that Oswald really was a demented assassin. And clearly this is what the Commission was trying to do. For in a secret cable to Russia from Anatoly Dobyrnin, the Soviet ambassador revealed that Dean Rusk had told him that the Warren Commission's preliminary investigation had dug a up a lot of data about Oswald's "mental instability." The Secretary of State then asked Dobyrnin if "that same data might be available in the Soviet Union when Oswald lived there."[57] If the Clinton-Jackson incident had achieved its probable objective, it would have been the icing on the Commission's case. The unanticipated problem was that the planners did not anticipate the large voter rally. Therefore, too many witnesses saw Oswald with Shaw and Ferrie.

At the time this inquiry was halted, Fruge and Dischler were still not done. They had many leads still to follow up on. But the State Police had now requested Fruge return to his regular position. What had happened is that Garrison was discovering too much for some quarters. A state legislator had called for the return of expenses made to a state police detective and a woman state employee working on a murder investigation.[58] This was clearly a political move, which shortchanged Garrison of one of the richest veins of evidence he had, and two of his best investigators.

Thornley: Oswald's False Friend

From looking through the Warren Commission testimony, for reasons stated in Chapter 7, Garrison became interested in the strange case of Kerry Thornley. Thornley was a Marine Corps buddy of Oswald's whose testimony to the Warren Commission was used to portray Oswald as a Communist loner. As Garrison noted in his book, Thornley's testimony is at odds with other service friends of the alleged assassin, who do not recall him as an ideologically committed Marxist.[59] Another important fact about Thornley is that he wrote *two* books about Oswald, one before and one after the assassination: the novel *The Idle Warriors* (unpublished until 1991), and *Oswald* (published in 1965). Both books accomplish the same end as Thornley's Warren Commission testimony: they portray Oswald as a committed and sociopathic communist. The 1965 work is a nonfiction tome that reads something like the Warren Commission witness, psychiatrist Renatus Hartogs' profile of Oswald. Consider the following line:

> I'm certain that in his own eyes Oswald was the most important man in the [Marine] unit. To him the mark of destiny was clearly visible on his forehead and that some were blind to it was his eternal source of aggravation.[60]

Later in the book, Thornley writes, "Frankly, I agree that the man was sick, but I further think his sickness was, in the long run, self induced in the manner previously outlined."[61] In the last three chapters of the book, Thornley basically traces the Warren Commission version of the last few days of Oswald's life. In the last chapter he lays all the blame for the murder at Oswald's feet—that is, there was no conspiracy, large or small. In fact, Thornley's early writings on the case are pretty much indistinguishable from what the Warren Commission pumped out. They are so similar that one wonders if the Commission borrowed its profile of Oswald from Thornley in the first place.

According to both Thornley and Jim Garrison, the Secret Service swept down on Thornley on November 23, and in short order he was on a plane to Washington with his manuscript of *The Idle Warriors.*[62] Thornley reveals in his later, nonfiction book that he talked to Warren Commission counsel Albert Jenner on a number of occasions about his testimony. According to Garrison, Thornley stayed in the Washington, D.C., area for almost a year. He then moved out to California where his parents resided. Ironically he worked at an apartment complex which housed, of all people, CIA-Mafia-Castro assassination plots intermediary Johnny Roselli. Around this time, David Lifton was going through the Warren Commission volumes and noted Thornley's testimony. He looked him up in person and they became friends. During the early part of Garrison's investigation, Lifton popped in to help out, and discussed Thornley with the DA. It was this event which marked the beginning of the falling out between Garrison and Lifton. For, from the evidence adduced by the new file releases, Thornley was a much more suspicious character than the one Lifton has always presented.

First, as should have been apparent from the beginning, Thornley was an extreme right winger who had an almost pathological hatred of Kennedy. This could have provided a reason for him to characterize Oswald as he did for the Commission. Thornley worked briefly for rightwing publisher Kent Courtney in New Orleans and was a friend of New Orleans-based CIA journalist Clint Bolton. According to an article in *New Orleans Magazine,* Thornley was also once employed by Alton Ochsner's INCA outfit, the CIA-related radio and audiotape outfit which sponsored Oswald's famous debate with Cuban exile leader Carlos Bringuier. According to former Guy Banister employee Dan Campbell, Thornley was one of the young fanatics who frequented 544 Camp Street.[63] Additional facts make the above acquaintances even more interesting. Thornley tried to deny that he knew Bringuier, yet his girlfriend Jeanne Hack described an encounter between Thornley and a man who fit Bringuier's description to Bill Turner in January of 1968. And as Thornley notes in his introduction to the 1991 issue of *The Idle Warriors,* he showed that manuscript to Banister *before* the assassination, back in 1961.

This last point brings up one of the most important issues concerning the whole Thornley episode: his early denials and later reversals. Two memos written by Andrew Sciambra in February of 1968 reveal that Thornley denied knowing Banister, Dave Ferrie, Clay Shaw, and Shaw's friend Time-Life journalist David Chandler. Garrison, however, had evidence that revealed the opposite to be the case. And years later, on the eve of the House Select Committee investigation, Thornley *admitted to knowing all of these shady characters.* Then, of course, there was the issue of Thornley's association with Oswald himself in the summer of 1963. Thornley denied before the New Orleans grand jury that he associated with Oswald in New Orleans in 1963. This seemed improbable on its face since, as noted above, both men knew each other previously and both men frequented some of the same places in 1963. But further, consider Thornley's rather equivocal denial on the witness stand:

> Q: Did she [Barbara Reid] see you with Oswald?
> A: I don't think she did because the next day I started asking people . . .
> Q: You don't think so?
> A: I don't know whether it was Oswald, I can't remember who was sitting there with me . . .[64]

The above statements earned Thornley a perjury indictment from Garrison. But there was much more. Garrison had no less than *eight* witnesses who said they had seen Oswald with Thornley in New Orleans that summer of 1963. An event denied by Thornley to both Lifton and to Garrison. And some of these witnesses went beyond just noting the association between the two. Two of these witnesses, Bernard Goldsmith and Doris Dowell, both said that *Thornley told them Oswald was not a communist.*[65] This is amazing since, as noted earlier, the Warren Commission featured Thornley as its key witness to Oswald's alleged commie sympathies. This indicates that Thornley himself 1.) knew the truth about Oswald's intelligence ties and 2.) was probably involved in creating a false cover—a "legend," in intelligence parlance—for the alleged assassin.

On top of these devastating admissions, there is the information from Mrs. Myrtle LaSavia, who lived within a block of Oswald in New Orleans. She stated that she, "her husband, and a number of people who live in that neighborhood saw Thornley at the Oswald residence a number of times—in fact they saw him there so much they did not know which was the husband, Oswald or Thornley."[66] In May of 1999, at the National Archives, Oswald author John Armstrong discovered FBI documents which show that other neighbors of Oswald picked out photos of Thornley as a frequent visitor to the Oswald apartment. According to a radio interview Garrison did in 1968, the DA had

witnesses who saw Thornley shopping with Marina Oswald. If this is so, not
only did Oswald encounter Thornley in New Orleans in 1963, but the two were
quite close.

This apparent closeness may have had a purpose beyond the framing of
Oswald as a leftist in the public mind. There are two indications of this. The
first is noted by Harold Weisberg in his book *Never Again:*

> When the New Orleans Secret Service investigation led it to the Jones Printing
> Co., the printer of the Fair Play for Cuba Committee handbills, and the Secret
> Service was on the verge of learning, as I later learned, that it was not Oswald who
> picked up those handbills, the New Orleans FBI at once contacted FBI HQ. The
> FBI immediately leaned on the Secret Service HQ and immediately the Secret
> Service was ordered to desist. For all practical purposes, that ended the Secret
> Service probe—the moment it was about to explode the myth of the "loner" who
> had an associate who picked up a print job for him.[67]

What Weisberg does not reveal in this passage is that the person who
picked up the flyers was identified as Kerry Thornley. In an interview with journalist Earl Golz in 1979, Weisberg stated that two employees at the print shop
picked out photos of Thornley, not Oswald, when he questioned them about
the "Hands off Cuba" flyers. Weisberg secretly taped one of the interviews
with the employees. When Weisberg informed Garrison investigator Lou Ivon
of this new development, Bill Boxley—a CIA plant in Garrison's office—tried
to distort what had happened. Weisberg pulled out the tape, quieting Boxley.
But later, the tape disappeared.[68]

The other 1963 incident that makes Thornley even more fascinating was his
trip to Mexico in July/August. As Jeanne Hack noted in an interview, Thornley was
usually a quite talkative individual, but when it came to this Mexico trip, he was
quite reluctant to speak about it.[69] According to his February 25, 1963 FBI statement, Thornley said "that he made this trip by himself and emphatically denied that
Oswald had accompanied him from New Orleans to California or from California
to Mexico." Doth Thornley protest too much? In another FBI memo written the
same day Thornley was interviewed, the following statement appears: "Thornley is
presently employed as a waiter in New Orleans and has recently been in Mexico
and California with Oswald. Secret Service has been notified." Again, if this is so it
is very interesting to say the least. But even if it were so, the Secret Service probably
followed up about as vigorously as it did the Jones Print Shop incident.

Thornley's behavior during the ongoing Garrison probe was strange, to say
the least. As noted above, he told the DA's representative he never met Shaw,
Ferrie, Chandler, or Oswald, at least not Oswald in New Orleans. He was a
bit hazy on Banister saying that he "may have met Banister somewhere around

Camp Street," but he was not sure. His equivocations on Oswald are even more striking. He told Andrew Sciambra the following:

> He also admits that there are some coincidences which have taken place which make it appear that he and Oswald were in contact with each other but he declares that these are only coincidences and that he has never seen Oswald since the days in the Marine Corps together.[70]

In a later interview with Sciambra, Thornley also denied knowing Bringuier and Ed Butler of INCA, even though he applied for a job at the latter. Every one of these denials turned out to be false and Thornley admitted to them later. But on *top* of this, there is the apparent element of the protection of Thornley when he became a hot item in New Orleans in 1968. For instance, according to Mort Sahl, Thornley insisted on meeting Sciambra at a curious location for one of their interviews: NASA. Sciambra recalled thinking as he entered the place that if someone like Thornley could command access to such a place then Garrison really didn't have a snowball's chance in Hades.[71] Several of Oswald's cohorts from Reily Coffee had gone to NASA before the assassination. It seems odd that a coffee company would be a training ground for such a scientifically oriented facility. Garrison camp infiltrator Gordon Novel also went there while on the lam from Garrison.

And then there was the problem of locating Thornley. Garrison investigator and former CIA agent Jim Rose took on that assignment. Through his network of Agency contacts he found Thornley was living in Tampa. The supposedly working class Thornley had two homes in Florida, one in Tampa and one in Miami. He lived at the Tampa residence, which, according to Rose's notes, was a large white frame house on a one acre lot. In addition, he owned two cars at the time.[72] All this from a man who had only been a waiter and doorman in civilian life up to that time.

After the Garrison investigation, Thornley slipped into obscurity. But he resurfaced in the late seventies around the time of the House Select Committee on Assassinations. Clearly fearing that the HSCA would take up where Garrison had left off, he now reappeared as a kind of stoned hippie who had a rather eccentric interest in aliens, Nazis, and the occult. He assembled a long narrative in which he now stated that, "I did not realize I was involved in the JFK murder conspiracy until 1975, when the Watergate revelations made it rather obvious." The reason it became obvious was that he now recognized Howard Hunt as one of the men who recruited him into the plot. In this new mode he even admitted that Oswald had been framed for the crime. Quite an admission from the author of the 1965 book which concluded the opposite.[73]

At around this same time, Thornley sent Garrison a long manuscript outlining the Kennedy plot as he saw it. This document is in the form of a long affidavit executed while Thornley was living in Atlanta. To anyone familiar with the true facts of the case and Thornley's suspicious activities, it is a long and involved and deliberate piece of disinformation.[74] In it, Thornley admits that he had met both Ferrie and Banister by the summer of 1962. But yet, they are not the true conspirators. The real ones are people named Slim, Clint, Brother-in-Law, and one Gary Kirstein—nameless, faceless nonentities. (Later, Thornley named one as Jerry M. Brooks, former rightwing Minuteman turned informant to Bill Turner.) Thornley's communications with the HSCA were frequent as he tried to rivet their attention on his new and improved JFK plot.

In 1992, Thornley was paid to make an appearance on the tabloid program *A Current Affair*.[75] Some of what Thornley said on camera is worth quoting:

> I wanted to shoot him. I wanted to assassinate him very much. . . . I wanted him dead. I would have shot him myself. I would have stood there with a rifle and pulled the trigger if I would have had the chance.

Clearly, Thornley's hatred of Kennedy is virulent. And, as some of Garrison's detractors try to imply, Thornley's hatred of Kennedy was not at all new in 1992. It was manifested back in the 1960s. For example, in a letter he wrote to Philip Boatwright in 1964 from Washington, he admits that there was reason for the FBI and Secret Service to suspect he played a role in Kennedy's death. And since he was in the Washington area, and after the Commission decided what to do with him, "I may yet go piss on JFK's grave, RIP."[76] Thornley also had some interesting comments about Garrison. Concerning the DA's indicting him for perjury, Thornley commented, "Garrison, you should have gone after me for conspiracy to commit murder." Of course, the conspiracy Thornley is hinting at is the later manufactured one with Slim, and Brother-in-Law, etc. He also insisted in 1992 that he had not betrayed his friend Oswald, even though he now thought the case was a conspiracy. Thornley was apparently doing his distracting limited hang-out number for bucks this time around. Thornley died in 1997 of a kidney ailment.

What is the sum total of the reliable evidence about Thornley available in the new files? First, Thornley lied about his relationship with the intelligence network surrounding Oswald. He knew all of these players. He also lied about not knowing Oswald in New Orleans in the summer of 1963. He even distorted their respective heights! He said Oswald was five foot, five inches, which was five inches shorter than Thornley. When in fact they were of nearly equal height.[77] The question of course is: Why did he lie about all these material issues? And the answer seems to point to some deeper involvement that he himself suggests in his 1964 letter quoted above. This seems to imply that the Weisberg investigation of the flyers at Jones print shop and the FBI telex about Oswald accompanying Thornley to California and Mexico have some validity to them. It also suggests that Thornley's admission about knowing Oswald was not a communist has some weight. That is, Thornley may have known the truth about Oswald all along and may have helped him construct his cover. Garrison went so far as to suspect that it was Oswald's head imposed on Thornley's body in the famous backyard photograph.[78]

The Baron, the Paines, and Dulles

In his 1967 *Playboy* interview, and then in his 1988 book, Garrison made some cogent remarks about George DeMohrenschildt. In his investigation, Garrison clearly was interested in the puzzling Oswald association into the Dallas White Russian community. As noted in Chapter 8, this was certainly an odd ideological connection. In contrasting the two men Garrison described the Baron as enigmatic and intriguing. He then continued:

> Here you have a wealthy, cultured White Russian émigré who travels in the highest social circles . . . suddenly developing an intimate relationship with an impoverished ex-Marine like Lee Oswald. What did they discuss—last year's season at Biarritz, or how to beat the bank at Monte Carlo?[79]

As noted, the Warren Commission accepted this relationship with nary a blink. Garrison did not. The DA then pointed out that the Baron had a tendency for turning up in some interesting spots at the right times, "for example, in Haiti just before a joint Cuban exile-CIA venture to topple Duvalier . . . and in Guatemala, another CIA training ground, the day before the Bay of Pigs invasion."[80]

Following this lead, the late Philip Melanson pointed out that many of the White Russians brought to the USA after the war came via the Tolstoy Foundation, which was in receipt of yearly subsidies from the CIA. In addition, the Russian Orthodox Church, which had a branch in Dallas also received CIA funds.[81] One only has to look at George's brother Dimitri to understand the CIA influence in the White Russian community. There is correspondence between Dimitri and Allen Dulles, going as far back as 1953.[82] Dimitri was involved with Radio Free Europe, the CIA sponsored propaganda arm which tried to broadcast anti-Communist programming into Eastern Europe. Dimitri was also the co-editor of a journal called *Russian Review* during the fifties and sixties. This appears to have been a CIA related endeavor. Dimitri's friend and co-editor for this publication was a man named William Chamberlin, a conservative columnist for the *Wall Street Journal*. Carol Hewett helped Bruce

Adamson trace the long correspondence between Chamberlin and Allen Dulles. It appears that Chamberlin was an informal adviser to Dulles on the Warren Commission. His area of specialty was advising Dulles on how to steer the Commission away from running into the intelligence ties of George and Dimitri.[83] Some of which led to himself. For in 1954, a young petroleum lawyer named Herbert Itkin attained a meeting with Dulles. Dulles referred him to George DeMohrenschildt. What is so interesting about this referral is that Dulles knew the Baron well enough to understand he used an alias in those days, namely Philip Harbin.[84] Itkin's relationship with DeMohrenschildt went on for a number of years.

As we saw in Chapter 8, George later admitted that he got into contact with Oswald at the request of Dallas CIA station chief J. Walton Moore. Moore was a man who actually dined occasionally at the Baron's home.[85] DeMohrenschildt also told author Edward Epstein that he had been "dealing with the CIA since the early 1950s."[86] George said that although he had never been a paid employee, he had done favors for the Agency and, in turn, he had been helped along in his business contacts. As an example, he pointed out a contract awarded him to do a geologic survey in Yugoslavia in 1957. He had attained this deal through CIA contacts. On his return, he then briefed the CIA about the officials he had met while abroad. Once Moore gave him the go ahead to meet the Oswalds, since Moore said that Marina only spoke Russian, he arranged to drop in when Lee was not there. He then spoke with her in her native tongue about his hometown of Minsk. By the time Oswald returned, he was in her good graces. He then offered to introduce them to the White Russian community in the Dallas area. Since they did not own a car, he offered to chauffeur them around.[87] Thus began the odd pairing referred to by Garrison above.

As many writers have pointed out, one of the most interesting things that the Baron did was to introduce the Oswalds to Ruth and Michael Paine. This occurred as George was preparing to leave the country for Haiti. It was arranged for the Paines to meet the Oswalds at a gathering at the home of Everett Glover on February 22, 1963. The official story has it that Ruth never met George until then, and she never had contact with him afterwards.[88] When Garrison questioned her on this point before a New Orleans Grand Jury, this previous tenet of hers was shown to be in error. Garrison managed to get her to admit that she and Michael were dinner guests at George's house in 1966. At that time, they talked about a copy of the famous backyard photograph which was found in DeMohrenschildt's possessions after the assassination.[89] As author Steven Jones notes: Why would George invite a couple to dinner in 1966, if he had only briefly met them once three years earlier? Further, in his manuscript *I'm a Patsy, I'm a Patsy*, George wrote that he only discussed this backyard photograph with close friends.[90] The question then seems to be: Why did it appear that Ruth was trying to conceal the true nature of her relationship with George DeMohrenschildt?

Before the milestone work of Hewett, Jones, and Barbara LaMonica appeared, very few authors noted the hidden associations of the Paines. They were painted as simply Good Samaritans doing William Penn's work by the Warren Commission. In fact, the only Commissioner who raised any questions about them at all was Richard Russell. For him, they were simply too good to be true. One of the oddest things about the Paines is that someone on the Commission, or with the Bureau, seemed to anticipate that "too good" image. For the Texas-based Quaker couple had high-level acquaintances in the Eastern Establishment vouching for their good character right after the Warren Commission opened shop. In December of 1963, the FBI interviewed a couple in Philadelphia who were friends of the Paines. Frederick Osborne Jr. and his wife Nancy testified to the Paines's "religiosity, good character, and innocence in having anything to do with the assassination of President Kennedy."[91] Frederick's father was a close associate of Allen Dulles. They both graduated from Princeton. In Osborne's personal papers at that Ivy League university are a number of letters between he and the Dulles brothers. After the war Osborne and Allen Dulles co-founded an organization called Crusade for Freedom. This was an early Agency effort resembling Radio Free Europe. And as one could predict, this organization merged with Radio Free Europe in 1962.

But this is not the only connection to Allen Dulles and his circle that the Paine family had. And, as we shall see, Dulles himself recognized this second one. As an OSS officer operating out of Switzerland during World War II, Dulles got to know a woman named Mary Bancroft. Both personally and professionally. That is, he ran her as an agent, and he had a continuing sexual affair with her.[92] Although the affair eventually cooled, they remained friends for decades after. Bancroft was also a friend of publisher Henry Luce.[93] Bancroft's best and longest lasting female friend was Ruth Forbes. Or as she said, she "knew the mother of Michael Paine where Oswald stayed. She was Ruth Forbes, a very good friend of mine."[94] When Ruth divorced Michael's father, George Lyman Paine, she married Arthur Young and now became known as Ruth Forbes Young. Ruth and Arthur now became intimates of Bancroft.[95] To show how this Eastern Establishment circle felt about the Kennedys, Bancroft wrote a letter to Norman Mailer in the seventies saying that "I might call a Kennedy 'trash'—but never my friend 'trashy.'"[96]

Arthur Young was a New Age type and also an inventor. He was one of the creators of the Bell Helicopter, which made him wealthy. Arthur was responsible for attaining a high tech/high security clearance job at Bell Helicopter in Fort

Worth for his son through marriage. Michael had previously worked for the Franklin Institute, a CIA conduit.[97] When Arthur got a clearance for Michael, the young couple moved to Irving, Texas and Michael got his job at Bell. When asked by the Commission about his security clearance, Michael said he did not know what the classification was.[98] This is another statement made by the Paines that lacks credibility.

Because Ruth was still interested in the Russian language, the Paines became part of the local Russian expatriate community. Which was quite conservative, anti-Soviet, and with a parish church, which, as noted, was reportedly CIA affiliated. As George Michael Evica notes, this was a curious fit. For Quakers are usually liberal and have their own special church customs, which are not at all like Russian Orthodox. As many have noted, one of the greatest failures of the American media was its showing in the Kennedy assassination: Its acceptance of Jack Ruby as a bar owner who felt homicidal pity for Jackie Kennedy, its failure to look into the mystery of 544 Camp Street, its lack of curiosity about Oswald, and also its acceptance of Ruth and Michael Paine at face value. The "Good Samaritan" Quakers were in fact extensions of the Eastern Establishment in Dallas.

Michael Paine's ancestors are Boston Brahmins of the Forbes and Cabot first families of America. Michael's grand uncle, Cameron Forbes, was both governor and later ambassador, to the Philippines.[99] Prior to his death in 1959 he joined his Cabot relatives on the board of United Fruit.[100] One of these relatives, Thomas Dudley Cabot, was Michael's cousin. Thomas was actually a former president of the United Fruit Company. In 1951 he was working in the State Department Office of International Security Affairs. Thomas' brother, John M. Cabot, was also in the State Department around this time, and was exchanging information with Maurice Gatlin about the preparations of the CIA-United Fruit overthrow of Jacobo Arbenz. In the early sixties, Thomas was president of the Gibraltar Steamship Corporation, which leased uninhabited land ninety miles off the coast of Honduras named Swan Island. Gibraltar was a CIA front. It owned no ships. But it was on that island, through the Gibraltar front, that David Phillips established Radio Swan, the CIA radio station broadcasting into Cuba, Mexico, and Central America. During the Bay of Pigs invasion, Radio Swan broadcast secret messages to certain people in the know about that operation.[101]

Ruth Paine's family originated from New York before moving to Ohio. Her father, William Avery Hyde, was a high executive for Nationwide Insurance. He had worked for the OSS in World War II.[102] He ended up becoming the Agency for International Development's (AID) regional director for all of Latin America. John Gilligan, a former AID director later said that AID was infiltrated from top to bottom by CIA agents. So that the CIA could plant operatives in all types of operations abroad.[103] And, in fact, as Steve Jones discovered, one of Hyde's reports went from the State Department to the CIA.[104] Ruth told Jim Garrison during her grand jury appearance that her father "was on leave to an agency called the International Cooperative Alliance." This may be one reason why Ruth tried to say she only met George DeMohrenschildt once. Because George told the Warren Commission that he also traveled abroad for the ICA.[105] Interestingly, William Avery Hyde got this contract with AID in 1964, the year after the Kennedy assassination.

It is important to establish this familial background for the Paines and to always keep it in mind. Because this intermingling of wealth, diplomacy, and intelligence work helps explain the remarkable occurrence of espionage employment in the family. In that summer of 1963, Ruth made a cross country trip visiting certain friends and relatives. Before Ruth came down to pick up Marina—and finally achieve her goal of separating Marina from her husband—she had been visiting her sister in Falls Church, Virginia. Falls Church adjoins Langley, which then housed the new headquarters of the CIA. When Ruth appeared before the New Orleans grand jury, Jim Garrison observed that her sister's occupation was being withheld by the government. The DA asked why that was so. Ruth replied she was not even aware it was classified. So Garrison asked her what agency of government her sister worked for. Ruth replied she did not know.[106]

This is the fourth sworn statement by the couple which begs credibility. But there is a reason for the evasiveness. Ruth Paine was the younger sister of Sylvia Hyde Hoke. In 1993, a CIA security file was declassified which revealed that Sylvia had been employed by the Agency for a number of years prior to 1963 as a psychologist. Ruth, who had just spent a couple of weeks with Sylvia, somehow never knew where her sister went to work in the morning and was not even curious enough to ask, even though Sylvia's association with the CIA had been printed in the City Directory.[107] And to top it off, Sylvia's husband John Hoke, like Ruth's father, worked for AID. Ruth did mention this fact in her appearance before the New Orleans grand jury, but this was just before the exposure of AID made it into the press. Odd that Ruth would know who her sister's husband worked for, but not her sister.

As noted previously, by his association with Chamberlin, Allen Dulles was aware of how compromising all these associations were to him and his service on the Warren Commission. In fact, according to one of his biographers, he actually joked about it:

> Dulles joked in private that the [JFK] conspiracy buffs would have had a field day if
> they had known . . . he had actually been in Dallas three weeks before the murder . . .

that one of Mary Bancroft's childhood friends had turned out to be a landlady for
Marina Oswald . . . and that the landlady was a well-known leftist with distant
ties to the family of Alger Hiss.[108]

This tantalizing quote does not just reveal that Dulles understood how
dangerous the exposure of all these associations were to his veneer as an impar-
tial investigator. But that last clause suggests that he understood how important
Ruth Paine's veneer as a "leftist" was in her association with the Oswalds. Yet
Dulles died in 1969. This extensive work on the Paines by researchers like Jones,
Barbara LaMonica, and Carol Hewett was not published until the nineties. It
is quite interesting that Dulles knew about it back then.

And let us make no mistake about it. As this background material on the
Paines indicates, a veneer is now what it appears to be. As Steve Jones and
Carol Hewett have pointed out, the ARRB declassified an interesting FBI
report about a man talking to certain college students at Luby's Restaurant
near SMU in Dallas. The man would accost certain students, and then praise
the Castro revolution to them, while protesting America's policies toward
Cuba. The man claimed to know a communist, an ex-Marine who had recently
returned to the USA with a Russian wife, clearly a reference to Oswald. This
event occurred in April of 1963. Someone thought this a little unusual for Dallas at that time. So an FBI agent came down and started interviewing some of
the students the man had talked to. After one student physically described the
man, the agent pulled out a picture of Michael Paine. The student said Paine
was the man.[109] So the question with Michael Paine is this: What would a man
living off of trust funds from the Cabot and Forbes families—which he was at
the time—and with a security clearance from Bell Helicopter, why would such
a man be promoting Castro in Dallas with college students?

The answer appears to be that he was doing the same thing Oswald was
about to do. For in *Brush With History*, Eric Tagg's book about sheriff's deputy
Buddy Walthers, he reports that Walthers was one of the officers at the Paine
household on the twenty-second. He was there to do a search and seizure since
the authorities learned that Marina Oswald was living there and her husband's
possessions were likely located there. Walthers later talked about finding several
"metal filing cabinets full of letters, maps, records, and index cards, with names
of pro-Castro sympathizers." Sheriff Decker mentioned the metal boxes in his
official report provided to the Warren Commission. This created quite a stir,
and therefore the Warren Commission made it go away in the Speculation
and Rumors part of its report.[110] One can safely guess that some of the SMU
students who agreed with Paine about Castro had their names inserted in those
file boxes.

Why is it a "safe guess?" Because the collecting of the names of leftist sympathizers continued with Ruth during the days of American involvement in the Contra War in Nicaragua. Sue Wheaton was a volunteer for a religious group who journeyed to Nicaragua to help the Sandinistas consolidate their leftist revolution. There she met Ruth as part of another group. But Ruth's group ran a sawmill project on the east coast of Nicaragua, a Contra holdout and nexus of CIA based activities. Further, Ruth was associated with a man names Jon Roise who was trying to recruit former Contra members to speak at Casa Ben Linder in Nicaragua. Whenever Wheaton would encounter Ruth, she said Ruth would be taking copious notes and be accompanied by others who would take snapshots and also tape record proceedings. Wheaton concluded that Ruth was taking down information about Americans in Nicaragua who opposed U.S. policy there and that she was probably then giving it to members of the American Embassy who she said she knew.[111]

This posturing as a liberal Quaker, but then acting as a surveillance agent, was not just vaguely suggested by Allen Dulles. It was clearly suspected by other intelligence agencies about the Paines. And again, it surfaced through Garrison's grand jury proceedings. When a member of the grand jury asked Marina Oswald if she still associated with Ruth Paine, Marina replied that she did not. When she was asked why she did not, Marina said that it was upon the advice of the Secret Service. She then elaborated on this by explaining that they had told her it would not look good if the pubic found out that, "she [Ruth] had friends over there and it would be bad for me if people find out connection between me and Ruth and CIA." An assistant DA then asked, "In other words, you were left with the distinct impression that she was in some way connected with the CIA?" To which Marina replied in the affirmative.[112]

In Nicaragua, because the situation was so confrontational and since there was no powerful mainstream media to protect her, the suspicion of Ruth being an asset of the Agency was widespread. Steve Jones followed up on Sue Wheaton's information with another female worker who knew Ruth in Nicaragua and befriended her. When Ruth's surveillance activities finally became too suspicious in Nicaragua, the two women drove to Costa Rica for some R&R. When they arrived near the Costa Rican camp, some people approached the car to help them out. When they saw it was Ruth, they walked away moaning, "Oh no, its Ruth Paine. Keep her away from us. She's CIA." It got so bad, the pair had to leave.[113]

When they got back to the USA they remained friends. The woman actually won Ruth's confidence. For Ruth admitted to her that her father, William

Hyde, had worked for the CIA. She even told her that she had an estranged daughter who would not talk to her until she came to grips with the evil she had done in her life. When the woman asked Ruth, "What evil?" she clammed up. But the friend is certain that she was talking about the Kennedy assassination since the assassination was the previous context of the discussion.[114]

If that is so, then what "evil" could Ruth be talking about? One instance could be her dubious testimony about the call from Robert Adams, which could have placed Oswald outside of Dealey Plaza on November 22. But Ruth also figured prominently in producing questionable evidence to help the FBI and Warren Commission finger Oswald for a previously unsolved rifle assault. This was an unsuccessful shooting attempt at General Edwin Walker back on the evening of April 10, 1963. It is important to note that in the entire nearly eight month span the Dallas Police had this case under inquiry, Oswald's name never surfaced in any part of their investigation. Let us now observe how a German newspaper and Ruth Paine combined to give the Commission and the Bureau pretexts to convict Oswald in the public mind in the Walker case.

On November 29, a reporter named Helmet Hubert Muench published an article for a conservative West German newspaper published out of Munich. There were actually two articles, one a straight story and one a transcript of an alleged conversation with Walker on the twenty-third—and perhaps a follow up on the next day—by what appears to be another German reporter named Hasso Thorsten.[115] Thorsten had called Walker when he was in Shreveport on a speaking engagement right after Kennedy's murder. The point of both articles was that Walker had told the paper that it was Oswald who had fired at him in April, that this was known earlier—that is, before the assassination—and yet nothing was done about it. But if something had been done then Oswald would not have shot Kennedy. The problem with this story is that Walker denied under oath saying this to Thorsten, and in no uncertain terms.[116] In fact, Walker said that the accusation against Oswald in his case was not made until after the interview, so he could not have said such a thing.

But then, a day later, on November 30, a piece of evidence emerged from Ruth Paine's home. The Dallas authorities had spent a large part of two days looking through Ruth's home for evidence against Oswald. Their inventory list was forty-nine pages long. Somehow they missed a note which was inside a book. It was a note allegedly written by Oswald in Russian which ominously tells Marina what to do if he was in jail, and how to find him there.[117] Why did Ruth produce this book at the time? She said Marina had to have two books with her. One was entitled *Our Child* and the other was *Book of Helpful Instructions*. She had to have them since Marina used them each day. (This while Marina was being detained at a hotel and under twenty-four-hour watch by the FBI and Secret Service.) The note was then found in the latter book by the Secret Service. The note was not dated and did not have Oswald's latent fingerprints on it.[118] This, even though the note took up almost one side of a sheet of paper. But also interesting is this: the FBI did happen to take seven latent fingerprints off the note; yet none of them matched Lee or Marina. Prior to this, the police had retrieved photos of the exterior of Walker's house from Ruth Paine's garage. It was the confluence of these three elements—the news article, the photo, and the note—that provoked the FBI to take a new look at the Walker case. Yet even Wesley Liebeler of the Warren Commission asked an obvious question: Why would Oswald keep the incriminating note and photos around for well over seven months?[119]

The problem with this odd evidence is that it does not at all fit the parameters of the crime. First, the shooting of Walker vitiates the marksmanship in the Kennedy case. In the latter, one has to believe that Oswald fired three shots from a manual bolt action rifle in six seconds and got two of three direct hits at a moving target from as far away as 270 feet. Something that the best Army snipers could not do.[120] In the Walker case, Walker was sitting at his desk in his study, a stationary target. The sniper had time to line up the still target. The distance was approximately 30 yards. And he missed. True, it was night, but Walker's house was illuminated by the lights from a church parking lot next door. In a discussion with the officers after a reconstruction, the police were stupefied as to how the gunman could have missed. Walker himself reportedly said that whoever it was had to have been a lousy shot.[121] There were two principal witnesses. The first was Robert Surrey, an aide to Walker. Surrey had told the police that four nights prior to the shooting he had seen two men sitting in a brown Ford behind Walker's house. They got out of the car and walked around Walker's home. When the car pulled out, he followed it. He could detect no license on the car. He lost the car near downtown Dallas.[122] The other witness was young Kirk Coleman. Coleman's testimony corroborated Surrey. He said that he saw two men drive off in separate cars from Walker's home after the shooting attempt. One of the men threw something down on the floor of his car before pulling away. Concurring with Surrey, Coleman said that neither man resembled Oswald.[123] Oswald, according to the Commission, did not drive, and did not own a car. Further, who could be his accomplice? The FBI agents in Dallas were particularly impressed with Coleman as a witness. But Coleman never testified to the Commision.[124] In fact, Walker complained to the Commission that he had been blocked from getting any info on the case since the FBI took it over. Also, that he could not talk to Coleman since the witness had been told to keep his mouth shut.[125] This makes perfect sense in light of Hoover's upcoming agenda on the Walker case.

For by June 10, Hoover—after leaking to the press that Oswald had shot at Walker—was shutting down the inquiry. Even though his agents in the field came to no conclusion in the case.[126] In fact, the chief suspect prior to the FBI taking over the case was a man named William Duff, a former employee of Walker. Walker's lawyer said that Duff had actually admitted to firing on Walker to a former girlfriend.[127]

Also, why would a communist be shooting at both a rightwing ideologue like Walker and the most liberal president since Franklin Roosevelt? Further, it was Kennedy who pushed Walker out of his command after a thirty year career in the service. This was for distributing rightwing, John Birch Society literature to his troops. No one from the Commission posed these obvious questions. The Commission was enthralled by Ruth Paine now producing questionable evidence to implicate Oswald in the shooting.

And the exhibits produced by Ruth, almost by necessity, had to be dubious. As mentioned above, the FBI cut off Walker from all communications about their investigation. In fact, it appears that they also deliberately misinformed him. During his testimony, Wesley Liebeler showed Walker many photo exhibits. Near the end of his testimony Walker said that he had heard the FBI had matched up the bullet fired at him with the alleged Oswald rifle.[128] This last statement explains why, among all the photos shown to him, Walker was never shown the most important one of all: The bullet the FBI said they had matched up to Oswald's rifle. For they were now saying that it was a 6.5 caliber, copper-jacketed bullet. One compatible with the alleged rifle in evidence. Yet, this was not the bullet the police retrieved from Walker's house that night and Walker had held in his hand. That bullet was a 30.06, steel jacketed bullet.[129] As the reader can see, the combination of Ruth Paine with the FBI allowed the Warren Commission to manufacture a case that likely did not exist. As we will see, this will recur.

The pictures of the outside of Walker's home, along with the famous backyard photographs—the ones depicting Oswald with a rifle and handgun plus communist literature in his hands—both were found at the Paine home. The official story maintains that both photos were taken with an Imperial Reflex camera. Now, during its two searches, the police confiscated three cameras. These were listed on their November 23 inventory report. One was an American made Stereo Realist. One was a 35 mm Russian camera called a Cuera 2. The third was listed as a small German camera with black case and chain.[130] This last was the miniature Minox spy camera which, as we shall see, the FBI desperately wanted to go away. There was an evidentiary problem here in relation to the photos. All three cameras produced pictures equivalent to 35 mm photos. Yet the photos in evidence were developed on 620 roll film.[131]

On December 8, two weeks after the Paine household search was concluded, with three cameras already in evidence, Robert Oswald picked up a box of Oswald's articles at Ruth Paine's house. Inside this box was the Imperial Reflex camera, which *did use* 620 roll film.[132] When the policemen who searched the house were asked about this camera, four of five said they did not see it during their search. And they did recall going through many boxes.[133] Robert kept the camera for over two months. On February 24 he turned it over to the FBI. On February 1, Marina said the Cuera and the Stereo Realist appeared to be Oswald's two cameras.[134] On February 19, Marina now said she could not recognize the Stereo Realist. Then on February 25, when shown the newly retrieved Imperial Reflex, she now said it was Oswald's.[135] In the interval between the February 1 and February 19 FBI interviews, Marina had temporarily lived with Robert Oswald who had the Imperial Reflex at that time.[136] On August 12, the Stereo Realist camera was finally given to Ruth Paine, who said it was hers.[137] Apparently, she never looked for it in that entire six month time span.

On December 4, five days after she delivered Oswald's "Walker Note" in Marina's book, Ruth Paine was visited by two Secret Service agents. They were returning the "Walker Note" since they thought *it was from her.* (Recall Marina's grand jury testimony about the Secret Service suspecting Ruth was associated with the CIA.) Ruth said she had not seen it before.[138] But she now used this opportunity to give the agents even more exhibits. As in the Walker instance, these would help the FBI and Warren Commission bolster another dubious part of their case: namely that Oswald had been to Mexico City prior to returning to Dallas in early October. Ruth said the following items were found in her home, more specifically in the chest of drawers used by Marina. One was a "Rules for Betting" card used at a thoroughbred racetrack. A second item was a Spanish-English dictionary with a handwritten notation "watch Jai-lai game." Yet when checking on this, the Commission learned that proper attire was required at these games, which Oswald did not have. Also in the Spanish-English dictionary were the accompanying flyleaf notations: "Phone embassy," "Get bus tickets," "Buy Silver Bracelet," and "Buy Record." Ruth also turned over a Merriam-Webster English dictionary and six picture postcards with no writing or stamps, but depicting Mexican tableaux.[139] And as noted above, Ruth gave the agents a silver bracelet which had "the name Marina written in a crude fashion on the name plate part of the bracelet."[140] The Commission noted that this last did not really prove anything since it could have been picked up in Dallas at a department store.[141] But further as Steve Jones noted in a talk at the COPA Conference in Washington in 1995, when Ruth picked up Marina in September of 1963, she said Lee did not say anything about going to Mexico. Once Oswald was apprehended, he never admitted to being in Mexico.[142]

While sequestered at the Inn of the Six Flags in Arlington, Marina was asked about her husband's activities after she left New Orleans. She first replied that she thought he stayed in New Orleans and looked for work.[143] She told the FBI the same thing on November 29. Oswald was going to stay in New Orleans to see if he could find work. If not, he would then return to Dallas. She then said she had no knowledge of any trip to Mexico by Lee in September, and she added that, to her knowledge, Oswald had *never* been to Mexico.[144] When they asked her why she made that last comment, she made a telling reply. She said that she figured they were interested in that topic since it had been on television. As we shall see later, the CIA had released information that said Oswald had been to Mexico City and visited both the Soviet and Cuban consulates there. Marina was repeatedly asked about this topic on six more occasions. But she continued to deny that Oswald had ever said anything about being in Mexico City.

In February she signed a deal with an entity called Tex-Italia films for the rights to her story. She would go on to make 132,500 dollars from this mysterious company, which never produced a film about her.[145] In February, before the Warren Commission, she now reversed her story: Oswald had told her he was going to Mexico.[146] And she now backed up what the CIA was saying: Oswald went to Mexico City to get a visa to Cuba. (Marina would eventually go overboard on this point when she said Oswald told her he was going to hijack a plane and make the pilot take him to Cuba.[147]) Again, the Commission now had some corroboration for a trip to Mexico that no one recalled Oswald mentioning, and he himself denied. And it began with Ruth Paine.[148]

Let us conclude this section on the Paines with what is perhaps the most ignored piece of key evidence in all of the literature on the JFK assassination. On November 23, 1963 mailman H. W. Reed was at Powell's Waffle Shop in Irving, Texas, for his morning cup of coffee. He was sitting with two colleagues named C. E. Vaughn and Ray Roddy, and they were talking about the assassination. As Roddy got up to pay the cashier, Reed overheard her say something to him about a package being held for Oswald.[149] This turned out to be true. But it is necessary to note that between the day Reed first heard about it versus the day he signed his affidavit constitutes a span of nine days. This may be important, because if one looks at this package today, there is something odd about it. Actually it may be unexplainable. At the bottom of the address, written directly on the parcel, are the words Irving, Texas. Yet, right above this—obliterating the rest of the Irving address—is a mail address sticker. The sticker reads as follows:

Lee Oswald, 601 West Nassau St., Dallas, Texas.

And here begins the mystery. For that particular address does not exist in Dallas. Now, what makes this doubly odd is that it would only appear logical that underneath the sticker with the new address, a legitimate address in Irving does exist. And this could be read if the new address sticker was removed. Therefore, why did the FBI not apply a chemical to peel the adhesive off the back of the sticker, thereby cleanly exposing any address below? There is no evidence this was done, or even contemplated.[150] Because it was not done, we do not know when the new address sticker was attached. It could have been attached afterwards in order to blot out the name and address of the person it was mailed to. But because this new sticker with a non-existent address is on the package, it eventually ended up in the "Nixie Section" of the post office— the place where undeliverable mail ends up.

As noted, it was nine days between when Reed first heard about this package and when he signed a legal affidavit concerning it. Therefore, on the twenty-third, at least four people had already heard about the package. And very likely more, since the cashier at the restaurant knew about it and was spreading the word about it that morning. Yet it was not until another ten days *after* Reed's affidavit, on December 12, that the post office turned over the parcel to the FBI. Again, no explanation is given as to why it took three weeks for the Bureau to get custody of the evidence. Especially since many people were talking about it both inside and outside the post office. When the FBI did get hold of the parcel, it was through Post Office Inspector Harry Holmes, who picked it up from the postmaster in Irving. As many authors have noted, Holmes was a prized FBI informant inside the post office who cooperated mightily with the Bureau in more than one way to help make the case against Oswald. Now, according to the FBI, Postmaster Twilley told Holmes the parcel was discovered in Irving on December 4.[151] In light of the fact that the cashier at Reed's restaurant had heard about it on November 23, this makes no sense. It boggles the imagination that a parcel with the name of Kennedy's alleged killer could lay around the post office unnoticed for twelve days. This is at the same time that Oswald's name was being broadcast on TV and radio throughout each and every day in that two week interval. But the fact that it was not in custody for twenty days, and it was given to Holmes at that time, allows us to question when the sticker was applied.

In an FBI Airtel of December 13, the Bureau says there is no indication the parcel was ever mailed. This is not really accurate. There is a postmark on the package, in which the date is not quite decipherable. There is no postage visible on the one side of the package we can see in photos. In the airtel, the Bureau says something else which is hard to swallow. It says that Twilley questioned

numerous persons at the Irving Post Office and could not find out any information about the parcel. Are we really to believe that no one recalled handling
the package? Even after the assassination? Why didn't the FBI itself do the
questioning about this important piece of evidence? Further, Holmes said that
when he got the package it had already been partly opened. Could someone
really have forgotten partly opening a parcel with Oswald's name on it? Inside
the parcel was found a sheet of brown wrapping paper. Although the FBI called
it a bag, it was described as being open at each end. Which would more closely
resemble wrapping paper. In the FBI photo exhibits there is no tape measure
next to the paper. Further, attorney Carol Hewett, who has actually handled
the package, states that it is actually cut off at one end, making it harder to
reconstruct how long both the envelope and the paper inside was.[152] The Bureau
tells us that the wrap is eighteen inches long. It generally recalls the brown
paper discovered in the Texas School Book depository that the police accused
Oswald of using to form a sack to bring his Mannlicher Carcano rifle to the
Depository on November 22, 1963. One last point to make about this parcel.
Not any part of it, the parcel itself, the paper inside, nor the corrugation, none
of it bore any latent fingerprints.[153]

How does this all relate to Ruth Paine? On November 20, a package was
sent from the Irving Post Office to Lee Oswald at 2515 W. Fifth Street, Irving,
Texas. This is the address of Ruth and Michael Paine. It was not delivered at
that time since there was postage due on it. On November 23, the Dallas Police
searched Ruth's house for a second time and found the postage due notice with
instructions to pick up and sign for the parcel.[154] A deputy was dispatched to
the Irving post office. According to Officer Gus Rose's HSCA deposition, the
deputy was told the parcel had been picked up.[155] As we have seen from the H.
W. Reed affidavit, this was false. And it began the cover up about this potentially crucial piece of evidence. In February of 1964, in an interview with postal
inspector Roy Armstrong, Ruth Paine tried to imply that this notice was for
magazines. Which it was not.[156]

On November 26, something startling happened. On the Property Clerk's
Invoice for the search of Ruth Paine's home on the twenty-third, the following
item appears, "Postal Form, label bearing name George A. Bouhe, 4740 Homer
St., Dallas, Tex., Postal Form bearing name Lee Oswald dated 11/20/63." This
perhaps means that the form for Oswald was then attached to one for Bouhe.
But what on earth would a postage due form for Bouhe be doing at Ruth
Paine's? And who would attach it to the form due for Oswald's mystery package? And why? Bouhe is the man who's name surfaced in Marina Oswald's
testimony to Garrison's grand jury in an odd way. Marina mentioned him as
one of her English tutors in Dallas. Garrison asked if she knew that Bouhe

lived a door down from Jack Ruby; that they knew each other, and shared a common swimming pool. Marina said she did know that. Because right after the assassination, Bouhe came to visit her. He told her that it was all just a coincidence that he happened to live next door to her husband's killer.[157] Bouhe was the "organization man" who kept the files for the White Russian community.

It is important to recall that the first attempt to mail the parcel was on Wednesday the twentieth. It failed for postage due. But Oswald was at the Paine home on Thursday, the twenty-first, the night before the assassination. If the mailing had been successful, Oswald likely would have opened the package and then handled the paper. He probably would have discarded it. If he had, one of two things would likely have followed: 1.) The police would have found the discarded wrapping paper, or 2.) Ruth Paine would have found it. Either way, the police now would have fresh fingerprints on wrapping paper resembling the sack allegedly used by Oswald to carry a rifle into the Texas School Book Depository. This is crucial because the official story states that Oswald stored the Mannlicher-Carcano murder rifle in the Paine garage. To have Oswald's prints, and only his prints, on a sheet of discarded wrapping paper would have been strong evidence that the alleged assassin had wrapped the murder weapon the night before.

The incredible thing about the above case against the Paines is this: this does not even come close to exhausting it. For example, to mention just two further instances, one could detail their role in attempting to make Oswald's Minox camera disappear—a project in which they cooperated again with the FBI—and in which, for all intents and purposes, they appear to be working as accessories after the fact in order to conceal who Oswald actually was.[158] One could discuss the truly bewildering markings on Ruth's pocket calendar—and her even more bewildering explanation for them—concerning when Oswald allegedly ordered the rifle in evidence.[159] One could mention more startling statements. Ruth's excuse for latching onto Marina Oswald was that she wanted to attain more fluency in the Russian language. Yet she had studied Russian since 1957, there were many Russian speakers in the White Russian community she frequented, and third, she had a Russian tutor in Dallas named Dorothy Gravitis, who had been born in the Soviet province of Latvia.[160] Finally, Ruth Paine *taught* Russian at St. Mark's School for Boys![161] So why on earth would she need Marina to teach her Russian?

Another instance, when Oswald requested Ruth to contact an attorney for him, she said she was stunned and appalled because he thought he was innocent and could ask anything of her.[162] Or Michael Paine's reversal of his Commission testimony about seeing Oswald at the police station the night of the assassination and his now revised statement about "he was proud of what he'd done. He felt that he'd be recognized now as somebody who did something."[163] Or Michael Paine's inexplicable mentioning to the *Houston Post* on November 23 that Oswald may have been involved in the Walker shooting.[164] What is stunning about the literature on the Kennedy case, nearly half a century of it, over one thousand books and innumerable articles, is that until the work of Hewett, Jones, and LaMonica appeared in the nineties, no writer had ever done a sustained inquiry into the Paines, their relationship with DeMohrenschildt, and their ties to the White Russian community in Dallas. Jim Garrison tried to explore it, but too much evidence was being concealed in 1967. As the reader can see, there is a veritable cornucopia of associations, statements, and circumstances that arouse suspicion about the couple. As we shall see, both the HSCA and the ARRB ignored them also. In light of the above, they are truly a charmed couple. Until now. Suffice it to say, if there is ever a reopening of the JFK case, the Paines should be on the short list to be sworn before a grand jury.

Shaw, Ferrie, and Banister: Friends and Partners

In Chapter 1 the author introduced Freeport Sulphur and its subsidiaries Moa Bay Mining and Nicaro Nickel. These companies all had large investments in Cuba prior to Castro's revolution. And this ended up being one of the ways that Garrison connected Clay Shaw with David Ferrie. This came about for two reasons. First, with Castro taking over their operations in Cuba, Freeport was attempting to investigate bringing in nickel ore from Cuba through Canada, which still had trade relations with Cuba. The ore would then be refined in Louisiana, either at a plant already in New Orleans or at another plant in Braithwaite. Shaw, an impresario of international trade, was on this exploratory team for Freeport. And he and two other men had been flown to Canada by Ferrie as part of this effort.[165] More evidence of this connection through Freeport was found during their investigation of Guy Banister. Banister apparently knew about another flight taken by Shaw with an official of Freeport, likely Charles Wight, to Cuba. Again the pilot was David Ferrie.[166] Another reason this Freeport connection was important to Garrison is that he found a witness named James Plaine in Houston who said that Mr. Wight of Freeport Sulphur had contacted him in regards to an assassination plot against Castro.[167] Considering the amount of money Freeport was about to lose in Cuba, plus the number of Eastern Establishment luminaries associated with the company—such as Jock Whitney, Jean Mauze, and Godfrey Rockefeller—it is not surprising that such a thing was contemplated within their ranks.[168]

The above is just one instance of Shaw being associated with Ferrie, a fact Shaw denied at his trial. As Jim Garrison revealed in his book, *On the Trail of the Assassins*, he had statements from a number of witnesses who had seen the two together. And this is besides the witnesses in Clinton and Jackson. These witnesses included Jules Kimble who took a plane trip with the two men; David Logan who, after being introduced to Shaw by Ferrie, had a homosexual tryst with Shaw; Nicholas and Mathilda Tadin, who saw Ferrie with Shaw at the New Orleans Airport where Ferrie was giving their son flying lessons; and Raymond Broshears who had a drink with Shaw and Ferrie, and later joined them for dinner.[169]

Today, there can be no doubt about this point. And the indications are that Shaw's lawyers knew he was committing perjury when he denied this. For in the files secured by the Assassination Records Review Board there are now contributions by Shaw's own defense team. This collection by attorneys Bill and Ed Wegmann includes a report by Wackenhut—a detective agency the Wegmanns hired—of an interview of a secretary who worked for attorney G. Wray Gill. Gill had employed David Ferrie as an investigator on some of his cases, including his work for Carlos Marcello. The secretary, named Sandra Anderson, told the detectives that she had seen a photograph depicting Shaw with Ferrie.[170] (The reader should note, along with the photo taken in Clinton, this makes two pictures of the pair.) In March of 1967, J. Edgar Hoover had similar information that contradicted Shaw's denials. Aura Lee was a former secretary to Shaw at the International Trade Mart. She was now employed by the Heart Fund at Ochsner Clinic. After watching a press conference by Shaw at which he denied knowing Ferrie, she stated to Dr. Charles Moore, among others, that she had seen Ferrie enter Clay Shaw's office at the Trade Mart several times. It happened so often that she thought Ferrie had privileged entry into his office.[171] Also, in one of Harold Weisberg's unpublished manuscripts called *Mailer's Tale*, Weisberg wrote that he knew about Shaw's sado-masochistic sexual activities through his brother-in-law, Jack Kety. Because Kety had Ferrie as a patient.[172]

Tommy Baumler would be interviewed by Harold Weisberg for Garrison. But later on, in 1981, he was interviewed by controversial attorney Bernard Fensterwald. At that time he told him that Banister and Shaw were quite close and that "Clay Shaw, Banister, and Guy Johnson made up the intelligence apparatus in New Orleans."[173] Johnson was a former Naval officer in World War II. By 1950 he had a Top Secret clearance granted by the Office of Naval Intelligence while working for the Chief of Naval Operations.[174] He was part of the effort to get Sergio Arcacha Smith flown out of Castro's Cuba and into New Orleans. And he was originally part of Shaw's defense team. Further certifying a Banister-Shaw nexus is information given by local New Orleans reporter Jack Dempsey to Bill Davy and the author. Dempsey had a deceased acquaintance named Jules Fontana, a lawyer from Metaire. Fontana knew Shaw and had seen Banister in Shaw's office more than once.[175]

Another witness who clearly connected Shaw and Banister was Joe Newbrough. Newbrough was one of the men in the office who Banister would use to do any of the private eye work that popped in. He told author William Davy that he recalled an instance with Ferrie being in Banister's office. Banister then called out to Newbrough and asked him to get Clay Shaw on the phone for him. So he called the Trade Mart and got through to Shaw. When he did, Banister told him to give the phone to Ferrie.[176]

The Search for Clay Bertrand

Garrison also became convinced that Clay Shaw was the mysterious Clay Bertrand who had first sent some young homosexual clients to Dean Andrews, and then called him to go to Dallas to defend Oswald. In his book, Garrison notes a number of witnesses in the French Quarter who stepped forward on this, but only after he himself stopped going on missions there seeking confirmation on the issue.[177] Once Garrison left it up to his lower profile staffers, they began to get results. The first place that gave them a positive ID on Shaw as Bertrand was a bartender at Cosimo's. Which makes sense since, in his Warren Commission testimony, Andrews described this as a "freaky little joint," which was the last place at which he saw Bertrand.[178] When pressed, the bartender there said that Bertrand was Shaw and he had seen him on local TV with some important people. Garrison then got two more confirmations on this in French Quarter bars. Finally, a man named William Morris signed an affidavit saying he knew Shaw as Clay Bertrand. And the underlying message was that this was common knowledge.[179]

Which it was. Something Garrison does not reveal in his book is a specific reason his staff did not want him to go into the Quarter with them in search of Bertrand. As detailed in the previous chapter, Garrison had done irreparable damage to the tourist business in New Orleans and forced many bar owners out of business during his raids on the B girl drinking rackets. Therefore, out of spite, many of these people who worked there did not want to cooperate with him. When Joan Mellen did the research on her biography of Garrison, she found two witnesses, Ricky Planche and Barbara Bennett, who admitted this to her. Namely, that they knew Shaw was Bertrand, but they would not tell Garrison because of the economic damage he had inflicted on the French Quarter.[180] The idea that this knowledge was widespread is also confirmed by a source from outside the area. When Edgar Tatro went down to New Orleans to attend the Shaw trial, he was a twenty-two-year-old first-year English teacher. He went out one night in the Quarter. Since Tatro was from Boston and spoke with a distinctive Boston accent, a native New Orleans resident asked him what he was in town for. He said he was there for the Clay Shaw trial. The man started to giggle. Tatro asked: What was so funny? The man replied, "Look, everyone down here knows that Shaw is Bertrand. But that poor devil Garrison can't prove it to save his soul."[181]

There were two other instances of Shaw using the Bertrand alias that were different in kind. In one case he wrote it himself, and in the other, he spoke it to a police officer. Since Shaw did much receiving of guests for his trade missions, he knew a place called the VIP room at the Moisant Airport. This was a lounge for customers who used Eastern Air Lines frequently. When Garrison's office heard that a customer had signed the name "Clay Bertrand" on the register, the DA sent his investigators there to locate and photograph the book—it was dated December 14, 1966—and Garrison later subpoenaed it for Shaw's trial. The VIP hostess, one Jessie Parker, also recalled a man who fit Shaw's description as being the one who signed as Bertrand.[182] Like many of Garrison's witnesses, Parker came under intense pressure to recant. This went as far as threats of losing custody of her little son. To her credit, she did not.[183]

When Shaw was booked after being arrested, the booking officer was a fifteen-year veteran of the force named Aloysius Habighorst. When the officer routinely asked if Shaw had ever used an alias Shaw, apparently disheveled, replied with the words "Clay Bertrand." Habighorst, without looking at any other documents, typed this on the booking card, which Shaw then signed. The alias also appeared on the arrest record.[184] As we shall see, this episode and this evidence ended up being a controversial turning point at Shaw's trial.

The reason Shaw would pick this particular name is very likely because it derives from Pope Clement V, whose surname was Bertrand D'Agout. (It would also explain why in some instances, he used the first name Clem.) This pope had sheltered homosexuals in the fourteenth century. His legacy lived on in the cloistered homosexual community. So much so that there developed a Clement Bertrand Society which helped homosexuals with legal problems. That Shaw/Bertrand sent the gay Latins to Dean Andrews suggests Shaw was aware of this bit of history.[185]

Jack Ruby and the Mob

Contrary to popular belief, Garrison never actually ruled out the Mafia as a suspect in the assassination. In fact, he distributed a summary of organized crime leads to his staff after talking to crime writer Ed Reid. In the summary Garrison wrote:

It cannot be denied, for example, that there is evidence which appears to indicate some involvement of individuals who seem to have organized crime connections. Furthermore, we cannot arbitrarily assume that, even if the militant right wing factor continues to develop effectively, involvement of organized crime elements may not be an additional factor as a product of joint interest.[186]

So the idea that Garrison never entertained any kind of Mafia involvement is one of the many canards passed around from book to book by authors who were all too eager to criticize the DA without even looking at his files. In that same year of 1967, there was a story in *Newsday* which stated that "Garrison is trying to learn whether the Cosa Nostra and anti-Castro Cubans may have been linked by mob-controlled gambling operations in pre-Castro Cuba . . . Garrison is trying to determine if there is a thread which binds the Cosa Nostra, anti-Castro groups, the late Dave Ferrie, Oswald, and Jack Ruby."[187] During his deposition for his unsuccessful libel suit against Garrison, Gordon Novel revealed that at one time Garrison was considering involvement by local don Carlos Marcello in the assassination.[188] The FBI also picked up information that Garrison was examining the Mafia angle when, in June of 1967, a Bureau source said that "Garrison believed that organized crime, specifically, 'La Cosa Nostra' is responsible along with other anti-Castroites for the assassination."[189]

In fact, in no less than *Harper's Weekly* of September 6, 1976, Garrison expounded on this concept in an interview with Dick Russell. He started off by saying, "It's really not all that complicated. Elements of the CIA utilizing anti-Castro adventurers and elements of the Lanksy Mob. It all revolved around Cuba, getting Cuba back." As Russell commented, very few people back in 1967 had knowledge of the long association between the CIA and the Mafia. Garrison discovered this by his own digging. But Garrison always felt that the CIA was the lead locomotive driving the train ahead of the Cubans and the organized crime elements. Clearly, through the work done on Rose Cheramie, Garrison understood that Jack Ruby knew Oswald. Further, that Ruby was also likely involved in a drug and prostitution chain stretching from Miami to Dallas. And this episode in and of itself implied a nexus of CIA associated Cuban exiles, with Mafia contraband. It also contains one other element of protection that Garrison was likely unawares. As author Douglas Valentine has noted, the CIA had infiltrated some offices of the Customs Department in order to protect anti-Castro drug smuggling groups in the USA. This is very likely because, as we have seen, Kennedy was cutting off the stipends for these groups. Valentine specifically mentions as being compromised the Galveston and Houston Customs offices. This would make the route followed by Cheramie, Santana, and Arcacha Smith quite informed and convenient.[190] Another very interesting record which indicated a

Ruby-Oswald connection happened to be lost. On a job application form, Oswald listed the name Jack Ruby as one of three references.[191] We know this because the information was given to an FBI agent by a mutual acquaintance who Garrison had shown this document to. This document does not exist today. And the author would be willing to wager that once the FBI found out about it, they alerted one of their plants in Garrison's office, through the likes of an intelligence asset like Hugh Aynesworth, to steal it. (This large aspect of any study of the Shaw prosecution—the deliberate destruction of the DA's case—will be addressed in the next two chapters.)

In Garrison's *Playboy* interview, he stated that Ruby was clearly involved in these kinds of anti-Castro exile activites through the Agency. But Garrison made a clear distinction in his discussion of Ruby and the Agency. He did not mean at all to say that Ruby was a CIA agent. In other words, he was not answering to a formal chain of command at Langley. He would do certain jobs under their auspices. In this interview, Garrison was saying that, in addition to the involvement with the drugs and prostitution ring noted above, Ruby was also smuggling arms for Cuban exile groups. This is an angle that has positively mushroomed in the Kennedy literature since Garrison first mentioned it in 1967. But what is remarkable today is that through the declassification process we now know that the Warren Commission was thinking the same thing. Warren Commission attorneys Leon Hubert and Burt Griffin ran the investigation of Ruby for the Commission. They wrote up an investigative plan in memorandum form in March of 1964. The memo reads in part, "The most promising links between Jack Ruby and the assassination of President Kennedy are established through underworld figures and anti-Castro Cubans and extreme right-wing Americans."[192] This was a prescient insight for that time. For there was evidence adduced early that Ruby, in addition to being involved with the Dallas Police, was also involved with this underworld aspect of extremist figures related to Cuba. Hubert and Griffin did not give up. Two months later they wrote another memo on the subject: "We believe that a reasonable possibility exists that Ruby has maintained a close interest in Cuban affairs to the extent necessary to participate in gun sales and smuggling . . ." This was clearly true and the Warren Commission had evidence of this in the memorable testimony of Nancy Perrin Rich.[193] But there was much more of it to be found in the future since it was laying around waiting to be discovered. And, in fact, Hubert and Griffin alluded to this next in their memo: "Neither Oswald's Cuban interests in Dallas nor Ruby's Cuban activities have been adequately explored . . ." There was an intriguing lead that the authors may be referring to here concerning Oswald and Cubans in Dallas. Manuel Rodriguez Orcarberro was a man who Garrison was very interested in. In November of 1963, he was reportedly the head of the Dallas enclave of Alpha 66, the Cuban exile terrorist group that intrigued Garrison the most.[194] After Kennedy's death, Deputy Sherriff Buddy Walthers learned from one of his informants that a group of Cubans had been meeting at a safe house at 3128 Harlendale on each weekend for months. About one week before the murder of JFK, the Cubans deserted that house. Finally, his information was that Oswald had been seen at this house.[195] The obvious question for Hubert and Griffin was this: Why would a communist be in the same safe house with some anti-Castro Cuban exiles shortly before Kennedy was to be killed?

The second Hubert-Griffin memorandum concludes with: "We believe the possibility exists, based on evidence already available, that Ruby was involved in illegal dealings with Cuban elements who might have had contact with Oswald. The existence of such dealings can only be surmised since the present investigation has not focused on that area." The authors then said that these questions should not be left "hanging in the air." Clearly, they were overruled since these areas were left hanging. But the point to be made is that even some of the investigators for the Commission understood that the most promising trail to a connection between Ruby and Oswald was through their common ties in the underworld surrounding Cuban-American relations. And, let us not forget, the CIA contact officer with Alpha 66 was David Phillips. Again, it appears that Garrison was one step away from the next level of the plot.

After reading her affidavit in the Warren Commission volumes, Jim Garrison had personally interviewed Julia Ann Mercer.[196] Mercer said she had been traveling west on Elm when she felt traffic being slowed by a stalled pick up truck. The truck was a Ford and it contained "what appeared to be tool boxes" in the rear. A man went to the rear of the truck and took out what appeared to Mercer to be a gun case. She continued to watch him as he then carried it up the grass to the top of the grassy hill. While still in traffic, she observed three policemen "standing talking near a motorcycle on the bridge just west of me." In an important difference with her November 22 affidavit, Mercer told Garrison that unlike what the affidavit implied, she got a good look at the man in the driver's seat. She also told the DA that the signature on the affidavit was not hers.[197] But further, when the FBI interviewed her the following day, they showed her a series of photos. She picked out the driver of the truck as Jack Ruby. When one of the agents turned the photo over, she saw the name of Jack Ruby on the back of the picture.[198] In other words, if this is accurate, Ruby should have been brought in for questioning on that day. The day before he shot Oswald. But also, this provided Garrison the rationale for why Ruby did what he did on the 24th in the basement of the Dallas jail. Garrison now theorized that Ruby must have been asked to do this job since he had such close ties to the Dallas Police. But further, if he hesitated, he would be reminded that he had played an earlier role, and if he refused, that earlier role could easily be revealed.[199] Garrison also speculated on the role of Eugene Hale Brading aka Jim Braden. Braden was a lower level courier for the Mafia, and he happened to be in Dallas on both the day before and day of the assassination, in close proximity to Ruby. Braden had a long criminal record for things like burglary, embezzlement, and illegal bookmaking. He was arrested and detained for acting suspiciously in Dealey Plaza after the assassination. He told the authorities he was there on oil business and he had ducked inside a building to make a phone call. He was released without being charged. Garrison thought that Braden was there as a diversion, that is to create a false sponsor: that is the Mob had actually been in charge.[200]

Did Ferrie and Shaw Plan a Murder?

As Garrison noted in his *Playboy* interview, one of the odd things that fascinated Ferrie was the ejection angle for cartridges from rifles. In a book on firearms found in his apartment was a section dealing with the distance and direction a shell travels after being ejected. In the margin Ferrie had scribbled the figures 50 degrees and 11 feet. In the newly declassified files produced by the Assassination Records Review Board, this detail gains a bit more prominence. Like many DA's, Garrison employed both street informants and undercover agents. In the Kennedy case, two he used on Ferrie were Max Gonzalez and Jimmy Johnson. Johnson was a parole violator in a vulnerable position who Garrison and his Chief Investigator Lou Ivon used on Ferrie. To the author's knowledge, not until the ARRB declassification process did anyone reveal Johnson's special status in Garrison's office. Johnson told Garrison that Ferrie kept a manila file folder he called "The Bomb." He bragged that it would tear the city apart if it ever became known. Johnson one day had access to Ferrie's files and found a notebook marked "Files, 1963." This included a piece of loose-leaf paper with a diagram on it. The diagram seemed to be a plan for some kind of assassination attempt. Johnson described it as a figure of a man with what looked like a bullet hole in the rear of his skull and one in his right shoulder. There was an accompanying diagram from the side with arrows pointing coming from the back and exiting the throat. There were two lines, one going up to a building, and one coming down from the top to form a triangle. The line going up had a marking of 60 feet high, the line coming down was marked 2,500 feet long. At the bottom of the diagram was an airplane. The line illustrated the plane coming down over the building. This would appear to be a diagram for a Castro plot, since it would be much to dangerous to use a plane in the USA for an assassination plot.[201]

To those eager to dismiss such illustrated evidence, there was another witness to Ferrie's diagrams of a long range assassination plot. Clara Gay was an antiques dealer in New Orleans. She was a friend of conservative congressman Edward Hebert, a vehement opponent of Garrison and his assassination probe. G. Wray Gill was Clara's lawyer. She was in Gill's office on November 26, right after Ferrie had been interviewed by both Garrison and the FBI. Clara had known Ferrie through Gill's office, and they had a friendship which had since cooled. When she heard about Ferrie being questioned by Garrison's office, she called up Gill and noted the tumult on the other end of the phone. One secretary said words to the effect that Mr. Gill knew nothing about this. She then went over to his office. Clara looked over at Ferrie's desk and she saw what looked like a diagram of Dealey Plaza: it was a drawing of a car from the perspective of an angle from above, the car was surrounded by high buildings, reminiscient of Dealey Plaza. After the secretary threw it out, Clara retrieved it. She said it should be given to the FBI or Secret Service. The secretary took it back and a pulling contest ensued. The secretary eventually won, but not before Clara saw the two words "Elm Street" on the diagram. She later reconstructed this experience for Garrison. She said she came forward because she considered herself a good citizen, and Ferrie must have been something evil.[202] It would appear that Ferrie's illustrations seemed to follow the thought line of others in the Cuban exile/CIA associated community: If we cannot take out Castro, let us take out Kennedy.

Brothers Samuel and Hugh Exnicios were New Orleans attorneys involved in the controversy surrounding the Shaw prosecution. Hugh represented Al Beaubouef—one of Ferrie's companions on his Texas trip the day of the assassination—and later, Gordon Novel. Samuel represented a man named Woodrow Hardy. Hardy worked for Clay Shaw. He supervised many of his French Quarter real estate renovations. By 1963, he had worked for Shaw for many years. For so long that he had his own key to his house. One day in that fateful summer of 1963, Hardy slipped his key in the patio door and walked in to see Shaw, Ferrie, and Oswald talking away. Shaw did not exchange pleasantries. Nor did he talk shop. He got up and escorted Hardy outside, making it clear he was preoccupied.[203] Reading that brother Hugh was involved in the Shaw case, Woodrow decided to tell his lawyer, Samuel, about the incident. But he was too afraid to come forward with the information at the time.

Garrison did get an anonymous letter about Hardy. It said that Hardy had seen many Cubans visiting Shaw. Including Emilio Santana, the man with Sergio Arcacha Smith and Rose Cheramie on the way to Dallas four days before the assassination.[204] But Garrison could not follow up on the letter. Which would have been interesting since before fleeing New Orleans,

Santana, who worked for both Clay Shaw—and also the CIA's Clandestine Services from 1960–63—had told Garrison that Shaw had been to Havana with Jack Ruby in 1959. They were there on a gun-smuggling mission. Santana said both men were involved in Cuban exile activities,[205] which is something that is certain today.

The Reverend Clyde Johnson was a rightwing extremist who ran for Governor of Louisiana in the sixties. He was also a vociferous and vehement critic of President Kennedy, especially over his Cuba policies. In 1963, while running his campaign, he was paged at the Roosevelt Hotel. Johnson placed this in either July or August. A man calling himself Alton Bernard met him in the lobby. Bernard told him that he had seen him on TV a few times and encouraged him to continue with his anti-Kennedy diatribes. He completely agreed that Kennedy had betrayed the Cubans at the Bay of Pigs. To show his appreciation, and his possible future value, Bernard gave the extremist 2,000 dollars. Bernard stayed in phone contact with Johnson, each time appreciative of his torching of Kennedy.

The two met again in September in Baton Rouge at the Capitol House Hotel. When Bernard arrived he was with a young man named Leon. A kind of grubby, unshaven, unkempt version of Oswald. (As we shall see, this Leon, is similar to the one Perry Russo recalled at David Ferrie's.) The two visitors were soon joined by a mysterious Cuban and a man known simply as Jack. The candidate left the room to go to the bathroom. He heard a discussion going on about "getting" someone. Bernard chimed in with words to the effect that others were working on this too. At first, Johnson thought they were talking about him. But, as he grew apprehensive and fearful, he then heard someone say something like, he has to come down from Washington, since the pressure is on. When Johnson came out, Jack said, pointing at him, "What about him?" Bernard said, "That's alright. He's one of my boys." The candidate would identify Jack as Jack Ruby, Leon as Lee Oswald, and Alton Bernard as Clay Shaw.[206] Johnon's story was partly corroborated by his running mate Edward McMillan. McMillan recalled a post-election celebration in January of 1964. Johnson was staying at the Monteleone Hotel and among the crowd in Johnson's room was Clay Shaw.[207] One of the more fascinating things in what is left of Garrison's file on Johnson is an address book found by the candidate which identifies Clay Bertrand as "Lay Out Man" in August of 1963. It also has the name of Jack Rubion, Dallas, Texas.[208] As William Davy notes, we will never know if Johnson was genuine or not. As we shall see, a sorry fate, little different than others in the Garrison case, awaited him.

In February of 1967, Perry Russo was a young insurance salesman living in Baton Rouge. He had also been a former friend of David Ferrie. Russo had written to Garrison when he became aware of his investigation, but the letter was never delivered. Russo then gave interviews to both a local TV station and a reporter from the *Baton Rouge State-Times*.[209] When the interviews appeared, Garrison immediately sent Andrew Sciambra, a young assistant DA, to take a deposition from Russo in Baton Rouge. Russo said he had known Ferrie fairly well and had attended a gathering at Ferrie's apartment in mid-September of 1963.[210] He revealed that, late in the evening, after most had left, he, Ferrie, two of Ferrie's friends, and several Cuban exiles remained. Russo had brought two friends to Ferrie's that night, Sandra Moffett and Niles Peterson. Both left early, but Peterson later remembered a man named Leon Oswald.[211] By the time the discussion took place, both of Russo's friends were gone. Almost everyone else had left except Ferrie, Leon Oswald, and a tall, distinguished, white-haired man named Clem Bertrand.

The group, reported Russo, discussed Cuban-American politics and everyone expressed their distaste for both Castro and Kennedy. Then, the assassination of Fidel Castro was raised, but Bertrand noted that there would be a real problem getting at him inside Cuba.

Around this time the Cubans left, and only Ferrie, Oswald, Bertrand, and Russo remained. Ferrie continued the conversation saying that if they could not get at Castro, they certainly had access to Kennedy. Russo said this was characteristic of Ferrie. Since he had known him, Ferrie had become more and more embittered at the President. Russo had no liking for Kennedy either. He was a Republican and a Goldwater supporter. Joined by their stated hatred of JFK, the men now turned to the details of a plot to do away with him.

Ferrie became intense. Pacing the floor, he expostulated on the way to do it: In a "triangulation of crossfire"—shooting at Kennedy from three directions. Ferrie insisted this would ensure that one of the shots would be fatal. As Ferrie became more excited and voluble, Bertrand remained calm, smoking, and added, coolly, that if it happened, they had to be away from the scene. Ferrie said he would be at Southeastern Louisiana campus in Hammond. Bertrand said he would be on a business trip to the West Coast.

Russo realized that the discussion had now transcended the hypothetical. They were talking about where they would be *when it occurred*. Indeed, on his way back from Texas the weekend of the assassination, Ferrie did go see a friend at the university in Hammond. And on November 22, Shaw did have a speaking engagement in San Francisco.

Ferrie kept on talking about a triangulated crossfire. But Russo was now tired and his memory weak. Ferrie drove him home that night.

When Sciambra showed Russo a photo of Clay Shaw, he identified him as Clem Bertrand. When shown photos of Oswald, Russo could not positively identify him. But when artists drew in renditions with whiskers, Russo made a positive ID.[212]

Garrison now thought he had a sufficient case to go forward. But not satisfied with Russo's memory, he decided to subject him to the tests of hypnosis and the so-called truth serum. Sodium Pentothal tests are not allowed in court but prosecutors often use them to check and corroborate testimony. Dr. Nicholas Chetta, the Orleans Parish Coroner, administered the Sodium Pentothal. Dr. Esmond Fatter, an expert in hypnosis and memory, coordinated the questioning.

The story held up to Garrison's satisfaction. Here was finally a gestalt that made sense. A group at the operational level—the Cuban exiles—with real reasons to want Kennedy dead. A group at the organizational level—the CIA—with resources and experience to plan and execute such an operation. Both had access to the kind of marksmen necessary to pull off the lethal, military-style ambush in Dealey Plaza. From this perspective, Oswald's odd associations with people like DeMohrenschildt, the Paines, and Ferrie fit in. So did the call from "Bertrand," and Ruby's final, culminating murder.

What Garrison did not know that this was as good as it was going to get. This was the peak of his inquiry. From this point on, his investigation would be a long toboggan slide toward ruination. The seeds of destruction had already been sown.

CHAPTER ELEVEN

Inferno

"Certain elements of the mass media have an active interest in preventing this case from ever coming to trial at all and find it necessary to employ against me every smear device in the book."

—Jim Garrison, Playboy, *October, 1967*

The conventional view of the beginning of the end of Garrison's Kennedy investigation is usually dated from February 17, 1967. On that day, the *New Orleans States-Item* published a story headlined, "DA Here Launches Full JFK Death Plot Probe," by a young reporter, Rosemary James. The story described how Garrison had funded his secret investigation through judicially approved vouchers from his fines and fees account. The vouchers included trips to Florida, Washington, San Francisco and Texas. James described this as "pouring out-of-the-ordinary sums of money into a probe of a possible assassination plot." Since the probe had been secret, a fact that James treated as scandalous, there was no indication of what the DA and his small staff had achieved with the minuscule 8,000 dollar expenditure.

Rosemary James maintained that she had shown the story to the DA before publication, and he had read part of it before responding with a "No comment." A tale which Garrison strongly disputed.[1] And his response to the newspaper and its reporter—locking them out of a press conference—would surely indicate his anger at the disclosure. James never revealed what had provoked her to begin looking through the vouchers. She later remarked in a book that there were rumors around town that Garrison was working on something big. She never got more specific than that. It turns out that James was blowing smoke about what really provoked the story.

Jack Dempsey KOs Rosemary James

At the time of that story, James was a young reporter who focused on maritime stories based upon New Orleans's importance as a port city. Meanwhile, Jack Dempsey was a veteran local reporter who usually covered the police beat and the court system. On January 23, 1967—over three weeks before the James story appeared on the front page—Dempsey had written a short notice in his *States Item* column entitled "On the Police Beat." It read as follows: "Did you know? At least five persons have been questioned by the District Attorney's office in connection with another investigation into events linked to the Kennedy assassination." From his courthouse beat, Dempsey had discovered sources who knew that Garrison was calling in witnesses about the Kennedy assassination. But because the story was so brief and because, unlike James, the modest and mild-mannered Dempsey was not out to make a name for himself, this initial exposure of Garrison's inquiry remained essentially unnoticed until the debut of Steven Tyler's documentary *He Must Have Something* in 1991. In that film, Dempsey briefly discussed this issue. His memory differed markedly from James', who was also in the film. So when the author journeyed to New Orleans in 1994, he made it a point to look up Dempsey. That interview, building on the snippets in Tyler's film, undermines and rewrites the standard reports about this issue.

Rosemary James was asked to come into the story by her editors only after Demspey's original story had run. The paper was planning to build on Dempsey's original discovery, but did not want to include Dempsey in that follow-up. One insight into why is his reply to a question by the author about his original brief notice in January. The question concerned if he got any feedback to the first story. He slowly shook his head from side to side: "Did I get feedback?" He stopped his head movement and repeated, "Did I get feedback?" He then proceeded to tell the author about an experience that was a little scary for him. When Garrison discovered the short notice, he called Dempsey into his office. He was obviously beside himself. He understood what this would do to his investigation. He wanted to know who had tipped him off. And he threatened to take Dempsey before the grand jury to find out who his sources were. Dempsey, who was very guarded on that issue, told the DA that he could not reveal that information. Further, if he was placed on the stand, he would not answer any questions. Garrison said that doing that would result in a contempt of court charge and a jail term. Dempsey replied with words to the effect that if that was the price he had to pay, then his children's friends could begin calling their father a jailbird.[2] Although Dempsey was trying to put up a brave front, it was clear to the author that the reporter felt Garrison was actually going to call him before the grand jury. Dempsey left the meeting with no clear indication of what the DA was going to do. But the *States-Item* was determined to unmask Garrison's inquiry. Realizing Dempsey was in trouble already, they gave the young woman the unenviable assignment of getting Garrison's comment before the longer story was to run. In Tyler's film, James gives her usual rendition of what Garrison said when she asked him about the story. She says that he replied with an emotionless, "No Comment." Meaning to her that this was a winking approval to print the story. When Dempsey comes on screen, we understand what actually happened. And its consistent with what the DA did to him. He says that when James returned from Garrison's office she said that the angry DA had asked her, "Who wrote this garbage?" Garrison then continued by calling the story completely false and that they would be "in trouble" if it ran. And what Garrison did after, is also consistent with Dempsey's version. Garrison was so angered that he went through a three-stage reaction to the James story. First, he issued a statement denying the story, saying it was based on rumor.[3] Then he swore at the press, before bursting out with, "I don't have to explain trips to any newspaper."[4] By February 20, he could deny the story no longer and called a press conference to detail how the story had already hindered his investigation. "[W]e were making progress until the newspapers revealed a number of details." He added that he did not plan to make the probe public "until the time came to make arrests."[5] All of the above demonstrates that James seems to have been less than honest about her "no comment" remark. And her subsequent tale about Garrison actually wanting her to run with the story, thereby implying he wanted publicity for his probe, is rendered absurd by Garrison's confrontation with Dempsey. But that meant nothing to the *States-Item*. The next day they made explicit what James was implying. They wanted to know what Garrison had uncovered, "or is he merely saving some interesting new information which will gain for him exposure in a national magazine."

Besides falsely picturing the DA as an ambitious and self-centered publicity seeker, the story now caused the klieg lights of the national media to descend upon New Orleans. As the second *States-Item* article revealed, the local media was not going to be in the DA's corner on this issue. And since the national media had bought into the Warren Report hook, line, and sinker, they were not going to be an easy sell either. At this point, an upper class envoy was sent to meet Garrison in an attempt to guide the DA to guard his own self-interests. The envoy had likely been briefed since he knew more about Garrison's inquiry than had been printed in the papers up to that point. In his book, Garrison disguises this person under the false name of John Miller.[6] But he does reveal his proper profession, a wealthy Denver oil man. His real name was John King. And his agenda was to first flatter the DA for his achievements, and then to essentially tell him that whatever he had done to that point had been high tide for him. It would all be downhill now that the media was on to him. With that dire prognostication in front of him—which happened to be accurate—King now magnanimously offered an escape passage to the DA. He offered him a lifetime appointment to the federal bench. As stated, it appears that King had been briefed about Garrison's inquiry. He had not been briefed about Garrison the man. As Governor McKeithen had found out, Garrison was not interested in a high-paying, cushy job over being an active DA. If he had, he would have accepted McKeithen's previous offers. And once Garrison was onto the Kennedy case, as Bill Alford's previous anecdote shows, he was totally committed to it. Whatever the personal price would be. And it turned out to be quite large. So Garrison told King what he later said to *Playboy* and to McKeithen: Nothing was going to divert him from his Kennedy investigation.[7]

The Last Days of David Ferrie

Ferrie had been placed under surveillance by Garrison in late 1966, and cameras had been fixed outside his apartment to record his comings and goings. A change had come over Ferrie. Two changes, to be exact. The first had come right after the assassination. In late November 1963, Ferrie dropped out of sight for awhile and seemed directionless. He quit his job with Banister and the two parted ways. This may have been because he was the only one of the group to be questioned by the FBI and the District Attorney.

In his own mind, according to what he told Lou Ivon, the next casualty of the story was Ferrie. He had become an emotional wreck, existing on coffee, cigarettes, and tranquilizers. His behavior toward Garrison was mercurial. Sometimes he would call and ask how the investigation was proceeding. Other times, he would tell him that he was now a marked man. But after Ferrie read the Rosemary James story, he now called Ivon and spoke rather prophetically: "You know what this news story does to me, don't you? I'm a dead man. From here on, believe me, I'm a dead man." When Ivon tried to reassure him that he was overreacting, Ferrie replied "You'll find out soon enough. You'll see."[8] He then tried a desperate two-track system. He leaked the story about his involvement in the probe to several reporters and, the day the story broke, Ferrie began to denounce Garrison to any reporter who would listen. He called the inquiry a "big joke," and said that he had been tagged "as the getaway pilot in a wild plot" to kill the President.[9] Ferrie seemed to be doing a good job in promoting his cause and deflating Garrison. *Washington Post* national security reporter George Lardner, Jr., referred to Ferrie as "an intelligent, well-versed guy on a broad range of subjects."[10]

Unfortunately, and apparently unawares, Garrison began to play into the media's hands. When New Orleans became a seething cauldron of publicity and reporters, he evaded reporters by using a back entrance to his office. There he read Ferrie's comments and an editorial criticizing him for spending the 8,000 dollars and implying he was using it for vacation trips for his staff and to get national publicity. Garrison was offended by these remarks because they were not just unfair, but completely mischaracterized what he was doing and why. So, smarting from the editorial, Garrison began to make statements that were, at best, ill-advised and, at worst, inflammatory:

> My staff and I solved the case weeks ago. I wouldn't say this if I didn't have *evidence beyond a shadow of a doubt*. We know the key individuals, the cities involved and how it was done. . . .

> We are building a case and I might add, it's a case *we will not lose*, and anyone who wants to bet against us is invited to. But they will be disappointed.

> There will be arrests, charges will be filed, and on the basis of these charges, *convictions will be obtained*.

> *We solved the assassination*. . . . We're working out details of evidence which will probably take months. We know that we are going to be able to *arrest* every person involved—at least every person who is still living.[11] (Emphases added.)

From his own perspective, these quotes were justified. But it was a mistake to issue these sweeping statements. First, his investigation had been exposed before it was finished, as some of the quotes indicate. Therefore, the collecting of evidence was by no means complete. Nor had Ferrie yet been indicted, or even called before a grand jury to testify. And equally, if not most importantly, this would be the first time Garrison had been exposed to consistent worldwide media attention. (The national coverage of his Bourbon Street clean up had been sporadic.) He had no experience in this arena and no advisers to help him. His candor, his way with words, his predilection for hyperbole, which may have worked locally, these all played into the worst aspects of global pack journalism: sensationalism and caricature. He was setting himself up for a fall. A conscious campaign by selected journalists to derail and discredit his case was gearing up.

As noted previously, Ferrie tried to fight back in the press through people such as Lardner. He also tried to laugh the whole thing off by calling it a "big joke." But, almost simultaneously, he also went to people in the DA's office like Lou Ivon. On February 18, Ferrie was interviewed by Andrew Sciambra and Ivon at his home. He was evasive and told them very little.[12] But the day after, Ferrie called Ivon at his residence. He was fearful for his life. After notifying Garrison, Ivon checked Ferrie into a hotel room under an assumed name. Ivon recalled to author William Davy that Ferrie appeared quite scared, almost like "a wild man." Ferrie now admitted he had worked for the CIA and that he knew Oswald. He also admitted to knowing Clay Shaw and that Shaw also worked for the Agency. And he added that Shaw despised President Kennedy.[13] But he as yet did not admit to any role in the plot to kill Kennedy. Ivon stayed with Ferrie in his hotel room until the early hours of the next morning. He then went home to sleep. When he returned the next morning, Ferrie was gone. Ivon and others on Garrison's staff now began to search the Cuban exile community on Decatur Street near the French Quarter where Ferrie often stayed.

The last person to have seen Ferrie alive was Lardner. He visited him very late on the evening of the twenty-first and stayed into the early hours of the twenty-second. On February 22, 1967, the same day Garrison had decided to call him before the grand jury, David Ferrie was found dead.[14]

The contents of Ferrie's apartment at the time of his death were unusual for a private investigator. They included a blue, 100-pound aerial bomb, a Springfield rifle, a Remington rifle, an altered-stock .22 rifle, 20 shotgun shells, two Army Signal Corps telephones, one bayonet, one flare gun, a radio transmitter unit, a radio receiver unit, 32 rifle cartridges, 22 blanks, several cameras, and three rolls of film.[15]

His body was found naked on his living room sofa; a sheet was pulled over his head. Two typed suicide notes were found. Neither one of them was signed.[16] The table next to his body was strewn with medicine bottles, several of them empty. Coroner Nicholas Chetta had the body moved out quickly, before Garrison and his staff arrived. Garrison took some of the medicine bottles in order to check them out. On February 28, Chetta ruled that Ferrie had died of natural causes, specifically, a berry aneurism or broken blood vessel in the brain.

Garrison had his doubts, especially in light of the two typed suicide notes. He had Proloid, one of the drugs found in the apartment, analyzed and discovered that with Ferrie's hypertension, this drug could cause death by brain aneurism without a trace.[17]

There are other mysteries beyond the two suicide notes and the deadly drugs. *Washington Post* reporter George Lardner, Jr., claims he was with Ferrie until 4:00 A.M., a time the coroner insisted was "absolutely the latest possible time of death." This means that Ferrie must have died, by whatever means, within minutes of Lardner's departure.[18] It could mean that, if Ferrie was murdered, the killers were waiting for Lardner to leave. And in fact, years later, when coroner Frank Minyard looked at the autopsy pictures of Ferrie, he noted contusions of the inside of the lower lip and gums. The day before he died, Ferrie had purchased 100 thyroid pills. When his body was discovered, they were gone. Minyard theorizes that if Ferrie was murdered, the killers may have mixed the pills into a solution and forced it down his throat with a tube. One of the contusions is on the inside of the lower lip where the tube may have struck during a struggle. With all these suspicious circumstances, why did Chetta rule as he did? In no one's memory had someone left a suicide note—in this case, what could be considered two of them—and then died of natural causes. But Chetta apparently wanted to play it safe in the face of the tremendous publicity focused on Ferrie's death.[19]

Further, Chetta had first set the time of Ferrie's death as *before* 4:00 A.M. But then Lardner came forward and said he had been with the man until about four in the morning. This is when Chetta revised his time of death until 4:00 A.M. as the absolute latest possible time of death. And further, Ferrie's doctor Martin Palmer told author Joan Mellen he thought the autopsy was "slipshod." He termed it not a full autopsy but a partial one.[20]

Ferrie's death was a staggering body blow to Garrison's inquiry. But his death was compounded by the death in that same twenty-four-hour period of Eladio Del Valle. As mentioned, Del Valle was a former congressman in Cuba under Batista. Once Castro took over, Del Valle joined the violent opposition to him. One of the things he did was to hire David Ferrie to run fire bomb missions over Cuba. Since Del Valle had run up a small fortune in smuggling contraband with mobster Santo Trafficante, he could afford to pay Ferrie well, 1,500 dollars per mission.[21] According to author Dick Russell, congressman Del Valle eventually became part of Batista's military intelligence forces in charge of narcotics south of Havana. And this is how he became involved with Trafficante.[22]

Bernardo DeTorres: The CIA's First Infiltrator

Garrison found out about Del Valle's murder through a man named Alberto Fowler. Fowler was a Cuban living in New Orleans who was an aide to Garrison's investigation, about whose loyalty some have suspicions about. But the man who told Fowler about Del Valle's death was undoubtedly a CIA agent masquerading as a Garrison aide.[23] In fact, one can make the case that Bernardo DeTorres was the first infiltrator into Garrison's assassination probe. And his early penetration dates from at least December of 1966, perhaps even a bit earlier.[24] Before Del Valle's death, DeTorres had told Fowler that Del Valle was willing to help him in his case.[25] Which seems odd since no less than Fabian Escalante, head of Castro's security services, thought Del Valle was a suspect in Kennedy's murder. The actual death report as it came to Garrison reads as follows: "He was shot in the chest and it appears 'gangland style' and his body was left in the vicinity of BERNARDO TORRES' apartment."

At the time Fowler turned his name over to Garrison as a possible aide in checking out leads in south Florida, DeTorres was working as a private eye in Miami. But this was likely at least a partial front. For as was later discovered, DeTorres began filing reports on Garrison with the Miami CIA station almost immediately.[26] This information was discovered through the HSCA, who later got onto the trail of DeTorres independently of Garrison. But they then discovered he was the first CIA agent to infiltrate Garrison's office. DeTorres was also cozy with Del Valle's pal Trafficante. Having been a veteran of the Bay of Pigs, DeTorres was associated with the CIA by 1961, and associated even closer in 1962. DeTorres's work in Florida was an expensive item for Garrison with very little, or nothing, to show for it. Except, perhaps, the dead body of Del Valle.

It is interesting to note Cuban intelligence chief Fabian Escalante's suspicions about Del Valle's role in Kennedy's murder. Especially in regard to the fact that certain members of the HSCA—Al Gonzalez, Gaeton Fonzi, and Edwin Lopez—all ended up believing that DeTorres was involved in Kennedy's assassination. By 1963, DeTorres was a full fledged CIA officer who was cross posted at times into military intelligence. In fact, Gerry Hemmings met Bernardo in just such an office in 1963.[27] Bernardo also became the Latin American representative for Military Armament Corporation, a firm run by Mitch Werbell. In the summary of his HSCA interview, Bernardo admitted to being both a visitor at Werbell's house and being enlisted by the Secret Service to guard Kennedy on his visit to Miami in November of 1963. The HSCA later wrote that "DeTorres has pictures of Dealey Plaza in a safe deposit box. These pictures were taken during the assassination of JFK. *Life* offered DeTorres twenty or thirty thousand dollars but he refused."[28]

How did the HSCA get a lead on DeTorres, thus throwing backward light on how worried the Agency was about Garrison at a very early date? It began with Fonzi talking to Cuban exile Rolando Otero. Otero had heard that there were five Miami men who were involved with the assassination. One of them was DeTorres, who was allegedly in Dealey Plaza posing as a photographer. Further, Otero said that DeTorres was actually *in contact* with Oswald prior to the assassination.[29] (This could have been at the Alpha 66 safe house at Harlendale referenced in Chapter 9 to the Buddy Walthers's report.) When Fonzi tried to find the source for Otero's information, this led him to an associate of Paul Bethel. Bethel was a longtime conservative operative for the United

States Information Agency in Cuba, and was a friend of Phillips. After Castro came to power, Bethel became associated with the Cuban exiles in Miami. Like Howard Hunt, he was a friend of William F. Buckley; and also like Hunt, he wrote for Buckley's *National Review*. In 1969 Bethel wrote a book called *The Losers*. In it he wrote that, after the Missile Crisis, "There is no doubt that President Kennedy and his brother . . . consciously set about the business of stopping all efforts to unhorse Fidel Castro—from outside exile attacks, and from Cuba's internal resistance movement."[30] These were the kinds of circles that DeTorres and his cohorts were fellow travelers in. When Fonzi talked to Otero's source, the DeTorres/Bethel colleague, the man was in jail for driving with a fraudulent driver's license.[31] Fonzi found out that he began his career as a likely plant on the liberal democratic side during President Johnson's invasion of the Dominican Republic in 1965. When he defected to the American side in that conflict, he made a beeline to none other than DeTorres's business cohort, the CIA weapons expert, Mitch Werbell. From here he quickly became a witness for conservative Kennedy nemesis Senator Thomas Dodd on the subject of Cuban exportation of subversion in the Caribbean. From there, he was sitting in on National Security Council meetings. This is how connected DeTorres, Werbell and Bethel were. Afterwards, he went to work for Werbell.

When Fonzi talked to him, Otero's contact revealed that DeTorres was working for Werbell in 1963. He then added that both Werbell and DeTorres were involved in planned assassinations of political targets. About Oswald, DeTorres had said he knew he had not killed Kennedy because DeTorres knew the people who were actually involved—and they were talking about it before it happened.[32]

I have detailed the DeTorres penetration at length since it is important in order to understand what really happened to Jim Garrison. And also to reveal just how much was at stake for suspects like Bernardo DeTorres and his allies. As Fonzi notes in his book, and as the author found out from an interview, when Victor Marchetti was executive assistant to CIA Director Richard Helms, Helms would run staff meetings about Agency operations. During these meetings, Marchetti would take the official notes. At times, Helms would indicate he wanted certain things not taken down. At other times, something would come up, and Helms would cut off any follow-up by waving his hand. He then would add that this subject would be pursued further in his office, or in the proper deputy's office, with Marchetti not there to take notes. Marchetti said that the Garrison inquiry and the Shaw trial came up more than once. Each time, Helms would ask what they were doing to help the defense.[33] Fonzi later found out that DeTorres's penetration was only the inception of the CIA's effort to torpedo Garrison. For the HSCA later discovered through CIA documents that there were nine undercover agents at one time or another in Garrison's office.[34] So, in addition to what Mr. King had warned Garrison about, that is the negativity of the media which would now plague him until the end, there was something that King left unsaid. But after he left, assistant Andrew Sciambra noted it to Garrison. He said, "Well, they offered you the carrot, and you turned it down. You know what's coming next don't you?"[35]

What we are about to describe in this chapter and the next is something that neither Garrison nor Sciambra could have likely imagined at the time. But with the aid of extensive interviews, plus declassified documents, for the first time we will now outline a three stage program to destruct Garrison's case and to make sure Shaw would be acquitted. This first stage began very early with DeTorres, a man who—while working with Mitch Werbell—may have been involved with Kennedy's murder. But it will continue with certain other "singleton" penetrations by people like William Gurvich and Gordon Novel. The second stage of the effort will center around the wider efforts of former National Security Agency officer Walter Sheridan in alliance with the CIA and NBC. That effort was coupled with the work of intelligence assets/journalists James Phelan and Hugh Aynseworth. When Garrison would still not give up, a third phase set in with two prongs to it. James Angleton's office took over in September of 1967, and, as we have previewed, Angleton's endeavor was then allied to and expanded all the way up to Director Richard Helms in 1968 and 1969. With operations that could not even be discussed in public or for the record. But which, as we shall see, HSCA Deputy Counsel Bob Tanenbaum saw certain documents about.

The Gurviches: P. I. Services for Free

After DeTorres, the next dubious aide who came into Garrison's office offering his investigative skills was William Gurvich. Gurvich and his brother Louis ran a private investigation service in New Orleans. It was one of the larger and more sophisticated offices in the city.[36] The Gurviches offered their clients services like witness location, photographic analysis, electronic surveillance and, significant to this instance, undercover infiltration. As Garrison told *Playboy* in his October 1967 interview, Bill Gurvich knocked on his door around Christmas of 1966 offering to work for the DA on his Kennedy probe for free. He also offered the services of his brother Louis, plus a local polygraph analyst Roy Jacob. Since Garrison was short-handed, and the probe was widening, he took up professional sleuth Gurvich on his offer without asking any questions.

From around December of 1966 to March of 1967, Garrison gave Gurvich some sensitive assignments which he performed adequately. But in March of

1967, when Shaw was arrested, a reporter asked him how long the inquiry would last. Gurvich replied, "Maybe thirty years."[37] When Gurvich was locating Eladio Del Valle in Florida, he worked with DeTorres. When Perry Russo went to see Gurvich's handpicked polygraph technician, Jacob tried to intimidate him *before* he took the test. Jacob later told Garrison's office that Russo was a "psychotic." In a key interview with Cuban exile Ricardo Davis, Gurvich's tape recorder just happened to malfunction. When Harold Weisberg reinterviewed Davis—who placed Shaw with militant Cuban exiles—Davis told Harold that there some interesting things he told Gurvich that were left out of the investigator's summary.[38] Like, for example, that the FBI had interviewed him the day after the assassination and showed him a picture of Shaw. As Weisberg noted, no such FBI interview was ever sent to the Warren Commission.[39] But yet, people like Bill Turner, even at this point, still believed in the Gurviches. For a positive *Ramparts* article about Garrison, Turner often quoted the brothers as believing in Garrison's case and frowning on what the FBI had done in New Orleans. Turner even quoted Louis Gurvich when he compared the Kennedy murder with the celebrated Dreyfus case in France.[40]

It was around late March of 1967, when Garrison heard that Gurvich had been talking to Walter Sheridan, that Garrison began to suspect Gurvich was a double agent.[41] Prior to this he trusted Gurvich implicitly. They shared an office, to which Gurvich had the keys, and Gurvich even used Garrison's car. (Gurvich later admitted to actually stealing things off Garrison's desk and copying them.[42]) But after Garrison heard what Sheridan was doing to some witnesses, he began to freeze Gurvich out of sensitive areas of the inquiry. Gurvich formally defected in late June of 1967. In fact, he called a press conference on the very day that CBS began to broadcast its four-part defense of the Warren Report. But what is also interesting is that, two weeks before he announced his defection, he had visited with Bobby Kennedy in New York City. Clearly, Sheridan was trying to influence and mold his former boss's opinion of Garrison.[43] While using his own efforts to give some ballast to CBS.

But Gurvich was not done dispensing his favors yet. Not by a long shot. For when Gurvich left, he took with him a copy of Garrison's master file. This is something he failed to admit to in public. But in an interview he did with Clay Shaw's lawyers, Ed Wegmann, and Irvin Dymond, he spoke of it like this: "I have it locked in a vault in a bank and you are welcome to have every bit of it as far as I am concerned."[44] So here you have the spectacle of a former aide decrying the DA's ethics while failing to admit he is a thief. On top of that, Gurvich asked to appear before the grand jury to testify about Garrison's unethical practices. In his first appearance, he testified that Garrison had forced certain witnesses into the office to be cross-examined and polygraphed. When asked who they were, he could not name anyone. He said he had to consult his records. Which he did not have with him, even though he had requested to take the stand.[45] When he appeared again he still could not name anyone. So he said that Garrison had ordered the arrest and physical beating of Walter Sheridan and Rick Townley. The only problem is neither man was ever arrested or beaten. And Gurvich could not name one police officer, assistant DA, or investigator who heard Garrison say this.[46]

Gurvich's father was a longtime FBI agent. His company, called Private Patrol, signed various contracts with shipping lines departing New Orleans for South America. The kind that Clay Shaw and his mentor Ted Brent monitored for the intelligence community. Gurvich later joined forces with the FBI to investigate CIA pilot Leslie Bradley's comings and goings at Lakefront Airport, and his possible connection to Shaw and Ferrie. Gurvich then worked directly for Shaw's lawyers on the eve of his 1969 trial. He was interviewing prospective witnesses with copies of his purloined documents from Garrison's master file. In fact, Gurvich worked for Shaw's defense all the way to 1971, when the perjury case against Shaw was thrown out.[47] All told, Gurvich worked almost five years on this case. Does anyone believe he did it for nothing?

In 1996, a resident from New Orleans got in contact with the author through researcher John Newman. He was a former veteran who had been through a bad experience in Vietnam. He was therefore living off his veteran's benefits. He said that, one summer in the early seventies, he was at a vacation spot on the Mississippi coast. He was at a four star hotel with a girlfriend of his. While relaxing at the pool he started up a conversation with the woman next to him. He discovered that she, like he, was from New Orleans. So he introduced himself by name and told her where he lived in New Orleans. She then did likewise, and said she was staying in a suite with a friend named Lou Gurvich and his family. At that time, that name did not ring a bell with him. As the sun began to die down, she invited him up to their room for a drink. When he got there, Gurvich's daughter, who had been poolside with them, went into the shower. The woman gave him a drink, and then the daughter emerged from the shower. But when she emerged, she had different color hair. The woman noticed the puzzlement on his face. She leaned over and whispered to him, "He does some work for the CIA. So he has his loved ones take precautions."[48] With that brief aside, a light went on in his head. He now recalled the Gurvich name from the Shaw prosecution.

Allen Dulles Recruits Gordon Novel

Gordon Novel was originally from the New Orleans area. As a teenager he was associated with a rightwing group called the Storm Troopers.[49] Because of this association, Gordon had some early problems with the law, when the group tried to derail a locomotive and blow up a theater. This is where Novel got his early skills not just in mixing explosives but in propelling them. After graduating from East Jefferson High in 1957, Gordon then briefly attended LSU. While there, he formally asked the administration to begin integrating the university. He dropped out of college in 1958 and resumed his high school relationship with Rancier Ehlinger. They got involved in a car theft ring specializing in swiping Corvettes. Ed Butler was Ehlinger's cousin. Therefore, Novel first met Butler at this time. Butler was then an advertising executive just getting into CIA related propaganda work. By 1959, Novel had encountered David Ferrie, Clay Shaw and Dean Andrews. The latter two he met through a business concession he wanted to open at the Trade Mart.

It is his friendly CIA relations with assets like Shaw, Ferrie, and Butler, which first brought him into preparations for the Bay of Pigs.[50] We have already seen how Novel was involved with the transfer of munitions from the Schlumberger bunker at Houma, and in preliminary talks for a city wide telethon involving Sergio Arcacha Smith and a CIA officer who has all the appearances of being David Phillips. But Novel then became owner of two private businesses: a speedway in Hammond (about forty-five miles north of New Orleans), and a bar off the French Quarter called the Jamaican Village. The speedway was at least partly used as a CIA cover in preparation for the Bay of Pigs. For on the speedway lot was a storage bunker for even more weapons for the Bay of Pigs. These particular munitions were to be used for the New Orleans based diversionary landing by Nino Diaz which never came to fruition.[51] But another one of his Bay of Pigs duties utilized his electronics skills. Novel operated a CIA front called the Evergreen Advertising Agency . This was used for embedding cryptographic messages to alert agents in the field about the invasion date. Novel claimed to have spent over 72,000 dollars of the CIA's money to buy ad time to convey these secret messages.[52]

Since Novel was an experienced Agency operative, and since he had excellent electronics skills, he became a good target for Allen Dulles to hire to infiltrate Garrison's office. Since, due to those skills, he could wire the office for surveillance as part of a counterintelligence program. Counterintelligence techniques were something Dulles was all too familiar with from his decades long espionage career. The two met sometime in late 1966.[53] Since Novel was from New Orleans and knew about Garrison's good reputation as a DA, he was reluctant to perform the assignment. Predictably, Dulles had a lot of money with him, so Novel took him up on the offer. Novel found a good way to snuggle up to Garrison. It was through, Willard Robertson, one of the organizers of a group of wealthy city residents called Truth and Consequences. This was a private group that decided to back Garrison because Rosemary James's story had made the DA's use of his fines and fees fund so controversial on the Kennedy case. (The group was rather short-lived, and Garrison ended up spending a lot of his own money financing the inquiry.)

Robertson, a wealthy car dealer in New Orleans, was also a personal friend of Garrison. Novel was introduced to the DA by Robertson as a skilled investigator with razor sharp electronics skills—which was accurate. But Garrison did not hire him until February of 1967.[54] So now, in addition to DeTorres and Gurvich, Allen Dulles had his own personal agent on Garrison's staff. And in fact, once on Garrison's staff, Novel promptly went to work secretly wiring Garrison's office for sound.[55] As Lisa Pease notes in her fine three part series based on Novel's deposition in his lawsuit against Garrison, Novel admitted that he and Dulles used to talk a lot about Garrison's case.[56] And Novel's communications were not just limited to Dulles. He also wrote letters to Richard Helms about Garrison.[57] What makes this so fascinating is that all three of these infiltrations began almost six months before Garrison even accused the CIA of being part of the assassination plot against Kennedy!

But Novel was also quite friendly with the FBI. In fact, when he returned from his first long discussion with Garrison, Novel described the front of his home looking like an armada of FBI agents had descended upon it: "They were across the street in the doorway. They were across the street in the alley, there was two or three of them dressed up as bums."[58] Gordon described the agents as "hungry wolves" who nevertheless addressed him politely with: "What has the Giant [Garrison] got on his mind tonight?" They asked if he could get close to the DA, and if he could would he help them? And Gordon agreed to cooperate with them.

But it did not take long for Novel to blow his cover. He began to meet with NBC producer Walter Sheridan. He met Sheridan through an old lawyer acquaintance who represented him in his dealings with Clay Shaw, Dean Andrews.[59] Sheridan actually met Novel in Andrews's office. One of the first questions Sheridan asked him was, "Tell me everything you know about Garrison. I've got to know." He also asked the Bay of Pigs accessory about various Cubans he knew.[60] At this point, although Novel stayed in touch with Dulles and Helms, he now also began to do paid work against Garrison for Sheridan and NBC. For instance Sheridan wanted to know where Sergio Arcacha Smith was; and he also requested that Novel photograph some of the exhibits Garrison held as evidence. Which Novel did with a Minox camera. As Novel admitted in his deposition, he gave Sheridan some of his surveillance tapes of Garrison's office.[61] The problem was that—New Orleans being the smallest big city in America—wind of Gordon's meetings with Sheridan got back to Garrison. And once the DA realized what Sheridan was up to, which did not take long, he immediately got suspicious of his newly hired "security expert."

As he should have. On March 7, 1967, Novel called up a policeman he knew, a Sergeant John Buccola.[62] He asked him if he had been assigned to Garrison's Kennedy probe yet. Buccola said he had not. Gordon said he would be soon. And when he was, he should call him. In the interim, Buccola found out that Novel was paying the police for information about Garrison's probe. Two days later, as Novel predicted, Buccola and his partner Thomas Casso were transferred to Garrison's office. Buccola called Novel and met him at the Jamaican Village. He asked him how he knew he would be transferred. Novel said he had connections everywhere. (Which he did.) He now began to ask Buccola questions about Garrison's probe, and he requested certain mug shots of Ferrie's friends from police files. He even made a telling remark to them about the case: "When Garrison opened up his case to you, weren't you amazed to hear about the Second Oswald?" He then made an even bolder comment. He asked about a student friend of Ferrie's ducking back to college "when Ferrie was killed." Buccola wrote to Garrison's Chief Investigator Lou Ivon that Novel did not say "when Ferrie died." He specifically used the work "killed." Novel added that he knew all the principals involved in Garrison's case and the exact location of Clay Shaw. This last seemed aimed at Buccola. Because the first assignment Ivon gave him was to find Shaw. Which he and his partner Casso had spent twelve days working on—without success. And vice-versa, Shaw knew Novel's phone number also, even when he was in Reno, Nevada. A number almost no one else had.[63]

After a couple of weeks of this kind of behavior, on March 16, 1967, Novel was subpoenaed to testify before the grand jury. He appeared with, not one, but two attorneys: Steve Plotkin and Eddie Sapir.[64] It was a week after this appearance, on March 23, that Novel sold his interest in the Jamaican Village. He then skipped town. Plotkin said his client was visiting Washington. He added that Novel would return in due course. He then said, "His absence from the state is not to avoid the subpoena, or not to cooperate with the district attorney's office, but for personal reasons."[65] This was a lie. Novel would not return to New Orleans until years later. And his intent was not just to avoid cooperating with Garrison. Now that he was out of his legal clutches, he was going to smear him in newspapers across the country. But especially by telephone and telegram to papers and magazines inside the

Crescent City. How? Because now, Dulles and the Agency would begin to connect the fugitive from New Orleans with over a dozen CIA friendly journalists who—in a blatant attempt to destroy Garrison's reputation—would proceed to write up the most outrageous stories imaginable about the DA.[66] For instance that Garrison had advanced a "bizarre plan" to Novel, which entailed shooting Ferrie with a tranquilizing dart, kidnapping him, and applying as much sodium pentothal as needed to get him to confess.[67] Later on he called Garrison "power-mad. . . . His mad ambitions have run away with him."[68]

To lend an air of credence to these wild charges, Walter Sheridan had arranged for Novel to take a polygraph test in McLean, Virginia. Novel then stated that he passed the test. This self-serving proclamation was also trumpeted in the media.[69] For example, Novel said that when he was asked by the polygrapher if Garrison's inquiry was a fraud, he answered "yes." And the machine revealed he was being truthful. What the media did not investigate is the man Sheridan had hired for the Novel polygraph. Lloyd Furr was a partner of Leonard Harrelson. Harrelson was later investigated and prosecuted for fraud in polygraphing a certain number of police officers in St. Louis. Neither Furr nor Harrelson was a member of the Academy for Scientific Investigation, a professional board group that critiqued polygraph technicians and pushed for higher standards in the field. In fact, this group specifically criticized the work of Harrelson in a previous case where he was also employed by Sheridan. They said he deliberately lied about a certain polygraph result.[70] After this dubious examination, Novel flew to Columbus, Ohio where he was safe housed. Governor James Rhodes did not sign the extradition papers from Garrison to allow him to be sent back to Louisiana. We will pick up this important strand in the next chapter.

As stated earlier, there were four stages enacted in the overall plan to subvert Garrison. What has been just described here is the first one, consisting of singleton type penetration operations by DeTorres, Gurvich, and Novel. It is important to note a certain crossover from phase one singleton operations to what can be called phase two: the Walter Sheridan assault. For William Gurvich was sent by Sheridan to visit with Bobby Kennedy. Clearly this was an attempt by Sheridan to prejudice Kennedy against Garrison.[71] Novel fleeing to Columbus, Ohio, and beginning an incessant media smear crusade against the DA is also important in the overall picture. Because as Paris Flammonde noted in his book *The Kennedy Conspiracy,* there was a long and intense media campaign that culminated in the last week of June with Walter Sheridan's Monday night program entitled "The JFK Conspiracy: The Case of Jim Garrison." What Novel's proclamations did was to begin this national propaganda barrage which would provide cover for certain governors not to honor extradition requests and for certain judges to decline to serve subpoenas.

Once Ferrie and Del Valle were dead, it became much more difficult for Garrison to proceed. The lawyers on his staff knew that. Garrison held a meeting to see what his employees wanted to do at this point. Assistant DA Charles Ward recommended he stop the inquiry. Garrison disagreed. After the meeting, Jim Alcock and John Volz, two of his best trial specialists, went into his office. They explained how difficult it would now be with his best witness gone. Volz pointed out how short they were of help and he also recommended halting the inquiry. Garrison would have none of it, although he did say that anyone who wanted off the Kennedy inquiry could leave.[72]

Garrison now decided to proceed against a second suspect he was building a case against. The man who he knew was Clay Bertrand. On March 1, 1967, at 5:30 P.M., Garrison issued an arrest warrant for Clay Shaw and a search warrant for his home in the French Quarter. When Garrison's investigators came back from Shaw's house, they had with them some strange artifacts: two large hooks that had been screwed to the ceiling of Shaw's bedroom, five whips, several lengths of chain, a black hood, a webbed hat, and a cape. Shaw passed this off as Mardi Gras attire.[73]

Explanations aside, it was clear that the fifty-four-year-old bachelor was into the nether regions of sado-masochist activity. In fact, Shaw's position as director of the International Trade Mart had caused him to come under the all-seeing eyes of J. Edgar Hoover. Hoover had in his Bureau files a report by an informant who stated that his homosexual relations with Shaw included sadism and masochism.[74] It all explained Shaw's use of Andrews to defend the "gay Mexicanos." It also may have accounted for his use of an alias. Shaw's homosexuality may also have provided a bond between the cool, wealthy, well-mannered Shaw and the excitable, rootless, eccentric Ferrie, a bond beyond their politics, and (as later revealed) their Agency ties.

The search of Shaw's home turned up another interesting tidbit. In his address book, there appeared the following entry:

Lee Odom, P. O. Box 19106, Dallas, Tex.
Garrison was aware that this same post office box number also appeared in Lee Oswald's address book.[75] Shaw's lawyers later produced a man named Lee Odom who said he was from Dallas. The box number, he said, was that of a company he once worked for, and that he had tried to contact Shaw about "promoting a bullfight" in New Orleans. To Garrison, this was all reminiscent of Ferrie's story about setting off for Texas to ice skate and hunt geese in a lightning storm.

But there was another entry in Shaw's book that was just as interesting. Although the entire book listed addresses and phone numbers, on one otherwise blank page were scrawled the two abbreviations "Oct." and "Nov." and next to these, the word "Dallas."[76]

On March 14, 1967, Garrison initiated a preliminary hearing against Shaw. This is a process usually requested by the defense, because it requires the DA to present a *prima facie* case to a judge or panel of judges. Prosecutors do not normally request it because, at such a hearing, the defense can cross-examine witnesses, which they cannot do in a grand jury proceeding.

At the hearing, Garrison presented as his main witnesses Perry Russo and Vernon Bundy. Bundy was a drug addict who testified to seeing Shaw meet with Oswald on the shores of Lake Pontchartrain and pass him money. After the hearing, a three-judge panel held that there was enough evidence to charge Shaw with conspiracy to murder John F. Kennedy. Then, Garrison took his case to a grand jury, and it issued the indictment.

"Big Jim Will be Dumped in the White Paper Can"

There can be little doubt that Garrison's success at the preliminary hearing drove Walter Sheridan into high gear. As we have seen, once Sheridan arrived in town he began to meet with some of Garrison's witnesses, like Dean Andrews. He then met with Gordon Novel (who later wired the above sub head message to *New Orleans Magazine*).[77] From the moment he arrived in town there was never any doubt about where Sheridan was headed. He had made up his mind about the DA within twenty-four hours of arriving in New Orleans.[78] He was going to turn the tables on him. Garrison was now going to become the defendant. Sheridan was going to achieve this by using four major techniques:

1. He was going to attempt to "flip" certain of the DA's witnesses.
2. He was going to accuse the DA of using unethical practices.
3. He was going to give his production a bare bones stage play look to make it appear like an informal hearing, with Garrison as the accused.
4. Offscreen, he was going to use certain allies of Shaw, his defense team, and the CIA to create his wildly skewed film.

Regarding the last, we have seen how Sheridan met up with and began to exchange information with Gordon Novel. Further, Sheridan was going to use people like Hugh Aynesworth, James Phelan, and Gurvich to aid his show. But Sheridan, through his lawyer Herbert Miller, was also in contact with the CIA. The earliest known declassified document in this regard is dated May 8, 1967. This is a summary of two phone calls between Miller and Richard Lansdale. Lansdale was the assistant to CIA Chief Counsel Lawrence Houston. The topic of conversation was the trip arranged to Washington by Sheridan for Al Beaubouef, one of Ferrie's companions to Texas the weekend of the assassination.[79] After talking to Sheridan and Miller, Beaubouef became quite malleable. For Miller advised Lansdale that, "Beaubouef would be glad to talk with or help in any way we want." This is an example of technique number one: the reversal, or flipping, of a Garrison witness. For as Garrison noted in his *Playboy* interview, after his trip to Washington, "a change came over Beaubouef; he refused to cooperate with us any further and he made charges against my investigators." The routing of this Lansdale memo prefigures the third phase of the subversive effort against Garrison by the Agency. For, among other places, the memo went to both the Office of Security and James Angleton's Counterintelligence unit. But, what makes this so interesting is that Angleton *already* seemed aware of Beaubouef's journey to Washington.

It appears he was tipped off to this by Sheridan. Angleton relayed this information to his FBI contact Sam Papich and expressed his view of the importance of Beaubouef to Garrison's case. The reason for the coziness between Angleton and Sheridan may be due to a fact revealed by Jim Hougan: Sheridan had worked for the National Security Agency prior to going to work for Bobby Kennedy.[80] Sheridan worked the counterintelligence unit at NSA, which would suggest he had previous liaison ties to Angleton.[81] Just seventy-two hours after this communication about Beaubouef, Miller wired another message to Angleton. Lansdale now wrote that Miller had told him that Sheridan would be willing to meet with CIA "under any terms we propose." Further, Sheridan would be willing to make the CIA's view of Garrison, "a part of the background in the forthcoming NBC show."[82]

From viewing the final product, there can be no doubt that this happened. And, in fact, because Sheridan's show took awhile to produce—it was actually once planned to be in two parts—the CIA seems to have been eager to help defray production costs. William Martin had learned from Clay Shaw's friend David Baldwin, that some of the money for Sheridan's show was being funneled through the large law firm of Monroe and Lemann in New Orleans.[83] This would seem natural since Stephan Lemann, a partner in the firm, was General Counsel for WDSU TV, the TV station Sheridan was working with in New Orleans. The owners of this station, Edith and Edgar Stern, were big backers of Shaw. There can be little doubt that 1.) Sheridan needed the covert money, and 2.) NBC had little problem with what Sheridan was doing. Regarding the former, Sheridan put Novel on a 500 dollars per day retainer.[84] Regarding the latter, Andrews was promised a recording studio if he cooperated with Sheridan. Andrews told British television he had been personally pledged this by Bobby Sarnoff. Robert Sarnoff was the NBC president, and son of the founder of the TV network, David Sarnoff.[85] Capping all this is information given to a local FBI agent by WDSU reporter Rick Townley. Townley also worked with Sheridan on the show. Townley said he had received instructions from NBC in New York that the special Sheridan had in preparation on Garrison had instructions to "Shoot him down."[86]

With this large budget, plus a rubber stamp from NBC, Sheridan began to utilize his skills as a former intelligence operative on Garrison's witnesses. But first, he understood that he had some natural allies to help him in the Crescent City. One was Shaw's lawyers. A second was the Metropolitan Crime Commission. The MCC was a private group of wealthy individuals who wanted to keep a vigilant eye on any spurt in crime in the area. Its director at this time was former FBI employee Aaron Kohn. Kohn was still close to the man he had worked for, J. Edgar Hoover. He also despised Italian-Americans.[87] Therefore he was eager to deflect attention away from any FBI failures in the Kennedy case, and to try and place culpability on the Mafia. He was also a close ally of Shaw's lawyers, and was willing to help Sheridan.

Now that we have noted this covert team assembled around Sheridan, and outlined their four techniques, let us now detail some of the things this motley crew did, all the time accusing Garrison of using unethical, extralegal methods.

Marlene Mancuso was Novel's estranged wife. She had been talking to Garrison. She had detailed knowledge of Gordon's Agency activities with people like Ferrie and Sergio Arcacha Smith. Plus she was fully informed about the transfer of arms from the Schlumberger bunker for the Bay of Pigs. In May of 1967, Townley found her working as a cashier in the Quarter at a place called Lucky Pierre's. Townley told her bluntly that Garrison was going down. They wanted her to say, on camera, that the DA had coerced her into giving him testimony about the Schlumberger munitions transfer. When that did not work, a friend of Gordon's called and warned her about facing federal perjury charges if she did not turn on Garrison. Finally, Sheridan showed up in person. He also said that Garrison was going down the drain, and she was going with him. But if she would talk to him, he would get her a job at NBC. This also failed. So Sheridan started following her around. Once he followed her to church. His excuse was that he wanted to say a prayer inside. One day both Sheridan and Townley showed up at her front door. They said they were looking for Gordon. The next day Townley called her and said if she did not get away from Garrison, she could get killed.[88] Mancuso did not turn on Garrison. She signed a statement for the DA revealing the threats and extortion by Townley and Sheridan.

Jules Ricco Kimble was a Garrison witness who said he traveled once on a flight to Canada with Ferrie as the pilot and Shaw as a passenger. Sheridan paid him 500 dollars for papers and tapes spirited out of Ferrie's apartment by Kimble's friend Jack Helms. Sheridan then told Kimble to stop talking to Garrison and go to Canada where he would be "safe." If he was subpoenaed by Garrison, the FBI would help him out in exchange for his cooperation with Sheridan.[89] According to former Banister investigator, and future Southern Research employee Joe Oster, Kimble actually did go to Canada.[90]

One of the more startling declarations that the ARRB uncovered was an affidavit by a man named Fred Leemans. Leemans was a Turkish bath owner who originally told Garrison that a man named Clay Bertrand had frequented his establishment. Leemans was the climactic interview for Sheridan's special. He testified on the show that the DA's office had actually approached him first, that he never knew that Shaw used the alias Bertrand, that everything he had previously said to the DA's office were things he was led to say by them, and that they had offered to pay him 2,500 dollars for his affidavit in which he would now say that Shaw was Bertrand and that Shaw came into his establishment once with Oswald. In other words, all the things Novel had been saying in his public declarations about Garrison were accurate. At the end of his interview, Leemans told Sheridan and the public that everything he had just revealed on camera was given to NBC freely and voluntarily. Leemans even said that he had actually asked Sheridan for some monetary help but Sheridan had said he did not do things like that.

In January of 1969, Leemans signed an affidavit in which he declared the following as the true chain of events:

> I would like to state the reasons for which I appeared on the NBC show and lied about my contacts with the District Attorney's office. First, I received numerous anonymous threatening phone calls relative to the information I had given to Mr. Garrison. The gist of these calls was to the effect that if I did not change my statement and state that I had been bribed by Jim Garrison's office, I and my family would be in physical danger. In addition to the anonymous phone calls, I was visited by a man who exhibited a badge and stated that he was a government agent. This man informed me that the government was presently checking the bar owners in the Slidell area for possible income tax violations. This man then inquired whether I was the Mr. Leemans involved in the Clay Shaw case. When I informed him that I was, he said that it was not smart to be involved because a lot of people that had been got hurt and that people in powerful places would see to it that I was taken care of. One of the anonymous callers suggested that I change

my statement and state that I had been bribed by Garrison's office to give him the information about Clay Shaw. He suggested that I contact Mr. Irvin Dymond, attorney for Clay L. Shaw, and tell him that I gave Mr. Garrison the statement about Shaw only after Mr. Lee [Garrison's assistant DA] offered me 2,500 dollars. After consulting with Mr. Dymond by telephone and in person, I was introduced to Walter Sheridan, investigative reporter for NBC, who was then in the process of preparing the NBC show. Mr. Dymond and Mr. Sheridan suggested that I appear on the show and state what I had originally told Mr. Dymond about the bribe offer by the District Attorney's office. I was informed by Mr. Dymond that should the District Attorney's office charge me with giving false information as a result of the statement I had originally given them, he would see to it that I had an attorney and that a bond would be posted for me. In this connection Mr. Dymond gave me his home and office telephone numbers and advised me that I could contact him at any time of day or night should I be charged by Garrison's office as a result of my appearing on the NBC show. My actual appearance on the show was taped in the office of Aaron Kohn, Managing Director of the Metropolitan Crime Commission, in the presence of Walter Sheridan and Irvin Dymond.[91]

This is one of the most revealing documents portraying the lengths to which Sheridan would go in tampering with witnesses. It also demonstrates that Shaw's lawyers—Bill and Ed Wegmann, Irvin Dymond, and Sal Panzeca—knew almost no boundary in what kind of help they would accept to win their case. Third, it reveals that Shaw's lawyers had access to a network of attorneys that they could hire at any time for any witness they could pry loose from Garrison. Because, as the declassified ARRB documents reveal, there was a CIA cleared attorneys' panel that was at work in New Orleans.[92] Attorneys that the Agency vetted in advance so they would be suitable for their covert use and could be trusted in their aims. The fact that Shaw's lawyers were privy to such CIA secret knowledge, and were utilizing it, shows just how willing and eager they were to indulge themselves in covert help—and then lie about it. For when the author discussed this issue with Irvin Dymond in his office in New Orleans, this is what he did. He tried to feign that he knew nothing about it. This is ludicrous. Because Shaw's boss, Lloyd Cobb, was given a Provisional Security Approval for this very panel at the time Sheridan's show was broadcast![93] In fact, Dymond knew so much about it that, as the Leemans affidavit shows, he used it. He even made referrals to it.[94] This important point, Shaw's lawyers' ties to the intelligence community, and their dissembling about it, will be returned to later.

With the above in mind, let us now note how Sheridan was intent on flipping Garrison's two preliminary hearing witnesses. Jane Lemann and Nina Sulzer were two New Orleans Parish prison workers. Lemann was related by marriage to Steven Lemann of the previously noted Monroe and Lemann, the

CIA related law firm funneling money to Sheridan and representing WDSU. Nina Sulzer knew Clay Shaw through her husband Jefferson Sulzer, a friend of Shaw's.[95] At the preliminary hearing, Bundy had noted that he had seen a man fitting Shaw's description meeting with a man he thought was Oswald near the Lake Ponchartrain seawall. The tall white haired man got out of his black sedan and walked in Bundy's direction. Bundy, who was about to inject himself with narcotics, started to walk away. But the man only said something about the weather to him. Bundy watched as the two men met. The man who Bundy identified as Shaw gave some money to the man who Bundy later identified as Oswald. Oswald put the money in his pocket, but as he did so, some leaflets fell out. After both men left, Bundy walked over and looked at the leaflets. They had something about Cuba printed on them and were yellow in color. And in fact, as assistant DA John Volz later discovered, some of the leaflets passed out by Oswald were yellow in color.[96] Of course, this would indicate that Shaw was involved with Oswald's agent provocateur activities that summer.

There were three people that Sheridan recruited to try and flip and discredit Bundy. They were Sulzer, plus convicts Miguel Torres and John Cancler. Cancler, a convicted burglar and pimp, was shown first on the show. He said that Bundy had previously told him he was going to lie to Garrison. Bundy even asked him for advice about the best story to tell. Miguel Torres had a record that included burglary, assault and suspected murder. He said pretty much the same thing: that Bundy told him he was going to make up a story about Shaw to get "cut loose." Towards the end, the men later returned on camera. Both now said that members of Garrison's staff had also tried to recruit them into their unethical crusade to convict Shaw. Cancler said he was supposed to "plant" incriminating materials in Shaw's house. Torres said he was supposed to say that Shaw made homosexual advances to him, and also that Shaw's alternate name was Clay Bertrand.[97]

As Garrison noted in his *Playboy* interview, Cancler and Torres were later called before the grand jury to repeat these charges under oath. They both declined and took the fifth amendment against self-incrimination.[98] Both were cited for contempt and got added time to their sentences. (Irvin Dymond got a former associate of his, Burton Klein, to represent Torres[99].)

But this was not all that Bundy had to endure. For Sulzer was also fully involved with Sheridan's efforts to subvert Garrison. From inside the prison, she began to talk to Bundy about his preliminary hearing testimony against Shaw. It was the same message that Sheridan had delivered to the others. As Bundy's cellmate told Garrison's office, Sulzer told Bundy "that he was riding the wrong horse, that he was on a losing team."[100] She then started giving Bundy magazines which featured anti-Garrison articles by people like Hugh Aynesworth. She then asked him what Garrison was doing for him, to which Bundy replied the DA was doing nothing for him. Sulzer then said that Bundy was going to get in trouble on the outside. She then went further by saying that someone was actually going to kill Bundy. She culminated this harangue with the threat that once Bundy got out, he would be as good as gone.[101] When Garrison put a tail on Sulzer, it was revealed that after one of her attempts to dissuade Bundy, she went to a residence at which Shaw was staying and spent about three hours with him.[102]

Alvin Beaubouef appeared on the program and, as predicted above—after his trip to Washington—said what Sheridan wanted him to say. On camera he said that he felt that Garrison's investigator Lynn Loisel had tried to bribe him for information that Garrison wanted to make his case. The problem is that in a sworn statement that Beaubouef signed predating the show he said that this was not the case. He wrote that "no representative of the Orleans Parish District Attorney's office has ever asked me to do anything but to tell the truth." What had happened was that Beaubouef had said that he could not spend any more time talking to the DA's office since he was in dire financial straits. Loisel said to him that if he told the whole truth about the case as he knew it, and if those facts led to the capture of the real killers of President Kennedy, then he probably would not have to worry about a job or money. This was then construed by the likes of Aynseworth and Sheridan as being bribery.[103] On the program, Sheridan tried to explain why Beaubouef had altered his story. The witness said that Garrison's staff had compromising photos of Beauboeuf and threatened to pass them out if he had done so. There is no evidence outside of Sheridan's fevered imagination that anything like this ever occurred.

James Phelan Declassified

Journalist James Phelan also appeared on Sheridan's program. In the May 6, 1967, issue of the *Saturday Evening Post,* Phelan wrote an article entitled "Rush to Judgment in New Orleans." From the title (borrowed from Mark Lane's book on the Warren Commission) on to the last sentence, the article was a one-sided attack on almost every aspect of Garrison's probe—written in a belittling, amused style that revealed the author's supercilious attitude toward the subject. Garrison, about whom Phelan had written a favorable piece in 1963, was pictured as an egocentric megalomaniac whom Phelan called a "one-man Warren Commission."[104]

Phelan's five-page article was filled with snide characterizations, half-truths, and innuendo. But he saved his harshest blast for the end. He wrote that when assistant DA Sciambra first interviewed Perry Russo, his notes made no mention of the party at Ferrie's. Phelan then suggested that all of Russo's testimony at the preliminary hearing had been pumped into him under drugs and hypnosis by Dr. Chetta and Dr. Fatter. It did not matter to Phelan that both Russo and Sciambra denied this to his face before he went to press. Nor that Russo had talked about the fateful party at Ferrie's to the Baton Rouge press and television before Sciambra had ever met with him.[105] When Phelan appeared on camera for Sheridan, he said essentially the same thing. He went on to say the same to James Kirkwood in his 1970 book on the Shaw trial, *American Grotesque*. And he repeated the same story in his 1982 book, *Scandals, Scamps, and Scoundrels*. What is astonishing about this is that not only did the mainstream media accept Phelan's story readily, but that even those in the Kennedy research community did so. Further, when asked, James Phelan never revealed his background as a compromised journalist who had ties to government agencies. The public had to wait for the declassification process of the ARRB to ascertain the facts about Phelan's checkered past.

Now that we know much more about him, there are many paths one can follow in order to understand what Phelan did in the Garrison investigation. A good place to start is his long association with Robert Loomis. Loomis was a former top editor at Random House who was known for sanctioning books that specialized in concealing the true facts about the assassinations of the sixties: in 1993 he sponsored Gerald Posner's infamous *Case Closed;* in 1970 it was Robert Houghton's book on the RFK case, *Special Unit Senator;* and then again, he helped publish Posner's 1998 book on the King case, *Killing the Dream.* The reader should note, not only did Loomis help get these spurious books published, he got them out at timely moments in history. The Houghton book was published right after the trial of Sirhan Sirhan. The John F. Kennedy book was out at the 30th anniversary of his death. The King book was also published at the 30th anniversary, and in the midst of a swirling controversy about that case due to legal proceedings instituted by attorney William Pepper in Memphis. Well, Loomis was the editor for Phelan's 1982 book which featured a long and derogatory chapter on the Garrison case.

Before Phelan ever got to New Orleans and Shaw's preliminary hearing, he had already done work for government agencies. In Garrison's files adduced for the ARRB, there is a report of a private investigator who went to visit Phelan unannounced. His pretext was that he wanted to ask him about an interview Phelan had done for *Penthouse Magazine* with Clay Shaw. The investigator asked Phelan if he was familiar with reporters being used by the CIA in planting stories. Phelan said he knew of this process of compromising journalists. But his personal ethics as a reporter would not allow him to compromise a story, or a source for a story. Further, he would never reveal the contents of any story prior to publication to anyone, especially to someone connected to a government agency. The visitor now showed Phelan declassified documents revealing two reporters, one working for the *Saturday Evening Post,* who were being used by the FBI in counterintelligence programs against the Klan. Since the *Post* had been Phelan's primary employer, Phelan now began to grow a bit uneasy and started stroking his arm.

The investigator now showed Phelan a photocopy of an article that appeared in the *Saturday Evening Post* in March of 1964. It was by Phelan about L. Ron Hubbard. The investigator then asked who the man at *Saturday Evening Post* was who assigned him the article about Hubbard. Phelan said he could not recall who it was. Phelan was then asked if he was ever assigned to write an article by the FBI, CIA, or the FDA. Phelan said this had never occurred. Phelan was then shown a copy of a letter from an editor at the *Post* consenting for the magazine to be used by the FDA for an attack on Hubbard. Phelan read the letter slowly and again got nervous. Phelan was then asked if he had ever been asked by an agency of government to furnish either his notes for a story or his interview notes to them before his article was published. Phelan denied this had ever happened. Phelan was now shown declassified documents revealing that this was precisely what he had done in relation to his Hubbard story. In his report, the PI writes, "As Phelan read the three documents he started breathing very heavily and started making some types of moaning sounds. He then grabbed one arm and stroked it."[106]

The reader should especially note here that not only was Phelan a willing conduit for a government agency, but then when asked if he was on a covert assignment, he continually lied about this aspect of his professional life. When, in fact, to anyone who carefully examined his career it would, at the very least, suggest itself. Needless to say, when the ARRB began to declassify documents on the Garrison investigation it was revealed that Phelan again did what he had denied he had done. He had gone to the FBI and turned over documents he had attained as a result of his interview with Garrison in Las Vegas in early 1967. In an April 3, 1967 FBI memo, it is revealed that R. E. Wick wrote to Cartha DeLoach that he had agreed to see Phelan reluctantly. Phelan was trying to pump Garrison for details about his investigation but was disappointed that the DA would return to criticism of the Warren Report.[107] Having had personal conversations with Phelan prior to the declassification of these FBI documents, the author can say that when asking Phelan these very questions about his dealings with Garrison, the pattern was repeated. That is, he denied informing to any government agency about the DA, and he also denied turning over any documents from his work product. In these FBI documents he requested that the Bureau not reveal his name. Therefore he probably thought he could maintain a false veneer of independence and deceive everyone about it. But after the ARRB review, Phelan was now exposed as lying about this crucial matter a second time. Needless to say, if the public had been informed about this past history, they likely would not have taken his writings about the DA at face value.

An important part of Phelan's rendition about his encounter with Russo in Baton Rouge was his asking him when he first mentioned the name of Clem Bertrand. For instance, Phelan told James Kirkwood that in Baton Rouge, Russo did not say anything about Clay Shaw as Bertrand, nor did he mention the gathering at Ferrie's home.[108] As the reader can see from the citation above, Russo did mention the gathering in a Baton Rouge newspaper. But further, there was a third party with Phelan when he went to see Russo for the first time after Garrison let him read Andrew Sciambra's memorandum about his Baton Rouge interview with Russo. This man's name was Matt Herron. Herron was a photographer for various large circulation magazines, including the *Post*. When Phelan discussed Herron with this author, he always clearly insinuated that it was no use talking to him, since Herron would back up Phelan's version of the encounter. That is, Herron also heard Russo say that the first time he had mentioned Bertrand at the gathering was in New Orleans.[109] In fact, in a phone conversation with the author, Phelan actually said that Herron had lost faith in Garrison after this.[110] Therefore, no one thought it was worth the trouble to find Herron. Even though he would be the deciding vote in the matter, because Sciambra and Russo disagreed with what Phelan had written about this issue.[111] In fact, Phelan actually told Kirkwood that after they left Russo's house, he told Herron to recall what Russo had just said since "someday you're going to be in court on this and I'm going to have to tell this story and you're my witness."[112]

Kirkwood was a lousy investigator. Because this is now exposed as another Phelan canard. After all these documents impeaching Phelan's credibility had now been exposed to the light of day, this author decided that if Phelan was willing to lie about such important matters as cooperating with the FBI and FDA, and turning over documents to them in advance of an article, then would it not be consistent that he would also lie about Matt Herron? That is, to camouflage his own story by discouraging anyone from communicating with the man. After all, contrary to what Phelan told Kirkwood, Herron was not called as a witness for the defense at Shaw's trial. Why would Dymond not call him if he bolstered Phelan's version of his encounter with Russo? So the author looked up Mr. Herron and talked to him on two occasions. On both occasions, Herron said that Russo had told them that he mentioned Bertrand in Baton Rouge. And further, that Russo's statements on this were very strong in 1967. Because of this, Herron was surprised when he read Russo's testimony at the Shaw trial. He felt that, for whatever reason, it was now diluted.[113] If you are counting, this is now three lies to three different people that Phelan told. Actually four lies, since he not only lied about Russo, but about what Herron would say about him. (As we will see in the discussion of the Shaw trial, Phelan told another lie about Russo in public.)

Let us address other misrepresentations by Phelan. The reason that Garrison met with Phelan and told him about his Kennedy inquiry in the first place is that Phelan had written a long story in the *Post* about Garrison's attempt to clean up the French Quarter. But as it turned out, Phelan did not write that story. It was written by local reporter David Chandler. Phelan changed it ever so slightly and then took the byline.[114] This might be the reason Garrison trusted Phelan and agreed to meet with him in Las Vegas to discuss the case with him at length. Also, on Sheridan's program, Phelan called Sciambra Garrison's first assistant. This was not accurate. John Volz was Garrison's first assistant at the time. In Kirkwood's book, Phelan describes Bill Gurvich as Garrison's chief investigator. Again, this is not true. Lou Ivon was Garrison's chief investigator. He then says that Gurvich was deeply troubled by what Phelan had learned about Russo and Sciambra. This is stage decoration by Phelan. Gurvich could not have been greatly disappointed since, as we have seen, he never believed in Garrison's case anyway. He was on assignment.

It is necessary now to explain why Phelan found it necessary to lie about Matt Herron. The strategy utilized by Phelan and Sheridan was to state that Russo had all these memories about Bertrand, Ferrie, Russo, and Oswald discussing an assassination plot drugged into him by Nicolas Chetta and Dr. Esmond Fatter. Chetta applied the sodium pentothal—commonly called truth serum—and Fatter conducted the hypnosis and then questioned Russo. When one reads these sessions in the correct order, one can see that there was no leading of the witness by Fatter. The author was fortunate enough to attain these transcripts directly from Garrison's files, even before the ARRB got hold of them.[115] When the two sessions are arranged in the correct order, as Garrison marked them, it is manifest that "Russo quite clearly and unequivocally describes Bertrand all by himself."[116] James Phelan and Shaw's lawyers quoted them out of sequence to make it seem that Russo had to be prompted to name Bertrand.

As both Bill Davy and Joe Biles accurately note, what Phelan always referred to as the "first memorandum" is actually the second memorandum. What happened is that when Sciambra went up to visit Russo, the witness orally sketched out the gathering at Ferrie's and named who was there. He also chose some photographs of the participants. But Sciambra thought it better for recall, and also for truthfulness, that Russo be put under sodium penothal and hypnosis for his actual description of the discussion. Therefore, he interviewed Russo about all the other things that ended up in the actual second memorandum, such as Russo's relationship with Ferrie, Ferrie's obsession with Kennedy, and the other times he saw Shaw/Bertrand, etc. As Biles points out, this is easy enough to discern by just looking at the signature block of the memo about the gathering at Ferrie's where an assassination was discussed. That date is February 28, 1967. The second memorandum, about the lesser details, was done about a week after Shaw's arrest, around March 6.[117] Further, it was this first memo, misrepresented by Phelan, that served as the basis for Lou Ivon's search warrant. In that warrant, Ivon writes about what Russo had said under truth serum and he adds the following: "That the said confidential informant while under the sodium pentothal verified, corroborated, and *reaffirmed* his earlier statements"[118] (italics added). Since Sciambra had still not finished his memorandum about the other things Russo had said to him, then clearly Sciambra had already related to Ivon what Russo had said in Baton Rouge about the gathering at Ferrie's apartment. That is why Ivon used the word "reaffirmed." And finally, as Biles points out: If all the things Russo had to say were really not that important, then why would Garrison OK the request by Sciambra to put him under hypnosis and truth serum?

The other objections to Russo's testimony are that in a TV interview he did before he was administered truth serum he was asked about Oswald and Ferrie. He said he did not recall Oswald being associated with Ferrie.[119] But the point is that the man Russo identified was Leon Oswald, not Lee Harvey Oswald. And in fact, the evidence today is pretty much decisive that there was a Leon Oswald in New Orleans around this time. For instance, Sylvia Odio, one of the best and most important witnesses in this case, said that two Cubans came to her house in late September of 1963 with a Caucasian man they called Leon Oswald.[120] Richard Case Nagell also said he knew a Leon Oswald in that summer of 1963. Nagell said that this Leon Oswald was meant as a Second Oswald and was working with the anti-Castro Cubans, he was not at all pro-Castro.[121] Raymond Broshears, a friend of Ferrie's, also spoke about a Leon Oswald. He described him as resembling Oswald.[122] Michael Kurtz interviewed rightwing witnesses in Baton Rouge who recalled meeting an Oswald who was introduced to them as Leon Oswald in July and August of 1963. This happened more than once, and on his last visit to the area, Leon Oswald was accompanied by two Latins.[123] David F. Lewis, who once worked for Banister, said that he was introduced to a man named Leon Oswald by Sergio Arcacha Smith's right hand man Carlos Quiroga at Mancuso's Restaurant in late 1962.[124] It is doubtful this was the real Lee Harvey Oswald since he was still living in the Dallas-Fort Worth area at the time. All of this testimony strongly suggests that there actually was a Leon Oswald who resembled Oswald. Niles Peterson, who was a friend of Russo's and briefly attended the gathering, told William Davy and Peter Vea that there was a Leon Oswald there.[125] This author believes that it was this man—not Lee Harvey Oswald—who was at Ferrie's the night of the gathering described by Russo.

In the light of all this new evidence, it is startling that some serious and intelligent people still take James Phelan seriously. Clearly, Phelan was on a mission. And like the intelligence assets they were, he and Sheridan were out to politicize, polarize, and propagandize Garrison's case any which way they could. What is surprising is that they were so successful for so long.

Hugh Aynesworth: CIA Applicant

Coordinated to appear in conjunction with Phelan's *Saturday Evening Post* piece, Aynesworth's article appeared nine days after Phelan's. On May 15, 1967, *Newsweek* published his "J.F.K. Conspiracy," the most violent attack on Garrison's investigation thus far. The first two sentences set the tone for what followed: "Jim Garrison is right. There has been a conspiracy in New Orleans—but it is a plot of Garrison's own making."[126] The piece made numerous bizarre accusations against Garrison: that the investigation had financially ruined several men; that the DA's office had offered a witness 3,000 dollars and a job to give false testimony; that Garrison's staff had threatened to murder a witness; that Garrison himself had threatened a man who tried to talk him out of his probe; that Russo had testified at the preliminary hearing under post-hypnotic suggestion; that Garrison was holding the citizenry of New Orleans in terror in order to manufacture more headlines; and that Garrison's theory of the assassination had gone through so many changes that his conspirator was now a composite of "Oswald, homosexual, rightwing extremist, FBI agent, Cosa Nostra hood, CIA operative and Russian double-agent."[127]

To understand how someone could conjure up such a fantasy—with utter disregard for the canon of reporting ethics—one has to understand who Aynesworth was and is, and how protected he was. At the time of the assassination he was a conservative reporter at the *Dallas Morning News*.[128] According to Hugh he was in Dealey Plaza on November 22. At times he says he was at the scene of Tippit's murder. He has also maintained he was at the Texas Theater when Oswald was arrested. Finally, he has written that he was in the basement of the Dallas Police Department when Oswald was killed by Jack Ruby. The problem is that its difficult to find evidence for him being at any of these places at the time he says she was—let alone all four of them. In spite of that, it seems that he quickly made the decision that he was going to make a career out of the Kennedy assassination. He also decided that he was going to try and keep the Commission honest. With Aynesworth that meant portraying Oswald as not just a lone assassin but as a serial political killer. On July 21, 1964, Aynesworth's colleague, rightwing syndicated journalist Holmes Alexander, wrote a revealing column about Hugh. The implication was that the local Dallas reporter did not trust Earl Warren to helm the Commission. He was therefore conducting his own inquiry. He had talked to Marina Oswald and she had told him that Oswald had also threatened to kill Richard Nixon. The portrait of Oswald slowly emerging from the small amount of information put out by the Commission was that "of a hard-driven, politically radical Leftist . . . If the full report follows the expected line, Oswald will be shown as a homicidal maniac." Alexander concludes with a thinly veiled threat: If the Commission's verdict "jibes with that of Aynesworth's independent research, credibility will be added to its findings. If [it] does not there will be some explaining to do." Clearly, Alexander had communicated with Aynesworth. And his view of the case, at this relatively early date, was as skewed as his friend's. For no objective person could possibly label Aynesworth's inquiry as "independent." To use one example: Aynesworth's story about Marina and Nixon was so far out that not even the Warren Commission bought into it.[129] For as the Commission noted, Nixon was not even in Dallas until several months after the alleged incident. And there was no announcement in the papers that Nixon was going to be there at this time period. Clearly, Aynesworth was manipulating a witness, in this case Marina Oswald, to achieve his own political agenda.

Not long after the assassination he was involved in the sale of Oswald's diary to the *News* for 50,000 dollars, and he became a close associate of Marina Oswald for about a month. The diary also appeared in *U.S. News and World Report*. There is a long FBI report on this subject. And although it does not come to any firm conclusions, it appears that the people involved in the heist of the diary from the police archives were assistant DA Bill Alexander and Aynesworth.[130] The diary ended up in *Life* and Alexander, Aynesworth and his then wife Paula ended up splitting tens of thousands of dollars. *Life* decided to pay Marina since it appears that Hugh originally tried to cut her out of the deal, even though she was the legal heir to the estate. In a follow up FBI report of July 7, it appears that the reporter was also using the diary as a way of career advancement. An informant told the Bureau that Aynesworth was trying to use the diary as leverage to become *Newsweek's* Dallas bureau chief. As the report notes, he did become a Dallas stringer for that publication afterwards.

In late 1966, somehow, some way, Aynesworth had became a part of the *Life* team reinvestigating the Kennedy case. This team was led by reporter Dick Billings and editor Holland McCombs (the latter was a friend of Clay Shaw's). Almost immediately, Aynesworth began informing on this inquiry to the FBI. On December 12, he told the Bureau that the team had discovered a witness who connected Oswald with Ruby. The inquiry eventually ran into the one being done by Jim Garrison.[131] Therefore, Aynesworth became one of the first to discover what Garrison was up to. The unsuspecting DA actually granted Aynesworth an interview. After which the FBI informant wrote a note to McCombs saying that they should not let the DA know they were playing "both sides" in the case. Again, this is insightful of Aynesworth's ethics. Since reporters are not supposed to be playing any sides. This was the first time Aynesworth had met Garrison. His reaction says all one needs to know about Aynesworth's objectivity in regards to the DA.

But the declassified files of the ARRB have now revealed something that presages all of this. In October of 1962, Aynesworth had applied for a visa to Cuba. He had heard nothing about it for eleven months. Then in September of 1963 he had gotten some news from Washington that it was now being considered. Shortly after he got this news, Aynesworth reported to J. Walton Moore of the Dallas office of the CIA. He told Moore that he was offering the Agency his services if he in fact got the visa. Moore noted in this document that he was now beginning to process a name check on Aynesworth and would keep his superiors informed of further developments.[132] In other words, Aynesworth had an application in with the CIA before the assassination. The paper trail indicates that Aynesworth was given the name of the CIA recruiter for the southwest area. But it ends there.[133] But there are many indications that Aynesworth ended up having a strong bond with the CIA.

As we have seen, Sheridan featured a segment on his program which centered on the accusations of Alvin Beaubouef. Well, in his May 15, 1967 article in *Newsweek*, Aynesworth did the same. Like Sheridan, Aynesworth ignored Beaubouef's previous statement in which he said all the DA's office ever stated to him was that they wanted him to tell the truth. Aynesworth also left out another significant factor. There are signs the tape originally made by Hugh Exnicios was later altered. For both Beaubouef and his new lawyer Burton Klein stated that several parts of the conversation seemed edited out from the original. These parts would all have disproved the notion of a bribe.[134]

It was therefore quite natural that Aynesworth became an informant for both J. Edgar Hoover and Lyndon Johnson on the Garrison case. In a document obtained through the Freedom of Information Act by Gary Mack from the Lyndon B. Johnson Library, Aynesworth reveals his intent with regard to Garrison in the following telegram to Johnson's Press Secretary, George Christian, at the White House. Attached to a draft of his upcoming article, it reads in full:[135]

> Here is the rough draft of the story we discussed this morning. It will be changed in a minor way, but for the most part will be just this.

The story will break late Sunday via the wire services. Naturally, the strength and seriousness of it will evoke considerable reaction. I thought the President might be interested in this advance version.

I am not offering this for comment of any kind, nor a check of the validity of any part. Simply, it's FYI . . . .

Naturally, I would expect this to go no further.

My interest in informing government officials of each step along the way is because of my intimate knowledge of what Jim Garrison is planning. The subpoena of two FBI agents Saturday (today) is another step in his plan to make it seem that the FBI and CIA are involved in the JFK "plot." He is hell-bent on involving several high officials, is considering embarrassing others. In his devious scheme he can—and probably will—do untold damage to this nation's image throughout the world.

I am well aware that Garrison wants the government to defy him in some manner or to step in to pressure a halt to his "probe," but, of course, this should not happen . . . for that is exactly what Garrison wants.

I intend to make a complete report of my knowledge available to the FBI, as I have done in the past.

                                                            Regards,
                                                            Hugh Aynesworth

The reader should note that, like Phelan, Aynesworth did not want the fact that he was a government informant revealed to the public. He wanted the benefits of being an informant, but none of the derogatory aspects associated with it. Like Phelan, he wanted to maintain the illusion of being an actual reporter instead of a government flack.

The declassified files of the ARRB reveal that once Aynesworth got to New Orleans, he wore at least three hats. He was ostensibly *Newsweek's* Dallas stringer, but he was also being paid by Time-Life for the work he did on their Kennedy probe. But almost immediately after he got there, Aynesworth went to work for Shaw's lawyers, undermining Garrison. This can be traced to at least February of 1967. We know this because a lawyer for Garrison, Jim Alcock, had gone to Dallas to try and interrogate the fascinating suspect Sergio Arcacha Smith. But Garrison made a mistake here. He assigned investigator Bill Gurvich to go with Alcock. Therefore, through Gurvich, Aynesworth likely learned of this crucial appointment. And he followed the events as they happened. On the evening of Friday, February 24, from New Orleans, Alcock tried to phone Arcacha Smith at his home. He left a message with his wife that Garrison would like to talk to her husband and he would wire him airfare to New Orleans. When she declined for him, Alcock said he would travel to Dallas then to question him.[136] When Alcock arrived the next morning and phoned him, Arcacha Smith got in contact with the police. Officers Cunningham and Rodgers now went to his home to await a further call.[137] That call did not come until 5:00 P.M., hours after the officers had left. Again, Alcock could not connect with Arcacha, even though he appeared to be home at this time. The Cuban suspect now called the police again. They were there when Alcock called at 9:15 P.M. Arcacha Smith asked Detective Rodgers to pick up the phone. Alcock said he wanted to question Arcacha Smith in the Kennedy case. Rodgers replied that the suspect did not want to talk to him. He then asked if Alcock had an arrest warrant with him. Alcock said he did not. Rodgers then arranged for Alcock to meet with Arcacha Smith at City Hall.[138]

At ten that evening, the two officers and Arcacha met Alcock and Gurvich on the third floor of the building. Gurvich plugged in a tape recorder and Alcock asked the policemen if they would leave so they could question Arcacha Smith alone. Arcacha did not like this and so the officers suggested an attorney be present. Arcacha requested Bill Alexander be in attendance. Alcock recognized Alexander as the assistant to DA Henry Wade. The conference therefore ended. Arcacha Smith was then escorted home and a security detail was stationed outside.[139]

The next day, Sunday the 26, Aynesworth appeared from his position off stage. He first called Arcacha Smith. He told him he was preparing a report for *Newsweek* that would attack Garrison's handling of this "so called conspiracy." The following Monday, the Dallas police now arranged a meeting between Aynesworth and Arcacha Smith. This meeting was held in the Criminal Intelligence Section of the Dallas Police offices. Aynesworth told the suspect that he had informants inside Garrison's office. He therefore had names of witnesses interviewed by the DA, and also persons who Garrison was trying to find in order to question.[140] What followed was clearly a sort of stage play between Aynesworth and Arcacha Smith. Superficially it was being done to inform the suspect about Garrison's inquiry. In reality it was being done to influence the Dallas Police against Garrison. Aynesworth said that Garrison's inquiry was based around David Ferrie. Arcacha now replied that although he knew Ferrie, he was never friendly with him. As we have seen, this reply does not align with the record. Since both men worked together on the Bay of Pigs, out of Banister's office, and Ferrie watched films of the ill fated CIA landing at Arcacha Smith's home in New Orleans. (Later, Arcacha Smith got even more ridiculous. He said he had never heard of Gordon Novel.[141]) Aynesworth now argued for Ferrie's innocence and told Arcacha that Garrison had gotten his unpublished phone number and address from his friend Carlos Bringuier. To show just how plugged into the DA's office he was, Aynesworth then listed the names and addresses of 19 people who Garrison's investigators had interviewed. The Dallas police now checked those names against their indices. Aynesworth concluded the meeting by saying that Garrison now considered Arcacha Smith as important a witness as the deceased

Ferrie had been.[142] It is this author's view that, tipped off by Gurvich, Aynesworth was in Dallas on Friday. And it was he who told Arcacha Smith to request the police to be at his home when Alcock called. It was also Aynesworth who suggested that Arcacha Smith not submit to questioning unless the police were there, knowing that Alcock would not accept those terms. Further, that it was Aynesworth, who was friends with Bill Alexander, who then suggested that Arcacha Smith name Alexander as the attorney he wished to be in the room with him during questioning.

This episode has been described in some length because it sets up a paradigm for what Aynesworth did for the next four years. Because, astonishingly, Aynesworth was in contact with Ed Wegmann, Shaw's personal lawyer, all the way until 1971.[143] Once he set up shop in New Orleans, Aynesworth spent much of his time writing up detailed reports for Shaw's lawyers about certain people involved in Garrison's inquiry. The breadth and depth of these reports suggests that Aynesworth was getting input from either very high level private intelligence networks or from the FBI and/or the CIA. For instance, in a report on Ferrie, Aynesworth mentioned that the CIA had tried to get former Nazi commando Otto Skorzeny to attempt a Castro kidnapping plot in 1963. Prior to reading these files, the author had never seen this written about anywhere. Yet somehow, Aynesworth got wind of it.[144]

But besides preparing these reports, Aynesworth's major function was as a counter intelligence operative for Shaw's defense team. Drawing on his undercover allies in Garrison's office, Aynesworth would then set about tracking down these prospective witnesses, often before Garrison did. Aynesworth even knew about certain witnesses who called into local papers, like the *States Item*. Cedric von Rolleston had called into that paper in October of 1967. Aynesworth knew about the call that week.[145] Rolleston was from Alexandria, northwest of New Orleans. He was one of several witnesses to an odd group of Oswald sightings in the Lafayette-Alexandria area in October of 1963. For instance a man calling himself Oswald had created a ruckus at a Holiday Inn in Lafayette. He had criticized the Kennedy family and then signed his bar slip, "Hidell."[146] Garrison had Francis Fruge and Anne Dischler check out these leads. But since he was short handed, he decided to switch Fruge and Dischler over to the Clinton-Jackson area. Well, when the Wegmanns got wind of Rolleston, they wrote Aynesworth about him. Aynesworth reassured the lawyers that he had already begun "a systematic checkout on him." He concluded his letter with, "Meanwhile, don't worry about Cedric. He's in the bag."[147]

What did the ubiquitous Aynesworth mean by that last comment? We can gain a measure of that by the trip northward to Clinton by Aynesworth and his partner Jim Phelan. Clearly, Shaw's lawyers were worried about these witnesses.

Therefore, the two colleagues went up to the rural area to practice some of the tricks that Walter Sheridan had used to reverse certain witnesses on his special. Aynesworth brought with him a copy of John Manchester's statement from Garrison's office, about him recognizing Shaw as the driver of the car. Aynesworth told the sheriff that he could have a job as a CIA handler in Mexico for 38, 000 dollars per year. All he had to do was not show up at Shaw's trial. Manchester was not at all malleable. He replied with, "I advise you to leave the area. Otherwise, I'll cut you a new asshole."[148]

Who was Walter Sheridan?

The conventional wisdom about Walter Sheridan places him as a former FBI man; reportedly he worked at the Bureau for about four years. He then went to Bobby Kennedy's Justice Department. There the Attorney General gave him more or less carte blanche over the "Get Hoffa" unit.[149] That summary is superficially accurate, but the picture it paints is both narrow and incomplete.

Sheridan's ties to the intelligence community, beyond the FBI, were wide, deep, and complex. He himself said that, like Guy Banister, he had been with the Office of Naval Intelligence.[150] Then, *after* he left the Bureau, Sheridan did not go directly to the Justice Department. He moved over to the newly established National Security Agency.[151] This was a super-secret body created by President Truman in 1952 both to protect domestic codes and communications and to gather intelligence through cracking foreign codes. It was so clandestine that, for a time, the government attempted to deny its existence. Therefore, for a long time, it operated in almost total secrecy. Neither the Congress nor any federal agency had the effective oversight to regulate it.

It is relevant to note here that General David Sarnoff, founder of NBC, worked for the Signal Corps during World War II as a reserve officer. In 1944, Sarnoff worked for the complete restoration of the Nazi destroyed Radio France station in Paris until its signal was able to reach throughout Europe. It was then retitled Radio Free Europe. He later lobbied the White House to expand the range and reach of Radio Free Europe.[152] At about this point, Radio Free Europe became a pet project of Allen Dulles. Sarnoff's company, Radio Corporation of America, became a large part of the technological core of the NSA. During the war, David's son Robert worked in the broadcast arm of the Office of Strategic Services (OSS), the forreunner of the CIA.[153] Robert was president of RCA, NBC's parent company, at the time Sheridan's special aired. David was chairman. As we have noted, according to Dean Andrews, Robert—who he called Bobby—made him certain promises during the production of that infamous special. In the sixties, David Sarnoff was also associated with the Rockefeller Brothers Fund panel on foreign policy. As a member of that panel he argued in an essay published in *Life*, that the USA must fight a stronger and more aggressive battle in the field of psychological warfare against the USSR.[154] With these kinds of connections, the reader can see why the Sarnoffs would have little problem relaying a "Shoot him down" order for their former intelligence cohort Sheridan.

It was only after his service with the Office of Naval Intelligence, the FBI, and at the secretive NSA that Sheridan joined forces with RFK. While at the NSA, Sheridan was Chief of Counterintelligence, Special Operations Division, working out of the Office of Security.[155] Later on, he became Assistant Chief of the Clearance Division. This is very close to what James Angleton's duties were at CIA. Therefore it is hard to believe that Sheridan and Angleton did not know each other or work together. Allegedly, at Sheridan's behest, Sheridan met Bobby Kennedy through a church friend. This was when Chief Counsel Kennedy hired him as an investigator for the McClellan Committee, which was surveying organized crime influences in labor unions.[156] At this time, that committee had just helped convict Teamster union president Dave Beck. RFK would now focus on Beck's successor, Jimmy Hoffa. The intelligence connections Sheridan garnered at NSA served him well in his new position. Both he and the Attorney General were on shaky ground with Hoover—Sheridan for quitting the Bureau and RFK for encroaching on the Director's turf.[157] As a result, Hoover extended minimal official help to the Hoffa effort. But, even then, Sheridan, "actually coordinated FBI agents with his own men—told them where to go, and they went."[158] But still, Hoffa proved so elusive that the tactics the pair used in his pursuit were legally questionable. They needed tough, experienced, wily veterans to get a solid indictment of the Teamsters' chief. Therefore, Sheridan and Kennedy availed themselves of another intelligence unit at their disposal.

In 1961, they began farming out the brunt of their investigatory work to a private proprietary, seemingly created for their own purposes. The company was International Investigators Incorporated, nicknamed "Three Eyes."[159] According to a Senate investigator, it was "owned lock, stock, and barrel by the CIA."[160] Two of the original principals, George Miller and George Ryan, were, like Banister, former G-men who later went to work for CIA cover outfits.[161] According to another source, not only was Sheridan the liaison to Three Eyes, he "disposed over the personnel and currency of whole units of the Central Intelligence Agency out of the White House."[162] By 1965, when the investigatory phase of the Hoffa case was complete, Three Eyes was taken over by two former CIA officers.[163] One of them, Beurt Ser Vaas, later purchased the *Saturday Evening Post*.[164]

This relates to another of Sheridan's skills, one that he honed to a needlepoint in his campaign against Garrison—the use of media assets. Hoffa always maintained that, because they could not beat him in court, Kennedy and Sheridan would try to win their case in the press.[165] As Jim Hougan pointed out, the pair assiduously cultivated a series of media contacts with whom they planted material for lurid exposés of Hoffa and his union. Two of the more cooperative contacts were Time-Life and NBC.[166] As we have noted, the former printed many pejorative articles about Garrison's inquiry. The latter sponsored Sheridan's special. Given his experience, connections, and influence, Sheridan, it is safe to assume, was the in-house ringleader and overall coordinator of the national media campaign that crested during the summer of 1967, leaving Garrison's credibility and reputation permanently scarred.

It is often stated, especially by Mafia did it theorists, that Walter Sheridan was really a "Kennedy man." And that everything he did had RFK's sanction. Yet, we know from Mort Sahl that Kennedy did not buy Sheridan's anti-Garrison special. In the summer of 1968, as RFK was campaigning in California, there was a gathering at the house he was staying at. Sahl, who was an investigator for Garrison, was there with his then wife China Lee. Sahl had a performance that evening and left early. When he got back, his wife said words to the effect that she wished he had not left. Sahl asked her: Why not? She replied that all Bobby did the rest of the night was ask her questions about what Sahl and Garrison were digging up.[167]

In this regard it is important to note a rather remarkable declassified CIA file on Robert Maheu. It states that in the fifties Maheu "rented desk space in a suite occupied by Carmine S. Bellino, a former Bureau agent, Certified Public Accountant, and currently employed on Capitol Hill with one of the Congressional Committees."[168] As the document notes, this is at the same time that Maheu had formed Robert A. Maheu and Associates in Washington, D.C. As a wide variety of authors have shown, this "company" was really a CIA "fix it" operation which provided cover for Maheu to migrate from the FBI to the CIA. One of the assignments the CIA eventually gave him was to recruit a team of assassins from the Mafia to kill Fidel Castro. In fact, Maheu was undergoing clearance procedures from the CIA to do this particular job at the time he was occupying space with Bellino.

Before Guy Banister moved south to New Orleans, he had been stationed in Chicago. More than one writer has speculated on whether or not Banister knew Maheu in Chicago. Whether or not this is true, Maheu's evolution from FBI agent to "private investigator" does recall Banister's similar evolution going on at around the same time. But another ARRB declassified document makes the seemingly odd pairing of Maheu and Bellino seem not so odd. Joe Oster had been an acquaintance and partner of Banister's in the late fifties. He later worked for Southern Research, which became the giant detective service Wackenhut Corporation. In Oster's interview with the HSCA, he revealed that one of the people who helped Banister get his "private detective" firm off the ground at the time was none other than Maheu's roomie, Carmine Bellino. Which is a coincidence of almost cosmic proportions. When Sheridan went to work for the McClellan Committee he met Bellino. It was Sheridan who wanted to bring in Bellino to the RFK Justice Department for the Hoffa investigation.[169] It seems a bit ironic that a trusted aide of Robert Kennedy had been the partner of the man who helped set up the fall guy in the murder of his brother.

As noted above, Sheridan did all he could to scuttle Garrison's investigation of what was, at the time, largely a CIA/Cuban exile conspiracy. Therefore one would think that Sheridan would probably favor a Mafia oriented conspiracy. After all, Sheridan and RFK accused Hoffa of being closely linked to the Mob. In fact, as mentioned above, the polygraph examination that Sheridan faked was done on Hoffa associate Edward Grady Partin. It concerned an attempt to assassinate Robert Kennedy by Hoffa. The final HSCA Report made all kinds of accusations about the Mob plotting to kill Kennedy. In fact, Robert Blakey, the HSCA Chief Counsel, even announced at a press conference that although the report was neutral, his opinion was that the Mafia, particularly Carlos Marcello and Santo Trafficante, had killed Kennedy. Since Sheridan was consulted by Blakey for the report, one would think that he would agree with that thesis. Not so. The day the report came out, Marcello's lobbyist Irving Davidson made a phone call. He said that he had just talked to Sheridan. Sheridan said that the report was all bullshit.[170] Which leaves us with a final question about Sheridan. If he wanted to scuttle Garrison's CIA oriented conspiracy, and he thought that Blakey's Mafia conspiracy was BS, did he really do what he did to Garrison because he thought the Warren Commission was right? Or was he not really a "Kennedy Man" after all?

The sustained media attack was not just jackal journalism. For Garrison— and the public's right to know—it went deeper than that. As in political campaigns, the person who attacks first has the advantage. The other is forced on the defensive and has to waste precious time denying absurd accusations. In Garrison's case, the story he had to relate was complex, long, and detailed and did not lend itself to TV sound bites as does political sniping. It is no coincidence that Garrison's most compelling appearance was in the long *Playboy* interview in October of 1967. Allowed the freedom of dialogue, the DA gave a tour-de-force performance—penetrating, comprehensive, masterful in detail, sardonically humorous about himself and his critics. But what chance did he have against the multinational forces of the networks, the newsweeklies, and the giant newspapers?

Garrison was also somewhat restricted because Edward Haggerty, the trial judge, limited his pre-trial comments in public in order not to prejudice the case, a stricture Garrison referred to often in the *Playboy* interview.[171] Sheridan, however, was not limited by any such order, and, since he was working with Shaw's lawyers, he could comment at will on the evidence in the upcoming trial.

Rosemary James's exposé provided an opening for those who wished to trash Garrison and hide the truth about the crime from the American public. After February 17, 1967, a pall was cast over the investigation that the DA could never dispel.

There were some liberal-left publications that came to Garrison's defense: *Ramparts*, the *New York Review of Books*, and *The New Republic*.[172] Of course, the combined circulation of those three magazines was about one-thirtieth that of just *Newsweek*. Garrison tried to press the case himself on July 15, 1967, by appearing on a thirty-minute "equal-time spot" ultimately granted him by the FCC to answer the hour-long NBC show. After this he appeared on TV's "Issues and Answers" and, on January 31, 1968, for forty-five minutes on Johnny Carson's "The Tonight Show." It was all too little, too late. Garrison had been seriously wounded. As we shall see, the bloodletting was not over. Not by a long shot.

CHAPTER TWELVE

"Shaw Will Never Be Punished"

"The Shaw case will end without punishment for him, because federal power will see to that"

—*Tommy Baumler*

Under the impact of the May-June media blitz, Garrison had fallen from a position of strength in early February of 1967 to a position of weakness by summer. The press disclosure of his secret investigation and the death of his prime suspect, David Ferrie, had been twin disasters. But some of his problems had been of his own making. Not arresting Ferrie earlier was a key error. In fact, Garrison's staff had been friendly with the pilot up to the day of his death. When Ferrie's behavior became erratic and manic, Garrison's assistants arranged for a room for him at the Fountainbleau Motel.[1] Had they taken him into custody, the entire case might have turned out differently.

Garrison's overstated remarks to the international press corps also served as ammunition to be shot back at him later. His precautions in verifying witnesses' testimony with the use of polygraphs, Sodium Pentothal, and hypnosis were successfully distorted as "mind control" by his attackers, and were much too exotic for the public to understand.

But, the press coverage notwithstanding, Garrison had done fairly well in spite of his missteps. He had convicted Dean Andrews of perjury for reversing his Warren Commission testimony and for denying that a Clay Bertrand existed or that he knew who he was.[2] He had won the preliminary hearing in the Clay

Shaw case and had obtained an indictment. He had discredited Aynesworth's May 15 *Newsweek* story by producing a retraction from Alvin Beaubeouf, who Aynesworth said had been bribed and intimidated by Garrison's staff. In fact, a subsequent police investigation demonstrated that a tape recording supposedly proving the bribery attempts had been doctored. He had secured contempt citations against two of the witnesses who appeared on the NBC show, and faced down Sheridan and Phelan by challenging them in court, the former for attempted bribery of witnesses.

One point man for the Johnson Administration in damaging Garrison's case was Ramsey Clark. In March of 1967, right after his confirmation as Attorney General by the Senate Judiciary Committee, Clark made an extraordinary intervention into the case: he told a group of reporters Garrison's case was baseless. The FBI, he said, had already investigated Shaw in 1963 and found no connection between him and the events in Dallas. When pressed on this, Clark insisted that Shaw had been checked out and cleared.[3]

But in his haste to discredit Garrison, Clark had slipped. The obvious question, though not pursued by the Washington press corps, was *why* back in 1963 the upstanding citizen Shaw had been investigated concerning the assassination. Shaw and his lawyers realized the implication of Clark's gaffe even if the Attorney General did not. When one of Shaw's attorneys, Edward F. Wegmann, requested a clarification of Clark's statement, a Clark subordinate tried to control the damage by asserting that the original statement was without foundation: "The Attorney General has since determined that this was erroneous. Nothing arose indicating a need to investigate Mr. Shaw."[4]

Things got even worse for Clark. The same day he made his original announcement, a *New York Times* reporter, Robert Semple, wrote that the Justice Department was convinced that "Mr. Bertrand and Mr. Shaw were the same man."[5] Semple had gone to the National Archives seeking Warren Commission references to Clay Shaw. Finding zero, he was told that the Justice Department believed that Bertrand and Shaw were actually the same person, and that this belief was the basis for the Attorney General's assertion.

Clark had come to praise Shaw but instead had implicated him. However, Clark was not through trying to aid Shaw and sandbag Garrison. The AG would have a surprise for the DA at the upcoming trial.

Although Garrison had been cut up and severely wounded, he was still walking. Like Gordon Novel had said, he had been dumped in the NBC White Paper can. But he was trying to fight his way out of it. For instance, on July 15, 1967, he had been granted 30 minutes by the FCC to respond to Sheridan's wildly one-sided program.[6] And he did a highly effective interview in *Playboy* in October of 1967. There he did much to refute the charges in the

NBC program. And he made some pungent remarks about the CIA being behind the assassination. He also made certain comments about the media, his inability to subpoena witnesses from out of state, and his suspicions about certain attorneys for both witnesses and suspects in his case.[7] The declassified files of the Assassination Records and Review Board make it hard to argue with him on these points.

"Clandestinely Renumerated"

As previously stated, when Gordon Novel fled to Columbus he made a side trip to Virginia. On this trip he was accompanied by Sheridan for the express purpose of finding a polygraph expert to administer his test. This was being done to give a baseline for the compromised journalists to carry the rest of his anti-Garrison stories with.[8] Novel and Sheridan first visited the offices of private investigator John Leon. Leon declined doing the test and referred them to the aforementioned Lloyd Furr in McLean. This was about two miles from CIA headquarters in Langley.[9] When Novel said he passed the test, and then called Garrison's inquiry a fraud, this declaration was broadcast on NBC and printed by Hearst Headline Services—who had shared the cost of the examination.[10] Novel was then safe housed in Columbus where he began working with numerous compromised reporters defaming Garrison. He was also guarded by an unmarked car outside which was monitoring what he said inside. Electronics expert Novel didn't like this. So he sent his patron out one night to get a list of electronics equipment. When he returned with the shopping list, in short order, the wizardry of Novel had put together a short range receiver set. They were now listening to the men in the car.[11]

In addition to being the source for bizarre stories about Garrison, Novel now served another purpose. Since Garrison's interview in *Playboy* was both highly effective and read by hundreds of thousands of people, the CIA wanted to counter it. Since Novel was mentioned in the interview, he was now pushed into filing a libel suit against the DA. In addition to Dulles, one of the people involved in this was James Angleton.[12] How intent was Angleton in trying to discredit Garrison through this lawsuit? According to Gordon, FBI Director Hoover did not want him to file the suit. In fact, he was strongly against it. He feared what the proceedings would expose what the FBI was doing to keep tabs on Garrison.[13] (We will discuss that operation next.) So Angleton gave Novel photos of Hoover and Hoover's assistant Clyde Tolson in a compromising sexual position. He told Gordon to show the photos to the pair at a restaurant they frequented. Novel did so. This was supposed to prove to Hoover that the CIA had something on him and he had better not interfere in any way with what Angleton and Dulles had planned for Garrison.[14] (Hoover got his revenge on Novel in 1970 by having him arrested in Reno, Nevada for transport of illegal eavesdropping devices across state lines.[15] Novel later explained how flimsy this was since the electronic devices were purchased at a department store in Columbus.)[16]

How could the out of work, itinerant Novel afford to finance an expensive civil suit against both a large company like *Playboy*, and a veteran attorney like Garrison? Especially since the suit would drag on for over three years, until 1971. David Krupp, attorney for *Playboy*, twice posed this question to Novel in the process of the legal proceedings. The second time, the plaintiff answered that his attorneys "refused fees for this matter, but it is my understanding that they were clandestinely renumerated by a party or parties unknown to me. . . ."[17] This is remarkable, because by the time his sojourn in Ohio was over, Novel had employed no less than four attorneys: Steve Plotkin, Jerry Weiner, Elmer Gertz, a libel specialist, and most importantly Herbert Miller. Previously, local New Orleans reporters Hoke May and Ross Yockey had reports that Weiner and Plotkin, Novel's lawyers in Columbus and New Orleans respectively, had been on CIA retainer.[18] But Miller and Gertz were qualitative leaps. For example, Miller founded the Washington law firm of Miller, McCarthy, Evans, and Cassidy. Miller knew Sheridan through their mutual work on, first the McClellan Committee, and then in the Justice Department.[19] (In fact, Sheridan had an office at this firm when it evolved into Miller, Cassidy, Larocca, and Lewin.[20]) Miller had been close to Sheridan throughout the making of his NBC program. In fact, former Justice Department lawyer Miller was communicating with the CIA about Alvin Beaubouef's upcoming visit to Washington in May of 1967.[21] Miller was also the attorney who successfully defended Novel against Garrison's attempts to extradite him back to New Orleans.[22] Throughout that process, Miller served as a conduit between Shaw's lawyers and the CIA. For example, he was dropping off documents from Ed Wegmann to Richard Lansdale at Langley.[23] Quite naturally, Novel was in almost continuous contact with the man who recruited him into this effort, Allen Dulles. When Miller helped rescue Novel from going back to New Orleans, Gordon forwarded Dulles the newspaper clipping and suggested the former CIA Director could use this precedent to prevent Garrison from requesting his appearance in New Orleans. (As we will see, Dulles used a different technique.) How "clandestine" were the calls between Dulles and Novel at this time? In February of 1969, Novel sued Ohio Bell so that Garrison could not get any of the conversations between Dulles and his Ohio asset.[24] As mentioned previously, Novel testified in his lawsuit that he and Dulles talked "a lot." Krupp then asked Novel if he was correct in assuming that Dulles was in private practice in New York at the time of the exchanges. Novel now showed how close he was to the spymaster. He said that Krupp was wrong. Novel knew for a fact that he had his office on Q Street in Washington.[25]

Hoover's Total Surveillance

As mentioned above, J. Edgar Hoover did not want Novel to file his lawsuit. Novel stated that the FBI Director was worried that a counterintelligence operation the FBI had going could be exposed. This likely did not just mean Novel's debriefing of numerous FBI agents at his home. It more likely referred to the fact that Hoover had more or less complete surveillance on Garrison's office. (In his *Playboy* interview, Garrison thought his phones were being monitored, but he did not know by who.) In 1973, former FBI employee William Walter called Garrison's Chief Investigator Lou Ivon and told him about some of the FBI subterfuges regarding the Kennedy case and Garrison. The reader will understand that it is Hoover's prime role in the cover up of the former, that caused his worries about Garrison's investigation.

Walter first said that he did not like Garrison personally. But he thought he was sincere since he knew what went on in the New Orleans FBI office concerning the JFK case. He said messages were sent to the office that FBI reports were to be altered so that there would be no questions about the conclusions of the Warren Report. He also stated that there "were complete statements from various individuals which were eliminated by the agents."[26] He then said that the Bureau had assigned ten to fifteen agents to follow Garrison's investigators to see what leads they were checking out. (The author should interject here to offer the following: this FBI detail may have been used by Aynesworth so that the Bureau could get to leads before Garrison actually did.[27])

In 1977, Garrison interviewed Walter in person, as he was contemplating filing a lawsuit against the federal government for illegal surveillance. Which is what Hoover likely feared Novel's lawsuit would provide an opening for. In this interview, since he was more professionally established, Walter went further than he had in 1973. He positively stated that Garrison's office was wired. He named several of the former FBI agents and an undercover agent who had been transferred to the phone company's security office. He then outlined a long standing agreement the Bureau had with the phone company in which the FBI could patch anyone's phone line into the Bureau's local cable to produce self-activated recordings.[28] This team was working under the supervision of a former technical wiretapping wizard for the Bureau. A man named Charles Carson. Carson was then employed by Wackenhut. And since the Wegmanns had hired Wackenhut to work for Shaw, it seems logical to assume that some of this illegal eavesdropping material was being relayed to them. Walter then revealed that these audio surveillance tapes were transcribed nearly every day in the New Orleans FBI office. He knew this as a fact because he later married the Bureau secretary who typed up the transcripts! Another Wackenhut agent, Bob Wilson, moved into a New Orleans hotel from his home in Mississippi as part of the surveillance operation. One of his duties was to personally tail Garrison.[29]

Walter then revealed how the FBI tried to cover their role in this, and at the same time, after numerous pleas, to help Shaw's lawyers. He said that originally the technical surveillance was done by Wackenhut on assignment for Aaron Kohn of the Metropolitan Crime Commission. Since Kohn was in alliance with the Wegmanns, some of this material had to be passed on to them. But Walter clarified this by saying that this Kohn/Wackenhut bonding was just a thin cover. (Kohn could be trusted since he had worked for the FBI in their fingerprint division.) Because all the conversations were monitored in the FBI's Technical Surveillance Room, the transcripts of Garrison's calls were typed in the FBI office, and these full file documents were kept in the office filing cabinets.[30] That was quite a lawsuit Garrison could have filed.

We have just described how Walter told Lou Ivon that the FBI at times just completely eliminated the testimony of a witness. And we have seen in the previous chapter how Ricardo Davis told Harold Weisberg the FBI had shown him a photo of Clay Shaw the day after the assassination, a report that Weisberg could not find. Well, in the wake of Garrison's investigation, Hoover also tried to deny any reports made by the witnesses in Clinton or Jackson. Even though Reeves Morgan said he had called the Baton Rouge office of the Bureau after the assassination. Garrison's office tried to get in contact with the agent there, a man named Elmer Litchfield. Andrew Sciambra wrote him letters. There was no reply. Alcock and Sciambra went to his office. He would not meet with them. In February of 1968, Sciambra wrote Hoover himself about the call by Morgan, and if the FBI had any reports about Oswald in the Clinton-Jackson area, Hoover referred him to the Warren Report and the 26 volumes. Years later, the FBI agent revealed that he and a cohort had driven by the Clinton Court House days after the assassination. The colleague said to him, "That must be where that guy thought he saw Oswald."[31] And in fact, an FBI agent was dispatched to the hospital in Jackson to check on Oswald's visit there.[32]

Loran Hall: "Play This if I'm Killed"

In a future chapter we will discuss the crucial Sylvia Odio incident. For now, we can say that when the Warren Commission asked the FBI to either prove or disprove that this incident had occurred, Hoover manufactured a fairy tale that fell apart upon the slightest examination. Hoover said that Odio had been visited by three men, but none of them was Oswald. The trio was made up of William Seymour, Lawrence Howard of Marydale Farms, and a man named Loran Hall.[33] This was simply not true, and Seymour was not a ringer for Oswald. As he had to have been according to Odio's testimony.[34] Further, the Commission had the FBI documents in hand that disproved their own fanciful thesis, *before* the Hearings and Exhibits were published.[35] Yet these documents were not included in the volumes.

It is true that all three men were involved in anti-Castro Cuban exile activities prior to the assassination. And, in fact, Hall had been arrested during a south Florida raid as part of Kennedy's crackdown on exile activities against Cuba in 1963.[36] Howard was exceptionally fanatical. He told the HSCA's L. J. Delsa that if the government asked him to swim to Cuba to kill Castro, he would do it. He said this with a loaded revolver on the table in front of him.[37] Garrison called Hall in for questioning. Afterwards he issued a statement that said Hall was not connected with the events in Dallas on November 22, 1963. He then added that "it is equally apparent that other individuals and agencies caused Mr. Hall's name to be injected into exhibits of the Warren Commission and into other statements so that any effort to investigate the assassination would cause his name to appear."[38] This would seem to indicate that it was Hoover who did this.

At the time of the Garrison investigation, there is very little doubt that Hall did not want to go to New Orleans at first. Hall was involved with three men at this time: Richard Billings of Time-Life, Jerry Cohen of the *LA Times*; and Art Kunkin of the *LA Free Press*. The first two were invariably critical of Garrison almost from the start. Even though Billings had cooperated with Garrison for a few months late in 1966 and early in 1967. But when Garrison indicted Shaw, the Time-Life inquiry began to noticeably cool. What else could have happened with both Aynesworth and Shaw's friend Holland McCombs as part of the team? The interesting part of the *LA Times* coverage was this: On the editorial board at the time was Ed Guthman. Guthman worked for Robert Kennedy's Justice Department in 1963 as the Public Relations officer. Later on, he would be part of Bobby's final campaign for the Democratic nomination for the presidency. During that campaign, Martin Luther King was assassinated in Memphis in April of 1968. In Los Angeles, in June of 1968, at the Ambassador Hotel, RFK was shot and later died. This was the last of the major assassinations of the sixties. The trial of Clay Shaw did not take place until over seven months later. Therefore, Guthman was in a position to do something about what was happening to America at the time.

When the news first broke about Garrison's inquiry, the first *LA Times* reporter in New Orleans was Atlanta based Jack Nelson. Since one of Nelson's specialties was the FBI beat, he naturally gravitated to former FBI employee Aaron Kohn. Who, as we have seen, was helping Walter Sheridan tamper with a witness—Fred Leemans—by coercing him to lie on camera. The result of Nelson's conversation with Kohn was predictable. For Nelson then told writer Eugene Sheehan that he thought Garrison had concocted a "hoax," and he was "exploiting all the doubts about the [Warren] Commission." He then told Sheehan how surprised Kohn was that Garrison would let himself get caught up in such a "bush league play." Nelson then made a highly revealing comment that speaks reams about the mainstream press and its reaction to the four major assassinations of the sixties: "You know how these things go. Every time some-body dies, this kind of thing feeds on itself." In other words, it didn't matter to Nelson how unusual the actual circumstances of Kennedy's death were. And he apparently didn't care to read the already published books of Mark Lane or Harold Weisberg which delineated just how suspicious those circumstances were. For Nelson there was nothing more unusual about Kennedy's death than there was about, say, Franklin Roosevelt's.

While Nelson was being plied by Kohn in New Orleans, Jerry Cohen was on the beat in Los Angeles. He was joined by Lawrence Schiller. There have been literally scores of pages declassified on Schiller, mostly by the FBI. It is not at all an exaggeration to say that Schiller acted almost as a quasi-FBI agent for the Bureau on the Kennedy assassination. In 1967 he co-authored a book called *The Scavengers and Critics of the Warren Report*. This book had an accompanying album with it. Both works heaped ridicule on the critics of the Commission. But in true undercover agent fashion, Schiller never revealed to the critics he interviewed—such as Weisberg, Lane, and Sylvia Meagher—what his intent was when he interviewed them for the book.[39] One of his favorite spying targets for the Bureau was Mark Lane. He spent a lot of time and effort tracking down Lane's informants for the Bureau. In one FBI interview he did on this subject, he explained himself as an "advocate of viewpoint of [the] Warren Commission and is opposed to 'irresponsible journalism' of writers such as Lane."[40]

When Garrison was trying to bring Loran Hall back to New Orleans for an interview, he sent investigator Steve Jaffe to Los Angeles to try and get him to show up voluntarily. It took awhile for Jaffe to find Hall. And in a hand printed note he wrote to Jim Rose, he told the former CIA agent he was being tailed.[41] When Jaffe tracked Hall down he asked him why he was reluctant to be interviewed by the DA. Hall replied that he had been visited by Cohen and Schiller the night before. They both told him he would be charged with contempt or perjury and thrown in jail for five years if he visited New Orleans.

They also told him "Garrison was some kind of nut" and urged him not to go to New Orleans under any circumstances.[42] Schiller even went to the FBI to track down the agent who had interviewed Hall about the Odio incident back in 1964.[43] Schiller kept informing the FBI of his efforts, along with Cohen, to keep Hall away from Garrison. He also told them that he would co-write a negative article with Cohen about Garrison's attempts to get Hall back to New Orleans. He asked the Bureau for help in showing Garrison had no case against Hall and that he was "grasping at straws."[44] What is notable about this is that, to this author's knowledge, Schiller did not work for the *LA Times* at that time. Just how close did Schiller keep the *LA Times* on Hall's tail? When Hall flew to Sacramento to talk to Ronald Reagan's Attorney General Edwin Meese, Cohen went with him. He even paid for the trip.[45]

Hall was very worried at first about going to New Orleans. He claimed there had been two attempts on his life at the time. One was done by poison and one was by sabotaging the steering mechanism on his car.[46] In fact, he was so worried about his untimely death that he created a tape recording in case he was killed. He turned this tape over to Art Kunkin. Kunkin was the creator, publisher, and editor of the *LA Free Press.* This was one of the very few papers which treated Garrison favorably. Kunkin told the author this was an old reel to reel tape, and Hall met with Kunkin privately at his home to give it to him. Hall gave Kunkin strict instructions. He was only to play the tape in case Hall met an untimely death under suspicious circumstances: a one car accident. He was then to publicize the transcript in his paper. When the author met Kunkin in the nineties, he asked the editor what he did with the tape.[47] Kunkin said that since Hall did not die at the time, he never played it. The author replied, "I would have played it for myself that night just to know what was on it." Kunkin was then asked where the tape was now. Kunkin said he thought he still had it in his attic. A mutual acquaintance then spent an afternoon looking through his attic in an attempt to find the potentially explosive tape. To no avail.

There is one more culminating fact that needs to be noted about this sorry tale concerning a frightened Hall, FBI asset Schiller, the compromised Cohen, the spoon-fed Jack Nelson, and RFK aide Ed Guthman. While Guthman was a chief editor of the *LA Times* at this time, he actually visited with Garrison ever so briefly in March of 1967.[48] He then helped coordinate the *Times* coverage of the DA. Which, as we can see with Schiller and Cohen, was so biased as to be worthless. When this author wrote to him about this in 1993 and asked him why it all seemed so one-sided, he sent a note back. He stated that the *Times* had a few experienced reporters covering the Garrison case. He conferred with them. They then decided "that there was no substance to Garrison's charges."[49] The former editor was very likely being disingenuous. Or the years had clouded his memory. Because this is not accurate. And Guthman apparently knew it at the time. There is an interesting revelation about Guthman in Richard Billings's journal about his involvement with Garrison's inquiry. He writes there that the prolific FBI informant Lawrence Schiller, who worked so hard with Guthman's newspaper, had garnered some interesting information about Guthman and Warren Commission counsel Wesley Liebeler. Namely this: Guthman had told Liebeler it had been known for two months that Clay Shaw and Clay Bertrand were the same man.[50] Which was one of the central tenets of Garrison's case. So much for Guthman's faux statement about there being "no substance to Garrison's charges." This is how compromised the mainstream press was on the issue. Even when they knew better, they said the opposite. In one of the *LA Times* anti-Garrison's editorials, the closing line was, "Whatever the outcome, the press will not be muzzled in its search for the truth in New Orleans."[51] As we have just seen, they most certainly were. But it took thirty years to find out about it.

The Garrison Group

The fact that Garrison would not go away, even after being bludgeoned in public, made his enemies ratchet up the weaponry in the war against him. At the same time, Shaw's lawyers kept on trying to get direct help from Washington. This is perhaps due to the Wegmanns understanding who Guy Banister really was and what he was doing in New Orleans. And therefore understanding that certain agencies in Washington had a lot to lose in this case. In September of 1967, Irvin Dymond and Ed Wegmann had a meeting with Nathaniel Kossack of the Criminal Division of the Justice Department. (Kossack was another previous acquaintance of Walter Sheridan through RFK's Get Hoffa team.[52]) The two lawyers impressed upon Kossack that if Shaw was convicted, the Warren Commission would be completely discredited and confidence in the American government would be undermined throughout the world. They were shocked that Washington could let a DA in a medium-sized city do such a thing. Further, even after Sheridan's special, Garrison's approval ratings were still sky high in the state. They then concluded by saying that the DA was "a dangerous, irresponsible man" and he had to be stopped.[53] Wegmann and Dymond wanted investigative assistance and cooperation. And they listed specific requests for information on Oswald, Ruby, and CIA files on Ferrie, Novel, their own client Shaw, and even themselves! (In the last chapter we will see why this was necessary.) They also wanted a formal investigation of Perry Russo in order to shake him up psychologically.[54] Two copies of this memo went to CIA General Counsel Lawrence Houston. In the second one, Kossack said that it seemed clear to him that Shaw had not told his lawyers of his own long involvement with the Agency. When Hunter Leake and Lloyd Ray of the New Orleans CIA station heard of this, they found it hard to believe that Shaw could be this secretive with his own defense team.[55]

Houston had been talking with Justice even earlier than this September meeting about their Garrison problem. Houston told Justice Department lawyers Kossack and Carl Belcher that they should carefully consider what to do about their mutual problem at their regular Wednesday morning meeting.[56] Right around the time of the Kossack meeting, September 21, 1967, two things happened. First, an internal memo went out suggesting that 1.) Director Richard Helms get the White House and Congress to attack Garrison in public, and 2.) CIA should have selected communications smear Garrison's case and his motives. In relation to this, one week later, Donovan Pratt of Jim Angleton's staff is suggesting using their press contacts to plant negative editorials in newspapers.[57]

The second thing that happened at this time occurred the day before Dymond and Wegmann appeared in Kossack's office to plead for help. There was a meeting of something called the Garrison Group. Chief Counsel Houston was there, as was Ray Rocca of Angleton's staff. (Rocca was Angleton's specialist on the Warren Commission and Jim Garrison.) And there were at least six other high level officers in attendance. They included the Director of Security, and Thomas Karamessines, the Deputy Director of Plans. Karamessines was commonly known as one of Helms's most trusted colleagues. Thus it was quite logical he was there since the meeting was called at Helms's request.[58] Helms wanted the group to "consider the possible implications for the Agency" of what Garrison was doing in "New Orleans *before, during, and after the trial* of Clay Shaw" (italics added). It is crucial to keep in mind that phrase: before, during, and after. As we will see, the effective administrator Helms was thinking not just of some short term fix, but of formulating a strategy for the long haul. According to the very sketchy memo about this meeting, Houston discussed his dealings with the Justice Department and the desire of Shaw's defense to meet with the CIA directly. Rocca then said something quite ominous. He said that he felt "that Garrison would indeed obtain a conviction of Shaw for conspiring to assassinate President Kennedy."[59] This must have had some impact on the meeting. Since everyone must have known that Rocca had developed, by far, the largest database on Garrison's inquiry at CIA. Perhaps in the world. To say it was voluminous does not even begin to describe its scope and size.[60] After this, it was decided that actions should be decided upon for performance before the trial, and then during and after the trial. This memo states that this was the first meeting of this group.[61]

The second meeting took place six days later. The same people were in attendance, with the addition of Donovan Pratt of Angleton's staff. The problem of the Agency's long history of contact with Cuban groups was posed, in that these groups could be implicated by Garrison.[62] Karamessines, speaking for Helms, said the Director needed some legal help since, although he wanted to fight, he also wanted to know how CIA could get in trouble in its quest to counter Garrison.

The third memorandum on this group's activities is confusing. First, the members of the meeting are not listed. Second, there is mention of a "policy meeting" held on the twenty-seventh, the day after the previous meeting. But there is no noting of what occurred at that meeting. Third, in the version this author has, there are still redactions—censored material—in this memorandum. Not just of what happened at the meeting, but even of who was there. Third, this memo is even shorter and sketchier than the first one. Finally, the title of "Garrison Group" is not on the memo. It is just titled "Garrison Investigation."[63] There is no real way to quantify what happened with this group. Except to add that Victor Marchetti, who eventually became Helms's executive assistant, stated that these discussions were eventually taken off the record and into certain offices.[64] As we will see, that does seem to have been the case.

No Subpoenas Honored

On March 27, 1967, Garrison's office issued a subpoena for Sandra Moffett, a girl Perry Russo said had gone with him to Ferrie's gathering on the night of the assassination discussion. The legal papers were signed by Judge Edward Haggerty, who would preside over the Shaw trial. Moffett had married and moved to Nebraska by this time. She said she was willing to testify, to take a polygraph test, or "anything else."[65] She was scheduled to appear in April and she was sent a check for her travel expenses. But two weeks before she was to arrive, Sandra Moffett got a lawyer. The lawyer now announced she was going to fight extradition and wanted to be under the protection of Nebraska courts.[66] Further, the county officials would not attempt to enforce the New Orleans order. Which was odd since Nebraska and Louisiana had a full extradition compact at the time. The officials then announced that their search for the now missing witness was being abandoned. Moffett had fled to Iowa, a state with no extradition agreement with Louisiana.[67]

After his attempt to question Sergio Arcacha Smith was derailed by Aynesworth and the Dallas Police, Garrison tried to extradite Arcaha Smith back to New Orleans. And, as we have seen, what a witness Arcacha Smith could have been. Here is a man who knew almost each and every important person in New Orleans: Ferrie, Shaw, Banister, Oswald, Carlos Quiroga, Emilio Santana, Ed Butler, and very likely Howard Hunt and David Phillips. A man who was associated with the CIA from the moment he left Castro's Cuba. A CIA agent who worked on the Bay of Pigs with Ferrie and even had films of the operation. And then, according to Richard Case Nagell, was likely involved in the setting up of Oswald; and through the statements of Rose Cheramie and Mac Manual, knew Kennedy was going to be killed in Dallas just days before the assassination. Here is a suspect who, by necessity, had to lie about almost everything. It would have been interesting to measure his complicity and knowledge by the depth and scope of his lies during questioning. For example Arcacha denied he knew Ferrie at first. He even said he knew no one who hated Kennedy for the Bay of Pigs failure. This was humorously contradicted when his wife told reporters that Ferrie had been at their house the day of the invasion.[68] But Arcacha Smith was not going to be subjected to such exposure under oath.

His attorney, William Colvin, commented, "Garrison is a man who is power mad! . . . [He] used the law like a damn club."[69] On July 5, 1967 Arcacha Smith was officially released from extradition hearings. The 90 day period for their completion had elapsed. Governor John Connally had refused to sign the transfer documents unless Arcacha Smith was guaranteed immunity from civil and criminal action—which was an untenable assurance for a DA to give in advance of questioning.[70]

With the declassified files, we finally get some insight into how the CIA was able to arrange some of these amazing feats of legal non-cooperation. In the summer of 1967, about a month before Sheridan's special was to appear on NBC, a CIA lawyer named Dennis O'Keefe met with a Judge Sinclair of Fairfax County, Virginia. Sinclair would be involved in the transfer of any subpoena from Garrison to Langley. O'Keefe briefed Sinclair on the Agency's views of any legal requests from Garrison. Afterward, the lawyer wrote:

> The Judge . . . promised to cooperate with us in every area whence in judicial and legal ethics would allow such cooperation. He said there would be no unnecessary publicity emanating from his court and stated that he would call Mr. Houston or myself if and when he heard anything relating to the service of Garrison's subpoena. I gave the Judge Mr. Houston's and my phone numbers and thanked him for his cooperation in this matter.[71]

At around this time, Garrison issued subpoenas for both Richard Helms and any photographs of Oswald in Mexico City that the CIA held. Counsel

Lawrence Houston promptly met with Carl Belcher at Justice, and called Louis LaCour the U.S. attorney in New Orleans, and Edward Hebert, the congressional representative from the area. Hebert was very close to the Agency, and in fact had met with Helms in May.[72] The meeting with LaCour was to prepare in case Garrison subpoenaed either Lloyd Ray or Hunter Leake from the local CIA office in New Orleans. Therefore, when Garrison's subpoenas arrived in Virginia, Houston and Belcher conferred and, "It was agreed that the subpoena would be returned as not having been properly served." In the memo, there were no legal grounds mentioned for returning the subpoena. The CIA did not want it served and Belcher, like Sinclair, complied. Simple as that. Houston then wrote a letter to New Orleans judge Bernard Bagert who had signed the subpoena. He denied there were photos of Oswald in Mexico City. This reply was run by Attorney General Ramsey Clark and White House adviser Harry McPherson. Hebert then called Bagert and the judge agreed to keep the returned, unanswered subpoena under wraps, with little or no publicity accorded. The judge was pleased to be part of such a covert little intelligence operation which made the Agency above the law. For Hebert informed the Agency that the judge had called him back after he got Houston's letter and "was very pleased with the letter and that he considered this 'privileged' information." How pleased was the judge? Hebert said Bagert "had turned the letter over to the foreman of the Grand Jury"![73] In other words the Agency not only had the thwarting of Garrison's subpoenas completely covered at both ends, they also had a cooperative judge signing them who was not going to reveal that secret operation to the press.

It is important to make a legal distinction here. Once a witness is served with a subpoena, he is legally obligated to appear in court. If he does not, he is in defiance of the subpoena. He then can be charged with contempt of court. This can lead to a jail term. With the CIA, Justice Department, and White House doing what they did—that is, interfering with the process ex parte— they saved the receiving parties the embarrassment of having to explain the judicial doctrine they were following by not complying with a legal subpoena.

This same interference was clearly at work when Garrison tried to subpoena both Commission counsel Wesley Liebeler and Warren Commissioner Allen Dulles. Liebeler complained that he had personal business to attend to at he time which conflicted with his New Orleans court date. Therefore, a district court judge then blocked a request to have Liebeler appear.[74] When Dulles was subpoenaed, the U.S. attorney David G. Bress refused to assist in the procedure. He wrote back to the DA that he did not care to assist him in this matter. He then returned both the documents and the check for Dulles's traveling expenses.[75] To say the least, these two men would have been very interesting witnesses to demonstrate how the Warren Commission actually worked. Or, more properly, didn't work. But it is clear that from the White House, to the halls of Langley, to Ramsey Clark at Justice, Washington was going to protect itself from being exposed in the court room. And they were going to get the issuing and returning judges to go along with it.

Cornering the Media

As mentioned above, when Irvin Dymond and Ed Wegmann met with Nathaniel Kossack, they pointed out to him that, even after the airing of Sheridan's special, Garrison's approval ratings within the state were still extremely high. What they were trying to suggest was that a jury of average people could still be swayed just by the DA's reputation and stature within the community. Something seems to have been done about this later in a clandestine manner.

In the spring of 1968, Harold Weisberg interviewed Tommy Baumler. Baumler had formerly worked for Guy Banister as part of his corps of student infiltrators in the New Orleans area.[76] Because of that experience, Baumler knew a lot about Banister's operation. For instance, that Banister's files were coded, and that Banister had blackmail material on the subjects he kept files on.[77] He also knew the intelligence network in New Orleans was constructed through Banister, Clay Shaw, and Guy Johnson; how close Shaw and Banister were; and that "Oswald worked for Banister."[78] In Weisberg's interview with Tommy, he would occasionally ask to go off the record by telling him to turn the tape recorder off. Clearly, there were things going on in New Orleans that Baumler considered too hot to be attributed to him.

At this time, April of 1968, Weisberg considered Baumler to be an "unabashed fascist." He explained this further by saying that Baumler was "aware of the meaning of his beliefs and considers what he describes as his beliefs as proper." He then explained to Weisberg the following, "that whatever happens, the Shaw case will end without punishment for him because federal power will see to that."[79] He further said that this would also happen to anyone else charged by Garrison. Baumler then started to describe "the activities of a man he said had to be CIA and engaged in what he wanted me to understand was a major propaganda campaign, designed to influence public opinion here, including that of jurors and about you personally." (Note, Weisberg's memo of this interview is being forwarded to Garrison, which is who "you" refers to.) Baumler went on to describe this man as outwardly "nondescript." But his knowledge of the case was "tremendous," and his attitude was "very antagonistic." Weisberg went on to note that Baumler said that about this man, "if the CIA could put 500 men like him working throughout the country, it would kill the probe. He is, according to Tommy, "fabulous."[80]

From this interview, what appears to have happened is that the CIA sent someone into New Orleans to impact public opinion about Garrison. This may have been occasioned by a letter forwarded to CIA HQ by Lloyd Ray of the local New Orleans office. In this letter, a lawyer friend in New Orleans named Charles Dunbar had written that, "From original skepticism, many people around town are beginning to think Jim might have something, in any event, I don't believe the CIA can play ostrich much longer."[81] This forwarded note seems to have marked a milestone in the Agency's reaction to Garrison. Prior to this, the CIA was being essentially passive. They were recording much material and monitoring events. Whenever they were asked for information or their attitude, as in the Sheridan case, they cooperated. But after this note was forwarded, John Greaney, Lawrence Houston's assistant, visited in New Orleans with Lloyd Ray to discuss the Garrison inquiry. Ray's memo on this meeting was still largely redacted, even at the time the ARRB was at work. But then something quite interesting happened. William Gurvich, now working with Shaw's lawyers, visited the offices of the *New Orleans States-Item*. Ross Yockey and Hoke May had been seriously investigating the Shaw case. And they had been doing that in a fair and judicious manner. They had uncovered some interesting facts about how Gordon Novel's lawyers were being paid. After Gurvich's visit, the *States-Item* pulled Yockey and May from the Garrison beat.[82] When this author interviewed Yockey in 1995, he said that after this, he was then assigned to covering high school football games.

With the *States-Item* now neutralized, the coverage in New Orleans now became imbalanced. Because the other major local reporters on the story were Rosemary James, David Chandler, and Dave Snyder. For instance, in the fall of 1968, Snyder told a potential witness for Garrison, "We want to talk to you because the *States-Item* was going to prove Garrison had no case and was on a witch hunt."[83] David Chandler would merit an entire chapter of his own. Briefly, Chandler had been a good friend of Jim Garrison prior to the DA's opening of his investigation of the Kennedy case. And his coverage of him as District Attorney had been balanced, that is, never getting wildly favorable, or extremely negative.

But something happened to Chandler after Garrison started investigating the JFK case. He had been one of the contacts for the team researching the JFK case for *Life*. Once this team got in contact with Garrison, Chandler immediately began to accent the role of Carlos Marcello in any kind of Kennedy assassination plot. Even though, at this point, late in 1966, there was very little, if any, evidence for which to make that case. So therefore Chandler began to just drop

Marcello's name into the investigation, once insinuating that Marcello had bribed someone in Garrison's office. Then in an interview with Garrison assistant Charles Ward, the reporter admitted he had nothing to base this upon.[84] Chandler, most likely at Dean Andrews's request, then began to state as fact broadly exaggerated and incomplete information he had from Garrison about the DA's investigation of the Clay Bertrand figure.[85] In a conversation with Tom Bethell of Garrison's staff, he once said that he would like to see Garrison behind bars.[86]

But Chandler's most serious blast against Garrison and his inquiry was a two part article written for *Life* in the fall of 1967. This appeared in the September 1 and 8 issues of the magazine. The pieces masqueraded as an expose of Mafia influence in large cities in America at the time. But the real target of the piece was not the mob, but Garrison. The idea was to depict him as a corrupt New Orleans DA who had some kind of nebulous ties to the Mafia and Carlos Marcello. There were four principal participants in the pieces: Chandler, Sandy Smith, Dick Billings, and Robert Blakey.[87] Smith was the actual billed writer. And since Smith was a long-time asset of the FBI, it is very likely that the Bureau was the originating force behind the magazine running the piece. The idea was that since Garrison had a hotel room paid for on a visit to Las Vegas, and he had a credit line there, he was somehow in the pocket of the Mafia. When Billings visited him about the article, Garrision explained the free room as a loss leader for the hotel—that is, by letting famous people stay there, they hoped to gain business and notoriety. Which is a common practice in the resort city. Further, the hotel *did not pay* for his phone bill or valet fee. Therefore, how could the Mafia have been behind such a thing?[88] When Billings then asked Garrison about a local bookkeeper in town, Garrison said he did not recall the name. Billings jumped on him for this lack of knowledge.[89] In the reissue of his Mafia did it book, called *Fatal Hour*, Billings wrote that the name he gave Garrision at this time was Marcello's. This is proven false by Garrison's contemporaneous notes of this discussion. The name is revealed there as someone called Frank Timphony.[90] But this is how badly *Life* wanted to smear Garrison.

It was the work of Chandler, a friend of both Clay Shaw and Kerry Thornley, which was the basis of the completely phony concept that Garrison was somehow in bed with the Mafia and his function was to steer attention from their killing of Kennedy. This ploy was not just damaging to Garrison, but it did much to confuse the true circumstances of the Kennedy assassination.[91] When Chandler was called before the grand jury to repeat the facts he used for the article, Garrison found that he had escaped his clutches by being hired as a state investigator by Governor McKeithen. Garrison must now have realized the meaning of the term hardball politics. McKeithen is the man who owed Garrison his office. The governor now sorrowfully explained to the DA that he couldn't support him anymore. He did what he did with Chandler because the editors at *Life* had threatened to do to him what they had just done to Garrison unless he went along with the scheme. Garrison told the governor, you know, we used to call Huey Long the Kingfish, we should call you the crawfish.[92]

Irvin Dymond Meets Lloyd Ray

As noted, in the summer of 1967, Shaw's defense team made all kinds of overtures, including trips to Washington, to enlist the aid of the federal government to help their client. As Tommy Baumler noted to Weisberg, this apparently happened in 1968. But there is an event that preceded the Baumler disclosure which may mark the moment in time that the Agency crossed over from lending aid and advice through fronts like Sheridan and Miller, to actually getting directly involved. This appears to have happened the same month that the Garrison Group met, September of 1967. At this point, Dymond's request for information was sent to CIA HQ in Langley. On September 26, in a cable marked "restricted handling" and "SECRET," this clandestine channel to Shaw's lawyers appears to be approved by Langley, Virginia. Upon this approval, the New Orleans station wired back, "I do not believe our contact with Dymond could possibly be twisted into a story of CIA association."[93] It is important to note that the request for approval came before the first meeting of the Garrison Group, but the actual approval came afterwards. There seems to be a connection between the two. Because in all the cable traffic prior to this, the disapproval of any meeting or direct contact was for the reason that if it was discovered, Garrison could use it to his advantage. (In August, Rocca requested that the local station be checked for implanted surveillance devices by the DA.) One has to suspect that it was Rocca's warning about Garrison being able to convict Shaw that somehow caused the reversal in policy. Once the commitment was made, it was really made. For a cable went out on January 8, 1968 which reads in part: "[Garrison] case is of interest to several Agency components covering aspects which relate to Agency . . . office heavily committed to this endeavor."[94] Another memo that was also partly declassified says, "This is an ongoing review. Recipients will receive updatings as the New Orleans cases develop. [Censored] is requested to carry out tasks stipulated in para. 5, 6 and 7. The New Orleans offices . . . will be *tasked* by separate memoradum per para. 8" (Italics added). This clearly suggests that there were task forces at work in the city to thwart the DA. Very likely the man Baumler was talking about was part of it. Another likelihood is that Gurvich's mission to remove Yockey and

May from the *States-Item* Garrison beat was a CIA ordered task. We will now describe what appears to be another.

We have already described the instance of the receptionist at the VIP Lounge for Eastern Air Lines telling Garrison that Shaw was there one day in December of 1966 and signed the register as Clay Bertrand. In addition to the identification, the handwriting clearly resembled Shaw's. There was a battle royal over the handwriting sample at the trial between two famous document examiners, Elizabeth McCarthy of Boston and the FBI's Charles Appel.

But something came up related to this incident way before the trial. And the local CIA office got involved in it. On November 15, 1967, Ray sent a memo to Langley. In it he told HQ that his colleague Hunter Leake had attended a party the night before at a friend's house. The friend, Alfred Moran, told him that Garrison's office knew of several individuals who were at the VIP Lounge when Shaw was there. The next sentence reads as follows: "Mr. Moran recalled the occasion and positively identified to the Assistant DA the presence of Clay Shaw at that time."[95] The next day, the CIA put Ray and Leake on the tail of Moran. It is important to note that Moran had been used as a contact by both the New Orleans and Miami offices. CIA HQ did extensive background checks on Moran. They then contemplated having Leake meet with him to get more on his story. This was then put off since Moran was ill. So another track was tried. The Agency decided that "it makes no sense for Clay Shaw to use the name Clem (sic) Bertrand at such a meeting," then there must have been two different people. Yet, no one in the city could turn up anyone else who used the name. Even though Shaw's lawyers placed an ad in the *States-Item* asking who signed the register as Clay Bertrand.[96] Houston told Leake that he should "casually" inquire of Moran along the line that he had suggested: That Shaw had no reason to sign the register as Bertrand and they were two different people. In other words, talk the man out of his story by employing false information. This ploy worked with the pliable Moran. In two weeks Moran admitted to everything he had said to Leake at the party with one exception: He had not seen Shaw at the VIP lounge on that occasion.[97] In other words, with some direction from the Agency, and implementation from Leake and Ray, the witness had reversed himself.

Bill Boxley aka William Wood

One of the most horrendous errors Garrison made was hiring a man named William Wood.[98] Wood told Garrison he had previously worked for the CIA, then quit due to an alcohol problem. He had then gotten into the newspaper business, where he had been successful. When Garrison doubted he had actually worked for the Agency, Wood told Lou Ivon to call the infirmary at the Agency and the managing doctor there would vouch for him. When this happened, Garrison decided to hire him since he felt that Wood, who Garrison renamed Bill Boxley, could help him understand intelligence operations better. Garrison did this even though Boxley had failed two polygraph tests.[99] Even though by the time he hired Boxley, in May of 1967, he had already experienced the likes of Gordon Novel, Bernardo De Torres, and Bill Gurvich. Something that Garrison did not know was that Boxley had tried to rejoin the Agency earlier in the year.[100] If he had known that, hopefully, he likely would not have hired him.

Having read several of Boxley's memoranda the author can vouch for what Vincent Salandria and Joan Mellen say about him. He specialized in writing long, detailed, complex memos that were really more like short essays. (The multi-paged one he wrote about Nina Sulzer, Ruth Paine, Ruth Kloepfer, and what he called the Quaker connection was a real doozy.) And since he was a good writer, these memos would generally be interesting. But in the end, all of his memos seemed to point to some kind of extraneous, isolated, sinister activity within say the Office of Naval Intelligence, the Quaker community, the FBI, etc. So when taken as a whole and read consecutively—then and only then—could one see what Mr. Wood was really doing. Which was leading Garrison to nowhere. As previously mentioned in Chapter 11, a complementary example of Boxley/Wood in the field would be when he tried to undermine Harold Weisberg at the Jones Printing Company by saying Weisberg really did not get identifications of Kerry Thornley as the man who actually picked up Oswald's flyers. When in fact he did.

As Harold Weisberg has noted, another aspect of Boxley's bizarre series of attempts to undermine Garrison from within was the Robert Perrin episode. Nancy Rich was one of the Commission's most memorable witnesses. She described aspects of Jack Ruby's association with the Dallas Police that showed just how enmeshed Ruby was with the force. She then described gunrunning activity in the Dallas-Fort Worth area that also featured Ruby and appeared to be sanctioned by the military. Nancy Rich also mentioned her husband in passing. Boxley tried to convince Garrison that somehow Nancy's husband, Robert Perrin, was the assassin who had shot Kennedy from the front.[101] Since some people in the office knew this was complete flim-flammery, they decided to set upon showing it as such. Boxley's idea was to indict Perrin for the fifth anniversary of Kennedy's murder. So Harold Weisberg set out to show this was completely misguided since Robert Perrin had died years earlier—in 1962 in New Orleans.[102] Boxley next said that he had not actually died, the authorities got the wrong body and Perrin lived

on. Harold Weisberg and Lou Ivon literally rebelled at this. And they kept
Garrison away from the precipice.[103]

But Boxley had an alternative for Perrin. It was Edgar Eugene Bradley.
Bradley was a forty-nine-year-old worker for fundamentalist evangelical Dr.
Carl McIntire, the president of the American Council of Christian Churches.
He was living in North Hollywood, California in 1967. Right before Christmas of that year Garrison filed an indictment against Bradley for conspiracy
to assassinate John F. Kennedy.[104] Bradley responded with disbelief. He said
Garrison was being mislead; whatever information he was using in the indictment must have been planted.[105] He then said that he was neither a rightwing
nor leftwing extremist and he knew nothing about either Jim Garrison or the
Kennedy assassination.[106] Bradley said he was in El Paso on the day of the
assassination, and had only been to New Orleans once in his life, and that
was in 1967.[107] Bradley was duly arrested on December 26, 1967. No bond
was set, and the case was adjourned until the extradition papers arrived. This
happened in March of 1968. Although Attorney General Edwin Meese recommended that Governor Ronald Reagan comply with the request, Reagan did
not.[108] It is not easy to comprehend how Bradley ever got injected into the
information bank at Garrison's office. The closest we can come to ascertaining
this key point is from Tom Bethell's diary entry of February 13, 1968.[109]

Since Bradley lived in California, William Turner—who lived in the San
Francisco area—worked on this case. But strangely, so did Boxley. Boxley was
supposed to be from Texas, but he was renting an apartment in New Orleans.
But as Lou Ivon has said, one of the strangest things about Boxley is that he
would just disappear for weeks at a time. What appears to have happened is
that a man named Thomas Thornhill had written a letter to one Mike Karma-
zin in April of 1967. Thornhill wrote that Edgar Eugene Bradley had tried to
hire a man he knew to murder John Kennedy. Apparently, Garrison did not
think very much of this lead or the information in it. But one day in September,
Turner had discovered it and decided to follow through.

In December of 1967, Turner and Boxley went to a house on Fulton Street
in Van Nuys, California. This was the home of one Carol Aydelotte. She lived
there with her husband and Thornhill. Turner then wrote a memorandum
saying that the woman knew Bradley, and that Bradley had said continually
that someone should kill Kennedy. There had been a civil suit filed between
the two over her accusations. Aydelotte then gave the investigators two names
of persons who would back up what she said, Dennis Mower and Wesley
Brice. When Mower was interviewed he said that Bradley had indeed solicited him to kill Kennedy when he was running for president in 1960. But he
had reported the solicitation to the FBI. The eventual Brice information said

nothing about New Orleans in connection with Bradley. There were supposed to be photos of Bradley in Dealey Plaza, but this was never actually confirmed. There was supposed to be some kind of connection between Loran Hall and Bradley. But this turned out to be quite tenuous also. Almost all of the Aydelotte and Thornhill information came through Boxley, and to a lesser extent Turner. What appears to have happened is that, on one of his California trips, Boxley and Turner presented Garrison with their work on Bradley. Garrison did not cross check it or bring it to one or more of his lawyers for a written critical analysis of its legal implications. For when the legal staff did finally get a hold of the Boxley/Turner evidence they realized that they actually had no case against Bradley, because 1.) There was no credible evidence Bradley was in New Orleans prior to the assassination. Therefore their office had no jurisdiction over any criminal acts as a result of his possible part in a conspiracy. 2.) Even if Bradley had solicited Mower, that solicitation was for an attempt in California before Kennedy became president, and Mower had turned it down. 3.) There was no credible evidence then linking Bradley to what happened in Dealey Plaza. After this was all out in the open, the criminal lawyers on Garrison's staff—Andrew Sciambra, Richard Burnes, Charles Ward, and Jim Alcock—made short work of it. They considered it lucky that Reagan had not signed and returned the extradition papers.

Then there was Boxley and the *Farewell America* hoax. This was a book published in Europe that ended up in Garrison's office. The publishing house was something called Frontiers Publishing in Geneva, Switzerland. One day, Garrison got a call from an alleged representative of Frontiers. He asked Garrison if he was interested in seeing the manuscript of a new book they were publishing on the Kennedy assassination. The DA said fine. In short order, the manuscript appeared and then a copy of the bound book followed.[110] Garrison then sent a copy of the typewritten manuscript to the editor of *Ramparts*, Warren Hinckle. Hinckle was astonished at how beautifully typed the manuscript was: not a word was spelled wrong, not one comma was out of place. This is what began his doubts about the efficacy of the book.[111]

There then were two overseas inquiries about the actual origins of the book. One was by Steve Jaffe, a young student who had volunteered for Garrison's staff. The other was by *Ramparts'* Larry Bensky who was sent to Europe by Hinckle. Both men were given the runaround by mysterious Kafkaesque characters. Jaffe was given a card by a French intelligence operative with Charles de Gaulle's name on it. This was supposed to certify that the book had the French premier's approval. In other words, the ostensible story was that de Gaulle had doubted the Warren Commission. He commissioned

French intelligence, the SDECE, to investigate the case. *Farewell America* was the product. Benksy met a mysterious man named Michael. Michael promised a closing chapter to the book which would reveal the true names of the killers. When that "final chapter" came, it was nothing but a half page long. And it named no one.[112] It turned out that there really was no Frontiers Publishing company. It was created as a front.[113] But a front for what? Neither Bensky nor Jaffe could actually find out. Then the book's alleged author arrived in New Orleans.

The book had been serialized in Germany and published in book form in France.[114] The supposed author was James Hepburn. This was a pseudonym for one Herve Lamarr. On his European tour, Jaffe had been introduced to Lamarr in one of the law offices which the young investigator had traced Frontiers to. In 1968, Lamarr turned up in New Orleans. He said he was the writer of the book. Garrison and Ivon wanted to know why they should believe that was the case. Lamarr only replied in generalities. Harold Weisberg was in the office at this time. He looked at the irregular legal pads which contained the manuscript. He was completely puzzled. Weisberg had been a government investigator as far back as World War II. The only place he had ever seen those irregular shaped legal pads was in the Pentagon. This made him quite suspicious about both the book and Lamarr.[115] So he began to tail Lamarr in order to find out who his associates were. And also who his sources were. He also began to ask some of his field contacts who he had developed while working for Garrison if they had encountered Lamarr. Some of them had. Many of these were in the oil business in Texas. But there was one other person who Harold discovered had been assisting Lamarr: Bill Boxley.[116] In fact, Boxley had actually penned a drawing of what the book was supposedly saying. It was written in typical Boxleyian language: All kinds of name dropping, putting together every possible associa-tion—Ruby, Shaw, Lee Odom, H. L. Hunt, the FBI, Earle Cabell, etc.—into a Rube Goldberg contraption that no one could believe. Or explain.[117] Even after Garrison fired Boxley, Boxley said that Garrision swore by the book. Which simply was not true at that time.[118]

After putting together an investigative dossier of what he had uncovered, Weisberg showed it to Lou Ivon. He explained that what Lamarr was presenting as a top secret French intelligence investigation of the JFK murder, done with the hidden approval of de Gaulle, was looking more and more like a home-grown American product. If this was so, then why was Lamarr not arrested for failure to register as a foreign agent operating in America? Would Hoover really be willing to have a foreign intelligence agency uncover the truth about the JFK case? The fact he was not arrested implied that either 1.) He was not really working for the SDECE, and/or 2.) His mission was being sanctioned by American intelligence. This, plus Boxley's role in the affair, led Harold to believe that the clandestine sponsor of the book was the CIA.[119] Or as he put it, "I think the probability they are in accord with the purpose of this is high, as is their involvement." One of the most remarkable things about Weisberg's memo is that he actually found out who the secret sponsor of the project was. He referred to him as "Philippe." He also suspected he was a double agent, that is, he was ostensibly with the SDECE, but really working for the CIA. He had also found out that he had once been stationed in Washington under diplomatic cover. Harold felt this was probably when Philippe was turned. Harold turned over his investigative file to Garrison. It is truly one of the most remarkable pieces of sleuthing this author has ever seen one man do in this case. Garrison's handwritten notes on this file, based on Weisberg's work, map out every contributor to the book in each subject area. But at the top of the annotated chart is this name: Philippe de Vosjoli. When the author first discovered this graph, that name was foreign to him. But it was part of Tom Mangold's biography of James Angleton. It turned out that Weisberg was correct. De Vosjoli was a double agent who had worked for Angleton. From what is contained in this file, Weisberg was not aware of that precise connection. He suspected that "Phillipe" had been turned by the "liberal" side of the Agency. Which Angleton certainly did not represent. But that appears to be the only thing that the indefatigable investigator got wrong. *Farewell America* offers up a mysterious Committee of Texas oil barons who put in the money to finance the murder of JFK. That scenario would be the kind of diversion that Angelton—and Boxley—would find useful. If it fooled the DA, perfect. If he spent valuable time and energy trying to figure it out, almost as good.

Armed with this new information about the book, Ivon and Garrison summoned Lamarr back for questioning. They demanded to know who his sources were for the tome. Predictably, Lamar was not forthcoming. Lucky for him, as he would have been challenged by Weisberg's work. They insisted again that he reveal his sources. Again, Lamarr would not cooperate. There are two versions of what happened next: Ivon's and Weisberg's. Ivon said that he told Lamarr he had no credibility and asked him to leave. When the author told Weisberg this, Harold replied, "Oh no Jim. That is not what Lou did. He grabbed Lamarr by the back of the neck, lifted him off his chair, and threw him out of the office. He then yelled at him something like, "Go out and mislead someone else!"[120]

The triple disasters of Perrin-Bradley-Lamarr made 1968 a bad year for Garrison. Toward the end of it, after the Perrin-Bradley false accusations, Garrison had confided in fellow Warren Commission critic Vince Salandria. He told him that he felt like his office was the object of some intricately designed counterintelligence operation.[121] On one of his visits to New Orleans, Salandria had listened to Boxley speak to the staff about one of his journeys to Dallas. Afterwards, Salandria asked to see some of Boxley's work product. The Philadelphia lawyer spent some time going through his memos. He had brought down a book that he wanted Garrison to read a chapter from. It was a chapter about how counterspies were used in the Russian Civil War against Lenin and Trotsky. Garrison read it. Salandria then handed him a small stack of Boxley's memos. Garrison had the same experience described above: an elegant and deliberate voyage to nowhere, coolly planned in advance. When Garrison was done reading he understood he had been taken. The pair then called up Lou Ivon and he drove over. They then phoned Boxley and asked him to come over to Garrison's home. Boxley said he would. They all waited. But he did not show. They called again. He said he would come over. They waited. He did not show. Ivon called a third time. Boxley now cackled into the phone: "Lou, tell Big Jim, we're coming after him—with it all!" He then laughed loudly and hung up.[122] All three men then drove over to Boxley's rented room. He was not there. They knocked on the landlady's door. The woman said she had not seen him since he first took a lease. Boxley just sent her a check each month. When she showed them Boxley's room, there was one folded shirt on the bed. That was it. When Garrison showed her the number he had given him, she said, "There's no phone with that number here." Garrison now realized why Boxley always brought a bigger and bigger briefcase to work. He was absconding with his investigative files.[123]

The aftermath of all this was that Garrison finally understood that he had made a huge error in accepting volunteers to work in his office. His excuse was that there were too many leads to follow and he could not pursue them all with the small staff he had. There was some truth to this of course. But the problem was that the Kennedy case was so politically charged that there was bound to be attempts at infiltration. Or as Ray Marcus once said to the author, "If the infiltration did not happen, then the critics were wrong."[124] Well, the critics were right. Except Garrison had handled it poorly. Once he realized what had happened he now asked every volunteer to turn in his deputy's badge.[125] From here on in, with few exceptions, Garrison stuck almost exclusively with his professional staff in the office.

There now began to be deep-rooted and bitter recriminations—which exist to this very day—about who had worked with Boxley and what they were up to. Because of the Bradley fiasco, the entire California contingent was now suspect by those from back East—that is, people like Weisberg and Salandria and Gary Schoener now had deep suspicions about Bill Turner and former CIA pilot Jim Rose, another volunteer who had worked with Turner.[126] At one point Jaffe was literally cross examined by Ray Marcus and Marjorie Field.[127] Steve Burton mailed back his credentials stating that certain actions of his cohorts had shown what inexperience can do to damage an investigation.[128]

There was also a further subdivision. Garrison had the utmost respect for both Salandria and Weisberg. But since it was Salandria who had smoked out Boxley, Garrison now started to favor him on the eve of the Shaw trial. And it was Salandria who now was chosen to design the Dealey Plaza part of the Shaw trial.[129] Thus began a falling out between Garrison and Weisberg.

All in all, the taking on of Wood/Boxley ended up being a first-class debacle.[130] All the worse since its denouement had not come until the eve of the Clay Shaw trial.

CHAPTER THIRTEEN

Anticlimax: The Shaw Trial

"Garrison had something big, high persons were involved in the assassination conspiracy. Shaw felt confident because he knew that these high persons would have to defend him."

—*Carlos Bringuier, April of 1967*

Clay Shaw was arrested in March of 1967. He was arraigned on April 5, 1967. His chief counsel, F. Irvin Dymond, entered a not guilty plea and asked for an expeditious trial so his client would have the opportunity to demonstrate his innocence. He requested thirty days to file pre-trial motions.

The motions dragged on for twenty more months.[1] The trial did not begin until January of 1969. Some of the delay was caused by prosecution motions, but, contrary to lingering claims that Garrison never really wanted a trial, most of it was due to the defense attorneys. Moreover, there was a critical difference between the two sets of pre-trial motions. Most of the prosecution's motions were filed in order to secure evidence or witnesses. Despite Dymond's original request to expedite the case, most of the defense motions were meant to delay or throw out the case.

For instance, in June the defense requested subpoenas for 32 witnesses. Included were Garrison; members of his legal and investigative staff; businessmen from Truth and Consequences; Albert LaBiche, the foreman of the Orleans Parish Grand Jury; and the entire grand jury itself.[2] The tactic was to subpoena many witnesses and much documentary material and then to file more motions based on anything discovered. In fact, Dymond subpoenaed the entire grand jury twice.[3] He also summoned seven criminal court judges. Sometimes, the defense would file a motion and then not show up to argue it.[4] Occasionally Dymond would file a motion on the last day of a sitting grand jury, so that the motion would· have to be tabled for thirty days until a new grand jury was seated.[5]

The longest delay, the one that postponed the trial for six months, came after the defense had exhausted all local and state pretrial appeals. In the summer of 1968, Dymond filed a petition in federal District Court asking that Shaw's indictment be overturned on the ground that the Warren Report was "legally valid, accurate, binding, and controlling upon all courts in the United States."[6]

In July of 1967, Garrison had tried to expedite matters by filing for an early trial date.[7] For one thing, he wanted to stop Phelan and Sheridan from tampering with, intimidating, and making offers to witnesses. But when he saw that the defense was determined to drag out the pre-trial phase, he decided to use the interval to secure more evidence from the government. Here, Ramsey Clark, his nemesis, blocked his path.

After the Attorney General had bungled his first attempt to discredit Garrison's case, he secretly tried another method. Garrison had been trying to secure the original JFK autopsy photos and X-rays to exhibit at the trial. They would form an important part of his case, since, to prove a conspiracy, he had to present evidence against the Warren Report, which maintained there was no conspiracy and that Oswald had acted alone. In 1968, Clark convened a panel of experts—which did not include any of the doctors who had performed the original examinations—to review the autopsy photos and X-rays. In early 1969, just a few days before he left office and on the eve of the trial, Clark announced that this panel had endorsed the findings of the Warren Report. The panel released its findings, but none of the original evidence on which it was based. This was clearly meant to influence public opinion before Shaw's trial began.

There was, of course, a method to the seemingly endless and frivolous attempts by the defense to delay the trial (they even attempted to subpoena Clark as a witness to support the Warren Report[8]). It was to gain more time for both the covert and overt arms of the Shaw defense team to weaken the prosecution's case. That is for people like Boxley to undermine Garrison from within, for Aynesworth to try and influence more witnesses, for the CIA to try and reverse testimony as it did with Mr. Moran and the VIP Lounge, and for media allies like Chandler and Snyder to influence the local jury pool. Judge

Edward Haggerty seemed to realize this when he commented from the bench in 1967:

> The key flaw in the system of free press versus free trial is the unchallenged chatter that hits the . . . media between the time of the arrest and the time of trial. Elaborate trial rules permit jurors to hear admissible evidence, subject to searching cross-examination; the whole system is subverted when the press, radio and television media fill jurors' heads with inadmissible evidence.[9]

Wise and fair words. But Haggerty did not seem to realize that his admonition was far more constraining for Garrison, isolated and under the judge's nose as he was, than for Shaw's attorneys, whose cooperative friends in politics and the media were not bound by Haggerty's warning. Further, Shaw's lawyers would forever deny that they were getting any such covert help. As we have seen, Dymond lied to this author about his knowledge and use of the CIA cleared attorneys panel. Dymond had to lie in order to conceal an attorney's knowledge and cooperation in an obstruction of justice.

One friend of the defense was Aaron Kohn, the managing director of the Metropolitan Crime Commission.[10] This was a private watchdog organization of business interests that kept an eye on the police and the DA's office. Under the influence of *Newsweek* and its point man Hugh Aynesworth, as well as Shaw's defense team, Kohn had sent an ominous letter to Louisiana Attorney General Jack Gremillion urging him to investigate charges of bribery and intimidation in the DA's office. Not content with this, Kohn went to the media and began to denounce Garrison: "What you are looking at is a budding new Huey Long. I'm no longer interested in if he's right. His course is a destructive one."[11] Kohn did not say what Garrison was destroying. And he did not seem to realize how serious it was for the Metropolitan Crime Commission to accuse the DA of such serious transgressions, especially since the grand jury and police department had already investigated the charges and found them false.

The defense also used their ally Dean Andrews. Andrews had stated on the NBC special that the mysterious Clay Bertrand was not Shaw, and that although he knew who Bertrand was, he could not disclose his real name. Later, after Sheridan's special, NBC gave what it said was the name, Eugene Davis, to the FBI. But when Andrews testified before the Warren Commission, he had stated that he had seen "Bertrand" only a few times. He had known Davis since law school, for seventeen years. He had seen him every few months during all that time. Moreover, Davis himself vehemently denied ever using the alias, and when he was separately questioned and investigated by both Garrison and the FBI, they concurred.[12]

This was a good example of how the media coverage delayed the trial and damaged the case. When Shaw's lawyers heard Andrews's new story, they asked for a dismissal because now Shaw could not be Bertrand. The judge had to wait for Davis to be checked out before throwing out the motion.[13] In the meantime, Garrison felt compelled to file perjury charges against Andrews for the games he was playing. He got the perjury conviction, but under Louisiana law a convicted perjurer can still testify at a trial while his conviction is being appealed. Andrews appealed, and Dymond went ahead and used him at the Shaw trial.

But Walter Sheridan had done even more to undermine Garrison's case. As stated before, former CIA agent, Jules Ricco Kimble, had been on a mysterious plane flight to Montreal in 1963 with Ferrie and Shaw. When Sheridan got wind of it, he intimidated Kimble first, into not talking, and then, into skipping town.[14] Emilio Santana, another important witness (especially in relation to Sergio Arcacha Smith and the Rose Cheramie story), also disappeared. Garrison's investigators felt that the ubiquitous Sheridan might have reached him also.[15]

That journalistic duo, Phelan and Aynesworth, were both on the scene: Phelan as a witness for the defense and Aynesworth to help Shaw's attorneys. An odd thing about this was that neither man had an ostensible writing assignment at the time. But it turned out that Phelan had a very special function for his backers. Most reporters in town to cover the proceedings rented a hotel room. But not Phelan. Phelan rented a house.[16] Why would he do such a thing if he was not there to write a story? Because his was a much bigger assignment. His job was to put the spin on each day's testimony for the residing press corps. Thereby controlling the entire national media reportage on the Shaw trial. How did he do such a thing? He would invite all the reporters over to his rented house at the end of each day. He would then serve them refreshments and snacks. He then would spell out the next day's story on a chalkboard. This is how some of the most interesting and important testimony presented during the proceedings got covered up by the media. On the day the Zapruder film was shown, Phelan had his work cut out for him. For the repeated showing of the film—depicting Kennedy's body being violently knocked back—really shook up the press. It appeared Garrison was right, it was a conspiracy. But when they arrived at Phelan's rented house, the reporter pulled a proverbial rabbit out of his hat. He took out his chalkboard, raised up his piece of chalk, and he began to outline the dynamics of the so-called "jet-effect" explanation for the action on the film. That is, if Oswald was firing from behind Kennedy, why does Kennedy's body recoil with tremendous force to the rear of the car? What Phelan and the jet effect proffer is that somehow the spurting of blood and brains served as a jet that drove

Kennedy's head backward with overpowering force.[17] This is how determined Phelan was to keep a lid on what came out of the trial. One can only assume where the reporter got his quick course in physics to dream up such a theory in a matter of hours.

Actually, we can do a bit more than assume. Decades later, David Chandler wrote an article for a small magazine in Denver, called *Westword*. Towards the end of the piece he wrote that, in early 1964, Phelan was in J. Edgar Hoover's office. There he overheard the Director talking about certain Oswald files. Phelan got the clear impression that Hoover was destroying all records of the FBI's contacts with Oswald. That Phelan was this close to the Bureau and Hoover, and that in his entire writing career he never revealed this fascinating episode of evidence destruction personally ordered by the Director, all this cogently sums up his work and writing on the JFK case.[18]

One of the attorneys who was originally announced for Shaw's defense team was the aforementioned Guy Johnson. As we have seen, Johnson was an important intelligence asset in New Orleans in more than one way. And he worked in that regard with Shaw and Banister. Therefore, it was not wise to keep him on the defense team. And in fact he was dropped from the team fairly early. When this author asked Sal Panzeca why he was dropped, the lawyer said it was because there was a personality conflict between Johnson and the Wegmanns.[19] At that time, this author did not know enough to realize this was another smoke screen by Shaw's defense. We will return to the real reason Johnson left in the last chapter. One which is only alluded at here.

But the worst for Garrison came from another surprise inside his own office. Tom Bethell had been one of the DA's key investigators and researchers. He was an Englishman, and an assassination expert. Since Garrison had designated him as his chief archivist, he had access to and control of both Garrison's files and his most recent witness list. He had always been a curious presence inside the office. Since he would argue about certain aspects of the case with people like Vincent Salandria, and invariably take the Commission's side of things.[20] Secretly, he met with Sal Panzeca, one of Shaw's attorneys, and gave him a witness list he had prepared, with summaries of each witness's expected testimony for the prosecution.[21] Years later, when writing about this betrayal, Bethell tried to insinuate that he had volunteered this information to Lou Ivon and Garrison.[22] This is misleading. There was an inquiry into how it happened. And when all the evidence pointed to Bethell as the culprit, then and only then, did he weepingly admit what he had done.[23]

If anything showed Garrison's desire to try this case, it was his response to Bethell's confession.[24] With it, Garrison could have called for a mistrial. He did not. He continued to press forward knowing the defense was lying in wait for him every step of the way. Whether this was nobility, stubbornness, stupidity, or a death wish, it is up to the reader to draw his or her own conclusion.

The Shaw case posed both tactical and strategic problems. Tactically, the classic way to crack a conspiracy is to isolate one of the conspirators and convince him to talk, either by offering immunity or presenting an overwhelming accumulation of evidence that targets him. This way, the code of silence can be broken. Once one yields, the dominoes fall one by one as the evidence begins to accumulate, and the convictions follow. Shaw understood that with Ferrie, Oswald, and Banister all dead, this tactic would be virtually impossible. As long as Shaw preserved his impeccably respectable exterior and denied everything, the true nature of his background and operations was shielded from Garrison's probing. And as long as his attorneys and the media pummeled Garrison, others would be discouraged from digging further into Shaw's background.[25]

But Garrison made a strategic error here. With Shaw and his attorneys taking a hunkered-down stance, while seeming to be above the fray, the only attack with any hope of success was to overwhelm them with so many witnesses, even minor ones, as to make that stance seem phony. If one could chip away at Shaw's testimony, his image might begin to crack and, along with it, the basic defense strategy. In other words, the "respectable" Clay Shaw would become the issue: his character, his life, his weird associations, his murky service record, his mysterious European jaunts. Who was he *really?* If that line could be crossed, Garrison could go on the offensive, and the wall might come tumbling down.

But for some reason, Garrison rejected this approach. He wanted to present a streamlined case against Shaw, using a few credible witnesses to expose his alias and his part in the conspiracy. He then hoped to launch a frontal assault against the Warren Report to prove that the assassination was the work of many, not of one man.

It was a mistake. And Garrison sorrowfully realized this mistake afterwards when he said, "one of my bad decisions was not to use all of our witnesses."[26] A letter from a source close to Garrison reveals more on this point: "Garrison, of course, knew how the American news media would treat the trial, so he did not use many of his witnesses and held back on much of his evidence. His strategy considered the trial to be only one step of many, leading to the conviction of all the assassins and the exposure of the top structure above them. However, the strategy backfired . . ."[27]

The prosecution also chose to ignore the issue of Shaw's homosexuality. But since one of the main points of the case was Shaw's use of an alias, this weakened their case. Since it seriously hurt the State's chances of proving Shaw's use of an alias. Given the prejudices of the establishment and Shaw's straight business ties, his homosexuality would have been a motive for using an alias. Garrison even had witnesses in the French Quarter who attested to its use.[28] But they were hesitant to violate Shaw's privacy and Garrison was reluctant to press them or Shaw on the issue. Except for one instance, not initiated by the prosecutor, whenever the point surfaced, it did so in veiled, indirect terms.

One failure that was not Garrison's fault was his inability to bring in the intelligence community and its ties to the assassination. In May of 1967, Garrison first openly attacked the CIA and accused it of complicity in the crime.[29] But many of the intelligence connections to the case, such as Banister, his former partner Hugh Ward, and Ferrie, had died, while some, like Novel, had fled, and others, such as FBI agents Regis Kennedy and Warren DeBrueys, initially refused to testify. This weakened the possibility of getting the intelligence community in the dock and really exposing how Oswald was used in the conspiracy and how and why the cover up was constructed. As we have seen the CIA arranged to not have subpoenas served on its officers.

Another prosecution error was in not calling enough witnesses to nail down the Shaw-Ferrie relationship. There were many witnesses who attested to this relationship. As noted above, Sheridan deprived Garrison of Jules Ricco Kimble, who had flown with the pair to Montreal.[30] We have previously noted the witnesses involved in the Freeport Sulphur connection and how Ferrie and Shaw figured in that episode. On rebuttal, Garrison did call two witnesses, Nicholas and Matilda Tadin, to link the pair and fortify Russo's statements, but there should have been more.[31]

Garrison's attack on the Warren Report was much better than the New Orleans side of the case. He attacked the Report on three levels. First, he called new witnesses or witnesses who had been ignored by the Commission, all of whom attested to a crossfire in Dealey Plaza and/or sightings of possible assassins. Second, he demonstrated how one shooter could not have performed the feat attributed to Oswald, because of the timing of the shots and the trajectory of the bullets. And finally, by obtaining the Zapruder film and by cross-examining Dr. Finck, he made public evidence which had never before been revealed, and changed the nature of the case forever.

Garrison himself did not appear very often at the trial. He made the State's initial presentation, outlining the case to the jury, and he made one of the final summations. He questioned few witnesses between. There has been all kinds of speculation down through the years, including by this author, as to why Garrison was not the lead lawyer for the prosecution. In the files contributed to the Review Board by Garrison's son, Lyon, the reason finally appeared. In a reply to a query by a supporter mailed to him after the trial, the DA explained that he was stricken by both his recurrent bad back and the Hong Kong flu at the time. His back bothered him so much that he could barely bend over. In fact, it was so bad that, at times he literally had to crawl across the floor to replace a file. But since he feared that Shaw's lawyers would delay the trial again, he decided to press forward with the proceeding anyway.[32]

The lead attorney for the State was young Jim Alcock. One of Garrison's few good choices during the trial, Alcock did a decent enough job with the materials available. He knew the nuances of the case, the constitutional issues involved, and his summation, before Garrison's, was simple, direct, and impassioned.

Alvin Oser, the assistant DA who handled most of the Dealey Plaza testimony, was just as good as Alcock. With the help of Vincent Salandria, he had mastered the technical aspects of the case: the autopsy report, the ballistics tests, the bullet trajectories, and more. Oser was confident, aggressive, and thoroughly convinced of and schooled in the fallacies of the Report. By the time he delivered his summation, the Warren Report lay in tiny pieces on the courtroom floor.

After a long jury selection process that entailed more than 1,200 interviews, the trial began on February 6, 1969. Including jury selection, it lasted thirty-nine days.[33] To say the CIA was ready for the proceeding is an understatement. As soon as the jury was selected, James Angleton began to run background checks on them through Agency computers. This information was then given to the Office of Security.[34] Certain of Garrison's witnesses were also afforded this treatment. For example Dr. John Nichols had been a deft critic of the Warren Commission's treatment of the ballistics evidence. Garrison had him testify about the dubiousness of the Single Bullet Theory. This was the Warren Commission's necessary concept that one bullet went through both Kennedy and Governor John Connally, making seven wounds and smashing two bones, yet remained almost unscathed when allegedly found at Parkland Hospital. Nichols was a pathologist from Kansas. After he testified, Angleton sent a request to the FBI for additional information on the doctor.[35] The FBI was ready for the requests, since after a series of meetings with Shaw's lawyers they had agreed to check out State witnesses, or potential witnesses, who would testify for Garrison.[36]

The CIA also decided it needed not just wall to wall coverage of the trial, but coverage in real time. Declassified internal memoranda reveal that the Agency subscribed to both local papers for the trial coverage: the *States–Item* and *Times-Picayune*. Hunter Leake of the New Orleans office would then forward clippings from the papers to Richard Helms' assistant at CIA HQ.[37] But then a teletype machine was actually moved into the New Orleans office to keep Langley aware of all developments in the trial as they occurred.[38] The Justice Department was also represented at the proceedings. Their official liaison with the court was a young lawyer named Harry Connick. Connick was the man who sat next to witnesses that the government deemed important and official, such as Navy pathologist Pierre Finck and FBI agent Regis Kennedy. He also was with them when there was any pre-trial questioning requested. For instance, when Finck flew into town, he was asked questions by both sides in their offices. Connick was by his side. As we shall see, this was a significant detail that had future large ramifications.

It is necessary to add one more important aspect to what happened at the trial. Before and during the trial, Garrison's witnesses were being surveilled, harassed, and physically attacked. For instance, Richard Case Nagell had a grenade thrown at him from a speeding car in New York. Nagell brought the remains of the grenade to Garrison and told him he did not think it wise for him to testify at Shaw's trial.[39] Even though Garrison had spirited Clyde Johnson out of town, and very few people knew where he was, the FBI's total surveillance evidently paid off. He was brutally beaten on the eve of the trial and hospitalized.[40] Aloysius Habighorst, the man who booked Shaw and heard him say his alias was Bertrand, was rammed by a truck the day before he testified. After he testified, Edwin McGehee found a prowler on his front lawn. He called the marshal, and the man was arrested. At the station, the man asked to make one phone call. The call he made was to the International Trade Mart.[41] After he testified, Reeves Morgan had the windows shot out of his truck.[42] What makes all this violent witness intimidation more startling is what Robert Tanenbaum stated to the author in an interview for *Probe Magazine*. He said that he had seen a set of documents that originated in the office of Richard Helms. They revealed that the CIA was monitoring and harassing Garrison's witnesses. As Tanenbaum stated it, he had a negative view of Garrison up until the time he became Deputy Counsel of the House Select Committee on Assassinations. Then he read "all this material that had come out of Helms's office, that in fact what Garrison had said was true. They were harassing his witnesses, they were intimidating his witnesses. The documents exist. Where they are now, God only knows."[43] As alluded to before, this was the escalating stage of CIA interference which could not be recorded by Marchetti. Where the top level of Angleton's office met CIA Director Richard Helms.

After opening presentations by Garrison and chief defense attorney Dymond, the prosecution led off with what many observers considered their best witnesses: the people from Clinton who had seen Ferrie, Oswald, and Shaw together in the late summer of 1963. Reeves Morgan, Edward Lee McGehee, John Manchester, Henry Palmer, Corrie Collins, and William Dunn made strong, simple witnesses. The prosecution bolstered their testimony with Bobbie Dedon and Maxine Kemp, two women from Louisiana

State Hospital in Jackson, the place where Shaw and Ferrie wanted Oswald to get a job. They testified that Oswald had indeed visited them to inquire about a position and had filled out an application, which had since been discarded.

Next on the stand for the State was Vernon Bundy, who linked Shaw to Oswald. Dymond warmed to the attack on this relatively easy target. Bundy was black, was a drug user, and had a police record, so Dymond scored some points here. But Bundy had a surprise in store for the crusty courtroom veteran. He asked the judge to have the defendant go to the back of the room while Bundy himself sat in an aisle seat. Judge Haggerty agreed, and Vernon Bundy now began his demonstration. He asked Shaw to walk toward him. As Shaw did so, Bundy stared at his feet. When he got close, he stopped, and after a pause, Bundy asked him to repeat the exercise. After the second time, Bundy returned to the witness stand and revealed how he knew he had seen Clay Shaw: "I watched his foot, the way it twisted that day. This is one way I identified this man the next time I saw him."[44] In fact, when John Volz interviewed Bundy, Volz took him to his office window, since he knew Shaw was coming into the court building that day. Bundy looked at him and told Volz that was him, he recognized the limp.[45] Shaw, in fact, did walk with a slight twist. He explained later how an old war injury to his back had caused this hitch in his gait. The irony was that this witness, whose status the defense had tried to belittle, had noticed something telling that no one else had.

The prosecution had quickly reached its zenith. The next witness for the State was a New Yorker named Charles Spiesel.[46] The DA had not uncovered Spiesel. He had called Garrison's office to enter the case.[47] Alcock went to New York to interview him and, according to the prosecutor, he seemed alright to him at the time.[48] Apparently what neither Alcock nor Garrison knew was that Spiesel's father was an FBI agent and was fully aware of what he was going to testify to on the stand.[49] The small, wiry New York accountant had been in Louisiana, he related, to visit his daughter who attended LSU, when he met Ferrie at a bar.[50] The two then went to visit Clay Shaw at a building in the approximate area where Shaw's home was located. They began drinking, and, testified Spiesel, Ferrie brought up the subject of a possible Kennedy assassination. Spiesel was surprised at this turn in the conversation but he chalked it up to the liquor. Spiesel recalled some talk about a high-powered rifle and a telescopic sight. Shaw had added that Ferrie would have to fly the assassins away after the crime.[51] He closed his direct testimony saying that he never saw Shaw again, though he did run into Ferrie a few times. Ferrie had suggested, he claimed, that Shaw could help set him up in business in New Orleans. Spiesel allegedly called Shaw's office on a few occasions, but those calls were never returned.[52]

Dymond now took over, asking the witness if he had tried to sell his story to the media. At first Spiesel resisted, but when Dymond challenged him, he admitted he had discussed the matter with CBS. When the attorney asked how much he was looking for, he replied, "I told him a couple of thousand."[53] Dymond then asked where Spiesel had stayed in New Orleans during the summer of 1963. He said it had been at a hotel and then two apartments. When asked to name the hotel and the location of the two apartments, Spiesel could not recall.[54]

Now Dymond closed in for the kill. He asked Spiesel if he had noticed anything unusual about David Ferrie. "No," replied the witness. This was amazing because everyone knew what a startling appearance Ferrie had possessed. Spiesel added that he was "fairly well-groomed," and the only unusual thing about his appearance was his rather thin eyebrows.[55] This about a hairless man who glued on a wig and pasted mohair above his eyes.

Dymond then asked Spiesel if he had ever been hypnotized, and Spiesel replied many, many times.[56] When asked by whom, he said it was the New York City Police who had tortured him while he was under hypnosis and made him give up his accounting work.[57] Dymond pursued this, asking if he had had trouble with a communist conspiracy, "people following you and tapping your phones?"[58] Spiesel tried to dodge this, and Dymond then asked if he had fingerprinted his daughter in New York before she left for LSU. Spiesel said he had. Did he also fingerprint her when she returned. Again, the answer was yes. When Dymond asked why he did this, Spiesel replied that he had been hypnotized so often he wanted to be sure it was her when she returned.[59] At this point, Garrison later recalled, "I was swept by a feeling of nausea."[60]

How did Dymond know precisely how to detonate the witness? The defense team's story about Spiesel was that a friend of Sal Panzeca's named Bill Storm informed him about the witness during cross examination. With the files adduced by the Review Board, this does not ring true today. For instance, there are newspaper clippings about Spiesel in the defense team's files. Aynesworth was asking questions about him ten days before he took the stand. And at that time he noted that the defense had *already* tried to call him.[61] Two days before he testified, the defense team's prime investigatory service, Wackenhut, had tracked down his daughter and her husband. Finally, in the Wegmann files turned over to the ARRB, there is a combined confidential report and a legal attachment, of which only a cover sheet remains. This report was assembled by a different detective agency. Either this file is missing or it was stripped before it was turned over to the Review Board.[62] With this new evidence, a question now appears as to how and when the defense really discovered Spiesel's questionable background.

The reason that Spiesel was so devastating was that his testimony directly struck the chords that Sheridan, Phelan, and Aynesworth had been harping upon. Namely that Garrison would use hypnotized, unstable witnesses to convict an innocent man. For this purpose, Spiesel was nearly perfect. And as he left the stand, so went Garrison's case against Shaw. After the trial, Ed Wegmann wrote, "Had we been unsuccessful in our efforts to secure information with regard to Charles I. Spiesel . . . the results could well have been a verdict of guilty."[63]

Perry Russo, a crucial witness, was next. And as Matt Herron later noted, his testimony, because of the two year battering he had taken, now seemed diluted.[64] During his two-and-a-half days on the stand, he admitted that the fateful discussion he overheard may have been just that, just talk, not an actual plan to commit a crime. Russo also said that no one except Ferrie ever told him they had decided to kill the President, and Ferrie told him this in private.[65]

Dymond tried to get Russo to say that he was not sure that the "Bertrand" at the meeting was actually Shaw. Earlier, journalist James Phelan had also tried this on Russo, implying he had actually seen Banister instead of Shaw. But Russo was ready this time. He denied it categorically, "No, that is absolutely false. . . . I am absolutely sure the defendant is the man who was there."[66] After two days of grilling, Russo got strained and edgy. His cross-examination ended in a shouting match between the witness, Dymond, Alcock, and the judge. Dymond closed his cross-examination by implying that Russo was mentally ill.[67]

Since the defense had impugned Russo's mental state, Alcock made a motion to read to the jury the testimony of Dr. Nicholas Chetta at the preliminary hearing. (Dr. Chetta had died in the interval.) The real reason for bringing in the testimony was to bolster Russo's credibility by showing there was no hanky-panky during the administering of the Sodium Pentothal. Alcock knew that Phelan would later be put on the stand by the defense to tell his story about Russo. Because of Dymond's references to Russo's mental state, Judge Haggerty allowed the reading of Dr. Chetta's testimony.[68] When Alcock tried to have Dr. Fatter, who had conducted the hypnosis, accepted as a witness, Dymond objected on the ground that most of what he had to say was hearsay; Judge Haggerty agreed. Alcock argued, with some logic, that this was inconsistent with the ruling on Dr. Chetta's testimony.[69]

After Russo, the most important witnesses relating to Clay Shaw were Richard Jackson and James Hardiman.[70] These two postal employees testified that for a time in 1966, Clay Shaw had redirected his mail to 1414 Chartres Street, home of a friend named Jeff Biddison. There was confusion over just when this had begun, but it ended on September 21 of that year. Jackson had handled the change of address card, whereas Hardiman actually delivered the mail to the house. He said that a few pieces of mail were in fact addressed to a Clem Bertrand at the Chartres house. When Alcock asked if any of the letters were given back because they were wrongly addressed, the letter carrier replied, "No, I don't recall getting any back."[71] This restored some of the lost credibility to Garrison's case, particularly as it related to the alias.

The only witness that Garrison was able to produce to inquire into the official investigation of the assassination in New Orleans was FBI agent Regis Kennedy. And even then, by prior arrangement with the Justice Department, Kennedy would only testify about a certain area of his inquiry, namely his interview with Dean Andrews and his consequent search for Clay Bertrand. This limitation hurt the DA since Kennedy was a relevant witness to other aspects of the case. For instance, along with several others, he had been a member of the Friends of Democratic Cuba group set up by Guy Banister and William Dalzell. Further, there were witnesses who put Kennedy in Banister's office.[72] Therefore, what Kennedy could have told the court about Banister, Ferrie, their association with the Cubans—especially Sergio Arcacha Smith—and Oswald, was very likely considerable. But he was not allowed to testify about any of those important matters. Consequently, when Alcock asked him if he was involved with the investigation into President Kennedy's death *prior* to his interview with Andrews, Kennedy said he was not sure if he could answer that question. He then conferred with Connick, who was a near constant presence in the courtroom. After doing that, Kennedy refused to answer. Then, with the jury escorted outside, a long discussion took place about whether or not Kennedy could answer the question. The discussion then went inside the judge's chambers. Connick then called Washington. After this, the jury was called back inside. Alcock then asked Kennedy if prior to his interview with Andrews, had he been engaged in the inquiry into President Kennedy's assassination. Kennedy replied in the affirmative. Alcock then was allowed to ask the follow up question, which related to the first: Was Kennedy seeking Clay Bertrand in connection with his overall investigation into the assassination. Kennedy said that he was.[73]

There was a coda to all this that Alcock could not have known about. But it was part of the reason that Attorney General John Mitchell severely curtailed Regis Kennedy's testimony in mid-trial. After Garrison's probe had been exposed in public, the FBI began to do a survey as to what their post-assassination investigation had revealed. William Branigan was the counter-intelligence chief in charge of the FBI's Oswald investigation. In the Bureau's 1967 review, he stated that all the information Regis Kennedy uncovered had been forwarded to the Warren Commission. But some of it had been sealed at the request of certain Commission members and McGeorge Bundy, Kennedy's national security adviser. (Bundy was a friend of Allen Dulles.) Parts of the report had been sealed because it pertained to "information showing certain people were homosexuals" and this was deemed as not important to the investigation.[74] Since the term "homosexuals" is in the plural, this almost has to be Shaw and Ferrie. Therefore it confirms what Ramsey Clark said about Shaw being part of the FBI's investigation back in 1963. It would also seem to affirm the Justice Department report in the *New York Times* stating that they were convinced that Shaw and Clay Bertrand were the same man.[75]

Alvin Oser then presented the prosecution's all-out attack on the Warren Report. It featured a scale model of Dealey Plaza, the Zapruder film shown at various speeds, photos and visual models, and compelling witnesses the Commission ignored. Well prepared by Salandria, Oser was particularly adept at demolishing the testimony of "experts" like Robert Frazier on ballistics and Dr. Finck on the autopsy. Oser got Frazier to admit that the tests conducted by the FBI did not replicate the conditions at Dealey Plaza. They were staged to produce a desired result, and even then, none of the marksmen could duplicate Oswald's alleged feat.[76]

Pierre Finck "Louses Everything Up"

Edward Wegmann first phoned Dr. Pierre Finck and requested that he testify at the Shaw trial on February 16.[77] This was likely in response to the effectiveness of the Alvin Oser/Vincent Salandria Dealey Plaza presentation of the trial. The conjunction of the Zapruder film with witnesses like James Simmons, who said he heard shots from the grassy knoll area and then saw smoke rising from there, was compelling.[78] Oser then called Dr. John Nichols, a pathologist, to offer commentary on the Zapruder film. Oser asked him to make a conclusion as to the source of the fatal shot to Kennedy's skull. Nichols replied, "Having viewed the Zapruder film, the individual 35 mm frames and the particular exhibits here, I would say that this is compatible with a gunshot having been delivered from the front."[79] Wegmann was going to bring in Finck to certify that all this testimony did not matter. Because the medical evidence convicted Oswald, and only Oswald. So after Finck got Wegmann's call, he phoned the Justice Department and met with Deputy Assistant Attorney General Carl Eardley. He then went to his office and reviewed numerous documents about the autopsy.[80] After organizing his trip, Eardley called Finck and told him he had a check and a D.C. court order for him to appear at the Shaw trial. Finck then flew down to New Orleans and met with Shaw's lawyers. Connick also called him at his hotel to offer him his help.[81]

Finck was fine under direct examination by Irvin Dymond. He recited the Warren Commission doctrine: Two shots from behind and above. And the bullet entering in the back performed the functions necessary for the Single Bullet Theory. The defense must have thought it blunted the previous week of testimony exposing a crossfire in Dealey Plaza. Likely, they did not remotely perceive all the myriad problems with the medical evidence in the Kennedy case. Problems which the Warren Commission had concealed or buried due to the adroit and studious censorship and dodges of Philadelphia lawyer Arlen Specter. It was Specter who controlled and choreographed the medical and ballistics evidence for the Commission. The problem for Wegmann and Finck is that Garrison, Oser, and Salandria had seen through the Specter smoke screen. For one of the memorable highlights of the trial was Oser's cross examination of Finck. Considering when this examination took place, and the information assistant DA Alvin Oser had to work with, he did a creditable job.

The official autopsy report holds that there were two bullets that struck President Kennedy. One came in at the bottom of the rear of the skull and exited the right side of the head, above and forward of the ear. This wound was fatal. A prior bullet entered the back and exited the throat. According to the Commission, this bullet proceeded forward to enter and exit John Connally twice, and then entered his thigh where it lodged. The debate about these wound locations, even in the period of 1966–69, was loud and quite heated. It was complicated by the fact that Dr. Malcolm Perry had cut a tracheostomy over Kennedy's throat wound to try and save his life. Many observers felt the back wound was too low to exit the throat. Therefore, the throat wound and the back wound were actually from two separate shots, which would betray a crossfire and therefore two assassins. Therefore, Oser explored this point. He tried to find out why Finck did not call the Dallas doctors that night to find out if there actually was an exit wound from the throat. Finck replied that he was not running the autopsy, it was Commander James Humes. When Oser asked if Humes was actually in charge, Finck made a disclosure which literally changed the face of the autopsy evidence forever. And it should have rocked the news media if Phelan had not been controlling it. Finck replied that Humes actually stopped and asked, "Who is in charge here?" Finck then said he heard an Army General say, "I am." Finck then added, "You must understand that in those circumstances, there were law enforcement officials, military people with various ranks, and *you have to coordinate the operations according to directions*" (Italics added).

This was the first time that any of the three autopsy doctors—Finck, Humes, or Thornton Boswell—had stated for the record that they did not actually control the proceedings at Bethesda Medical Center that night. Which meant that the doctors were being limited in their practice by the many military higher-ups in attendance. (Finck stated that the autopsy room was "quite crowded" with top brass.) When Oser asked if Finck recalled the name of the Army General who replied to Humes, Finck said he did not. When Oser asked if Finck felt he had to take orders from this Army General, the pathologist replied with: "No, because there were others, there were Admirals. . . . And when you are a Lieutenant Colonel in the Army you just follow orders." He then testified that at the end of the procedure they were told not to discuss what had happened that night.

Oser then got Finck to make another telling admission. Finck tried to imply that he had seen the autopsy photographs before he signed the official autopsy report. This was not true. And Oser had a document which Finck had signed in which the doctor himself stated that he had not seen the photos until January 20, 1967, over three years later. Impeached by his own document, Finck did something strange. He tried to deny he had said what he just said. Namely he *had* seen them before he signed the autopsy report. Oser had the stenographer read back the question and answer. Which showed that he had said just that. Desperate to show he had not just committed perjury, and his autopsy was haphazard at best, Finck actually said *the stenographer had made a mistake.* He finally amended his answer to, "I was there when the photographs were taken, but I did not see the photographs of the wounds before I signed the autopsy report." Which begs the question of why they were taken in the first place. He then testified that the doctors did not have the photographs or X-rays when they were writing their final draft of the autopsy report. They were relying on their memories and notes. When, of course, the pictures and X-rays would be more reliable.

Oser then asked Finck when he first saw the Zapruder film. Finck replied he first saw it in March of 1964 before he testified to the Warren Commission. Oser then pointed to page two of the autopsy report, which is titled Clinical Summary. In the second paragraph it reads that "Three shots were heard and the President fell *forward*" (Italics added). This, of course, is contradicted by the Zapruder film which shows Kennedy's body moving backward with incredible speed. The summary then quotes two newspaper reports which stated that "a rifle barrel disappeared into a window on an upper floor of the nearby Texas School Book Depository Building." It also states that Governor John Connally, riding in the same car in a jump seat in front of Kennedy was wounded "by the same gunfire." What this all did of course, was to frame the very questionable circumstances of the assassination into a setting which favored Oswald as the assassin. That is, it dictated how many shots were fired, from where, and that the same bullet went through Kennedy and Connally. It also lied about in which direction Kennedy fell. A lie Finck had to have understood when he saw the film in March. These were unsubtle stage directions for the pathologists to follow. Oser then showed that the pathologists had not verified any of this information before they committed to it. In fact, Finck had told the Warren Commission he really did not think that CE 399, the bullet that allegedly went through Kennedy and Connally, could have done so.

Oser then moved on to another key issue that exposed the pathologists as pawns. A very important point about the autopsy is its failure to convincingly prove directionality. That is, from which direction did the bullets enter the body. There have always been serious queries about whether the wound in Kennedy's throat was an entrance or exit wound. If that wound was one of entrance, then Kennedy was shot at least once from the front. That shot could not have been from Oswald, therefore the murder was a conspiracy. What makes this possibility very real is that Malcolm Perry said during a televised press conference on November 22 that the throat wound was one of entrance. He repeated this three times that day.[82] Since he did the tracheostomy right over that wound, he should certainly know. The best way to have proven this point once and for all was to have dissected the wound track. Amazingly, this elementary and integral procedure was not done. When Oser tried to find out why it was not done, Finck used every evasion he could to avoid answering the question. Going over the transcript of this exchange is a bit startling. The reader will find that Oser had to pose the question *eight* separate times. It got so bad that Oser even had to request that the judge direct the witness to answer the question. Finck finally answered with, "As I recall I was told not to but I don't remember by whom." Again, someone was controlling the pathology team in a way that prevented them from doing a full and correct autopsy. The invisible subtext of this exchange was this: If the wound was not tracked, how did Finck know it was a through and through wound? That is, if the two wounds did not meet, then they were caused by different bullets. Ergo, the killing was a conspiracy. Further, the fact the doctors were ordered not to track the wound indicated the military brass may have been trying to cover this point up.

If this was the case, then a piece of evidence the ARRB did not locate may be crucial. As we have seen, one of Kennedy's chief antagonists during the Missile Crisis was General Curtis LeMay. In the recorded calls between the White House and Air Force One on its return from Dallas to Washington for the autopsy, there had always been some missing tape. Clearly, this tape had been edited. But a fuller version was located in 2011. On this newly restored tape there is a stunning request that General LeMay should be located! All references to LeMay had previously been cut. But on this version, LeMay's aide wants to locate him badly and interrupts the dialogue in order to try and find him: "This is Colonel Dorman, General LeMay's aide. . . . General LeMay is in a C140. Last three numbers are 497. . . . He is inbound. His code name is Grandson. And I want to talk to him." This places LeMay in the air on the way to Washington three hours after the assassination.[83] When this author interviewed the late Paul O'Connor, who was at the autopsy that night, he related an unforgettable story. He said that there were dozens of military brass in the gallery, the likes of which he had never seen. Someone was smoking a cigar. Dr. Humes called him over and said, "Please go tell than man to stop smoking." O'Connor went over, and as he approached him, he saw it was LeMay. Needless to say, he was not going to tell the Air Force Chief to stop anything.[84] If this information is accurate, then it casts the darkest aspersions over why the doctors were not allowed to proceed normally. And shows how close Oser was to uncovering a huge cover up.

Oser then deftly moved to the size of the back wound versus the reported diameter of the throat wound. He was trying to show, from the information in the autopsy report, that the wound in the back was larger than the wound in the throat. But how could an entrance wound be larger than an exit wound? Again this would suggest two bullets: One from the front and one from the back. And further two different caliber bullets. Dymond strenuously objected to this line of questioning on the grounds that this made Finck respond with information he did not experience firsthand. Dallas physician Malcolm Perry had partly obscured the throat wound by cutting a tracheostomy over it. So the information as to the size of the throat wound was garnered from his memory as conveyed to Humes via telephone the next day. But clearly, according to the measurements in the autopsy report, the back wound was larger than the throat wound. Which is almost unheard of in wound ballistics. With a path paved by Dymond, Finck managed to dodge the question by saying he really did not know since he was relying on someone else's information.

Oser then asked Finck why he signed a review of the autopsy pictures and X-rays in January 1967 at the National Archives. Finck replied that he thought the idea was to correlate the photographs and X-rays with the report, and since the pathologists had not seen the photos before, and only saw the X-rays that single night. Oser asked Finck who asked him to do this. Again, Finck clearly did not want to answer the question. There was a long pause. So long that Judge Haggerty asked Oser, "Are you waiting for an answer?" Finally, the reluctant witness responded as to *when* he saw the photos for the first time. The judge then said the question was not when he saw them, but who asked him to go. Finck now finally came across with the name of Carl Eardley at the Department of Justice.[85]

Unbeknownst to Oser, he was now scratching the surface of the years old, large, and multi-leveled cover up about the medical evidence in the JFK case. One that was ongoing at that very instant. Because, through Connick, Eardley was following and monitoring Finck's historic, landmark testimony. As Eardley read it, he went into a panic. In fact, Finck's appearance had backfired so badly that Eardley did something very odd. He called fellow autopsist Thornton Boswell to prepare him to go to New Orleans to counter and discredit his own witness, Finck. In sworn testimony, Boswell told the ARRB's Chief Counsel Jeremy Gunn that Eardley was "really upset" about the Shaw trial. Particularly about Finck's testimony saying that it was the military, and not Humes, controlling the procedures performed during the autopsy. Eardley told Boswell that he had "to get somebody to New Orleans quick. Pierre is testifying and he's really lousing everything up."[86] Eardley wanted Boswell to go down and testify that Finck was a "strange man" in order to discredit him.[87] It is important to recall, it was Wegmann and Eardley who had called the "strange man" to the stand in the first place. Apparently, they did not anticipate Oser would be so acute, or that Finck would testify honestly under cross-examination.

Boswell then flew to New Orleans and went to a reserved hotel room. Connick had left a note there telling him to meet someone down around the wharfs. Boswell did so. The two proceeded to the federal building. Connick now showed Boswell Finck's disastrous two days of testimony.[88] Boswell spent the whole night studying it. But, in the end, Boswell did not testify. Perhaps because it would have looked silly to hear a clinical pathologist—Boswell—who had not done a gunshot autopsy in years, try to discredit a forensic pathologist like Finck, who was called into Bethesda for the very reason that he had vast experience in doing gunshot autopsies. During his ARRB testimony, Jeremy Gunn asked Boswell a rather logical question about this strange and previously concealed episode: "What was the United States Department of Justice doing in relationship to a case between the district attorney of New Orleans and a resident of New Orleans?" To which Boswell replied that clearly, "the federal attorney was on the side of Clay Shaw against the district attorney."[89] About that, there can be no doubt. As we will see, that federal attorney was marked out to do more than just help acquit Shaw.

What Finck and Boswell were doing with Eardley, and his Justice Department colleague Carl Belcher, was participating in Ramsey Clark's cover-up of the medical evidence in the JFK case. This started in November of 1966, with the release of Edward Epstein's critical book *Inquest*. It would continue until Clark's Garrison-directed, strategic release of his aforementioned panel review of the autopsy photo and X-rays. In fact, the Justice Department had sent Boswell a letter to sign which would request that very review. They sent it to him in order make it appear that it was Boswell's idea in the first place. It was not. Boswell was serving as a stage prop in order to make it look like it was not Ramsey Clark's idea.[90] Which it was. But Boswell signed the letter anyway. Which shows just how much in the pocket of the government the three pathologists were. That review was always meant to reaffirm the verdict of the Warren Commission. That particular review panel was convened in February of 1968. They did less than a week of work. Yet Clark held back on the public release of that report for eleven months. That is, until two days before jury selection began for the Shaw trial.[91] The other part of this Clark directed cover-up was to get Humes and Boswell, the autopsy photographer, John Stringer, and radiologist John Ebersole, to sign sworn statements that the autopsy photos and X-rays they saw at the National Archives in late 1966 and early 1967 corresponded to the exact number and views that were taken during the autopsy in 1963. The four signed false statements. Because there were pictures missing at this time. And the signatories knew it.[92] Then in January, Finck was brought back to sign another statement, along with Humes and Boswell. This one said that the newly reviewed photos and X-rays supported their original autopsy report. This is the document Oser showed Finck on the stand which proved the doctor had not seen the photos in 1963. And he had not consulted them in the writing of the autopsy report. Which is a bit startling. And it is why Eardley and Belcher, at Clark's request, wanted these two new statements issued. Clearly, Clark was responding to pressure brought by the combination of critical books being published about the assassination and also to the furor around Garrison's inquiry. We know that this was a conscious and coordinated effort on his part since declassified memos reveal that Clark was in communication with former Warren Commission lawyers David Slawson and Wesley Liebeler in November of 1966, when this process began. Slawson wrote to Clark that there was a reasonable chance of stopping the growing movement for a complete reopening of the Kennedy case "by a re-investigation limited to aspects of the autopsy." And Clark complied with that request.[93]

On January 14, 1967, the *Saturday Evening Post* ran a cover story previewing Josiah Thomspon's upcoming book, *Six Seconds in Dallas*. The director of the 1968 panel was Dr. Russell Fisher. He later stated that Ramsey Clark got hold of the proofs of Thompson's book after this article appeared. The contents clearly upset the Attorney General. Because, as Fisher related, one reason that the Clark Panel was convened, was to "partly refute some of the junk" in that book.[94] The release of its findings were then delayed in order to be timed with the opening of the Shaw trial. In other words, Washington was countering the critics through concealed and controlled means. This multi-staged, intricate, ongoing Justice Department cover up of the medical evidence was the tip of the iceberg Oser was touching on in his milestone examination of Dr. Finck. Naturally, it drove Eardley up the wall.

The final witnesses during the prosecution's direct case also dealt with Shaw's use of the Bertrand alias. Mrs. Jessie Parker, hostess at the exclusive VIP Room at the New Orleans Airport, said she had seen Shaw sign the guest register as "Clay Bertrand" in 1966. She described his appearance and pointed to his signature in the book. She then pointed to Shaw as the man who signed in. She said she remembered him because of his striking appearance and because very few people used the room. One needed a pass key. The handwriting expert for the DA was the illustrious Elizabeth McCarthy. She was a graduate of Vassar and Portia Law School. She had been a leading authority in the field for over thirty years who had testified in many high profile cases, including that of Alger Hiss. She had been employed as a document examiner for both the Boston Police and the Massachusetts State Police. She stated the writing was Shaw's. The authority that Irvin Dymond first announced in court to dispute that expert finding was New Orleans handwriting analyst Gilbert Fortier. But this was soon changed to longtime former FBI employee Charles Appel.[95] When this author asked Dymond how this switch occurred, he said it was because Appel called and volunteered his services. Appel concurred with this.[96] This was another smoke screen. For under cross-examination, Appel admitted he was actually contacted by Lloyd Cobb, Shaw's former boss. As we have seen, Cobb had applied for membership on the CIA's cleared panel of New Orleans attorneys. In keeping with that, Appel was one of Hoover's closest and most trusted FBI colleagues; so close that he often had dinner with him at his favorite restaurant in Washington.[97] So, predictably, Appel contested McCarthy's analysis and said the handwriting was not Shaw's.

Haggerty Vetoes Habighorst

Then came the second and final turning point in the trial. Jackson, Hardiman, and Parker had been good witnesses. The Zapruder film was shocking. Finck's cross-examination was riveting. Garrison had actually recovered a bit from the Spiesel disaster. To try to clinch the case that Shaw was Bertrand, Garrison called to the stand policeman Aloysius Habighorst.[98] When Shaw was first arrested in March of 1967, Habighorst had handled the booking. Before having him sign the fingerprint card, the officer had routinely asked if the defendant had ever used an alias. Apparently unsettled by his arrest, Shaw had replied "Clay Bertrand." Habighorst typed this on the card and Shaw signed it. Alcock now wanted to admit both the card and the officer's testimony as evidence into the trial. This seemed powerful, damning evidence because it came right out of Shaw's mouth and hand. It would lend credence to Garrison's claim that Shaw really had called Dean Andrews to defend Oswald, and that Andrews had indeed perjured himself to protect Shaw.

Aloysius Habighorst joined the police force at 21; he was a fifteen-year veteran when he appeared at the Shaw trial.[99] In 1967, at the time of Shaw's arrest, he had been receiving three letters of commendation a year for his work.[100] He had been taking FBI classes in fingerprinting and would often take cards home with him to practice identification techniques.[101] The day after he had booked Shaw, he and his wife, Elsie, were home watching television when they heard a news commentator mention Garrison's contention that Shaw had used the alias Clay Bertrand. Habighorst jumped out of his chair and told his wife that that was just what Shaw had said to him the night before, at the routine booking procedure.[102] He ran to his room and showed her the three copies of Shaw's card, which listed the alias and had Shaw's signature. The alias also appeared on the arrest record.[103]

Habighorst hardly knew Garrison when he went to him with the cards. Garrison realized how critical this was to his case, and, with witnesses disappearing right and left, he placed Habighorst under protective surveillance.[104] Two days before he was to testify, a man called his house and asked Elsie if "Al" was there. She thought this odd, since all her husband's friends called him by his boyhood nickname: "Hotsie." The caller asked when he would be getting off work. She said it would be late that evening and asked if there was any message. The man said no. The next day, Mardi Gras, Garrison decided to take the surveillance off Habighorst since he would be with other officers guarding the parade. Unexpectedly, however, Habighorst was relieved early, and headed home. As he was driving, a yellow truck pulled out of an alley near his house and tried to ram him.[105] Habighorst suffered facial lacerations in his attempt to avoid the truck.

Dymond would have had a tough time belittling Habighorst, given his performance record. He could hardly have attacked his character. Habighorst came from a religious family, and served still, on occasion, as an altar boy. He had once leapt into a river to rescue a drowning man. He was so well-regarded by his superiors he was used in training films.[106] It would have been difficult for Dymond to convince the jury that Habighorst was perjuring himself to help Garrison or to harm Shaw.[107]

Consequently, he took a different tack. Dymond decided to challenge the admittance into evidence of both Habighorst's testimony and the card. Haggerty excused the jury. Shaw took the stand and told the judge he had never told Habighorst he used an alias. He also said he had signed a blank card that was filled in later.[108] Shaw's attorneys at the time of the arrest, Sal Panzeca and Edward Wegmann, testified that neither was at Shaw's side at the time of the booking.[109] The defense argued that this violated the *Miranda* and *Escobedo* rules, which require police to inform a suspect of his rights to remain silent and to have an opportunity to consult with an attorney.[110] Invoking *Miranda* was stretching things, since Shaw had already been read his rights before he was brought to the booking room.[111] As for *Escobedo,* New Orleans police procedure has always required that a suspect's counsel be *nearby* when routine booking was taking place, which was in fact the case at Shaw's booking.[112] This had been standard practice since before *Miranda* and *Escobedo* were decided by the Supreme Court.[113]

The prosecution's protestations fell on deaf ears. Judge Haggerty would not allow the evidence. He held that Shaw's constitutional rights were violated because his attorney was not standing right next to him during his fingerprinting. Habighorst had no right to ask Shaw if he used an alias without Panzeca or Wegmann in his presence.[114] But the judge went further. He said, "If Officer Habighorst is telling the truth, and I seriously doubt it . . ."[115]

Alcock leaped out of his chair. His face was red, and his voice cracked with emotion. "Your Honor. Are you ruling on the credibility of Officer Habighorst?"

Peering over his spectacles, Haggerty replied, "No jurors are present."

"But you are passing on the credibility of a witness before the press and the entire world."

"I don't care," Haggerty responded. "The whole world can hear that I do not believe Officer Habighorst. I do not believe Officer Habighorst."

"I demand a mistrial," Alcock shouted. "A judge's unsolicited comment on evidence . . ."

"Denied," said Haggerty. "I rule this evidence is inadmissible before the jury."

Alcock did not file for a mistrial. Instead he tried to get a twenty-four-hour stay of the judge's ruling from the State Supreme Court. The motion was denied.[116] The next day he asked Haggerty to reconsider the ruling. Haggerty refused.[117]

If the defense had made a wish list before the trial, they could not have asked for a better witness than Spiesel or a better ruling than Haggerty's exclusion of Habighorst's testimony. Indeed, the judge had now deprived the prosecution of their best hope of linking Shaw to a conspiracy. The jury would not get to pass on the credibility of the officer. The judge had already done so.

Dymond's defense case included Dean Andrews and James Phelan. Andrews changed his testimony yet another time to say that there was no such person as Clay Bertrand. It had all been a figment of his imagination. Alcock was not allowed to bring up Andrews's perjury conviction directly because of the pending appeal,[118] although the defense later mentioned it.

Phelan had been cooperating with Sheridan, Aynesworth, and Shaw's attorneys almost since he arrived in New Orleans. It was only natural that the journalist was happy to testify for Shaw. Phelan was used to attack both Russo's testimony and Sciambra's memorandum of his first interview with Russo in Baton Rouge.[119] But after Dymond took him through his paces, Alcock showed him the obstacle course. Phelan had been on local television, the Sterns' WDSU, and stated that he had a taped interview with Perry Russo in which he contradicted his original Baton Rouge statements to Sciambra. Alcock asked him if he did, indeed, have such a tape. He replied he did not. Alcock then asked him if his statement on television was a lie. Phelan replied diffidently, "If you wish to call it that."[120]

Alcock then asked Phelan about his visit to Russo before he had submitted his *Saturday Evening Post* story. He asked how long he had been with Russo at that time, and Phelan replied more than two hours. Alcock asked him why the very last thing they discussed, literally as he was walking out the door, was the Sciambra memorandum. Phelan said that once he got going, Russo was a talkative young man.[121] But, Alcock asked, if Russo had not mentioned any meeting at Ferrie's apartment, why did he leave that fact out of his article? Phelan replied it was because of space limitations.[122] When Alcock asked Phelan if he had tried to convince Russo that Shaw was really Banister, Phelan agreed. Alcock then asked if Phelan had ever seen Banister. He had not. Then how did he know what the now dead Banister had looked like? Phelan replied that Banister had been described to him by *Sheridan*.[123]

What should have been a bombshell went off right after Phelan stepped down, but it was so subtle that almost no one noticed. Alcock seemed to be tiring and was unable to take advantage of it. The self-confident, clever Phelan had once told author James Kirkwood that Garrison did not have a bad case *without* Russo. But Garrison needed Russo because he "is the only man on this planet who puts Dave Ferrie and Oswald together, the only one."[124]

This was false on its face. There were witnesses who had seen the pair together in New Orleans from 1956 to 1963. But grant that Phelan believed it. Right after he stepped off the witness stand, the defense called Mrs. Jessie Garner. She had been Oswald's landlady in the summer of 1963 in New Orleans. The defense had called her to say that she had only seen Oswald clean-shaven and neatly dressed. Her testimony was supposed to rebut Russo's testimony that, at Ferrie's party, Leon Oswald had been whiskered and scruffy in appearance. She was shown some photos of Oswald, and with these photos there was a picture of Ferrie. Surprised, she quietly and unexpectedly said that she knew "that man" too. She spoke so softly that almost no one heard her utter the sentence.[125] She added that he was at her house shortly after the assassination.

In the aftermath of the assassination, many government agents had come to her home. But Ferrie was also there. When she realized he was not an agent, she asked him to leave. Incredibly, the prosecution did not press this issue. Alcock did not even mention it until his summation, and then he made almost nothing of it. But several researchers did talk to Mrs. Garner afterwards. She said that Ferrie had returned to search for his library card.[126] He thought he had given it to Oswald and wanted to retrieve it from his room. Right then, two months after Oswald had left town and immediately after the assassination. So much for Phelan's assurance that "no one on the planet" could put Oswald and Ferrie together. No one except Ferrie himself.

The last defense witness was Shaw himself. He did not have to take the stand, but his attorneys had a good feeling about his performance and the way the trial was proceeding. They wanted a complete vindication, for Shaw to deny all charges and to paint the Garrison case as a slimy sham motivated by the basest political and personal opportunism. A motive so reckless and a DA so driven by the lust for power that he would wreck the life and reputation of a completely innocent citizen.

Shaw did just that. He denied ever knowing Oswald or Ferrie. He denied attending any meeting at Ferrie's apartment. He denied using an alias. He denied ever working with the CIA. He even denied the Clinton trip. He said he was a believer in what Jack Kennedy stood for and harbored no ill feeling toward him.[127]

The last to testify were rebuttal witnesses, called by both sides to counter specific testimony already presented. The most important rebuttal testimony in Garrison's favor was delivered by Mr. and Mrs. Nicholas Tadin. They had called the DA after reading that Shaw denied ever knowing David Ferrie. Both testified that in the summer of 1964, they had taken their sixteen-year-old son to Lakefront Airport, to get a flying lesson from Ferrie. Mr. Tadin stated that previously he had seen Clay Shaw around town and knew from the papers who he was. When he and his wife brought their son to the airport, he saw Ferrie emerge from the hangar door with a tall, white-haired man. As they got closer, he recognized the second man as Shaw. As Shaw walked off, Tadin asked Ferrie if he had a new student. "No," he replied. "He's a friend of mine, Clay Shaw. He's in charge of the International Trade Mart."[128] His wife testified to the same incident. She also knew who Shaw was. The last question Alcock asked Matilda Tadin was, "Are you telling the truth?" The woman immediately snapped, "Of course I'm telling the truth."[129]

The trial was now over. Closing arguments were presented. Alcock tried to counter Dymond's admission from Russo that the discussion at Ferrie's had the characteristics of a "bull session." Alcock stated that the "bull session" was carried out precisely on November 22: Oswald was in Dealey Plaza, Shaw had an alibi on the West Coast, and Ferrie made his trip to Texas in case he was needed as a getaway pilot.[130] Alcock also accused Shaw of lying in the face of the number and credibility of the Clinton witnesses.[131] Oser went through the impossibility of any single person performing the feat of marksmanship achieved during the assassination. He insisted that there must have been at least three assassins in Dealey Plaza. And that, he concluded, brought us to a conspiracy and David Ferrie's "triangulation of fire" concept at the meeting at his apartment.[132]

Dymond cast doubt on all the prosecution witnesses, even the Tadins and the people from Clinton. He said it was ludicrous to think that someone as well-known as Shaw would really attempt to use an alias. He added that much of Garrison's entire theory came from the mind of Dean Andrews, who had only once told the truth. And that was when on the stand in this case. Could they really convict Shaw on such questionable testimony?[133]

Garrison spoke last and bitterly attacked the testimony of Frazier and Finck to illustrate what a colossal fraud the Warren Report was. He tried to get the jury to be courageous enough to overrule the experts and the Report and to begin to tell the truth about the assassination.[134]

The four summations began at about 2:30 P.M. Friday afternoon, February 28. They ended about 11:30 P.M. that night.[135] The judge charged the jury and they went in to deliberate. The jurors asked the two alternates to vote and leave their ballots with a deputy. Interestingly, they both voted guilty.[136] The jurors who counted did not see it that way. In an hour, a not-guilty verdict was returned. Thus ended the only trial ever conducted for the murder of John F. Kennedy.

As Gordon Novel later testified, when Shaw was acquitted, his lifestyle greatly improved. For instance, he went from driving a seven-year-old Lincoln to leasing a brand new super luxurious Continental Mark III for which he did not have to lay out a down payment.[137]

CHAPTER FOURTEEN

Garrison Must Be Destroyed

*"This thing, I have to do all the way. They'll have
to kill me so stop me."*

—*Garrison to author Paris Flammonde*

The first business day after the verdict, March 3, 1969, Garrison filed perjury charges against Shaw for denying that he ever knew Ferrie or Oswald. In light of the Clinton witnesses and the Tadins, Garrison seemed to have a good case. And in fact, by looking over the DA's briefs for the perjury action, Garrison had learned his lesson. He was now going to throw every witness he had on this point against Shaw. The total number was over ten.[1] Shaw's lawyers tried to go before state court judge Malcolm O'Hara to get the charges thrown out. This did not work. The judge set a trial date for January 18, 1970.[2] The Wegmanns continued to appeal the charges through each and every possible avenue. This delayed the trial for a full year.[3]

While this was ongoing, the other side continued their covert defense of Shaw. In August of 1969, the mass circulation magazine *Look*, ran a long article entitled "The Persecution of Clay Shaw." This piece appears to be a joint operation between Hoover and Cartha DeLoach in Washington, and locally, Aaron Kohn and Bill Gurvich. The information in the article is essentially all the phony Mafia smears that David Chandler and Aaron Kohn had manufactured and utilized to tar Garrison. The photographs accompanying the article were taken by Bill Gurvich.[4] The man who officially received the byline for the article, but who really served as a figleaf for Kohn and Gurvich, was Warren Rogers. This could not be known at the time of publication. But Rogers, like Phelan and Sandy Smith, was a reliable asset of the FBI. That is he could be contacted to do favors for them when called upon. The public did not know this until the 1979 posthumous publication of William Sullivan's book about the FBI called *The Bureau*. Sullivan had been a top echelon officer in the FBI for many years. In his book there is a chapter entitled "Flacking for the Bureau." Listed as one of the reporters who would often write articles with information fed to them by the FBI was Warren Rogers.[5] In addition to the FBI, the CIA was also on the ready. Headquarters in Langley wanted to remove the teletype machine from the local station after the trial was over and Shaw had been acquitted. But Hunter Leake requested that the communications keystone stay in New Orleans until after the Shaw perjury trial was complete. Leake got his request fulfilled.[6]

After having been in receipt of Garrison's briefing papers for the perjury trial, Shaw's attorneys finally tried for a temporary restraining order to stop Garrison's case from proceeding. This was initially denied. But then, on January 18, 1971, the day the state trial was to begin, a motion for emergency relief was granted.[7] This was unusual because the federal judiciary does not often intervene in state prosecutions.[8] But Shaw's lawyers wrote that Shaw would suffer "grave and irreparable injury" as the result of the state perjury case which had been brought in "bad faith" and "in furtherance of Garrison's scheme of harassment and intimidation." A hearing on whether or not to grant the preliminary injunction was set for January 25, 1971. Just one week after the state trial was to begin. In other words, Shaw's lawyers needed almost no preparation time for the new venue and the new hearing. Which they likely had been preparing for in advance. Since they had an intimation that they would be successful in switching the venue.

They were counting on Herbert Christenberry. Christenberry was the federal judge who presided over this hearing. To understand what happened there, one must understand who Christenberry was. It was not possible to do that before the releases of the ARRB or the work of Professor Donald Gibson. Attorney Christenberry had been a political operative in the state since the 1930's. As Professor Gibson made the case in the pages of *Probe Magazine*, it appears that Christenberry and his brother Earle were undercover agents in the camp of populist Senator Huey Long. Herbert Christenberry was the source for a story that has been repeated many times over the years about a plot to kill Long by state backers of Franklin Roosevelt. Long was planning to run for president in 1936. Roosevelt's state backers had a meeting in July of 1935 at the DeSoto Hotel in New Orleans. Somehow, some way, Herbert Christenberry and two friends knew when and where this meeting was to take place. They even knew the room where it was held. One of them got a job as a desk clerk and booked the room next door. Christenberry said he placed a dictograph to the wall and managed to overhear the meeting, which he took down in short-hand.[9] Long was assassinated on September 8. The day after the shooting, Earle Christenberry declared that his assassin, Carl Weiss, was at the DeSoto Hotel meeting.

The reason this story has been recycled is that, as Gibson notes, there was a huge cover-up of the true circumstances of Long's murder. As he writes, "Almost all of the records disappeared for almost 60 years. In 1991 the gun allegedly used to kill Long and a 600 page police report turned up. . . . A complete reconstruction of the events on the night of the assassination is now—for the above reasons—impossible."[10] Because of this evidentiary vacuum, historians like Arthur Schlesinger have utilized the DeSoto story as a way to explain Long's murder. Therefore, according to Christenberry's eavesdropping, Carl Weiss was part of a plot to kill Long arranged by in state Democrats. Therefore it was part of an internecine party feud. Christenberry had given his transcription to a Long Democrat who was under indictment at the time of the assassination. Yet, after Long's murder, the indictment was suddenly dropped. Earle Christenberry had been Long's secretary. He was also in charge of Long's treasury. Which disappeared after Long's death. Further, Earle insisted that Weiss's name actually appeared on his brother's transcript. But when Long's biographer, T. Harry Williams, found the man who had it, he refused to show him the transcript. He then said, no one would ever see it. But he had told someone else that Weiss's name *was not* in the transcript.[11] If this is so, then Herbert Christenberry probably put out a cover story. The purpose of which was to confuse what actually happened to Long. For the really vicious enemies of Long, who had actually hatched a plot to take over the state capitol and kill Long, was a group from Standard Oil.[12]

Gibson's thesis gains credibility when he traces what happened to Herbert Christenberry after Long's murder. One would expect that since he allegedly exposed a plot by backers of Roosevelt to kill a state legend, FDR's administration would blackball him forever. One would be wrong. In 1937, Christenberry became U.S. attorney for the Eastern District of Louisiana. In 1942, he was nominated to be U.S. attorney at New Orleans. He was quickly confirmed in January of that year. As Gibson notes, "Apparently, no one asked him to explain his role in blaming Roosevelt supporters for murder." Then, in 1947, he was elevated to U.S. District Judge. The position he held when the Shaw perjury case arrived in front of him.[13] As Gibson notes, this would seem to suggest that Christenberry was not really a Long loyalist. This is especially likely since a true Long follower, Sidney Songy, went to jail after he exposed the Standard Oil plot to kill Long.[14]

The other piece of information that helps elucidate what Christenberry did was found in the National Archives as part of Shaw's personal papers. It is a letter from Christenberry's wife Caroline to Shaw which was sent a week after his acquittal. It begins like this: "Our most sincere congratulations! We shared your anxieties over the past two outrageous years." The reader should note the plural pronoun which denotes that Herbert is in complete agreement with his wife's sentiments. The note goes on with: "Should your case have eventually found its way to Federal Court and been allotted to my husband you most certainly would have had a fair trial. He felt we should not risk the possibility of being considered "prejudiced" in advance. This is our reason for not openly expressing these sentiments earlier." As if Shaw did not have a fair trial the first time around? The reader should note the quotes around the word prejudiced. That usage and the sentence's meaning clearly denotes that Christenberry was ferociously biased for Shaw and against Garrison. But he did not want anyone to know that. And surely, Shaw was not going to reaveal this letter since it would have forced Christenberry to recuse himself from his case. Which is the last thing Shaw and his lawyers wanted. But the fact this was sent in 1969 clearly influenced his lawyers' strategy for the perjury case. Which was likely done with former political operative Christenberry's connivance. As one could predict from all this, once the case got to Christenberry's court, this hidden bias manifested itself throughout the proceeding.

That three day hearing might have been scripted by Hugh Aynesworth. This proceeding was not in any way a preliminary hearing on the viability of the perjury charges. In other words, the many witnesses to Shaw's perjury statements were not called and cross-examined. If that had occurred, a trial would have to have been held. This hearing was a review of both Shaw's trial and Garrison's investigation. Except, as indicated in Caroline Christenberry's letter, the review was as wildly biased as Walter Sheridan's special. For example, William Gurvich was allowed to testify as to the fraudulence of Garrison's investigation.[15] Perry Russo's meeting with Andrew Sciambra in Baton Rouge and his subsequent sodium pentothal session was presented exactly in James Phelan's terms. In fact, in some ways, Christenberry went beyond Phelan. Consider: "A fair inference to be drawn is that these ex parte procedures were used to implant into Russo's mind a story implicating the plaintiff in an alleged conspiracy plot. This could have been accomplished by post-hypnotic suggestion."[16] Garrison, not Shaw, was actually placed on the witness stand and asked to explain why he ever called in Shaw for questioning in the first place. In other words, at the Wegmanns' request, Christenberry was asking the DA to give away his planned upcoming case against the defendant. As the reader can see, in Christenberry's court, Garrison was now the defendant, the Wegmanns were the prosecutors, and Christenberry was sitting at their table. Christenberry, well-schooled in political subterfuge, turned his court into a political arena. But he still had one serious problem. He had to find a way to characterize the bringing of the perjury charges as an act of bad faith. He ended up lying on his point. He wrote that after Shaw's acquittal, Garrison charged Shaw with perjury without any other witnesses except those had used at the trial.[17] This was not accurate. To use just one example, Garrison had an interview of a man named David Logan who had told his office that he had met Ferrie at a gathering at Shaw's home.[18] Logan did not appear at the conspiracy trial. As the author has made clear, a mistake Garrison made at the trial was not to use all of his witnesses against Shaw.

The man who may have misled the public about the conspiracy to murder Senator Huey Long, was now ending the first and only criminal prosecution of the conspiracy to murder President John F. Kennedy.

In relating the following sorry story, one should remember the directions for the Garrison Group. The CIA was making long-term plans that went to the point of *beyond* the Shaw trial. We should also recall, that in particular CIA cases, the attempt is not just to jail or assassinate a target, but to destroy its reputation so no one will ever follow that person or trail again. This is why the Helms-Angleton plan was always contingent on continuing after the Shaw trial. The strategy was not devised just to end Garrison's case against Shaw. That was just the beginning. The overall objective was multi-leveled. It was to end Garrison's career, ruin his reputation, place him in jail, take over his office, and then incinerate his evidence. All this to guarantee that no indictments would ever come out of New Orleans again. How was this accomplished?

After Garrison charged Shaw for perjury, Aaron Kohn and the Justice Department went to work to manufacture a criminal case against the DA. Kohn began to send over material from the Metropolitan Crime Commission files about alleged laxity by Garrison over crime in Orleans Parish. But even the attorney who would prosecute the case against the DA, Gerald Gallinghouse, complained to Kohn about the quality of the material he had been sent. He characterized it as weak.[19] Therefore, the Justice Department recruited Pershing Gervais, a former friend of Garrison and a man who had worked in his office as an investigator. But who Garrison had later fired. The charge was that Garrison was participating in a kickback scheme from illegal payoffs for pinball machines. There was a legitimate case in all this. A group of pinball operators were bribing a police officer to let them get away with their illegal payoffs on machines. This was done by alerting the operators as to when the machines would be checked.[20] These funds were then secretly forwarded to the police superintendent.[21] But Garrison was not involved in the scheme at all. And as the trial dragged on, this became obvious. Garrison, who decided to defend himself, would question each operator on this point. And each testified that not only did they never pay him or his assistants any money for this protection racket, they did not even know him.[22] The closest association Gallinghouse could get was that the operators had donated to Garrison's campaigns. But they had also donated to the campaigns of other DA candidates who were not involved.[23]

Realizing they had a large problem in this case regarding Garrison, the Justice Department had tried to solve it in two ways. They first organized a phony task force they called Strike Force and moved some men into New Orleans. This was to give the illusion that crime was running rampant there and they had to take care of it since Garrison could not. Second, they put pressure on Gervais to turn state's witness against Garrison. Gervais had been running a little private business by telling family members who were indicted that he could fix their cases for them. He was actually playing a little gamble on which cases were strong and which were weak. When he guessed correctly, he would collect a fee which he said was used in part to pay off the lead attorney. Since this was a form of fraud, Gervais could not report the money on his taxes. When the Justice Department found out about this, they turned him over to the IRS.[24] They now had leverage over Gervais to become their witness against the man they wanted out of the DA's office: Garrison. With Gervais in tow, Garrison was charged on June 30, 1971. He pleaded not guilty on December 15, 1971. In the meantime, one month after Garrison's arrest, Gervais was shipped to Canada and given a job doing very little with General Motors.

By September of 1971, Gervais was in Vancouver. In the local newspaper there, Gervais had confessed that he was recruited to frame Jim Garrison.[25] In fact, to reporter Rosemary James he stated that he was picked to go to Canada and get a fake job since he was the one who could get Garrison.[26] He was employed under the assumed name of Paul Mason. And he showed up at "work" and signed in once a week. When the *Vancouver Sun* called General Motors in Canada about this arrangement, they refused to answer any questions.[27] In addition to getting a salary from GM, he was also given a company car and an annual stipend from the Justice Department. Apparently, Gervais did not like Vancouver. After he gave out interviews to both James and the Canadian papers, he decided to sneak back into the United States. Which defeated the purpose of the subterfuge. The original idea was to get him out of the country under an assumed name so that Garrison could not find him or question him. Therefore, his appearance at the trial would be a total surprise. The exposure of all this skullduggery created a mini-scandal in Canada. Prime Minister Pierre Trudeau ordered an investigation of the whole affair.[28] At the end of May, many Canadian newspapers were running summaries of Gervais's exposure of Canada's role in a scheme to place Jim Garrison behind bars.

Garrison was allowed to listen to the undercover tapes Gervais had made of him in advance of the trial. He deduced that the Justice Department was arranging a charade in which Gervais would drop by his house to repay money he had borrowed from Garrison. He would be wired for sound. The bug in his pocket was personally authorized by Attorney General John Mitchell, who apparently did not like having to limit the testimony of Regis Kennedy at the Shaw trial.[29] The bills returned would be marked.[30] But since Garrison had no part in the scheme, the tapes had to be altered. Which they were.[31] The effect was to transform the debt being repaid to Garrison into a payoff for his complicity in the pinball protection racket.

In addition to not being able to get the pinball operators to link him to the scheme, Garrison brought in people from his office, and formerly with his office, to testify that they knew nothing about this kickback affair. Also that Gervais had been fired for trying to sell off a case, and he owed Garrison money.[32] So Gallinghouse's case against Garrison rested on the tapes and the testimony of Gervais. Gervais created a problem for himself by saying that Garrison had collected 150,000 dollars in the scheme. This did not correspond with what was on the tapes. As Garrison had loaned him just 5000 dollars.[33]

Armed with the previous disclosures in the Canadian and local newspapers, Garrison gave Gervais a blistering cross examination. The witness was read back a transcript in which he stated he had been forced to lie for the Justice Department. And that the whole point of him being pressured into being a witness and then exiled to Canada was to silence Jim Garrison. Gervais even admitted that he had participated in a frame up. And he called the case against Garrison a fraud based purely on politics.[34] Garrison even got Gervais to admit he had offered a lawyer friend of the DA's to "write the script" for the trial for 50,000 dollars.[35]

With Gervais reduced by his own words, Garrison now turned to exposing the tapes. He called Dr. Louis Gerstman, a professor of speech and hearing science at City University of New York. Gerstman found technical disparities and inconsistent noise levels on the tapes which showed that Garrison's voice had been spliced into certain conversations from elsewhere.[36] The DA concluded his case by calling other law enforcement officials who testified that his office had done as much or more to prosecute pinball operators than other DA's in the past, or others in neighboring areas.[37]

Garrison's summation lasted for three hours. He was acquitted on the first ballot. Even though the judge was Herbert Christenberry. Referring to that ironic fact, Gervais said "You can bet it's not an accident."[38] The Strike Force now left the state. This is how badly Washington wanted to punish Garrison for bringing a criminal case for the murder of President Kennedy. They were willing to send a DA who never had any record of bribery, not even a trace of it, to jail on completely manufactured charges.

But it was a winning plan anyway. Because the actual priority was to get Garrison out of office and the man they had wanted into office. A man who they could rely upon never to bring any charges in the Kennedy case. Even though, if one looked for it, New Orleans was honeycombed with evidence of Oswald being manipulated in the summer of 1963. But if you had a man who was actually part of the Justice Department that covered up that case, who was actually aiding Shaw's defense, then you could rest assured: No case would ever be brought. That man, of course, was Harry Connick.

Connick began to gear up for his first race against Garrison after Shaw's acquittal. Because of the fact that both major newspapers continually pilloried Garrison over the Shaw trial, much of the power elite in the city backed and contributed to Connick's campaign. Along with allies of Shaw. For instance, the Gurvich brothers, William and Louis, both gave Connick 10,000 dollars each. About a month before the election, a poll put Garrison ahead by a wide margin, more than thirty percentage points. About three weeks later, on the eve of the election, a St. Louis company called DeWitt announced the results of another poll. This one would put Connick ahead by twenty points. WDSU television, severe critics of Garrison's prosecution of Shaw, did a much publicized segment trumpeting that poll's results. Garrison won handily. The day after the election, even the *Times-Picayune*, wondered if the poll was a hoax intended to help Connick.[39]

Five months after Christenberry stopped Garrison's further prosecution of Clay Shaw, Garrison was arrested on the phony pinball protection charges. Gallinghouse, who worked in the same office as Connick, was in no hurry to go to trial. In fact, the trial did not occur until two years after Garrison's initial arrest. In the interim, Connick again challenged Garrison. This time around, Garrison's name was now in the news in a derogatory way for an extended period of time. Connick again began to raise a war chest to retire Garrison. The backers of the Superdome project were all on board, since Connick's brother was the secretary for that fund drive. Among others, Clay Shaw and Carlos Bringuier also contributed.[40] Since the trial dragged on well into the election season of 1973, Garrison was still getting bad publicity into the campaign. Then, after he was acquitted, he only had about two months to put together a positive push. The compacted time frame caused him to lose the election by a bit more than 2,000 votes. Connick now took office.

During the 1969 race, when asked about Garrison's inquiry into Kennedy's assassination, the challenger replied that although he tended to think there was little value to Garrison's assassination probe, he would evaluate each case on its individual merits.[41] There is no evidence that this happened. In fact, thanks to a hearing in New Orleans by the ARRB, we know what one of Connick's prime objectives was once he got into office. It was to literally set fire to the evidence Garrison left behind. Therefore, the world would never see the primary documents of the only criminal prosecution ever brought in the JFK case.

On June 28, 1995, Connick testified before the Review Board in New Orleans. He said he felt they were doing the right thing by putting all the records of the JFK assassination in one place. Therefore scholars of the future could clarify "clouded areas of the past and make sense of what happened."[42]

Connick's carefully scripted performance was blown to bits two weeks later. A former Connick staffer named Gary Raymond told a TV reporter friend of his that, once Connick had taken over the office, he almost immediately set about incinerating Garrison's leftover files. Connick packed up the testimony of over forty Clay Shaw grand jury witnesses and told Raymond to incinerate it. This included testimony from Dean Andrews, Perry Russo, and Marina Oswald. When Raymond hesitated on the grounds that this material had historical value, Connick replied, "Burn this sonofabitch, and burn it today!" Fortunately for history, Raymond kept the boxes in his garage. When the ARRB came to town, he finally had an official agency to turn the records over to. Not wanting to get involved personally, he called up his friend, reporter Richard Angelico. He told Angelico to turn them over for him. But before doing so, Angelico decided to interview Connick and confront him with the dichotomy between what he told the Review Board and what had actually happened. Connick had told the Board that his collection of Garrison's assassination records was not complete because Garrison had taken parts of it with him. This was accurate as far as it went. But it was not the whole truth. For Raymond had signed a sworn affidavit saying that he and two or three others were ordered by Connick to incinerate anything Garrison left behind. Trapped on camera with Raymond's affidavit, Connick at first tried to deny he had done what Raymond said he did. He then said, "I, I don't recall that. I don't recall that. But if I did do it, so what, its done."[43] The day after Connick tried to deny he had burned the records, another former staffer, Ralph Whalen, told the local papers, that he recalled that Connick burned a "bunch of Garrison stuff . . . some things that related directly to the Shaw case."[44] The idea seems to have been that, without the actual evidence, the media could ridicule Garrison's case based on the likes of Aynesworth, Phelan, and Walter Sheridan. In fact, Connick and Aynesworth had been friends for decades.[45]

It's hard to believe but even after Garrison was acquitted on the pinball protection scam, he was indicted again on a directly related charge. Namely, for not paying taxes on the money he never got in the first place.[46] Garrison was acquitted again. Yet, this hurt his chances in his run for the State Supreme Court.[47] Then there was a civil suit filed by Shaw in 1970. In this lawsuit, Shaw alleged that Garrison entered into a conspiracy with some of the leaders of the Truth and Consequences group in order to conduct a "fraudulent investigation for the assassination solely for the personal and political aggrandizement of the conspirators, particularly Garrison, Robertson, Rault, and Shilstone."[48] (Willard Robertson, Joe Rault, and Cecil Shilstone were the leading members of the Truth and Consequences organization.) It is hard to find these accusations credible since none of these men got any bit of aggrandizement out of the Shaw case. In the case of Garrison, one could effectively argue the opposite: it unraveled his life and career. Sal Panzeca told Harold Weisberg that the main targets of the lawsuit were: 1.) The money of the Truth and Consequences members, and 2.) To humiliate Garrison. The problem for the plaintiffs, as Weisberg stated to Panzeca, is that Shaw actually did perjure himself at the trial.[49]

The trial was set for November of 1974. But Shaw died in August of that year. That did not stop Shaw's lawyers, particularly Ed Wegmann. Contrary to what some have written, the case was not dismissed upon the plaintiff's death. For Ed Wegmann filed a motion to have it continued in his name. Even though state law specifically stated that an action like this would survive "only in favor of a spouse, children, parents, or siblings. Since no person with the requisite relationship to Shaw was alive at the time of his death, his action would have abated had state law been adopted as the federal rule."[50] Surprisingly, Wegmann's motion was allowed by the Christenberry influenced state court in 1975. As the U.S. Supreme Court eventually wrote, the Louisiana federal court refused to apply the specific state law in this particular case. Instead, it created "a federal common law of survival in civil rights actions in favor of the personal representative of the deceased." In this case, Ed Wegmann. That decision was reversed by the United States Supreme Court in May of 1978.[51]

As the reader can see, the legal actions were meant to put Garrison in prison, remove him from the DA's office, ruin his personal reputation, and to hurt him financially. But as pointed out, once Connick took office, his particular aim was not just to halt forever any investigation of the evidence rich New Orleans. Connick was intent on shoveling Garrison's evidence into the incinerator. The author can attest to this from firsthand experience. Having seen an

index of Garrison's files done by the HSCA, this author visited Connick's office
in 1994 to ask if these files were still there. Connick called in an assistant and
queried him about this single file cabinet. The assistant said it was still there.
Connick's eyes bulged and he said in exasperation, "We still have that stuff?"
Clearly, the DA thought he had burned it all previously.[52]

Accompanying the attempt by Connick to unseat Garrison, there was a
supplementary propaganda war through the media conducted by Shaw's allies.
Aynesworth, Phelan, and their young protégé, playwright James Kirkwood,
implanted their biased view of Garrison's case onto the New Orleans public
consciousness. Quite literally. At the close of the Shaw trial, local television
station WYES, Channel 8, aired an hour long discussion of the Shaw case by
those three men.[53] This was on top of the reporting in the local papers by the
likes of Chandler, James, and Snyder. And editorials demanded that Garrison
resign.[54] Kirkwood then went on to write a long book about the Shaw trial called *American Grotesque*. The idea for this book started with Clay Shaw himself.
Shaw wanted a book which depicted Garrison as homophobic; the underlying
thesis being that this caused him to go after the homosexual Shaw. He first
asked novelist James Leo Herlihy to write it. He turned it down. But Herlihy
got in contact with his friend Kirkwood and he took up the assignment.[55] To say
that Kirkwood came through for Shaw does not begin to do his book justice.
One only has to read his descriptions of the trial presentation of the Zapruder
film, and the testimony of Pierre Finck to understand what the man was up to.
But the point is that, until Jim Garrison published *On the Trail of the Assassins*,
Kirkwood's book was the standard reference work for the Shaw trial. Mainly
because no one had access to the trial transcript. The impression one would
get from reading Kirkwood's solipsistic work is that the transcript would not
be worth reading, which of course, was the intended result. The combination
of Phelan's daily spin meetings, with the publication of Kirkwood's book left
the message that there was nothing of any value that came out of Shaw's trial,
which as we have seen, was far from the truth.

In 1973, the federal government made sure no one would ever inspect the
site from which Oswald carried out his anti FPCC campaign for Phillips and
McCord in the summer of 1963. Sam Newman had sold the 544 Camp Street
building in July of 1965. It was a weird transaction. It appears to have been
sold for 58,000 dollars, and then resold on the same day, for a significantly
lower price of 34,800 dollars. That price ended up being a steal. Because in
1973, Gerald Gallinghouse, the man who was prosecuting Garrison at the time,
filed a motion for the federal government to purchase the building. The offer
was one the present owner could not refuse. It was over four times the last
sales price: 141,162.50 dollars. The motion was filed in the U.S. Eastern District

Court for Louisiana. The court Christenberry was serving on at the time. The case was handled by Judge Edward Boyle. The Camp Street building was now razed. And the ultimate irony is that the new building was named the Hale Boggs Building, in honor of the local congressional representative who had served on the Warren Commission.

The last stroke in creating a morass of doubt and confusion in the JFK case at this time was constructed in 1970. According to David Copeland, a rather obscure lawyer in Waco, Texas, he was then visited by two men who said they were from the Secret Service and the FBI.[56] Why these men appeared to Copeland has never been explained. And Copeland never seems to have asked them to prove if they were really from the FBI and Secret Service either. For some bizarre and inexplicable reason they revealed to him one of the most wild, untenable and unsupportable tales ever related about the JFK case. One that makes *Farewell America* and its southwest oil million-aire assassination Committee look rather staid and conservative. According to Copeland's retelling, the conspiracy to kill Kennedy was truly an interdisciplinary affair. One that involved scores of people beforehand, in addition to several different organizations. Including some rather overlooked ones like the American Council of Christian Churches, the security division of NASA, and something called DISC, Defense Industirial Security Command. There were also some overlooked personages involved: attorney Roy Cohn, General John Medaris, and mobster Joe Bonanno. In one of the most incredible statements in the entire fantastic essay, it is held that President Kennedy's murder was planned and supervised by the domestic intelligence branch of the FBI.[57] Incredibly, the essay then says that all the major tenets included were "established and documented by overwhelming evidence beyond a reasonable doubt."[58] Which is nothing more than a self serving lie.

Under the alias of William Torbitt, Copeland actually typeset this fantasy and published it. The title was "Nomenclature of an Assassination Cabal." It became popularly known as the *The Torbitt Document*. Which is a very misleading title, since it is not a document at all. And it contains little documentation to support its grandiose claims. It does allude to documents, which it says will back up its spurious claims. But those references are often to the files of New Orleans DA Jim Garrison. Having searched through many of those remaining files, this author can certify that little, if any, of the acts described by Copeland are attested to by Garrison's files. And why Copeland would write that they were, without seeing the actual evidence, shows how careless and irresponsible he was to accept what the two men told him. For instance, Copeland actually names William Seymour and Gordon Novel as Oswald impersonators. He then says that these claims are backed up by Warren

Commission evidence. They are not. Novel is not mentioned in the Commission volumes. And, as shown previously, Seymour was proven not to have been at Sylvia Odio's apartment impersonating Oswald.

Once Copeland printed this spurious tale, it was then distributed by Texas based researchers like Penn Jones. In the vacuum which existed after Shaw's acquittal, it took on a life of its own. The sheer volume of names in the essay, plus its intimations of a colossal conspiracy between so many different public and private organizations, plus its dubious claims of supporting documentation, all this managed to hypnotize people into overlooking one crucial fact. Although Copeland wrongly used Garrison as a source, and although he often referred to his inquiry, if one looks at the list of people accused by him, there is one group that is missing. It happens to be Garrison's number one suspect: the CIA. Like Bill Boxley, Copeland's work was pointing people almost everywhere: the Mafia, President Johnson, the FBI, Texas oil millionaires, DISC, NASA, John Connally, the Tyrall compound in Montego Bay. All this misdirection, this creation of a colossal and multi-faceted Rube Goldberg conspiracy, this was all a foreshadowing of what was laying ahead in the road. For now would come an outpouring of books and essays which would indicate a laundry list of suspects with very little evidence to back the assertions. The cabal that was arranged to release Shaw and bury Garrison had succeeded. At least temporarily.

CHAPTER FIFTEEN

Blakey Buries the Case

*"No, no, no. You don't have time to do that! Like
I said, that's the real world. That's irrelevant."*

—*HSCA Deputy Counsel Gary Cornwell*

When Garrison subpoenaed the Zapruder film from Time-Life, he said that it would show that President Kennedy was killed from the front, not from behind.[1] The night before the Zapruder film was shown at the Clay Shaw trial, he told his assistants the same. There is no doubt that the jury felt the film was compelling, since they asked to see it several times. The problem was that the American public had not seen the film. In 1975, they finally did see it. This was on an ABC television program, hosted by Geraldo Rivera, in prime time. Robert Groden and Dick Gregory were the only guests. The showing of the film on network television was, in a word, electric. The day after, the Kennedy assassination was a hot topic around the office water cooler. Further, since the film was shown in the midst of Senator Frank Church's investigations into the crimes of the CIA and FBI, popularly known as the Church Committee, that created the proper background to the inquiry into possible intelligence community malfeasance in the JFK case.

One of the people who got his own private screening of the Zapruder film was Representative Tom Downing of Virginia. His son obtained a copy of the film to show to his father.[2] This galvanized Downing into action. He placed a bill on the floor of the house to create a special committee to reopen the murder case of John F. Kennedy. In a tactical move, he later added the murder of Martin Luther King to get the support of the Black Caucus. It took over a year, but Downing finally got his bill passed in September of 1976.[3] Celebrated Philadelphia prosecutor Richard Sprague was nominated as Chief Counsel and Executive Director. Sprague then picked New York homicide prosecutor Robert Tanenbaum to be his Deputy Counsel for the John F. Kennedy probe. One could hardly ask for two more successful lawyers to helm the case. As interested parties like Church Committee investigator Gaeton Fonzi and pathologist and Commission critic Cyril Wecht stated, Richard Sprague was a perfect fit to helm this inquiry.[4] Both Sprague and Tanenbaum had tried scores of homicide cases. And Sprague had supervised a long and complex special prosecutor investigation into the murder of labor reform leader Jock Yablonski. After a series of trials, Sprague convicted corrupt United Mine Workers boss Tony Boyle, the man Yablonski was trying to unseat.

Downing was going to be the chair of the committee, and was prepared to back Sprague in his 6.5 million dollar budget request. This was submitted at the end of 1976. It marks the high water mark of the HSCA. Two things were clear from this budget request. First, Sprague was going to do a real investigation over every aspect of the Kennedy case. He was going to start anew, and not rely on any previous precedent. He wanted to hire people like document experts, and handwriting analysts. Second, unlike the Warren Commission, there was going to be no reliance on the FBI, Secret Service, or the CIA for any services. Sprague said that he could not do this since, if he was to do a thorough inquiry, the actions of those agencies would be part of that inquiry.[5] Or as Bob Tanenbaum said more colorfully when the FBI wanted to review their applications for positions, "I'll be damned if I will let them investigate us before we investigate them!"[6] As Sprague later said, he was determined to do this as purely and as professionally as possible. For he felt that this was very likely the last opportunity for the American public to find out the truth about the Kennedy case.[7]

The truly remarkable thing about all this is that Downing was in wholehearted support of what Sprague and Tanenbaum were going to do.[8] And as he took Sprague around to visit the committee members, they all embraced him. Looking back at it, Sprague felt he should have questioned two things. First, Downing had announced he was going to retire at the end of his term. Which meant he was not going to be around once the actual investigation began. Sprague felt that Richardson Preyer of North Carolina would have been a good choice to succeed him. That was not to be. Second, Sprague did not talk to anyone higher up in the leadership than Downing. That is, he was not aware that Downing's level of commitment to the inquiry was not reflected in say, Speaker of the House Tip O'Neill or Majority Leader Jim Wright. In retrospect, Sprague said those were errors of judgment on his part. He should have checked on those contingencies in advance.[9] Because as it turned out, the fact that Downing left ended up being a tipping point. And the support from the higher level of the Democratic leadership could not fill that breach.

But in the interim, Sprague did some decent enough work. In addition to hiring some of the staff, he was interested in redoing some experiments in public. For instance, testing the Single Bullet Theory. He was interested in investigating Oswald's mysterious journey to Mexico City in September and October of 1963.[10] He was also interested in the physical evidence, namely the Zapruder film, the photographs taken in Dealey Plaza, and the autopsy evidence. They were also going to review the methodology and conclusions of the Warren Commission. When these seasoned professional prosecutors began to look at these things, they were literally taken aback by what they saw. For example, committee lawyer Al Lewis could not even describe in words his impression of the state of the medical evidence in this case.[11] As Tanenbaum began to review the Warren Commission volumes he was appalled at the holes in the case against Oswald. And also, by how much evidence exculpatory of Oswald was left out of the Warren Report.[12] After viewing a lengthy slide show on the assassination by three different photographic authorities from the critical ranks, Lewis stated that, of the 13 staff lawyers in attendance, only one still supported the Single Bullet Theory.[13] After multiple viewings of the Zapruder film, Tanenbaum felt that the fatal shot came from the front and to the right of the president.[14] His chief detective in New Orleans, based on Kennedy's differing reactions, felt the president was was hit by two different caliber weapons.[15] All this, combined with the fact that Sprague was going to perform a no holds barred investigation, leaving no stone unturned, no path untrodden, all this promised that the Kennedy assassination was finally going to be addressed as it should have been back in 1963. For instance, Tanenbaum told photographic analyst Bob Groden that he had concluded the Warren Report was an untenable cover-up, and he and Sprague were going to blow that cover-up sky high.[16]

Tanenbaum had been influenced by his discussion of the issue with Senator Richard Schweiker of the Church Committee. Schweiker and Senator Gary Hart had helmed a sub-committee, which investigated the performance of the intelligence agencies in support of the Commission. But it actually had gone further than just analysis of documents. Pennsylvania's Senator Schweiker had hired Philadelphia journalist Gaeton Fonzi to do some field investigation. And he had come up with some very interesting results concerning a mysterious personage named Maurice Bishop. Tanenbaum had visited Schweiker with Detective Cliff Fenton. After discussing a few things with the pair, the senator asked Fenton to leave the room. Schweiker then turned over Fonzi's Maurice Bishop file to the HSCA Deputy Counsel. Schweiker then looked at Tanenbaum and told him that the Central Intelligence Agency had killed President Kennedy.[17] Etched in those grave terms, the Deputy Counsel read the file carefully. On the strength of it, he hired Fonzi. There is little doubt that the conversation with Schweiker and the research file on Bishop combined to make a strong impression on Tanenbaum and Sprague. As Tanenbaum later stated, from what he was able to discern, there were certain rogue elements of the CIA, in union with Bishop, who were involved with both Oswald and the Cuban exiles. And he felt that these exiles were involved in the assassination.[18] Tanenbaum has always qualified this as a working hypothesis he had. Not an ultimate conclusion. Since, as we will see, he was not around long enough to prove that thesis.

In addition to Fonzi, Tanenbaum hired a detective named L. J. Delsa. Tanenbaum knew Delsa from a previous case they had worked on together.[19] Delsa was a resident of New Orleans. He recommended the hiring of New Orleans police investigator Robert Buras. Tanenbaum also hired attorney Jonathan Blackmer.[20] While Tanenbaum was running the Kennedy inquiry, these three men formed his New Orleans team. While Fonzi and Al Gonzalez, another detective Tanenbaum brought with him from New York, investigated South Florida. To say that this network got compelling results does not begin to do them justice.

As we have seen, it was Fonzi who discovered the wider story about the first CIA infiltrator into Garrison's camp, Bernardo DeTorres. And how DeTorres may have been associated with Oswald before the assassination, and allegedly had photos of what went on in Dealey Plaza. Further, DeTorres was associated with Mitch Werbell in 1963, the CIA weapons expert who some believe may have designed the weapons used in Dealey Plaza.[21] When Blackmer was interviewing Francis Fruge about his work on the Rose Cheramie case and the Clinton witnesses, he retraced how Garrison had sent Fruge back to the bar that Rose and her two companions had stopped at and where they had forcibly bid her adieu. Fruge went on to relate how the bartender there had identified the two men with Rose as Sergio Arcacha Smith and Emilio Santana, both seen at 544 Camp Street, and both friends of Clay Shaw. As we have seen, Santana provided a link between Shaw and Ruby; Rose provided a link between Oswald and Ruby. But in a separate interview with investigator Bob Buras, Fruge dropped in a bombshell that connected the New Orleans aspect of the case, that is the setting up of Oswald, with the actual mechanics of the murder in Dealey Plaza.

At the time of Kennedy's death, Arcacha Smith had been living in Dallas. Probably because—due to embezzlement accusations—he had been deprived of his leadership role in the local branch of the CRC. But he kept close tabs on his friends in New Orleans and visited the city. Arcacha Smith appears to have gotten into the lucrative transportation of contraband from Florida to Texas, specializing in drugs, guns, and even prostitution.[22] And this is how he may have gotten involved with Ruby, since Ruby had been in the gun running business with, among others, CIA contract agent, Thomas Eli Davis. In fact, Ruby even said that if he was acquitted for killing Oswald, he hoped to get back in business with Davis.[23] While incarcerated, Ruby made one of his most memorable utterances: "They're going to find out about Cuba. They're going to find out about the guns, find out about New Orleans, find out about everything."[24] As we have seen in abundance, Arcacha Smith was directly involved with Banister, Ferrie, and Shaw. Recall, Carlos Quiroga was polygraphed by Garrison, and he reportedly was deceptive when he said that Arcacha Smith did not know Oswald and that he, Quiroga, had not seen the weapons used in the assassination prior to Kennedy's murder.

To top this all off, in a summary of an interview that Bob Buras did with Fruge, the former state trooper casually interrupted the investigator and asked him if the Committee had discovered "that diagrams of the sewer system in Dealey Plaza were found in Arcacha Smith's apartment in Dallas." Buras goes on to write that Fruge thought it was Will Fritz who mentioned this to him, but he was not sure on that point.[25] In Arcacha Smith, you have a man who, one can make a case, seems to have been involved in nearly every aspect of the assassination. No wonder Aynesworth did not want Garrison to question him. But also incriminating is this: Arcacha Smith strongly resisted a formal deposition by the HSCA. His interview was done on a moment's notice by Fonzi himself. It should have been done by someone on the New Orleans team: Buras, Delsa, or Blackmer. Further, not only did Fonzi not have enough time to prepare properly, Arcacha Smith's attorney insisted the interview *not be done under oath.*[26]

Further research by Bob Dorff has shed light on an apparently inaccurate aspect of the famous HSCA report on Cheramie. In that report, written by Pat Orr, it states that the doctor who Cheramie told in advance about the JFK assassination was a man named Dr. Bowers.[27] Bowers then relayed this information to Dr. Victor Weiss. Weiss then talked to Cheramie on the twenty-fifth, and did a brief interview with her on that date. Weiss had been the source to Garrison for this information way back in 1967. In that rendition, Weiss had said it was *he* who first interviewed Rose. But, similar to Fruge, he said, "he didn't really pay much attention to a woman of this type until after the assass-

ination occurred."[28] When Dorff tracked down Dr. Bowers, Donn Bowers said
that the HSCA report on this is wrong. It was *Weiss* to whom Rose predicted
the assassination in advance, not him. He never actually talked to her. Weiss
told Bowers what she said on Sunday, November 24. Bowers then heard that
Oswald had been killed by Ruby after he had talked to Weiss.[29] The HSCA
never talked to Bowers. Therefore they did not know that Weiss was not an
indirect witness to what Cheramie said, but a direct witness, as Fruge was.
Clearly, Weiss did not want to be involved in a formal way with the Kennedy
assassination.

Gaeton Fonzi started reinvestigating Garrison's leads on Freeport Sulphur.
He felt it was a nexus point for many suspicious people prior to the Kennedy
assassination. And not just people like Shaw and Ferrie, or even David Phillips.
For the executive board of Freeport Sulphur went all the way up to the top
of the Eastern Establishment at the time.[30] It included people like Godfrey
Rockefeller, Admiral Arleigh Burke, and the Chairman of Texaco, Augustus
Long. The founder of Freeport Sulphur was John Hay Whitney, Ambassador
to England under President Eisenhower. As Donald Gibson later wrote, four of
the directors of this rather medium sized company were members of the Council on Foreign Relations, that very exclusive and elitist based New York City
organization which strongly influences the government and media agenda.
Indeed, Freeport had as many directors in the CFR as did giant transnationals
like DuPont and Exxon.[31] Further, there were other Rockefeller originated globalist organizations in New Orleans that Shaw was associated with, namely
International House and the Foreign Policy Association of New Orleans. For
instance, Shaw's International House runs a student exchange program worldwide, an effort to seemingly spread the concept of globalization, sometimes
called "one worldism." A director of Freeport Sulphur, and its Vice-President,
was E. D. Wingfield, a native of New Orleans who had been with the company
since 1933. Wingfield was a director of International House, and Shaw served as
its acting manager in 1961–62.

Jock Whitney, publisher of the *New York Herald Tribune*, and a firm
Rockefeller ally, was Chairman of the Board of Freeport from 1936–57. In an
authorized biography of Whitney, the following passage appears: "On November 22, President Kennedy was killed. Whitney, who *was pressed* into emergency service that tumultuous night as a copy reader, had a speaking engagement four days later"[32] (italics added). As Professor Gibson notes, the idea that
Whitney—the publisher of the *Herald Tribune*, a man worth several hundred
million dollars, and a leading Establishment figure—could be "pressed" into
anything is ridiculous. If Whitney was at his newspaper office reading copy the
night President Kennedy was killed, its because he wanted to be there.

What makes all this interesting is that the *Herald Tribune* published an editorial the next morning entitled, "Shame of a Nation-History of Assass-inations." There was no source or author given. This article stated that, although in some European states assassination had been a weapon of power politics, in America that pattern had not been historically followed. It then specifically mentioned a book called *The Assassins* by former *Herald Tribune* reporter Robert Donovan to back up this thesis. Quoting Donovan, the piece then reads that previous American assassination attempts did not attempt to shift political power, they did not attempt to alter a policy of government, nor did they try to resolve ideological conflicts. An accompanying editorial then said that in America, assassinations have almost always been the work of "crazed individuals representing nothing but their own wild imaginings. . . . The heat of normal politics has its reflex on the lunatic fringe."[33] In other words, on the night of the assassination, Whitney's newspaper—with him reviewing the content—had predicted what the Warren Commission would conclude ten months later. That Oswald was a disturbed killer, a sociopath. At the same time it was pushing for a "crazed individual" solution to the case, Whitney's paper was deliberately pushing away from any kind of poli-tical policy reason for the murder. But yet, at this time, Oswald was being branded a communist in the press. And at no time when he was allowed to appear in public that day, did he appear to be a "crazed individual." If that is not prescient enough, consider the following. The very book that the *Herald Tribune* was quoting from, *The Assassins,* is the same book that Allen Dulles would be passing out to fellow members of the Commission at their first meeting, just two weeks later.[34] This was a clear attempt by the former spymaster to influence the Warren Commission members. Just as Whitney's paper, under his direct supervision, was trying to inculcate the public. And there can be no doubt that Whitney knew Dulles.[35]

In this first phase of the HSCA, one of the personages who genuinely interested Tanenbaum and Fonzi was David Phillips. While working for Schweiker, Fonzi had done some good work on the militant Cuban exile group Alpha 66. The file he had turned over to Tanenbaum contained that work. During his field investigation, Fonzi had interviewed the Alpha 66 exile leader Antonio Veciana. Veciana had been part of a 1961 attempt to assassinate Castro. One which the CIA had not reported to the Church Committee. Veciana had also visited the Alpha 66 safe house in Dallas, the one that Oswald had repor-tedly been at.[36] It should be noted here that Alpha 66 was a group of particular focus to Jim Garrison. In fact, some who worked with Garrison actually said he was a bit obsessed with this group.[37] We should keep that point, plus the mysterious Mr. Phillips in mind—the man who was going to arrange the New

Orleans telethon for Sergio Arcacha Smith—as we detail the following. For Alpha 66 seemed especially intent on violating Kennedy's policies in the Caribbean. In fact, by raiding Russian supply ships, Alpha 66 was bent on provoking a direct conflict between America and the USSR. The man who supervised all of Veciana's thirteen years of anti-Castro activity, and who orchestrated the violations of Kennedy's Cuban policy, was a man he called Maurice Bishop. In fact, according to Veciana, Alpha 66 was essentially Bishop's creation.[38] It was he who had directed the Alpha 66 attempt to kill Castro in Cuba in 1961.[39] Veciana told Fonzi he had seen Oswald in Dallas with Bishop in early September of 1963. It was at the Southland Center, a 42 story office complex built in the late fifties. When Veciana entered the lobby, he saw Bishop talking with Oswald off in a corner. When Veciana approached, Bishop ended the conversation. The three walked out of the lobby and onto the sidewalk. Bishop then dropped back with Oswald, exchanged some words with him and Oswald left.[40]

There is very little doubt today that Bishop was Phillips.[41] And for him to meet Oswald at this time and place would make perfect sense. For two reasons. First, after all the activity that Oswald had just performed in his public discrediting of the Fair Play for Cuba Committee, Phillips was likely now instructing him on what the next step would be. We can say this because we know something today that neither Fonzi nor Garrison knew at the time. Namely that Phillips was supervising the CIA campaign to counter the FPCC. Secondly, because Oswald now had a rather high profile in New Orleans, it was safer to meet somewhere else. Especially since Phillips had been at Guy Banister's office to organize the New Orleans telethon.

After a series of conferences in the late summer of 1977, between Fonzi, Delsa, Blackmer, Garrison, and others, Blackmer authored a long memo which included the following statement, "We have reason to believe Shaw was heavily involved in the anti-Castro efforts in New Orleans in the 1960s and [was] possibly one of the high level planners or 'cut out' to the planners of the assassination."[42] By the time this memorandum was written, the participants in this series of meetings didn't really understand that everything had been changed. Whether or not Shaw was a planner or "cut out" for the assassination did not really matter. Because both Sprague and Tanenbaum were now gone. Beginning in January of 1977, an unrelenting press campaign had been revved up. The twin objects were to get Sprague removed as Chief Counsel, and to derail the committee. Sprague had made too many public comments about conducting a real investigation. And, as mentioned above, his first budget submission of December, 1976 proved that was his aim.[43]

The first attacks on Sprague began with the *Los Angeles Times*. These were then picked up and amplified by the *New York Times*. And then the *Washington*

Post jumped into it. Their reporter was Walter Pincus, who called the HSCA in February of 1977, "perhaps the worst example of Congressional inquiry run amok."[44] The man who led the charge at the *LA Times* was, predictably, Jack Nelson.[45] The reporter who previously went after Jim Garrison. At the *New York Times,* something very revealing occurred. The first reporter that the *Times* had on the beat was Ben Franklin. Franklin had covered the prosecution of Tony Boyle by Sprague.[46] And he had given Sprague some fair press so far.[47] But at about the time of Sprague's budget submission, they replaced Franklin with David Burnham. Burnham went to the newspaper morgue in Philadelphia and wrote a long series about Sprague's career in the Philadelphia DA's office. He picked five small points of controversy in Sprague's illustrious eighteen-year career. When the series was over, the *Times* ran an editorial asking Sprague to resign.[48] Once this happened, Burnham was rotated out of this assignment.[49]

The other problem was that after Downing stepped down, there began to be a feud between Sprague and the new chairman Henry Gonzalez. This was very likely egged on by two assistants on the staff of Gonzalez, Gail Beagle and Edyth Baish. Baish admitted to being a mole inside of Sprague's office for Gonzalez.[50] Baish once reported back to Gonzalez that Sprague had poked fun at him at a meeting. Which Sprauge denied. After this, on February 10, 1977, Gonzalez tried to fire Sprague. But the committee rallied to Sprague's side. Gonzalez then tried to shut down the committee by depriving them of certain functions, like franking privileges. He then began to denounce Sprague on the floor of Congress. Finally, at the end of February, sick and exhausted, he resigned and went back to San Antonio for care. But not before calling Sprague an "unconscionable scoundrel."[51]

At this point, Representative Louis Stokes of Ohio was brought in as Chairman. Stokes measured the way the votes were lining up in lieu of the incessant newspaper attacks on Sprague, and the embarrassing verbal fisticuffs of Gonzalez. The latter started up again once Gonzalez got his health back and returned to Washington. Stokes decided that if the committee was to survive, it would have to be without Sprague. Therefore Sprague resigned on the evening of March 29, 1977. Here it is interesting to note something. Very few people would dispute that, at the time he was appointed Chief Counsel, Sprague was one of the finest prosecutors in the country. Since he left Washington, he has had a distinguished career in private practice. The only time he ever had his professional credentials questioned was during the six months he agreed to serve as counsel to the HSCA. And that is simply because he was going to supervise a real investigation of the JFK case. Yet, the same thing happened to him as happened to Jim Garrison. In fact, like Garrison, Sprague was also even accused of being in bed with the Mafia![52] When the first press attacks began, HSCA staffer Chris Sharrett remembers thinking, "It's Garrison all over again."[53] Or, as Joe Rauh, who knew Sprague from Philadelphia and had a front row seat to the controversy in Washington, said, "You know, I never thought the Kennedy case was a conspiracy until now. But if they can do that to Dick Sprague, it must have been." With Sprague's resignation, the House Select Committee survived. The interim Chief Counsel was Tanenbaum with Al Lewis, a friend and colleague of Sprague's, as his deputy.

Death in Manalapan

During the tumultuous twenty-four hour period that Sprague left and the HSCA was renewed, another jarring event happened in Florida. George DeMohrenschildt died of a shotgun wound to the head. He had just been served with a subpoena from the committee by Fonzi. It is relevant to note that DeMohrenschildt's attitude toward Oswald seemed to change over the years. The Baron and his wife Jeanne had been accusatory witnesses for the Warren Commission against Oswald. But by the time they returned from Haiti, this seemed to have changed. The Baron now told author Dick Russell that the Warren Commission had railroaded Oswald and that he was sure that Oswald had not killed Kennedy. His wife added, "Of course, the truth has not come out. We know it was a vast conspiracy."[54] Toward the end of his life, DeMohrenschildt became an instructor at a local college teaching French. He seemed to be having emotional problems. He exhibited some of this imbalance when Russell visited him again in July of 1976. During the interview, when his wife stated that Oswald had been sent to the Soviet Union at the request of the CIA, George began pacing across the room. He then started shouting, "It is defiling a corpse! Defiling a corpse! I don't want to talk about it, it makes me sick!"[55] This is around the time that DeMohrenschildt began to see a mysterious Dr. Mendoza. George suffered from chronic bronchitis. He did not like going to hospitals. He was persuaded to see a newly arrived physician in Dallas named Charles Mendoza. Although his physical health improved, he began to show symptoms of paranoia and a nervous breakdown.[56] Jeanne accompanied George on one of his visits to Mendoza. She discovered he was giving her husband injections and expensive prescription drugs. She confronted the doctor as to why he was doing this and what was in the drugs and chemicals he was administering to her husband. Mendoza got angry and upset. Jeanne eventually came to believe that it was Mendoza who was behind George's nervous breakdown.[57] Jeanne eventually had George placed under observation at Parkland Hospital. The couple then split up.

At this point, December of 1976, Dutch television journalist Willem Oltmans, who had known the Baron since 1967, got in contact with him. When Oltmans encountered the Baron after his hospital stay, he talked him into traveling with him to Amsterdam. There they were to film a series of interviews on NOS television, a large network in the Netherlands. But before the pair departed from Dallas, DeMohrenschildt got a phone call from author Edward Epstein. Epstein was offering the Baron money to be interviewed for his upcoming book about Oswald, entitled *Legend*.[58] The Baron decided to leave anyway with Oltmans. They departed from New York on March 2.[59] When they arrived in Amsterdam, Oltmans began negotiating a book and television deal for DeMohrenschildt.[60] After a few days in Amsterdam, Oltmans decided to go to Brussels. He was meeting with an old acquaintance named Vladimir Kuznetzov, the Soviet charge d'affaires. According to Oltmans, when they met the Russian, DeMohrenschildt talked to him for awhile in Russian. Oltmans did not understand anything they said. The Baron excused himself to take a walk, and he said he would return in an hour.[61] This was the last time Oltmans saw DeMohrenschildt.

The Baron went back to America and stayed with his daughter Alexandra in an affluent Florida town called Manalapan, just south of Palm Beach. Alexandra was staying with her aunt, Mrs. C. E. Tilton. George stayed in touch with Oltmans. And Oltmans, who had been in contact with the HSCA, told Robert Tanenbaum that George was in Florida. While in Manalapan, Epstein tracked down the Baron. They then agreed that DeMohrenschildt would do a series of four interviews with Epstein. The deal was a thousand dollars for each interview session. On March 29, 1977, Epstein was in his second day of interviews with George at the luxury hotel The Breakers in Palm Beach. Gaeton Fonzi was alerted to where DeMohrenschildt was staying and he left his card with Alexandra that day. He said he would call back in the evening. Epstein and DeMohrenschildt then took a lunch break. The Baron drove back to Manalapan in a car rented by Epstein. When he arrived, Alexandra showed him Fonzi's card, to which George showed no reaction.[62] He then went to his bedroom on the second floor to rest. At 2:21 P.M., he was dead from a shotgun blast. His body was discovered by Alexandra at 2:45 P.M.[63]

It is important to note here that, after DeMohrenschildt's death, Oltmans seemed to want to write the public epitaph to his life in relation to the Kennedy assassination. For example, within forty-eight hours of his death, Oltmans was testifying in front of the HSCA. Emerging from that testimony, he immediately began giving interviews to the press. (In fact, he had actually been on the ABC show *Good Morning America*, before he appeared in front of the HSCA.[64]) At his request, Oltmans', HSCA testimony had been in executive session—

that is, it was secret.[65] But now, as he emerged from that secret testimony, he had no qualms telling the public the substance of what he had just said. In a complete reversal of what the Baron had told Dick Russell several months previous, Oltmans now said on camera that DeMohrenschildt had instructed Oswald in his killing of Kennedy. The two had discussed the matter from A to Z. Therefore, DeMohrenschildt knew Oswald was going to kill Kennedy.[66] But he immediately added that Oswald was among four of the assassins of Kennedy. Oswald had apparently arranged with some other Cubans for there to be a crossfire in Dealey Plaza.[67] DeMohrenschildt also claimed to Oltmans that he knew Jack Ruby and had been in his saloon.[68] He seemed to imply that DeMohrenschildt, in turn, had gotten his instructions from Texas oil men Lester Logue and H.L. Hunt. He knew this since Oswald had told DeMohren-schildt that he had written to Hunt.[69] Again, this is another reversal. Because when Oltmans asked DeMohrenschildt on camera in 1968 if Texas oil money financed the assassination, the Baron said no it had not.[70] Further, when Robert Tanenbaum asked Oltmans if the Baron had told him how he instructed Oswald to arrange the crossfire, he said no he had not. When he asked him if DeMohrenschildt told him what Hunt's instructions were to him, he said no he had not.[71] Oltmans then seemed to try and discredit his own story. He quoted DeMohrenschildt as saying that he only made up a story about Oswald because everyone makes money off the Kennedy assassination. Except him. So now it was his turn to do so.[72] What makes all this even more odd is that in the manuscript he was working on, *I am a Patsy, I am a Patsy,* DeMohrenschildt wrote that Oswald actually admired Kennedy, specifically for his attempts to break down segregation in the south, and his efforts to wind down the Cold War.[73] DeMohrenschildt also wrote that Oltmans, who visited him often, by 1976 believed he had nothing to do with the assassination.[74]

Then, a year later, Oltmans took another pass at the JFK case. In a much heralded article for *Gallery,* he came up with a new key witness. A man named General Donald A. Donaldson. Oltmans claimed Donaldson had been instructed by President Kennedy to investigate any plots against his life. After the Dallas assassination, Donaldson kept quiet about this investigation. But years later he confided to Oltmans because of his work with DeMohren-schildt. In this new updating of Oltmans's JFK conspiracy, the Dutchman cooperated with Japanese writer Nobuhiko Ochiai. This time, the plotters were not Texas oil men. They were Allen Dulles and J.Edgar Hoover with the approval of Richard Nixon.[75] Near the end of the story, Oltmans tells us that Donaldson is now missing.[76] Therefore, for any interested parties, it would be difficult to check the information. Or even find out if the man really was who Oltmans said he was. In a last minute insert at the beginning of the magazine the publisher tells us that, as the issue went to press, they learned through "extremely reliable sources" that Donaldson had been killed in December of 1977. The cause of death was a rather improbable 17 bullets to the skull. This made it impossible to ever check on the Oltmans revision.

Even though a coroner's inquest ruled his death as self-inflicted, there are some serious questions about DeMohrenschildt's demise. First, according to the crime scene report and the autopsy, there was not any exit wound to the rear of the skull. Yet DeMohrenschildt allegedly placed a shotgun in his mouth and pulled the trigger. Its true that shotgun shells disperse more quickly than jacketed bullets. But this shot was almost within contact distance. Neither the maid nor the cook heard the shotgun blast, even though both women were right below the room that DeMohrenschildt was in at the time.[77] The police also had problems explaining the blood spatter pattern on the wall. When a blood spurt hits a flat surface it creates a different pattern than if it hits a surface that is perpendicular to it. In looking at photographs of the spatter pattern, it appears that the bathroom door was closed at the time the shooting took place. Because the blood pattern looked continuous. But the police said this was not the case. The bathroom door was open at the time. The testifying officer demeaned the jurors for asking this question and then jumped to a new topic.[78] But it would appear that someone altered the crime scene afterwards. The final oddity about the scene is the position of the weapon after death. It fell trigger side up, parallel to the chair DeMohrenschildt was in, with the barrel resting at his feet and the butt of the rifle away from him and to his left. The police had a problem with this issue and so did the inquest jurors.[79] As author Jerry Rose has noted, this strange positioning of the rifle suggests it was "placed" by someone.

Ms. Tilton was not at home at the time of DeMohrenschildt's death. But she had left strict instructions for the maid to record her favorite TV programs. The home had an alarm system which caused a quiet bell to ring anytime an outside door or window was opened. During the hearing, the tape of the program was played. When it was, the alarm bell went off and then the gun blast was heard.[80]

Mark Lane was at the coroner's inquest. He interviewed local DA David Bludworth. Bludworth was greatly concerned about the tragedy. And he was waiting for the HSCA to send down an investigator to talk to him. Bludworth brought up a point that Jerry Rose also found curious. Why did Epstein have DeMohrenschildt leave so early if he was paying him so much money? Couldn't George have rested in Epstein's room? Further, Bludworth told Lane that Epstein said he had no notes or tape recordings of the interview session. The DA did not believe that, not at the price he was paying. Bludworth then brought up a curious point. He told Lane that his office had records of all long distance calls, including Epstein's. Bludworth then said that Epstein showed DeMohrenschildt a document, "which indicated that he might be taken back to the Parkland Hospital in Dallas and given more electroshock treatment." Bludworth stared at Lane and then added, "You know, DeMohrenschildt was deathly afraid of those treatments. They can wreck your mind. DeMohrenschildt was terrified of being sent back there."[81]

There are three ways to look at DeMohrenschildt's death today. Perhaps distraught by the fact he was going to be called before the HSCA, he took his own life. The second way to look at his death is that he may have been murdered. The third way to view it is that he was hounded and harassed into taking his own life by the combined actions of Mendoza, Oltmans, and Epstein. In this last regard, it is interesting to note that Epstein's book *Legend* posited the idea, however vaguely, that Oswald killed Kennedy while working as a Russian agent. Because he was Russian by birth, DeMohrenschildt has a very large role in that book. While working on the book, one of Epstein's consultants was James Angleton.[82] Angleton pushed the myth that Oswald was a Russian agent until he died. Although George revealed to Epstein that he was instructed by Dallas CIA station chief J. Walton Moore to first visit Oswald, that fact is not in the original 1978 edition of the book. Finally, once DeMohrenschildt was in Florida, he told Mrs. Tilton he was being harassed by Oltmans.[83] He also wrote a statement saying that while in Amsterdam, he felt Oltmans was trying to drug him, and also exchange his traveler's checks. He also felt that Oltmans was making homosexual overtures to him. All this in order to make him admit things that he did not do. He also feared that his family lawyer, Patrick Russell, was collaborating with Oltmans against him.[84]

Reporter Jerry Policoff also got copies of the statements that DeMohrenschildt had written in Amsterdam concerning Oltmans's tactics and objective. He wrote about them in an article for *New Times*. When he saw that article, Oltmans called Policoff and told him to meet him in the lobby of an apartment building near the United Nations in New York. When they met, Oltmans claimed that the DeMohrenschildt documents that Policoff based his article on were not genuine. Policoff said he did not believe that at all. He thought they were real. When Policoff said this, Oltmans put on an entirely different face and demeanor than that of the cheery and articulate television reporter. He became extremely menacing and intimidating. He began to say things that were threatening and designed to scare Policoff. It got so bad that Policoff decided to get up and leave. Clearly, Oltmans did not want the fact that he was attempting to undermine DeMohrenschildt to gain currency. Then no one would buy his steady stream of disinformation anymore. They would wonder where he was getting it.

Blakey Takes the Helm

It is not an exaggeration to say that a sea change overtook the House Select Committee once G. Robert Blakey filled the Chief Counsel position. It was not easy to find a replacement once the spectacle of the removal of Dick Sprague was complete. Former Justice of the Supreme Court Arthur Goldberg was one candidate who turned down the job. Al Lewis had talked Goldberg into filling the position. But Goldberg had one reservation. He wanted to know if the CIA would cooperate with him. Lewis suggested calling up Stansfield Turner, President Carter's CIA Director. So Lewis called him and told him Goldberg wanted to talk to him. He put Goldberg on the line and the candidate asked Turner if he could guarantee the Agency would cooperate if he became Chief Counsel. A long silence ensued. It got so long and so quiet that Goldberg turned to Lewis and said, "I'm not sure if he's there anymore." Lewis suggested that he say something. So Goldberg asked if he was still on the line and Turner said he was. Goldberg asked him for an answer to his question. Turner said, "I thought my silence was my answer."[85] Goldberg decided to bow out.

Apparently, this kind of attitude did not deter Blakey, the organized crime authority. Blakey had served in Robert Kennedy's Justice Department and played a leading role in drafting the Racketeer Influenced and Corrupt Organizations Act, commonly referred to as RICO. Blakey later helped draft a wiretapping law as part of the Omnibus Crime Control and Safe Streets Act of 1968. He was a law professor at Notre Dame from 1964–69. He then worked as a Chief Counsel to Senator John McClellan on a subcommittee of the Senate Judiciary Committee dealing with Criminal Laws and Procedures. At the time he was offered the HSCA position, he was a law professor at Cornell.

Just from this brief background one can discern two things about Blakey. Unlike Sprague, he had some experience in the ways of Washington. Secondly, he had spent a large part of his career up to that time focusing on the way that organized crime worked. In America, at that time, this meant the Mafia. Before we detail some of the controversial things that Blakey did once he became Chief Counsel, it is important to ask if he came to Washington with any kind of preconceived ideas about Kennedy's assassination and who was behind it. Jim McDonald was a lawyer Blakey recruited to serve on his Organized Crime team. McDonald was reluctant to go to Washington. But Blakey intimated that he had some new evidence. He then asked McDonald who he thought killed Kennedy. McDonald said he didn't know. Blakey told him to think, since it was obvious. But McDonald still could not guess the right answer. Finally Blakey declared, "Organized crime killed Kennedy!"[86] In a conversation that William Davy and the author had in Virginia with committee investigator

Bill Triplett, Triplett said that if the suspect's name did not end in a vowel—meaning it sounded like he was in the Italian Mafia—Blakey wasn't interested in him.[87] When the author talked to Gaeton Fonzi, he said that from the beginning Blakey was centered on the Mafia as his main suspect. And it became an obsession as more evidence came in that pointed elsewhere.[88]

But there was a complement to this focus on the Mob. And that was a feeling of protectiveness towards the CIA. When a manuscript written in Spanish allegedly based on a secret Cuban intelligence report came into the committee, it was given to the Spanish speaking Eddie Lopez to read and summarize for Blakey. Later, reporter Jack Anderson learned that Blakey had turned it over to the Agency. Blakey called Fonzi one evening and told him that if Anderson or one of his cohorts told Fonzi that he had done that, it wasn't true. The problem is that it was true. And Blakey knew that when he told Fonzi he hadn't.[89] When confronted with skepticism over the Bureau's and Agency's true intentions with his committee, Blakey replied with, "You don't think they'd lie to me, do you? I've been working with these people for twenty years."[90] Toward the end, when CIA liaison Regis Blahut was caught mishandling Kennedy's autopsy photos while they were secured in a safe, the Agency offered Blakey four ways to do an inquiry of what had happened. The main object being to see if Blahut was part of a larger operation to undermine the HSCA. One option was to do the inquiry through the D.C. police, another was through the FBI, and the third was an internal HSCA inquiry. The last was to have the CIA do it. Even though the Agency officers at this meeting strongly encouraged Blakey not to choose them to do the investigation, he still did.[91] The reporting officer, Haviland Smith, made the only conclusion he could from this meeting. He wrote that his interpretation of what Blakey wanted was the Agency "to go ahead with the investigation of Blahut and that he expects us to come up with a clean bill of health for the CIA."[92] Which, of course, they did despite the fact that Blahut flunked three polygraph tests.[93] When the author talked to HSCA staffer Eddie Lopez about this matter, I told him that in reading these memoranda, I was struck by how friendly Blakey was with these CIA officers. That is, what a seemingly easy rapport he had with them. I said, "You know Eddie, he talks to them . . ." Lopez interrupted me in mid-sentence and completed the thought for me: "He talks to them like he's one of them."[94]

When Blakey was trying to make his argument that the Mafia killed Kennedy with Oswald as their hit man, he maintained that Dutz Murrett knew and worked with Sam Saia. Murrett, Oswald's uncle, had run a bookmaking operation in New Orleans for a number of years. According to information Blakey attained through unreliable Garrison antagonist Aaron Kohn, Saia was a gambler and a close associate of Carlos Marcello. Yet, in interviews the HSCA did with Murrett's wife and son, it became clear that Murrett had gotten out of the bookmaking business prior to 1959.[95] Therefore, the Marcello-Saia-Murret connection would not have been viable in 1963.[96] The HSCA report on this issue is careful not to be blunt with this information, which is clever of Blakey, since his staff was unable to provide credible evidence of a direct relationship between Dutz Murrett and Marcello[97]—that is, one without Saia. In fact, in a later book co-authored by Blakey, he admits this by saying the Committee could not find any other underworld figures associated with Oswald besides Murrett.[98] The above testimony, closely held by Blakey, is probably the reason why most of the members of the Organized Crime team did not think they had connected Oswald to the Mob. But it became clear by Blakey's attitude at meetings that "Blakey wanted that. He wanted to make the link more than anything else."[99]

Blakey did the same thing, except in an inverse sense, with information that pointed in a direction he did not want to follow. He either eliminated it, or abridged it to soften its impact. For instance, in the discussion of Oswald at 544 Camp Street, the Committee briefly discusses Kerry Thornley. These statements are included: "Thornley firmly denied contact with Oswald at 544 Camp Street in New Orleans or at any time since his Marine Corps days. His statements have been corroborated and no evidence has been found to contradict him."[100] As we have seen, this is simply false. And the original New Orleans team knew that. If one can believe it, this report actually uses the Secret Service interview with James Arthus in a way to neutralize the fact that Oswald was at Banister's office.[101] Yet the Committee had information in its files which said that Arthus used to kid Banister about Oswald by laying his FPCC literature on his desk.[102] (As we have also seen Arthus wanted to send a dead pigeon to the White House.) This report also quotes the original FBI interview of Sam Newman saying that he denied ever renting space to Oswald, which of course, did not mean Oswald was not at 544 Camp Street. In an interview with the HSCA, Newman denied seeing Oswald at the building.[103] But the staffers considered Newman to be an untruthful witness with a lot to hide.[104]

This report then quotes Delphine Roberts and Jack Martin as saying they had seen Oswald at Banister's. But it does not quote them fully, and then says more corroboration would be necessary, since, at first, neither disclosed Oswald was at 544 Camp Street. But they both had good reasons for doing that. Martin feared Banister because of the pistol whipping, which is likely why he shifted the focus to Ferrie in his later talks with the DA's office. And Banister had sworn Roberts to secrecy. He had told her that she should not talk to anyone about Oswald or any of the anti-Castro activities she had seen.

Another thing that frightened the woman was that she felt that both Banister and Ferrie had been murdered.[105] But before he died, Banister correctly predicted to her that the Warren Report would not tell the truth about what happened.[106] For the Oswald scheme to hold, it was important for Roberts to be quiet for, as mentioned previously, she actually saw the second floor room that Oswald used to assemble his pro-Castro literature. And, showing that the HSCA staff was right about Sam Newman's dissembling, she told Bob Buras that Newman brought these things to Banister's office to "get rid of them after Oswald left New Orleans."[107] She also said that she thought that Martin was actually trying to get at Banister's Oswald file on the day of the assassination. And this is why Banister erupted at him.[108] Like others who worked for Banister, she said he had frequent visits by men from the CIA and FBI. She said something else that was fascinating: Ferrie had shown her and Banister photos of Shaw in full drag. Banister then took the photos from him and placed them in the file he had on Shaw.[109] One last point of interest: She had seen Regis Kennedy in Banister's office. As had former Banister partner Joe Oster.[110]

One can see why Blakey would not want to reveal the full contents of this interview. So he kept it classified for over fifteen years. But as far as not having enough corroboration for a Banister/Oswald relationship, in the HSCA Report itself, CIA agent William Gaudet states that he had seen Banister speaking to Oswald on a street corner.[111] Later, in an interview with Tony Summers, Gaudet stated that "I did see Oswald discussing various things with Banister at this time and I think Banister knew a whole lot of what was going on."[112] In addition we have seen others like Dan Campbell who also place Oswald inside Banister's office. For Blakey to say there was not enough corroboration for this is simply disingenuous. As we have seen, there was plentiful corroboration for it.[113]

According to New Orleans investigators Delsa and Buras, Blakey placed severe restrictions on the re-investigation of the Clinton-Jackson incident. They were only allowed to speak to the witnesses already interviewed by Garrison's team. Buras and Delsa were not allowed to go to the area together. And they were not given the previous witness statements for comparison purposes. When Patricia Orr, a favorite of Blakey, arrived in town, she had the list of witnesses Buras was supposed to interview. And it was Orr who made the journey north with Buras, not Delsa or Blackmer.[114]

Eventually, even this ended up being too much for Blakey. Since he and his newly hired colleague Dick Billings, had already been part of the anti-Garrison crusade for *Life,* they were not going to risk being part of any developments that showed they had been wrong. When Delsa, Buras, and Blackmer found a New Orleans witness who said he knew something about a New Orleans based conspiracy along the lines outlined by the DA, they decided to polygraph him using their own money. When the session was over, the technician said that he had passed the test.[115] When word of this got back to Washington, Blakey, Billings, and Deputy Counsel Gary Cornwell decided the New Orleans team was going to be put out to pasture. Delsa and Buras were placed on informal suspension. Blackmer was shipped out to other areas. According to researcher Wallace Milam, Blackmer ended up working on aspects of the medical evidence.[116] And in fact, according to writers who have tried to contact him, Blackmer will not talk about his HSCA experience today.[117] Young people, like Orr, were now placed in New Orleans from Washington, people that Blakey could control. Amazingly, Blakey even assigned investigators from the Martin Luther King side of the HSCA to interview witnesses in New Orleans.[118]

This was really all part of a plan. For when Blakey first replaced Sprague in the late summer of 1977, he called in some of the veteran Kennedy researchers who had been working with Tanenbaum and Sprague. He told them, "You guys are thinking too big. You've got to get your conspiracy smaller." When asked how small it should be, the new Chief Counsel said, "Five or six people."[119] By severely curtailing the New Orleans investigation, by focusing an incredible amount of work and effort on Oswald's gossamer thin ties to the mob, and by never calling in Ruth or Michael Paine for a deposition, Blakey's team managed to achieve this small conspiracy.[120]

The other way they achieved this was by accepting the quite dubious ballistics evidence at the so-called "Oswald sniper's nest" on the sixth floor of the Texas School Book Depository building. Namely the Warren Commission's three shells at the sixth floor window.[121] Work by authors Allan Eaglesham and Michael Kurtz has shown this three shell scenario to be filled with the gravest doubt. Eaglesham interviewed WFAA-TV newsreel cameraman Tom Alyea, perhaps the first non-police witness on the sixth floor.[122] According to Alyea, who was there to photograph the scene, the boxes in the so-called "sniper's nest" were not arranged in the Dallas Police "three sided shield" manner as shown in the Warren Commission.[123] It was more of an L shaped configuration. But even worse, the Dallas Police rearranged the configuration of the three shells found there. According to Alyea, when they were first discovered, the three shells were lying within the diameter of a hand towel, a distance of no more than two feet. The shells were then picked up by Captain Will Fritz and placed in his pocket. The circumstantial evidence indicates that either Fritz, or police photographer Robert L. Studebaker, then rearranged the shells in a much more dispersed pattern for the photos included in the Warren Commission.[124] A man experienced with weapons, as Fritz was, would know that the Mannlicher Carcano rifle found on the sixth floor would simply not eject shells in that orderly a pattern. When FBI technician Robert Frazier tested this manual bolt action rifle for an ejection pattern, he found that the shells first landed in a 47 inch circle, at right angles to the ejection port. The distance they flew in the air was 80 inches. But once they bounced off the floor they flew anywhere from 8 inches to 15 feet.[125] As Fritz likely anticipated, the idea that they would all be neatly arranged near each other was not borne out by the FBI's experiments. And further, one of the shells, labeled Commission Exhibit CE 543, was almost certainly not fired that day. Because it "lacks the characteristic indentation on the side made by the firing chamber of Oswald's rifle." One forensic pathologist has stated that CE 543 was probably "dry loaded." This is revealed through the deeper and more concave indentation made at its base when being struck by the firing pin. Only empty shells show that characteristic.[126]

Ignoring all these problems with this warmed over evidence, Blakey then strongly relied upon the Neutron Activation Analysis testing of Vincent Guinn to state that the Magic Bullet, Commission Exhibit 399, actually inflicted all the damage to Governor Connally and President Kennedy.[127] This test, and Guinn's qualifications to conduct it, have since been shown to be without foundation. Two peer-reviewed studies by two teams of scientists, each made up of a metallurgist and statistician, have invalidated the NAA test to the point where the FBI will not use it anymore in court.[128] Blakey's other method of endorsing the Magic Bullet, the backward tracing of the bullet's trajectory by NASA scientist Thomas Canning has also been shown to be nothing more than "junk science."[129] But this shows how determined Blakey was to go with the Single Bullet Theory. Which is what he told Andy Purdy behind closed doors once Tanenbaum and Lewis were gone and he was in control.[130] This then was step number one in shrinking the conspiracy.

Ken Brooten was an attorney for the HSCA while Sprague was in command. He resigned in March of 1977. He wrote to Harold Weisberg that the committee "had compromised itself to such an extent that their final product has already been discredited. I simply refused to compromise my personal and professional integrity for a group of politicians and accordingly have returned to the practice of law here in Florida."[131] As Buras later wrote, the "HSCA report did not settle anything." He then added that it "did not get the autopsy and crime scene straightened out and it accepted the magic bullet theory."[132] Tanenbaum came to believe that the House of Representatives was not the place to find out who killed President Kennedy.[133] It was not, in any sense, the place to conduct a homicide investigation. And that is what the Kennedy assassination is really about. If Downing had not retired, and Sprague had managed to stay on, would things have been different? Perhaps. But probably not. After years of studying what happened to Jim Garrison and then the House Select Committee, this author has concluded that the Kennedy assassination is simply a bête noir of the entire American establishment, including the mass media and the political establishment, both then and now. It is simply a national Bermuda Triangle, where the laws of science and logic are suddenly ripped loose from their moorings. And therefore the subject cannot be dealt with in any rational, objective way in the mode of public discourse. And the proof is that both the Warren Commission and the HSCA signed onto the ludicrous Single Bullet Theory. A theory that has been rendered even more risible today than it was in the sixties and seventies. For researcher John Hunt has proven with declassified documents that the so-called Magic Bullet was at the FBI lab in Washington at 7:30 P.M. on the night of the twenty-second. But how could this be if that bullet was not turned over by the Secret Service to FBI agent Elmer Lee Todd until 8:50 P.M.? In other words, lab technician Robert Frazier had booked CE 399 into his records one hour and twenty minutes *before* it was given to him by agent Todd.[134] But further, Todd's initials were said by the FBI to be on this bullet he dropped off with Frazier that night. Hunt saw the blow up photos of the entire circumference of CE 399 at the National Archives. The FBI lied on this key issue. For Todd's initials are not on the bullet.[135]

All one needs to know about the efficacy of the HSCA is that it never took the time to do what John Hunt did. It never sent someone over to the National Archives to look at Frazier's work product, or to inspect the markings on CE 399. This is surprising, because most researchers consider CE 399 the single most important piece of evidence in the Kennedy case. Of course, if Blakey *had* done this, it would have blown apart his attempt to revive the Magic Bullet. The public had to wait for John Hunt and his 2006 milestone essays for the final burial of that pernicious myth.

CHAPTER SIXTEEN

Mexico City and Langley

"All information re LHO in Mexico City is clouded with a mist, as if it were something that happened about the time of the Druids. This place is the thing wherein we'll catch the conscience of the Queen Bee."

—*Jim Garrison to Lou Ivon, January 19, 1968*

Garrison, who always harbored literary aspirations, was borrowing from William Shakespeare's *Hamlet* for the above literary allusion.[1] In that play, Prince Hamlet suspects that his stepfather, King Claudius, has killed his real father. He alters a play to be performed at court. In his version, he includes matters related to him by the ghost of his father as to how Claudius had killed him and then attained the throne. Upon seeing these matters visualized in the play, Claudius becomes visibly upset and stomps out. Hamlet is now convinced that Claudius killed his father.

To my knowledge, no critic or commentator before Garrison ever seriously questioned the Warren Commission's version of Oswald's alleged journey to Mexico City. And no one before him ever attached the above kind of weight to that event. Today, with the declassified documents secured by the ARRB, it appears that Garrison was correct about both the importance of and deliberate mystery surrounding Mexico City. The declassified record suggests that, seven weeks before the assassination, certain individuals in the CIA were manipulating either Oswald or an imposter in Mexico City. And it appears to have been done for a diabolically clever purpose that was planned out and prepared for in advance.

The Warren Report deals with Oswald and Mexico City at three intervals within its 888 pages.[2] Almost all the information the Commission received came from the CIA and the FBI. And it arrived in heavily censored form. For instance, the CIA decided as early as three weeks after the Commission was created that they would not mention any of the phone taps they had on either the Russian or Cuban consulate to the Commission.[3] Further, it does not appear that the Commission even knew who did the translations for the Russian embassy intercepted phone calls. Since that married couple, Boris and Anna Tarasoff, were never even approached by the Commission or the FBI.[4] So what information did the Commission use about Oswald being in Mexico City? It was not until August of 1996, thirty-four years later, that the ARRB declassified the Slawson-Coleman Report. This was the report written by Warren Commission lawyers David Slawson and William Coleman describing their journey to Mexico City to investigate what Oswald did there. The excursion was actually suggested to them by Deputy Director Richard Helms.[5] Helms had advised the Commission that if they had any questions or problems while in Mexico, the best way to achieve their goals would be to rely on their CIA representative on the spot.[6] Once in Mexico City, the two Commission representatives were guided around by Clarke Anderson, the FBI legal attaché there, who happened to be a close friend of David Phillips.[7] The lawyers ended up taking Helms's advice. They trusted everything their official envoys showed them. Part of the reason for this was that Slawson developed a personal affinity for the Agency representatives he worked with while on the Commission— Allen Dulles and James Angleton's assistant Ray Rocca. For instance, he said about the former, "Allen Dulles and I became fairly close, I think . . . he was very smart and I liked him very much."[8] Slawson was so taken with his brief association with Dulles and Rocca that working for the CIA "was something I briefly considered myself."[9] This is important because, as we have seen in our study of Oswald, it was Angleton's and Rocca's counterintelligence unit that held the pre-assassination file on Oswald with all the attendant mysteries surrounding it. And in the entire 888 pages of the Warren Report, you will see not one reference to that file, or even the noting of James Angleton's name.

One reason for the Commission's ignorance about the Oswald file—and the subsequent importance of Mexico City—is that Helms actually appointed Angleton to be the main liaison to the Commission. Unlike his predecessor in that spot, John Whitten, Angleton tried to accent Oswald's Russian period for the Commission. Whitten wanted to highlight the Cuban connection. It

appears Helms did not wish that dangerous ground to be explored.[10] He there-
fore brought in Angleton to be the CIA's chief interface for the Commission.[11]
Since Angleton and Dulles were close colleagues from the 1940s, Dulles tipped off his friend as to what queries they would get about Oswald from the
Commission. Since there had been a rumor that Oswald was an FBI agent,
Dulles informed Angleton in advance as to what the Commission queries
would likely be about Oswald's possible intelligence ties. Then Angleton and
William Sullivan of the FBI rehearsed and unified their responses to deny any
intelligence connection to the alleged assassin.[12] This was an important part
of the cover up since it curtailed any inquiry into the question of whether or
not agent Oswald was completing a mission in Mexico that he began in New
Orleans. That is, was he further discrediting the FPCC by associating with
communist foreign consulates and trying to gain transport to Cuba? What
made this even more crucial is the fact that there was an "operational interest"
in Oswald held by a handful of officers in the Special Affairs Staff (SAS) of the
CIA just weeks before the Kennedy assassination.[13] This group was involved
with what was left of the Kennedy campaign against Cuba, which was not very
much. But as far as the Warren Commission inquiry into Mexico City goes,
we have established two key points: 1.) Slawson was much too trusting of the
Agency, and 2.) Angleton and Dulles were determined to keep clues about any
preexisting relationship between Oswald and the CIA concealed.[14]

Before going any further, it is necessary to outline what Oswald was
allegedly doing in Mexico City. The story assembled by the Commission was
that he was there to get something called an "in transit" visa. This would get
him to Russia by going through Cuba first. So Oswald was visiting both the
Cuban and Soviet consulates in Mexico City to arrange for two visas. But
neither consulate would immediately cooperate in getting him that type of
visa. So he left on the morning of October 2. As John Newman notes, on the
surface, the whole thing makes no sense. Because the State Department had
approved his passport to Russia that summer. But they had stamped it with
the warning that a person traveling to Cuba could be prosecuted.[15] Therefore,
if Oswald wanted to get back to Russia he could have traced the same route he
had followed in 1959. But to go through Cuba risked legal action against him.
Predictably, this problem is not addressed in the Warren Report.

The Commission was reliant on the CIA and FBI for its information on
this issue. Therefore, when staff lawyers David Slawson and William Coleman
visited Mexico City, they bought Clarke Anderson's story about Oswald being
at the Hotel del Comercio, even though his name on the register was incorrect
and, during the first round of witness interviews, no one in the hotel recalled seeing him there.[16] Eventually Anderson came up with two witnesses, one

who he himself did not trust. In his trip report, Slawson cites the signature on the hotel register as evidence Oswald was there. Even though his name appears there on the first day of his visit as "Lee, Harvey Oswald." In other words, each name is in the wrong placement order.[17] Slawson then found out that the FBI could not find one shop owner who recalled selling Oswald the silver bracelet he brought back for Marina. Even though they visited 300 merchants.[18] Slawson also found out that an alleged witness to Oswald being inside the Cuban embassy failed to identify a photo of Oswald leafleting in New Orleans.[19] Incredibly, Slawson and Coleman never interviewed Sylvia Duran, the secretary at the Cuban embassy who had the most contact with Oswald.[20] But the two did talk to CIA station chief Winston Scott. According to Slawson's report, Scott's evidence "was unambiguous on almost all crucial points."[21] But yet, this is not what Slawson said on the 1993 *Frontline* program "Who Was Lee Harvey Oswald?" In 1993, he said that the tape he heard of Oswald inside the Cuban compound was of poor quality, difficult to understand, and he could not confirm it was Oswald's voice. Slawson may have amended his answer for two related reasons. He understood that, in 1993, he was not taking evidence back to be rubber stamped by the likes of Allen Dulles, John McCloy, and Gerald Ford. There was too much out now in the record which raised many doubts about Oswald in Mexico City—and also upon the efficacy of the tapes. Yet it was this 1964 Slawson-Coleman report that the Warren Commission largely relied upon for its evidence of what Oswald did in Mexico City.

Its fairly obvious from the above that the Commission did not do any real investigation of what Oswald was doing in Mexico City. For instance, they never discovered that Duran did not describe Oswald accurately. She originally described the man she dealt with as being short, about five foot, six inches, blond, and over thirty years old. Oswald was five foot, nine inches, dark haired, and twenty-four years old. This problematic information from Duran was deleted from the ten-page report of her testimony transferred by the CIA to the Warren Commission.[22] Another inaccuracy by the Commission was stating that Oswald visited the Cuban compound twice on September 27. In fact, he was there three times that day.[23] If they had interviewed Duran they would have discovered something that made her suspicious of Oswald. She had prior experience with communists from America coming to Mexico City for travel to Cuba. They usually followed a procedure, arranged for by the American Communist Party, which allowed them to obtain a visa in advance through the Cuban Communist Party. That way, "The American would then come to Mexico, visit the Cuban Consulate, and receive his visa immediately."[24] This process would have eliminated all the trouble Oswald had in his failure to attain his in transit visa to Russia through Cuba.[25] The fact Oswald did not do this was revealing. It seemed to suggest that either Oswald was not a real communist, or that people inside the communist circles in America thought he was an agent provocateur.[26] They therefore did not trust him.

Another part of the CIA report of Duran's testimony was altered for the Commission. Duran stated firmly that after the twenty-seventh, when Oswald had failed to secure his special visa, he did not call her back.[27] Again, someone embroidered this for the Commission. For in the Warren Report she is quoted as saying ". . . she does not recall whether or not Oswald later telephoned her at the Consulate number she gave him."[28] This was an important discrepancy in testimony. Because, as we shall see, there was another call to the Russian consulate on Saturday the twenty-eighth. The CIA claims this call was by Duran, with Oswald also on the line. But if Duran's recall is correct, then the CIA evidence is spurious.

When Robert Blakey took charge of the House Select Committee on Assassinations he agreed to do something that Richard Sprague would not. In return for access to classified materials, members and employees of the committee signed agreements pledging not to disclose any information they garnered while doing their work. Then, when Blakey, Gary Cornwell, and Dick Billings edited the report and volumes, the agencies they made agreements with were allowed to veto what information was included in the published volumes. This is the reason that the HSCA report on Mexico City—assembled by two law students of Blakey's from Cornell—was not part of the published volumes in 1979. For when it came time to vet the report for release, Blakey, Ed Lopez and Dan Hardway met with the CIA representatives. The Agency made so many objections, it took four hours to get through the first two paragraphs.[29] The report is over 300 pages long. It was therefore classified until the ARRB was created. And then it had to go through several reviews. But even today, an annex to the report, "Was Oswald an Agent of the CIA" has not been released.[30] This long classified report confirms that, as Garrison wrote in 1968, the Commission version of what happened in Mexico City was deliberately covered in mist.

Even before Hardway and Lopez began their report, Sprague and Bob Tanenbaum understood that something was wrong with what the CIA was presenting. For it is not possible to consider Oswald's trip to Mexico without linking it to the Sylvia Odio incident. After having read the Warren Report, Sprague wondered why the Commission chose to discount the testimony of Silvia Odio.[31] Odio stated that two Cuban exiles appeared at her apartment door in Dallas on or around the night of September 26.[32] They were with a third man named Leon Oswald. They said they were from New Orleans. They also said they were looking for a Sarita Odio. That fact should have raised some suspicion. Sarita was attending college. She was the Odio sister *not* living with Sylvia or her sister Annie at the time.[33] This implies that the three men were not traveling on their own personal knowledge, but on some (faulty) instructions from someone else. As Silvia recalled in 1993, the taller Latin called himself Leopoldo. He then introduced both Leon Oswald and Angelo, a Latin she thought spoke with a Mexican accent. The men wanted help in raising money for the Cuban exile cause. Since Silvia was associated with the group JURE, and her father was famous for being imprisoned at the Isle of Pines by Castro, they decided to come to her. Since the sisters did not know the men, and since it was clear the two Latins were there under false "war names," the sisters were suspicious and decided not to help.[34] Further, the men did not know any of the local JURE leaders, or Manolo Ray, the leader of JURE. Ray, as we have seen, was Howard Hunt's nemesis in the Cuban exile community.[35] And Odio knew Ray very well, "He was a very close friend of my father and mother. He hid in my house several times in Cuba."[36] Therefore, the end implication of this occurrence is that Oswald was meeting with a JURE representative less than two months before shooting Kennedy.

Two days after the impromptu meeting, Leopoldo, who had a Cuban accent, called her back. He was very friendly and wanted to know what she thought of the American. Since he had said so little, she had no opinion of him. In furtherance of the implication outlined above, Leopoldo was now trying to sell Oswald as a marksman, an ex-Marine, someone who could be used by any organization. Leopoldo added, "Well, you know he is—we don't know what to make of him. He's kind of loco. He's been telling us the Cubans should have . . . assassinated President Kennedy right after the Bay of Pigs, and they didn't have any guts to do it. They should do it and it was a very easy thing to do, at the time." Leopoldo then closed with, "We probably won't have anything to do with him."[37]

The Odio incident created manifold problems for the Commission. The first being that Odio was a credible witness who had corroboration for her testimony. When she first heard of Oswald's involvement with the Kennedy assassination, she immediately recalled the visit of the three men. That afternoon she became very fearful, so much so that she fainted.[38] She then met with her sister, and as they had both been watching television with Oswald's photo on the screen, they both realized he was the man who thought the Cubans should have killed Kennedy after the Bay of Pigs. In addition to Annie, Sylvia had written to her father about the episode three days after the visit. She also told her psychiatrist about the strange visit the same week it happened.[39] The second problem was the incident seemed designed to make an indelible impression upon her about this Leon Oswald who came from New Orleans. Leopoldo introduced him to her twice. He added that Leon was an American "who was very much interested in the Cuban cause."[40] Leopoldo had called her back and described him as a former Marine who resented Kennedy and was a good shot—which Oswald was not. Remarkably, this is how the Warren Report would characterize Oswald one year later. So the Odio incident clearly suggested that Oswald was being set up nearly two months in advance of the assassination.

The third problem, the one that bothered Sprague, was that the dates of the visit clashed with the dates that Oswald was supposed to be going to Mexico. Odio twice told the Commission that, to her best remembrance, the men were there on a Thursday or Friday in the last week of September.[41] This would mean either the twenty-sixth or twenty-seventh. Even if we choose the earlier date, this contradicts the Commission. For they state that, on the 26th, Oswald was on a bus headed from the Mexican border town of Nuevo Laredo to Mexico City.[42] This is why pro-Commission authors—like Vincent Bugliosi—try to move the date to the twenty-fifth. But even if one does that, it creates a problem for the official story since the Warren Report has Oswald in Houston that night calling the socialist editor of a magazine.[43] The Odio incident took place around 9:00 P.M.[44] Yet the alleged call to the editor came either at that time, or a bit later. And the drive time from Dallas, where Odio was located, to Houston is about four hours. And as the report reads, there is no indication of this being a long distance call.

Because of all these problems, the Commission decided that Odio's story could not be accepted. At any cost. So in addition to having Hoover concoct a jerry rigged cover story about William Seymour, Loran Hall, and Lawrence Howard being the three men at her door—which they were not—the Commission did something else. After Wesley Liebeler took her testimony in Dallas, he invited her out to dinner with an acquaintance of his. He kept on threatening her with a polygraph test.[45] He then stated something that Odio found unforgettable. He said, "Well, you know if we do find out that this is a conspiracy you know that we have orders from Chief Justice Warren to cover this thing up."[46] When Gaeton Fonzi heard this from her his eyebrows arched. He asked, "Liebeler said that?" To which Odio said, "Yes sir, I could swear on that." Liebeler then invited her up to his room at the hotel on the pretense of looking at some pictures. Odio described what happened next to Fonzi and the Church Committee:

> Not only that, he invited me to his room upstairs to see some pictures. I did go, I went to his room. I wanted to see how far a government investigator would go and what they were trying to do to a witness. . . . He showed me pictures, he made advances, yes, but I told him he was crazy.[47]

Liebeler wasn't through. To show her what kind of operation the Commission really was, he told her that they had seen her picture and joked about it at the Warren Commission. They said things like what a pretty girl you are going to see Jim. Besides the professional ethics involved in such a thing, this points to a tactic used by the Commission to discount Odio. For HSCA staff lawyer Bill Triplett told this author that the reason that chairman Earl Warren did not believe Sylvia Odio is that she was some kind of a "loose woman."[48] As the reader can see, this was not the case. Yet this was the tactic Liebeler was going to use. This is how desperate the Commission was to discredit a dangerous witness like Odio.

The Commission thought that the Odio episode—with its depiction of Oswald with Cuban exiles and the mentioning of the murder of Kennedy over the Bay of Pigs—was much too suggestive of a logical conspiracy angle. Further, it even showed Oswald in the company of like-minded men. They therefore decided to favor the Oswald in Mexico City angle. To them, this depicted the communist Oswald: A man apparently dissatisfied with America, trying to escape to a Marxist state. This was much more favorable to their predetermined conclusion. The problem with this was the one that Garrison pointed out. The information the Warren Report assembled seemed to barely scratch the surface of what Oswald did while he was there. In addition to all the problems named above—the witnesses and signature at the hotel, the silver bracelet purchase, the lack of witnesses at the Cuban consulate, Duran's wrong description of Oswald, his complete lack of preparation to attain his visa, and the apparently false September 28 call—there is much more. Just one example: There is no chart in the Warren Report denoting the number of visits or phone calls made by Oswald to each compound, or from where they were made, or what language was spoken.

This seems to have been part of the Helms-Angleton agenda. For Lopez and Hardway *did* put together a chart of the phone calls attributed to Oswald. One look at the chart, which lists the languages spoken, and it immediately raises questions about who made them. For it has Oswald speaking fluent Spanish,[49] which no one has ever said Oswald did. Further, the HSCA report says that Oswald spoke poor, broken Russian.[50] Yet both Marina Oswald and George DeMohresnchildt said Oswald spoke Russian quite well upon his return to the United States. Further, professional translator Peter Gregory thought Oswald was fluent enough to give him a letter certifying Oswald's ability to serve as a translator.[51] But if that were not enough, there is a serious problem that Garrison spoke about in his *Playboy* interview. The CIA had multiple still cameras set up outside the Cuban embassy in Mexico City to catch everyone coming out of and going inside in order to secure a visa to Cuba. When, at the request of the Commission, the FBI asked the CIA for a photo of Oswald entering the consulate, they got Commission Exhibit 237. This is a picture of a husky six footer with a crew-cut. Obviously not Oswald. He is not identified in the photo so he came to be known as the "Mystery Man."[52] The Commission just printed the picture as "Photograph of an Unidentified Man" in Volume 16. In other words, we are supposed to believe the following: In Oswald's combined five visits to the Cuban consulate and Soviet consulate, the battery of CIA cameras failed to get even one picture of him entering or leaving. In other words, they went zero for ten. And the camera right outside the Cuban consulate was pulse activated. That is it was, "A camera with a shutter that is automatically tripped by a triggering device activated by changes in light density."[53] How could a camera that sensitive miss Oswald six times?

David Phillips's assistant Anne Goodpasture was in charge of the "daily take" from both target embassies.[54] That is the photographs taken from outside and the clandestine tape recordings made from inside the compounds. This is important because she then would have been the first person to see a photo of Oswald. Therefore, she should have sent for a photo of Oswald from Langley in a timely manner while Oswald was still in Mexico City. She did not. And this is one reason why she tried to lie to Lopez and Hardway about who was responsible for the daily surveillance and notes. She tried to say it was not her. But it was.[55]

The work of Lopez and Hardway also caught David Phillips in another lie. Another because when Tanenbaum questioned Phillips early on, he asked him about the audio tapes of Oswald and any pictures of Oswald from Mexico City. Phillips said that they had no audio tapes because they "recycled their tapes every seven or eight days."[56] The tapes were actually recycled every ten days. But they were held for a longer time if so requested.[57] Further, if any American citizen spoke broken Russian inside the Soviet consulate, the tape would be sent to Washington.[58] Because he would be considered of possible operational interest to the Soviets. Oswald allegedly did speak broken Russian. But the tape was not sent back. Phillips also told Tanenbaum that the reason the CIA did not have a photo of Oswald was because their camera was out that day.[59] This appears to be another lie. First of all, Oswald went to the Soviet consulate on two different days, the twenty-seventh and twenty-eighth. So all three of the cameras covering that site would have had to have been out on both days.[60] When one adds in the coverage of the Cuban compound, the number of mechanical breakdowns gets excessive. But further, the HSCA report found no evidence of any of the cameras being broken at the time Oswald was there.[61]

The new lie that Hardway and Lopez caught Phillips in was about a cable sent to CIA HQ. The surveillance of the Russian consulate revealed that by October 1, the CIA knew that Oswald was in direct contact with those who worked there, such as Valery Kostikov of the KGB. But yet, the cable alerting headquarters to this fact did not arrive until a week later, October 8. Phillips tried to explain this delay by blaming the translators for slow work. He then said he knew that was the case since he signed off on the cable.[62] Hardway and Lopez found out that Phillips did not sign off on the cable, since it did not deal in any way with Cuban matters. But even worse, he *could not* have signed off on it because he was not in Mexico City at the time.[63] The likely reason the cable was sent out so late was to keep Oswald's profile low while he was allegedly in Mexico City. For although the October 8 cable says Oswald spoke with Kostikov, the description of Oswald is wrong, and there is no hint as to who Kostikov really was. It only says he was an embassy consul. Therefore, based on this, there would be no scrutiny of Oswald while he was there. This was a principal goal of the plot.

The phrase, "the dog that didn't bark" became famous through its usage by Arthur Conan Doyle in his Sherlock Holmes story *Silver Blaze*. The idea was that a watchdog did not bark while a racehorse was being abducted because the abductor was not a stranger but a person the dog knew and was familiar with. The main thesis of John Newman's important book *Oswald and the CIA* is very similar to Doyle's in *Silver Blaze*. And this is why it was necessary for Helms and Angleton to guide the Warren Commission very carefully through its Mexico City investigation. The aim was to avoid the question: Why didn't the dog bark? For as Newman points out, if everything had been working normally—that is if Goodpasture had sent for Oswald's photo the first day, if the cable about Oswald being at the Russian consulate was sent on October 2 instead of 7, if the audio tape of Oswald speaking broken Russian in the Soviet consulate had been sent to Washington—if all these things had occurred, the sirens would have been sounding throughout the intelligence community as Oswald left Mexico City. After all, you had a former Russian defector communicating with the Russian consulate in broken Russian. And one of the consulate employees, Kostikov, was suspected of being a KGB agent. This should have posed the question: Was Oswald sent back to the USA as a KGB "sleeper" agent? That is, was he to be activated by a Russian contact for a specific assignment? But yet, in spite of all these circumstances that seem so alarming, the alarms did not go off. They remained silent. Why?

There were three more elements to the plot that guaranteed Oswald would land safely in Dallas and Ruth Paine would aid him into being present on Kennedy's motorcade route. The first one actually began before Oswald left for Mexico. On or about September 23, Angleton began to bifurcate Oswald's file. The FBI reports on Oswald's Fair Play for Cuba Committee activities in New Orleans went into a new operational file, separate from his 201 file.[64] Therefore, the bizarre things Oswald was doing in New Orleans—the leafleting on Canal Street and in front of Shaw's ITM, the fracas with Bringuier, his arrest and jail time and court hearing—these were all kept out of his 201 file. So when the late arriving cable finally did come into CIA HQ from Mexico City about Oswald in the Soviet consulate, this was kept separate from his New Orleans activities. Then two different cables went out on October 10. One was sent to the Bureau, the State Department, and the Navy, describing a man who doesn't fit Oswald's description: he is thirty-five years old, has an athletic build, and stands six feet tall.[65] This description resembles the wrong Mystery Man photo. At almost the same time, another cable is sent to Mexico City. This one has the right description, but was missing key information: it said that the latest information that HQ had on Oswald was a State Department memorandum from 1962. This was false: the FBI report and other materials about Oswald in New Orleans were in the other file. Ann Egerter, Angleton's trusted assistant signed off on both phony cables. Which means that he did not inform her of this deliberate internal deception. One which he had to have known about. Since he was the one man at CIA HQ who had access to all of the Oswald files.[66]

But even so, by October 18, the FBI had sent a memo from Mexico City saying that Oswald had met and talked with Kostikov.[67] Yet, Oswald was not placed on the FBI's Security Index list which was passed on to the Secret Service in advance of Kennedy's visit to Dallas. If he had been on that list, the Secret Service would have made sure he was not on the motorcade route, since he constituted a clear risk to President Kennedy. One reason he was not on the list is because the FBI "FLASH" on Oswald, which had been in effect since his defection in 1959 was removed. This warning required any information or inquiry on the subject to be immediately forwarded to the Espionage Section of Division Five, the Domestic Intelligence unit. Incredibly, the "FLASH" was canceled on October 9, 1963. In other words, after being attached to Oswald's file for four years, it was removed just hours after the cable from Mexico City arrived in Washington reporting Oswald's visit to the Soviet compound and meeting with Kostikov. The day before the CIA sent out the misleading memo about Oswald. But in addition to that, on September 16—the day Oswald stood in line to attain a tourist card to Mexico at the New Orleans consulate—the CIA sent a memorandum to the Bureau saying that the Agency was considering taking action against the Fair Play for Cuba Committee in foreign countries. That is, they were going to plant "deceptive information which might embarrass" the FPCC.[68] In other words, since Oswald had been doing that already in New Orleans with Banister as part of the Phillips-McCord program, his trip to Mexico City may well have been an extension of that street theater. Therefore it was an ongoing charade, and Oswald was just an actor in a continuing discreditation ploy. The implication being, the FBI should steer clear of this continuing CIA operation.

The last part of this scheme took place on the day of the assassination. For it was on that day that it was discovered that Kostikov was part of the lethal Department 13.[69] In an after action CIA report it is revealed that the FBI called the Agency when Oswald's name first was mentioned on the radio. That call was then passed on to Angleton's office.[70] And now, Kostikov's true identity was revealed. His was the KGB unit responsible for assassinations in the Western Hemisphere. After being methodically lulled to sleep, in the Holmes parallel, not barking, this information must have felt like a hard punch to the jaw. Oswald had met with the KGB representative for assassination seven weeks before Kennedy arrived in Dallas. Yet, he was allowed to be in the building behind where the president's limousine would be driving. And no one in the FBI or Secret Service did anything for nearly two months. The diabolical trap had been sprung. Hoover had no choice. He went into CYA overdrive. He eventually punished 17 agents for not properly surveilling Oswald on his return from Mexico to Dallas. And therefore not placing him on the Security Index.[71]

Yet, something very odd happened the day after the assassination. When the FBI agents who had been questioning the detained Oswald heard one of the tapes of the accused in Mexico City, they said the voice on the tape was not Oswald's. J. Edgar Hoover communicated this fact loud and clear twice. Once in a memorandum, and once in a taped phone call to President Johnson. Within twenty-four hours after Kennedy's murder, Lyndon Johnson had already heard about Oswald's alleged visits to the two communist consulates in Mexico City. He was clearly worried about them. In a phone call on the twenty-third he asked Hoover, "Have you established any more about the visit to the Soviet Embassy in Mexico City in September?" Hoover replied that this was all very confusing. He said that they had a tape and a photo of a man who was at the Soviet consulate using Oswald's name. But, "That picture and the tape do not correspond to this man's voice, nor to his appearance. In other words, it appears that there is a second person who was at the Soviet Embassy down there."[72] On that same day, Hoover wrote a memorandum in which he said that two FBI agents who had been questioning Oswald heard this tape and concluded that the voice on the tape was not Oswald's.[73] This false tape and photo had been transferred from Anne Goodpasture to FBI agent Eldon Rudd on the evening of the twenty-second.[74]

After Hoover exposed this material as being phoney, thereby endangering the conspiracy, something remarkable happened. A cover story was set in motion. The cover story was that the tapes had been destroyed *prior* to the assassination. If the reader recalls, this was what Phillips told Tanenbaum in one of his first interviews with the HSCA. In fact, both Goodpasture and Rudd played roles in the cover up. Goodpasture started it on November 23 by sending a cable to Langley saying that the tape of the call made by Oswald on the 28 was recycled before the tape of his October 1 call was secured.[75] This, of course, is false. As we have seen, tapes were kept for at least ten days. On that same day, the twenty-third, Rudd then chimed in by saying that tapes of Oswald in Mexico City had been erased.[76] Then Gordon Shanklin, the Special Agent in Charge at Dallas, notified Hoover "the actual tape from which this transcript was made has been destroyed."[77] The cover up then deepened. On November 24, Mexico City advised Langley, "Regret complete recheck shows tapes for this period already erased." In other words, the story now was that not one single tape of Oswald in Mexico City survived.[78] The CIA then provided FBI agent Clarke Anderson with *transcripts* of Oswald, claiming the original tapes had been destroyed. Anderson then advised the Bureau that the recordings of Oswald's voice had been erased prior to the assassination.[79] For all intents and purposes, the tapes that had just been listened to on the twenty-third, ceased to exist on November 24.

Which is simply not true. In addition to Hoover's memorandum and phone call—based on the testimony of two agents—FBI agent Burt Turner wrote a memo on November 25 stating that the tapes had been previously reviewed in Dallas. CIA officer and Deputy Station Chief Stanley Watson testified to the HSCA that at least one recording existed after the assassination.[80] Further, the man who was first in charge of the CIA's inquiry for the Warren Commission, John Whitten, wrote that while some tapes had been erased, some of "the actual tapes were also reviewed," and that another copy of the October 1 "intercept on Lee Oswald" had been "discovered after the assassination."[81] This may be why Whitten was removed by Helms from this position and replaced by Angleton. Further, Whitten's preliminary report on Mexico City stated that Oswald entered and exited Mexico by car. When, in fact, the Commission said Oswald could not drive. This therefore suggested someone was escorting him and he therefore had accomplices in Mexico. This report also admitted the CIA had no photos of Oswald, and the one they produced was not him.

It was important, actually it was crucial, to cover up this hole in the plot. Not just to sustain the frame-up of Oswald, but also to allow President Johnson to invoke a national security cover up while recruiting the Warren Commission. For it was this threat of nuclear war against Russia that Johnson used on both Chief Justice Earl Warren and Senator Richard Russell to overcome their reluctance to join the Commission he was constructing. When Russell resisted, Johnson told him "we've got to take this out of the arena where they're testifying that Khrushchev and Castro did this and did that and kicking us into a war that can kill forty million Americans in an hour. . . . Now you put on your uniform in a minute." Realizing that Hoover was already part of the cover-up, he told Russell, "All you're going to do is evaluate a Hoover report that he's already made."[82] When Warren also resisted, Johnson used the same tactics with him. He said he was greatly disturbed by the rumors going around involving Castro and the Russians in Kennedy's murder. These rumors, if not abated, could catapult the world into nuclear war. Johnson then told Warren he had talked to Secretary of Defense Robert McNamara. McNamara said a nuclear strike by the USSR would cost the USA as many as sixty million lives. He then said he had the Commission all set up. But there was one thing missing, the imprimatur of the highest judicial officer in the country. He then added, "You've worn the uniform; you were in the Army in World War I. This job is more important than anything you ever did in the uniform."[83] According to some reports, Warren left this meeting with tears in his eyes.[84]

In his later talk with Russell, LBJ went into a bit more detail about the process. He said that once Warren was in his office, he refused the offer two times. Johnson now decided to play his ace card. He said he pulled out a piece of information given to him by Hoover. It concerned Oswald in Mexico City. Johnson said, "Now, I don't want Mr. Khrushchev to be told tomorrow and be testifying before a camera that he killed this fellow . . . and that Castro killed him." Johnson then confirmed that Warren started to weep.[85]

To say this deception about Oswald in Mexico worked well does not begin to do it justice. For at the first meeting of the Warren Commission the former DA of Alameda County California, Earl Warren, came out as meek as a lamb:

1. He did not want the Commission to employ any of their own investigators.
2. He did not want the Commission to gather evidence. Instead he wished for them to rely on reports made by other agencies like the FBI and Secret Service.
3. He did not want their hearings to be public. He did not want to employ the power of subpoena.
4. Incredibly, he did not even want to call any witnesses. He wanted to rely on interviews done by other agencies.
5. He then made a very curious comment, "Meetings where witnesses would be brought in would retard rather than help our investigation."[86]

In other words, as Johnson told Russell, they were to ratify the FBI's inquiry. There was to be no real investigation by anyone. The Mexico City charade, with its threat of atomic holocaust, had secured the cover up of Kennedy's murder. But although Hoover went along with that cover up, he later realized that he had been snookered by the CIA. Just seven weeks later, while reading a memo about CIA activities in the USA, he scrawled on the margin: "OK, but I hope you are not being taken in. I can't forget the CIA withholding the French espionage activities in the USA and the false story re Oswald's trip to Mexico, only to mention two instances of their double-dealing."[87]

As John Newman notes, the plotters were absolutely desperate to get the names of Oswald and Valery Kostikov together on one call. This is why the October 1 call with the impersonated voices of both Oswald and Duran had to be made. Recall, Duran said that the short, blonde Oswald did not come back after the twenty-seventh. He had lied to her about the fact that he had attained a Soviet visa. He had not. When Duran called the Russian consulate, Kostikov said they would have to wait for word from Washington about his visa in four months. The problem with this in relation to the plot is that neither Duran nor Kostikov mentioned Oswald by name on this call. So there was no direct relationship between the two.[88] Consequently, whoever was handling this charade, knew there had to be one more call made to establish direct contact between the two. Therefore, the October 1 call, in which Oswald is mentioned by name twice, was faked. And his name was actually spelled out in letters. The impersonator then said he could not remember the name of the counsel he had spoken with previously. At this point the voice on the other end said, "Kostikov."[89] Everything was now in place for the delayed doomsday scenario. Although the Dallas FBI had information about Oswald calling and meeting Kostikov, they did not know his KGB covert role.[90] Therefore, when the FBI called the CIA, and this was revealed on November 22, the natural reaction was for Hoover to blame it all on the subordinate agents. Which, as we have seen, he did. The letters of censure went out about three weeks after the assassination.[91] When the Warren Report was published, another round of even harsher disciplinary action was issued by the FBI.[92]

After the FBI and CIA decided to lie about the tapes being erased prior to the assassination, there was one last bit of evidence that had to be deep-sixed for the plot to stay secret. CIA station chief Winston Scott had told Slawson and Coleman that he had photographs and an audio recording of Oswald in his safe. And he played a recording for the two. There was a big problem with this. If Scott had such things before the assassination, and they were genuinely of the real Oswald, why did he not forward these materials to the Commission immediately? Perhaps right after the Commission was created on November 29. And why would he sit by quietly while the CIA sent up the wrong picture of Oswald to the Commission, and then read stories about the tapes being erased before the assassination? As long as Scott held those materials in his safe, the threat existed that a future investigation would later find them and compare them to what the CIA sent to Texas on the night of the twenty-second for the Dallas FBI agents to look at and listen to.

April 28, 1971 was the day after Janet Scott buried her husband Winston Scott.[93] When she heard of Scott's death, Anne Goodpasture told James Angleton about the contents of the former Mexico City station chief's safe.[94] On that day, on a mission approved by Richard Helms, James Angleton flew to Mexico City. He was in such a hurry that he forgot his passport.[95] And if the recordings were of the same false Oswald's voice on tape, it would endanger the cover story about those tapes being destroyed prior to the assassination. After entering the house, Angleton vaguely threatened Janet's widow benefits. He then had Scott's safe emptied. The contents were shipped by plane to Langley, Virginia. The man most responsible for creating first, the Oswald legend, then the design of the doomsday scenario to the plot had now disposed of a last obstruction to his handiwork. In fact, the recordings apparently were of the false Oswald, since in an inventory Scott made of calls he had, the speaker talked in broken Russian and he also made a call on September 28 that Duran said he could not have made, since he never returned to the Cuban consulate after the 27.[96]

As Jim Garrison said in 1968, the deliberate mist around Mexico City disguised the last masterstroke of the conspirators. And reading his comments about Mexico City back in January of 1968, its hard not to be impressed by how forward his thinking was on the subject. He writes that he was reading Commission volume 24 well into the wee hours of the morning. He is puzzled by the inability of the CIA to produce a photograph of Oswald entering or exiting the Cuban or Russian consulate. He writes that if the CIA did have such a photo, it would be on the front cover of the Warren Report.[97] He also notes that one of the Cuban consulate employees the FBI talked to could not recognize Oswald's photo leafleting in New Orleans. He therefore doubts if Oswald ever really talked to Sylvia Duran. He thinks it may have been an imposter there. He acknowledges that Duran's name is in Oswald's notebook, but he writes that it is *printed*. He also notes that the bus manifest for Oswald's trip south is missing. He further notes that although Oswald allegedly signed his tourist card, there are no latent fingerprints on it. The reader will search in vain for any other critic to exhibit anywhere near this level of sophistication or acuteness about Mexico City at this time. After this quantum leap forward, Garrison concludes, "There's something malodorous in Mexico."

That bad odor also tends to tinge the plot with an anti-Castro spin. As Dan Hardway and Ed Lopez sorted through the information, they began to see that there was even more of an attempt to connect Oswald with Cuba after the assassination. For instance, the Monday after Kennedy died, a man named Alvarado walked into the U.S. Embassy in Mexico City. He said that, in September, he had had been at the Cuban consulate in Mexico City. He said that there, he watched as Oswald was given some money to allegedly kill Kennedy.[98] This story was soon detonated by the FBI. They found that Oswald was in New Orleans on the days Alvarado said he witnessed the incident. Another example is the false information that Oswald had defected to Cuba in 1959 and was a card carrying member of the Communist Party. This information was sent by cable on November 22 to the U.S. Strike Command at Fort MacDill in Florida. This base was in the forward phalanx of any retaliatory attack on Cuba.[99] When Lopez and Hardway digested all these false stories, they discovered that most of them came from assets of David Phillips. In fact, they assembled a color coded chart in which each story was summarized, the asset was named and his connection to Phillips was outlined.[100] So it would seem that the actual managers of the plot tried to stage an invasion of Cuba in order to head off Kennedy's attempt at détente with Castro. With his fear of World War II, Johnson put the brakes to this. In fact, through his aide Cliff Carter, it appears he got the local authorities not to charge Oswald as being part of a communist conspiracy because it could cause World War III.[101]

It took fifteen years for Lopez and Hardway to begin to scrape away the bad odor. It took another fifteen years for the public to see that report. By that time, Angleton had passed away. But during the so-called "season of inquiry," that is the investigations of the Church Committee and the HSCA, his name finally became popular with the press in a way it never had been before. As mentioned previously, Angleton always wished to portray the Kennedy murder as the product of the KGB. And this is what he—with the help of David Phillips—had arranged for with the soufflé they had cooked up in Mexico City. But when, after the anesthesia of the Warren Commission finally began to wear off, and questions about the Kennedy assassination began to be asked, Angleton's extensive but submerged role in all this began to be exposed. The surprising thing is that, even after his role in the case was finally revealed, he *still* insisted that the Russians had killed Kennedy. But during his all too brief inquisition—at the time of the Church Committee and HSCA—two famous incidents of resonance took place. In 1974 Director William Colby dismissed Angleton because of his zealous insistence that Russian defector Yuri Nosenko was not genuine. Nosenko gravely wounded Angleton's KGB case since he said the Russians never seriously thought of employing Oswald. The dispute over Nosenko partially paralyzed the CIA. Colby fired not just Angleton, but his trusted assistants Ray Rocca and Scotty Miler. In the midst of the formation of the Church Committee, which would soon question him, and the possibility of a reopening of the Kennedy case, Angleton uttered his now famous and provocative phrase: "A mansion has many rooms . . . I'm not privy to who struck John."[102] Angleton had dabbled in writing poetry for many years, and was a friend of T. S. Eliot. Therefore he knew how to be precise with words. What many thought he was suggesting was the following: Since he was now cut loose from any formal protection by the Agency, if they had any ideas about pinning the assassination on him, he was not going down by himself.

This suspicion was furthered over the brouhaha over the so-called Hunt memorandum. In 1978, former CIA officer Victor Marchetti wrote an article saying that the Agency had decided on a limited hang out on the JFK murder. They would surrender Howard Hunt to the HSCA. The basis for this was the alleged surfacing of a 1966 internal CIA memo from Angleton to Richard Helms saying that no cover story had been constructed for Howard Hunt's presence in Dallas on the day Kennedy was killed. No one had seen the memo prior to Marchetti writing his story in 1978. But Angleton did show it to author Joe Trento in that year. As he did, he told Trento, "Did you know that Howard Hunt was in Dallas on the day of the assassination?"[103] Although the HSCA never did get this memo, a subsequent trial over Marchetti's article did show that Hunt indeed had no alibi for where he was on the day Kennedy was killed.[104] As Lisa Pease maintains in her two part essay on Angleton, this whole memo issue seems part of Angelton's attempt to repeat his "Who struck John" warning.[105] For Howard Hunt was not a part of Angleton's unit of over 200 employees. As we have seen, Hunt was associated with Allen Dulles, Tracy Barnes, and later Richard Helms. The memo to Helms—whether real or con-cocted later—would insinuate Hunt's covert action group in the assassination. Again, if Angleton was going to take the fall, he was going to bring others with him.

Angleton died in 1987. A year later, David Phillips also passed away. Phillips spent a large part of the last decade of his life defending himself against accusations of his involvement in the Kennedy assassination. In fact he founded a group called CHALLENGE to help finance lawsuits against publications and authors like Donald Freed and Anthony Summers who advanced the work of official investigators like Fonzi, Lopez, and Hardway. The litigation took place not just in America but in foreign countries like England. Phillips took the work of these investigators both seriously and personally. After the HSCA report came out, which described Veciana's sighting of Phillips with Oswald, and after various authors began to write about his role in the classified Mexico City report, Phillips spent a lot of time in litigation. He also did research on people like Ed Lopez and A. J. Weberman. When Tony Summers called *Washington Post* editor Ben Bradlee to see if Bradlee could further investigate Veciana's story about Phillips as Bishop, Bradlee put a young English intern on the assignment. Bradlee told him to see if he could discredit the story. David Leigh came back and told Bradlee that he couldn't discredit it. From what he could dig up, the story looked genuine.[106] What Summers and Leigh didn't know was that Phillips had also called Bradlee to investigate the Veciana story. And that is why Bradlee wanted that particular spin from Leigh.[107] In fact, in the last two years of his life, Phillips was hard at work courting famous prosecutor Vincent Bugliosi to take up the cause of writing a book on the JFK case to counter the work of the likes of Fonzi and Weberman. While Phillips was in England involved in litigation against Summers, he was planning on meeting with Bugliosi while the attorney was filming a British television program called "The Trial of Lee Harvey Oswald." Phillips was clearly hoping Bugliosi would write a book based on this experience. In fact, in preparation for that effort, he was recommending Bugliosi read the works of Warren Commission advocates like Priscilla Johnson and Jean Davison.[108]

Before he died on July 7, 1988, he called his estranged brother James Phillips. James knew how much his brother disliked Kennedy. And he always suspected he had played a role in his assassination. Phillips/Bishop knew he was dying. So the brothers understood this was probably the last time they would ever speak. At the end of the call, James asked David if he had been in Dallas the day Kennedy was killed. The longtime Cold Warrior started to weep. He then said that, yes, he had been. This confirmed what James had long suspected. James then hung up.[109]

CHAPTER SEVENTEEN

Washington and Saigon

*"The American cold warriors' view . . . I learned, was that
under no circumstances could the U.S. lose control of Vietnam
and its valuable natural resources."*

—Jim Garrison, On the Trail of the Assassins

Whether or not one agrees that Lyndon Johnson was a part of the conspiracy to kill John F. Kennedy, there can be little doubt that, by any objective analysis, once he became president, American foreign policy now reverted back to where it had been before Kennedy's inauguration. This happened on multiple fronts and with great alacrity. As many writers have shown, unlike President Kennedy, Lyndon Johnson was a dyed in the wool Cold Warrior. He believed in the Domino Theory, and he had very little insight or interest into the struggles of the Third World to be free of European colonialism. Nowhere was this split between the two men better illustrated than in Vietnam.

As noted in Chapter 2, in November of 1961, there was a decision made by Kennedy after a two week long debate in the White House. The decision was that the president would send in 15,000 more advisers to help Ngo Dinh Diem win his war against the Viet Cong in South Vietnam. In his three years in office, this was as far as Kennedy would go in committing direct American forces into that theater. During that November debate, Kennedy was virtually the only one in the room opposed to sending in combat troops.[1] It was a line he would not cross at any time during his presidency. Learning his lesson well from Edmund Gullion ten years previous, he understood that if he committed American combat troops to Vietnam, he would be repeating the mistake France had made in the first Vietnam War.

But, at almost the same time that Kennedy was signing NSAM-111, the order to affirm 15,000 advisers to help South Vietnam fight the war, he was also arranging for Ambassador to India John Kenneth Galbraith to make a trip to Saigon. Whereas Deputy National Security Adviser Walt Rostow and General Maxwell Taylor had returned from a trip to Vietnam with a recommendation of inserting combat troops, Kennedy knew Galbraith disagreed with that position. So he sent Galbraith to Vietnam for a second opinion.[2] This particular trip, and the report made from it, was kept more low key than the much publicized Taylor-Rostow Report requesting the insertion of combat troops. Upon his return, Galbraith was sent to talk to Secretary of Defense Robert McNamara.[3] McNamara now understood that Kennedy was not going any further than sending in advisers. Today, there are two sources from McNamara's side who verify that Kennedy had told the Secretary to begin to wind the war down: Roswell Gilpatric and John McNaughton.[4] For all intents and purposes this marks the beginning of Kennedy's plan to withdraw from Vietnam. And we should note an important fact about it here. During the November debate in the White House, Kennedy apparently realized just how hawkish the rest of his cabinet was. And this is what appears to have caused him to make an end run around them with the Galbraith-McNamara back channel. McNamara then spent the next year coaxing the Joint Chiefs into presenting a plan for withdrawal of all American forces.

This plan was finally presented to McNamara at the May 6, 1963 SecDef meeting in Hawaii. This was an annual meeting in which McNamara called in all military and agency chiefs and their deputies representing all American forces in South Vietnam. This document was declassified by the ARRB on December 22, 1997. The record of this meeting leaves it all but certain that Kennedy's plan worked from Galbraith to McNamara. Because all the agency heads from the armed forces are presenting plans for withdrawal from the theater. On page after page of these documents, at every upper level of the Pentagon, everyone seems aware that Kennedy's withdrawal program will begin in December of 1963 with a pullout of 1,000 men, and that this would be the beginning of an eventual complete withdrawal by 1965. As young Kennedy learned in his visit to French Indochina, the possibility of any American "victory" was virtually non-existent anyway. In 1963 Kennedy pegged the chances of winning the war at 100 to 1.[5] When McNamara was presented with these plans his reaction was that they were not fast enough. He wanted the turnover to the South Vietnamese accelerated "to insure that all essential functions . . . now performed by U.S. military units and personnel, can be assumed properly by the Vietnamese by the end of calendar year 1965." In fact, on one document General Adams wrote that he would draw up training plans for the South Vietnamese army "that will permit us to start an earlier withdrawal of U.S. personnel than proposed under the plan presented."[6]

Once this plan was in place, Kennedy decided to activate it in the fall of 1963. In September, he sent McNamara and Taylor to Saigon in order to make a report about the progress of the war. Their observations that all was going well was a mask for the fact that it was not going well. This false rosy scenario would be used by Kennedy as a pretext for his withdrawal plan: If the war was going well, then the USA was not really needed. Kennedy was so intent on using this report as support for his plan that he would not even allow Taylor or McNamara to actually write it. It was actually written in Washington while the two men were in Vietnam. And the final arbiter of what went into it was Kennedy. Instead of Taylor and McNamara presenting their findings to the president, the president presented his report to his two envoys.[7] Once the report was presented in turn to his Washington advisers objections were heard about announcing the thousand man withdrawal, and completing it by 1965. Kennedy overrode them. He then sent McNamara out to announce the withdrawal plan to the awaiting press. As McNamara proceeded outside to address the media, Kennedy opened his door and yelled at him, "And tell them that means all of the helicopter pilots too!"[8] Consequently, the report secretly edited by Kennedy became his basis for National Security Action Memorandum 263, Kennedy's order for the withdrawal plan to begin. NSAM 263 was signed and entered into the record on October 11, 1963.

LBJ vs. JFK in Vietnam

The withdrawal never happened. Kennedy's assassination made sure it would not occur. In fact, Lyndon Johnson looked askance at it as Kennedy was putting it together. In the summer of 1961, Kennedy sent Vice-President Johnson to visit South Vietnam. Even at this early date, Johnson was working closely with the Pentagon on escalating the war. He was privy to a secret message from General Lionel McGarr in Saigon in advance of his meeting with President Ngo Dinh Diem. The message was to encourage Diem to request American combat troops for the war.[9] And during Johnson's second meeting with Diem, with McGarr in the room, Johnson did suggest that Diem needed American troops to defeat the Viet Cong insurgency.[10] As noted above, this is in direct opposition to what Kennedy wanted. But this episode shows that LBJ was much more in tune with what the Pentagon wanted than the president was. Secondly, it shows how comfortable Johnson was with the United States committing combat troops halfway across the globe in very difficult terrain to fight a guerrilla war. This presaged what would happen once Kennedy was murdered.

In November of 1963, Kennedy had recalled American ambassador Henry Cabot Lodge back from Saigon for the purpose of firing him.[11] After this, a long review was going to take place on how the USA ever got involved in Vietnam, what the original intent was, and what the purpose was in staying there.[12] Clearly, now that the withdrawal was imminent, Kennedy was going to try and get the rest of his administration on board to his way of thinking. Not only did this not happen once Kennedy was dead, but the first meeting on Vietnam afterwards was a strong indication that things were now going to be cast in a sharply different tone. This meeting took place at 3:00 P.M. on November 24. The hawkish Lodge told Johnson, "If Vietnam is to be saved, hard decisions will have to be made. Unfortunately, Mr. President, you will have to make them." This was clearly meant as a push for a wider war, with more American involvement. And Johnson accepted the invitation. He replied with: "I am not going to lose Vietnam. I am not going to be the president who saw Southeast Asia go the way China went." He then added, "Tell those generals in Saigon that Lyndon Johnson intends to stand by our word."[13] This is remarkable, since Kennedy's last word to the generals—through McNamara at the May SecDef meeting—was that they were withdrawing from the country. Johnson then said that he was unhappy with our emphasis on social reforms, he had little tolerance for the United States trying to be "do-gooders." He then added that he had "never been happy with our operations in Vietnam."[14] Johnson's intent was clear to McNamara. He was breaking with the previous policy. The goal now was to win the war.[15] LBJ then issued a strong warning: He wanted no more dissension or division over policy. Any person who did not conform would be removed. (This would later be demonstrated by his banning of Hubert Humphrey from Vietnam meetings when Humphrey advised Johnson to rethink his policy of military commitment to Vietnam.[16]) When this meeting was over, Johnson's assistant Bill Moyers remained in the room with his boss. LBJ said, "So they'll think with Kennedy dead we've lost heart . . . they'll think we're yellow . . ." Moyers asked whom he was referring to. Johnson replied the Chinese and the Russians. Moyers asked the new president what he was going to do now. Johnson said he was going to give the generals what they wanted, more money. And he now repeated that he was not going to let Vietnam slip away like China did. He was going to tell those generals in Saigon "to get off their butts and get out in those jungles and whip the hell out of some Communists."[17] The reader should recall, this meeting took place just *forty-eight hours after Kennedy was killed.*

It is important to note that Johnson never wavered from his comparison of losing Vietnam with losing China. Towards the end of his life, when he was preparing to write his memoirs, he actually compared withdrawing from Vietnam with what Neville Chamberlain did with Hitler at Munich. He then added, "And I knew that if we let Communist aggression succeed in taking over South Vietnam, there would follow in this country an endless national debate . . . that would shatter my presidency, kill my administration, and damage our democracy."[18] The reader will search in vain trying to find anytime during his presidency where Kennedy talked like this about Vietnam. To say the least, it was a huge miscalculation on Johnson's part.

But the drastic change in style and tone signaled to the hawks and closet hawks that, unlike with JFK, they would now have Johnson's ear. And further, this is what LBJ wanted to hear. Dean Rusk wrote that "The President has expressed his deep concern that our effort in Vietnam be stepped up to he highest pitch and that each day we ask ourselves what more we can do to further the struggle."[19] Johnson then told McNamara that America was not doing all it could in Vietnam. He sent McNamara to Saigon in order to give him a ground level report. Right before Christmas of 1963, McNamara returned with a bad depiction of what was happening.[20] The South Vietnamese had been lying about their progress in the war. A month after that, the Joint Chiefs sent a proposal to the White House recommending bombing of the North and the insertion of American combat troops. As authors like John Newman explained, Kennedy knew the intelligence reports painting a benign picture of battlefield progress were false. But he used them as a pretext for his withdrawal plan. That is, since the South was doing so well, they did not need the Americans. And McNamara understood this. But realizing what Johnson wanted, McNamara now began to give him the real battlefield conditions, which showed that South Vietnam was losing the war against the Viet Cong.[21] Therefore, on March 2, 1964, the Joint Chiefs passed a new war proposal to the White House. This was even more ambitious than the January version. It included bombing, the mining of North Vietnamese harbors, a naval blockade, and possible use of tactical atomic weapons in case China intervened.[22] Johnson was now drawing up a full scale battle plan for Vietnam. In other words, what Kennedy did not do in three years, LBJ had done in three months.

Johnson said he was not ready for this proposal since he did not have congress yet as a partner and trustee. But he did order the preparation of NSAM 288, which was based upon this proposal. It was essentially a target list of bombing sites that eventually reached 94 possibilities. By May 25, with Richard Nixon and Barry Goldwater clamoring for bombing of the north, LBJ had made the decision that the U.S. would directly attack North Vietnam at an unspecified point in the future.[23] But it is important to note that even before the Tonkin Gulf incident, Johnson had ordered the drawing up of a congressional resolution. This had been finalized by William Bundy, McGeorge Bundy's brother. Therefore, in June of 1964, Johnson began lobbying certain people for its passage in congress. On June 10, McNamara said, "that in the event of a dramatic event in Southeast Asia we would go promptly for a congressional resolution."[24] But William Bundy added, the actual decision to expand the war would not be made until after the election.[25]

And that is what happened. Johnson seized upon the hazy and controversial events in the Gulf of Tonkin during the first week of August to begin the air war planned in NSAM 288. Yet the Tonkin Gulf incident had been prepared by Johnson himself. After Kennedy's death, President Johnson made a few alterations in the draft of NSAM 273. An order which Kennedy had never seen but was drafted by McGeorge Bundy after a meeting in Honolulu, a meeting which took place while Kennedy was visiting Texas. In the rough draft prepared by Bundy, it allowed for maritime operations against the North, but only by the government of South Vietnam.[26] This was changed by Johnson. Realizing that, as written, this would take time—since South Vietnam had no Navy to speak of—he allowed these missions to be performed by American ships. This resulted in what was called OPLAN 34A. These were hit and run attacks done by small, fast patrol boats manned by South Vietnamese sailors. But all the support and preparations were done by Americans. This included American destroyers offshore of North Vietnam monitoring enemy action through electronic intelligence in order to collect data on where things like North Vietnamese radar installations and torpedo boat harbors were located. It was these patrols, codenamed DESOTO, that resulted in the American navy violating Vietnamese territorial waters. On August 2, the destroyer *Maddox* was attacked by three North Vietnamese torpedo boats. Although torpedoes were launched, none hit. The total damage to the *Maddox* was one bullet through the hull. Both Johnson and the Defense Department misrepresented this incident to congress and the press. They said the North Vietnamese fired first, that the USA had no role in the patrol boat raids, that the ships were in international waters, and there was no hot pursuit by the *Maddox*. These were all wrong.[27] Yet Johnson used this overblown reporting, plus a non-existent attack two nights later on the destroyer *Turner Joy,* to begin to push his war resolution through congress. He then took out the target list assembled for NSAM 288 and ordered air strikes that very day. After the air reprisals for the one bullet of damage to an American hull, the government of North Vietnam met. They decided that direct American military intervention in Vietnam was on its way. That a continuous air war was imminent and the public had to be made aware of this. The next month, they began sending the first North Vietnamese regulars down the Ho Chi Minh trail into South Vietnam.[28] They were right about the continuous air war. For on August 7, Johnson sent a message to General Maxwell Taylor. He wanted a whole gamut of possible operations presented to him for direct American attacks against the North. The target date for the systematic air war was set for January 1965.[29] This was called operation Rolling Thunder and it ended up being the largest bombing campaign in military history. The reader should note: the January target date was the month Johnson would be inaugurated after his re-election. As John Newman noted in his masterful book *JFK and Vietnam*, Kennedy was disguising his withdrawal plan around his re-election; Johnson was disguising his escalation plan around *his* re-election.

But there is today new evidence that makes Johnson look even worse on this issue. This new evidence more than suggests that not only did Johnson know he was breaking with Kennedy's policy, but he tried to disguise that break. In a declassified phone call of February 20, 1964, Johnson told McNamara, "I always thought it was foolish for you to make any statements about withdrawing. I thought it was bad psychologically. But you and the president thought otherwise, and I just sat silent."[30] In other words, Johnson was aware of what Kennedy and McNamara were planning. He was opposed to it but suffered in silence. But that would now be changed with Johnson in charge. The policy split between Kennedy and Johnson depicted in this call clearly harks back to Johnson's visit with Diem in 1961 and his cooperation with the Pentagon in trying to get Diem to request combat troops.

In another conversation, less than two weeks later, Johnson actually tries to make McNamara take back what he said in 1963 about the initial thousand man withdrawal and the complete withdrawal in 1965. He begins to formulate excuses to say that NSAM 263 didn't really mean that "everybody comes back, that means your training ought to be in pretty good shape by that time." When McNamara is silent over this contradiction being imposed on him, Johnson tries to soothe him by saying there is not anything really inconsistent in these new statements he wanted McNamara to make.[31]

LBJ Restores the Cold War Consensus

The reversal pattern illustrated in Vietnam was repeated elsewhere. As we saw in Chapter 2, in Congo, Kennedy had sided with the Dag Hammarskjold led United Nations in order to stop Moise Tshombe from breaking away the mineral-rich Katanga province from the newly independent Congo. In this, Kennedy had threatened to use economic warfare against England and

Belgium, the former colonizer. He had also denied granting Tshombe a visa to argue his case before the American public.[32] Meanwhile, Kennedy had invited Cyrille Adoula, the Congolese leader he favored, and a follower of Lumumba, to speak before the United Nations where he paid tribute to "our national hero Patrice Lumumba."[33] To show Kennedy's support for him, Adoula was then invited to the White House.

Kennedy understood that Tshombe would essentially be a front man for England and Belgium to exploit Katanga for their benefit. And that Congo would be a poorer nation without Katanga. Therefore Kennedy now pushed hard to stop the splitting away of Katanga from Congo. In the face of this resistance, Tshombe asked for talks. These proved futile. Therefore, Kennedy backed a United Nations military force to prevent the secession of Tshombe's Katanga. The hostilities began on December 24, 1962. By January 22, Katanga's secession effort was over. A few months later, after Tshombe had fled to rightwing Rhodesia, the United Nations wanted to withdraw because of the large expense of the operation. Kennedy realized this was dangerous because the actual Congolese army was not stable or reliable. And also because, unlike Lumumba, Adoula was not a charismatic, dynamic leader. Kennedy decided the U.S. was not quitting. He even did something relatively rare. He flew to New York to address the United Nations himself. On September 20, 1963 he addressed the General Assembly on this subject. He urged the UN not to abandon a viable project when it got tough, since this would jeopardize the difficult gains already made. He said they should all "protect the new nation in its struggle for progress. Let us complete what we have started."[34] The General Assembly voted to keep the peacekeeping mission in place for another year.

But in October and November, things began to fall apart. Kennedy wanted Colonel Michael Greene, an African expert, to train the Congolese army in order to subdue a leftist rebellion. But General Joseph Mobutu, with the backing of the Pentagon, managed to resist this training which the United Nations backed. In 1964, the communist rebellion picked up steam and began taking whole provinces. The White House did something Kennedy never seriously contemplated: unilateral action by the USA. Johnson and McGeorge Bundy had the CIA fly sorties with Cuban pilots to halt the communist advance. Without Kennedy, the UN now withdrew. America now became an *ally* of Belgium and intervened with arms, airplanes, and advisers. Mobutu now invited Tshombe back into the government. Tshombe, perhaps at the request of the CIA, now said that the rebellion was part of a Chinese plot to take over Congo. Kennedy had called in Edmund Gullion to supervise the attempt to make the Congo government into a moderate coalition, avoiding the extremes of left and right. But with the Tshombe/Mobutu alliance, that was now dashed.[35] Rightwing

South Africans and Rhodesians were now allowed to join the Congolese army in a war on the "Chinese-inspired left." And with the United Nations gone, this was all done under the auspices of the United States. The rightward tilt now continued unabated. By 1965, Mobutu had gained complete power. And in 1966, he installed himself as military dictator.

To put it mildly, the end result was not what Kennedy, Hammarskjold, Lumumba, or Adoula had envisioned. Mobutu now allowed his country to be opened up to loads of outside investment. The riches of the Congo were mined by huge Western corporations. Their owners and officers grew wealthy while Mobutu's subjects were mired in poverty. Mobutu also stifled political dissent. And he now became one of the richest men in Africa, perhaps the world. His holdings in Belgian real estate alone topped one hundred million dollars. One Swiss bank account held 143 million dollars.[36] Mobutu then stayed in power for over thirty years.

In Indonesia, after President Kennedy helped negotiate the return of the last vestige of empire to nationalist leader Achmed Sukarno in 1962, he then issued NSAM 179. In this directive, he specifically wrote that he wanted a new and better relationship with Indonesia. And he urged all agencies to review their programs for aid to Sukarno to see "what further measures might be useful."[37] Kennedy had his aid bill based on NSAM 179 approved in November of 1963. Sukarno appreciated his new friendship with the American president so much that he invited him to visit his country in 1964. He even began building a new estate for him to stay in while he was there. But this new and warm American/Indonesian relationship was not going to last long.

If we recall, Freeport Sulphur had been kicked out of Cuba after Castro's revolution there. But in 1959, Freeport engineer Forbes Wilson made a potential billion dollar discovery. Buried in a library in the Netherlands was a geologic study of the Erstberg. This was a mountain in West Irian province that contained huge deposits of iron, copper, silver, and gold.[38] With the permission and cooperation of the Dutch, Freeport had been doing a lot of exploratory work on opening a giant mine there. The Board of Directors had decided to approve a large construction bill to erect such a mine. But this all changed when Kennedy became president and worked on returning West Irian to Sukarno. As Forbes Wilson wrote, after this Sukarno made a series of moves which strongly discouraged all outside investment in Indonesia. He ordered all U.S. agencies, including the Agency for International Development, out of Indonesia. He then "cultivated close ties with Communist China and with Indonesia's Communist Party, known as the PKI."[39]

Two things happened in the space of two years that lifted Wilson's fortunes, and Freeport's. First, President Kennedy was assassinated. Shortly after, his aid bill landed on Johnson's desk. The new president refused to sign it.[40] The next year, Robert Kennedy visited Indonesia in place of his brother. When a journalist asked Sukarno what he thought of Bobby, he replied that he liked him very much. He reminded him of President Kennedy. Speaking of JFK he said, "I loved his brother. He understood me. . . . John F. Kennedy promised me he'd come here and be the first American President ever to pay a state visit to this country." He then fell silent. "Now he'll never come." Sukarno now started to perspire. He mopped his brow and then asked, "Tell me, why did they kill Kennedy?"

In return for not signing the aid bill, in 1964 LBJ received support from both Augustus Long and Jock Whitney of Freeport Sulphur in his race against Barry Goldwater.[41] In fact, Long established a group called the National Independent Committee for Johnson. This group of wealthy businessmen included Robert Lehman of Lehman Brothers and Thomas Cabot, Michael Paine's cousin.[42] Unlike Kennedy, Johnson now supported England in the creation of the new state of Malaysia on the Indonesian border. Sukarno then threatened to pull out of the UN if Malyasia was admitted. It was, and Sukarno made good on his threat. He then went to work on building an alliance of non-aligned Third World countries. Indonesia then quit the World Bank and International Monetary Fund. Then, in early 1965, Augustus Long was rewarded for helping Johnson get elected. LBJ appointed him to the Foreign Intelligence Advisory Board. This is a small group of wealthy private citizens who advises the president on intelligence matters. The members of this group can approve and suggest covert activities abroad. This appointment is notable for what was about to occur. For with Sukarno now unprotected by President Kennedy, the writing was on the wall. The Central Intelligence Agency now began to send into Indonesia its so called "first team."[43]

What happened next can be looked upon two ways. If one thinks that nationalism in a formerly colonized Third World country is good, and one wants to see these countries find their own way independently, what followed was a calamity of immense proportions. If one has the mindset of say a David Phillips or Allen Dulles, it was a multi-layered, interlocking masterpiece of a clandestine operation. A coup d'etat that was so well designed, so beautifully camouflaged, so brilliantly executed that—like the Kennedy assassination—writers are still putting pieces of the jigsaw puzzle together today. In fact, the Agency was so proud of it, that it recommended it as a model for future operations.[44] And there is no doubt that it was a CIA operation because it was predicted almost a year in advance. In December of 1964, a Dutch intelligence officer attached to NATO said that Indonesia was about to fall into the hands of the West like a rotten apple. For "Western intelligence agencies . . . would organize a 'premature communist coup' [which would be] foredoomed to fail, providing a legitimate and welcome opportunity to the army to crush the communists and make Sukarno a prisoner of the army's goodwill."[45] This is just what happened. On the morning of October 1, 1965, a group of young Army colonels banded together to attack and kill a group of generals who they feared were about to overthrow Sukarno. Somehow the young officers did not attack General Suharto. Even though one of them had visited him the night before.[46] This was odd since Suharto had a reputation for collaborating with colonizing countries like the Netherlands and Japan. Suharto then led the Indonesian Army's counter attack which crushed the colonels within forty-eight hours. Suharto now manufactured a military propaganda campaign to blame the killing of the generals on the Indonesian communists, the PKI. He then used that emotionally charged campaign to create what is probably the greatest anti-Communist pogrom in twentieth-century history. No one knows how many perished in the slaughter that followed. Estimates range from 200,000 to over 500,000. But because the PKI was central to Sukarno's coalition, he had now suffered a mortal blow. Within one year, much of Sukarno's power was given over to Suharto and the parliament. In 1967, Sukarno was stripped of his remaining powers and Suharto was made Acting President. Sukarno was then placed under house arrest. Like Mobutu, Suharto now began a thirty-year dictatorial reign. Like Mobutu, and unlike what Kennedy and Sukarno envisioned, Suharto now began to sell off Indonesia's riches to the highest bidder. Including Freeport Sulphur, which opened what were perhaps the largest copper and gold mines in the world there.[47] And in fact, revealing just how close Freeport was involved with the coup, in November of 1965, just one month after the counter attack by Suharto, with Sukarno still ostensibly in charge, Forbes Wilson got a call from the Freeport board about reopening their plans to take over the Erstberg. Wilson, the technical minded outsider, was surprised by the call.[48] Freeport, along with several other companies, now harvested billions from the Suharto regime. Meanwhile the citizens of Indonesia remained quite poor. Many of them made about a dollar per day at the time Suharto was finally forced from office in 1998.

In Laos, the CIA had never been happy with the truce and then the coalition government arranged by President Kennedy and his envoy to the Geneva Conference Averill Harriman. In fact, Harriman told Arthur Schlesinger in May of 1962, before the coalition government agreement was signed, that JFK's Laos policy was being "systematically sabotaged" from within the government by the military and the CIA. He said, "They want to prove that a neutral solution is impossible, and that the only course is to turn Laos into an American bastion."[49]

In large part this was done through Air America, the CIA's covert Air Force operating in Southeast Asia out of countries like Thailand and Taiwan. According to Christopher Robbins' study of Air America, the CIA and Pentagon obeyed the truce by moving cross border into Thailand. From there, forces were flown into Laos by Air America "whose entire helicopter operation was based in Udorn, [Thailand]."[50] Then, in April of 1964, the coalition government was overthrown by the rightwing, with the CIA's favorite Phoumi Nosavan in charge of a conservative government. The Pathet Lao, representatives of the leftists, were now left standing outside the door, hats in hand. They were pushed too hard and now the fighting was reignited at a more intense level. For all intents and purposes a civil war broke out. The Pathet Lao began to score some significant victories.

Now, a similar thing happened in Laos that happened in Vietnam. Because the CIA could not field a nativist army strong enough to fight the leftist rebels, the decision was made to resort to an air campaign, with heavy bombing.[51] All kinds of incendiary devices were used. According to one witness, "Village after village was leveled, countless people burned alive by high explosives, or burnt alive by napalm and white phosphorus, or riddled by anti-personnel bomb pellets."[52] And as with Johnson and Vietnam, the bombing policy reduced to a logic that destroying the country was necessary in order to save it. One Senate report stated that "The United States has undertaken . . . a large scale air war over Laos to destroy the physical and social infrastructure of Pathet Lao held areas and to interdict North Vietnamese infiltration."[53] The report continued that this had been done by subterfuge and in secrecy, "through such things as saturation bombing and the forced evacuation of population from enemy held or threatened areas—we have helped to create untold agony for hundreds of thousands of villagers."[54]

In the late 1960s much of the two million tons of bombs dropped over Laos were dropped over the Ho Chi Minh Trail in the southern part of the country. And it was not just bombs that Air America dropped in Laos. The CIA dropped millions of dollars in forged Pathet Lao currency in order to wreck the economy of the areas the leftists controlled.[55] The CIA even bombed its own Meo tribesmen, people who were supposed to be their allies in the war against the Pathet Lao. Their offense was that some of them did not want to give up their young sons to fight in the CIA's war. And it was from this war that the heroin trade in the Golden Triangle was now facilitated by Air America. According to Dr. Alfred McCoy, in the sixties and seventies, 70 percent of the world's supply of heroin had its origins in this area. As one reporter wrote, "It is transported in the planes, vehicles, and other conveyances supplied by the United States. The profit from the trade has been going into the pockets of some of our best friends in Southeast Asia."[56] One of those "best friends" was Vang Pao, a Hmong leader who rose to become a general in the Royal Lao Army.

When a settlement was reached in Vietnam, the Ho Chi Minh Trail was not needed anymore by the North Vietnamese for infiltration purposes. Therefore a cease fire was arrived at in Laos in 1973. Another coalition government was formed. This one lasted until 1975. At that time, the Pathet Lao took control of Laos. But what was left of the country? As one writer has stated, "Laos had become a land of nomads, without villages, without farms; a generation of refugees; hundreds of thousands dead, many more maimed."[57] Yet, unsparingly, when the U.S. Air Force shut down its radio station, the sign off message was, "Good-bye and see you next war."[58]

As with Mexico City, Jim Garrison was the first critic of the Warren Commission to understand that the Kennedy assassination was not just about bullet trajectories or firing positions in Dealey Plaza. There was much more to it than that. To understand this aspect of the case, Garrison began to accumulate a large library about the creation and maintenance of the military industrial complex. One of his favorite authors was Seymour Melman.[59] But beyond that, Garrison's investigation attracted many private citizens who understood something was really wrong with the Warren Commission. Therefore, in 1968, a professor from Ohio University mailed him a twenty-five-page handwritten treatise on how the Vietnam War was escalated after Kennedy's assassination.[60] And this allowed the DA to see at an early date that the reason for the assassination was a fundamental shift Kennedy was making in his approach to the Cold War. In addition to the above changes which took took place in Vietnam, Congo, Indonesia, and Laos, we have seen how Kennedy's attempt for a détente with Castro died on the vine once Johnson became president. We could mention other places where this pattern was repeated, for example in Dominican Republic, Brazil, Iran, and Greece. In the last case, President Johnson memorably told the Greek ambassador, "Then listen to me, Mr. Ambassador, fuck your Parliament and your Constitution. America is an elephant. . . . If your Prime Minister gives me talk about Democracy, Parliament, and Constitutions, he, his Parliament, and his Constitution may not last very long."[61] And, of course, because of these reverses, Kennedy's attempt at a relaxation of tensions with Moscow, so beautifully expressed in his commencement speech at American University on June 10, 1963, also ended up being stillborn.

In fact, through William Walton's mission to Moscow in early December of 1963, we know what Robert and Jacqueline Kennedy thought about the assassination. And also what they thought about Johnson's ability to keep the attempt at American-Soviet détente going. Walton, a painter, was visiting Moscow on a mission to meet various Soviet artists. But this ended up being a cover for him to convey two important messages through an intermediary to Chairman Khrushchev. The first message was that "despite Oswald's connections to the communist world" the Kennedys believed there was a large conspiracy behind JFK's murder. A conspiracy that was domestic and rightwing in its orientation, not communist. Secondly, they advised that the Soviets should not trust that President Johnson would continue in President Kennedy's tradition in working for world peace. Walton said that LBJ would be "incapable of realizing Kennedy's unfinished plans." Johnson's close ties to big business would bring their representatives into the White House and they would have an adverse impact on the quest for a winding down of the Cold War. And, in fact, Johnson was much closer to both the Rockefellers and Texas oil tycoons than Kennedy ever was.[62] To the point that he even thought of nominating Nelson Rockefeller as his Vice-President in 1968. Walton's message finished by saying Bobby Kennedy would resign as Attorney General in 1964. He then would run for a political office. This would be in preparation for a run for the presidency. Walton said that only RFK could then complete what his brother had started after Johnson induced a cooling down period.[63] So what the Kennedys had communicated to the Soviets in secret after the assassination, Jim Garrison understood by late 1967.

But there was one person who understood all this way before Jim Garrison. And he actually sat on the Warren Commission.

On December 22, 1963, Harry Truman wrote an editorial that was published in the *Washington Post*. The former president wrote that he had become "disturbed by the way the CIA had been diverted from its original assignment. It has become an operational and at times a policy-making arm of government." He wrote that he never dreamed that this would happen when he signed the National Security Act. He thought it would be used for intelligence analysis not "peacetime cloak and dagger operations." He complained that the CIA had now become "so removed from its intended role that it is being interpreted as a symbol of sinister and mysterious foreign intrigue—and a subject for Cold War enemy propaganda." Truman went as far as suggesting its operational arm be eliminated. He concluded with the warning that Americans have grown up learning respect for "our free institutions and for our ability to maintain a free and open society. There is something about the way the CIA has been functioning that is casting a shadow over our historic position and I feel that we need to correct it." This column was published on December 22, 1963, one month to the day after Kennedy was killed. Ray Marcus first brought this editorial to relevance in his self-published monograph entitled *Addendum B*. He called it the "least known important public policy statement by a president or former president in the twentieth century." There was even more to the story than anyone thought. Marcus, through the Truman Library, has filled it in.

Through the acquiring of Truman's notes, it turns out that the first draft of this editorial was completed on December 11. But the rough draft was started on December 1, which brings the provenance of the piece to about one week after Kennedy's murder. On December 27, Admiral Sidney Souers congratulated Truman on the editorial by calling it a "splendid statement." Souers had been part of Naval Intelligence and Truman picked him to head the Central Intelligence Group in 1946. From 1947–50 he served on the National Security Council and later was a consultant to the White House on military and foreign affairs. Souers wrote to Truman that Allen Dulles "caused the CIA to wander far from the original goal established by you, and it is certainly a different animal that I tried to set up for you."

But someone else saw the column and had a different reaction. In April of 1964, while serving on the Commission, Allen Dulles arranged to meet Truman at his home. After exchanging formalities, Dulles had arranged for his assistants to leave the room. Dulles then did two things: 1.) He tried to soften Truman up by telling him how much he admired him for setting down the Truman Doctrine after World War II, and 2.) He tried to say that what he covertly did as CIA Director was only a natural evolution of the Truman Doctrine. In short: guilt by association. Dulles then pulled out the real reason for why he was there. He took out the December 22 editorial and said that, consequently, Truman's editorial "seemed to be a misrepresentation of his position." In Dulles's April 21, 1964, memo to CIA counsel Lawrence Houston, he says that Truman then studied his essay, and seemed "quite astounded at it. In fact, he said that this was all wrong. He then said that he felt it had made a very unfortunate impression. He asked me if he could keep the article." Dulles then continues with: "At no time did Mr. Truman express other than complete agreement with the viewpoint I expressed and several times said he would see what he could do about it, to leave it in his hands. He obviously was highly disturbed at the *Washington Post* article."

As the meeting ended and his associates rejoined the two men, Dulles explicitly praised John McCone, the man JFK picked to succeed to his office after Kennedy fired him. But as of yet, there had been no explicit mention of

President Kennedy himself. Dulles now did so. And in a truly startling way. As he was leaving, Dulles mentioned the "false attacks" on CIA in relation to Vietnam and how Kennedy had repudiated those attacks.

Dulles concludes the memo by saying he was not sure "what will come of all this. It is even possible, maybe probable, that he will do nothing when he thinks it over." He then suggests that Houston get the president's old pal Clark Clifford to contact Truman and perhaps even McCone should do so himself. He then tells Houston to show the memo to Richard Helms and Cord Meyer and perhaps they can do something with the Director.

The clear implication is that Dulles wanted Truman to either take back or soften his December editorial. If he didn't succeed, he wanted a phalanx of people to intervene: Clifford, Helms, Cord Meyer, even John McCone if necessary. Secondly, this author doubts the description of Truman's reaction. Does anyone think Truman actually asked for a copy of a column he already wrote? Further, Truman worked on the piece for at least ten days. According to a memo he wrote on December 1, he called Souers for his input. So how could he later be "quite astounded" at his own column's contents? The crafty CIA Director was likely leaving a disinformation trail back at CIA HQ. One for others to pick up on later.

We now come to the utterly fascinating parting shot: Dulles bringing up the recent "false attacks" on CIA in relation to Vietnam. He's probably referring to the now-famous columns published in October of 1963. The October columns were penned by Arthur Krock and Richard Starnes for the *NY Times* and *Washington Daily News*. Krock's piece mentioned a source in Vietnam who likened the CIA's growth "to a malignancy," which even the White House could not control. His source added that if the USA ever experienced a coup it would come from the CIA and not the Pentagon. Starnes's source said the same: "If the United States ever experiences a *Seven Days in May* it will come from the CIA, and not from the Pentagon." Contravening Dulles's final comment, this author knows of no place where Kennedy repudiated the October columns. In all probability, Dulles was trying to dupe Truman into issuing a retraction. But his actions are even more suggestive if he was referring to those columns; especially when one adds in the fact that he specifically mentioned Kennedy to Truman in regards to them. Dulles's comments imply that he thought Truman wrote the column due to his suspicions about the CIA, Kennedy's murder, and the Vietnam war—which Johnson was now in the process of escalating. What makes this even more fascinating is that if one looks at the very first wave of Kennedy assassination books and essays, no one connected those dots—Vietnam, those columns, JFK's death—that early. By getting Truman to retract, was Dulles trying to prevent anyone from doing so in the near future? If so, as prosecutors say, it reveals "consciousness of guilt."

On December 29, 1967, Pacifica Radio did an hour long interview with Josiah Thompson. His book, *Six Seconds in Dallas*, had just been published. It is subtitled "A Micro Study of the Kennedy Assassination." And it certainly is. It's chockful of trajectory configuration, wound examination, frame by frame Zapruder film study, ballistics analysis and so on and so forth. It is a font of technical sophistication deconstructing the Warren Report. On this program, Thompson said that on the way to the studio he heard Jim Garrison had "announced that the assassination was in fact a coup d'etat—a shift in power in this country. And this was the proper grounds for understanding it." He went on to say that at the present time there was precious little evidence for that. And a good reporter could make Garrison look foolish by questioning him on this point. The implication being that a responsible critic would never say anything like that.

Recall, at this time the coup in Indonesia was completed. After the slaughter of at least 200,000 communists, Kennedy's friend Sukarno was now under house arrest and Suharto was selling off the country. In Africa, the Kennedy-Hammarskjold attempt at preserving Congo for its citizens was now completely shattered. The USA had actually joined up with the former colonizer Belgium to stop an alleged "Chinese inspired" rebellion. The target of the Kennedy backed UN action, Moise Tshombe, was now part of the Congo government. The dictator Mobutu was in power and siphoning off the resources of his incredibly rich nation for himself. Kennedy's neutralization of Laos had been broken, and the Air America air war was now pounding its citizens daily. While their planes carried heroin back to addict Americans while enriching Laotian generals. There were 540,000 combat troops in Vietnam. And Operation Rolling Thunder was in the process of exploding more bombs in South Vietnam than were ever dropped on Nazi Germany. Approximately 20,000 Americans were dead, and about a million Vietnamese had perished. Finally, Kennedy's attempt to work toward diplomatic recognition of Castro had been cast adrift by Johnson. And Bobby Kennedy had told the Soviets that, with Johnson in power, their attempt at détente would have to be placed on hold.

Thompson was missing the forest for the trees. While he was counting bullets on Elm Street, the rivers in Indonesia were being dyed red with the blood of the PKI massacre. Garrison didn't miss the trees, but he had his eye on the forest. It took the rest of the critics decades to catch up with him. Some of them still haven't.

CHAPTER EIGHTEEN

Denouement

"I suppose I'd describe myself as a Wilsonian-FDR-Kennedy liberal."

—*Clay Shaw to James Kirkwood*

Once Clay Shaw was acquitted and Herbert Christenberry threw out Garrison's perjury case against him, Shaw began to visit college campuses and give his spin as to what motivated Garrison on such a misguided legal action, and just how flimsy the DA's case against him was.[1] Other surrogates—such as James Phelan, local attorney Milton Brener, and James Kirkwood—also helped in this effort. Brener had served as counsel to both Walter Sheridan, and Ferrie's good friend Layton Martens. Kirkwood had worked with both Phelan and Hugh Aynesworth throughout the trial and, as we have seen, Shaw had actually enlisted him to write the book *American Grotesque*. Because the covert apparatus employed to undermine Garrison would remain hidden, and because the mainstream press was so biased against him, even many Warren Commission critics ended up sounding like Phelan, Aynesworth, Sheridan, and Kirkwood on the subject. To use one example, David Lifton actually spoke at FBI asset James Phelan's wake.[2] When Phelan passed away, Paricia Lambert told the *Los Angeles Times* that, "He was a dying breed" and the world was a sadder, barren place without him.[3] Neither one of these writers have ever detailed the sorry record revealed in this book concerning Phelan's munificent cooperation in doing assignments for government agencies and his later lies about these assignments. So when Lambert says Phelan was a dying breed, it is hard to understand what she is talking about. Especially in light of the now declassified record. Government assets are always common on the journalistic scene. And that kind of career sell out usually benefits the reporter by getting him more work and a higher profile. This is why Phelan was chosen by Bob Loomis to do a quickie biography of the CIA associated Howard Hughes after his death, and he also wrote several essays for the *New York Times*. And if America did not have so many compromised journalists, it would probably be a better country and not be in a state of decline.

One thing Phelan never did was admit the truth about Clay Shaw. Even though Phelan did not pass away until September of 1997, he always resisted admitting Shaw's ties to the CIA as much as he did his own ties to the FBI. Today, with the declassification process of the ARRB, these are simply undeniable. And Shaw's misrepresentation, as quoted above to James Kirkwood, is simply part of the deception set forth by himself, his lawyers, and compromised journalists like Phelan and Aynseworth. This deception can begin to be exposed just by looking at who Shaw worked for and with: the International Trade Mart and its sister organization, International House. As the author has shown in this book, one of Kennedy's largest splits with the Eastern Establishment was that he was a proponent of Third World nationalism. Shaw's two agencies were early advocates for what we term today as globalism, or the One World free trade doctrine. That is, the idea that American companies can take advantage of "free trade" in order to develop business connections overseas that allow them to exploit foreign workers at low prices, and then bring the profits back to corporate headquarters.

When Shaw returned from his intelligence duties in World War II, he went to work at the New Orleans branch of International House.[4] International House was founded by the Rockefellers and spread worldwide. It was a way of doing both student and cultural exchanges in order to advance the whole globalist, One World doctrine. Both David and William Rockefeller III served as trustees of International House, and David was chairman of the executive committee at one time. The chairman of the board of trustees in New York in the fifties and sixties was John McCloy who was very close to the Rockefeller family and later served on the Warren Commission.[5] As Donald Gibson noted, the first managing director in New Orleans was Herman Brock of Guaranty Trust Company of New York. Brock was followed by J. Stanton Robbins, a special assistant to Nelson Rockefeller.[6] The New Orleans branch of International House was important because the port of New Orleans served as a gateway into Latin America. Considering the fact that American businesses had many holdings south of the border, International House and the ITM were important envoys into Latin America for the elite families who controlled so much of the energy, stocks and bonds, and banking industry. And this is why Shaw not only figured in their globalist trade design, but as we have seen, as an agent of Freeport Sulphur (later Freeport McMoran) a company which Gibson notes was controlled at that time by the Rockefellers, Whitneys, and Harrimans.[7] So just from this, its clear to see that—as David Ferrie said—politically Shaw and Kennedy were opposed to each other.

His overt work for the globalist designs of the Eastern Establishment was the visible complement to his covert intelligence work. Shaw began his intelligence career in the Army during World War II. As he admitted in his entry in *Who's Who in the Southwest* for 1963–64, Shaw served as aide-de-camp to General Charles Thrasher. As discovered in an Army manual by the superb archives researcher Peter Vea, Thrasher's unit fell under Special Operations Section, or SOS, a branch of military intelligence.[8] When he returned to New Orleans after the war, Shaw became a friend of Ted Brent a self-made millionaire and "Queen Bee" of the local homosexual underground.[9] It was Brent who became Shaw's benefactor and aided him in his move up into the business world in New Orleans. That is from International House to Mississippi Shipping Company to the founding of the International Trade Mart. And it was in this phase of his career where Shaw's association with the CIA began. As Jim Garrison once noted, the CIA used Mississippi Shipping as a conduit for intelligence gathering into Latin America. Once the ITM was established, Shaw began his work as an overseas informant to both Latin America and Eastern Europe. This part of his Agency career lasted—officially at least—from 1948–1956. I use the phrase "officially at least" because the CIA considered Shaw such an important and valued asset that they created a "Y" file for him. William Davy discovered a handwritten note in the CIA declassified files saying that one of those files had been destroyed.[10]

Opponents of Garrison, like Robert Blakey and Vincent Bugliosi, reply to this by saying that Shaw was like over 100,000 Americans who were routinely interviewed by the CIA on their return from abroad. There are two serious problems with this line of defense. First, how many of those citizens had a "Y" file? Second, Shaw was not routinely debriefed after he returned from overseas. He was briefed *before he left*. He then filed written reports on both the political and economic climates in places like Peru. The intricacies of these reports are well beyond the scope of any routine business traveler. In fact, Shaw conferred with very high officials to gain this valuable information. For instance, while in Nicaragua, Shaw spoke to both the Minister of Finance and the President. While in Argentina, he spoke with the Minister of Public Works.[11] Few routine businessmen have that kind of access.

Peter Vea discovered a very important document while at the National Archives in 1994. Attached to a listing of Shaw's numerous contacts with the Domestic Contact Service, a listing was attached which stated that Shaw had a covert security approval in the Project QKENCHANT.[12] This was in 1967 and the present tense was used, meaning that Shaw was an active covert operator for the CIA while Garrison was investigating him. When William Davy took this document to former CIA officer Victor Marchetti, an interesting conversation ensued. As Marchetti looked at the document he said, "That's interesting . . . He was . . . He was doing something there." He then said that Shaw would not need a covert security clearance for domestic contacts service. He then added, "This was something else. This would imply that he was doing some kind of work for the Clandestine Services."[13] When Davy asked what branch of Clandestine Services would that be, Marchetti replied, "The DOD (Domestic Operations Division). It was one of the most secret divisions within the Clandestine Services. This was Tracey Barnes's old outfit. They were getting into things . . . uh." The former CIA officer stopped to seemingly catch himself. "Uh . . . exactly what, I don't know. But they were getting into some pretty risky areas. And this is what E. Howard Hunt was working for at the time."[14] And in fact, Howard Hunt did have such a covert clearance issued to him in 1970 while he was working at the White House.[15]

The next step in the CIA ladder after his high-level overseas informant service was his work with the strange company called Permindex. When the announcement for Permindex was first made in Switzerland in late 1956, its principal backing was to come from a local banker named Hans Seligman. But as more investigation by the local papers was done, it became clear that the real backer was J. Henry Schroder Banking Corporation.[16] This information was quite revealing. Schroder's had been closely associated with Allen Dulles and the CIA for years. Allen Dulles's connections to the Schroder banking family went back to the thirties when his law firm, Sullivan and Cromwell, first began representing them through him.[17] Later, Dulles was the bank's General Counsel. In fact, when Dulles became CIA Director, Schroder's was a repository for a fifty million dollar contingency fund that Dulles personally controlled.[18] Schroder's was a welcome conduit because the bank benefited from previous CIA overthrows in Guatemala and Iran.[19] Another reason that there began to be a furor over Permindex in Switzerland was the fact that the bank's founder, Baron Kurt von Schroeder, was associated with the Third Reich, specifically Heinrich Himmler.[20] The project now became stalled in Switzerland. It now moved to Rome. In a September 1969 interview, Shaw did for *Penthouse Magazine*, he told James Phelan that he only grew interested in the project when it moved to Italy.[21] Which was in October of 1958. Yet a State Department cable dated April 9 of that year says that Shaw showed great interest in Permindex *from the outset.*

One can see why. The Board of Directors was made up of bankers who had been tied up with fascist governments, people who worked the Jewish refugee racket during World War II, a former member of Mussolini's cabinet, and the son-in-law of Hjalmar Schact, the economic wizard behind the Third Reich, who was a friend of Shaw's.[22] These people would all appeal to the conservative Shaw. There were at least four international newspapers that exposed the bizarre activities of Permindex when it was in Rome. One problem was the mysterious source of funding: no one knew where it was coming from or going to.[23] Another was that its activities reportedly included assassination attempts on French Premier Charles de Gaulle. Which would make sense since the founding member of Permindex, Ferenc Nagy, was a close friend of Jacques Soustelle. Soustelle was a leader of the OAS, a group of former French officers who broke with de Gaulle over his Algerian policy. They later made several attempts on de Gaulle's life, which the CIA was privy to.[24] Again, this mysterious source of funding, plus the rightwing, neo-Fascist directors created another wave of controversy. One newspaper wrote that the organization may have been "a creature of the CIA . . . set up as a cover for the transfer of CIA . . . funds in Italy for illegal political-espionage activities."[25] The Schroder connection would certainly suggest that.

To even more clearly characterize Shaw's association with Permindex, let me note a witness who would know, since it was his job to ascertain such things. Let's use a very credible observer with his guard down: New Orleans FBI agent Regis Kennedy, the man who, officially at least, could not find Clay Bertrand. Shaw's active association with the Permindex organization lasted about five years. In 1967, after Permindex had moved to South Africa, a Garrison informant reported that Regis Kennedy had confirmed that "Shaw was a CIA agent who had done work, of an unspecified nature, over a five-year span in Italy."[26] This is an almost perfect match all the way around: in time, in location, and in Shaw's true association.

About three weeks before the assassination Clay Shaw called J. Monroe Sullivan, director of the San Francisco World Trade Center. Sullivan had never met Shaw before this phone call. Shaw asked him to put on a luncheon for November 22. He had a program to obtain tenants for the International House in New Orleans, the sister organization to the Trade Mart. Shaw said he would send out invitations and pay the costs of everything involved. Shaw then arrived at the San Francisco World Trade Center at around 9:00 A.M. on the twenty-second. As the two men were talking, a bulletin came on that Kennedy had been shot in Dallas. Sullivan was emotionally shocked. Yet, according to Sullivan, Shaw exhibited no reaction at all to the news. A few minutes later, news arrived that Kennedy was dead. Sullivan turned to Shaw and asked him if he still wanted to go through with his luncheon. Shaw replied that he did. So they proceeded to do so. Sullivan called for a moment of silence for the dead president. He then introduced Shaw, who made his pitch for International House. Sullivan was struck by Shaw's apparent lack of empathy for Kennedy's death.[27]

The next day, Shaw/Bertrand then called his lawyer friend Dean Andrews to go to Dallas to defend Oswald. There is no doubt that the FBI and Secret Service wanted this call to go away. The FBI interviewed Andrews about it six times, and the Secret Service three times.[28] Andrews was deathly afraid of what would happen to him if he revealed the true identity of Clay Bertrand. As Jim Garrison said in his *Playboy* interview, when Mark Lane tried to interview Andrews in 1964, he found him visibly scared. He told Lane, "I'll take you to dinner, but I can't talk about the case. I called Washington and they told me that if I said anything, I might get a bullet in the head." In that same interview, Garrison said Andrews felt he was being tailed at the time of his investigation. These were good reasons not to talk.

As we have seen, there were several witnesses that certified that Shaw was Bertrand. For example, William Morris, Ricky Planche, Barbara Bennett, and Aloysius Habighorst, and Edgar Tatro received the comment from a local that it was common knowledge that Shaw used that name. In addition, we have also seen that the Justice Department told the *New York Times* that Shaw and Bertrand were the same man. But Garrison's investigation found several more witnesses in this regard. William Turner talked to a man named Thomas Breitner who said that, on Shaw's trip to San Francisco, he visited the University of California and he introduced himself as Clay Bertram.[29] Virginia Johnson had been Shaw's maid for several years, until 1965. A man who stayed with Shaw on several occasions told her that Shaw had used the name of Bertrand.[30] Dr. Jacob Hety knew a gay man named Greg Donnelly. Donnelly had known Shaw for many years, and he had referred to him as Clay Bertrand.[31] In an utterly fascinating interview, a man named Leander D'avy told Garrison's investigators that he had once worked at a restaurant called The Court of the Two Sisters. One night, a man he identified as Lee Oswald walked into the place. He asked for Clay Bertrand. Gene Davis came out and talked to him. After Oswald left, Davis told Leander, "that kid had been behind the Iron Curtain." D'avy remembered that both Dean Andrews and Clay Shaw both frequented the establishment.[32] Then there was Mrs. Jessie Parker who was the hostess of the Eastern Air Lines VIP Room at Moisant Airport. This was a lounge where customers of the airline could have drinks and watch television while waiting for a flight. There was a guestbook which Parker tried to get customers to sign. On December 14, 1966, a man signed the guest book as Clay Bertrand. Parker identified Shaw as the man who signed the book with that name.[33] After HSCA investigator Lawrence Delsa investigated this issue he too agreed that Shaw's use of the Bertrand alias was an open secret.[34]

But beyond this, there are other sources that also reveal the same thing. In an FBI report about Shaw, it is revealed that as of February 24, 1967, the Bureau "received information from two sources that Clay Shaw reportedly is identical with an individual by the name of Clay Bertrand."[35] (This is likely where Ed Guthman, formerly of the Justice Department, got his confirmation that Shaw was Bertrand.) In another FBI report from 1967, it is revealed that informant Lawrence Schiller knew three homosexual sources in New Orleans and two in San Francisco who indicated that Shaw was known by other names, including that of Clay Bertrand.[36]

And finally there is Andrews himself. What he told Harold Weisberg makes all the above sleuthing a bit irrelevant. While working for Jim Garrison, Weisberg talked to Andrews several times and developed a friendly relationship with him. In an unpublished book written much later, Weisberg revealed that Andrews told him that Shaw was Bertrand.[37] So today, in the face of all this, there can be no doubt that Shaw called Andrews on November 23 to go to Dallas to defend Oswald. And this is why Ramsey Clark stumbled over the truth when he told the press on March 2, 1967 that Shaw had been investigated back in 1963. Clark's statement, of course, caused consternation at FBI HQ. Hoover had done all he could to snap the cover up on immediately. But Clark's slip up revealed that Shaw's name *had* come up back in November and December of 1963. In response to Clark's faux pas, Cartha DeLoach wrote to Hoover's deputy Clyde Tolson that Shaw's name had surfaced in December of 1963 as part of the original FBI inquiry. He then added that "several parties" had furnished "information concerning Shaw."[38] One has to ask: 1.) Why was Shaw being investigated in 1963? 2.) Did the FBI ever turn over this information to the Warren Commission? They sure as heck never admitted it to Jim Garrison.

Of all the things that the ARRB declassified about the Garrison investigation, one of the most fascinating aspects has been the solicitation and cooperation of Shaw's lawyers with the national security state. And, just as interesting, their attempts to cover up that symbiotic relationship. As the author has noted, Shaw's lawyers began accepting help from the likes of Walter Sheridan, Hugh Aynesworth, and James Phelan almost as soon as Shaw was indicted. They then worked with agents in Garrison's camp like Bill Gurvich. The associations with government asset Aynesworth and undercover agent Gurvich went on for years. But even that was not enough. They then solicited even more help from the Justice Department, FBI, and the CIA. In this incontinent quest for aid, they then visited Washington and wrote letters to people like Allen Dulles.[39] As we have seen, eventually the help came from all three agencies. To give this covert aid time to set in and work at undermining Garrison, Shaw's lawyers used every device at their disposal to postpone the trial.

In addition to this, through their own inquiries, and what the agents infiltrated into Garrison's office pilfered, the Wegmanns had in their hands some very interesting information. Much of which was compromising to their client. In a stolen December 14, 1966, Garrison memorandum, Jack Martin revealed that David Ferrie had introduced him to Oswald in Banister's office. With Ferrie at the time was Sergio Arcacha Smith.[40] They also had a memo from the previous day in which Martin revealed that Oswald had an office at 544 Camp Street. In a memo from their own detective agency, they discovered the same information from a different source inside Banister's office. Namely that Oswald had been seen with Ferrie and Banister.[41] In another report from their own detectives, a photo of Shaw with Ferrie is alluded to.[42] From this and more, it is obvious that Shaw's lawyers, at the very least, knew about the association between Oswald and Banister, and Shaw and Ferrie. And in fact, when Irvin Dymond put Shaw on the stand, he apparently knew he would commit perjury. For many years later, this author saw an e-mail from the late David Chandler's son. Chandler had been the best man at Garrison's wedding, but had turned on him over the Shaw case. It turns out that the journalist had revealed a secret to his offspring. Chandler had told him that Shaw admitted he had known Ferrie. But he lied about it to avoid "tossing Garrison too big a bone."[43] Since Chandler was working closely with Shaw's lawyers, how can one believe he would know this but they would not?[44]

As seen in these pages, and noted by other authors, Clay Shaw told numerous lies under oath at the Shaw trial. But what is not noted by many is the fact that his lawyers continuously lied about the secret help they were getting. We have seen how Irvin Dymond lied about not knowing about a CIA cleared attorneys panel in New Orleans. But also, when the author asked him if he was curious about all the help he was getting, Dymond replied, "It's the Kennedy assassination."[45] As revealed here, this was a deception. Apparently, like Phelan, Dymond never counted on the release of so many documents revealing his incessant quest for more and more help from the CIA and FBI. We have seen how Sal Panzeca was less than truthful about how and when the defense found out about Charles Spiesel. Let us recall something else that Panzeca told the author. Namely that even though Guy Johnson was an excellent lawyer, he left the defense team over a personality conflict with the Wegmanns. This is an odd statement. Because many years before Shaw was indicted, Johnson was a law partner of Bill Wegmann in the firm of Racivitch, Johnson, Wegmann and Moledeaux.[46] Are we to believe that in 1967 the two didn't know they had this personality clash extending back to the fifties? Further, Panzeca himself joined this law firm when he graduated from law school in 1959.[47] He didn't notice the problem prior to 1967 either? Guy Johnson left the team for a different reason. Because he was too close to Guy Banister. So close that the two worked together as part of the intelligence apparatus of New Orleans. Banister sent prospective undercover agents to Johnson for approval to penetrate the National Students Association, which was part of a CIA sanctioned project.[48] And this happened *when Johnson was at this law firm with Bill Wegmann*. At that firm, Johnson and Banister exchanged letters on certain prospects. There is even evidence that Johnson was in receipt of some of Banister's files after he died.[49] Therefore, the record indicates that Johnson had to have been aware of the reality of what was going on at Banister's in the summer of 1963. But further, it would seem that the Wegmanns did also. For in an ARRB declassified CIA document it is revealed that the articles of incorporation for Banister's so-called detective agency were notarized on January 21, 1958 by none other than William Wegmann.[50] This is when both he and Johnson were at Racivitch, Johnson, Wegmann and Mole-deaux. Why would Johnson trust Wegmann to do such a thing if Wegmann was not aware of what Banister and Johnson were up to?

Bill Wegmann knew. His knowledge was revealed during a very long interview by Shaw's lawyers with Bill Gurvich. After he "defected," the double agent was asked what Garrison knew about Banister's operation. Gurvich answered with some gibberish about Garrison not knowing that Banister existed. Bill Wegmann's reply undermined the efficacy of Panzeca's statement to this author. Bill Wegmann said that this issue—Garrison's knowledge of the inner workings of Banister's operation—had been a point of contention between Johnson and himself.[51] So far from being a personality clash, the issue was how much could Garrison dig up about Banister's CIA-FBI operation. In which Guy Johnson was implicated. If Garrison had discovered the documents mentioned here, showing Johnson and Banister working hand in hand, and then been able to expose just what Oswald was doing at Banister's through say Delphine Roberts or Dan Campbell, then that would have been bad for Shaw. Because it would have cast the worst aspersions on his own defense team. But in light of what they discovered during their own inquiry, plus this declassified background of Johnson and Bill Wegmann, plus Wegmann asking this question about Banister, it is very hard not to conclude that Shaw's lawyers understood just what Garrison had stumbled onto. Namely that Oswald was working out of Banister's office in the summer of 1963 as an agent provocateur for the CIA. And that Banister connected to both Ferrie and and Shaw. Johnson had to have known this since he was in the midst of it. For the point is this: If Shaw's lawyers were secure in their case from the start, and convinced of their client's innocence, then why did they go to these extreme lengths described here to get all the help they could from Washington? Shaw was so worried about his past CIA work that he did not even level with his own lawyers about that issue. When the local CIA station found out about Shaw's silence in this regard, they were quite surprised. But further, when Ed Wegmann and Irvin Dymond visited the Justice Department in September of 1967, they asked not just for files on Shaw—since they knew he was not leveling with them—but they also wanted files on themselves![52] This is how closely they were involved with the CIA at this early date. And from their later deceptions about this deep and hidden relationship, one can fairly speculate that with all they knew— including Shaw's initial refusal to come clean with them—they suspected their client may have been guilty. Or else why did they request so much help?

About the other aspects of the Kennedy case, that is Oswald's role in either the murder of Officer J. D. Tippit or the assassination of President Kennedy, today the Warren Commission looks even worse than it did in 1967. On the JFK case, the work of Robert Harris complements the discoveries of John Hunt. Harris has done some fine work in showing that, contrary to what the Warren Commission concluded, a bullet did fall out of Connally's body as they transferred him to an examining table. It made a noise and the bullet was picked up by a nurse and given to officer Bobby Nolan, who then dropped it off at the Dallas Police Department. From there, the FBI made this bullet disappear by deliberately confusing it with an envelope of fragments scooped up by Nurse Audrey Bell.[53] The work of Hunt and Harris completely and totally obliterates both the Warren Commission's three bullet scenario and the Single Bullet Theory. They show that neither one of them ever existed. And the long debate over them has been a pointless distraction. Which is what it was intended to be from the start.

As per the case against Oswald for the Tippit murder, a truly startling piece of evidence surfaced when FBI agent James Hosty published his book *Assignment: Oswald* in 1996. Hosty wrote that fellow FBI agent Bob Barrett drove to the scene of the Tippit murder at tenth and Patton once he heard that a policeman had been shot. When he got there, Captain Westbrook of the Dallas Police found a leather wallet near the puddle of blood where Tippit's body had been lying. He showed the wallet to Barrett and asked if he knew anyone by the name of Lee Oswald or Alek J. Hidell.[54] Barrett said he did not. But films taken by WFAA-TV cameraman Ron Reiland show that prior to Westbrook getting the wallet, it had been handed to Sergeant Kenneth Croy by an unidentified civilian. Croy then gave it to Sergeant Calvin Owens who opened the wallet as Captain George Doughty looked at the items inside. Later on, Patrolman Leonard E. Jez arrived at the scene. Through a confidential source, Jez insists that this wallet had Oswald's ID inside.[55] In addition to the witness statements, this cannot be Tippit's wallet since when his body was taken to Methodist Hospital, his wallet was removed and his belongings delivered to the DPD identification department at 3:25 P.M. One of the items delivered was a black wallet.[56] The monumental problem with this is that the Warren Commission tells us that Oswald's wallet was removed from his pants pocket on the way to the police station after he was arrested.[57] And further, Oswald supposedly left a wallet in his dresser at the Paine's home the morning of the assassination.[58] This new evidence indicates that someone dropped a mock up of Oswald's wallet, including ID, at the scene of the Tippit shooting.

That someone was not Oswald. In his book, *The Girl on the Stairs*, Barry Ernest interviewed a witness who no FBI agent ever talked to. Her name was Mrs. Higgins, and she lived very close to the crime scene. When she heard the shots, she ran out her door to see Tippit lying in the street. Barry asked her what time it was. She said it was 1:06. He asked her how she recalled that specific time. She said because she was watching TV and the announcer said it. She automatically checked her clock when he said it and he was right. Since Oswald had left the scene of his rooming house by, at the latest, 1:03, it would be physically impossible for him to traverse the nine-tenths of a mile in three minutes. Mrs. Higgins said she also got a look at a man running from the scene with a handgun. She told Mr. Ernest that it was definitely not Oswald.[59] Clearly, the FBI and the Commission deliberately avoided witnesses who would exculpate Oswald in the Tippit case. They don't come much better than Mrs. Higgins. With the discovery of the dropped wallet and the testimony of Mrs. Higgins, the case against Oswald in the Tippit shooting, which even some critics bought into, is now gone.[60]

In December of 1995, in the Bahamas, a group of American researchers met with General Fabian Escalanate. Escalante was the former chief of G-2, the Cuban security forces assigned to protect Fidel Castro. This conference was designed to share information between the two groups. Escalante was joined by his longtime assistant Arturo Rodriguez and Carlos Lechuga, Cuba's former ambassador to the United Nations. Lechuga was the man whom William Attwood had been working with to develop an accommodation between Castro and the United States.

Escalante was now the director of Havana's Institute for National Security Studies. In that position he had spearheaded a three year long investigation into the JFK murder. It is interesting to note how closely much of what he presented coincides with the best of what the American researchers had concluded. Escalante had Lechuga there because he believed that the motive for the assassination was to halt the attempt to establish diplomatic recognition of Cuba once an accommodation had been worked out. He presented evidence that two Cuban exiles—Felipe Vidal Santiago and Tony Cuesta—told him that the anti-Castro Cubans had gotten wind of this secret diplomacy and were furious about it. Escalante said that to prevent this, a plot was hatched. It had two objectives: 1.) To eliminate Kennedy, and 2.) To place the blame on Cuba. Vidal told his CIA handler, Colonel William Bishop, about Kennedy's treachery. Once this word spread, "A CIA official came to a safe house in Miami and said to a group of Cuban exiles, 'You must eliminate Kennedy.'"

It is not known if this man was David Phillips. But Escalante said that through their infiltration of exile groups they knew that Maurice Bishop was Phillips. Tony Veciana had told one of Escalante's informants that the HSCA had pushed him to identify Phillips. But since Philips had threatened him, he stopped short. But he told Escalante's spy that Bishop was Phillips. Further corroboration came from another informant who had delivered messages from Phillips to Veciana in 1959, when Veciana was still in Havana. Also, Escalante had an informant inside the camp of Eladio Del Valle. According to this man, Del Valle had told him in 1962 that Kennedy must be killed in order to solve the Cuban problem.[61]

The attempt to forestall the back channel is echoed at a much higher level. As Jim Douglass reveals in his fine book *JFK and the Unspeakable*, Richard Helms was monitoring the progress of the secret talks.[62] Helms understood that one of the conditions that Kennedy had set was for Castro not to export communist revolution into South America, especially on the eve of the upcoming Venezuelan elections. In mid-November of 1963, Helms got word of a large arms cache that had landed in Venezuela from Cuba. It was allegedly shipped there to aid communist guerrillas. In other words, the evidence indicated Castro was exporting revolution into South America, thereby breaking conditions in the negotiations that Helms knew about. Alarmed, the Deputy Director of Plans went over to see Robert Kennedy and argued his case for emergency action. For according to Helms, it was three tons of armaments. RFK passed on it and sent him to see President Kennedy. Which he did. Helms even brought one of the rifles that was captured from the cache. Presumably to impress upon the president the urgency of the situation. After all, here was the casus belli to end the back channel. Yet, like his brother, President Kennedy was non-plussed.[63] Either the Kennedys did not buy the arms cache story, or JFK was determined to see his plan for normalization of Cuban relations realized. The date of this meeting was November 19, 1963.[64]

Was the arms cache planted to force Kennedy's hand and dissolve the back channel? Former CIA officer Joseph B. Smith seemed to think so. In his book, *Portrait of a Cold Warrior*, he refers to the seizure of his arms cache. He apparently got some reports on it. Skillful and veteran analyst that he was, he quickly deduced it was planted.[65] This is how much Helms wanted to derail the Attwood-Lechuga attempt at accommodation. He surely must have realized after the nineteenth that Kennedy was not going to be deterred from this path.

One of the main tenets of this book is that Allen Dulles was one of the top level active agents in both the conspiracy to kill Kennedy and the disgraceful official cover up of his death. As Walt Brown demonstrates in his book *The Warren Omisision,* Dulles was, by far, the single most active member of that body. Through a series of detailed matrixes, which measure attendance at hearings and number of questions asked, Brown proves that Dulles took full advantage of being the one member of the Commission who did not have a full-time job. He made the Warren Commission his full-time job. Brown's book also proves that Dulles, John McCloy, and Gerald Ford controlled that body.[66] These three members of the Eastern Establishment thoroughly dominated what this author calls the Southern Wing. That is, Senator Richard Russell, Senator John S. Cooper, and Representative Hale Boggs. And this is why the three southerners ended up abandoning the Commission in public within a few years of its closing.

Why Lyndon Johnson appointed Dulles to the Warren Commission remains a mystery that has never been satisfactorily solved. As mentioned in the previous chapter, Johnson had a rather hidden relationship with the Rockefellers, especially Nelson. As revealed by Donald Gibson in a groundbreaking essay, he was also badgered into creating the Commission by other Eastern Establishment stalwarts like Eugene Rostow, Joe Alsop, and Dean Acheson.[67] Therefore, the idea may have come in in some secret way from one of these men, who all knew Dulles. However it happened, from Johnson's declassified phone call with Senator Russell , there is little doubt that Johnson understood from the beginning that the Commission was designed to endorse a cover up begun in Washington by his friend J. Edgar Hoover. Johnson also knew the problems with the Single Bullet Theory. And in a taped conversation with Russell he said he didn't buy it.[68] But apparently neither man realized that it was the keystone to the report. Without the Single Bullet Theory, you had to have a second assassin.

Johnson knew how bad the Commission was. Apparently, it didn't bother him. As long as it cleared him—and every other suspect—of any suspicion in the Kennedy case. It therefore helped him win a huge landslide victory in 1964. A victory he would soon squander by stupidly escalating a senseless war in the jungles of Vietnam. The evidence adduced here indicates that Kennedy would not have done this. As we have also seen, Johnson then made an attempt to distort this record by inducing Robert McNamara to take back what he had said about Kennedy's withdrawal plan. Thereby disguising Johnson's escalation as an extension of Kennedy's policy instead of the radical break that it was.

Johnson did the same with his hapless Commission. In 1969, when he was beginning work on his memoirs, he recorded a tape about the formation of the Commission. On that tape, he muses that it was Robert Kennedy's idea to appoint Dulles to the Warren Commission. As we have seen in Chapter 3, this is nonsense. Bobby Kennedy was the chief antagonist for Dulles during the Taylor Report hearings. When those were completed, Robert Lovett was brought in to recommend the firing of the CIA Director. But that was not enough for RFK. He then began searching for any leftovers from the Dulles debacle. He found out that one of the Dulles family was still around in the administration. Allen's sister Eleanor worked under Dean Rusk at State. RFK then insisted to Rusk that she be fired too because "he didn't want anymore of the Dulles family around."[69] So the idea that he would then want Dulles brought back to investigate his brother's suspicious death, after he had exposed the treachery Dulles had perpetrated with the Bay of Pigs, this all seems ridiculous. It appears that Johnson was doing here what he did with Vietnam. That is, he was switching the responsibility for a debacle of his own creation onto a Kennedy. And in both cases the tactic was quite convenient. Because both men were dead when Johnson did the dirty work.[70] Its easy to walk over someone when they are lying under a gravestone.

Another underlying tenet of this book is that Jim Garrison was one step away from the next level of the conspiracy. As outlined in this book, that would include people like David Phillips and Howard Hunt. As we have seen, Phillips was managing the CIA's anti-FPCC program, of which Oswald was a part of, operating out of Banister's office. Howard Hunt was instrumental in setting up the CRC, of which Sergio Arcacha Smith was the New Orleans representative. He was also worked closely with Allen Dulles from 1962 to 1963. Phillips also had a role in the Mexico City part of the plot, about which Garrison was quite acute about back in 1968. And it was because of Garrison's closeness to this second level that the CIA and its allies decided he had to be stopped. And he was. But not before shedding much needed light on what had happened to this country in 1963.

And make no mistake, something did go wrong with this country in 1963. As Kevin Phillips demonstrated in his book *Arrogant Capital*, in 1964, the year the Warren Report was issued, the percentage of people who said they trusted Washington to do the right things most of the time was almost 80 percent. But in that year, a toboggan slide began which resulted in the dwindling of that figure to below 20 percent by 1993. And one of the worst things about this slide into cynicism, that it began with President Kennedy's murder, is well known in Washington—at the very top. In 1992, attorney Dan Alcorn called Ross Perot's presidential campaign office. Reflecting the unconventionality of that quixotic venture, Perot himself answered the phone. Alcorn asked him if he had any campaign position on the Kennedy case. Perot replied matter of factly, "Oh, you'll never get to the bottom of that one."[71] Al Gore's well-off Tennessee family was friendly with the well-off Fensterwald family, also from Tennessee. So Gore knew attorney Bud Fensterwald who ran the Assassination Archives and Research Center in Washington. When Gore first arrived there as a congressman, Fensterwald asked him to stop by each Friday for a couple of hours before returning home for the weekend. He wanted to show the congressman documents for his reading on the JFK case. So every Friday afternoon, Fensterwald would stack a pile of papers on a desk for him to read. Gore did this for about a year. At the end of this education process Gore told Fensterwald, "You're right, it was a conspiracy."[72] Gore maintained that thesis while he was in the White House.[73]

In 1977, Edward Epstein was preparing his CIA friendly book about Oswald called *Legend*. The CIA backing came through James Angleton who was a prime consultant for the work.[74] Billy Joe Lord had been a passenger on the same ship that Oswald took to Europe in 1959. Epstein wanted to interview him. Lord was reluctant to do so. Over lunch he was told by one of Epstein's assistants that he knew someone who could convince him to talk to Epstein. That person was George W. Bush, son of the CIA Director at the time.[75]

Finally, there is the startling revelation by Webb Hubbell in his book *Friends in High Places*. Lawyer Hubbell had known Governor Bill Clinton for many years in Arkansas. They were close enough that Clinton appointed him to be Chief Justice of the Supreme Court of Arkansas in 1983. When Clinton became president, he told Hubbell that once he was installed in the number three position at Justice, he wanted him to find out who killed President Kennedy— meaning that Clinton didn't think it was Oswald. Hubbell regretted that he was forced to resign before he could find out the answer to that question.[76] The reader can see that the question about what happened to President Kennedy has been a plague upon the collective conscience of the nation since 1964. And that psychic plague extends from the bottom all the way to the top.

Like other things, Jim Garrison predicted this in January of 1968. At the public request of Mort Sahl, Johnny Carson invited Garrison on his show. Sahl had been working for Garrison as a volunteer. And with his show biz connections, he had previously gotten him an interview in *Playboy*. He now got him on *The Tonight Show*. The problem was that Carson was employed by the Sarnoff owned NBC network. The previous year, the Sarnoffs had approved the Walter Sheridan-CIA hatchet job documentary on Garrison. They were not going to reverse field and give the DA a free and fair platform to educate millions of Americans on the JFK case. Therefore they had rehearsed Carson to play the Hugh Aynesworth-James Phelan antagonistic role. Further, NBC had asked Garrison to arrive early at the studio. They then sent lawyers to interview him for hours when he arrived.[77] They recorded his answers. When Garrison walked onstage, he noted that Carson had cards typed up in front of him with his recorded answers plus their rejoinders attached. Consequently, instead of being a free and open forum done to educate the public about the Kennedy case, it turned into a preview of the adversarial, and thankfully cancelled, CNN program *Crossfire*. And it began with Carson's very long first question. In which he accused, not the Warren Commission, but Garrison of confusing the American public. Carson did not come off well. Realizing this, he angrily confronted Sahl afterwards and said that it would be a long time before he ever appeared on his show again.[78] Sahl's career went into serious decline after this.

At the end of the program, Garrison managed to invoke a Cassandra-like warning about the future. In the face of Carson's non-chalance about the cover up of Kennedy's murder, Garrison said that he was there to tell the people that the honor of this country was at stake. And if they do not demand to know what happened to President Kennedy, the country as they knew it would not survive. Everyone, including Al Gore, Ross Perot, George W. Bush, and Bill Clinton understands that today.

Jim Garrison understood it in 1968.

Notes

In the notes that follow, references to the Report of the Warren Commission appear as WR. References to the Commision volumes are cited by the volume and page number. References to the Final Report of the House Select Committee on Assassinations appear as HSCR. Citations to the 12 volumes of appendices and hearings appear as HSCA and the volume and page number.

Books cited in these endnotes are listed by author(s) only, unless an author has written more than one work, in which case titles are added. If a book is used for only one or two footnotes, the full citation is given in the footnotes. If a book is referred to only in the footnotes, the author and title are given. The full citations to all other books appear in the Bibliography. Full citations for regularly used periodicals are also in the Bibliography.

One of the great contributions of the Assassination Records Review Board is the recovery of part of the records of the Garrison investigation. These references are cited with the acronym of NODA, meaning New Orleans District Attorney's office.

When an article from *Probe Magazine* is sourced, the author and title appear only the first time the essay is referenced.

Chapter 1

1 Britain's request for an American takeover of its imperial role allowed the Truman administration to implement a Cold War policy of American leadership which was long in the planning. The British step-down was a necessary component of American leadership. See Jezer, p. 43.
2 Cabell B. Phillips, pp. 167–168. Acheson became a leading architect of American Cold War policy, a proponent of the view that unlike America, the Soviet Union was not entitled to a postwar sphere of influence over other nations. See Jezer, p. 41.
3 In congressional testimony, Acheson described the domino theory in terms of "rotten apples": "Like apples in a barrel infected by one rotten one, the corruption of Greece would infect Iran and all to the East. It would also carry infection to Africa through Asia Minor

and Egypt, and to Europe through Italy and France, already threatened by the strongest Communist parties in Western Europe. The Soviet Union was playing one of the greatest gambles in history at minimal cost.... We and we alone were in a position to break up the plan." Acheson, p. 219.

[4] Bernstein and Matusow, pp. 182–184.

[5] The Marshall Plan was tailored to American export needs and well–based fears of a return to prewar depression conditions. The plan, known as the European Recovery Act, made the U.S. dollar the standard of international trade, provided U.S. companies with significant foreign markets, and integrated European recovery into America's industrial and banking system. Jezer, pp. 45–48.

[6] The Plan did not pass easily. Its major corporate and political supporters had to overcome determined opposition from then powerful isolationist, nationalist Congressmen. The communist takeover in Czechoslovakia (Stalin's response to America's rebuilding West Germany) created the crisis atmosphere necessary for its passage. Jezer, pp. 47–48.

[7] Ranelagh, pp. 748–749; and Ellis, p. 37.

[8] Ellis, p. 36. Indeed, there was fierce bureaucratic infighting, "probably orchestrated by J. Edgar Hoover." Ranelagh, p. 114.

[9] The act denied the CIA any "internal police and security functions," although the term was not defined. National Security Act, Sec. 102(d)(3). In fact, the CIA conducted many domestic operations, some, such as Operation CHAOS against opponents of the Vietnam War, quite extensive.

[10] Ellis, p. 37.

[11] Prados, p. 21.

[12] In one early, major covert operation, the CIA intervened decisively in Italy's 1948 elections to prevent a likely Communist victory. Men like Allen Dulles, James Jesus Angleton, Frank Wisner, and William Colby combined in "a crash program of propaganda, sabotage and secret funding" which was "run out of the [Wall Street law] offices of Allen and John Foster Dulles at Sullivan and Cromwell." Simpson, p. 90.

[13] Prados, pp. 15, 40–43.

[14] After Chiang Kai–shek's defeat by Mao Tse–tung in 1949, several thousand of his troops remained in Burma perched on China's southern border. There they were regrouped and supported by the CIA as contras for some seven or eight military incursions into Mao's mainland China. While the CIA armed and maintained these forces, they also developed into an opium army that would control the so–called Golden Triangle, the poppy–rich area spanning the borders of Cambodia, Thailand, and Burma, which became the world's (and America's) chief supplier of raw opium from the early 1970s to the mid–1980s. See McCoy, pp. 162–192. This may have been the organization that Gary Underhill referred to and that JFK had gotten wind of and would use in his upcoming shake–up of the Agency (see Chapter 5).

[15] Ellis, p. 38.

[16] For general details regarding Gehlen, see Simpson, and Reese. For many of the specifics discussed here, see Scott, "Allen Dulles"; and Oglesby, "Gehlen"

[17] During the time of Soviet–American wartime alliance, Dulles was harboring, then implementing, virtually treasonous plans for a postwar anti–Soviet alliance. Dulles conducted his own private negotiations with Nazi General Kurt Wolff for a separate German surrender to Americans in northern Italy, to head off Germany's full–scale surrender to the joint allied command—obviously including Americans and Russians. Dulles's dogged efforts—Operation Sunrise—which he secretly continued despite direct orders to stop them, sowed enormous distrust between the Americans and the British on the one hand, and the Russians

who feared a separate surrender deal behind their backs, on the other. See Scott, "Allen Dulles," p. 6.

[18] According to Scott, "There seems no question that by April 1945, the OSS was recruiting Nazis and fascists to help mobilize against postwar Communism." Scott, "Allen Dulles," p. 14.

[19] Oglesby, "Gehlen," pp. 14–15.

[20] Bird, p. 353.

[21] Ibid., p. 354.

[22] For a recounting of the deal, see Oglesby, pp. 13–15. For the escapes of Mengele and Barbie, see Scott, "Allen Dulles," p. 10. A future member of the Warren Commission, John J. McCloy, was U.S. High Commissioner for Germany, and played a role in Klaus Barbie's escape. Brussell, p. 105.

[23] As chief of Eastern Front intelligence, Gehlen played a signficant role in what Christopher Simpson calls "one of the most terrible atrocities of the war": namely, "the torture, interrogation and murder by starvation of some 4 million Soviet prisoners of war." Simpson, p. 44.

[24] Simpson, p. 53. In light of Allen Dulles's anti–Soviet efforts during wartime, his links, and those of his brother, John Foster Dulles, with German financial interests, before, during, and after the war, bear scrutiny. For considerable details, see James Stewart Martin, pp. 67–68; Higham, pp. 22, 112–113.

[25] Ambrose, *Eisenhower*, p. 548; Bernstein and Matusow, pp. 293–295.

[26] Lisagor and Lipsius, p. 129.

[27] Kahin and Kahin, p. 8.

[28] Ambrose, *Eisenhower the President*, see Chapters 5 and 8, also pp. 210, 214–215; Prados, pp. 133–138 for Sukarno operation.

[29] Blum, pp. 174–181.

[30] Morley, p. 32.

[31] Ibid, ps. 34–35.

[32] Ibid, pp. 35.

[33] Ibid, pps. 35–36.

[34] Ibid p. 36.

[35] Ibid, p. 39, p. 55.

[36] Ibid p. 49.

[37] Ibid, p. 50.

[38] Ibid.

[39] Ibid, p. 51.

[40] Ibid.

[41] Ibid, p. 53

[42] Ibid.

[43] Ibid, p. 56.

[44] Pease, Lisa. "David Atlee Phillips, Clay Shaw and Freeport Sulphur." *Probe Magazine*, Vol. 3 No. 3, p. 18.

[45] Ibid, p. 19.

[46] Fonzi, pps. 133, 265.

[47] HSCA interview of November 3, 1978.

[48] Morley, p. 57.

[49] Ibid, p. 58.

[50] Ibid, p. 61.

[51] Ibid, pps. 63–64.

[52] Szulc, p. 81.

[53] Morley, p. 75.
[54] Hinckle and Turner, pps. 56–57.
[55] Ibid, pps. 56–61.
[56] Morley, pps. 76–78.
[57] Ibid, p. 79.
[58] Ibid, p. 80.
[59] Ibid, p. 81.
[60] Ibid.
[61] Ibid, p. 82.
[62] Ibid, p. 84.
[63] Ibid.
[64] NODA memorandum of October 9, 1968.
[65] Ambrose, *Eisenhower the President,* pp. 556–557.
[66] Morley, p. 85.
[67] Ibid, p. 94.
[68] NODA memorandum of 2/13/67 from Sgt. F. Sedgeber to Jim Garrison.
[69] HSCA interview with Jack Martin, 12/5/77.
[70] Summers, p. 440.
[71] Inspector General Report, p. 15. Hereafter designated as IG Report.
[72] Ibid, p. 19.
[73] Ibid, p. 32.
[74] Morley, p. 80.
[75] Ibid, p. 95.
[76] Ambrose, *Eisenhower the President,* p. 557.
[77] Dulles was right. Nixon was so wedded to toppling Castro that after failure of the Bay of Pigs, he reportedly answered Kennedy's request for advice by saying "I would find a proper legal cover and go in." Hinckle and Turner, p. 97.

Chapter 2

[1] Parmet, *Presidency of JFK,* p. 31.
[2] Markmann, p. 26.
[3] Parmet, *Struggles of JFK,* pp. 175–180.
[4] Ibid., pp. 310, 368.
[5] E. O'Ballance, *The Red Army,* (New York: Praeger, 1964), p. 199; Michio Kaku and Daniel Axelrod, *To Win A Nuclear War* (Boston: South End Press, 1987), p. 11.
[6] Parmet, *Presidency of JFK,* pp. 45–46.
[7] Ibid., p. 46.
[8] Ibid., pp. 46–47.
[9] Morley, p. 95.
[10] Parmet, *Presidency of JFK,* pp. 47–48.
[11] As Eisenhower said of the Vietnam of 1954–5: You have "what you would call the 'falling domino principle.' You have a row of dominos set up, you knock over the first one, and what will happen to the last one is the certainty that it will go over very quickly. So you could have the beginning of a disintegration that would have the most profound influences." Quoted in Jezer, p. 64.

[12] More than any other country in World War II, the Soviet Union suffered unprecedented destruction of its people and economy from the German invasion: over 20 million Soviets, and one–third of its total wealth and infrastructure destroyed.

[13] Not only "by itself," but against Stalin's express policy. Stalin had long tried to control, curb, even destroy any independent Chinese communism. Indeed, when WWII ended, Stalin signed the Sino–Soviet Treaty of 1945 with Mao's sworn enemy Chiang Kai–shek promising to aid Chiang's troops exclusively and to recognize Chiang's authority even in an area like Manchuria where neither he nor the U.S. then had any forces. Stalin's position was for Mao to at most accept a junior role in a government under Chiang Kai–shek—definitely not to pursue victory in a civil war. Snow, pp. 227–228.

[14] Ambrose, *Eisenhower the President,* p. 183.

[15] Ibid., p. 197.

[16] Ibid., p. 236. In 1955, the Communist Chinese began to shell two offshore islands, Quemoy and Matsu, which were still run and occupied by Nationalist Chinese troops under Chiang Kai–shek. This caused a brief crisis which not only did the Russians refuse to fuel, but which Communist minister Chou En–lai finally resolved by giving up the islands to the Nationalists.

[17] Ambrose, *Eisenhower the President,* p. 180.

[18] In the early 1950s, the Democrats were pilloried for having "lost China" since it happened on Harry Truman's watch.

[19] Some of the more courageous include scholars such as William Appleman Williams, Bertrand Russell, and Peter Dale Scott; politicians like Senators Wayne Morse, Ernest Gruening, Mike Gravel, and William Fulbright; and independent journalists like I.F Stone and George Seldes.

[20] Parmet, *Struggles of JFK,* p. 226.

[21] DiEugenio, James. "Dodd and Dulles vs. Kennedy in Africa." *Probe Magazine*, Vol. 6 No. 2, p. 18.

[22] Mahoney, pps. 14–15.

[23] Ibid, p. 12.

[24] DiEugenio, James. "Dodd and Dulles vs. Kennedy in Africa." *Probe Magazine*, Vol. 6 No. 2, p. 18.

[25] Ibid.

[26] Mahoney, p. 15.

[27] Ibid.

[28] Blum, p. 135.

[29] Mahoney, p. 16.

[30] Ibid.

[31] Ibid, p. 15.

[32] Ibid, p. 16.

[33] Ibid.

[34] Blum, p. 137.

[35] Ibid, p. 138.

[36] Ibid, p. 139.

[37] Ibid.

[38] DiEugenio, James. "Dodd and Dulles vs. Kennedy in Africa." *Probe Magazine*, Vol. 6 No. 2, p. 19.

[39] Ibid.

[40] Ibid.

[41] Ibid.

[42] Mahoney, p. 19.

[43] Nevins, p. 67.

[44] Ibid, p. 72.
[45] Ibid, p. 77.
[46] Ibid, p. 80.
[47] *Probe Magazine*, op. cit. p. 20.
[48] Mahoney, p. 20.
[49] Ibid.
[50] Ibid.
[51] Ibid, p. 23.
[52] *Toldeo Blade*, 7/15/57.
[53] Hurt, p. 415.
[54] Ibid, p. 416.
[55] DiEugenio, James. "Dodd and Dulles vs. Kennedy in Africa." *Probe Magazine,* Vol. 6 No. 2, p. 20.
[56] Ibid.
[57] Ibid.
[58] Ibid, p. 21.
[59] Ibid.
[60] Kaiser, p. 31.
[61] Ibid.
[62] Schlesinger, p. 163.
[63] Hilsman, p. 130.
[64] Schlesinger, p. 329
[65] Ibid, p. 332.
[66] Ibid, p. 337.
[67] Ibid, p. 516.
[68] Newman, *JFK and Vietnam*, pps. 3–4.
[69] Goldstein, pps. 53–66.
[70] Blight, pps. 282–83.
[71] Goldstein, p. 101.
[72] Ibid, p. 162.
[73] Pease, Lisa. "Indonesia, President Kennedy and Freeport Sulphur." *Probe Magazine*, Vol. 3 No. 4, p. 19.
[74] Ibid, p. 20.
[75] Ibid.
[76] Kahin and Kahin, p. 179.
[77] Ibid, p. 181.
[78] *Probe Magazine*, op. cit. p. 21.
[79] Ibid.
[80] *Probe Magazine,* op. cit.
[81] Schlesinger, p. 535.

Chapter 3

[1] Hancock, *Nexus*, p. 52.
[2] Ibid.
[3] Ibid.
[4] Ibid, p. 53.
[5] Ibid.
[6] Kornbluh, p. 81.

[7] Ibid, p. 48.

[8] Ibid, p. 58.

[9] Ibid, p. 99.

[10] Ibid., pps. 283–84.

[11] Ibid, p. 94.

[12] Davy, pps. 30–31.

[13] Kornbluh, pps. 97, 122.

[14] Ibid., p. 303.

[15] Ibid., pps. 120–123.

[16] Ibid, p. 291.

[17] Schlesinger, p. 249.

[18] Higgins, p. 102.

[19] Ibid., p. 103.

[20] Kornbluh, pps. 294–95.

[21] Ibid.

[22] Schlesinger., p. 250.

[23] Ibid., p. 257.

[24] Kornbluh, p. 125.

[25] Ibid., p. 288.

[26] Ibid.

[27] Ibid, p. 126.

[28] Ibid, p. 296.

[29] Ibid, p. 126.

[30] Prados, pp. 183, 188–189, 191.

[31] Kornbluh, p. 295.

[32] Ibid, pps. 227–28.

[33] Ibid, p. 307.

[34] Ibid., p. 321.

[35] Hunt, pps. 22–23.

[36] Ibid.

[37] Szulc, p. 72.

[38] Hunt, p. 38.

[39] Ibid., p. 16.

[40] Hancock, op. cit., pps. 22–23.

[41] Ibid., p. 25.

[42] Ibid., p. 26.

[43] Kornbluh, p. 72.

[44] Ibid., p. 73.

[45] Schlesinger, p. 260.

[46] Ibid., p. 264.

[47] Kornbluh, p. 70.

[48] Ibid., p. 73.

[49] Ibid.

[50] Hunt, p. 41.

[51] Ibid., p. 97.

[52] Ibid., pps. 172–176.

[53] Ibid., p. 185.

[54] Kornbluh, p. 321.

[55] Ibid, p. 310.

[56] Ibid., pps. 311–12.
[57] Ibid., pps. 321–22.
[58] Arboleya, p. 85.
[59] Ibid.
[60] Kornbluh, p. 313.
[61] Ibid., pps. 312–15.
[62] Ibid.
[63] Author's 1995 interview with Marchetti at his office in Virginia.
[64] Kornbluh, p. 314.
[65] Ibid., p. 313.
[66] Ibid., p. 319.
[67] Ibid., p. 320.
[68] Hinckle and Turner, p. 122.
[69] Morrisey, *The Fourth Decade*, Vol. 1 No. 2, p. 20.
[70] Ibid.
[71] Ibid.
[72] Ibid.
[73] Ibid., p. 21.
[74] Ibid.
[75] Ibid.
[76] Ibid., p. 22.
[77] Ibid.
[78] Ibid., p. 26.
[79] Ibid.
[80] Ibid, pps. 25–26.
[81] Kornbluh, p. 319.
[82] Talbot, pps. 48–49.
[83] Hancock, op. cit., p. 54.
[84] Ibid.
[85] Kornbluh, pps. 41, 52.
[86] Ibid., pps. 125–27.
[87] Ibid., p. 262.
[88] The Fourth Decade, op. cit., p. 23.
[89] Schlesinger, p. 273.
[90] DiEugenio and Pease, p. 324.
[91] Grose, p. 522.
[92] Ibid., p. 521.
[93] Ibid., p. 522.
[94] Ibid.
[95] Johnson, p. 74.
[96] Fay, p. 189.
[97] Morris, p. 36.
[98] The following account is taken from Arthur Schlesinger's *Robert Kennedy and his Times* (Boston: Houghton Mifflin, 1978), pps. 474–78.
[99] Kornbluh, p. 73.
[100] Schlesinger, p. 279.
[101] Ibid., p. 284.
[102] Hancock, *Someone Would Have Talked*, p. 131.
[103] Howard Hunt, pps. 97, 185.

[104] Higgins, p. 92; Hinckle and Turner, p. 53.
[105] Kornbluh, pps. 1, 3.
[106] *New York Times,* April 25, 1966, p. 20.
[107] Schlesinger, pps. 426–27.
[108] Newman, *JFK and Vietnam,* p. 98.
[109] Ibid.
[110] Ibid.
[111] Ibid., p. 99.
[112] Ibid.
[113] Lane, *Plausible Denial,* p. 94.
[114] Hancock, *Nexus,* p. 81.
[115] Howard Hunt, p. 13.
[116] Ibid., p. 15.
[117] Ibid., p. 213.
[118] Ibid., p. 215.
[119] Ibid., p. 216.
[120] Murphy, pps. 92–93.
[121] Ibid., p. 93.
[122] Ibid., p. 230.
[123] Howard Hunt, p. 196.
[124] Murphy, p. 223.
[125] Ibid.
[126] Ibid., p. 234.

Chapter 4

[1] Record of Actions at the 483d Meeting of the National Security Council. Unless, otherwise noted, this and other memorandum discussed in this section are taken from the State Department Volume X, Foreign Relations of the U.S.
[2] Hinckle and Turner, p. 122.
[3] Ibid, p. 126.
[4] Morley, pps. 147–48.
[5] Ibid., pps. 148–49.
[6] Ibid., p. 149.
[7] Hinckle and Turner, pps. 134–35
[8] Morley, p. 150.
[9] Talbot, p. 98.
[10] Morley, p. 150.
[11] Ibid.
[12] Ibid., p. 151.
[13] Talbot, p. 103.
[14] Hancock, *Nexus,* p. 80.
[15] IG Report, p. 41.
[16] Hancock, *Nexus,* p. 65.
[17] Ibid., p. 66.
[18] IG Report, p. 49.
[19] Ibid., p. 53.
[20] 3/13/62 JCS letter to McNamara, p. 5.

[21] Ibid., pps. 7–13.
[22] May and Zelikow, p. 35.
[23] Ibid, p. 36.
[24] Ibid., p. 37.
[25] DiEugenio, James. "Introduction to the Kennedy Tapes." *Probe*, Vol. 5 No. 4, p. 16.
[26] Besides *The Kennedy Tapes*, the other volume is called *Averting "The Final Failure"* by Sheldon Stern.
[27] May and Zelikow, p. 54.
[28] *Probe*, Vol. 5 No. 4, p. 20.
[29] May and Zelikow, p. 59.
[30] Ibid., p. 177.
[31] Ibid, p. 178.
[32] Ibid, p. 182.
[33] Ibid, p. 186.
[34] Ibid., p. 188.
[35] Op. cit., *Probe*, pps. 22–23.
[36] May and Zelikow, pps. 342–44.
[37] Ibid., p. 628.
[38] Ibid., p. 478.
[39] Ibid., p. 485.
[40] Ibid., p. 343.
[41] Hancock, *Nexus*, p. 70.
[42] Talbot, p. 169.
[43] Op. cit. Hancock.
[44] Op. cit., Talbot.
[45] Talbot, p. 170.
[46] Op. cit. *Probe,* p. 17.
[47] Hancock, *Nexus*, p. 86.
[48] May and Zelikow, p. 664.
[49] Talbot, p. 173.
[50] *Probe*, Vol. 7 No. 1, p. 8. This essay is a summary of Kornbluh's article in the October 1999 issue of *Cigar Aficiando*.
[51] Hancock, *Nexus,* p. 97.
[52] Op. cit., *Probe Magazine*.
[53] Op. cit., Hancock.
[54] Ibid.
[55] Fonzi, p. 132.
[56] Ibid.
[57] Douglass, p. 58; Garrison pps. 34–35.
[58] Ibid, Douglass.
[59] Davy, William. "File Update: Notes on Some Recent Releases." *Probe Magazine*, Vol. 7 No. 2, p. 5.
[60] Ibid.
[61] *NY Times* April 18, 1963
[62] Op. cit., *Probe Magazine*.
[63] Letter from Fitzgerald to McGeorge Bundy of 3/6/64.
[64] Letter from Fitzgerald to Bundy of 6/18/64.
[65] DiEugenio, James. "Kennedy's Quest for Détente with Castro." *Probe Magazine*, Vol. 7, No. 1, p. 9.
[66] Ibid.
[67] Hancock, *Nexus*, pps. 105–06.

[68] Ibid, p. 107; Summers, p. 402.
[69] Ibid., p. 114.
[70] Ibid., p. 123.
[71] Ibid., p. 115.
[72] Ibid., p. 85.
[73] FBI memorandum 109–584–39.
[74] JM/WAVE report on Pawley Relationship 7–25–63.
[75] IG Report, p. 78.
[76] Ibid., p. 85.
[77] Ibid., p. 87.
[78] Ibid., p. 89.
[79] Ibid., pgs 93–94.
[80] Summers, p. 401.
[81] Ibid., p. 402.
[82] Op. cit., *Probe Magazine*.
[83] Lechuga, pps. 197–200.
[84] Attwood, pps. 259–60.
[85] Daniel, *Unofficial Envoy*, pps. 16–17.
[86] Ibid.
[87] Daniel, *When Castro Heard the News*, p. 7
[88] Summers, p. 394.
[89] Mangold, p. 45.
[90] Ibid., p. 50.
[91] Ibid., photograph 20 in the picture section.
[92] Hancock, *Nexus*, p.61.
[93] Ibid., p. 111.

Chapter 5

[1] DiEugenio, James. "Rose Cheramie: How She Predicted the JFK Assassination." *Probe Magazine*, Vol. 6 Number 5, p. 1.
[2] Ibid.
[3] HSCA Vol. X, p. 200.
[4] Op. cit., *Probe*.
[5] Ibid. Fruge's part of the story was told to the HSCA in a 4/18/78 deposition.
[6] Jim Olivier, 2003 Lancer Conference.
[7] Op. cit., HSCA Vol. X.
[8] Mellen, p. 222.
[9] *Madison Capital Times*, February 11, 1968.
[10] Fruge's HSCA deposition, p. 12.
[11] Op. cit., *Probe*, p. 3.
[12] Ibid.
[13] Ibid., p. 5.
[14] Ibid., p. 4; see also FBI Memo of 12/2/61 written by Special Agent J. Edward Kern.
[15] Mellen, p. 72.
[16] Ibid,.
[17] Ibid.
[18] HSCA Vol. X, p. 130.

[19] NODA affidavit of Martin and David Lewis, 2/30/68.

[20] Garrison, p. 5.

[21] Mellen, p. 71.

[22] NODA memorandum from Sciambra to Garrison, 10/28/68.

[23] HSCA interview of 4/6/78.

[24] Martin to Trosclair, 11/23/63.

[25] Martin letter to FBI of 11/25/63.

[26] Davy, p. 48.

[27] NODA memorandum from Sciambra to Garrison, 3/1/68.

[28] New Orleans FBI report of 11/27/63.

[29] Unless otherwise noted, this biographical background is taken from the report assembled by Southern Research Company for Eastern Air Lines during FAA hearings to have Ferrie dismissed from his pilot job. It was filed in December of 1963.

[30] Popkin, "Garrison's Case," p. 28.

[31] Ibid.

[32] Armstrong, p. 122.

[33] Davy, p. 6.

[34] Ibid., p. 4.

[35] Ibid., p. 5.

[36] HSCA interview of 10/17/78.

[37] Davy, p. 6.

[38] HSCA interview of 12/15/78.

[39] HSCA interview of 1/3/79.

[40] Armstrong, p. 123.

[41] HSCA interview of 12/9/78.

[42] NODA affidavit of Thomas Lewis Clark, 3/1/567.

[43] Davy, p. 7.

[44] Hinckle and Turner, p. 233, *Probe* Vol. 5, No. 5. p. 26.

[45] This incident is related in Ed Haslam's *Dr. Mary's Monkey*, (Walteville, Oregon, TrineDay, 2007) p. 101.

[46] The Andrews account is from WCH XI, pp. 325–39.

[47] Ibid., p. 326.

[48] Ibid., p. 328.

[49] Ibid., p. 331.

[50] Ibid.

[51] Ibid., p. 332.

[52] Ibid., p. 334.

[53] Ibid.

[54] Ibid., p. 337.

[55] McGehee's description is taken from his HSCA interview of 4/19/78 and his testimony at the Clay Shaw trial on 2/6/69.

[56] Morgan's description is taken from his HSCA interview of 4/19/78 and his testimony at the Clay Shaw trial on 2/6/69.

[57] Interview of Mary Morgan by the author and William Davy, 9/4/94. She insists to this day that this was Oswald.

[58] Interview of Van Morgan by the author and William Davy, 8/26/94.

[59] These date from August 8–22 and are quoted in Davy, p. 103.

[60] Collins' description is taken from his affidavit for the HSCA dated 11/7/78, and his testimony at the Clay Shaw trial, 2/6/69.

[61] Davy, p. 299.

[62] NODA Memoranda from Andrew Sciambra to Jim Garrison of 1/9/68 and 1/17/68.

[63] Mellen, p. 219.

[64] Palmer's description is taken from his HSCA interview of 4/19/78, and his testimony at the Clay Shaw trial, 2/6/69.

[65] This is from a documentary film in progress, *Rough Side of the Mountain*.

[66] Ibid.

[67] The Thomas testimony is from an NODA memo of 1/29/68; the Spears information is from an NODA memo of 1/31/68.

[68] NODA affidavit of Clark, 2/12/67.

[69] Ibid.

[70] NODA memoranda from Andrew Sciambra to Jim Garrison of 5/29/67 and 8/31/67.

[71] HSCA testimony of Manchester, 3/14/78.

[72] Palmer HSCA testimony, op. cit.

[73] Ibid.

[74] Billings journal, pps. 81–81.

[75] HSCA document number 006098.

[76] Davy, p. 300.

[77] Author's interview with New Orleans scholar and archivist Arthur Carpenter, 1/22/92.

[78] Davy, p. 111.

[79] Author's interview with Butterworth, 4/29/94.

[80] NODA memoranda of 1/10 and 1/22/68.

[81] Davy, p. 300.

[82] Palmer testimony, op. cit.

[83] Palmer's HSCA deposition of 4/19/78.

[84] HSCA memorandum of interview with Ronald Johnston, 3/10/78.

[85] Testimony of Dedon at Shaw trial, 2/7/69.

[86] Testimony of Kemp at Shaw trial, 2/7/69.

[87] Kemp interview by HSCA 2/16/78. When phoned by the HSCA, Booty said he could not recall this and said, "I prefer not to get involved." (Ibid.)

[88] NODA memorandum by Andrew Sciambra to Jim Garrison of 2/29/67.

[89] DiEugenio, James. "The Life and Death of Richard Case Nagell." *Probe Magazine*, Vol. 3 No. 1, p. 1.

[90] Ibid.

[91] FBI Report of David Reid, 12/20/63.

[92] Op. cit., *Probe Magazine*.

[93] Russell, p. xvii, and see photo section.

[94] Ibid, p. xviii.

[95] Ibid, p. 2.

[96] Ibid., pps. 46–47.

[97] Ibid., p. 54.

[98] Ibid., p. 263.

[99] Davy, p. 196

[100] Letter to Eleanore Gambert of 10/7/66.

[101] Russell, pps. 147–48.

[102] Ibid., p. 152.

[103] Ibid., p. 154.

[104] Ibid., p. 160.

[105] Ibid., p. 164.

[106] Ibid., p. 182.

107 Ibid., p. 210.
108 Letter to Garrison of 3/23/67.
109 Russell, p. 211.
110 Nagell letter to Greenstein 10/8/67, *Probe* Vol. 3 No. 1, p. 6.
111 Russell, pps. 240–41.
112 Op. cit., *Probe*.
113 Report from Roy Jacob to William Gurvich of Garrison's office dated 4/15/67.
114 *Probe*, Vol, 6 No. 5, p. 23. NODA memorandum of 4/1/6/67, from William Martin to Garrison.
115 Nagell letter to Greenstein 10/8/67, *Probe* Vol. 3 No. 1, p. 6.
116 Russell, p. 265.
117 Ibid., p. 287.
118 Ibid., p. 278.
119 Ibid., p. 283.
120 Ibid., p. 291.
121 Details about Underhill's arrival at the Fitzsimmonses' are from a letter by Robert Fitzsimmons to John Donovan, June 21, 1964.
122 The conversation between Underhill and Charlene Fitzsimmons is reconstructed from the above letter and a letter from Mr. Fitzsimmons to Jim Garrison, May 3, 1968. Friends' opinions of Underhill's "rational and objective" demeanor are found in Turner, "Inquest," p. 29.
123 Underhill's background is taken from the Fitzimmons letter to Donovan and a Donovan letter to Jim Garrison of April 29, 1967; also Turner, "Inquest" pps. 28–29; David Cort, *The Sin of Henry R. Luce* (Seacucus: Lyle Stuart, 1974)
124 Underhill's influence on Luce is noted in an internal *Ramparts* magazine memorandum by Edward Cohen dated May 15, 1966. The magazine researched Underhill for its two articles on the Garrison inquiry, one in June of 1967 and one in January of 1968.
125 Turner, "Inquest," p. 28; also Fitzsimmons's letter to Garrison, Donovan's letter to Garrison, and *Ramparts* memorandum by Cohen dated June 21, 1966.
126 Cohen memorandum, May 15, 1966.
127 For Brynes's long relationship with Underhill, see Donovan letter to Garrison.
128 Cohen memorandum, May 15, 1966.
129 Ibid.; also Turner, "Inquest," p. 29.
130 Ibid.; Cohen memorandum.

Chapter 6

1 Hurt, p. 19.
2 WR, p. 744.
3 Weisberg, *Oswald,* p. 335.
4 Ibid., p. 331.
5 FBI draft message from New Orleans to FBI director, NARA JFK files RIF 124–10248–10191.
6 Summers, *Official and Confidential,* p. 325.
7 WC Volume 26, p. 783.
8 This information is drawn from an autobiographical sketch located at the AARC in Washington.
9 Ibid.
10 *New Orleans Times Picayune*, March 3 and 4, 1957.

[11] Davy, p. 281.
[12] FBI memorandum 105–70374–1949.
[13] HSCA interview of Oster, 1/27/78.
[14] NODA memorandum of 9/30/68.
[15] Op. cit., Oster interview.
[16] Hinckle and Turner, p. 231.
[17] A. J. Weberman, online at "The 544 Camp Street Nexus, NoduleX19" p. 16. The page numbers to this source refer to the PDF printed out version.
[18] Ibid., p. 17.
[19] NODA memorandum of 10/30/68.
[20] FBI interview of David Ferrie, 8/22/61.
[21] "The JFK Conspiracy" broadcast, 4/15/92; interview with Oster by A. J. Weberman, 11/22/93.
[22] Research notes of journalist Scott Malone, interview with Newborough of August 16, 1978.
[23] Pease, Lisa. "Novel and Company: Phillips, Banister, Arcacha and Ferrie." *Probe*, Vol. 4 No. 6, p. 32.
[24] Ibid; see also Davy, pps. 22–24.
[25] HSCA interview with John Irion, 10/18/78.
[26] Kornbluh, p. 39.
[27] CIA Memorandum for Chief CI, document # WH/C 67–336, October 1967.
[28] Hinckle and Turner, p. 233.
[29] Weberman online at p. 40; *Baton Rouge States Times*, 2/27/67.
[30] NODA Memorandum of 3/23/67.
[31] *Probe*, Vol. 4, No. 6, p. 33.
[32] Ibid.
[33] Garrison, p. 40.
[34] NODA Memorandum of 1/31/67.
[35] Op. cit., *Probe*, pps. 32, 34.
[36] DiEugenio, James. "The Wegmann Files, Part 2." *Probe*, Vol. 4, No. 5, p. 19.
[37] Author interview with Allen Campbell, August of 1994.
[38] *Probe*, op. cit.
[39] Ibid.
[40] Ibid.
[41] FBI memorandum of 1/17/61.
[42] Ibid.
[43] Weberman online, at p. 61.
[44] Garrison, p. 37.
[45] This information was contained in an essay written by Haslam to the original publisher of this book, Sheridan Square Press.
[46] Author's 1993 phone interview with Haslam.
[47] "Novel and Company." *Probe* Vol. 4, No. 6, p. 32.
[48] Interview with former FBI agent Warren DeBrueys at his home in Metaire LA. in 1994.
[49] Garrison, p. 182.
[50] NODA memorandum of 4/1/67.
[51] HSCA deposition of Pena dated 6/23/78.
[52] FBI teletype of 1/15/76.
[53] NODA memoranda of 5/9/67 and 2/14/68, interviews with Sewall.
[54] For the form, see Summers, p. 382.
[55] See CD 75, pps. 677–78.
[56] *Back Channels Magazine*, Volume 3, Numbers 1 and 2.

57 NODA Memorandum of 4/1/67.
58 Letter from Arcacha Smith to Eddie Rickenbacker, 7/18/61.
59 Weberman online at p. 14.
60 Summers, p. 294.
61 HSCA interview of Roberts by Buras, 7/6/78.
62 Summers, p. 292.
63 Weberman online at p. 16.
64 Summers, p. 296. Years later, discredited writer Gerald Posner tried to discount Roberts's testimony to Summers. Posner said that she told him that she had lied to the British author. What Posner did not reveal is what Allen Campbell told me in a personal interview in 1994. By the time Posner interviewed her, the woman was suffering from senility and living in an assisted living center.
65 Kurtz, *The JFK Assassination Debates*, pgs 159–61.
66 Author's 1994 interviews with Campbell in New Orleans and Los Angeles.
67 Ibid.
68 Author's 1994 interview with Allen Campbell in New Orleans.
69 DiEugenio, James. "The Wegmann Files, Part 1." *Probe*, Volume 4, Number 4, p. 8.
70 NODA interviews of Martin on 12/13 and 12/14/66.
71 *Probe,* op. cit, p. 16.
72 HSCA report, p. 219.
73 Summers, pps. 364–65.
74 Hurt, p. 337.
75 NODA memoranda of April 12, and 16–17, 1967.
76 William Davy on *Black Op Radio*, archived program of 3/17/11.
77 Paul Wallach memorandum for Church Committee, 12/2/75.
78 NODA Memorandum of 11/7/67.
79 HSCA Document number 180–10101–10379.
80 Roberts' interview with HSCA on 7/6/78.
81 Hinckle and Turner, p. 233; *Probe* Vol. 6, No. 2, p. 26.
82 Hinckle and Turner, p. 233.
83 Popkin, "Garrison's Case," p. 18.
84 Davy, p. 29.
85 NODA memorandum of 12/6/67.
86 Research notes of journalist Scott Malone, interview with Joe Newbrough of August 16, 1978.
87 Summers, p. 318; Hinckle and Turner, pps. 224–27; Davy, p. 30.
88 *New Orleans Times–Picayune* of 8/1/63.
89 Hinckle and Turner, pps. 225–28.
90 Michael Kurtz, *Crime of the Century* (Knoxville: University of Tennessee Press, 1982) p. 203.
91 Summers, p. 304.
92 Mellen, p. 48.
93 "The Probe Interview: Bob Tanenbaum." *Probe*, Volume 3, Number. 5, p. 24.
94 Two other witnesses to this film who were interviewed by author Joe Biles were HSCA investigator L. J. Delsa, and photo analyst Bob Groden. Biles interviewed both in September of 2000 for his confirmations of Phillips, Oswald, and Banister. See Biles, p. 227.
95 Kirkwood, p. 263.
96 Record of Ferrie's Grievance Hearing against Eastern, p. 858.
97 Davy, p. 29.
98 NODA Memorandum of 12/30/66.

[99] Summers, p. 300.

[100] HSCA contact report of June 1, 1978 by Robert Buras, based upon information given him by Joe Newbrough and Jack Martin.

Chapter 7

[1] WR, p. 292.

[2] CE 826, p.12.

[3] Newman, *Oswald and the CIA*, p. 337.

[4] Ibid.

[5] WR, p. 292.

[6] CE 1414.

[7] CE 3119.

[8] See footnote 441, on p. 837.

[9] WR, p. 669.

[10] Ibid.

[11] WR, p. 670.

[12] Ibid.

[13] Ibid., p. 671–72.

[14] Armstrong, p. 22.

[15] WR, p. 672

[16] WR, p. 673.

[17] WR, p. 674.

[18] WR, p. 675.

[19] Armstrong, p. 41.

[20] WR, p. 675.

[21] WR, p. 676.

[22] WR, p. 379.

[23] Armstrong, p. 51.

[24] WR, p. 676.

[25] WC, Carro Exhibit No. 1, Vol. 19, p. 309.

[26] Armstrong, pps. 59–60.

[27] WR, p. 678.

[28] Armstrong, p. 66

[29] ARRB memo from Buttimer of 9/8/1995.

[30] Armstrong. p. 62.

[31] Ibid.

[32] Armstrong, John. "Harvey and Lee: The Case for Two Oswalds." *Probe*, Vol. 4 No. 6, p. 20.

[33] Ibid., p. 21.

[34] FBI report of 12/2/63.

[35] Op cit. *Probe*, p. 19.

[36] WC Vol. 1, p. 301; *Fort Worth Star Telegram*, 10/29/59; and 6/8/62.

[37] WR, p. 679.

[38] Galindo's phone conversation with John Armstrong in January of 1994.

[39] Armstrong, pps. 97–103.

[40] Kudlaty sat for a long interview with Armstrong in 1996 which is excerpted on You Tube.

[41] WC Vol. 1, p. 198; WR p. 679.

[42] WC Vol. 8, p. 12.

[43] WR, p. 679.

[44] WC Vol. 8, p. 14, and pgs 29–32, the witnesses were Voebel and Fredrick O'Sullivan.

[45] Marrs, p. 99.

[46] WR, p. 680.

[47] Davy, p. 6.

[48] WR, p. 680.

[49] Davy, p. 17.

[50] WR, p. 681.

[51] WC Vol. 8, p. 81.

[52] WC Exhibit 635.

[53] WR, p. 682.

[54] Ibid.

[55] WR, p. 683.

[56] Ibid.

[57] Prados, p. 69.

[58] *New York Times*, 5/17/60.

[59] Marrs, p. 114.

[60] Prouty, p. 353.

[61] Ranelagh, p. 318.

[62] Prouty, p. 381. In a You Tube segment, Prouty makes a notable argument about whether or not the U–2 was shot down.

[63] *Boston Globe*, 12/10/10

[64] Newman, *Oswald and the CIA*, p. 28.

[65] Ibid., p. 29.

[66] Weisberg, *Oswald in New Orleans*, p. 91.

[67] Newman, op. cit., pps. 30–31.

[68] Szulc, pps. 72–74.

[69] Russell, p. 71.

[70] Ibid., p. 72.

[71] Lane, *Rush to Judgment,* p. 123.

[72] Ibid., p. 124.

[73] Captions in photo section of Hurt's book.

[74] Hurt, p. 198.

[75] WR, p. 191.

[76] Ibid., p. 192.

[77] WR. p. 683.

[78] Ibid., p. 684.

[79] Ibid., p. 685.

[80] Ibid.

[81] Melanson, p. 10.

[82] Ibid.

[83] Garrison, p. 22.

[84] WR, p. 685; Melanson, p. 11.

[85] Melanson, p. 12.

[86] Russell, p. 44.

[87] 1994 Dan Campbell interview with author in New Orleans and Los Angeles. Both John Armstrong and Alaric Rossman have set forth the idea that the man who met with Quinn was in fact a Second Oswald. One from Eastern Europe who knew the language much better

than the Oswald born in New Orleans. The work of Armstrong's which I have noted so far builds that idea. See Armstrong, *Harvey and Lee*, p. 226.

[88] Garrison, p. 47.
[89] Marrs, p. 110.
[90] Ibid., p. 111.
[91] WC Vol. 11, p. 96.
[92] Ibid. p. 87
[93] Ibid., p. 90.
[94] Armstrong, p. 227.
[95] Letter from John Lathrop to Friends of Albert Schweitzer College issued in September of 1953.
[96] Armstrong, John and James DiEugenio. "The Albert Schweitzer Documents." *Probe Magazine*, Vol. 3 No. 3, p. 7.
[97] Ibid.
[98] Ibid., p. 26.
[99] Evica, *A Certain Arrogance*, p. 65.
[100] Ibid., p. 21.
[101] Ibid, p. 78.
[102] Ibid., p. 116.
[103] Evica, p. 223; Armstrong, p. 229.
[104] Op cit, *Probe*, p. 26.
[105] WR, p. 688.
[106] Ibid.
[107] Hurt, p. 205.
[108] WR, p. 689.
[109] Hurt, op. cit.
[110] Armstrong, p. 240.
[111] Injury report by Liberty Insurance Company dated 12/11/58.
[112] Letter from Goldberg to Liberty Insurance Company dated 1/26/59.
[113] FBI report of 11/23/63, by Jack French and Robley D. Madland, CD 5, p. 298.
[114] Armstrong, p. 243.
[115] HSCA interview of Kozak, 8/2/78
[116] WC, Vol. 8, p. 257.
[117] WR p. 689.
[118] Armstrong, p. 251.
[119] WR, p. 689.
[120] WR, p. 690.
[121] WC Vol. 8, p. 257.
[122] Melanson, p. 13.
[123] WR, p. 690.
[124] WC Exhibit 946.
[125] Armstrong, p. 254.
[126] Griggs, p. 123.
[127] Ibid., pps. 124–26.
[128] Armstrong, p. 254.
[129] Letter from Richard Helms to Warren Commission Chief Consul J. Lee Rankin of 7/31/64.
[130] Armstrong, p. 255.
[131] WR, p. 690.
[132] *New York Times*, June 30, 1959.

[133] Pease, Lisa. "What Did Otepka Know about Oswald and the CIA." *Probe*, Vol. 4, No. 3, p. 9.
[134] Melanson, p. 25.
[135] Newman, *Oswald and the CIA*, p. 172.
[136] Melanson, op cit.; Marrs, p. 116.
[137] Marrs, p. 116.
[138] Armstrong, pps. 256, 267; based on an interview with Webster by author Dick Russell.
[139] Marrs, p. 117.
[140] CD 5, p. 259, FBI interview of Katya Ford of 11/24/63.
[141] Titovets, p. 8.
[142] WR, p. 691.
[143] Titovets, the letter appears on pps. 5–6.
[144] Summers, p. 153.
[145] Armstrong, p. 264.
[146] CE 895.
[147] Titovets, p. 13.
[148] Ibid, p. 6.
[149] CIA document #609–786 says that Snyder joined the CIA in 1949. According to a CIA memo, on September 26, 1950, Snyder resigned from the CIA to work for the High Commissioner's Office in Germany. (Melanson, p. 135.) Yet, Julius Mader's 1968 *Who's Who in CIA,* published in East Germany, lists Snyder as still in the Agency. In any event, the High Commissioner, whom he either worked for or used as a cover, was future Warren Commissioner John McCloy.
[150] Simpich, "12 Who Built the Oswald Legend," Part One.
[151] CE 914; WR, p. 693.
[152] Newman, *Oswald and the CIA*, p. 6. This visit by Oswald took place on a Saturday. In the Warren Report it says that the embassy was closed on Saturday, (p. 705). Yet John Newman states in *Oswald and the CIA* that the embassy always closed at noon on Saturday (p. 1). Presumably he got this information from interviews with Snyder or McVickar. Either the report is in error, or someone lied to Newman so as not to make this Saturday visit more unusual and staged than it was.
[153] Titovets, p. 19.
[154] Newman, p. 6.
[155] Ibid., p. 19.
[156] Ibid., p. 25.
[157] Ibid., p. 27.
[158] Ibid., pps. 28, 33–34.
[159] Ibid., p. 43.
[160] Ibid., p. 46.
[161] Ibid., p. 48.
[162] Ibid., p. 47.
[163] Ibid., p. 52.
[164] Ibid., p. 54.
[165] Ranelagh, p. 271.
[166] Author's 1994 interview with Newman at a researcher meeting in San Francisco.
[167] WR, p. 697.
[168] Titovets, p. 47.
[169] WR, p. 698.
[170] WR, p. 695.
[171] WC Exhibit 1385, typed notes of reporter Mosby.

172 Ibid.
173 Ibid.
174 Newman, *Oswald and the CIA*, pps. 9, 67.
175 Armstrong, p. 285.
176 Titoverts, p. 62.
177 This KGB summary is taken from Peter Wronski's web site, "Lee Harvey Oswald in Russia."
178 PBS 1993 *Frontline* special "Who was Lee Harvey Oswald?"
179 Op. cit., Wronski, "Minsk Part 2, Oswald and the Minsk KGB."
180 Titovets, p. 195.
181 Ibid, p. 202.
182 CE 92 and 94 for the descriptive notes, *Probe* Vol. 5 No. 1., p. 22, for the quote.
183 Mellen, *Jim Garrison: His Life and Times,* pps. xi–xiii; Op. cit., 1993 *Frontline* special.
184 WR, p. 699.
185 Ibid.
186 Ibid, p. 701.
187 The above details about Marina's life are from Hosty, pps. 111–12.
188 FBI interview of Martin, 7/13/67.
189 HSCA document number 180–10083–10193, interview of Martin. This aspect of Marina's life is also mentioned in Titovets, pps. 246–47.
190 WR, p. 703. In Ernst Titovets's book, *Oswald: Russian Episode*, he makes a very interesting argument that this meeting was subtly orchestrated by the KGB. From the eavesdropping at Oswald's apartment to learn about the plans, to having Yuri Merezhinksi and Kostya Mandarin act as agents in the actual meeting (See pps. 248–60).
191 Hosty, p. 113.
192 WR, p. 704; Armstrong, p. 335.
193 Interview by John Armstrong with Ana Ziger, 10/98.
194 WC Vol. 8, p. 368.
195 WC Executive Session, 12/16/63, p. 41.
196 WC Vol. 5, p. 589.
197 Ibid., p. 590.
198 Ibid., p. 592.
199 Ibid., p. 604.
200 Ibid., pps. 606–07.
201 Ibid., p. 600.
202 Armstrong, p. 340.
203 Ibid., p. 256.
204 Ibid., p. 341.
205 James Hosty also advanced this concept of Marina as a sleeper agent in his *Assignment: Oswald.* He also reveals that there was an FBI tap on Marina's phone at the request of the Commission. Perhaps Rankin was impressed by Russell's questioning. See p. 110.
206 WR, p. 706.
207 Ibid.
208 WR, p. 711.
209 Ibid., p. 712.
210 Newman, op. cit., p. 249.
211 Ibid.
212 Melanson, p. 22.
213 Mellen, op cit pps. xi–xiii.
214 Author's interview with Newman at a 1994 researcher meeting in San Francisco.

[215] Internal CIA memo of 11/25/63, CIA document 435–173A

Chapter 8

[1] WR, p. 714.
[2] Report of John Fain, Dallas FBI office, 7/10/62.
[3] WR, p. 716.
[4] WR, pps. 716–17; Benson, p. 80.
[5] WR, p. 717.
[6] Baker, pps. 72, 75.
[7] Bill Simpich, "Twelve Who Built the Oswald Legend, Part 7" at OpEd News.com
[8] Moore interview with the HSCA of 3/14/78; HSCA Vol. 12, pps. 54–55.
[9] WC Vol. 9, p. 235.
[10] Epstein, *The Assassination Chronicles*, p. 558. It should be noted that Moore denies ever instructing DeMohrenschildt about Oswald.
[11] Ibid., pps. 558–59.
[12] Douglass, p. 49; Russell, p. 169; Douglass notes that Henry Hurt interviewed an employment counselor who disputes that DeMohrenschildt had a role in securing the position.
[13] Ibid., Russell.
[14] WC Vol. X, p. 208.
[15] Ibid.
[16] Summers, p. 230.
[17] Hurt, pps. 219, 221.
[18] Melanson, p. 86.
[19] Newman, op. cit., p. 271.
[20] Dallas Police Report of 2/17/64, part of CD 950. See also, Garrison, p. 54, Benson p. 290.
[21] Douglass, p. 168.
[22] Ibid., p. 48.
[23] Garrison, p. 56.
[24] Douglass, p. 168; See also Ruth Paine's testimony before the New Orleans Grand Jury of 4/18/68, pps. 2–4.
[25] WR, p. 718.
[26] Hewett, Carol, Jones, Steve and Barbara LaMonica. "The Paines: Suspicious Characters." *Probe* Vol. 3 No. 4, p. 15.
[27] Ibid. Much of the material I will use in this book about the Paines originates in a series of landmark articles written for *Probe Magazine* by Carol Hewett, Steve Jones, and Barbara LaMonica. This series was so compelling that Thomas Mallon wrote a book—*Mrs. Paine's Garage*—in which he tried to counter their work by, in part, ridiculing the authors. In his mammoth book *Reclaiming History*, Vincent Bugliosi characterizes this series as "slim pickings." Yet, the series went on for five installments, and Bugliosi could not counter any evidence or tenet therein.
[28] Ibid.
[29] Ibid.
[30] WR, p. 725.
[31] Davy, p. 35.
[32] Ibid; Garrison, p. 27. ARRB declassified files show that INCA's tapes were distributed into South America by the Agency, *Probe Magazine*, Vol. 3 No. 6., p. 13.
[33] Davy, p. 78.

[34] CIA Memorandum from Domestic Contacts Division, 5/23/68.

[35] Summers, p. 313; Garrision, pps. 115–16; Davy, p. 36.

[36] CIA memo to file from M. D. Stevens, dated January 11, 1964.

[37] WR, p. 726.

[38] HSCA Report, pps. 193–94.

[39] CE 2718, see pps. 94–95.

[40] CE 793, p. 680.

[41] CE 2966A originally contained Oswald's address. It was altered to resemble CD 1370, a stampless Oswald handbill. See Newman, p. 316.

[42] Newman, op. cit., p. 300.

[43] Author's interview with DeBrueys in 1994 at his home in Metairie.

[44] Newman, op. cit., p. 95.

[45] Ibid., p. 236

[46] All this information is in the author's first edition of this book, pps. 218–19.

[47] Church Committee Report, Book Five, p. 66.

[48] WC Vol. X, p. 61.

[49] WC Vol. XX, p. 524.

[50] CE 3120, p. 783.

[51] Mellen, *A Farewell to Justice*, p. 59.

[52] Davy, p. 287; Mellen, ibid., pps. 59–60, based on interviews with Walter in 2000 and 2001.

[53] Summers, p. 281.

[54] DiEugenio, James. "FBI vs. ARRB: Heading into Overtime." *Probe Magazine*, Vol. 2, No. 6, p. 1.

[55] FBI teletype of 2/10/64.

[56] Summers, p. 280; Newman, p. 334.

[57] On the notes being destroyed, WC Vol. 4, p. 433; the actual report is in CE 826.

[58] See page 2 of Quigley's 8/15/63 report.

[59] Newman, *Oswald and the CIA*, p. 337.

[60] Melanson, p. 66.

[61] NODA memorandum of interviews with Higginbotham, April 12, 16–17, 1968.

[62] Peter Model and Robert Groden, *JFK: The Case for Conspiracy* (New York: Manor Books, 1976) p. 77.

[63] Armstrong, p. 568.

[64] NODA Memorandum of interview with Mrs. Carlos Marquez, 2/14/67.

[65] WC Vol. X, p. 269; Davy, p. 38.

[66] Letter and enclosure from Roy Jacob to William Gurvich of Garrison's office dated 4/15/67.

[67] WR, p. 729.

[68] Summers, p. 279.

[69] WR, p. 729.

[70] WC Vol. 21, Stuckey Exhibit 3; audio of the debate is at the Mary Ferrell web site.

[71] WC Exhibit 2124.

[72] WR, p. 730.

[73] WR, p. 738.

[74] WR, p. 737.

[75] WC Vol. 11, p. 481, affidavit of Robert Adams.

[76] WC Vol. 9, pps. 389–90.

[77] WC Vol. 1, p. 68.

[78] *Probe Magazine*, Vol. 4, No. 3, p. 9.

[79] Ibid., p. 10.

[80] Newman, *Oswald and the CIA*, p.172.

[81] Op cit, *Probe*.

[82] Ibid., p. 11.

[83] Ibid., p. 12.

[84] Proctor, Grover B., Jr., "Oswald's Raleigh Call," *The Third Decade*, Vol, 5 No. 3, p. 5.

[85] Ibid.

[86] Ibid., p. 6.

[87] Ibid., p. 7.

[88] Ibid., pps. 7–8.

[89] Szulc, p. 95.

[90] Davy, p. 196.

Chapter 9

[1] This idea is prevalent in the Rosemary James-Jack Wardlaw book, *Plot or Politics?* In fact, it is clearly suggested in the very title.

[2] *New York Post*, 2/23/67.

[3] Mellen, *Jim Garrison: His Life and Times*, p. 5.

[4] Ibid., p. 225.

[5] Garrison, p. 9.

[6] Op cit. Mellen pps. 21, 25.

[7] Garrison, p. 10.

[8] Op cit. Mellen, pps. 35–36.

[9] Ibid., p. 41.

[10] Ibid., p. 44.

[11] Ibid.

[12] Garrison, p. 262.

[13] Op cit, Mellen, pps. 44–45.

[14] Ibid., p. 61.

[15] Ibid., p. 71.

[16] Ibid., p. 81.

[17] *Probe*, Vol. 2 No. 5, p. 4.

[18] Op cit Mellen, pps. 98–100.

[19] *Washington Post*, 2/10/63.

[20] Op cit Mellen, pgs. 112–14; See also Savage, p. 11. The latter book is biased, both on Garrison's inquiry, and the Supreme Court case of *Garrison vs. Louisiana*. But it does contain some useful information about the latter case.

[21] *Saturday Evening Post*, "The Viceman Cometh," 6/8/63.

[22] *New Orleans Times Picayune*, 12/4/62.

[23] Mellen, *Jim Garrison*, p. 116.

[24] Savage, p. 16; Mellen, pps. 125–28.

[25] Savage, pps. 16, 19; Mellen, p. 128.

[26] *New Orleans States Item*, 11/2/62.

[27] Op cit Savage, p. 17.

[28] Mellen, op. cit., p. 129.

[29] Savage, p. 21.

[30] Mellen, op. cit., p. 151.

[31] Savage, p. 25.

[32] *New Orleans Times Picayune*, 1/9 and 1/13/63; 3/29/64; 4/11/64.

[33] Mellen, op. cit., p. 173.

[34] *Washington Post*, 2/10/63.

[35] Mellen, op. cit., pps. 158–59.

[36] Ibid.

[37] Ibid, p.173.

[38] Flammonde, p. 10.

[39] Mellen, op. cit., pps. 211–12.

[40] Ibid, p. 217.

[41] Ibid, p. 208.

[42] Author's interview with Mort Sahl in 1998. Sahl was once married to former Playmate China Lee who lived in the New Orleans area when Garrison was elected DA.

[43] Garrison, p. 11.

[44] Mellen, op. cit., p. 236.

Chapter 10

[1] Melanson, p. 42.

[2] Ibid.

[3] Ibid; See also HSCA Vol. 10, p. 113.

[4] HSCA Vol. 10, p. 113.

[5] Garrison, p. 7.

[6] Ibid.

[7] Melanson, p. 42; Garrison, pp. 7–8.

[8] Turner, "Garrison Commission," p. 47.

[9] CD 75, pps. 285–97. FBI interview of Ferrie by agents Wall and Shearer on 11/25/63.

[10] Author's phone interview with Lou Ivon, 1996.

[11] Mellen, *A Farewell to Justice*, p. 1.

[12] Garrison, *Playboy* interview.

[13] Popkin, "Garrison's Case," p. 26. Andrews's testimony about encountering Oswald is also corroborated three times: by Springer, by Davis, and by a Secret Service interview November 25, 1963. He could not have been aware of so many facts about Lee and Marina unless Oswald had revealed them to him at an earlier date. Meagher, pp. 375–376.

[14] Weisberg, *Oswald,* p. 335.

[15] Garrison, pp. 37–38. For reference to the Shaw file, see Turner, "Garrison Commission," p. 48.

[16] Newman, *Oswald and the CIA*, pps. 236–44.

[17] CD 75, pps. 309–11, FBI report of agents Schlager and Kennedy of interview of Jack Martin.

[18] Garrison, pps. 31–32.

[19] *New Orleans Times Picayune*, August 1 and 2, 1963.

[20] Handwritten notes of Jim Garrison, December 13 and 14, 1966.

[21] WC Vol. 11, pps. 331, 34.

[22] WR, p. 325.

[23] WC Vol. 11, p. 31; Flammonde, p. 47.

[24] Davy, p. 52.

[25] Garrison, pps. 80–82.

[26] See Turner, "Inquest," p. 24; Summers p. 340.

[27] Memorandum of 2/23/67 from Detective Meloche and Sergeant Sedgebeer to Jim Garrison.

[28] *Probe Magazine*, Vol. 6 No. 5, p. 5.

[29] Ibid., p. 21.

[30] Ibid., p. 27.

[31] Flammonde, p. 119.

[32] Russell, p. 2

[33] Ibid., p. 3.

[34] Ibid., p. 7.

[35] Interview with William Turner in 1997. The office address is noted in letters Martin wrote to Nagell in the summer of 1967.

[36] Letter from Maurice Gatlin to William Martin, 11/21/61.

[37] CIA Memorandum from New Orleans office to Director of Domestic Contacts Service, 1/3/68.

[38] NODA Memorandum of 4/18/67, Martin to Garrison.

[39] Ibid.

[40] NODA statement of Newman to Garrison, 1/24/68.

[41] *Probe Magazine*, Vol. 6, No. 5, p, 27.

[42] Letter from Martin to Nagell, 6/20/67.

[43] Letter from Martin to Nagell, 8/7/67.

[44] Op. cit *Probe*, p. 25.

[45] Mellen, *A Farewell to Justice,* pps. 208–10.

[46] Ibid., p. 215.

[47] Ibid., p. 217.

[48] Ibid., p. 219.

[49] DiEugenio, James and William Davy. "False Witness: Aptly Titled." *Probe*, Vol. 6 No. 4, p. 25.

[50] Mellen, op. cit., p. 230.

[51] HSCA interview with McGehee, 4/19/78.

[52] HSCA interview with Morgan, 4/19/78.

[53] HSCA interview with Palmer, 4/19/78.

[54] Benson, p. 200.

[55] *Probe*, Vol. 4 No. 5, p. 18.

[56] Author's 1994 interview with Morgan in Jackson.

[57] Titovets, p. 365.

[58] Mellen, op. cit. p. 231.

[59] Garrison, pps. 46–47.

[60] Thornley, p. 19.

[61] Ibid., p. 69.

[62] Garrison, p. 75.

[63] Author's interview with Campbell in 1994.

[64] Biles, p. 64.

[65] NODA memos of 3/12/68 concerning Goldsmith, and 11/6/67 concerning Dowell. The affidavits and statements of most of the witnesses Garrison had to impeach Thornley are in Appendix B of the Biles book.

[66] Letter from John Schwegmann to Jim Garrison, 2/22/68.

[67] Weisberg, *Never Again* (New York: Carroll and Graf, 1995), p. 19.

[68] Author's 1997 phone interview with Weisberg. See also Mellen, p. 273.

[69] *Probe Magazine*, Vol. 6, No. 4, p. 28.

[70] Ibid.

[71] Author's 1997 conversation with Mike Willman who was friends with Sahl at the time.

[72] Author's 1998 interview with Jim Rose in San Luis Obispo. Rose brought his notes, which contained this information.

[73] Op cit, *Probe*, p. 29.

[74] Garrison, p. 76. The author has read this manuscript and Garrison's characterization of it is accurate.

[75] Broadcast of 2/25/92.

[76] Garrison, p. 78.

[77] WC Vol. XI, p. 89.

[78] Garrison, pps. 74–75. Former *Probe* writer David Manning told the author in 1992 that this point, about Thornley posing for the backyard photographs, was confirmed to him by Breck Wall, an acquaintance of Jack Ruby while Manning was living in Las Vegas in the seventies and Wall was a choreographer there. When Manning and the author visited Wall in 1993 for an on camera interview, Wall reneged on the claim.

[79] *Playboy*, October 1967.

[80] Ibid., *Playboy*.

[81] Melanson, p. 79.

[82] Jones, Steve. "Friends in High Places." *Probe*, Vol. 5, No. 3, p. 9.

[83] Ibid.

[84] Simpich, "The Twelve Who Built the Oswald Legend," part 6.

[85] Ibid. This closeness of this relationship was lied about by Moore. (See Epstein, p. 564)

[86] Epstein, *The Assassination Chronicles*, p. 558.

[87] Ibid., p. 559.

[88] WC, Vol. 9, p. 396.

[89] Grand Jury testimony of Ruth Paine 4/18/68.

[90] Op cit, *Probe*.

[91] This is based on an FBI interview of 12/14/63.

[92] Ibid., p. 234.

[93] Op cit *Probe*.

[94] *Oral History of Mary Bancroft* (Columbia University, 1972, p. 24)

[95] Evica, p. 234.

[96] Hewett, Carol. "The Paines Know." *Probe*, Vol, 5 No. 1, p. 17.

[97] Ibid., p. 235.

[98] WC, Vol.2, p. 385.

[99] *Probe*, Vol. 3 No. 4, p. 15.

[100] *Probe*, Vol. 5 No. 5, p. 7.

[101] Ibid.

[102] *Probe*, Vol. 3 No. 4, p. 16.

[103] Douglass, p. 170.

[104] Ibid, p. 243.

[105] *Probe*, Vol. 5 No. 3, p. 30.

[106] Ruth Paine's grand jury testimony of 4/18/68. See pages 57–58.

[107] Security File on Sylvia Hyde Hoke of 7/30/71, File Number 348 201.

[108] Evica, *A Certain Arrogance*, p. 230.

[109] *Probe* Vol. 3 No. 4, p. 16; also Vol. 5 No. 1, p. 14.

[110] Hancock, *Someone Would Have Talked*, (Southlake Texas: JFK Lancer Productions and Publications, 2006) pps. 552–54.

[111] Hewett, Carol, Jones, Steve and Barbara LaMonica. "Ruth Paine: Social Activist or Contra Support Networker." *Probe*, Vol. 3 No. 5, p. 9

[112] Marina Oswald's grand jury testimony of 2/8/68. See pages 69–70.

[113] Steve Jones, "The Confessions of Ruth Paine" at the web site *Deep Politics Quarterly*.

[114] Ibid.

[115] WC Vol. 11, pps. 425–27.

[116] Ibid., p. 427.

[117] Armstrong, p. 512.

[118] McKnight, p. 56.

[119] Armstrong, p. 509.

[120] Meagher, pps. 107–10.

[121] WC Vol. 11, pps. 409–10.

[122] Benson, p. 440; Armstrong, p. 505; WC Vol. 11, pps. 412–13.

[123] Benson, p. 84; McKnight, pps. 57–58.

[124] McKnight, p. 58.

[125] WC Vol. 11, pps. 416–17.

[126] See J. Edgar Hoover memo to Rankin of 6/16/64, and the Lee/Barrett Report to Hoover of 6/10/64 on the Walker shooting.

[127] WC Vol. 11, p. 414.

[128] Ibid., p. 428.

[129] Dallas Police Report by officers Van Cleave and McElroy of 4/11/63; *Dallas Times Herald* 12/7/63.

[130] WC Stovall Exhibit A.

[131] Armstrong, p. 492.

[132] See Camerapedia Web Site, 620 film page.

[133] CE 2557, pps. 4–5.

[134] CE 1155, p. 2.

[135] CE 2557, p. 3.

[136] Armstrong, p.493.

[137] Ibid., p. 495.

[138] CE 1403, p. 1.

[139] Ibid., pps. 4–6; See also, Armstrong, p. 695.

[140] Ibid., p. 7.

[141] WR, p. 736.

[142] The only witness who said Oswald admitted to being in Mexico City while in detention was postmaster Harry Holmes, who also doubled as an FBI informant. Holmes' testimony on this point was so at odds with everyone else that not even the Commission could accept it. See Armstrong, p. 941.

[143] CD 344, p. 18.

[144] CE 1781, pps. 4–5.

[145] Armstrong, pps. 977–78.

[146] WC Vol. 1, p. 23.

[147] CE 1404, FBI report of 2/25/64, p. 4.

[148] There is also another piece of evidence that Ruth turned over to the Commission that bolstered the CIA's version of Oswald in Mexico City. This is the handwritten draft, and handwritten copy of that draft, of a letter allegedly sent by Oswald to the Russian Embassy in Washington. This letter mentions his visit to the Cuban consulate and the Russian consulate in Mexico City. There have been four valuable discussions of this letter and its versions: by Carol Hewett in *Probe*, Vol. 4 No. 3, p. 16; by Jerry Rose, in *The Fourth Decade*, November of 1999, p. 5; by John Armstrong in *Harvey and Lee*, pps. 760–62; and by Jim Douglass, in *JFK and the Unspeakable*, pps. 227–234. As John Armstrong notes, whoever wrote the letter had access to information that it is difficult to believe Oswald could have

known, like the transfer of personnel from the Cuban consulate 7 weeks before it happened. Another notable oddity mentioned by Hewett is that the FBI returned the alleged Oswald handwritten draft to Ruth Paine! While, as Hewett also notes, Ruth's handwritten copy of the first Oswald draft has disappeared from the National Archives. The Russians felt the letter was a forgery, or it was dictated to Oswald, in order to lay the blame for the assassination at their feet.(Douglass, p. 230). Recall, when the KGB first met with Richard Case Nagell, this is what they feared most about the rumors they had heard.

149 Affidavit of H. W. Reed dated 12/2/63.
150 FBI Airtel of 12/13/63, which suggests how to proceed with the package.
151 Ibid.
152 Author's 2012 interview with Carol Hewett.
153 FBI Memorandum of 12/16/63 by Sebastian LaTona.
154 Stovall Exhibit B, WC Vol. 21, p. 593.
155 Interview of 4/13/78, pps. 23–25.
156 FBI Series 62–109090, WC HQ File, Section 28, pps. 2,3. Available at Mary Ferrell Foundation Web Site.
157 Jones, Steve. "The Testimony of Marina Oswald before the Orleans Parish Grand Jury." *Probe*, Vol. 7 No. 3, p. 3.
158 See, Carol Hewett's two part essay in *Probe*, Vol. 4 No. 1, p. 21, and Vol. 4 No 2, p.12.
159 See CE 401 for her calendar, note especially the month of March; see WC Vol. 9, pgs 358–59 for her bewildering explanation, see also an article by Jerry Rose in *The Third Decade*, January 1990, p. 14, on this subject which casts aspersions on her strained explication.
160 *Probe*, Vol. 5 No. 1, p. 14.
161 Hosty, p. 38.
162 WC Vol. 3, pps. 85–86.
163 CBS News, *Who Killed JFK? The Final Chapter*, broadcast in 1993.
164 *Probe op. cit.* , Vol. 5 No. 1, p. 11.
165 NODA Memorandum of 6/27/67, interview of Ken Elliot.
166 NODA Memorandum of 10/9/68, by Andrew Sciambra to Garrison.
167 Ibid.
168 *Probe*, Vol. 3 No. 3, p. 24.
169 See Garrison, pps. 118–20.
170 *Probe*, Vol. 4 No. 4, p. 8.
171 FBI Teletype of 3/5/67, from New Orleans to the Director.
172 This book is at the Harold Weisberg collection at Hood College online.
173 Interview with Baumler by Fensterwald and J. Gary Shaw of 12/30/81.
174 From CIA Memo of Marguerite Stevens to Deputy Chief, SRS, of 9/12/67.
175 Dempsey interview with Bill Davy and the author in New Orleans in 1994.
176 Interview of Newbrough by Bill Davy on April 3, 1995.
177 Garrison, p. 84.
178 WC Vol. 11, p. 335.
179 Garrison, pps. 85–86.
180 Mellen, *Jim Garrison: His Life and Times*, p. 117.
181 *Probe*, Vol. 6 No. 4, p. 4.
182 Garrison, pps. 86–87. Garrison's critics have used every angle to discount this written evidence. One of them is that the signature was written on the last line of the register, therefore it could have been added later. This overlooks the fact that unless each line on a page is full, there is always an extra line available to "add on" a signature.
183 Interview of Joan Mellen with Garrision investigator Numa Bertel, 10/9/2000.

[184] The cards were made exhibits at the trial. For the arrest record, see Hurt, p. 275.

[185] Joan Mellen notes some of the factual basis for this legacy in her book *A Farewell to Justice*. See p. 122 in the text, and p. 429 in her End Notes.

[186] NODA Memorandum of 12/24/67 from Garrison to staff.

[187] *Newsday*, March 7, 1967.

[188] Novel vs. Garrison et al; deposition by Gordon Novel, p. 713.

[189] FBI memorandum of 6/10/67.

[190] Valentine, *The Strength of the Wolf* (London: Verso, 2004), pps. 312–14.

[191] FBI Memorandum of 3/5/67.

[192] Memorandum of 3/20/64 from Hubert and Griffin to Chief Counsel J. Lee Rankin.

[193] WC Vol. 14, p. 330 ff.

[194] Author's 1991 phone interview with Gary Schoener, who worked for Garrison.

[195] Walthers's Supplementary Investigation Report of 11/23/63

[196] WC Vol. 19, pps. 483–84.

[197] Corrections to original affidavit by Mercer for Garrison, dated 1/18/68.

[198] Corrections to the FBI report by Mercer for Garrison, dated 1/15/68.

[199] See the DVD *The Garrison Tapes* by John Barbour. Near the end of the film, Garrison discusses this point.

[200] Garrison, pps. 205–06.

[201] Mellen, *A Farewell to Justice*, p. 83.

[202] Memorandum from Jim Garrison to L.J. Delsa and Bob Buras, 10/20/77.

[203] Interview with Samuel Exnicios by Joan Mellen, 1/8/02.

[204] Mellen, op. cit., p. 95.

[205] Flammonde, p. 167.

[206] Statement of Clyde Johnson to Lou Ivon and Jim Alcock, 4/5/67.

[207] Statement of Edward McMillan to Lou Ivon, 4/11/67.

[208] DiEugenio, James. "What Harry Is Hiding." *Probe*, Vol. 3 No. 6, p. 18.

[209] February 24, 1967; the station was WAFB, also on February 24.

[210] The Russo episode is from Garrison, pp. 151–56.

[211] Popkin, "Garrison's Case," p. 25.

[212] Ibid. The man Russo said he saw was not clean–shaven. This is why he asked that whiskers be added to the picture. See also Kirkwood, pp. 144–145.

Chapter 11

[1] Phelan, "Rush to Judgment," p. 22

[2] Author's interview in New Orleans with Dempsey in 1994.

[3] *Baton–Rouge State–Times*, February 18, 1967.

[4] Ibid.

[5] Ibid., February 20, 1967.

[6] Garrison, pps. 132–36.

[7] Stone and Sklar, pgs.96–99.

[8] Garrison, p. 138.

[9] Flammonde, p. 33.

[10] Hurt, p. 264.

[11] The first and last quotes are from Milton Brener, *The Garrison Case* (New York: Clarkson N. Potter, 1969) p. 84; the second quote is from Garrison's *Playboy* interview, p. 60; the third

quote is from Rosemary James and Jack Wardlaw, *Plot or Politics?* (New Orleans: Pelican Publishing House, 1967),p.39.

[12] NODA Memorandum of Ivon and Sciambra to Garrison, dated 2/28/67.

[13] William Davy interview with Lou Ivon 4/7/95.

[14] Marrs, pp. 502–503.

[15] *Baton Rouge State–Times*, 2/28/67.

[16] Garrison, p. 141.

[17] NODA Memorandum of 12/11/67, Garrison to Alcock.

[18] Flammonde, p. 36.

[19] Author's interview with Frank Minyard, 1/31/92. That controversy engulfed even Robert Kennedy. He called the Chetta residence and wanted to speak to the coroner about Ferrie's death. See Talbot, p. 322.

[20] Palmer letter to Mellen of 6/18/01, and her interview with him of 8/9/02. Dr. S. Pittelli also questions Chetta's autopsy. See the exchange between him, Stephen Roy, and Dave Reitzes at Greg Parker's "Reopen Kennedy Case" web site.

[21] Hinckle and Turner, pps. 270, 321.

[22] Electronic Assassinations Newsletter, Issue No. 2, "JFK and the Cuban Connection" by Dick Russell.

[23] *Probe* Vol. 3 No. 6, p. 20.

[24] Epstein, *The Assassination Chronicles*, p. 195.

[25] NODA Memorandum of 2/26/67, from Ivon to Garrison.

[26] Author's 1995 interview with the late HSCA investigator Al Gonzalez in Los Angeles.

[27] Op cit, *Probe*.

[28] Ibid. In Fonzi's book, he does not get this detailed about the photos. But the HSCA summary written by the staff interrogating DeTorres, led by attorney Bill Triplett, did go further.

[29] Fonzi, p. 234.

[30] *The Losers*, p. 398, Arlington House, New Rochelle, NY,1969.

[31] Although, through the work of ace archives researcher Peter Vea, I know this man's name; in deference to the wishes of Fonzi and Gonzalez, I will not reveal it here.

[32] Fonzi, p. 239.

[33] *True Magazine*, April 1975; 1995 author interview with Marchetti in his Virginia office.

[34] *Inside Edition*, February 5, 1992. Bill O'Reilly's report on this was furnished to him by Fonzi. (Author's 1993 interview with Fonzi.)

[35] Garrison, p. 136.

[36] Peter Vea sent me an ad in one of the local papers that Garrison clipped.

[37] DiEugenio, James. "Connick to Turn over the Garrison Files?" *Probe,* Vol. 3 No. 4, p. 3.

[38] Ibid.

[39] Harold Weisberg letter to Andrew Sciambra, 12/28/68.

[40] *Ramparts,* April of 1976, p. 8.

[41] Garrison, *Playboy* interview.

[42] *Probe*, Vol. 4 No. 4, p. 11.

[43] Ibid, p. 17.

[44] Ibid.

[45] Gurvich's grand jury testimony of June 28, 1967.

[46] Gurvich's grand jury testimony of July 12, 1967.

[47] Op cit, *Probe*.

[48] Author's 1996 interview with a confidential source. He is confidential for reasons stated in the text.

[49] This early information about Gordon Novel is from the Novel file of Jim Garrison, plus an unpublished manuscript called *The Mysterious Mr. Novel* co–authored by Irv Yarg. Both use Lou Ivon's extensive check of Novel's police record.

[50] See FBI memorandum of 4/20/67 in which Novel explains more about the Houma raid being Agency sanctioned as a lease deal between Schlumberger's oil exploration company and the CIA. In this report, Novel states that both he and Sergio Arcacha Smith are still employed by the CIA in 1967.

[51] Interview with Novel in Los Angeles in early 2007; Yarg, p. 5.

[52] Flammonde, p. 102.

[53] The information about this recruitment meeting by Dulles was conveyed to the author in a 1997 interview with Lars Hansson at the Beverly Hills Hotel. In the 80s Hansson became a companion of Novel and his friend John Lear in Las Vegas. Lars talked about his relations with both men in a 1993 issue of *Steamshovel Press*, No. 8.

[54] Pease, Lisa. "Gordon Novel: Agent Against Garrison." *Probe*, Vol. 5 No. 5, p. 10.

[55] Pease, Lisa. "Gordon Novel: My Dinner with Allen." *Probe*, Vol. 4 No. 5, p. 26.

[56] This important series appeared in *Probe*, Vol. 4 No. 5 and No. 6, and concluded in Vol. 5 No. 5.

[57] Researcher Michael Levy discovered these at the AARC and showed them to me on a 1993 visit to his home in Washington, D.C. Novel admitted he also communicated with Richard Helms by telegram in his deposition for his lawsuit. He would sometimes request his salary be forwarded. See *Probe*, Vol. 4 No. 5, p. 27.

[58] *Probe*, Vol. 5 No. 5, p. 11.

[59] Ibid; See also Flammonde, p.97.

[60] Ibid, *Probe*, p. 12.

[61] *Probe*, Vol. 4 No. 5, p. 26.

[62] *Probe,* Vol. 5 No. 5, p. 12.

[63] Ibid, p. 34.

[64] Flammonde, p. 97.

[65] *New Orleans States–Item*, 3/22/67.

[66] This CIA orchestrated journalistic campaign in smearing Garrison was revealed in Novel's private correspondence with a deceased Kennedy researcher.

[67] *New Orleans States–Item*, 3/27/67.

[68] Ibid., 6/28/67.

[69] *New Orleans States–Item*, 3/27/67.

[70] *Probe*, Vol. 4, No. 4, p. 10.

[71] *Probe*, Vol. 3 No. 4, p. 17.

[72] Joan Mellen interviews with Lou Ivon 5/27/01, and John Volz, 5/21/98.

[73] *New Orleans States–Item*, 3/2/67; Hurt p. 281.

[74] Hurt, p. 281.

[75] On the controversy over P.O. Box 19106, see Flammonde, pp. 227–31. The entry in Oswald's book was most intriguing, since Dallas did not have post office box numbers that high in 1963. Garrison, p. 147.

[76] Garrison, p. 148. This ties in with Ferrie's comment to Russo in October 1963, "We will get him and it won't be long." Popkin, "Garrison's Case," p. 28.

[77] *New Orleans Magazine*, July, 1967, p. 59.

[78] Talbot, p. 326.

[79] *Probe*, Vol. 4 No. 5, p. 21.

[80] Hougan, *Spooks*, p. 124.

[81] Author's interview with Steinberg at his home in Virginia in 1993. In his book *Kennedy Justice*, Victor Navasky also mentions this point on p. 456.

[82] *Probe*, op cit.

[83] NODA Memorandum of 5/24/67, Martin to Garrison.

[84] Case of Novel vs. Garrison and *Playboy*, his deposition at page 534.

[85] See William Davy's article at ctka.net, "Shoot Him Down." This promise appears to have been a cruel joke, since there is no evidence this gift was ever transferred.

[86] Ibid.

[87] Author's 1994 interview with Sal Panzeca in New Orleans.

[88] NODA affidavit of Marlene Mancuso, 5/20/67; Mellen, pps. 192–93.

[89] NODA Memorandum of Kimble, 10/10/67. Also William Turner, "The Garrison Commission," *Ramparts*, January 1968, p. 68.

[90] Oster interview with Joan Mellen, 10/01/2001.

[91] *Probe*, Vol, 4, No. 4, p. 10.

[92] *Probe*, Vol. 4 No. 5, p. 18.

[93] Ibid.

[94] Ibid.

[95] NODA Memorandum from Bill Boxley to Jim Garrison, undated.

[96] Author's 1994 interview with John Volz at his office in New Orleans. Volz wanted to test Bundy, so he asked him what color the pamphlets were. Bundy came up with this rather unusual color. Volz later found out that, indeed, some of the flyers that Oswald distributed were yellow. Today, they are preserved as an exhibit at the Royal New Orleans Collection.

[97] "The JFK Conspiracy: The Case of Jim Garrison" is on You Tube.

[98] For an overview of what happened to Sheridan's witnesses after the program aired see Garrison, pps. 169–71; Flammonde pps. 304–14; and Garrison's *Playboy* interview.

[99] *Probe op. cit.*, Vol. 4 No. 5, p. 18.

[100] New Orleans Police Department statement of Bundy's cell mate Arthur King, May 22, 1967.

[101] Ibid. It should be noted that although Bundy had a probation record for breaking into cigarette machines for petty change for narcotics, at this point, he was in jail voluntarily since he feared consequences of his addiction. This would appear to further undercut the accusations of Cancler and Torres. (NODA memorandum of 3/16/67).

[102] Op cit, NODA memorandum from Boxley to Garrison.

[103] Affidavit of Beaubouef, April 12, 1967. When I interviewed Beaubouef's attorney Hugh Exnicios in New Orleans in 1995, he told me that he allowed Shaw's lawyers into his office to transcribe the tape he had made of the Loisel–Beaubouef discussion. He then made a mistake and left the office to get something to eat. When he returned, both the tape and the lawyers were gone.

[104] Phelan, *Rush to Judgment,* p. 22.

[105] *Baton Rouge Morning Advocate,* February 25, 1967.

[106] *Probe*, Vol. 6 No. 4, p. 5 and p. 32. A much longer version of this report was in this issue.

[107] *Probe*, Vol. 3 No. 3, p. 24.

[108] Kirkwood, pps. 161–73.

[109] Ibid.

[110] Author's 1993 phone interview with James Phelan.

[111] Davy, pgs.121–22.

[112] Op cit., Kirkwood.

[113] E mail message from Matt Herron in 2009.

[114] Mellen, *A Farewell To Justice*, p. 144.

[115] Lyon Garrison let the author copy these and many other exhibits in 1994.

[116] *Probe*, Vol. 6 No. 5, p. 26. At a meeting in San Francisco, I showed these Garrison–marked transcripts to a gathering of Kennedy researchers. They all agreed that Russo was not being prompted and were surprised that Phelan would present it as otherwise. What Phelan and Shaw's lawyers did was use the March 12 hypnosis session as the first one, where Dr. Fatter refers to a "TV screen," in order to leave the impression that he is leading Russo. But the first session was March 1, where Russo came up with all the details of the date, place, and people including the "big guy" with "white hair," "Clem Bertrand." Again, these documents are all right out of Garrison's files—before anyone else could adulterate them for their own agenda.

[117] Biles, p. 44.

[118] Ibid. Biles brief but incisive discussion of this issue is one of the best in the literature.

[119] See the You Tube series, "The JFK Conspiracy: The Case of Jim Garrison."

[120] WC Vol. 11, pps. 370–71.

[121] Russell, pps. 288–89.

[122] Ibid., p. 367.

[123] Kurtz, "Lee Harvey Oswald in New Orleans: A Reappraisal," p. 17.

[124] Flammonde, pps. 23–24.

[125] Interview by Peter Vea and William Davy in 1994 of Niles Peterson in New Orleans. Michael Kurtz in his book *The JFK Assassination Debates*, notes that a Cuban he encountered, Santos Miguel Gonzalez, recalled the gathering at Ferrie's. He also said that Shaw, Ferrie, and Oswald were there. But he denied there was any discussion of assassinating Kennedy that night. Which is not necessarily inconsistent with Russo's recall since he said this discussion occurred when almost everyone was gone (Kurtz, p. 164).

[126] "The J.F.K. Conspiracy," *Newsweek*, May 15, 1967, p. 36.

[127] Ibid., p. 40.

[128] Material on Aynesworth's activities in Dallas are primarily from Joesten, *Garrison*, pp. 100–5.

[129] WR, pps. 187–88.

[130] *Probe*, Vol. 4 No. 4, p. 12.

[131] Ibid.

[132] Confidential CIA memorandum of October 10, 1963.

[133] Davy, p. 133.

[134] New Orleans Police Report of June 12, 1967. As noted in the footnote above, Exnicios told me that Shaw's lawyers absconded with the tape. If this is accurate, then they may have had it altered.

[135] The Western Union teletype is dated May 13, 1967, and it includes a "rough draft copy" of the piece that appeared in the May 15 *Newsweek*. The elipses are in the original.

[136] Detective D. K. Rodgers report to Captain W. F. Dyson, of 2/27, in Dallas Police files.

[137] Ibid.

[138] Ibid.

[139] Ibid.

[140] Detective D. K. Rodgers report to Captain W. F. Dyson of 3/3, in Dallas Police files.

[141] Flammonde, p. 97. There is a CIA memorandum of June 6, 1967, based on an FBI report, which says that "Other sources have stated that Gordon Novel and Arcacha Smith have 'marque' letters granting them immunity and are allegedly employed by the CIA." A letter of marque is one which grants the bearer immunity from committing a crime since it is in his line of duty.

[142] Op. cit., Rodgers report of March 3.

[143] *Probe op. cit.,* Vol. 4 No. 4, p. 11.

[144] Ibid., p. 13.

[145] Ibid., p. 14.

[146] NODA Memorandum of July 13, 1967, from Andew Sciambra to Jim Garrison.

[147] Op cit, *Probe*, p. 14.

[148] Mellen, *A Farewell to Justice*, p. 235.

[149] Navasky, p. 405.

[150] Garrison, p. 166.

[151] Hougan, *Spooks*, p. 124.

[152] *New York Times*, May 16, 1947.

[153] *New York Times*, February 24, 1997.

[154] *New York Times*, June 2, 1960.

[155] Navasky, p. 456.

[156] *New York Times*, January 15, 1995.

[157] Navasky, pp. 412–413.

[158] Ibid., p. 457.

[159] Op cit., Hougan.

[160] Ibid.

[161] Ibid., p. 126.

[162] Ibid., p. 128. It is important to recall that RFK had a supervising role in Operation MONGOOSE at this time, which explains his access to the CIA.

[163] Ibid., p. 126.

[164] Ibid.

[165] Ibid., p. 129.

[166] Ibid., p. 128. As we shall see, the first tarring of Garrison's name with Mob connections, particularly Carlos Marcello, began with a story in the September 8, 1967, issue of *Life*. Not only did Sheridan have ties to the magazine, so did another Shaw ally, reporter David Chandler. Sheridan uses the Marcello tactic in his book, *The Fall and Rise of Jimmy Hoffa*, on page 417.

[167] *Probe*, Vol. 4, No. 5, p. 24.

[168] Ibid.

[169] Ibid.

[170] Vincent Bugliosi, *Reclaiming History*, (W.W. Norton and Company: New York, 2007) p. 1175.

[171] The judge's order is in Flammonde, p. 212.

[172] Two favorable articles are Turner and Popkin, already noted; Powledge is also favorable.

Chapter 12

[1] Garrison, p. 139.

[2] Popkin, "Garrison's Case," p. 19. Andrews appeared on the NBC show to deny that Clay Shaw was Clay Bertrand, after which NBC narrator Frank McGee intoned that NBC knew the "real" Clay Bertrand and was withholding his identity for his own protection. Andrews was soon pushed to reveal his identity and said Bertrand was New Orleans barkeeper, Eugene C. Davis, who vehemently denied the charges and gave Garrison a sworn statement to that effect. See Flammonde, pp. 307–8.

[3] *New York Post*, March 2, 1967.

[4] *New York Times*, June 3, 1967.

[5] *New Orleans Times–Picayune*, May 6, 1967.

[6] This program in on You Tube.

[7] This interview is available at the JFK Lancer web site.

⁸ It is important to note here that Allen Dulles was one of the originators of Operation Mockingbird, the CIA's program to control the media. Therefore, he knew how to develop a program for his asset Novel.

⁹ Some residents of McLean today are Elliot Abrams of Iran/Contra fame, Frank Carlucci of the Carlyle Group, former Vice–President Dick Cheney, Newt Gingrich, conservative political operative Bill Kristol, former Secretary of State Colin Powell, and Supreme Court Justices Anthony Scalia and Anthony Kennedy.

¹⁰ From the reporting notes of Julian Granger of Scripps Howard News Service.

¹¹ From a 1994 interview with a source who knew the man who owned the house.

¹² See Anthony Summers, *Official and Confidential*, p. 244. According to Novel, there were also people in the White House who wanted him to puruse this lawsuit.

¹³ Gordon Novel interview by Dave Emory of 10/29/84, on *The Expressway Show*. This interview is available at Spitfire.list.com as program number 253. The title is "The Watergate Tapes Revisited."

¹⁴ Ibid. This lawsuit failed. But as we shall see it was part of an endgame strategy that the Agency had to ultimately destroy Garrison both personally and professionally. The overall strategy largely succeeded.

¹⁵ *New Orleans States–Item*, March 11, 1970.

¹⁶ Op Cit, Dave Emory tape.

¹⁷ *Probe* Vol. 4 No. 5, p. 18.

¹⁸ Journal of *Life* reporter Richard Billings, p. 82.

¹⁹ Navasky, pps. 456–57.

²⁰ Ibid., p. 491.

²¹ CIA Memorandum of May 8, 1967 by Richard Lansdale.

²² Op. cit, *Probe*, p. 21.

²³ Note from Miller to Lansdale to cover document enclosures, May 31, 1968.

²⁴ Novel Chronology accompanying the unpublished manuscript "The Mysterious Mr. Novel."

²⁵ *Probe op. cit.,* Vol. 4 No. 5, p. 26.

²⁶ NODA Memorandum of May 11, 1973, Ivon to Garrison.

²⁷ One example of this is Ferrie's friend and Bay of Pigs veteran Julian Buznedo. When I contacted him in Denver, he told me that he was interviewed by two government agents in 1967 *before* Garrision called him.

²⁸ *Probe,* Vol. 4 No. 5, p. 16.

²⁹ Ibid.

³⁰ Ibid.

³¹ Litchfield interview with Joan Mellen, January 30, 2002.

³² Merryl Hudson interview with Joan Mellen, February 3, 2001.

³³ WR p. 324.

³⁴ See Meagher, p. 387; Gary Shaw with Larry Harris, *Cover Up* (Cleburne, Texas: privately published, 1976) p. 109.

³⁵ CD 1553; also Fonzi, pps. 114–15.

³⁶ Fonzi, p. 114.

³⁷ Author's interview with Delsa in 1994 in New Orleans.

³⁸ Benson, pps. 168–69.

³⁹ Author's 1998 interview with Ray Marcus in Los Angeles.

⁴⁰ FBI Memorandum of March 23, 1967 from Los Angeles office. Schiller lived there at the time.

⁴¹ In one of David Lifton's derogatory articles about Garrison written at the time, he ridiculed a meeting he had with Garrison in Los Angeles. (June 6, 1968 in the journal *Open City*) Lifton

met Garrison at the Century Plaza Hotel in October of 1967 and he said he had "never seen a man so utterly frightened, and so convinced that he was constantly followed, bugged, etc." This shows how uninformed Lifton was about Garrison. For Hall told Jaffe that the LAPD had recruited an employee of the Century Plaza Hotel to spy on Garrison when he was there on investigatory trips to Los Angeles. (Memo from Jaffe to Garrison of 4/30/68).

[42] Memorandum from Jaffe to Garrison of March 20, 1968.

[43] FBI Airtel of January 15, 1968.

[44] *Probe*, Vol. 5 No. 3, p. 7.

[45] Memorandum from Jaffe to Garrison of 4/30/68.

[46] Op Cit, *Probe*, p. 33.

[47] Author's 1997 interview with Kunkin in Los Angeles.

[48] *Ramparts*, April 1967, "The Plot Thickens" p. 8.

[49] Letter from Guthman to this author dated August 8, 1993.

[50] Billings Journal, p. 20.

[51] *Los Angles Times*, July 14, 1967, "New Orleans: Justice is on Trial."

[52] Navasky, pps. 468–69.

[53] Justice Department Memorandum of September 22, 1967.

[54] *Probe*, Vol. 4 No. 5, p. 20.

[55] Ibid., p. 21.

[56] Ibid., p. 22.

[57] Ibid.

[58] CIA Memorandum for the Record of the Garrison Group dated Septemeber 20, 1967.

[59] Ibid.

[60] Bill Simpich has surveyed the Rocca collection on Garrison. In an e-mail communication with the author on April 21, 2012, he said it would take a person a number of years, perhaps a decade, to read the library of documents Rocca eventually collected on the Garrison inquiry.

[61] When the author characterizes the memo of this meeting as "sketchy," he is being generous. The notes of this meeting take about one minute to read.

[62] Memorandum for the Record, Garrison Group, 9/26/67.

[63] Memorandum for the Record, 9/29/67. It is surprising that the ARRB could not get CIA to completely declassify this document, follow the chain of these memoranda to their conclusion, or interview anyone who was at these meetings.

[64] Marchetti said this on more than one occasion, including an aforementioned interview with this author.

[65] *New Orleans States–Item*, April 10, 1967.

[66] Ibid., April 11, 1967.

[67] Ibid., April 25, 1967.

[68] *Baton Rouge States–Times*, February 27, 1967.

[69] Flammonde, p. 120.

[70] Ibid.

[71] *Probe op. cit.*, Vol. 4 No. 5, p. 25.

[72] Ibid.

[73] Ibid.

[74] *New Orleans States–Item*, August 8, 1967.

[75] Ibid., May 22, 1968,

[76] Interview of Baumler by Bud Fensterwald and J. Gary Shaw, December 30, 1981.

[77] Interview of Baumler by Harold Weisberg, April 9, 1968, forwarded to Jim Garrison.

[78] Op. cit., Interview of Baumler by Fensterwlad and Shaw.

[79] Op. cit., Weisberg's interview of Baumler.

[80] Ibid.

[81] *Probe op. cit.*, Vol. 4 No. 5, p. 22.

[82] Ibid.

[83] NODA Memorandum of interview of Daphne Rosen to Garrison, September 16, 1968.

[84] In a January 26, 1967 interview with Garrison assistant Charles Ward, Chandler essentially admitted this.

[85] Flammonde, pps. 60–62.

[86] Tom Bethell diary entry of October 6, 1967.

[87] Davy, p. 154; Mellen, *A Farewell to Justice*, pps. 255–59.

[88] Davy, p. 153.

[89] Garrison, p. 164.

[90] See unpublished manuscript by Garrison called *Coup d'Etat* p. 16ff; also quoted in Mellen, op. cit., p. 255.

[91] This "Mob influenced" myth was finally demolished by the author at a talk he did at the 1995 COPA Conference in Washington called "Garrision, the Media, and the Mob." That talk is repeated and amplified by William Davy in his book *Let Justice be Done* on pages 153–67.

[92] Author's 1997 interview with Mort Sahl in Los Angeles.

[93] *Probe op. cit.* Vol. 4 No. 5, p. 25.

[94] Ibid.

[95] Ibid.

[96] Ibid, p. 32.

[97] Ibid.

[98] Garrison, p. 173.

[99] Interview with Boxley by George Rennar in 1971.

[100] CIA Memorandum 4/26/68, Domestic Contacts Service.

[101] Author's 1996 phone interview with Harold Weisberg.

[102] Ibid.

[103] Ibid.

[104] Flammonde, p. 198.

[105] *New York Post,* December 21, 1967.

[106] Flammonde, p. 200. For the record, there is little doubt that McIntire's group was very conservative.

[107] Ibid.

[108] *Probe,* Vol. 3 No. 6, p. 19.

[109] For reasons to be stated in the next chapter, I do not like using Bethell or his diary for anything on the Garrison case. But in this instance, this entry seems well–documented and it jibes with other information and interviews I have done on the subject of Bradley.

[110] Hinckle, p. 268.

[111] Ibid.

[112] Ibid, pps. 282–83.

[113] Author's 1991 interview with Steve Jaffe in Dallas.

[114] Hinckle, pps. 272–73.

[115] Author's 2000 interview with Harold Weisberg.

[116] Letter of January 4, 1969 by Paul Rothermel. Rothermel worked for H. L. Hunt.

[117] In that respect, it resembles a forerunner of the infamous Torbitt Document.

[118] File memorandum of Paul Rothermel, January 19, 1969.

[119] File memorandum of Harold Weisberg, January 9, 1969.

[120] Author's 1996 interview with Ivon; author's 2000 interview with Weisberg.

[121] Garrison, p. 190.

[122] Author's interview with Lou Ivon, 1994; author's interview with Vince Salandria in 1995. As expressed to me by Salandria, the problem Garrison had with the saboteur Boxley was simple: Garrison actually liked Boxley personally. This blinded him to what the man was doing to him. From studying Garrison's life, this was a serious character fault he had.

[123] Garrison, p. 192; DVD, *The Garrison Tapes*.

[124] Author's conversation with Marcus in Los Angeles in 1997.

[125] Author's 1991 interview with Steve Jaffe in Dallas.

[126] To show just how bad this all got, in a letter to Joan Mellen dated April 29, 1998, Weisberg claimed he saw Rose manufacturing evidence.

[127] Author's 1996 interview with Ray Marcus and Maggie Field in Los Angeles.

[128] NODA Memorandum of December 20, 1968, Burton to Garrison.

[129] Author's 1992 phone interview with Vince Salandria.

[130] In his 1971 interview with Rennar, Boxley revealed that there was a "Garrison desk" at CIA. This very likely was the previously described Garrison Group.

Chapter 13

[1] Flammonde, p. 213.

[2] Ibid., p. 233.

[3] Ibid., p. 239.

[4] Ibid., p. 240.

[5] Ibid., p. 241.

[6] Ibid., pp. 244 ff. At this time, Dymond actually had his picture taken clutching the Warren Report to his chest. Joesten, "Highlights," p. 54. For a complete chronicle of the incredible delaying tactics of the defense, see Flammonde, pp. 233–246.

[7] Flammonde, p. 235.

[8] Ibid., p. 244.

[9] Ibid., p. 212.

[10] The Kohn episode is described in Flammonde, p. 235.

[11] Ibid., p. 299.

[12] Ibid. In his statement to the DA's office on charges that he was Clay Bertrand, Davis characterized them as "utterly and completely false and malicious and damnable." Ibid., p. 308.

[13] Popkin, "Garrison's Case," p. 20.

[14] Turner, "Garrison Commission," p. 68.

[15] Author's 1992 phone interview with Lou Ivon.

[16] Author's 1997 interview with Art Kunkin in Los Angeles.

[17] Ibid.

[18] *Westword Magazine*, Volume 16 No. 13, November 25, 1992, p. 21.

[19] Author's 1994 interview with Panzeca in New Orleans.

[20] Author's 1992 phone interview with Vincent Salandria.

[21] Kirkwood, pp. 246–47.

[22] *National Review*, December 16, 1991.

[23] Author's 1992 phone interview with Lou Ivon.

[24] Bethell also disparagingly wrote about his experiences with Garrison case in his book *The Electric Windmill* (pp. 60–71). One has to wonder just why Bethell joined Garrison's staff in the first place.

[25] In a generally faultless performance, Shaw slipped only once. At a very early press conference he referred to the alleged assassin as "Harvey Lee Oswald." As researchers know, the only instances in which Oswald had been referred to in this way were two cases of Oswald impersonations and in some intelligence files. See Weisberg, *Oswald,* p. 233; and Melanson, pp. 124–25.

[26] Kirkwood, p. 491.

[27] Joesten, "Highlights," p. 48.

[28] Garrison, p. 85. Other witnesses included William Morris, who was introduced to Shaw by Eugene Davis.

[29] Joesten, *Garrison,* p. 80.

[30] Garrison, pp. 117–119.

[31] Having been through most of Garrison's surviving files the author can attest to the fact that the DA could have called more witnesses on each of these evidentiary points. For instance, in William Davy's accumulated archives, he now has marked a combined total of 16 witnesses who say that Shaw used the Bertrand alias.

[32] From what we know today about the electronic monitoring of Garrison's office by the FBI, it would not be surprising if Shaw's lawyers knew this about Garrison's health and decided to press for a trial at that appropriate time.

[33] On the number of jurors, see the *New Orleans States–Item,* February 5, 1969; on the number of days, see the *New Orleans Times–Picayune,* March 1, 1969. Most prospective jurors were dismissed for one of two reasons: financial duress (jurors were not paid) or bias toward one side or the other.

[34] CIA Memorandum from CI/R & A to Sara Hall, Security, February 11, 1969,

[35] CIA memo from Angleton to Hoover and Sam Papich, February 28, 1969.

[36] *Probe,* Vol. 4 No. 5, p. 21.

[37] CIA routing sheet of February 12, 1969.

[38] *Probe op. cit.,* Vol. 4 No. 5, p. 32.

[39] Russell, p. 436.

[40] Davy, p. 310; Mellen, *A Farewell to Justice,* p. 301.

[41] Author's 1994 interview with McGehee in Jackson.

[42] Davy, p. 301.

[43] *Probe,* Vol. 3 No. 5, p. 25.

[44] Kirkwood, p. 228.

[45] Author's 1994 interview with Volz in New Orleans.

[46] The Spiesel appearance is described in Kirkwood, pp. 231–242, and Garrison, *On the Trail,* pp. 236–237. This testimony does not have a stenographic transcription available.

[47] *Probe,* Vol. 4 No. 4, p. 13.

[48] Author's 1991 phone interview with Jim Alcock.

[49] Ibid.

[50] Kirkwood, p. 231.

[51] Ibid., pp. 231–232.

[52] Ibid., p. 232.

[53] Ibid., p. 233.

[54] Ibid.

[55] Ibid., p. 235.

[56] Garrison, p. 236.

57 Ibid, p. 237.
58 Ibid.
59 Ibid.
60 Ibid.
61 *Probe,* op. cit.,
62 Ibid.
63 Letter from Ed Wegmann to Elmer Gertz, March 12, 1969.
64 This actually understates Herron's reaction to Russo's testimony.
65 Kirkwood, p. 276.
66 Garrison, pp. 237–238.
67 Kirkwood, p. 295.
68 *New Orleans States–Item,* February 13, 1969; Kirkwood, pp. 296–298.
69 Kirkwood, pp. 308–309.
70 Ibid., pp. 306–308.
71 Ibid., p. 306.
72 HSCA interview with Joe Oster, January 27, 1978.
73 Shaw trial transcript of February 17, 1969.
74 FBI Memorandum of May 10, 1967.
75 *New York Times,* March 3, 1967.
76 *New Orleans Times–Picayune,* February 23, 1969.
77 Memo by Finck to Director of Air Force Institute of Pathology, dated March 11, 1969.
78 Shaw trial transcript; Zapruder testified on February 13, Simmons on the fifteenth.
79 Shaw trial transcript, February 17, 1969.
80 Op. cit., Finck memo of 3/11/69.
81 Ibid.
82 McKnight, p. 166.
83 See the web site JFKcountercoup, entry dated February 12, 2012.
84 Author's 1991 interview with O'Connor in Dallas.
85 Except where noted, the above material about Finck's appearance at the trial is from Finck's testimony of February 24–25, 1969, Shaw trial transcript.
86 Biles, p. 151; Boswell's ARRB testimony of February 26, 1996.
87 Boswell's ARRB testimony of 2/26/96.
88 Ibid.
89 Ibid.
90 Ibid.
91 *Probe,* Vol. 3 No. 1, p. 13.
92 Two good discussions of Clark's attempts to uphold the collapsing official story at this time are the essay by Gary Aguilar and Cyril Wecht in the book *Trauma Room One,* pps 214–26; and the discussion in Doug Horne's book, *Inside the ARRB,* Vol. 1, pps.143–51.
93 *Probe,* Vol. 4 No. 4, p. 19.
94 *Maryland State Medical Journal,* March 1977.
95 Kirkwood, pp. 348–349.
96 Author's 1994 interview with Irvin Dymond in New Orleans. For Appel's story see the Shaw trial transcript of February 25, 1969.
97 Davy, p. 181.
98 The Habighorst episode is in Kirkwood, pp. 353–359; and Garrison, pp. 145, 159, 242–243.
99 Author's 1992 phone interview with Habighorst's widow, Elsie.
100 In Elsie Habighorst's possession. She has sent the author samples.
101 Op. cit., Habighorst interview. Habighorst's captain confirmed this.

[102] Ibid.

[103] Hurt, p. 275.

[104] Op. cit., Habighorst interview.

[105] Ibid.

[106] Habighorst interview.

[107] Habighorst was the kind of policeman who brought home stray animals and lost children; he would then make phone calls until he located the pet's owners and the children's parents. Letter from Habighorst's daughter, Karla Kemp, to the author, February 27, 1992.

[108] *New Orleans Times–Picayune,* February 20, 1969.

[109] Ibid.

[110] Ibid.

[111] Author's 1992 phone interview with Lou Ivon.

[112] *New Orleans Times–Picayune,* February 20, 1969.

[113] Ibid.; see also Garrison, p. 242.

[114] *New Orleans Times–Picayune,* February 20, 1969.

[115] Colloquy from *New Orleans Times–Picayune,* February 20, 1969.

[116] Garrison, p. 242. Haggerty himself seemed confused by his decision. The day after he made it, when Alcock asked him to reconsider, he based his continued stance on *Miranda,* not *Escobedo.* Yet, the day before, when it was explained that Shaw had his rights read to him *before* Habighorst interviewed him, Haggerty seemed to base his ruling on *Escobedo.* See Kirkwood, p. 360.

[117] *New Orleans Times–Picayune,* February 21, 1969. Habighorst took Haggerty's rebuke hard. He could not understand why his word was being questioned. Within a year of the trial, he retired from the force, and became a private investigator. When his vision began to fail, he became a steamship dispatcher out of his home. In 1980, he died of a heart attack, aged 47.

When I asked William Wegmann about Judge Haggerty's hostility to Habighorst's testimony, he referred me to Irvin Dymond. When I took it up with Dymond, he told me Haggerty knew Habighorst because he grew up in the same neighborhood as the judge's family. This is correct, but Haggerty may have made a grave error. Habighorst had two uncles who lived within two blocks of Haggerty. When they got in trouble, they asked Haggerty to bail them out. But Habighorst himself lived *two miles* from Haggerty and had no such history of run–ins with the law. Wegmann interview, February 18, 1992; Dymond interview, February 20, 1992; Elsie Habighorst interview, February 29, 1992.

Haggerty's attitude is even more odd in light of the fact that he did not believe Shaw. In an interview he did for a New Orleans documentary filmmaker shortly before he died, Haggerty said he thought "Shaw lied through his teeth" at the trial, that he did "a con job on the jury." The documentary, "He Must Have Something," by Stephen Tyler, was broadcast on WLAE–TV, February 9, 1992.

[118] *New Orleans Times–Picayune,* February 26, 1969; Popkin, "Garrison's Case," p. 20. By this time, Andrews had been willingly coopted by the defense. On the day he testified, he was accompanied to court by Phelan. (See photo, front page, *New Orleans Times–Picayune,* February 26, 1969.) It should be recalled that Andrews's original testimony about the Bertrand call, as well as his saying he feared for his life if he revealed the information, were corroborated by three sources. He told it to Mark Lane before he told it to Garrison, and he told it to Anthony Summers after he had told it to Garrison. See Turner, "Inquest," p. 24; Summers, p. 340. The fear explains why he would rather commit perjury than divulge Bertrand's real name.

[119] Kirkwood, p. 399.

[120] *New Orleans Times–Picayune,* February 27,1969.

[121] Ibid.

[122] Ibid.

[123] Ibid. Early in the trial, one of the Clinton witnesses, Henry Palmer, revealed that he had known Banister *before* the Clinton trip. When asked if Banister was with Ferrie and Oswald that day, Palmer said no. *New Orleans Times–Picayune,* February 7, 1969. Coupled with the sheriff's testimony about his conversation with the driver of the car (see Chapter 3), can there be any doubt the third man was Shaw?

[124] Kirkwood, p. 173.

[125] Ibid., pp. 400–401

[126] Marrs, p. 100.

[127] Shaw's testimony is from the trial transcript and *New Orleans Times–Picayune,* February 28, 1969.

[128] *New Orleans States–Item,* February 28, 1969.

[129] Kirkwood, p. 420.

[130] *New Orleans Times–Picayune,* March 1, 1969.

[131] Ibid.

[132] Ibid.

[133] Kirkwood, pp. 454–460.

[134] *New Orleans Times–Picayune,* March 1, 1969.

[135] Ibid.

[136] Kirkwood, p. 462.

[137] *Probe,* Vol. 5 No. 5, p. 34.

Chapter 14

[1] For a partial listing of these witnesses, see Davy pps. 185–86, Biles, pps. 124–25, and Mellen pps. 320–21.

[2] Biles, p. 120.

[3] Ibid.

[4] See the entry for this article at the Library of Congress for the Gurvich photo credit.

[5] See Sullivan, *The Bureau* (New York: W. W. Norton and Company, 1979), p. 93.

[6] CIA Memorandum of May 23, 1969.

[7] Shaw vs. Garrison, US Court of Appeals, Fifth Circuit, November 20, 1972.

[8] Garrison, p. 253.

[9] *Probe,* Vol. 4 No. 5, p. 13.

[10] Ibid., p. 14.

[11] Ibid., p. 15.

[12] Ibid., p. 13.

[13] Ibid., p. 15.

[14] Ibid., p. 13.

[15] Op. cit., Shaw v. Garrison.

[16] Ibid.

[17] Biles, p. 124.

[18] Ibid.

[19] Mellen, *A Farewell to Justice,* p. 334.

[20] Garrison, p. 264.

[21] Mellen, op. cit., p. 335.

[22] Garrison, p. 264.

23 Mellen, op. cit., p. 335.

24 Garrison, p. 258.

25 *Vancouver Sun*, May 24, 1972.

26 Tatro, Edgar, "The HSCA's Birth: An Outsider's View," *The Fourth Decade*, Volume 1, Number 4, p. 4.

27 Ibid.

28 Ibid.

29 Dick Russell, *On the Trail of the JFK Assassins,* (Skyhorse Publishing: New York, 2008) p. 103.

30 Garrison, p. 259.

31 Ibid.

32 Mellen, op. cit., p. 336.

33 Garrison, p. 266.

34 Ibid, pp. 269–70.

35 *New Orleans Times Picayune*, September 23, 1973.

36 Garrison, p. 271.

37 Ibid.

38 Mellen, op. cit., p. 334.

39 DiEugenio, James. "Connick vs. Garrison: Round Three." *Probe*, Vol. 2 No. 5, p. 3.

40 Ibid.

41 Ibid.

42 Ibid.

43 Ibid, p. 6.

44 Ibid, p. 3.

45 Ibid, p. 4. Luckily, after a protracted legal battle, the Review Board was able to get the Garrison files left in the office from Connick and into the National Archives.

46 Garrison, p. 271.

47 Russell, op, cit., p. 104.

48 Shaw versus Garrison, United States District Court, Eastern District of Louisiana, March 4, 1975. Since this was Christenberry's court, the panel used his dismissal of the Shaw case as a characterization of Garrison's investigation.

49 Letter from Weisberg to Joe Rault, January 7, 1973.

50 Robertson v. Wegmann, May 31, 1978, U.S. Supreme Court decision.

51 Ibid.

52 Author's 1994 interview with Connick in his New Orleans office.

53 *New Orleans States–Item*, October 29, 1969.

54 Garrison, p. 146.

55 Mellen, op. cit., p. 236.

56 Post by Jim Marrs on November 1, 2005 at JFK Assassination Forum on the Spartacus web site. Marrs interviewed Copeland in the seventies while he was a reporter in Fort Worth. It is interesting to note that in the online edition of this essay at the Mae Brussell Archive, Copeland actually refers to the two men as being from the Customs Department and Bureau of Narcotics.

57 See Chapter 1 of the online version of the essay at Mae Brussell Archive.

58 Ibid.

Chapter 15

1 *New Orleans States-Item*, March 15, 1968.

[2] DiEugenio, James. "The Sins of Robert Blakey: Part 1." *Probe*, Vol. 5 No. 6, p. 13.

[3] Ibid.

[4] Ibid., p. 14.

[5] Williams, John. "Interview with Richard Sprague." *Probe*, Vol. 7 No. 2, p. 17.

[6] Author's 1996 interview with HSCA lawyer Al Lewis in Lancaster, Pennsylvania.

[7] Op. Cit., *Probe*, p. 19.

[8] Ibid., p. 18.

[9] Ibid.

[10] Ibid., p. 22.

[11] *Probe*, Vol. 5 No. 6, p. 14.

[12] Ibid; also Tanenbaum interview on *Radio Parallax*, April 8, 2004.

[13] Op. Cit., *Probe*, p. 15.

[14] *Probe*, Vol. 3 No. 5, p. 23.

[15] Author's 1994 interview with L. J. Delsa in New Orleans.

[16] Bob Groden at the 1993 JFK Midwest Symposium in Chicago.

[17] Op. Cit., *Probe*, p. 24. In fairness to Schweiker, when I interviewed him in Washington in 1995, he said he did not recall saying this to Tanenbaum. He said his staff lawyer, Dave Marston, may have. Yet Tanenbaum states that when the information was revealed to him, only he and the senator were in the room.

[18] Ibid.

[19] This case was depicted in Tanenbaum's book *Badge of the Assassin*, which was made into a television film of the same name.

[20] Author's 1996 interview with Robert Tanenbaum in Beverly Hills.

[21] Werbell was an expert at designing what he called "suppressors" for rifles. See Hougan, *Spooks*, pps. 34–48, especially the footnote on page 36.

[22] *Probe*, Vol. 6 No. 5, p. 27.

[23] Hurt, p. 402.

[24] *Probe*, Vol. 2 No. 5, p. 13.

[25] *Probe*, Vol. 6 No. 5, p. 28.

[26] Fonzi's letter to the editor of Tony Summers' book, *Conspiracy*, dated October 1, 1979.

[27] HSCA Vol. 10, p. 200.

[28] Statement to Jim Garrison by A. H. Magruder, February 23, 1967.

[29] Bob Dorff at 2003 Lancer Conference; Dorff's private e–mail to the author in 2010.

[30] Author's 1995 phone interview with Gaeton Fonzi.

[31] Gibson, Donald. "Clay Shaw, Freeport Sulphur and the Eastern Establishment." *Probe*, Vol. 4 No. 1, p.17.

[32] Ibid, p. 20.

[33] Ibid.

[34] Lifton, David, ed., *Document Addendum to the Warren Report*, (El Segundo, CA. :Sightext Press, 1968), pps. 89–90.

[35] In fact, there is a photo of Whitney with John Foster Dulles taken in the fifties in the referenced Gibson article. Further, Whitney was the cousin and close friend of Tracy Barnes, Dulles' Golden Boy in the CIA, the man he entrusted the overthrow of Arbenz to in 1954.

[36] Fonzi, pps. 118–19.

[37] Author's 1991phone interview with Gary Schoener.

[38] Fonzi, p. 131.

[39] Ibid., p. 125.

[40] Ibid., p. 141.

[41] In his fine book, *The Last Investigation*, Fonzi builds a very good case for this through numerous witnesses who identify an artist's rendering of Bishop and others who knew that Phillips used that alias.

[42] HSCA memorandum by Jonathan Blackmer to Robert Blakey, dated September 1, 1977.

[43] *Probe,* Vol. 5 No. 6, p. 15.

[44] See the Walter Pincus entry at the Spartacus Educational web site.

[45] Ibid.

[46] *Washington Post*, November 21, 2005.

[47] Op. cit., *Probe.*

[48] Lane, *Plausible Denial*, p. 31.

[49] Dick Russell, *On the Trail of the JFK Assassins*, (New York, Skyhorse Publishing, 2008), p. 53.

[50] *New Orleans States–Item*, March 5, 1977.

[51] Op. cit., *Probe.*

[52] Congressional Record, April 5, 1977. This was part of the vigorous attempt by Sprague's defenders to correct the record after he resigned.

[53] Op. Cit., *Probe.*

[54] Russell, op. cit., pps. 170–71.

[55] Ibid., p. 172.

[56] Marrs, p. 285.

[57] Ibid, p. 286. Jim Marrs discovered that Mendoza got registered to practice in Dallas in April of 1976, two months before he treated DeMohrenschildt. He left in December, leaving the Medical Society a false forwarding address. See Marrs, p. 286.

[58] *Gallery*, November, 1977, "The Mysterious Death of a Key JFK Witness" by Mark Lane, p. 112.

[59] Op. Cit., Oltmans HSCA testimony, p. 37.

[60] Ibid., pps. 45, 68.

[61] Ibid., p. 56. It is pretty obvious by this point in Oltmans's deposition that Tanenbaum does not believe him.

[62] Op. Cit., Gallery, November, 1977.

[63] Rose, Jerry, "Loose Ends in the Death of George DeMohrenschildt," *The Third Decade*, Vol. 1 No. 1, p. 22.

[64] HSCA testimony of Willem Oltmans, April 1, 1977, p. 75.

[65] Ibid.

[66] Ibid., p. 73.

[67] Ibid., p. 51.

[68] Ibid., pps. 41–42.

[69] Ibid.

[70] *CBS Evening News* segment of April 1, 1977. Almost all the above claims made by Oltmans are in this report.

[71] Op. Cit., Oltmans HSCA testimony, p. 51.

[72] *Time Magazine*, April 11, 1977.

[73] HSCA Vol. 12, pps. 132–33.

[74] Ibid, p. 287.

[75] *Gallery*, April, 1978, pps. 43ff.

[76] Ibid., p. 103.

[77] Op. Cit., *The Third Decade*, p. 25.

[78] Ibid., p. 27.

[79] Ibid.

[80] Op. Cit., *Gallery*, November, 1977. p. 112.

81 Ibid., p. 114.

82 Author's 1992 interview in Cincinnati with Jerry Policoff who talked to Angleton about this matter.

83 Op. Cit., *The Third Decade*, p. 24.

84 Russell, p. 173.

85 Author's 1996 interview with Lewis in Lancaster, Pennsylvania.

86 Fonzi, p. 256.

87 Interview by the author and William Davy of Triplett in Falls Church, Virginia in 1994.

88 Author's 1993 interview in Dallas with Fonzi.

89 Fonzi, p. 231.

90 Author's 1995 telephone interview with Eddie Lopez. According to Lopez, when this quote was leaked to the press, Blakey was furious.

91 CIA Memorandum of July 17, 1978.

92 Ibid. It turned out that a congressional committee later found out that Blahut *was* part of a larger CIA operation code–named MH/Child. (*Washington Post,* 6/28/79.)

93 DiEugenio, James. "The Sins of Robert Blakey: Part 2." *Probe*, Vol. 6 No. 1, p. 32.

94 Op. cit., Lopez interview.

95 HSCA interview of Mrs. Murrett on November 6, 1978. See especially pages, 7–9, 15–16, and p. 23.

96 HSCA interview of Eugene Murrett on Novmeber 7, 1978. See especially pps. 3, and 9–12.

97 HSCA Vol. 9, pps. 95–99. In a long discussion I had with Lamar Waldron and Giorgio DiCaprio in 2011 at Leonardo DiCaprio's Appian Way production office, they both mightily resisted this new information, which tells me they were not familiar with the HSCA declassified files.

98 G. Robert Blakey and Richard Billings, *Fatal Hour* (Berkley Books: New York, 1992) p. xxvii.

99 Fonzi, p. 255.

100 HSCA Vol. 10, p. 125.

101 Ibid.

102 HSCA interview of Delphine Roberts by Robert Buras, August 27, 1978.

103 HSCA Vol. 10, p. 128.

104 Journalist Scott Malone's research notes on his August 14, 1978 interview with Newman.

105 Op. cit., Roberts interview by Buras.

106 Ibid.

107 Ibid.

108 Ibid.

109 Ibid.

110 HSCA interview of Oster by Bob Buras, January 27, 1978. The presence of Kennedy at Banister's does much to explain Hoover's almost immediate FBI cover up of the Kennedy assassination.

111 HSCA Report, p. 219.

112 Melanson, p. 93.

113 In addition to Roberts, Martin, Campbell, and Gaudet putting the two together, there are the two INS agents, Smith and Roache, Roberts's daughter, and Vernon Gerdes, who told Gordon Novel's lawyer Steve Plotkin he had seen the two together with Ferrie. (Wackenhut Memorandum of 4/7/67).

114 Mellen, A *Farewell to Justice,* p. 347.

115 Author's 1994 interview with L. J. Delsa in New Orleans.

116 Author's 1995 phone interview with Wallace Milam.

[117] This includes authors Bill Davy and Joan Mellen.

[118] *Probe*, Vol. 6 No. 1, p. 32.

[119] Author's 1993 interview with photoanalyst Richard E. Sprague in Alexandria, Virginia.

[120] Ruth Paine fully expected to be deposed by the HSCA. She was seen at the National Archives at the time going through her files (Author's 1996 phone interview with Jerry Policoff).

[121] HSCR, p. 50.

[122] See Eaglesham's web site, "The Sniper's Nest: Incarnations and Implications."

[123] WC Vol. 7, p. 46.

[124] See, for example, Commission Exhibit 512.

[125] WC Vol. 3, pps. 401–02.

[126] Michael Kurtz, *Crime of the Century*, (Knoxville, Tenn: University of Tennessee Press, 1982), pps. 50–51.

[127] HSCR, p. 45.

[128] See the *Contra Costa Times*, August 21, 2006, for the study done by Pat Grant and Rick Randich; see *Washington Post*, May 17, 2007 for the study conducted by Cliff Spiegealman and William Tobin.

[129] HSCR, pps. 44, 48. For critiques of Canning, see Chapter 15 at patspeer.com, and *Probe*, Vol. 6 No. 1, pps. 10–11. Blakey and Richard Billings, one of the main authors of the HSCA report, also relied upon the HSCA medical panel chaired by Michael Baden. The findings of Baden and his panel have been shown by several authors to be dubious. Some good critiques of this subject are by Gary Aguilar and Cyril Wecht in the book *Trauma Room One*, pps. 170–264; two separate essays by Gary Aguilar and David Mantik in the book *Murder in Dealey Plaza*, pps. 175–297; and David Mantik's essay in the book *Assassination Science*, pps. 93–139.

[130] Author's 1994 interview with Lopez in Rochester, New York.

[131] Letter from Brooten to Weisberg dated April 7, 1977.

[132] Biles, p. xii.

[133] Robert Tanenbaum, 2003 Duquesne Symposium at the Cyril Wecht Institute of Forensic Science in Pittsburgh.

[134] See John Hunt's, "The Mystery of the 7:30 Bullet" at the JFK Lancer site.

[135] See John Hunt's "Phantom Identification of the Magic Bullet" at the JFK Lancer site.

Chapter 16

[1] The actual quote is "The play's the thing, wherein I'll catch the conscience of the king." *Hamlet*, Act 2, Scene 2.

[2] See the WR, pps. 299–311, 658–59, 730–36.

[3] CIA cable of December 20, 1963.

[4] HSCA Memorandum of interview of the Tarasoffs by Ken Brooten and Jonathan Blackmer dated December 5, 1976.

[5] Slawson Trip Report, p. 5.

[6] *Probe*, Vol. 4 No. 1, p. 14.

[7] Ibid.

[8] HSCA Vol. 11, p. 149.

[9] Ibid.

[10] Helms's dissatisfaction is expressed in a memo Whitten wrote after a meeting with the Deputy Director on December 24, 1963. Yet Whitten was puzzled as to what Helms objects

to in his initial reports, because Helms would not reveal to him the precise problems he had with them.

[11] McKnight, pps. 347–49.

[12] Ibid., p. 323, also pps. 366–68. This turned out to be a mangled story. When the FBI tracked this rumor down, the actual substance of it was that Oswald was a *CIA agent* masquerading as a communist, not an FBI operative. (See *Probe* Vol. 3, No. 6, p. 15).

[13] McKnight, p. 347.

[14] In 1994, Slawson was asked by the ARRB if he would discuss certain aspects of his Mexico trip. He said he "was not at liberty to discuss that." This was thirty years later, and a law had made the ARRB the governing authority on JFK records. Yet, Slawson was still loyal to the CIA and Warren Commision. (See Newman, *Oswald and the CIA*, p. xiv.)

[15] Newman, *Oswald and the CIA*, p. 615.

[16] *Probe*, Vol. 4 No. 1, p. 15.

[17] Armstrong, p. 628.

[18] Op. cit., *Probe.*

[19] Ibid.

[20] *Lopez Report,* pps. 191–92.

[21] Op. cit., *Probe,* p. 28.

[22] *Lopez Report*, p. 190; Armstrong, p. 646.

[23] *Lopez Report*, p. 192.

[24] Ibid., p. 193.

[25] WR, p. 301.

[26] *Probe*, Vol. 3 No. 6, p. 15.

[27] *Lopez Report*, p. 190.

[28] WR, p. 302; *Lopez Report*, p. 190.

[29] Author's 1994 interview with Ed Lopez in Rochester, New York.

[30] This annex is referred to in the text of the report. And it was confirmed to me by Lopez in my 1994 interview with him.

[31] *Probe*, Vol. 7 No. 2, p. 21.

[32] WR, p. 322.

[33] Gaeton Fonzi interview of Odio, January 16, 1976 for the Church Committee.

[34] PBS 1993 *Frontline* special, "Who Was Lee Harvey Oswald?"

[35] WC Vol. 11, pps. 370–71.

[36] Ibid, pps. 369, 375.

[37] Ibid., p. 377.

[38] Op. cit., Fonzi interview.

[39] WC Vol. 11, p. 373.

[40] Ibid., p. 371.

[41] Ibid., pps. 370, 386.

[42] WR, p. 733.

[43] WR, pps. 731–32.

[44] WC, Vol. 11, p. 372.

[45] Op. cit., Fonzi interview with Odio. Liebeler was referring to a speech Warren gave the Commission staff at their first meeting of January 20, 1964. In a memo by Melvin Eisenberg, he writes that Warren said "this was an occasion on which actual conditions had to override general principles.... He placed emphasis on the importance of quenching rumors, and precluding future speculations such as that which has surrounded the death of Lincoln."

[46] Ibid.

[47] Ibid.

48 Author's 1994 interview with Triplett in Falls Church, Virginia.

49 *Lopez Report*, p. 117.

50 Ibid., p. 121.

51 Bill Simpich, "Twelve who Built the Oswald Legend, Part 7," at OpEd News.com

52 Hardway and Lopez identified this person as KGB officer Yuri Moskalev. Anne Goodpasture lied about the day this photo was taken. It was taken on October 2, not the October 1. The authors also conclude that Goodpasture knew this man was not Oswald well before the assassination, by October 11 (See *Lopez Report*, pps. 139–41, 159, and 179).

53 Ibid., p. 303.

54 Ibid., pps. 47, 70; Author's 1994 interview with Lopez in Rochester, New York.

55 *Lopez Report*, p. 47.

56 Tanenbaum speech at Midwest Symposium in Chicago, 1993.

57 *Lopez Report*, p. 63.

58 Ibid, p. 133.

59 Op. cit., 1993 Tanenbaum speech.

60 Armstrong, p. 659.

61 See, for example, the *Lopez Report*, pps. 18, 40.

62 Ibid., p. 128.

63 Ibid.

64 Newman, *Oswald and the CIA*, p. 393.

65 Ibid., p. 398.

66 Ibid., p. 636.

67 Newman, John. "Oswald, the CIA and Mexico City: Fingerprints of Conspiracy." *Probe*, Vol. 6, No. 6, p. 4.

68 Ibid.

69 Ibid, p. 29.

70 CIA Summary Report of December 13, 1963, prepared by John Whitten.

71 Hurt, p. 252.

72 Transcript of phone call at 10:00 A.M. on the twenty-third, available at Mary Ferrell Foundation. As Rex Bradford notes, although there is a transcript of this call, for some reason, the actual tape of the call is not available.

73 FBI memorandum from Hoover to James Rowley of November 23, 1963.

74 December 15, 1995 ARRB deposition of Anne Goodpasture, excerpted in Newman's *Oswald and the CIA*, p. 653.

75 Mexico Station cable 7023 to CIA HQS of November 23, 1963.

76 FBI memo of November 23rd, from Rudd to Gordon Shanklin.

77 Armstrong, p. 651.

78 *Lopez Report*, p. 164.

79 Armstrong, p. 652.

80 Ibid., p. 659.

81 CIA internal memo by John Whitten, December 13, 1963.

82 Transcript of phone call of November 29, 1963. This audio tape is now on You Tube.

83 Transcript of Earl Warrren's Oral History interview of 9/21/71 at the LBJ Library at University of Texas.

84 Lane, *Plausible Denial*, p. 42.

85 Transcript of November 29th call between Johnson and Russell is at the *History Matters* web site.

86 Executive Session transcript of the Warren Commission, December 5, 1963, pgs, 1–3.

87 *Probe*, Vol. 6 No. 6, p. 29.

[88] Newman, *Oswald and the CIA*, p. 616.

[89] Ibid., p. 618.

[90] Hosty, p. 48.

[91] Ibid., p. 101.

[92] Ibid., pps. 166–67.

[93] Jefferson Morley, *Our Man in Mexico* (Lawerence, Kansas: University of Kansas Press, 2008) p. 1.

[94] Ibid., p. 286.

[95] Pease, Lisa. "James Jesus Angleton and the Kennedy Assassination: Part 2." *Probe*, Vol. 7 No. 6, p. 29.

[96] CIA Memorandum of November 27, 1963 from Winston Scott to Clarke Anderson. Not only does one have the voice problem and language problem and Duran's testimony that Oswald was not there on the twenty-eighth, but this call is just silly. Oswald says he is calling from the Cuban consulate because he forgot his own address and had to go retrieve it.

[97] NODA Memorandum of January 18, 1968, from Jim Garrison to Lou Ivon.

[98] McKnight, p. 72.

[99] JFK Countercoup blog dated June 8, 2012.

[100] Author's 1994 interview with Lopez in Rochester, New York.

[101] Op. cit., JFK Countercoup.

[102] Op. cit., *Probe*, p. 30.

[103] Ibid.

[104] This was the famous legal proceeding depicted in Mark Lane's book *Plausible Denial*, Spotlight v. Howard Hunt.

[105] Pease's milestone essays appeared in *Probe* Vol. 7, Nos. 5 and 6.

[106] Anthony Summers at the Chicago Midwest Symposium in 1993,

[107] Letter from David Phillips to Vincent Bugliosi, July 1, 1986.

[108] Ibid. Phillips' hopes were posthumously realized when Bugliosi published his mammoth book, *Reclaiming History* in 2007.

[109] Russell, p. 272.

Chapter 17

[1] Newman, *JFK and Vietnam*, p. 138.

[2] Blight, p. 129.

[3] Newman, *JFK and Vietnam* pps. 236–37; Blight, p. 129.

[4] For Gilpatric's comments on the withdrawal issue, see Blight, p. 371; McNaughton's are mentioned in Roger Hilsman's letter to the *New York Times* of January 20, 1992.

[5] Goldstein, p. 239.

[6] Records of eighth SecDef conference held in Hawaii, published in *Probe Magazine*, Vol. 5, No. 3, pgs 20–21.

[7] Newman, *JFK and Vietnam*, pps. 401–02.

[8] Ibid., p. 407.

[9] Ibid., p. 69.

[10] Ibid., p. 72.

[11] Douglass, pps. 374–75.

[12] Goldstein, p. 239.

[13] Douglass, p. 375; Newman, op. cit., p. 442.

[14] Newman, op. cit., p. 443.

[15] Robert McNamara, *In Retrospect: The Tragedy and Lessons of Vietnam* (New York: Vintage Books, 1995), p. 102.

[16] Blight, p. 321.

[17] *Newsweek,* February 10, 1975.

[18] Doris Kearns, *Lyndon Johnson and the American Dream*, (New York: Harper and Row, 1976), p. 264.

[19] Goldstein, p. 105

[20] Ibid., pps. 106–07.

[21] Newman, op. cit., pps. 425, 441.

[22] Goldstein, p. 108.

[23] Moise, p. 26.

[24] Ibid., pps. 26–27.

[25] Ibid., p. 44.

[26] Newman, op. cit., p. 440.

[27] Moise, p. 87.

[28] Ibid, p. 251.

[29] Ibid, p. 244.

[30] Transcript of Johnson–McNamara phone call of February 20, 1964.

[31] Transcript of Johnson–McNamara phone call of March 2, 1964.

[32] *Probe*, Volume 6 No. 2, p. 24.

[33] Ibid.

[34] Ibid.

[35] Ibid., p. 25.

[36] Ibid.

[37] *Probe*, Vol. 3 No. 4, p. 21.

[38] Ibid., p. 20.

[39] Ibid., p. 21.

[40] Ibid., p. 22.

[41] Ibid., p. 22; Vol. 4 No. 1 p. 16.

[42] Ibid., p. 22.

[43] Ibid., pps. 24, 26.

[44] Ibid., p. 24.

[45] Ibid., p. 23.

[46] W. F. Wertheim, "Suharto and the Untung Coup–the Missing Link", *Journal of Contemporary Asia* 1 No. 1, pps. 50–57

[47] Freeport Sulphur later became a multi–billion dollar company, largely off its Indonesian mines. It later switched names to Freeport McMoran and was intricately entwined with Suharto's dictatorship. The company has been accused of committing various crimes in that country.

[48] *Probe* op. cit. Vol. 3 No. 4, p. 24.

[49] Douglass, p. 118.

[50] Blum, *The CIA: A Forgotten History*, p. 160.

[51] Ibid.

[52] Ibid.

[53] Ibid.

[54] Ibid.

[55] Ibid., p. 161.

[56] *New York Times*, July 21, 1972.

[57] Blum, op. cit., p. 161.

⁵⁸ Ibid.
⁵⁹ Lyon Garrison allowed the author to look over some of what was left of his father's collection in 1994.
⁶⁰ This long essay was in the collection of papers Lyon Garrison allowed the author to look at and copy in 1994.
⁶¹ Blum, op. cit., p. 244. For a discussion of the Dominican Republic see Gibson, pps. 78–79. For Iran, see James Bill's *The Eagle and the Lion*, pages 131–182. The Kennedy State Department actually did a cost–benefit analysis of bringing back Mossadegh. For Brazil see Gibson pps. 79–80, Bird, pps. 550–53, and also A. J. Langguth's *Hidden Terrors* (New York: Pantheon Books, 1978) pps. 103–04. As Kai Bird notes, the man who David Rockefeller and the CIA sent in to first, negotiate with the government, and then begin the coup was John McCloy.
⁶² See Robert Dallek, *Flawed Giant* Vol. 2 (New York: Oxford University Press, 1998) pps. 544–45. By 1968, LBJ and Nelson Rockefeller were quite close. Johnson wanted Rockefeller to run for the GOP nomination since he thought he could beat Bobby Kennedy. Rockefeller took his advice and announced he was running in April of 1968. Another book that details the close relationship between the Rockefellers and Johnson is *Thy Will Be Done* by Gerard Colby and Charlotte Dennett (New York: Harpercollins, 1996). See pages 588, 711. As Donald Gibson notes, pps. 73–74, the Kennedys were not close to the Rockefellers. This Johnson/Rockefeller nexus was influential in what later happened in Indonesia and Brazil.
⁶³ Douglass, pps. 380–81.

Chapter 18

¹ For an example of this, one can listen to the *Black Op Radio* broadcast of August 14, 2009, Show No. 436 for a talk Shaw did at Moorpark College on October 17, 1970.
² This information was relayed to the author by Lisa Pease who had a conversation with Lifton about this in 1998..
³ *Los Angeles Times,* September 10, 1997.
⁴ *Probe*, Vol. 4 No. 1, p. 17.
⁵ Gibson, Donald. "Kennedy vs. the Early Globalists." *Probe*, Vol. 5 No. 2, p. 12.
⁶ *Probe*, Vol. 4 No. 1, p. 17.
⁷ Ibid., p. 16. Few giant corporations represent the bad side effects of globalism more than Freeport McMoran does today. For a good overview of how Suharto and Freeport benefited from each other, see Denise Leith's *The Politics of Power: Freeport in Suharto's Indonesia* (Honolulu: University of Hawaii Press, 2002).
⁸ It is silly for Patricia Lambert to deny this fact today. Shaw's lawyers knew about it through an inquiry by Wackenhut. See *Probe* Vol. 4 No. 4, p. 8.
⁹ Author's 1992 interview with New Orleans historian Arthur Carpenter.
¹⁰ Davy, p. 200.
¹¹ Ibid., p. 198.
¹² CIA Memorandum of March 1967, review of Marguerite D. Stevens's summary of Shaw's work.
¹³ William Davy interview with Victor Marchetti, April 26, 1995.
¹⁴ Ibid.
¹⁵ CIA Memorandum of October 27, 1970.
¹⁶ State Department Memorandum of October 8, 1957.
¹⁷ Grose, pps. 102, 111, 265.

[18] Hinckle and Turner, p. 83.

[19] Ibid.

[20] Davy, p.97.

[21] In this interview by Phelan, entitled "Clay Shaw: An Exclusive Penthouse Interview," Shaw also said he was never associated with the CIA. So much for his credibility.

[22] Garrison, pps. 87–88; Flammonde, pps. 216–18.

[23] Flammonde, pps. 216, 220.

[24] Davy, p. 99.

[25] Flammonde, p. 221.

[26] NODA Memorandum of April 1, 1967.

[27] This account is from William Turner's *Rearview Mirror* (Granite Bay, California: Penmarin Books, 2001), pps. 178–79. At his trial, Shaw lied about this by saying that Sullivan *approached him* about speaking in San Francisco. Transcript of February 27, 1969.

[28] FBI Memorandum of March 6, 1967.

[29] NODA Memorandum of September 23, 1967. Since Shaw never used that last name, Breitner likely recalled Bertrand wrongly.

[30] NODA report of interview of March 22, 1967. This man's last name is likely Formydahl, and he is named in Shaw's will.

[31] NODA Memorandum of February 14, 1968.

[32] NODA Memorandum of November 29, 1967. Davy later repeated this story to the HSCA. He also told them that Garrison had him polygraphed and he passed. See HSCA report of December 16, 1977. Davis clearly knew who Bertrand was, but he would not talk. One reason may be fear. Another reason may be that he appears to have been Shaw's pimp.

[33] Affidavit of Jessie Parker dated September 12, 1967.

[34] William Davy's 1995 interview with Delsa.

[35] FBI Airtel of March 2, 1967.

[36] FBI Teletype of March 23, 1967.

[37] The unpublished book is *Mailer's Tale*. See Chapter 5, page 11 for the information. It is available at the invaluable Weisberg Archives at Hood College online. In light of this accumulation of evidence, for Shaw to deny he ever used the alias, as he did at his trial, is simply not credible.

[38] FBI Memorandum of March 2, 1967 from DeLoach to Tolson.

[39] Letter from Edward Wegmann to Allen Dulles dated March 11, 1968.

[40] *Probe*, Volume 4 No. 4, p. 8.

[41] Ibid.

[42] Ibid.

[43] *Probe*, Vol. 6 No.4, p. 3

[44] Mellen, *A Farewell to Justice*, p. 293.

[45] Author's interview with Dymond in New Orleans in 1994.

[46] *New Orleans Times Picayune*, July 7, 2011.

[47] Ibid.

[48] Letter from Banister to Johnson dated January 5, 1959; See March 1967 *Ramparts* for an article by Sol Stern for the background on this CIA project.

[49] *Probe*, Vol. 4 No. 4, p. 16.

[50] Ibid.

[51] Ibid., p. 14.

[52] *Probe*, Vol. 4 No. 5, p. 20.

[53] The Harris article, called "The Connally Bullet," is at the web site ctka.net.

[54] Hosty, p. 62.

55 Armstrong, pps. 856–57; Confidential source who knows Jez and says he does not want to be formally interviewed on the subject. But he told her, "You can bet your life that was Oswald's wallet."

56 Dallas Municipal Archives Box 9, Folder 1, Item 17.

57 WC Vol. 7, p. 58; CE 2003, p. 78.

58 WR, p. 15.

59 Barry Ernest, *The Girl on the Stairs,* e–book version, pps. 58–59.

60 For instance, at a critics' conference in Washington in 1995, William Turner said that Oswald shot Tippit.

61 This material is taken from Dick Russell's article "JFK and the Cuban Connection" at his site dickrussell.org. It was originally published in *High Times* in March of 1996.

62 Douglass, p. 61.

63 Richard Helms with William Hood, *A Look Over My Shoulder,* (New York: Random House, 2003) pps. 226–27.

64 The timing of this incident makes pablum out of the thesis of the Lamar Waldron–Thom Hartmann book *Ultimate Sacrifice.* This unwieldy and fantastic contraption of a book theorizes that somehow the back channel was just a mirage, the Kennedys were planning an invasion of Cuba on December 2. And that Helms knew about it. Helms did not know about it. If he had, he would not have been pressing Kennedy with this phony arms cache story. When I confronted Waldron with this compelling information at a meeting at Leonardo DiCaprio's office in 2011, he gaseously escaped by making ad hominem attacks on Helms' character. He never confronted the information itself. Unfortunately for us all, DiCaprio and his father Giorgio plan on making a film out of the (even worse) sequel to this horrendous book, *Legacy of Secrecy.*

65 Joseph B. Smith, *Portrait of a Cold Warrior* (New York: Putnam, 1976), p. 383.

66 Walt Brown, *The Warren Omission* (Wilmington, Delaware: Delmax, 1996), pps. 83–87.

67 *Probe,* Vol. 3 No. 4, pps. 27–30.

68 Transcript of Johnson–Russell call of September 18, 1964, declassified by LBJ Library.

69 Mosley, p. 473.

70 Johnson claimed this on a tape from August 19, 1969 released by the LBJ Library in 2001. Much ballyhooed biographer Robert Caro actually used this in his recent best seller *The Passage of Power.* Apparently, Caro did not do his homework on the Bay of Pigs.

71 Author's 1994 phone interview with Alcorn.

72 Author's interviews with Peter Vea and Dan Alcorn in Washington in 1995.

73 Author's 1993 phone interview with Patricia Orr.

74 *Probe,* Vol. 7 No. 1 p. 25.

75 Ibid., p. 26.

76 Webb Hubbell, *Friends in High Places* (New York: William Morrow and Company, 1997), p. 282. The other question Clinton wanted investigated was if there were really UFOs.

77 Garrison, pps. 210–11.

78 Author's 1996 conversation with Mike Willman, who was friends with Sahl at the time.

Bibliography

Government Reports

CIA Inspector General's Report on Plots to Assassinate Fidel Castro. Written in 1967, declassified for the public in 1993 under the CIA Historical Review Program.

Oswald, the CIA, and Mexico City, more commonly referred to as "The Lopez Report." The HSCA report on Oswald in Mexico City was written in 1978 by Dan Hardway and Ed Lopez. It was almost fully declassified in 2003. Yet the appendix titled "Was Oswald an Agent of the CIA" is not available.

Report of the President's Commission on the Assassination of President John F. Kennedy (the *Warren Report*) (Washington, D.C.: U.S. Government Printing Office, 1964), with accompanying 26 volumes of exhibits and testimony.

U.S. Senate, Select Committee to Study Governmental Operations with Respect to Intelligence Activities, *Final Report, Book Five, The Investigation of the Assassination of President John F. Kennedy: Performance of the Intelligence Agencies,* 94th Congress, 2nd Session, 1976, S. Rpt. 94–755. (This body is more commonly referred to as the Church Committee.)

U.S. *House, Select Committee on Assassinations, Report,* with twelve accompanying volumes of hearings and appendices (material on Kennedy case as opposed to Martin Luther King, Jr., case) (Washington, D.C.: U.S. Government Printing Office, 1979), 95th Congress, 2nd Session, 1979, H. Rpt. 1828.

Periodicals

Daniel, Jean, "When Castro Heard the News," *New Republic,* 12/7/63.
Daniel, Jean, "Unofficial Envoy," *New Republic,* 12/14/63.
Garrison, Jim, interview in *Playboy,* October 1967.

Goldman, David, and Jeffrey Steinberg, "Special Report," *Executive Intelligence Review,* November 14, 1981.

Hilsman, Roger, Letter to the Editor, *New York Times,* January 20, 1992.

Joesten, Joachim, "Highlights and Lessons of the Clay Shaw Trial," *Truth Letter,* June 15, 1969.

Kurtz, Michael, "Lee Harvey Oswald in New Orleans: A Reappraisal," *Louisiana History,* Winter 1980.

Morrisey, Michael, "The Bay of Pigs Revisited," *The Fourth Decade*, Volume 1, No. 2.

Murphy, Charles, "Cuba: The Record Set Straight," *Fortune*, September, 1961.

Oglesby, Carl, "Reinhard Gehlen: The Secret Treaty of Fort Hunt," *CovertAction Information Bulletin,* No. 35, Fall 1990.

Phelan, James, "Rush to Judgment in New Orleans," *Saturday Evening Post,* May 6, 1967.

Popkin, Richard H., "Garrison's Case," *New York Review of Books,* September 14, 1967.

Powledge, Fred, "Is Garrison Faking?" *The New Republic,* June 17, 1967.

Simpich, Bill, "12 Who Built the Oswald Legend" at *OpEdNews.com.*

Scott, Peter Dale, "How Allen Dulles and the SS Preserved Each Other," *CovertAction Information Bulletin,* No. 25, Winter 1986.

Tatro, Edgar F., "Clay Shaw and Me," *The Continuing Inquiry*, August 22, 1983.

Turner, William, "The Inquest," *Ramparts,* June 1967.

————, "The Garrison Commission," *Ramparts,* January 1968.

Unpublished Manuscripts

The Richard Billings Journal

Carpenter, Arthur E., "Gateway to the Americas," unpublished dissertation, Tulane University, New Orleans, Louisiana, 1987.

Mailer's Tale by Harold Weisberg

"The Mysterious Mr. Novel"

Books

Acheson, Dean. *Present at the Creation* (New York: W.W. Norton, 1969).

Ambrose, Stephen. *Eisenhower* (New York: Simon and Schuster, 1983).

————, *Eisenhower the President* (New York: Simon and Schuster, 1984).

Arboleya, Jesus, *The Cuban Counterrevolution* (Athens, Ohio: Ohio University Press, 2000).

Armstrong, John. *Harvey and Lee* (Arlington, Tex. Quasar, Ltd, 2003).

Attwood, William. *The Twilight Struggle* (New York: Harper and Row, 1987).

Baker, Russ. *Family of Secrets* (New York: Bloomsbury Press, 2008).

Benson, Michael. *Who's Who in the JFK Assassination* (Citadel Press: New York, 1993)

Bernstein, Barton J., and Allen J. Matusow. *The Truman Administration: A Documentary History* (New York: Harper & Row, 1966).

Bethell, Tom. *The Electric Windmill: An Inadvertent Biography* (Washington: Regnery Gateway, 1988).

Biles, Joe G., *In History's Shadow* (Lincoln, Nebraska: Writer's Club Press, 2002)

Blight, James, and Janet M. Lang, David A. Welch, eds., *Virtual JFK: Vietnam if Kenendy had Lived* (Lanham Maryland: Bowman and Littlefield Publishers, 2009).

Blum, John Morton. *Years of Discord* (New York: W. W. Norton, 1991).

Blum, William. *The CIA: A Forgotten History* (London: Zed Books, 1986).

Brussell, Mae, *A Mae Brussell Reader* (Santa Barbara, Calif.: Prevailing Winds Research, 1991).

Bird, Kai, *The Chairman*, (New York: Simon and Schuster, 1992).

Davy, William, *Let Justice Be Done* (Reston, Va.: Jordan Publishing, 1999).

DiEugenio, James and Lisa Pease, eds., *The Assassinations* (Los Angeles: Feral House, 2003).

Douglass, James, *JFK and the Unspeakable*, (Maryknoll, New York: Orbis Books, 2008).

Ellis, Rafaela, *The Central Intelligence Agency* (New York: Chelsea House Publishers, 1988).

Epstein, Edward Jay, *The Assassination Chronicles* (New York: Carroll and Graf, 1992).

Evica, George Michael, *A Certain Arrogance* (Hartford: Iron Sights Press, 2006).

Flammonde, Paris, *The Kennedy Conspiracy* (New York: Meredith Press, 1969).

Fonzi, Gaeton, *The Last Investigation* (New York: Thunder's Mouth Press, 1993).

Garrison, Jim, *On the Trail of the Assassins* (New York: Sheridan Square Press, 1988).

Gentry, Curt, *J. Edgar Hoover* (New York: W. W. Norton, 1991).

Gibson, Donald, *Battling Wall Street* (New York: Sheridan Square Press, 1994)

Goldstein, Gordon, *Lessons in Disaster* (New York: Times Books, 2008).

Grose, Peter, *Gentleman Spy: The Life of Allen Dulles* (Boston: Houghton Mifflin, 1994)

Griggs, Ian, *No Case to Answer* (Southlake, Tex.: JFK Lancer Productions and Publications, 2005).

Hancock, Larry, *Nexus: The CIA and Political Assaassination* (Southlake, Tex.: JFK Lancer Productions and Publications, 2011)

Hancock, Larry, *Someone Would Have Talked* (Southlake, Tex.: JFK Lancer Productions and Publications, 2006)

Hepburn, James, *Farewell America* (Vaduz, Liechtenstein: Frontiers Publishing, 1968).

Higgins, Trumbull, *The Perfect Failure* (New York: W. W. Norton, 1989).

Higham, Charles, *Trading With the Enemy* (New York: Delacorte, 1983).

Hilsman, Roger, *To Move a Nation* (New York: Doubleday, 1967).

Hinckle, Warren, *If You Have a Lemon, Make Lemonade* (New York: Bantam Books, 1976).

Hinckle, Warren, and William Turner, *Deadly Secrets* (New York: Thunder's Mouth Press, 1993).

Hosty, James, *Assignment: Oswald* (New York: Arcade Publishing, 1996).

Hougan, Jim, *Spooks* (New York: William Morrow, 1978).

Hunt, Howard, *Give Us this Day* (New Rochelle: Arlington House, 1973).

Hurt, Henry, *Reasonable Doubt* (New York: Holt, Rinehart & Winston, 1985).

James, Rosemary, and Jack Wardlaw, *Plot or Politics?* (New Orleans: Pelican Publishing House, 1967).

Jezer, Marty, *The Dark Ages* (Boston: South End Press, 1982).

Joesten, Joachim, The Garrison Enquiry (London: Peter Dawnay, 1967).

Johnson, Haynes, *Bay of Pigs* (New York: W. W. Norton, 1964).

Kahin, Audrey and George, *Subversion as Foreign Policy* (New York: The New Press, 1995).

Kaiser, David, *American Tragedy* (Cambridge, Mass: The Belknap Press, 2000).

Kennedy, John F., *Why England Slept* (New York: W. Funk, 1940).

Kirkwood, James, *American Grotesque* (New York: Simon and Schuster, 1970).

Kornbluh, Peter, ed., *Bay of Pigs Declassified*, (New York: The New Press, 1998).

Kurtz, Michael, *Crime of the Century* (Knoxville, Tenn.: University of Tennessee Press, 1982).

Kurtz, Michael, *The JFK Assassination Debates* (Lawrence, Kans University Press of Kansas, 2006).

Lane, Mark, *Rush to Judgment* (New York: Holt, Rinehart & Winston, 1966).

———, *Plausible Denial* (New York: Thunder's Mouth Press, 1991).

Lechuga, Carlos, *In the Eye of the Storm* (Melbourne: Ocean Press, 1995).

Lifton, David S., ed., *Document Addendum to the Warren Report* (El Segundo, Calif.: Sightext Press, 1968).

———, *Best Evidence* (New York: Macmillan, 1980).

Lisagor, Nancy, and Frank Lipsius, *A Law Unto Itself* (New York: Paragon House, 1989).

Mahoney, Richard, *JFK: Ordeal in Africa* (Oxford Univeristy Press: New York, 1983).

May, Ernest and Philip Zelikow, *The Kennedy Tapes* (Belknap Press: Cambridge, Massachusetts, 1997).

McCoy, Alfred, *The Politics of Heroin,* 2d ed. (New York: Lawrence Hill, 1991).

Mangold, Tom, *Cold Warrior*, (New York: Simon and Schuster, 1991).

Markmann, Charles, *John F. Kennedy: A Sense of Purpose* (New York: St. Martin's Press, 1961).

McKnight, Gerald, *Breach of Trust* (Lawrence, Kans: University Press of Kansas, 2005).

Marrs, Jim, *Crossfire: The Plot That Killed Kennedy* (New York: Carrol and Graf, 1989).

Martin, James Stewart, *All Honorable Men* (Boston: Little, Brown, 1950).

Meagher, Sylvia, *Accessories After the Fact* (New York: Bobbs-Merrill, 1967).

Melanson, Philip, *Spy Saga* (New York: Praeger, 1990).

Mellen, Joan, *A Farewell to Justice* (Dulles, Virginia: Potomac Books, 2005).

Mellen, Joan, *Jim Garrison: His Life and Times* (Southlake, Texas: JFK Lancer Productions and Publications, 2008).

Moise, Edwin, *Tonkin Gulf and the Escalation of the Vietnam War* (Chapel Hill: Univeristy of North Carolina Press, 1996).

Morris, Willie, *New York Days* (Boston: Little Brown, 1993).

Morley, Morris H., *Imperial State and Revolution: The United States and Cuba, 1952–1986* (New York: Cambridge University Press, 1987).

Mosley, Leonard, *Dulles* (New York: The Dial Press, 1978).

Navasky, Victor, *Kennedy Justice* (New York: Atheneum, 1971).

Nevins, Allan, ed., *The Strategy of Peace* (New York: Harper and Row, 1960).

Newman, John M., *JFK and Vietnam* (New York: Warner Books, 1992).

Newman, John M., *Oswald and the CIA*, (New York: Skyhorse Publishing, 2008)

Parmet, Herbert S., *Jack: The Struggles of John F. Kennedy* (New York: Dial Press, 1980).

————, *J.F.K.: The Presidency of John F. Kennedy* (New York: Dial Press, 1983).

Phillips, Cabell B., *The Truman Presidency* (New York: Macmillan, 1966).

Prados, John, *Presidents' Secret Wars* (New York: William Morrow, 1986).

Prouty, L. Fletcher, *The Secret Team* (Englewood Cliffs, N.J.: Prentice-Hall, 1973).

Ranelagh, John, *The Agency: The Rise and Decline of the CIA* (New York: Simon and Schuster, 1987).

Reese, Ellen, *General Reinhard Gehlen: The CIA Connection* (Fairfax, Va.: George Mason University Press, 1990).

Russell, Dick, *The Man Who Knew Too Much* (New York: Carroll and Graf, 2003).

Russell, Dick, *On the Trail of the JFK Assassins* (New York: Skyhorse Publsihing, 2008).

Savage, James, *Jim Garrison's Bourbon Street Brawl* (Lafayette LA: University of Louisiana at Lafayette Press, 2010).

Schlesinger, Arthur, *A Thousand Days* (New York: Houghton Mifflin, 1965).

Simpson, Christopher, *Blowback* (New York: Weidenfeld and Nicolson, 1988).

Snow, Lois Wheeler, ed., *Edgar Snow's China* (New York: Random House, 1981).

Stone, Oliver, and Zachary Sklar, *JFK: The Book of the Film, A Documented Screenplay* (New York: Applause Books, 1992).

Summers, Anthony, *Conspiracy* (New York: McGraw-Hill, 1980).

Summers, Anthony, *Official and Confidential* (New York: Putnam, 1993).

Szulc, Tad, *Compulsive Spy* (New York: Viking Press, 1974).

Talbot, David, *Brothers: The Hidden History of the Kennedy Years* (New York: Free Press, 2007).

Thornley, Kerry, *Oswald* (Chicago: New Classics House, 1965).

Titovets, Ernst, *Oswald: Russian Episode* (Belarus: MonLitera Publishing House, 2010)

Tully, Andrew, *CIA: The Inside Story* (New York: William Morrow, 1962).

Weisberg, Harold, *Oswald in New Orleans* (New York: Canyon Books, 1967).

Index

Acheson, Dean, 1, 22, 33, 394, 398n2
Agency for International Development
(AID), 196–197
Air Force (U.S.), 83, 376
Alameda County, California, 359
Alba, Adrian, 157–158
Alcock, Jim, 182, 236, 252–254,
281, 293, 295, 297–298, 306–311,
427n206
Alexander, Bill, 250, 253–254
Algeria, 18
CIA in, 107
independence, 26
Algerian War, 27
alopecia disease, 85
Alpha 66, 68, 95, 96, 112, 214,
331–332
Alvarado, Ramon, 361–362
American Friends of Bolshevik
Nations, 150
American Grotesque (Kirkwood), 244,
322, 382
American University, 377
Andrews, Dean, 86–88, 93, 178, 180–
181, 210, 232, 233, 236, 237,
239, 255, 260, 288–289, 298,
307, 308, 311, 320, 387–388
"Angelo," 351
Angleton, James Jesus, 60, 75–76, 106,
142–144, 164, 179, 229, 238,
256, 262–263, 283, 293, 338,
347–348, 358, 361–363, 396
Another Country (Baldwin), 173
Anticommunism. *See* containment
policy
Anti-Communist League of the
Caribbean, 107

antiwar protests, 110
AP (Associated Press), 69, 159
Arbenz government, 7, 20
Arcacha Smith, Sergio, 14, 56, 80, 86,
92, 96, 97, 105–114, 177, 182,
184–185, 232, 252–254, 272,
329
Army (U.S.)
General at autopsy, 299–302
Army Map Service, 154
Assassination Archives and Research
Center, xii, 94, 396
Associated Press. *See* AP
Atsugi Air Base, Japan, 127, 143
Attwood, William, 71, 73–75, 392
audio-tape evidence, 101, 265, 354,
360
Australia, 20
autopsy
Army General's role, 300–301
Attorney General coordination
needed, 287
at Bethesda Naval Hospital, 300
Boswell's role, 300, 304–305
bullet trajectory, 292, 344
Connally's wounds, 293, 300,
301–302
and Dealey Plaza witnesses, 292,
293, 299
Dymond's comments, 286–287,
303
Eardley's role, 299, 303–304
FBI agents' role, 294,
Finck cross-examined, 292, 299–
306
Finck on Zapruder film, 299, 301
hearsay evidence, 297

Humes's role, 300–301, 303, 304, 305

Judge Haggerty's comments ("The Court"), 288, 295, 297, 303, 308

Justice Department's role, 293–294, 304–305

Kennedy family's role, 301, 350–351n48

Kennedy's wounds, 290–291, 293, 299, 300, 301–302, 325

and National Archives, 303, 305, 345

and news reports, 296, 301

number of shots, 300, 301

Oser's cross examination of Finck, 292, 299–306

panel review, 287

photographs, 287, 299, 301, 303, 305, 337, 340

reports, 293, 300, 301, 303, 305

Secret Service agents' role, 188, 341, 345

Specter's questioning, 300

State exhibits, 292

and Warren Commission, 293

Warren Commission Report, 291, 292

Wegmann's comments, 290, 297

X-rays, 136, 287, 301, 303, 305

Aynesworth, Hugh, 213, 237, 242, 249–255, 288, 296, 315

Baldwin, James
Another Country censorship case, 173

Banister, Guy,
in Anti-Communist League of the Caribbean, 107

and Arcacha, 110

as editor of Louisiana Intelligence Digest, 104

assault on Martin,180

and CIA, 105, 106, 107–108

and clearinghouse for Cuban exiles, 180

and Clinton trip, 93

death, 110

explosives from raid stored at office, 106–107

and Ferrie, 113, 342

in Friends of Democratic Cuba, 109

and Gatlin, 107

and Mafia, 15

and Maheu, 257

and Marcello, 115

Nagell testimony, 183

in Naval Intelligence, 209

and Oswald, 56, 80, 88, 92–93, 97, 102–103, 108–115

Palmer on, 93

Phelan on, 297, 309

Barbie, Klaus, 4

Batista, 8–12

Baton Rouge, Louisiana, 246–247

Baton Rouge States-Times, 90, 128

Bay of Pigs invasion, 18, 34–56, 65, 66, 69, 74, 86, 105, 106, 166, 196, 232

Beaubeouf, Alvin, 261

Belgium, 2, 28, 372

Bell Helicopter, 195

Bernstein, Barton J., 399n4, 400n25

Bertrand, Clay. See Shaw, Clay

Bertrand, Clem. See Shaw, Clay

Bethell, Tom, 276, 280, 290

bibliography, 453–458

Biddison, Jeff, 297

Billings, Richard, 91, 266, 269

"Bishop, Maurice" (CIA man), 53, 68–69, 96, 327, 332

Bissell, Richard, 16, 35–37, 40, 44–48

blacks, 90

Blakey, G. Robert, 258, 325–345, 350

Boggs, Hale, 147, 323, 3994

Boswell, J. Thornton, 300, 304–305

Bowers, Lee, 329–330

boys, proclivity for, 113

"Braden, James," 215
See also Brading, Eugene Hale

Bradley, Eugene, 280–281

Brading, Eugene Hale, 215

Brener, Milton, 382

Brent, Ted, 231, 384

Bringuier, Carlos, 118, 159, 161–162, 184, 188, 286

Broshears, Raymond, 209, 248

Brussell, Mae, 400n22

Brussels Pact, 2
Bundy, McGeorge, 31, 46, 62, 67–68
Bundy, Vernon William, Jr., 237,
    242–243, 295
Burke (Naval Chief of Staff), 41, 42
Burma
    CIA in, 399n14
Butler, Ed, 105, 108, 157, 162, 191,
    232
Cabell, Charles, 41, 44, 46, 54
Cabell, Earle, 282
California, 131, 188, 190, 257
Cambodia, 399n14
Camp/Lafayette Streets address, 102,
    110–114, 118, 161, 178, 179–
    180, 322, 341
Canada, 208, 240, 317–318
Cancler, John, 242
Caribbean,
    CIA in, 134
Carson, Johnny, 259, 397
Castro, Fidel, 11, 14–16, 36 ,40, 53,
    392
    assassination plot, 15, 61
    freeze of rapprochement with, 65,
        67–76, 97
    and John Kennedy, 17, 18–19, 35,
        66, 67–76
Castro, Raul, 62
CBS (Columbia Broadcasting System),
    27, 230, 296
censorship, 173, 300, 347
Central Intelligence Agency. See CIA
Central Intelligence Group, 379
Chandler, David, 161, 189, 247, 275–
    277, 290
Charity Hospital, 78, 80
Cheramie, Rose, 77, 78–79, 98, 181–
    182, 272, 329–330
Chetta, Nicholas, 219, 225, 226, 247,
    297
Chiang Kai-shek, 399n14
China, 3, 16, 18, 124, 368, 369
    CIA in, 127
Chou En-lai, 402n16
Christian, George, 251
Church Committee investigation, 15,
    71, 113, 325, 362
Church, Frank, 15, 325

CIA (Central Intelligence Agency)
    and Agency for International
        Development, 196–197
    and Alpha 66, 95–96, 112
    AM/LASH, 73,
    and Angleton, 60, 76, 142, 144,
        179, 229, 256, 294, 347–348,
        396
    and Anti-Communist League of the
        Caribbean, 107
    and Arcacha, 15, 105–107, 157,
        328
    and Arbenz's overthrow, 38, 107,
        196
    in Argentina, 384
    arms smuggling, 213
    Atsugi base, 127, 143
    and Banister, 15, 80–81, 105–107,
        112, 116, 157
    and Bay of Pigs. See Bay of Pigs
        invasion
    and Bishop, 328, 393
    and Bissell, 35
    and Blakey, 258, 339–345
    and Bringuier, 188
    censorship, 347
    in China, 127
    Church Committee investigation,
        15, 113, 325, 331
    on communist media, 102,
    on communist sympathies, 76, 154
    conduit for funds, 105, 116
    creation of, 5–7, 53
    and Cuban Embassy, 349, 353
    and Cuban exiles, 14, 34–35, 50,
        71, 328
    and Cuban Revolutionary Council,
        39
    and Cubela, 73
    and de Gaulle, 107
    and DeMohrenschildt (George),
        153, 155
    directors (DCI), 2, 5, 6, 24, 35, 44,
        50, 52, 62, 70, 143, 228, 263,
        270, 294, 339, 379, 385, 395,
        396
    on Dreyfus case, 230
    and Duran arrest, 349
    and Duvalier, 193

on Epstein, 153, 194, 396
and Evergreen Advertising Agency, 232
in Far East, 3
and Ferrie, 35
and Gaudet, 112
and Gehlen, 4
and Golden Triangle, 376
in Guatemala, 35, 106
and Harvey, 59
and Helms, 60
and Hoover, 2
and House Assassinations Committee, 10
and House Assassinations Final Report, 398
in Indonesia, 32
Inspector General's report, 15
and International Investigators Incorporated, 256
and Joint Chiefs of Staff, 57
Joint Technical Advisory Group, 127
on Jones, 197
on journalists, 229, 235, 383
and KGB, 98
and Kimble, 289
and Lansdale, 24
in Laos, 29
in Lithuania, 3
and Lumumba, 28
and the Mafia, 15, 68, 188
and Maheu, 15, 257
on Manchester, 255
and Marchetti, 41
and National Security Act of 1947, 2–4, 378
and National Security Memoranda, 367
and Nazis, 4
in Nicaragua, 44
Operation AJAX,
Operation CHAOS, 399n9
Operation MONGOOSE, 58
Operation SUCCESS, 7
and Permindex, 385
and Phelan, 229
and Phillips, 14
poison pen, 73

radio broadcasts, 19
and Russian Orthodox Church, 193
Senate Committee censures, 164
and Ser Vaas, 164
and Shackley, 51
and Snyder, 141
and Soviet Embassy, 95
in Taiwan, 376
and Tolstoy Foundation, 193
training of Cuban exiles, 34–35
and Underhill, 99
and Veciana, 331
on Weisberg, 190
civil rights, 89, 104
Clark, Ramsey, 261, 273, 287
classified files, 45, 46, 128, 140, 143, 158
Clifford, Clark, 59, 380
Clinton, Louisiana, trip, 88–93
Cold War, 2, 5–7, 21–25, 28–33, 74, 173, 336
Coleman, William T., Jr., 347, 348
Columbus, Ohio, 83, 235, 262
Colvin, William, 272
Communist Party, U.S.A., 123, 154, 349
communists, 122, 375
Congo,
    CIA in, 372
Congolese Army, 372
Connally, John, 182, 272
    CIA on, 315
    refuses Arcacha extradition, 272
    on single bullet theory, 301–302
    wounds, 293, 300
constitutional rights, 308
containment policy, 5–6, 18–20,
Cooper, John Sherman, 147–148, 394
Costa Rica, 69, 199
coup attempts, 32, 49
Crescent City Garage, 157
"Crime Against Cuba, The," pamphlet, 102, 118, 158
Crossfire (Marrs), 457
Crossfire (TV program), 397
Cuba
    Bay of Pigs invasion reaction, 53
    Castro's policies, 12
    Embassy in Mexico City, 353

House Assassinations Committee on, 68
missile crisis, 65, 115–116
political prisoners, 43
Soviet ships in, 69
U.S secret war against, 14
Cuban exiles, 14, 34–35, 50, 71, 328
Cuban Revolutionary Council, 39, 58, 107
Cubela, Rolando, 73
Dachau, 168
Dallas Morning News, 249
Dallas, Texas
image of, 101
Oak Cliff section, 163
Paine in, 156
Parkland Hospital, 293
Texas Theatre, 76, 78
White Russians, 96, 147, 152, 153, 193, 208
Dallas Times Herald, 425n129
Davis, Eugene, 288
Davis, Preston, 179
Davis, Ricardo, 230, 265
Davis, Thomas Eli, 329
de Gaulle, Charles, 25
assassination plot, 27, 107, 386
and Kennedy (John), 282
and Permindex, 386
Dealey Plaza, 56, 75, 200, 215, 227, 249, 281, 292, 299, 311, 377
DeBrueys, Warren, 80, 109, 158, 160, 292
declassification, ix, 38, 61, 109, 197
defections, 96, 117, 132, 143, 230
Defense Department, 62, 95, 370
del Valle, Eladio, 85, 96, 114, 226–227, 393
Democratic Party, 5
Democrats, 17, 18, 24
DeMohrenschildt, George, 152–153, 155, 194, 334–338
deportation, 140
Deslatte, Oscar, 109
Diem government, 7, 24
Document Addendum to the Warren Report (Lifton), 442 n.34
Dominican Republic, 228
domino theory, 2, 6, 19, 33, 365

Donnelly, Greg, 387
Donovan, William ("Wild Bill"), 4, 67, 68, 130, 142–143
Downing, Thomas, 325–327
Dreyfus case, 230
drug smuggling, 212
Dulles, Allen, 3–7
ousted as CIA Director, 52
and German financial interests, 400n24
law firm, 6
and Lumumba, 7
and Nazis, 4
and Operation Sunrise, 399n17
and Schroder, 385
Dulles, John Foster, 5–7, 14, 23, 25, 32
Duran, Silvia, 349–350, 360–361
Dymond, F. Irvin, 169, 230, 241–242, 269, 274, 277–278, 286–288, 295
Eardley, Carl, 299, 303–304
Eastern Air Lines, 83
dismissal of Ferrie, 86
Eastern Europe, 4, 193
Eisenhower, Dwight David, 4, 5–6, 11, 16, 17–19, 20, 23, 28, 75, 84, 127–128
El Paso, Texas, bank robbery, 98, 183
El Toro, California, Marine base, 127, 135
Electric Windmill, The (Bethell), 437n24
electronic surveillance, 145
Epstein, Edward Jay
and DeMohrenschildt (George), 153, 194, 335
Inquest, 304
Esquire magazine, 178
Escobedo decision, 308
Estonia, 3
Evergreen Advertising Agency, 232
Evica, George Michael, xi, 134, 196
extradition, 182, 235, 271
Fair Play for Cuba Committee, 96, 102, 118, 158, 162, 332, 355
fascist paramilitary groups, 4
Fatter, Esmond, 219, 244, 247, 297
FBI (Federal Bureau of Investigation),

and autopsy, 299, 340
Aynesworth as informant, 213
ballistics tests, 299
and Banister, 103
Cuban exiles, 80, 110
and DeBrueys, 80, 109, 292
Division Five, 356
documents, xv, 87, 189, 245, 265, 266
and Ferrie investigation, 103
and Garrison, 104, 109, 110, 177
Hoffa investigation, 256–257
in Mexico, 183
and Newman, 102
and Oswald, 80–82, 94, 103, 109
and Oswald as suspected informant, 109, 158, 160
and Paines, 156, 198
Sheridan and, 238
on Tippit, 122
and Warren Commission, 102, 109
See also Hoover, J. Edgar
FCC (Federal Communications Commission), 259, 261
Federal Bureau of Investigation. See FBI
Federal Republic of Germany, 4
Fensterwald, Bernard ("Bud"), xii, 94, 112, 209, 396
Fenton, Cliff, 328
Ferrie, David W.
    and Andrews, 260
    and Arcacha, 86, 92, 106
    autopsy, 226
    and Banister, 81
    Bay of Pigs connection, 84, 86, 105
    Broshears on, 209
    death, 175–176
    and del Valle, 85, 96
    dismissed from Eastern Air Lines, 86
    and Gill, 115
    instructor at CIA camp, 105, 115
    and Kimble, 209
    and Lardner, 224
    library card, 88
    and Martens, 106
    Martin on, 81
    in Montreal, 289

and Novel, 106
and Oswald, 81, 82–86, 92, 112
and pills, 226
planning of assassination, 116
proclivity for boys, 113
Russo on plot, 217–218
and Shaw, 91, 312
Tadins on, 312
Finck, Pierre A.
    background, 299
    cross-examination by prosecution, 292
fingerprinting, 307, 308
Fisher, Russell S., 305
Fitzsimmons, Charlene (Charlie), 98–99
Fitzsimmons, Robert (Bob), 98–99
Flammonde, Paris, 235, 312
Florida, 14, 18, 61, 77
    See also Miami, Florida
Fonzi, Gaeton, 68–69, 71, 227–228
Foreign Policy Association, 330
Fort Worth, Texas, 27, 120
Fortune, 46, 54, 99
France, 21, 22, 25, 127
Frazier, Robert, 299, 344
Freedom of Information Act, xv, 251
French Quarter, 83, 103, 113, 210, 247
French intelligence cover, 281
French Resistance, 5
Friends of Democratic Cuba, 109
Fritz, Will, 79, 329
Fruge, Francis, 78–79, 182, 185
Gallery, 336
Galveston, Texas, 79, 176
Garner, Jessie, 162, 309
Garrison Case, The (Brener), 427n11
Garrison, Jim
    acquittal in cases, 173
    with Alcock, 182
    Alcock's summation, 293
    and Alpha 66, 214
    Andrews perjury, 86–87, 181
    assistant District Attorneys, 93, 169
    Bethell's role against, 276
    Brener on, 382
    bribery allegations, 173
    Clark and, 91

death of Ferrie, 175–176
as District Attorney, ix, 167
extradition requests denied, 182,
    235
on Finck, 292
on Frazier, 311
Fruge testimony, 182
and Gervais, 174
and Gurvich, 182, 229
and Habighorst, 307
and House Assassinations
    Committee investigation, 189
on Huey Long, 277
and Johnson, 215
and Justice Department, 270
kickbacks trial, 316–317
and Kimble, 209
Kirkwood on, 246, 247
in Korean War, 130
law and order stance, 173
Lemann attack on, 241
Marachini subpoena, 157
and Marcello, 171
and Martin, 175–176
National Guard service, 168
Newman Building, 110
and Novel, 106
and *On the Trail of the Assassins*, ix,
    209, 322
Playboy interview, 238
and *Ramparts* article, 230
in San Francisco, 220
Santana testimony, 217
with Sciambra, 80
state Supreme Court decision, 171
support from Truth and
    Consequences fund, 233, 286,
    321
Tadins' testimony, 312
Townley on, 231, 239
at Tulane, 168
U.S. Supreme Court decision, 171
and Ward, 236
and Whalen, 320
and witness resistance, 238
in World War II as pilot, 168
and Zapruder film, 289
Gatlin, Maurice, 107–108, 183, 196
Gaudet, William, 112, 342

"gay Mexicanos"/Latinos, 87, 211, 236
Gehlen Organization, 4
Gehlen, Reinhard, 3–5
Geneva Accords, 7, 23
Geneva, Switzerland, 30, 281
German military intelligence, 4
Germany, 4, 282, 381
Gervais, Pershing, 174, 316–317
Gestapo, 11
Giancana, Sam, 15
Gill, G. Wray, 115, 209, 216
Golden Triangle, 376
Goldwater, Barry, 218, 369
Gonzalez, Henry, 333
Goodwin, Richard, 39, 50, 57
grassy knoll, 299
Greece, 1, 2, 377
Gremillion, Jack, 288
Groden, Robert, 325, 327
Guatemala, 35, 36, 51, 116, 385
Guinn, Vincent, 344
Gulf of Tonkin incident, 370
Gurvich, William (Bill), 182, 229–
    231, 247, 252
Habighorst, Alyosius, 211, 294, 306–
    308, 387
Habighorst, Elsie, 438n99
Haggerty, Edward, 171, 259, 271, 288,
    297
    and Finck testimony, 303
    and Habighorst testimony, 306–308
Haiti, 153, 155
Hall, Loren, 265–269, 281
Hammond, Louisiana, 218
"Hands Off Cuba" leaflet, 102, 190
Hardiman, James, 297
Hart, Gary, 327
Harvard University, 2, 99
Harvey, William, 59, 60–61, 65–66
Havana, Cuba, 10, 39, 217
"He Must Have Something"
    (documentary), 221
Helms, Richard McGarrah, 59, 60, 70,
    143, 150, 228, 270
Hidell alias, 94, 158
Hillenkoetter, Roscoe, 3, 6
Hilsman, Roger, 448n4
Hinckle, 281
Hitler, Adolf, 5, 63, 369

Ho Chi Minh, 21–24
Hoffa, James (Jimmy), 256–257, 258
Hoover, J. Edgar, 2, 102, 103 134,
    201–202, 236, 262, 264–265,
    352, 357
Hotel del Comercio, 348
Hougan, Jim, 165, 238, 257
Houma arms raid, 106, 182
House Select Committee on
    Assassinations investigation
  on Arcacha, 109
  on Banister, 116
  Billing's role, 350
  Bishop's role, 68
  Blakey's role, 339, 350
  on Camp street address, 110
  and CIA, 143, 294
  on Clinton trip, 209
  on De Mohrenschildt, 153
  Downing's role, 326
  Fenton's role, 328
  on Ferrie, 81
  and FBI, 85
  Final Report, 258
  Fonzi's role, 68
  and Garrison, 93, 294, 334
  Gonzalez's role, 333
  and Justice Department, 258
  Marchetti on, 228
  on Odio, 186
  on Oswald, 116, 136
  Sprague's role, 334, 350
  Stokes's role, 333
  Veciana's role, 68
Houston, Texas, 79, 175, 352
Howard, Larry, 159
Howard, Lawrence, Jr., 186
Howard, Lisa, 70
Hughes, Howard, 383
Humes, James, J., 300–305
Humphrey, Hubert, 18, 368
Hungary, 6, 122
Hunt, E. Howard, 10, 37–40, 51, 53,
    191, 336
Hurt, Henry, viii, 27, 129, 154
hypnosis, 219, 247, 297
immigration work, 87
Indochina War, 21, 22
Information Council of the Americas

(INCA), 105, 157
Inn of the Six Flags, 204
Inquest (Epstein), 304
International Investigators
    Incorporated, 256
International Trade Mart, 91, 112,
    161, 236, 294
Inverchapel, Lord, 1
Iowa, 168, 271
Iran, 385
Irving, Texas, 156, 163, 196, 204–206
Isle of Pines, 43, 351
"Issues and Answers" (TV program),
    259
Italy, 65, 385
Ivon, Lou, 178, 182, 190, 215, 225,
    234, 247
Jackson, Louisiana, 78, 88–89, 182
Jackson, Richard, 297, 306
Jaggars-Chiles-Stovall, 153, 154
James, Rosemary, 220–221, 259
Jenner, Albert E., Jr., 188
Jewish refugee racket, 386
JFK and Vietnam (Newman), 371
JFK (film), xi
JM-WAVE (CIA Miami station), 59,
    61, 65, 71
Johnson, Louis A., 83
Johnson, Lyndon Baines, 20, 27, 29,
    31, 75, 228, 251, 357, 358–359,
    365, 368 –372
Joint Chiefs of Staff (JCS), 29, 57, 63
JURE, 351
Justice Department, 69, 255, 261, 298,
    304–305
KGB, 64, 95, 97, 98, 134, 140, 141,
    144–146, 148–50, 166, 354,
    355, 357, 360, 362
Katzenjammer Bar, 80
Kemp, Karla, 439n107
Kennedy family, 254
Kennedy, Jacqueline (Jackie), 26, 152,
    196, 377
Kennedy, John Fitzgerald
  assassination of: arrival in Dallas,
    66, 67; autopsy evidence, 300,
    327; ballistics evidence, 293,
    300, 343; and Cheramie, 181,
    212, 216, 272; CIA link, 380;

conspiracy theory, x; Cuban exiles' role (*see* Cuban exiles); Ferrie connection, 81–88, 91–94, 97; FBI investigation, 160, 181; grassy knoll, 299; Mafia theory (*see* Mafia); medical evidence (see autopsy); Oswald as patsy, 77, 99, 185, 194, 336; researchers, xii, 310, 324, 343, 345, 392–3, 431n.116, 437n25; single bullet theory, 293, 300, 327, 344, 345, 391, 394; Stone movie, xi; Thompson on, 305, 381; and Underhill, 77, 98–100; Zapruder film, 289, 292, 299, 301, 306, 322, 325, 327, 381; *See also* autopsy; Garrison, Jim; House Select Committee on Assassinations investigation; Warren Commission

and Bay of Pigs (*see* Bay of Pigs invasion)

and Cabell, 42

and Castro, 17–19, 66–76

as Cold Warrior, 28, 364

and colonialism, 21–27

compared with Johnson, 365

and the Congo, 28–9, 33, 371–3, 377, 381

and Cuba, 34–56, 62 (*see also* Bay of Pigs invasion)

and Cuban exiles, 67, 97, 110, 111

and de Gaulle, 282

and debate with Nixon, 18

dismantling of Operation MONGOOSE, 61, 67–9

compared with Eisenhower, 19, 29, 33

election as president, 16¬–19

and ExComm, 64–65

foreign affairs background, 20

and France, 22, 25, 26

Groden on, 327

and intervention, 61

and investigation of labor, 18

and Joint Chiefs of Staff, 61, 63

and Laos, 375–7, 381

and Mafia, 68, 258, 381

and missile "gap," 18

and National Security Action Memoranda, 52

and Nixon, 18, 19, 24–26, 30, 39

and Nuclear Test Ban Treaty, 67

and paramilitary operations, 52

rhetoric, 19

compared with Roosevelt, 202

and Soviet Union, 62

and Vietnam War, 31, 366

and Vietnam withdrawal, 65, 366–9, 371, 395

and *Why England Slept*, 20

Kennedy, Regis, 80, 109, 110, 292, 294, 298, 318, 342, 386

Kennedy, Robert, 21, 33, 42, 48, 53, 58, 62, 63, 65–7, 69, 73–4, 258, 266, 339, 374, 393, 395

Khrushchev, Nikita, 63–7, 70, 74, 127–8, 358–9, 378

Kimble, Jules Ricco, 209, 240, 289, 292

King, Martin Luther, Jr. assassination, 266, 326, 343

Kirkpatrick, Lyman, 35, 38–41, 45, 46, 50

Kirkwood, James, 382–3, 244, 246, 309, 322

Kohn, Aaron, 173, 239, 241, 265, 267, 288, 312, 313, 316, 340

Korean War, 3, 95, 130, 168

Kostikov, Valery, 354–7, 360

Krock, Arthur, 380

Kurtz, Michael, 116, 248, 343

LaBiche, Albert, 286

Lacombe, Louisiana, 115, 116, 180

Lake Pontchartrain training camp, 115

Lakefront Airport, 83, 231, 310

Lamont, Corliss, 102, 111, 158, 159, 161

Lane, Mark, 129, 132, 178, 181, 243, 267, 337, 387

Langley, Virginia, 197, 213, 262, 263, 272, 274, 277, 278, 293, 313, 361

Lansky, Meyer, 9

Laos, 29–30, 33, 54, 375, 376, 377, 381

   CIA in, 375, 376

Lardner, George, Jr., 224–6

Las Vegas, Nevada, 245, 247, 276
Leemans, Fred,240, 241, 267
LeMay, Curtis, 57, 63, 302
Lemnitzer, Lyman, 29, 42, 43, 52
"Leopoldo," 351, 352
Lesar, James H., xii
Levy, Michael, 429n57
Lewis, David, 108, 113
libel, 212, 262, 263
Liebeler, Wesley J., 87, 88, 123, 155,
    178, 181, 201, 202, 269, 273,
    305, 352, 353
Life magazine, 72
Lifton, David, 188, 189, 382
limited warfare, 99
Lithuania, 3
London, England, 138
Long Island, New York, 98, 152
Long, Huey, 277, 288, 313, 316
Long, Russell, 177
Look magazine, 71
Lopez, Edwin, 227
Los Angeles, California, 17, 95, 96,
    134, 266, 267
Los Angeles Times, 332, 382
Louisiana, 14, 15, 77–9, 83, 86, 88,
    103, 106, 115, 171, 172, 175,
    178, 186, 208, 217, 235, 272,
    288, 295, 314, 321, 232
    law of, 289
Louisiana Intelligence Digest, 104
Louisiana State Hospital, 89, 92, 93,
    181
Louisiana State University (LSU), 78,
    103, 232, 295–6
Luce, Henry, 55, 99, 195
Lumumba, Patrice, 7, 28, 29, 372, 373
Luxembourg, 2
Mack, Gary, 251
Mader, Julius, 417n149
Mafia, 15, 68, 116, 172, 188, 211,
    212, 215, 239, 257, 258, 276,
    312, 324, 333, 339, 340
Maheu, Robert, 15, 257, 258
Mancuso, Marlene, 239, 248
Mao Tse-tung, 399n14
Marachini, Dante, 157
Marchetti, Victor, 166, 228, 271, 294,
    363, 385

Mardi Gras, 236, 307
Marine Corps, 120, 125, 126, 129,
    187, 191, 341
Marrs, Jim, 441n56, 443n57
Marshall, George, 1
Marshall Plan, 2, 399n5
Martens, Layton, 106, 382
Martin, Jack, 20, 102, 108, 112–4,
    119, 175, 177, 180, 341, 389
Matsu,18, 20, 402n16
McCarthy, Joseph, 18, 19, 38, 103,
    130, 306
McCloy, John J., 3, 4, 148, 349, 383,
    394
    and Barbie, 4, 400n22
    as High Commissioner in occupied
        Germany, 400n22, 417n149
McCone, John J., 52, 62, 65, 68, 70,
    379, 380
McGee, Frank, 432n2
McGehee, Edward Lee, 88, 89, 185,
    186, 294
McLaney, Bill, 115, 180
McLean, Virginia, 235, 262
McNamara, Robert S., 31, 42, 46, 57,
    58, 63, 64, 359, 366–71, 395
McWillie, Lewis, 15
Meagher, Sylvia, 267
Melanson, Philip, 130, 137, 154, 193
Mengele, Josef, 4, 400n22
Mexico
    CIA in, 71, 73–9, 196, 255, 272
    Eisenhower on, 20
    Oswald trip, 94–7, 156, 163, 193,
        203, 204, 327, 346–54
Mexico City, 272, 273, 377, 395
Miami Herald, 37, 72
Miami, Florida, 50, 51, 59, 65, 69–73,
    96, 106, 108, 112, 182, 191,
    212, 227–8, 278
    CIA station, 51, 227
    del Valle murder, 227
micro dot technology, 154
military industrial complex, 377
Miller, George, 256
Minox camera, 207, 234
Minyard, Frank, 242, 428n19
missile "gap," 18
Mob, the. *See* Mafia

Moffett, Sandra, 218, 271
Monterey School, 95, 131
Montreal, Canada, 289, 292
Moore, J. Walton, 153, 338
Moore, Joseph, 109
Morgan, Reeves, 89, 90, 186, 265, 294
Morris, William, 210, 387, 437n28
Morrison, DeLesseps, 103, 168
Morse, Wayne, 418n19
Moscow, U.S.S.R., 2, 62, 76, 96, 138–
    42, 144–6, 149, 159, 377, 378
Mossadegh government, 7, 14
Moyers, Bill, 368
Murret, Dutz, 340, 341
Nagell, Richard Case, 93–8, 128, 129,
    131, 183, 184, 248, 272, 294
Nagy, Ferenc, 386
NASA (National Aeronautics and
    Space Administration), 157, 191,
    323, 324, 344
National Archives, xii, xv, 189, 261,
    303, 305, 315, 345, 385,
    426n148, 441n45, 445n120
National Broadcasting Company. See
    NBC
National Guard, 168
National Review, 228
national security, 2–5, 33, 52, 158,
    224, 299, 358, 388
National Security Action Memoranda
    (NSAMs), 52, 366, 367, 369–71,
    373
National Security Agency, 71, 229,
    238, 255
National Security Council, 2, 3, 49,
    58, 228, 379
NATO (North Atlantic Treaty
    Organization), 2, 375
Navy (U.S.),
    Naval Intelligence, 15, 80, 142,
    165, 209, 255, 256, 279, 379
NBC (National Broadcasting
    Company), 229, 233, 238–41,
    255, 263, 272, 288, 397, 432n2
Nebraska, 271
Netherlands, The, 2, 31–33, 149, 335,
    373, 375
Neutrality Act, 115
"New Frontier" theme, 17

New Orleans, Louisiana
    Airport, 82, 209, 306
    Banister assault of Martin, 81, 180
    Banister in police force, 103, 104
    Camp Street address, 102, 110, 111,
        114, 161
    Cheramie case, 328
    Civil Air Patrol, 81, 83, 125
    Crescent City Garage, 157
    Criminal Court judges, 287
    Cuban exiles in, 111, 159
    Cuban Revolutionary Council, 96
    Fair Play for Cuba Committee, 96,
        102, 118, 158, 179, 190, 332,
        355, 356,
    Guy Banister Associates, 104,
    International Trade Mart, 91, 112,
        137, 161, 183, 186, 209, 236,
        294, 310, 383, 384
    Katzenjammer Bar, 80,
    police, 80, 81, 113, 308, 328,
    Reily Coffee Company, 157
    Spiesel in, 295–7,
    See also Oswald, Lee Harvey: in
        New Orleans
New Orleans States-Item, 161, 220, 275
New Orleans Times-Picayune, 172
New Republic, The, 99, 259
New Times, 338
New York City, New York, 102, 103,
    121, 123, 145, 150, 159, 161,
    230, 296, 330,
    police, 296
New York Council to Abolish the
    House Un-American Activities
    Committee, 162
New York Review of Books, 259
New York Times,10, 25, 37, 50, 52, 69,
    171, 261, 299, 332, 383, 387
Newman, John, 348, 355, 360, 369,
    371
Newman, Samuel, 102
Newman's office building (Camp/
    Lafayette Streets), 102
Newsweek, 249–53, 259, 261, 288,
Ngo Dinh Diem, 7, 24, 30, 54, 365,
    367,
Nicaragua, 44, 46, 108, 199, 384,
Nixon, Richard Milhouse, 6, 10, 16,

18, 19, 23–6, 30, 39, 44, 250,
    336, 369
North Atlantic Treaty Organization.
    See NATO
Novel, Gordon, 101, 105–8, 162, 191,
    212, 216, 229, 232–5, 237, 239,
    240, 253, 261–4, 269, 275, 279,
    292, 311, 323
    and Andrews, 233
    and Arcacha, 105–108
    explosive munitions raid, 232
    extradition denied, 235
    and Ferris, 216, 232, 235
    Grand Jury appearance, 234
    and Martens, 106
Nuevo Laredo, Mexico, 352,
OAS. *See* Secret Armed Organization
Ochsner, Alton, 92, 157, 188
Odio, Sylvia, 56, 96, 97, 186, 248,
    265, 266, 268, 324, 350–3
Odom, Lee, 236, 282
Office of Strategic Services. *See* OSS
Ofstein, Dennis, 153, 154
Ohio, 82, 83, 196, 235, 263, 333, 377
On the Trail of the Assassins (Garrison),
    ix, xi, 209, 322, 365
opium, 399n14
O'Reilly, Bill, 428n34
Orleans Parish Grand Jury, 286
Oser, Alvin, 293, 299, 300
    cross-examination of Finck, 300
O'Sullivan, Frederick, 178
OSS (Office of Strategic Services), 4, 5,
    6, 76, 134, 139, 195, 196, 255
"Oswald," 109
Oswald, June, 149
Oswald, Lee Harvey, 10, 53, 56, 76,
    89, 95, 117, 118, 120, 122, 124,
    164, 248, 349, 364
    alias Hidell, 94, 158, 160, 254, 391
    alias Leon Oswald, 97, 218, 248,
        249, 309, 350, 351
    Andrews and, 86–88, 93
    arrest at Texas Theater, 249, 392
    ballistics evidence, 343
    and Banister, 116, 291, 389
    and Bertrand (Shaw), 93, 294
    birth, 120
    birth of daughter, 149, 151, 163

    and Bishop, 332
    and Bringuier's assault, 118, 161
    in the Bronx, 121, 123
    and brother Robert, 203,
    at Camp Street address, 102
    and CIA, 143
    in Civil Air Patrol, 81, 125
    Clinton trip, 93, 310
    comparison with image of Dallas,
        101
    cover as leftist, 152, 250
    cover as Marine, 91, 112
    in custody, 205
    in Dallas, 150, 153, 213
    "defection," 87, 96, 117, 124, 132,
        139, 142, 143, 162, 164, 356
    disturbing the peace plea, 159
    diary sold, 250
    doubles (*see* "Oswald," "Oswald,
        Lee," "Oswald, Leon")
    enlists in Marines, 125–7
    and Fair Play for Cuba Committee,
        96, 102, 118, 158, 179, 190,
        332, 355
    as FBI informant (suspected), 158
    and Ferrie, 84, 85, 112, 177, 178,
        248, 310
    in Fort Worth, 124, 135, 136, 151,
        153
    hawking "Hands Off Cuba" leaflet,
        102
    in high school, 124
    in Houston, 352
    at Jaggars-Chiles-Stovall, 153, 154
    killing by Ruby, 117, 156, 182, 214,
        249, 330
    and landlady Garner, 162, 309
    and library card of Ferrie, 81, 88,
        98, 310
    Marine discharge, 87, 132, 135,
        136, 144, 150
    as Marine in Philippines, 142, 196
    marksmanship, 129,131
    marriage to Marina Prusakova, 147
    Marxist angle, 353
    "Mexico trip, 190
    and Minox camera, 207
    in Minsk, 151, 153, 154
    and Nagell, 95

in New Orleans, 118, 119, 189, 190, 192, 256
in Nuevo Laredo, 352
as patsy, 77, 99, 185, 194, 336
and Phillips, 116
postal box link to Shaw, 236
and Raikin, 149, 150
at Reily Coffee Company, 157, 191
rifle mail order, 160
and Ruby, 79, 214, 328
Russian language fluency, 207
and security clearance, 127, 128
seeks attorney, 87
and Shaw, 93, 294
in Soviet Union, 102, 153, 154, 187
in Texas, 94
at Texas School Book Depository, 156, 163, 206, 207, 301, 343
and Tippit, 391, 392
and uncle Murret, 340
and U–2, 127, 128, 141, 142, 143, 154
and Veciana, 332, 363
and Warren Commission, 76, 94, 102, 103, 113, 118, 119, 122, 123–5, 130, 131, 132, 134, 136, 138, 142, 147, 153, 156–62, 178, 179, 184–9, 193, 198, 200–4, 210, 265, 327, 331, 334, 343–353, 355, 358, 359, 392
witnesses, 84, 88, 93, 116, 125, 186, 187, 189, 190, 201, 248, 254, 294, 309, 334, 353, 392
"Oswald, Leon," 97, 218, 248, 249, 309, 350, 351
Oswald, Marguerite, 120–126,
Oswald, Marina Prusakova, 139–140, 146–147, 149, 155, 190, 206
Paine, Michael, 155, 194, 195, 206, 343
Paine, Ruth, 148, 155–157, 163, 193–201, 343
Palmer, Henry, 90–93, 185
Panzeca, Sal, 290, 296, 308, 321, 389
Paris, 73, 107
Parker, Jessie, 211, 306, 387
Parkland Hospital, 156, 293, 334
Parmet, Herbert, 20
PBS (Public Broadcasting System), 84, 108
Permindex, 385–386
Peru, 384
Peterson, Niles, 218, 248
Phelan, James 243–248, 289–290, 309, 382–383
Phillips, David Atlee, 10, 35, 53, 69, 95, 105, 272, 332
Playboy, xi, xv, 105, 193, 213, 215, 258, 262
Plotkin, Steve, 112, 234
Poland, 63
Policoff, Jerry, 338
Powers, Gary Francis, 127, 142
prostitution, 9, 77, 87, 212
Prouty, Fletcher L., 52
Puerto Rico, 44, 113
Quemoy, 18, 20
Quiroga, Carlos, 97, 161–162, 184, 329
radio broadcasts, 19, 162, 196
Radio Free Europe, 3, 193, 255
Raikin, Spas, 149–150,
Ramparts, 230, 281
Rankin, J. Lee, 123, 131, 183
Rault, Joseph M., 321
Ray, Manolo, 39, 43, 58
Reagan, Ronald, 280
Reily, William, 157
Reily Coffee Company. *See* New Orleans
Republican Party, 5
Rhodes, James, 235
Rich, Nancy Perrin, 213, 279
Roberts, Delphine, 80, 110–111, 116, 341
Robertson, Willard, 233
Rodriguez, Manuel, 213
Rogers, Warren, 313
Rome, Italy, 65, 385
Roosevelt, Eleanor, 18, 202
Roosevelt, Franklin Delano, 4, 313
Rose, Jerry, viii, 337
Roselli, Johnny, 15, 60, 65, 188
Rubenstein, Jacob. *See* Ruby, Jack
Ruby, Jack
    Cheramie connection, 78–79,
    CIA on, 196
    at *Dallas Morning News*, 249

Fruge on, 79
Garrison investigation, 182
House Assassinations Committee
    on, 78
McLaney friendship, 115
Rich connection, 279
and Tippit, 249
and Warren (Earl), 250
in Warren Report, 117
Rusk, Dean, 30, 42, 58, 369
Russell, Patrick, 338
Russell, Richard B., 64, 147, 195
Russian Civil War, 284
Russo, Perry, 217–219, 230, 237, 243,
    246–249, 269, 297, 309
Ryan, George, 256
Saigon, South Vietnam, 21, 30, 365–
    369
Salandria, Vincent, 178, 279, 284–
    285, 293
San Francisco, California, 280
Santana, Emilio, 182, 216, 289
Saturday Evening Post, 243, 245, 305
Scandals, Scamps and Scoundrels
    (Phelan), 244
Schoener, Gary, 284
Schroder, J. Henry, 385
Schweiker, Richard, 150, 327–328
Secret Armed Organization (OAS), 27,
    107, 386
Seligman, Hans, 385
Semple, Robert, 261
Senate Judiciary Committee, 261, 339
Ser Vaas, Buert, 256
Seymour, William, 266, 323
Shackley, Theodore, 51, 59, 61, 72
Shah of Iran, 7
Shaw, Clay
    acquittal, 304, 311
    alias Clay Bertrand, 180, 210–211,
        236, 240, 242, 269, 278, 387
    alias Clem Bertrand, 211, 218
    and Andrews, 93, 180, 210, 236,
        288, 307
    in Argentina, 384
    arrest, 211, 230, 236
    and Banister, 15, 92
    and Biddison, 297
    and Brent, 231, 384

Bundy on, 237, 242, 295
and CIA, 110, 157, 166, 183, 217,
    232
and Clark, 91, 261, 287
in Clinton, 93, 209, 311
death of, 321
District Court decision, 287
and Ferrie, 92, 93, 110, 185, 187,
    208–210, 215–219
FBI file, 179
Habighorst on, 211, 294
and International Trade Mart, 112,
    183, 209
Kirkwood on, 244
Nagell on, 183–184, 294
and Novel, 232, 240
Parker on, 211, 306, 387–388
perjury charges, xiii, 289, 312
and Permindex, 385–386
Phelan on, 244, 246–248, 289, 309
and Ruby, 217, 328
Russo on, 218, 237, 247, 309
in San Francisco, 218
and Santana, 216, 217, 328
and Sheridan, 233, 239, 269
and Spiesel, 295,
Tadins on, 311, 312
and Thrasher, 384
trial of, 93, 161, 209, 266, 270–
    271, 278, 286–311, 389
on Warren Report, 137
See also Garrison, Jim
Sheridan Square Press, xi
Sheridan, Walter, 229, 233, 235, 255–
    259, 289
Shreveport, Louisiana, 200
Shilstone, Cecil, 321
Sichell, H.M., 1
Simmons, James, 299
Sirhan, Sirhan, 244
SIS, 3, 5
Six Seconds in Dallas (Thompson), 305,
    381
Sklar, Zachary, xi
Skorzeny, Otto, 254
Smathers, George, 85
Smith, Earl, 9
Smith, Walter Bedell, 4, 6
Snyder, Richard E., 141

Souetre, Jean, 27
South Africa, 386
South America, 4, 9
Southeastern Louisiana University, 218
Soviet Union, 4, 5, 7, 13, 18, 62, 128, 141, 164, 334
Spain, 98
Specter, Arlen, 300
Spiesel, Charles, 295–297
Sprague, Richard A., 326, 332, 333–334, 350
Springer, Eva, 179
Stalin, Josef, 2, 19
Standard Oil, 9, 32, 314
State Department, 6, 11, 49, 67, 124, 139, 348
Stern, Edgar, 161, 238
Stern, Edith, 161, 238
Stevenson, Adlai, 18, 24, 46, 101
Stokes, Louis, 333
Stone, Oliver, xi
Sukarno, 7, 32–33, 374
Sullivan and Cromwell, 6, 49, 385
Summers, Anthony, 111, 115, 160, 363
Supreme Court (U.S.), 171, 321
Switzerland, 133, 195, 385
Tadin, Matilda, 292, 310
Tadin, Nicholas, 209, 292, 310
Tanenbaum, Robert, 116, 294, 326
Taylor, Gen., 31, 41, 63, 366
Teamsters union, 256
Texaco, 330
Texas School Book Depository, 156, 163, 206, 207, 343
Thailand, 29, 376
Third Reich, 385
Third World, 6, 19, 24, 365
Thrasher, Charles, 384
Tippit, J.D., 249, 391, 392
Tolstoy Foundation, 193
"Tonight Show, The," 259, 397
Torres, Miguel, 242
Townley, Richard, 231, 239
Trafficante, Santos, 9, 15, 85, 226
Trento, Joseph, 363
Truly, Roy, 163
Truman Doctrine, 2
Truman, Harry S., 2, 3, 4, 6, 22, 48, 255, 378
Tulane University, 84, 92
Turkey, 1, 2, 65
Turner, William, 51, 280
Tyler, Texas, 182
Underhill, John Garrett (Gary), 98–100
Underhill, Patricia, 99, 100
United Fruit, 6, 7, 196
United Nations, 28, 33, 371
Varona, Antonio, 15, 51, 72
Veciana, Antonio, 10, 53, 68, 95, 331, 393
Vietnam, 20–25, 173, 366
Vietnam War, 22, 31, 370
Voebel, Edward, 83, 125, 178
Wade, Henry, 253
Walthers, Buddy, 198, 227
Ward, Charles, 236, 276
Ward, Hugh, 179, 292
Warren, Earl, 80, 250, 358
Warren Commission
    Andrews testimony, 181
    autopsy, 293, 300
    and Aynesworth, 250
    CIA and, 134, 188, 270
    and DeMohrenschildt, 194
    Dulles's role, 5, 194, 195, 347
    FBI's role, ix, 94, 102, 158, 178
    Ford's role, 394
    Groden on, 327
    Johnson's role, 358
    Liebeler's role, 87, 178
    magic bullet theory (see Warren Commission: single bullet hypothesis)
    and Marina Oswald, 147
    McCloy's role, 349, 383
    perjury, 260
    and Phillips, 347
    Rankin's role, 123, 131
    Report; Aynsworth on, 297; and Dymond, 287; on Ferrie, 118; and Lewis, 327; on Oswald, 80, 102, 157, 265, 327, 353; and Shaw, 137, 157, 287
    Schweiker on, 327
    single bullet hypothesis, 293, 300, 327
    Specter's role, 300

and subpoena power, 359
on Tippit, 391–392
Warren's role, 250
and Zapruder film, 292, 301, 327
Washington, D.C., 188, 257
Washington Post, 170, 363, 378
WDSU-TV, 161
Wecht, Cyril, 326
Wegmann, Edward, 209, 241, 254,
    261, 269
Wegmann, William (Bill), 209, 241,
    390
Weisberg, Harold, 131, 190, 209, 274, 321

Why England Slept (Kennedy), 20
Wicker, Tom, 52
Wood, Dr., 279
World War I, 55
World War II, 3, 5, 19, 36, 63, 195,
    379
Yarborough, Ralph, 160
Yugoslavia, 153, 194
Zapruder film, 289, 292, 299, 306,
    325, 381
Zelden, Monk, 88, 179
Compiled by Daniel C. Tsang